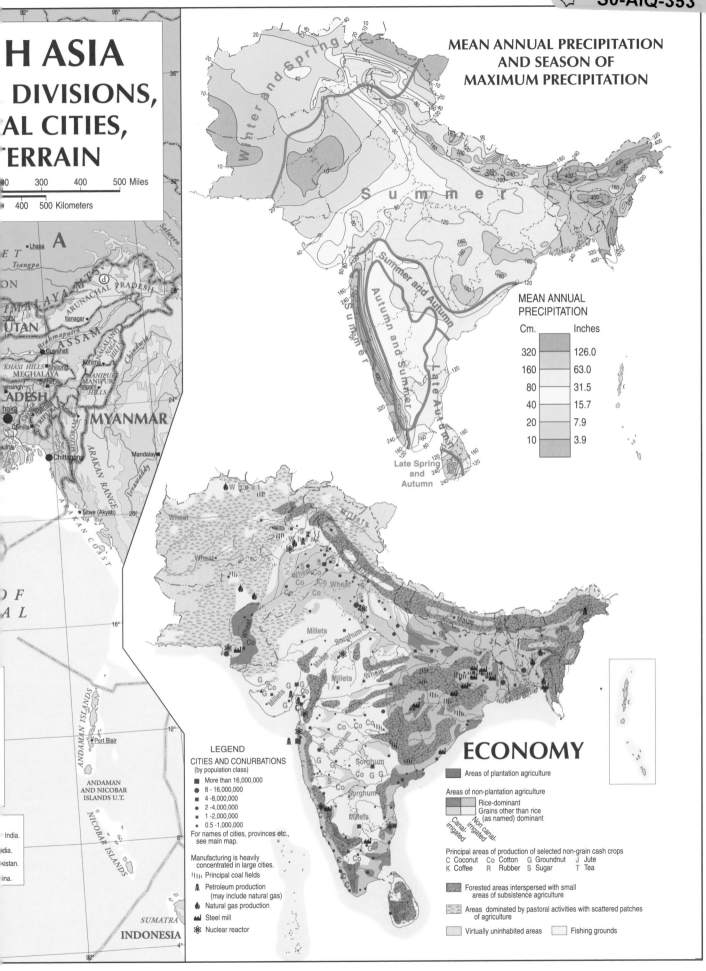

H ASIA

DIVISIONS,
AL CITIES,
ERRAIN

0   300   400   500 Miles

400   500 Kilometers

MEAN ANNUAL PRECIPITATION AND SEASON OF MAXIMUM PRECIPITATION

Winter and Spring

Summer

Summer and Autumn

Autumn and Summer

Summer

Late Autumn

Late Spring and Autumn

MEAN ANNUAL PRECIPITATION

Cm.		Inches
320		126.0
160		63.0
80		31.5
40		15.7
20		7.9
10		3.9

Lhasa

Tsangpo

HIMALAYA MTS.

ARUNACHAL PRADESH

Itanagar

ASSAM

Guwahati

NAGALAND NAGA HILLS

Kohima

KHASI HILLS *Shillong*
MEGHALAYA *Sylhet*

MANIPUR
MANIPUR HILLS
Imphal

ADESH

MYANMAR

TRIPURA

MIZORAM

Comilla

Chittagong

ARAKAN RANGE

Mandalay

ARAKAN COAST

Sitwe (Akyab)

Irrawaddy

Wheat

Wheat

Wheat

Wheat

Wheat

Co Wheat

Millets

Co

Co

Co Wheat

Co

Maize

Millets

Sorghum

Wheat

Millets

Maize

G Co G

Millets Co

G

G Co

Co Co Co

Co

Sorghum

Co

Sorghum

S

S G

Co G G

Co

Sorghum

S Co

Millets

G

Co

ECONOMY

Areas of plantation agriculture

Areas of non-plantation agriculture

Rice-dominant

Grains other than rice (as named) dominant

Canal-irrigated Non canal-irrigated

Principal areas of production of selected non-grain cash crops
C Coconut Co Cotton G Groundnut J Jute
K Coffee R Rubber S Sugar T Tea

Forested areas interspersed with small areas of subsistence agriculture

Areas dominated by pastoral activities with scattered patches of agriculture

Virtually uninhabited areas   Fishing grounds

LEGEND
CITIES AND CONURBATIONS
(by population class)

■ More than 16,000,000
● 8 - 16,000,000
● 4 -8,000,000
● 2 -4,000,000
● 1 -2,000,000
● 0.5 -1,000,000

For names of cities, provinces etc.,
see main map.

Manufacturing is heavily
concentrated in large cities.

ıllı Principal coal fields

⚑ Petroleum production
(may include natural gas)

♦ Natural gas production

⚒ Steel mill

※ Nuclear reactor

ANDAMAN ISLANDS

Port Blair

ANDAMAN AND NICOBAR ISLANDS U.T.

NICOBAR ISLANDS

SUMATRA

INDONESIA

India.
dia.
kistan.
ina.

OF
AL

ENCYCLOPEDIA OF *India*

editorial board

ENCYCLOPEDIA OF *India*

VOLUME 2

E–J

Stanley Wolpert

Editor in Chief

CHARLES SCRIBNER'S SONS
An imprint of Thomson Gale, a part of The Thomson Corporation

Detroit • New York • San Francisco • San Diego • New Haven, Conn. • Waterville, Maine • London • Munich

Encyclopedia of India
Stanley Wolpert, Editor in Chief

LIBRARY OF CONGRESS CATALOGING-IN-PUBLICATION DATA

Encyclopedia of India / Stanley A. Wolpert, editor in chief.
    p. cm.
      Includes bibliographical references and index.
      ISBN 0-684-31349-9 (set hardcover : alk. paper)—ISBN 0-684-31350-2 (v. 1)—ISBN 0-684-31351-0 (v. 2)—ISBN 0-684-31352-9 (v. 3)—ISBN 0-684-31353-7 (v. 4)
      1. India—Encyclopedias.   I. Wolpert, Stanley A., 1927–
DS405.E556 2005
954'.003—dc22
                                                 2005019616

This title is also available as an e-book.
ISBN 0-684-31512-2
Contact your Thomson Gale representative for ordering information.

Printed in the United States of America
10 9 8 7 6 5 4 3 2 1

table of contents

Volume 1

List of Maps ix
Preface xi
List of Articles xv
Thematic Outline of Contents xxiii
Directory of Contributors xxxiii
Chronologies xlvii
A–D
Color Insert: Art, Architecture, and Sculpture

Volume 2

List of Maps vii
List of Articles ix
E–J
Color Insert: Contemporary Life

Volume 3

List of Maps vii
List of Articles ix
K–R
Color Insert: Handicrafts

Volume 4

List of Maps vii
List of Articles ix
S–Z
Color Insert: Physical Environment
Primary Source Documents 261
Glossary 287
General Bibliography 295
Index 299

list of maps

Volume 1

The Mughal Empire, 1525–1707 30
The Empire of Alexander the Great 35
The Bengal Partition and Related Changes,
  1905–1912 132
The Revolt of 1857–1859 170
The Advance of British Power, 1766–1857 . . . 178

Volume 2

Guptan Empire, c. 300–550 163
Invasions from the Northwest, 330–1 B.C. . . . 209
Indus Valley Civilization, c. 2800–1600 B.C. . . . 260

Volume 3

Jammu and Kashmir 12
The Marathas, 1646–1819 95
Mauryan Empire, 321–185 B.C. 104
Muslim Expansion, 8th–15th Centuries . . . 199
Territorial Changes, 1947–1955 304
Territorial Changes, 1956–2000 305
European Commercial Contacts, 16th–18th
  Centuries 321

list of articles

A

Abdul Kalam, Avul Pakir Jainulabdeen (A.P.J.)
Advani, Lal Krishna
Aesthetics
Afghani, Jamal-ud-din
Afghanistan
Afghanistan, Military Relations with, 1994–2001
Agni
Agra
Agricultural Growth and Diversification since 1991
Agricultural Labor and Wages since 1950
Agricultural Prices and Production, 1757–1947
Agricultural Wages, Labor, and Employment since 1757
Ahmedabad
AIDS/HIV
Ajanta
Akbar
Akkamahādēvi
Ālāp
Albuquerque, Afonso de
Alexander the Great
Allahabad
All-India Muslim League
Ambedkar, B. R., and the Buddhist Dalits
Amritsar
Anand, Mulk Raj
Āndāl
Andhra Pradesh
Andrews, C. F.
Andy, S. Pulney
Anglo-Afghan Wars: War One (1838–1842)
Anglo-Afghan Wars: War Two (1878–1880)
Anglo-Afghan Wars: War Three (May–August 1919)
Armed Forces

Artha Shāstra
Arunachal Pradesh
Āryabhata
Āryabhatīya
Ārya Samāj
Ashtādhyāyī
Ashvamedha
Asian Development Bank (ADB), Relations with
Asiatic Societies of Bengal and Bombay
Assam
Astronomy
Auckland, Lord
Aurangzeb
Aurobindo, Sri
Avatāras of Vishnu, Images of
Ayodhya
Āyurveda
Azad, Maulana Abul Kalam
Azariah, Vedanayakam Samuel

B

Babur
Bactria
Bahadur Shah I
Balance of Payments: Exchange Rate Policy
Balance of Payments: Foreign Investment and the
   Exchange Rate
Bālasarasvati, T.
Ballistic and Cruise Missile Development
Ballistic Missile Defenses
Baluchar Sari
Baluchistan and the North-West Frontier
"Bande Mataram"
Bandhani

Banerjea, Surendranath N.
Bangalore
Bangladesh
Bank and Non-Bank Supervision
Banking Sector Reform since 1991
Barahmasa
Baroda
Bene Israel
Bengal
Bentinck, Lord William
Bhabha, Homi
Bhagavad Gītā
Bhāgavata Purāṇa
Bhajan
Bhakti
Bharat
Bharatiya Janata Party (BJP)
Bhave, Vinoba
Bhopal
Bhubaneswar
Bhūta
Bhutto, Zulfikar Ali
Bihar
Bimbisara
Biotechnology Revolution
Bombay
Bonnerji, Womesh C.
Bose, Subhas Chandra
Brahmacarya
Brāhmaṇas
Brahmo Samaj
Brazil–India Relations
British Crown Raj
British East India Company Raj
British Impact
British India Office, The
Brocade
Bronzes: Early Images
Bronzes: South Indian
Buddha, Life of the
Buddhism in Ancient India
Buddhist Art in Andhra up to the Fourth Century
Burma

C
Cabinet Mission Plan
Calcutta
Capital Market
Caste and Democracy
Caste System
Central Banking, Developmental Aspects of
Chaitanya
Chalcolithic (Bronze) Age
Chandigarh

Chatterji, Bankim Chandra
Chaudhuri, Nirad C.
Chelmsford, Lord
Chidambaram
China, Relations with
Chola Dynasty
Christian Impact on India, History of
Cinema
Civil-Military Relations
Clive, Robert
Commodity Markets
Common Property Resources, Past and Present
Congress Party
Contract Farming
Cornwallis, Lord
Cripps, Sir Richard Stafford
Curzon, Lord George

D
Dalhousie, Marquis of
Dalits
Dance Forms: An Introduction
Dance Forms: Bharata Natyam
Dance Forms: Kathak
Dance Forms: Kathakali
Dance Forms: Koodiyattam
Dance Forms: Kuchipudi
Dance Forms: Manipuri
Dance Forms: Mohini Attam
Dance Forms: Odissi
Das, Chitta Ranjan
Debt Markets
Deccani Painting
Demographic Trends since 1757
Demography and Census-taking
Desai, Morarji
Development of Commercial Banking 1950–1990
Development Politics
Devī
Devi, Siddheshvari
Dharma Shāstra
Dhrupad
Diaspora: Economic Impact
Diaspora: History of and Global Distribution
Dīkshitar, Muttusvāmi
Dīvālī
Dravidian Parties
Dubois, Jean-Antoine
Dufferin, Lord
Dundas, Henry
Dupleix, Joseph François

E
Early Maritime Contacts

Economic Burden of Defense
Economic Development, Importance of Institutions in
  and Social Aspects of
Economic Policy and Change, 1800–1947
Economic Policy Under Planning, Aspects of
Economic Reforms and Center-State Relations
Economic Reforms of 1991
Economy Since the 1991 Economic Reforms
Educational Institutions and Philosophies, Traditional
  and Modern
Elephanta
Ellenborough, Earl of
Ellora (Elura)
Elphinstone, Mountstuart
Employment Structure
Energy Politics and Policy
Environmental Consciousness since 1800
Ethnic Conflict
Ethnic Peace Accords
European Union, Relations with
External Debt Policy, 1952–1990

F

Family Law and Cultural Pluralism
Famines
Federalism and Center-State Relations
Feminism and Indian Nationalists
Feudalism
Filmīgīt
Film Industry
Finance Commission
Fiscal System and Policy from 1858 to 1947
Fiscal System and Policy since 1952
Fitch, Ralph
Folk Art
Folk Dance
Food Security
Foreign Resources Inflow since 1991
Forster, E. M.
French East India Company
French Impact
Fundamental Rights

G

Galbraith, John Kenneth
Gama, Vasco da
Gandharan Art and Architecture
Gandhi, Indira
Gandhi, Mahatma M. K.
Gandhi, Rajiv
Gandhi, Sonia
Gandhinagar
Gaṇesha
Gat-Tora

Gender and Human Rights
General (National) Elections
Geography
Globalization
Goa
Goddess Images
Gokhale, Gopal Krishna
Government of India Act of 1919
Government of India Act of 1935
Gujarat
Gujral, Inder Kumar
Guptan Empire
Guptan Period Art
Guru Nanak

H

Haq, A. K. Fazlul
Harappa
Hardinge, Lord
Harsha
Hastings, Warren
Health Care
Health Care for Tourists
Hindu Ancestor Rituals
Hindu and Buddhist Thought in Western Philosophy
Hinduism (Dharma)
Hindu Nationalism
Hindu Nationalist Parties
Hindu Tantric Deities
Hindutva and Politics
History and Historiography
Human Development Indicators
Human Rights
Humayun
Hyderabad

I

Indian Institutes of Technology (IITs)
India Office and India Office Library
India's Impact on Western Civilization
Indo–U.S. Relations, Cultural Changes in
Indra
Industrial Change since 1956
Industrial Growth and Diversification
Industrial Labor and Wages, 1800–1947
Industrial Labor Market, Wages and Employment, since
  1950
Industrial Policy since 1956
Indus Valley Civilization
Informal Credit Markets
Information and Other Technology Development
Infrastructure and Transportation, 1857–1947
Infrastructure Development and Government Policy
  since 1950

Insurance Industry
Insurgency and Terrorism
Intellectual Property Rights
Internal Public Debt, Growth and Composition of
International Monetary Fund (IMF), Relations with
Iqbal, Muhammad
Irwin, Lord
Islam
Islam's Impact on India
Israel, Relations with
Ivory Carving

J
Jahangir
Jain and Buddhist Manuscript Painting
Jainism
Jain Sculpture
Jamdani
Jammu and Kashmir
Jammu and Ladakh
Jamshedpur
Japan, Relations with
Jewelry
Jews of India
Jinnah, Mohammad Ali
Jodhpur
Judicial System, Modern

K
Kabir
Kālidāsa
Kāma Sūtra
Kanpur
Karachi
Karaikkāl Ammaiyār
Kargil Conflict, The
Karnataka
Kashmir
Kashmir Painting
Kashmir Shawls
Kayasths
Kerala, Coalition Politics
Kerala, Model of Development
Kerkar, Kesarbai
Khajuraho
Khan, Abdul Ghaffar
Khan, Ali Akbar
Khan, Liaquat Ali
Khan, Vilayat
Khayal
Khusrau, Amir
Kipling, Rudyard
Kīrtana
Krishna in Indian Art

Krishnamurti, Jiddu
Kriti

L
Land Tenure from 1800 to 1947
Land Tenure since 1950
Languages and Scripts
Lansdowne, Lord
Large-scale Industry, 1850–1950
Leaders, Christian
Liberalization, Political Economy of
Linlithgow, Lord
Literature: Modern
Literature: Tamil
Love Stories

M
Macaulay, Thomas Babington
Mādhaviah, A.
Madras
Madurai
Magadha
Mahābhārata
Maharashtra
Maldives and Bhutan, Relations with
Mandal Commission Report
Mangeshkar, Lata
Manipur
Maritime Commerce, 1750–1947
Mauryan Empire
Media
Medical Science Education
Medieval Temple Kingdoms
Meghalaya
Menon, V.K. Krishna
Metalware
Military Interventions in South Asia
Miniatures: Bikaner
Miniatures: Bundi
Miniatures: Central India
Miniatures: Harem Scenes
Miniatures: Kishangarh
Miniatures: Kotah
Miniatures: Marwar and Thikanas
Minto, Lord
Mīrabai
Mizoram
Modern and Contemporary Art
Mohenjo-Daro
Monetary Policy from 1952 to 1991
Monetary Policy since 1991
Money and Credit, 1858–1947
Money and Foreign Exchange Markets
Montagu, Edwin S.

Monuments: Eastern India
Monuments: Mughal
Monuments: Southern India
Monuments: Western India
Morley, John
Mountbatten, Lord
Mughal Painting
Mughal Painting, Later
Music: An Introduction
Music: Karnātak
Music: South India
Muslim Law and Judicial Reform
Muslims
Mutual Funds, Role of
Mysore

N
Nabob Game
Nagas and Nagaland
Naidu, Sarojini
Nainsukh
Naoroji, Dadabhai
Narayan, Jaya Prakash
Narayan, R. K.
Narayanan, K. R.
National Security Decision-Making
Nātya Shāstra
Nehru, Jawaharlal
Nehru, Motilal
Neolithic Period
Nepal
Nepal, Relations with
New Delhi
Nightingale, Florence
Nizam of Hyderabad
Nobili, Robert de
Non-banking Financial Institutions, Growth of
Northeast States, The
Nuclear Programs and Policies
Nuclear Weapons Testing and Development
Nyāya

P
Paithani
Pakistan
Pakistan and India
Palaeolithic Period
Pandit, Vijaya Lakshmi
Pandita Ramabai
Pānini
Pant, Govind Ballabh
Papermaking
Paramilitary Forces and Internal Security
Parsis

Patanjali
Patel, Sardar Vallabhbhai
Patna
Patola
Paul, K. T.
Pension Funds and Social Security
Peshwai and Pentarchy
Pillai, Samuel Vedanayakam
Pingala
Planning Commission
Political System: Cabinet
Political System: Constitution
Political System: Parliament
Political System: President
Political System: Prime Minister
Population, Gender Ratio of
Portuguese in India
Poverty and Inequality
Prasad, Rajendra
Premchand
Presidents of India
Price Movements and Fluctuations since 1860
Prime Ministers of India
Princely States
Private Industrial Sector, Role of
Public Debt of States, since 1950
Public Expenditures
Punjab

Q
Qawwālī

R
Rabban, Joseph
Radhakrishnan, Sarvepalli
Rāga
Rāgamālā
Rahman, Sheikh Mujibur
Rajagopalachari, Chakravarti
Rajneesh, Osho
Rajput (Western, Central, and Hill) Painting
Ramananda
Rāmānuja
Rāmāyaṇa
Rāmāyaṇa and Mahābhārata Paintings
Ranade, Mahadev Govind
Rangōli
Ray, Satyajit
Reading, Lord
Reddi, Muthulakshmi
Reserve Bank of India, Evolution of
Ripon, Lord
Rishi
Rock Art

Roy, Ram Mohan
Rural Credit, Evolution of since 1952
Russia, Relations with

S
Sabhas and Samitis
Saṃskāra
Sānkhya
Sarod
Sassoon, David
Satyagraha
Saving and Investment Trends since 1950
Sayyid Ahmed Khan and the Aligarh Movement
Scheduled Tribes
Science
Scientists of Indian Origin and Their Contributions
Sculpture: Buddhist
Sculpture: Kushana
Sculpture: Mauryan and Shungan
Sculpture and Bronze Images from Kashmir
Secularism
Securities Exchange Board of India (SEBI)
Selected Macroeconomic Models
Shah Bano Case
Shah Jahan
Shankar, Ravi
Shankara
Shiva and Shaivism
Shivaji Bhonsle and heirs
Shiv Sena
Shore, Sir John
Shrauta Sūtras
Shreni
Shulba Sūtras (Vedāngas)
Shyāma Shāstri
Sikh Institutions and Parties
Sikhism
Simla
Sind
Singh, Bhagat
Singh, Maharaja Ranjit
Singh, Manmohan
Singh, Sadhu Sundar
Sirohi School Painting
Sitar
Size and Capital Intensity of Indian Industry since 1950
Small-Scale and Cottage Industry, 1800–1947
Small-Scale Industry, since 1947
Soma
South Asian Association for Regional Cooperation
  (SAARC)
South Asian Economic Cooperation
Southeast Asia, Relations with
Space Program

Sri Lanka
Sri Lanka, Relations with
State Finances since 1952
State Formation
State-Level Performance since Reforms of 1991
Step-Wells of India
Stock Exchange Markets
Strategic Thought
Subbalakshmi Ammal, R.S.
Subbulakshmi, M. S.
Subsidies in the Federal Budget
Sultanate Painting
Sultante-Period Architecture of South Asia

T
Tabla
Tagore, Rabindranath
Tāla
Tanchoi
Tansen
Tantric Buddhist Images
Tapas
Tata, Jamsetji N.
Taxation Policy since 1991 Economic Reforms
Technical Change in Agriculture, 1952–2000
Temple Types (Styles) of India
Textiles: Block-Printed
Textiles: Early Painted and Printed
Textiles: Karuppur
Theater
Theosophical Society
Thumrī
Tibetan Buddhists of India
Tilak, Bal Gangadhar
Trade Liberalization since 1991
Trade Policy, 1800–1947
Tribal Peoples of Eastern India
Tribal Politics
Tripura
Tyāgarāja

U
Underground Economy, Dimensions of
United States, Relations with
Upanishadic Philosophy
Urbanism

V
Vaisheshika
Vajpayee, Atal Bihari
Varanasi
Varuṇa
Vedānga Jyotisha

Vedic Aryan India
Vina
Vishnu and Avatāras
Vishwa Hindu Parishad (VHP)
Vivekananda, Swami

W
Wars, Modern
Wavell, Lord
Weapons Production and Procurement
Wellesley, Richard Colley
Women and Political Power
Women's Education
Women's Indian Association

World Bank (WB), Relations with
World Trade Organization (WTO), Relations with

X
Xavier, Francis

Y
Yajña
Yājnavalkya
Yajur Veda
Yoga

Z
Zoroastrianism

EARLY MARITIME CONTACTS Conventional studies have tended to categorize maritime trade in the Indian Ocean in the pre-colonial period into ethnic networks, such as Roman trade, Arab trade, and European trade in the western Indian Ocean, as well as Indian trade across the Bay of Bengal. The basis for these identities was inevitably the nature of sources available. For example, the first century A.D. text, the *Periplus Maris Erythraei* (Periplus of the Erythraen Sea) provides the most comprehensive account of trade and trading commodities between the Red Sea and the west coast of India. The text itself nowhere refers to "Roman trade," though it does mention a diverse range of communities involved, including the Ichthyophagoi, or coastal fishing communities, the Nabateans, Sabaeans, Homerites, Arabs, and Indians. Nevertheless, in historical writing, references to Roman trade supplying the markets of the Empire with luxury items such as Indian muslin continue.

Contrary to such assumptions, the archaeological data indicate that the initial stages of the maritime system in South Asia may be traced to around 10,000 B.C., when fishing and sailing communities settled in coastal areas and exploited a diverse range of marine resources. These communities formed the bedrock of maritime travel and often combined fishing with trading ventures, especially in regions such as Gujarat, where fishing grounds are located at some distance from the coast.

By the third millennium B.C., these local and regional fishing and sailing circuits had evolved into trade networks between the Harappan settlements on the Makran and Gujarat coasts of the subcontinent and the Persian Gulf, as evident from finds of Harappan ceramics and seals at sites in the Gulf. A triad of names that figures consistently in Mesopotamian texts of the third to second millennium B.C. includes those of Dilmun (the Bahrain archipelago), Magan (the Oman peninsula) and Melukkha (identified with the Harappan settlements). Around the beginning of the common era, this network had expanded to include large parts of the western Indian Ocean extending from the Red Sea to the east coast of India, as described in the *Periplus Maris Erythraei*.

A corresponding network extended across the Bay of Bengal to incorporate large parts of island and mainland Southeast Asia. However, the distribution of a range of ceramics such as the rouletted ware, a fine textured pottery with rouletted decoration, at archaeological sites from lower Bengal to Sri Lanka, the north coasts of Java and Bali, and as far as Vietnam indicates several regional and transoceanic circuits.

The Sassanians ruled Iran and adjacent countries from A.D. 226 to 651 and were active participants in the trade of the Indian Ocean, with Siraf, located in the Persian Gulf, an important center of trade. After a break in settlement, Siraf reemerged as a major center around A.D. 700 and, together with Sohar, its location close to the mouth of the Gulf on the coast of Oman enabled it to participate in a regional trade network in the ninth to eleventh centuries A.D. that extended to settlements in the Indus delta, such as Banbhore, several centers along the west coast of India, and Mantai on the north coast of Sri Lanka. One of the characteristic features of maritime trade from the ninth and tenth centuries onward was the location of markets in fortified settlements along the Indian Ocean littoral, as in the interior. Rules governing the payment of taxes and regulating the functioning of the markets were often inscribed on copper plates and provide useful insights into the organization of the trade network.

Trade and Exchange

The commodities involved in maritime trade in the Indian Ocean may be divided into various broad categories, such as aromatics, medicines, dyes and spices; foodstuffs, wood, and textiles; gems and ornaments; metals; and plant and animal products. These categories find mention in a range of textual sources from the first-century *Periplus Maris Erythraei* to the Geniza documents of the eleventh to thirteenth centuries, Chinese accounts, and medieval Arab writings.

Textiles were a major commodity involved in the Indian Ocean trade and included a wide range, from coarse cottons to fine silks and from dyed cloth to embroidered material. Furniture in Asia consisted mostly of various types of carpets, cushions, canopies and draperies—all produced by the textile industry. The value attributed to these varied not only temporally but also spatially in the different regions of the Indian Ocean littoral. It is suggested that textiles in Southeast Asia were recognized as a means of storing wealth, whereas in India domestic surplus income was traditionally stored in the form of gold and silver jewelry.

Gold, silver, and copper were the main traded metals, exchanged both as currency and bullion. Though sources of copper and lead are available in the subcontinent, the *Periplus* refers to the import of copper, tin, and lead to Kane, Barygaza, and Muziris on the west coast. This is repeated in the Geniza documents, which refer to trade in metals from south India and the regular export of iron and steel, brass, and bronze vessels. In return, copper, tin, and bronze vessels were imported into the south, where new ones were created and old ones repaired.

These commodities were exchanged through a complex diversity of transactions including gifts, barter, and trade. There are several references in the *Periplus* to presents given to the elite—for example, wine and grain in considerable quantity imported into the region of the Barbaroi in east Africa was "not for trade but as an expenditure for the good will of the Barbaroi." Similarly, in the region of Barygaza, or Bharuch, on the west coast of India, the king imported slave musicians, beautiful girls as concubines, fine wine, expensive clothing with no adornment, and choice unguent.

In addition to these gifts, the elite constantly tried to control trade. The *Periplus* refers to a customs officer and a centurion being dispatched to the harbor of Leuke Kome on the east coast of the Red Sea. The island of Socotra at the mouth of the Red Sea was under the control of the king of the frankincense-bearing land, who had leased it out; the island was hence under guard. Somewhat later in the text, there is reference to the harbor of Moscha Limen in the region of Omana, where frankincense was guarded by some power of the gods.

Organization of Trade

In the early centuries of the common era, Buddhist texts and inscriptions recording donations at early Buddhist monastic sites provide data on the organization of trading activity into guilds, in addition to the presence of individual merchants. The state no doubt derived revenue from taxing trade transactions at entry points to cities and towns. From the middle of the first millennium A.D. there are several instances of these taxes being transferred to religious establishments. The charter of Visnusena, dated to A.D. 592 from Lohata in the Gujarat-Kathiawar region, provides a detailed list of seventy-two trade regulations or customary laws to be followed by the "community of merchants" (*vaniggrama*) established in the region. For example, it is specified that merchants staying away for a year were not required to pay an entrance fee on their return. Other clauses specify duties that were to be paid. A boat full of vessels had to pay twelve silver coins, but if the vessels were for a religious purpose, then it was only one and a quarter silver coins. In the case of a boat carrying paddy, it was half this amount. Other commodities mentioned as being carried on boats included dried ginger sticks and bamboo.

From the ninth to the mid-fourteenth centuries, two of the merchant guilds that dominated economic transactions in south India were the Manigramam and the Ayyavole. Associated with these two merchant guilds were associations of craftsmen such as weavers, basket makers, potters, and leather workers. Though these two guilds originated independently, from the mid-thirteenth century onward, the Ayyavole association became so powerful that the Manigramam functioned in a subordinate capacity. Not only did these merchant associations develop powerful economic networks, they also employed private armies.

The range of their operations extended well beyond the boundaries of the Indian subcontinent into Southeast Asia. Several clusters of Tamil inscriptions have been found on the eastern fringes of the Indian Ocean from Burma to Sumatra. In contrast, the major states of Java and Bali reacted somewhat differently to the advent of Indian merchant groups. In the tenth century, local versions of these merchant guilds termed the *banigrama* appeared in the north coast ports of both the islands. While some foreign merchants may have been included in these groups, these appear largely as indigenous organizations associated with the local economic networks as tax-farmers.

Around the turn of the second millennium, there was increasing evidence of fortified settlements in coastal areas and of attempts by the state and religious institutions to localize the sale and exchange of goods, either within the fortified precincts or in the vicinity of a Hindu temple. The tenth-century Siyadoni inscription from Gujarat records donations made to a temple of the god Vishnu between 903 and 968 by merchants and artisans and the endowment of shops in the textile market, main market, and so on.

Along the Konkan coast, there are references to the fortified market center of Balipattana. The Kharepatan plates of Rattaraja, dated to A.D. 1008, lists gifts to the temple of Avvesvara built by Rattaraja's father and situated inside the fortifications. Also located within the fortifications were settlements of female attendants, oilmen, gardeners, potters and washermen, and also some land.

Farther south is the Piranmalai inscription of the thirteenth century from the Sokkanatha temple, built like a fortress. The importance of the temple lay in its strategic location astride routes crossing the southern part of the peninsula from the Malabar coast to the east. The record lists a range of commodities on which a tax was levied for the benefit of the temple. These included cotton, yarn, thick cloth, thin cloth, and thread.

Aggression and Sea Battles versus Ritual and Ceremony

The establishment of fortified coastal settlements is matched by references to settlements across the Bay of Bengal. In one of his inscriptions dated A.D. 1025, Rajendra Chola enumerates thirteen port cities of island Southeast Asia and the Nicobar islands, which were raided by the South Indian maritime force. Sastri used this reference to conclude that the Chola navy had conquered parts of the Malay Peninsula and Sumatra, and this is a trend found in subsequent writings.

These references should, however, be reexamined within the overall developments in peninsular India and the increasing emphasis on the cult of the hero. Elaborately carved memorial stones have been found extensively in peninsular India, dating from the first to the twelfth centuries. These provide abundant information on the cult of the hero and are also significant indicators of sea battles, especially those from the region of Goa dating to the period of the Kadambas (950–1270). From the eleventh century onward, representations on memorial stones depict planked vessels, sharp-ended with a long projecting bow strongly raked, in addition to canoe-shaped craft.

In contrast to this emphasis on sea battles and aggression along the west coast are the iconographic illustrations from Orissa and Bengal. A ceremonial barge is prominently depicted on the eleventh-century Jagannatha temple at Puri on the Orissa coast, stressing the ritual and ceremonial aspects of the boat. It is evident that several

networks overlapped in the Indian Ocean in the ancient period and brought together interest groups ranging from boat-building communities to religious functionaries, traders as well as armed groups. As the focus shifts from national histories to maritime history, researchers are only now unraveling the intertwined history of these communities.

Himanshu Prabha Ray

See also **Chola Dynasty**

BIBLIOGRAPHY

Abraham, Meera. *Two Medieval Merchant Guilds of South India.* Delhi: Manohar, 1988.
Casson, Lionel. *The Periplus Maris Erythraei.* Princeton, N.J.: Princeton University Press, 1989.
Christie, Jan Wisseman. "Asian Sea Trade between the Tenth and Thirteenth Centuries and Its Impact on the States of Java and Bali." In *Archaeology of Seafaring: The Indian Ocean in the Ancient Period,* edited by Himanshu Prabha Ray. Delhi: Indian Council of Historical Research Monograph Series I, 1999.
Deloche, Jean. "Iconographic Evidence on the Development of Boat and Ship Structures in India (2nd century BC–15th century AD)." In *Tradition and Archaeology: Early Maritime Contacts in the Indian Ocean,* edited by Himanshu Prabha Ray and Jean-François Salles. Delhi: Manohar Publishers, 1996.
Jain, V. K. *Trade and Traders in Western India (AD 1000–1300).* Delhi: Munshiram Manoharlal Publishers, 1990.
Mirashi, Vasudev Vishnu, ed. *Inscriptions of the Silaharas.* Delhi: Archaeological Survey of India, 1977.
Ray, Himanshu Prabha. *The Winds of Change: Buddhism and the Maritime Links of Early South Asia.* Delhi: Oxford University Press, 1994.
———. *The Archaeology of Seafaring in Ancient South Asia.* Cambridge, U.K.: Cambridge University Press, 2003.
Sastri, K. A. Nilakantha. *The Colas.* Chennai: University of Madras, 1955.
Spencer, George Woolley. *Royal Leadership and Imperial Conquest in Medieval South India: The Naval Expedition of Rajendra Chola I, c. 1025 AD.* Ann Arbor, Mich.: University Microfilms, 1968.
Tampoe, M. *Maritime Trade between China and the West.* Oxford: BAR International Series 555, 1989.

EAST INDIA COMPANY. *See* **British East India Company Raj.**

EAST PAKISTAN. *See* **Bangladesh; Pakistan and India.**

ECONOMIC BURDEN OF DEFENSE The question of "how much is enough" when addressed to estimating the optimal defense expenditure of nations

Border Security Force Patrolling the Indo-Pakistan Border in Punjab. A large part of the defense budget is spent on maintaining the Indo-Pakistan Border Fencing. INDIA TODAY.

yields no easy answers. Peace and disarmament lobbies argue that outlays on defense and social welfare by the state embody zero sum games; increases therefore in defense expenditure must inevitably lead to reductions in social welfare, and vice versa. This is a maximalist position, since the maintenance of armed forces and paramilitary units is essentially intended to ensure national security. Modern defense forces should be able to deter inimical nations from eroding a state's territorial integrity or abridging its national sovereignty. A new dimension to the need for greater defense expenditure to protect India from disruption is added by the increasing dangers arising from the menace of international terrorism.

India's Defense Budget in Context

Allocations for the defense budget in India are made in terms of "current rupees," which is the usual practice followed across the world. For comparative purposes and for long-term planning, defense expenditure can be designated in terms of "constant rupees," which has the advantage of discounting the inflationary factor. Assessing defense expenditure in "real terms" allows other deflators to be applied, like currency fluctuations that would allow the actual value of the defense rupee to be informed. For making comparisons between the economic burdens on defense accepted by different nations, some generally accepted means of comparison are possible, notably by denoting defense expenditure as a percentage of either the gross domestic product (GDP) or the central government expenditure (CGE). The Indian Constitution envisages the legislative, administrative, and financial control over the armed forces in India vesting in the central government; thus, including therein expenditures by the state governments for comparison purposes is inappropriate, although some analysts in India have found this useful. There are other parameters that can be used to express the defense burden, like its per capita amount or the size of the armed forces in relation to the population of the country, but they are not helpful for making comparative studies.

Characteristics of the Indian defense budget. The Indian government deprecates its need to incur expenditure on defense by rather self-consciously suggesting that it is only providing the minimum irreducible outlays required. The official explanations are: "The endeavour of defence planners is to balance the minimum maintenance requirements of defence forces and the need to modernize them, without unduly straining the economy" (Ministry of Defence, Annual Report, 1997–1998, p. 12); and "Given India's size and security concerns, the outlay on Defence, assessed either as a percentage of the total Central Government expenditure or of the Gross Domestic Product, continues to be one of the lowest among neighbouring countries" (Ministry of Defence, Annual Report, 1999, p. 16).

India's defense expenditure since the 1960s does not reveal any pattern of incremental growth, but rather suggests that periodic increases have been reactive to external conflicts and internal dynamics. The most important external factors were the wars that India fought with China and Pakistan: the Sino-Indian border conflict (October 1962); the Second Indo-Pak War (September 1965, preceded by the Kutch operations in April 1965), the Third Indo-Pak War (December 1971), leading to the creation of Bangladesh; and the Kargil conflict (May–July 1999). The yearlong Kashmir Line of Control buildup and border confrontation between India and Pakistan (December 2001–October 2002) also led to dramatic accretions in the defense budget. These periodic additions to India's defense budget occurred in the years following these conflicts, and relected high costs to replace lost equipment, make up for perceived deficiencies in weapon systems, and heighten defense preparedness. The major internal factors bringing dramatic increases in defense allocations were required to implement the awards of the Pay Commissions of 1974, 1986, and 1996.

Personnel and personnel-related military costs have radically increased over the years due to the generosity of successive Indian Pay Commissions. Recruiting suitable young persons for the armed forces in India has become progressively more difficult for various reasons, primarily the availability of attractive job opportunities in civil avocations and the disincentives of hard living conditions and inherent risks in the military profession. At the same time, the high value and complexity of modern weapon systems makes it imperative for the armed forces to recruit a fair share of the available talent by offering larger compensations and more attractive perquisites; these have added to manpower costs that approximated over 40 percent of the defense budget in India. Military pensions have also increased exponentially over the years due to the cumulative effects of the Pay Commission awards and the rapidly growing longevity of pensioners due to improved health conditions in India. Since 1984–1985, military pensions have been debited to civil estimates, but they now amount to around 20 percent of defense expenditure.

India's major weapon systems were long of Soviet origin, available at "political prices," and still comprise some 70 percent of the weapons in the armed forces. Over the years, the spares and ancillaries needed to keep these systems operational have progressively become more difficult to procure, and also much more expensive, as they are now only available at market prices. India is now diversifying its sources for procuring military supplies by turning to Western countries, and increasingly to Israel. These procurements, available only at commercial and market prices, add considerably to defense costs and spending.

Factors Influencing Defense Allocations

Defense expenditure in India is predicated on the threat perceptions of its strategic elite, who influence the decision-making process. These special interest groups include the three Services Headquarters (Ministry of Defence, Ministry of Finance, Finance Division of the Ministry of Defence), the Standing Committee of the Parliament on Defence, and the political parties. Other, but less significant, groups are the voters, foreign arms suppliers, and domestic contractors supplying defense requirements. There are, moreover, a steadily growing number of retired civil and military officials, media personalities, and academics who are active in the seminar circuit, and in print or electronic media. The official articulation of India's national security threats emphasizes its external dimensions and the dangers emanating from its strategic location in the northern Indian Ocean littoral, as well as its proximity to the volatile Gulf, Central Asian, and Southeast Asian regions. But the primary military threat is seen to arise from Pakistan, with its support of Islamic militancy and terrorism in Kashmir, and from China.

A cross-border security threat is increasingly perceived, especially by the nongovernmental components of India's strategic elite, as emanating from nonmilitary sources of insecurity, including international terrorism, arms and drug smuggling, organized crime, and money laundering, apart from forced migration and environmental decay. These threats require regional and global solutions. Furthermore, major threats to Indian security arise from internal factors, including ethno-nationalist upsurges, communal and caste conflicts, and the growing menace of indigenous extremist movements that have spread across several parts of the country.

Cumulatively, these threat perceptions guide the defense planning process. Its basic determinants have been identified to be the need for a two-front defense to secure the borders with Pakistan and China; the need to acquire an independent deterrent capability, since it runs counter to India's foreign policy to join any military alliance or strategic grouping; the inevitability of large-scale involvement by the armed forces in internal security functions; and India's strategic interests in the northern Indian Ocean, its Exclusive Economic Zone, and defending its island territories, highlighting its need for a blue-water navy.

Categorization of Indian defense budget. Expenditure estimates in the defense budget are classified under five major demands; four are on the revenue account (for the army, navy, air force, and ordnance factories), and the fifth on capital account. Military expenditures can be divided into six broad categories: pay and allowances of the personnel of the armed forces; payments to industrial establishments employed by stores, depots, and factories; transportation and miscellaneous expenditure; stores purchases; works expenditure; and capital outlays such as capital works, purchase of vessels, plants, and machinery.

The distinction made between revenue and capital expenditure in the Indian defense budget is an inherited British practice, which is not very satisfactory. In theory, revenue expenditure must not result in creating any permanent assets. Capital outlays are expended on acquiring lands, buildings, and machinery. This distinction is artificial, as expenditures on small and temporary buildings were classified under the revenue head. But it also included outlays on aircraft, aero-engines, and the naval fleet, which were anomalous. After 1987–1988, these latter outlays were classified under the capital head, which also includes expenditure on heavy and medium vehicles, equipment, and buildings that have a value of more than 200,000 rupees and a life of more than seven years.

Yet another manner of classifying the defense budget is to differentiate between outlays on personnel and personnel-related costs, maintenance costs, and modernization costs. This classification disaggregates the defense expenditure in terms of its major functions, allowing its utilization for comparative purposes and more purposeful orientation. The empirical experience regarding the utilization of the Indian budget reveals that any reduction therein or any unforeseen expenditure requiring accommodation in the defense budget results in a negative effect on the modernization effort. (Personnel costs are sacrosanct and remain unaffected.) This leads to a diminution in the operational capabilities of the Indian armed forces, due to weapons systems becoming obsolete, the unavailability of essential equipment due to the shortages of spares and ancillaries, and inadequate training of the forces.

Can economy and efficiency be achieved in the defense budget? The answer to the above question must be unequivocally affirmative. The major reasons given for increasing India's defense budget include such arguments as: no real increase in defense outlays has

occurred if inflationary factors over the years are discounted; allocations made to the army might have increased, but those for the navy and air force have remained almost static; capital outlays of around 30 percent of the budget are inadequate to cater to even high-priority modernization programs; and the financial implications of the Pay Commission reports are not being configured into the defense budgets. Moreover, a recurring complaint is that the defense plan is never finalized in time because of interminable bureaucratic delays, which disrupt the reequipment plans of the three services, adding to the cost of these acquisitions and ultimately to the defense burden.

There are large areas, however, where economies can easily be effected in defense expenditure that could, paradoxically, also improve efficiency in the armed forces. These include: the scaling down of authorized unit holdings of tanks, heavy vehicles, and other equipment; reducing the consumption of fuel, oil, and lubricants by imposing quantitative restrictions on their issue; renovating the ordnance depots and achieving better inventory management in stores holdings; and effecting greater capacity utilization in the ordnance factories and defense public sector undertakings. More radical steps could also be taken to reduce defense expenditure, such as reviewing the manpower holdings of the armed forces and locating areas of wasteful use. This could also be achieved by integrating similar administrative functions that are being separately performed by the three services headquarters, such as the procurement of stores. The possibility of using civilians in place of uniformed personnel could also be accelerated for tasks like the manning of general and logistics establishments. Civilian personnel may be employed at less than half the cost of uniformed personnel in terms of compensation and perquisites. A more professional system for the procurement of indigenous stores or acquiring weapon systems from abroad could also ensure economies. Large economies can thus be effected in defense expenditure without jeopardizing the operational efficiency of the armed forces.

Effect of nuclearization. The nuclearization of India has not led to any reduction in defense expenditure, though India's bomb protagonists had earlier argued that this would lead to a reduction in outlays on conventional weaponry. This reduction has not happened; instead, India's defense expenditure has almost doubled since the nuclear tests in May 1998. India's commitment in its Nuclear Doctrine to deploying the strategic triad of land-based missiles, long-range bombers, and submarine-launched missiles, apart from establishing the requisite command and control arrangements, and early warning systems to achieve assured second-strike capability, will add considerably to the defense budget. The prevailing thesis is that outlays on conventional forces will simultaneously have to be increased to "raise the nuclear threshold," so that conditions are not created that predicate the early use of nuclear weapons in any conflict.

Interservice rivalries also increase expenditures, since each service chief would like to be remembered for the perquisites he wrested for his own service and the weapon systems acquired during his tenure. Establishing the strategic triad has much to do, therefore, with satisfying the aspirations of the army, air force, and navy to acquire their individual nuclear forces. For this reason it seems inevitable that expenditure on nuclear weapons and their delivery systems will grow over time, as will the outlays on conventional forces. Therefore, no economies will be possible in the allocations made for defense.

Does defense expenditure strain the Indian economy? As a percentage of the GDP, the defense budget hovers between 2 and 3 percent, and between 13 and 16 percent of the CGE. This is by no means an insupportable economic burden for India. Nonetheless, it must be remembered that between a third and a fourth of India's population (approximately 300 million) live below the poverty line and are deprived of the most basic needs for food, housing, education, and public health. Viewed from this perspective, defense expenditure, which has been steadily rising, preempts funds required for meeting the basic needs of India's poor, representing significant lost opportunity costs.

P. R. Chari

See also **Armed Forces; Wars, Modern**

BIBLIOGRAPHY

Defence Services Estimates, 2003–2004. New Delhi: Government of India, 2003.
Kargil Committee Report, published as *From Surprise to Reckoning.* New Delhi: SAGE Publications, 2000.
Ministry of Defence. *Annual Report, 1999–2000.* New Delhi: Government of India, 2000.
Ministry of Defence. *Annual Report, 2002–2003.* New Delhi: Government of India, 2003.

SECONDARY SOURCES

Chari, P. R. "Defense Expenditure in India: Can It Be Reduced?" In *Defence Expenditure in South Asia: India and Pakistan.* RCSS Policy Studies 12. Colombo: Regional Centre for Policy Studies, 2000.
Ghosh, A. K. *India's Defence Budget and Expenditure Management in a Wider Context.* New Delhi: Lancer, 1996.
Rao, P. V. R. *Defense without Drift.* Mumbai: Popular Prakashan, 1970.
Singh, Jasjit. *India's Defense Spending: Assessing Future Needs.* New Delhi: Knowledge World, 2000.

Thomas, Raju G. C. *The Defense of India: A Budgetary Perspective of Strategy and Politics.* Delhi: Macmillan, 1978.

ECONOMIC DEVELOPMENT, IMPORTANCE OF INSTITUTIONS IN AND SOCIAL ASPECTS OF

A recent major advance in the analysis of economic development is the recognition of the importance of institutions. This has moved us beyond sterile debates such as whether the economy should be left to the market or should be thought of as the responsibility of government. It is now recognized that government and markets are not alternatives between which we choose, but that government—in particular, good governance—is a prerequisite for the market to function effectively; and that, for an economy to progress, it may not be enough to raise savings and investment rates, improve trade policy, and control fiscal deficits if we do not have good institutions.

One has to be careful about this kind of analysis because "institution" is not a well-defined term. In this article, "institutions" will refer to the social and political settings within which the economy is embedded. Thus the word will encompass not only the structure of government and its legal institutions but also the cultural and social norms within which the human beings of a nation function, and which can be even more important than the formally enacted laws of a nation.

The significance of institutions thus defined is easy to see. Trade, exchange, investment, and business almost always involve transactions performed over time. You supply a commodity today, and your trading partner will pay for it tomorrow or may have paid for it yesterday. You, as the owner of an enterprise, send a salesperson to market your good in distant lands, and the salesperson is expected to pay you back on his or her return. Even when you take a taxi, you usually pay after you have taken the ride. If traders and ordinary citizens did not feel confident that, after they had done their share, their trading partners or business associates would fulfill their obligations, they would refuse to do business or make investments. In such a nation, the market would be stunted and development would remain a distant dream.

If, on the other hand, a society's laws are effective, and contracts are enforced by the state without individuals having to incur too large a cost, then trade, business, and investment will grow, leading to greater economic prosperity. Even in the absence of law enforcement, if a nation's citizens are naturally trusting of one another, or its social norms are such that individuals keep their promises, then this society could also progress. Indeed, a disposition toward keeping one's promise could be even

Mother and Children in Front of Public Health Poster. Mother and her children front of sign proclaiming, "you can save your beloved child's life by timely inoculation against fatal diseases." The consistent underfunding of public health services by both central and state governments, which share responsibility for the provision and financing of health care, remains a major problem in India—with its infant and child mortality rates among the highest in the world. POPULATION COUNCIL.

better than the case in which contracts are enforced by formal legal machinery, which requires costly courts and enforcement bureaucracies.

One of the basic premises on which a market economy is founded is the principle of free contract. The principle asserts that adults who voluntarily agree to a contract, which has no negative impact on others, should not have the contract nullified by the government and, in an ideal situation, should be able to seek governmental or societal help to prevent anyone from reneging on the contract. A major role of institutions is to provide a setting in which the principle of free contract is upheld.

For India, it can be argued that the roots of its prolonged economic stagnation (and the optimism observed in recent years) cannot be fully understood if one ignores such variables as the social norms, collective beliefs, and the structure of polity and law—basically, the range of

institutions. An understanding of the role of culture and institutions in the life of a nation can help in the design of better and more appropriate economic policy. In the case of Russia, for example, it is now recognized that standard economic policies designed to speed transition did poorly because they amounted to changes that Russian society was not prepared to accept; the requisite culture and institutions for the market economy were not in place. The failure to adopt recommended economic policies (as in Tanzania or Venezuela), or the abortion of economic polices due to social instability (as in Indonesia or Yugoslavia), is often caused by a lack of understanding of the social and political context in which the policies were implemented.

It is also arguable that a nation's collective beliefs shape what is politically and economically feasible. In the case of independent India, the early economic policies

Prem Chand Gupta, Minister for Company Affairs. Gupta at opening session of the First National Conference on Corporate Governance Trends, 18 October 2004. Corporate governance is increasingly recognized as an important aspect of sustainable economic growth, and the government in New Delhi, in partnership with several Indian institutions, has established the National Foundation for Corporate Governance (NFCG) to lead the way. INDIA TODAY.

were marked by deep mistrust of the market and big business. In a democracy, one cannot simply overrule such popularly held views, and it is not surprising that until quite recently, India remained burdened by a gargantuan bureaucracy appointed to plan and control the economy but which in reality had become the cause of India's stagnation.

Centuries earlier, the British had come to India not to rule but to trade. The initial contact that India had with Britain was not with the Crown but with one of the earliest multinational corporations of the world, the British East India Company. Later, British commercial interests merged with imperial conquests that proved more lucrative, and gradually, without much serious resistance, a huge subcontinent passed into the control of the British Empire, the center of which was thousands of miles removed from South Asia. Thenceforth, the Indians would be relieved of their resources not only through asymmetric trade and currency exchange, but also by

taxation and state-sponsored extortion. Fears of multinationals and a general mistrust of business and trade were soon deeply etched into India's collective memory. Independent India would design its economic policy in the shadow of this memory. And it is not surprising that it took decades of debate and ultimately the shock of recession in the early 1990s to shake the country out of its policy stupor.

India's policy was born out of two conflicting systems of beliefs and ideas—those of Mahatma Gandhi and Jawaharlal Nehru—held together precariously, their differences often denied. The differences had roots that go back to well before 1947. Nehru's education at Harrow and Cambridge helped forge his commitment to Fabian socialism; Gandhi's ideas emerged from his grassroots struggles and his experiments in alternative communal village (ashram) lifestyles. The economic policies they envisaged for India were very different. In the 1930s and even the early 1940s, Nehru was enamored of Karl Marx and

V. I. Lenin (though not of Russian Communism), referring to their works repeatedly in his diary and in letters to friends. He had shed his Marxism-Leninism, and even socialism, by the time India attained independence, but his faith in planning, heavy industry, modern science and technology would persist. Along with Prasanta Mahalanobis, he would try to give shape to those ideas in the form of what came to be called the Mahalanobis-Nehru strategy of development. Gandhi's vision, on the other hand, was deeply rooted in rural hand labor, primarily cotton spinning and weaving, and the revitalization of India's village handicrafts.

The actual policy regime that India followed in its early days of independence was a mixture of these two competing institutional visions. A Soviet-style planning system was developed, but without the state having a monopoly of control over resources. Capitalism was allowed to flourish, but a large bureaucracy was nurtured. Huge investments were made in basic industries, but at the same time, several sectors were protected as belonging to the small-scale "Gandhian" sector. Capitalism was criticized, but it was at the same time relied upon. Socialism was never practiced, but the rhetoric of socialism was constantly reiterated. A burgeoning bureaucracy became the surrogate for socialism.

Advisers from Washington and many economists recommend that Third World nations must have democracy and that they must open up their economy and privatize, oblivious of the fact that to ask for a democracy and then to insist what the democracy should choose could amount to a contradiction. Since most developing countries are not democracies they did not face the problem, but India did. Once people's opinion had been shaped (and Nehru was instrumental in this), there was no way that policies could be easily dictated to them. Opinion would have to be molded before major policy shifts were possible.

Institutional changes are probably the hardest policies to effect. When India's reforms started in 1991, they began with standard economic policies. Thus ceilings on import tariffs were first brought down to 150 percent, and thereafter reduced steadily, virtually every year. The industrial licensing system was dismantled, fiscal deficits were curtailed, and controls on foreign exchange transactions were eased. Economic reforms, however, have not been able to alter India's legal system and other institutions.

Consider India's labor laws, especially those enshrined in the Industrial Disputes Act of 1947. This law was a direct outcome of India's mistrust of the market and a result of its own historical experience. When can a worker be fired, under what conditions can workers be retrenched, when can a firm be closed down? These were all matters that were written down as law, leaving very little room for the principle of free contract by which workers and employers could use their own judgment, bargaining power, and information about their specific industries to reach independent agreements. This has now become a handicap. A fashion industry with variable demands may want to pay its workers more than the "market" but retain the freedom to close down its operations at short notice. The workers themselves may agree to such terms, but Indian law makes such a contract difficult to uphold, thereby having a dampening affect on the demand for labor, and thereby holding wages down. Clearly, in the next generations of reforms, India will need to take on these institutional matters, amending many of its labor laws, rent control laws, and contract legislation, and reducing delays in its courts and the bureaucracy. Such reforms could bolster economic growth, even without raising investment and savings or reducing the fiscal deficit.

There is another class of policies, which only partly entail institutional change, but which should not be omitted from a discussion of development policy. This is what Jean Drèze and Amartya Sen broadly define as "social opportunity." In order to be able to partake in market activities, individuals need a minimal amount of education (and what constitutes "minimal" is steadily increasing in today's world of advanced technology) and to be in reasonably good health. Government has a major responsibility in ensuring that people are able to have access to basic health care and education. These are domains in which markets function poorly. In some sense, these are the prerequisites for the market to function well, rather than being what the market can deliver on its own. Hence, along with the role of providing good governance and better laws, a government has the responsibility to provide certain basic needs of its population, especially its poor, who are unable to marshal these for themselves.

Kaushik Basu

BIBLIOGRAPHY

Basu, Kaushik. *Prelude to Political Economy: A Study of the Social and Political Foundations of Economics.* Oxford and New York: Oxford University Press, 2000.

Basu, Kaushik, ed. *India's Emerging Economy: Performance and Prospects in the 1990s and Beyond.* Cambridge, Mass.: MIT Press, 2004.

Clifford, Mark. *Troubled Tiger.* London: M. E. Sharpe, 1994.

Drèze, Jean, and Amartya Sen. *India: Economic Development and Social Opportunity.* Oxford: Oxford University Press, 1995.

Granovetter, Mark. "Economic Action and Social Structure: The Problem of Embeddedness." *American Journal of Sociology* 91 (1985): 481–510.

North, Douglass. *Institutions, Institutional Change, and Economic Performance.* Cambridge, U. K.: Cambridge University Press, 1990.

Platteau, Jean-Philippe. *Institutions, Social Norms, and Economic Development.* Amsterdam: Harwood Academic Publishers. 2000.

Wolpert, Stanley. *Nehru: A Tryst with Destiny.* Oxford: Oxford University Press, 1996.

ECONOMIC POLICY AND CHANGE, 1800–1947

India, by the end of the eighteenth century, had attained a high degree of development not only in agriculture but also in a wide variety of industries. Spinning and weaving remained the major industries, but iron manufacture, shipbuilding, and several other industries were also flourishing by 1800. India produced manufactured goods not only for home consumption but also for export.

However, by about 1858, there was a marked decline in the output of the manufactures. In 1880 the Famine Commission noted that agriculture formed almost the sole occupation of the mass of the population, and that any remedy for India's predicament must include the introduction of diversity of occupations. The agricultural sector by 1881 employed more than 70 percent of the male working force; this proportion did not change until 1931. Employment in manufacturing declined from about 25 to 30 percent of the workforce in 1800 to 18 percent in 1881, and further to 15 percent in 1931. Varying estimates of per capita income from 1850 to 1900 show that the average annual per capita income did not change much during 1867 to 1882, then declined somewhat by 1900. On the basis of the most reliable estimate for the years 1900 to 1947, there was an increase of about 12 percent in per capita income during this period.

According to Simon Kuznets, et al. (1955), international differences in per capita income were not significant by about 1800. Colin Clark's estimate (1957) of the per capita income of the United Kingdom, in international units, was 378 in 1688. India's per capita income for that year was probably not different from that of the United Kingdom. Even assuming that India's per capita income was 25 percent lower than that of the United Kingdom, it could not have been less than 284 in international units. India's per capita income was about 200 in international units in 1925–1929, according to Clark. By these estimates, India's per capita income declined by about 30 percent between 1688 and 1925–1929. The decline probably was much greater. All the available data suggest that India passed through a phase of economic stagnation, or even decline, for the 150 years before independence.

Aspects of Economic Policies

Alexander Gerschenkron's research suggests that, during the period from 1800 to 1914, the role of the state in economic development was an increasing function of the relative backwardness of a country, on the basis of the experience of France, Germany, and Tsarist Russia. In India, the state was not only passive but even inimical to development. However, it did create important prerequisites for development. It brought about political and administrative unity and established an administrative, legal, and judicial system. It developed the railways and communications and introduced modern education. In spite of these real achievements, its policies not only lacked an orientation toward development but were such as to retard economic progress. The capacity of Indian farmers to improve the productivity of land was hampered by excessive and uncertain land taxes. These excessive land taxes would not have brought about the deterioration of agriculture if a part of them had been spent in improving agricultural techniques, as in Japan. Nor were these tax receipts used for starting an iron and steel industry to provide inputs for railways, which would have reduced the need for imports. The development linkages of iron and steel would have stimulated industrial developments in general; the building of railways produced a great momentum to industrialization in Europe, Japan, and the United States. Far from fostering an iron and steel industry, the state prevented Indians from starting one; Indian entrepreneur J. N. Tata was denied permission to manufacture iron in the central provinces in the 1880s.

Land revenue financed the export of capital to the United Kingdom for the payment of home charges (which included the expenses of the India office in London, and other commitments of the British government of India to England), interest on and repayment of avoidable and unproductive foreign debt, and some private remittances. The average annual level of this economic drain, on a conservative estimate, was about 2 to 3 percent of national income from 1800 to 1947. So India had to generate an export surplus of this magnitude. Thus, if the economic drain were excluded, India had a surplus on government as well as on external trade account. These surpluses could have been used for capital formation in India; they were actually used for the economic development of the United Kingdom.

British commercial policies were such as to adversely affect Indian exports, particularly textiles. From 1800 to 1850, there was in force an elaborate network of mercantilist provisions designed to aid British textiles, which penalized Indian textiles and industrial products in British markets, in foreign markets, and even in Indian markets. Further, Indian shipping was hampered by the policy of not permitting Indian ships to participate in the trade between the United Kingdom and India. Even the government stores' purchase policy discriminated against Indian industries, to the advantage of manufacturers in the United Kingdom. British industries, particularly the textiles industry, developed as a result of this protectionist policy, particularly against Indian imports, until 1858. Though all contemporary advanced countries protected their industries during the nineteenth century, India was unable to follow suit. Consequently, India's manufacturing sector experienced a significant decline.

The British government's policy did change after World War I, with the adoption of discriminating protection to Indian industries; government purchasing procedures too were reorganized to allow potential Indian suppliers to bid on equal terms with British suppliers. However, the shift in policy was piecemeal. Tariff protection was granted only to existing industries; there was no provision for new industries such as chemicals and machine tools. Furthermore, the shift came when the major railway construction was already completed. Despite such halting tariff protection, India was able to develop industries that included steel, cement, sugar, matches, and textiles.

Urgency of Planned Process of Development

Because of what has been described as a period of arrested economic development from 1800 to 1947, India faced tremendous problems of dire poverty, unemployment, and acute economic backwardness at the time of independence. Among the fifty-five countries for which the United Nations published per capita income data for 1952–1954, India's per capita income was one of the lowest. All these problems were aggravated by its large population, increasing at the rate of 2 percent per annum.

If a social catastrophe were to be avoided, India had to accomplish in a few decades the degree of economic development that had taken other countries more than a century. Under the circumstances, it was clear to the Indian leadership, even before independence, that there was an urgent need for initiating a planned process of development. In fact, the president of the Congress Party appointed a National Planning Committee in 1938 to create a program for planned development. The interrupted work of the committee was taken up by the Planning Commission of the Government of India in 1950. The era of planning thus began with the first Five-Year Plan (1951–1956) and still continues.

Vinayak Bhatt

See also **British Crown Raj; Land Tenure from 1800 to 1947; Maritime Commerce, 1750–1947; Trade Policy, 1800–1947**

BIBLIOGRAPHY

Bhatt, V. V. *Aspects of Economic Change and Policy in India 1800–1960.* Bombay: Allied Publishers, 1963.

Clark, Colin. *The Conditions of Economic Progress.* 3rd ed. London: Macmillan, 1957.
Dutt, Ramesh. *The Economic History of India in the Victorian Age.* 6th ed. London: Routledge and Kegan Paul, 1950.
———. *The Economic History of India under Early British Rule.* 7th ed. London: Routledge and Kegan Paul, 1950.
Gerschenkron, Alexander. *Economic Backwardness in Historical Perspective.* Cambridge, Mass.: Harvard University Press, 1962.
Kuznets, Simon, et al., eds. *Economic Growth: Brazil, India, Japan.* Durham, N.C.: Duke University Press, 1955.

ECONOMIC POLICY UNDER PLANNING, ASPECTS OF Economic development in India was initiated in 1952 through the formulation of Five-Year Plans, which set the direction of growth for the Indian economy. The government's economic policy under planning was predicated on four basic premises. First, the economy would not achieve rapid growth and egalitarian income distribution under free markets; therefore, the state must intervene in multiple ways. As a consequence, a comprehensive regulatory apparatus whose wings spread to all sectors of the economy emerged. Second, the economy should pull itself up by its own bootstraps, which meant in practice that it should operate almost as a closed economy, producing as many products as possible domestically and assigning a marginal role to foreign trade. Third, the public sector should occupy a commanding height in the economy, producing basic goods like steel and machinery, with consumer goods playing a complementary role. Fourth, the growth should benefit the most disadvantaged classes of society, affording them more employment opportunities and more equal income distribution.

Instruments of Economic Policy

The instruments devised to ensure the outcome of the economic policy according to the plan priorities were—apart from the fiscal, foreign exchange, trade and monetary policies (which are discussed separately in related entries): domestic industrial licensing, foreign investment licensing, price controls, and regulation of monopolies. All these instruments except the last one originated with the Industrial Development and Regulation Act of 1951, although their nature and coverage changed over time.

Industrial licensing. Industrial licensing was directed toward creating capacity in existing lines of manufacturing and in intended new areas. As a priority, small-scale industries with fixed capital below 50 million rupees were exempted from licensing and labor legislation in order to increase employment through less capital-intensive methods of production. In addition, production of certain goods was reserved for this sector, which was also given a credit subsidy. The issue of a letter of intent, which was only the first step in a series under the licensing procedure, often went through a bureaucratic tangle involving various ministries of the government of India and other concerned agencies. By the time a license was translated into concrete action, a considerable amount of time was spent, and in many cases, the investor either lost interest and withdrew or held the license without actually using it to start production. This dilatory procedure often ended in the hoarding of licenses for approved projects by influential producers, solely with a view to preventing their competitors from entering the field. Since 1985 there has been considerable relaxation of the regulations. Some categories of manufactures were completely delicensed, and industrial licensing was made more flexible by allowing additional capacity under different provisions of the act, like "automatic growth," "unlimited growth," and so on. However, the liberalization of industrial licensing remained half-hearted, with uncertainty hanging over its possible future reversal.

Foreign investment control and licensing of foreign technology. Being concerned about the free entry of foreign capital into the country, many restrictions were imposed on foreign investment on the grounds of foreign exchange scarcity and the need to promote domestic enterprise and indigenous technology suited to India's resource endowment. India opted for the purchase of foreign technology and minority foreign participation in equity during the 1960s. Royalty rates and fees were prescribed, and the conditions for Indianization of management and proportion of equity participation were set forth. The most restrictive policy was introduced through enactment of the Foreign Exchange Regulation Act in 1973, under which maximum equity participation by foreign investors was limited to 40 percent, except in export-oriented and high-technology industries, and the royalty rates were lowered. In terms of the impact on industrial growth, however, these restrictions were less onerous because foreign investment, both in stock and flow terms, had been modest and the domestic industrial policy's bias against competition and high profits hardly excited foreign firms.

Price controls. The government maintained comprehensive price controls on commodities, varying from essential consumption goods like sugar and gram to intermediate goods and even capital goods, accounting for about sixty-five individual goods or groups of commodities. Prices were usually set on a cost-plus basis, derived from technical relationship and the norms for reasonable rate of return on capital employed. The coverage of commodities was altered from time to time, depending on which prices needed to be raised or lowered. This mode of determining prices was not uniform and varied from industry to industry. As a result, there were anomalous situations, such as uniform pricing for all plants for a given product like steel, regardless of the cost conditions in each, or different prices for different plants for the same product, depending on the obsolescence of the plant, or different prices for the same product from a given plant. On many occasions, the prices of products manufactured by public enterprises were raised only to wipe out their losses or to increase their profits. It was overlooked that the policy of jacking up prices of intermediate goods helped raise resources for financing public sector investment only in the short term, while creating a resource crunch in the medium and long run with higher intermediate goods prices. The chaotic and counterproductive price control regime was continued, despite a severe indictment of this regime by various official committees. The government did, however, eventually recognize the complexity and irrationality of price controls, though it persisted with the core of the administered price control system to accommodate populist opinion and the vested interests.

Regulation of monopolies. Whenever the industrial licensing mechanism failed to accomplish what it was designed to do, other regulatory measures, often draconian, emerged from its womb. One such was the Monopoly and Restrictive Trade Practice Act (MRTP) to control the size of firms. One of the committees of the government of India, set up in 1969 to evaluate the effectiveness of the licensing policy, concluded that the prevailing licensing framework did not succeed in regulating the growth of industrial output in the right direction and in fact facilitated concentration of economic power and monopolistic practices. The MRTP Act was passed to prevent this outcome by restricting the expansion of large industrial firms with gross assets exceeding 200 million rupees in interlinked undertakings, or of "dominant" undertakings with assets over 10 million rupees. Since 1985, however, the asset limit to be exempt from the application of MRTP was raised to 1 billion rupees. As a result, the large firms had to overcome more obstacles than other industrial firms to raise the production capacities or to introduce new products. Paradoxically enough, the MRTP-induced restrictions on large firm entry or expansion accentuated the prevailing market concentration and led to excessive profits, as the threat to the existing dominant firms from new competitors was substantially reduced.

Implications of Economic Policy

The implications of economic policy, vaguely perceived initially by the government and the intelligentsia, became clear with the passage of time. If the public sector was to be the promoter of heavy industry, the private sector must be denied entry into that field. If employment-generating and quick-yielding small-scale industries were to be encouraged, large industries in the private sector must be prevented from encroaching on the areas reserved for small industries. If egalitarian goals were to be attained, luxury goods must not be allowed to be produced domestically or imported from abroad. These "don'ts" rather than "dos" received prominence in fashioning industrial policy as well as trade policy design. Initially, the government's objectives were confined to steering investment allocation where it would yield maximum benefits, but once the regulatory machinery was set in motion, it developed a life of its own, with constricting impact on growth in industrial production, efficiency, and trade promotion, thereby creating opportunities for corruption.

Indian economic policy under planning, often buffeted over the years for ideological reasons, can best be characterized as "unlearning by learning." Right from the beginning, the basis of economic policy and the instruments of its implementation were influenced by a strong perception that there was a pervasive market failure and that salvation lay in frequent and decisive government intervention. The effectiveness of this interventionist approach was judged in terms of its "first impact effects." If industrial licensing was used to determine the output pattern, import quantity, and composition of imports, it was believed that the final outcome would conform to the original intention. If foreign exchange was allocated according to a scale of priorities, it was assumed that it would go to the sectors that were designated as high priority. If bank credit was selectively channeled to what were designated as essential sectors, like agriculture, small-scale industries, and so on, it was concluded that the earmarked sectors would be the real beneficiaries.

As it turned out, the actual effects of the remedies directed toward eliminating market failure were vastly different from the intended ones. Although impressive progress was achieved by the late 1960s in diversification of output and development of infrastructure, and in industrial and agricultural technology, there was widespread inefficiency in the use of labor and capital. Industrial production was of low quality and high cost; small-scale industry used more capital than labor; and the public enterprises, which were heralded as the instruments of resource mobilization and income distribution, drained away, instead, the resources mobilized by the government through massive tax efforts. The only beneficial consequences were discerned in several infrastructure activities and public distribution of essential supplies to the low-income population—the areas that were well suited to government intervention. However, such was the mesmerizing appeal of state intervention that it took several decades before the targeted groups could realize its pernicious effects and utter futility. In the meantime,

parasitic middlemen mushroomed to appropriate the gains flowing from the interventionist policies.

The importance of competition and efficiency was recognized at times, as reflected in marginal changes in the economic policy frame in 1964 and 1965, 1981 to 1985, and 1989, but there were quick retreats from action to promote them at the slightest sign of protest from not only the left but the center and the right political parties as well. Despite the superficial diversity in political ideology, India's political parties were usually in agreement with regard to the core of economic policy. Both those who advocated liberalization and those who urged interventionist policies held that the state should not abdicate its responsibility in economic management. If there was any difference among the various ideological camps, it was only about the degree of intervention. Though the parties rationalized their advocacy of state intervention by invoking the poor and downtrodden, the real reason lay in the enormous power that they wielded and the patronage they dispensed when the state remained strong and centralized.

Political Economy Perspective of Economic Policy

The inability of a democratic polity and its highly modernized political leadership to pursue a growth-promoting and welfare-enhancing policy has to be seen from a political economy perspective. Policy instruments under planning, though designed as promotional measures, bred proliferating rent-seeking activities. The initial controls were the product of ideas and ideology, but they later created the interests that stalled a shift in strategy, even when ideas and ideology changed. As Jagdish Bhagwati (1988) argued, the regime of controls yielded a society with entrepreneurs enjoying squatters' rights, "which created a business class that wanted liberalization in the sense of less hassle, not genuine competition. The bureaucrats, however idealistic at the outset, could not have noticed that this regime gave them the enormous power that the ability to confer rents generate. The politics of corruption also followed as politicians became addicted to the use of licensing to generate illegal funds for election. The iron triangle of businessmen, bureaucrats and politicians was born around the regime that economists and like-minded ideologues had unwittingly espoused."

The condition for such an "iron triangle" was made possible by the existence of a proprietary coalition of the industrial-capitalist class, white-collar bureaucrats, and rich farmers, all of whom belonged to the top percentile of the population, as propounded by Pranab Bardhan (1984). There have been continuing conflicts among these proprietary classes—conflict between urban industrial and professional classes and rural classes of rich farmers, between the professional class in the public sector and the other proprietary classes in industry and trade, and so on. The consequences of these conflicts were seen in the deceleration of public investment and the decline in the productivity of capital, which largely accounted for the slowdown of economic growth. The resources raised were frittered away through the competing demands of these various classes, entailing uncontrollable expansion of the government's nonproductive current expenditure.

In the name of social welfare, the proprietary groups created a regime that protected the administrative power of a literati bureaucratic power group, the business class, which easily manipulated its way through the maze of regulatory controls, being insulated from foreign and domestic competition, and the rich farmers who benefited from massive subsidies. This configuration of power derived legitimacy from the populist rhetoric of national self-reliance, the role of the benign state in providing distributive justice, and the need for protection from the greed of the unbridled private sector. In such a conjuncture, the economy that evolved only culminated in waste of resources, not to speak of lack of economic growth and poverty alleviation. The answer to the intriguing question of why the proprietary classes could exploit the state machinery with impunity for their parochial interests could be sought in the role of the prevailing political system in economic decision making. The weaknesses of the ineffective economic policy had its genesis in the inner workings of the political system, which operated in such a manner that, at one extreme, economic policy had punishment as its basis, but without any sanctions for enforcing it, and at the other, incentive as its basis but without any built-in mechanism to reward success. The omnipresent physical and price controls and licensing procedures, though motivated by the desire to punish the defaulters, left enough loopholes to render them ineffective. The announcement of penalties was more often than not in a nature of a quietus to hold in check the restiveness of the electorate. The reason for this opportunistic nature of economic policy lay in the concentration of political power at the center and the dominant role of the state in decision making.

The economic reforms unleashed in 1991 transformed the Indian political landscape and consequently the framework of economic policy making. Through liberalization, the iron grip of the state on the economy was loosened, and this process was strengthened by changes in center-state relations induced partly by the economic reforms but more importantly by the eclipse of the dominant one-party rule at the center and its substitution by a coalition of different political parties. The economic policy making therefore tended to become less dependant on the arbitrary decisions of the bureaucracy and vested interests of all hues and was governed more by the impersonal judgments of the market.

Deena Khatkhate

See also **Fiscal System and Policy since 1952; Industrial Growth and Diversification; Monetary Policy from 1952 to 1991; Private Industrial Sector, Role of**

BIBLIOGRAPHY

Bardhan, Pranab. *The Political Economy of Development in India.* Oxford and New York: Basil Blackwell, 1984.

Bhagwati, Jagdish. "Poverty and Public Policy." *World Development* (May 1988): 539–555.

Bhagwati, Jagdish, and Padma Desai. *India: Planning for Industrialization.* London and New York: Oxford University Press, 1970.

Bhagwati, Jagdish, and T. N. Srinivasan. *Foreign Trade Regime and Economic Development: India.* New York: Columbia University Press, 1975.

Desai, Ashok. "Market Structure and Technology." Paper presented at the Conference on Technology Transfer and Investment, European Community, Berlin, 1984.

———. "Technology Acquisitions and Applications: Interpretations of the Indian Experience." In *The Indian Economy: Recent Development and Future Prospects*, edited by Robert Lucas and Gustav Papanek. Boulder, Colo.: Westview Press, 1988.

Khatkhate, Deena. "Restructuring of the Political Process: Agenda for the New Government." *Economic and Political Weekly* (2 July 1977): 1057–1062.

———. "National Economic Policies in India." In *National Economic Policies*, edited by Dominick Salvatore, vol. 1. New York: Greenwood Press, 1991.

———. "India on an Economic Reform Trajectory." In *India Briefing, 1992*, edited by Gordon Leonard and Philip Olderburg. Boulder, Colo.: Westview Press, 1992.

ECONOMIC REFORMS AND CENTER-STATES RELATIONS The founders of modern India set themselves the task of devising a Constitution that would suit India's "unity in diversity," adopting a federal Constitution with some unitary features. The states of the Indian Union have been vested with jurisdiction over important areas and assigned independent sources of tax and other revenues and are fairly autonomous within their spheres. However, the states' powers are circumscribed by: a list of concurrent powers; powers given to Parliament to legislate with respect to any matter in the state list under certain conditions (Article 250); a requirement to obtain the president's approval of proposals for state legislation in areas of concurrency before they can be enacted; and the placing in Entry 52 of the Union list "Industries, the control of which by the Union, is declared by Parliament by law to be expedient in the public interest." With respect to a subject in the concurrent list, supremacy is given to the law passed by Parliament. Furthermore, the president can supersede a state government if he or she determines that there is a breakdown of the Constitution or a financial emergency subject to the approval of Parliament.

These provisions make the Indian Constitution a quasi-federal one. To be sure, these Consitutional powers given to the Union (central) government in this regard are in the nature of enabling provisions, to be used when necessary in the national interest. So in practice, states could have had autonomy over broad areas of policy. Even powers in the concurrent list were, for the most part, introduced only to enable the central government to lay down the broad framework of policy, with the states formulating and implementing programs within that framework. Had the central government followed this policy in general, the states would have been autonomous with respect to the major part of governmental activities.

Economic Planning and Centralization

However, the adoption of centralized economic planning with a large role assigned to central public enterprises led to considerable augmentation of the powers and responsibilities of the central government. For purposes of planning, the central government extended its activities and control to most of the important sectors of the economy. Using powers given under Entry 52 in the Union List, the Industrial Development and Regulation Act was passed which conferred on the central government the power to control all important industries. Establishing the Planning Commission within the central government gave it considerable power over the entire planning process, including the allocation of plan expenditures. The introduction of physical controls such as licensing of industries, import control, and control over foreign investment, intended to regulate the market, simultaneously diminished the area of autonomy of the states. The nationalization of large private banks by the central government added considerably to the process of centralization. Overwhelming economic power thus came to be wielded by the central government.

Such centralization of economic decision making had led to inefficiencies in the allocation of resources, since market forces were suppressed. Also, the subnational governments found their freedom of action greatly diminished, and felt that the Indian Constitution had lost much of its federal character.

Liberalization and the Enlargement of States' Area of Activities

Economic reforms launched in 1991 were mainly designed to convert India's economy into a market-oriented, open economy. This transition involved the gradual removal of most of the physical controls such as industrial licensing, exchange control and import controls over a wide area, and the phased abolition of price controls. Another important aspect of liberalization has been a steep reduction of investment in public enterprises, public sector disinvestment, and the opening of most industries to the private sector.

As a result of these policy changes, state governments, no less than private enterprises, have had their spheres and freedom of action enhanced. Each state now is free to develop its economic, social, and intellectual infrastructure in such a way as to attract and develop industries best suited to its natural and human endowments and geographic location. With the abolition of industrial licensing by the central government, states now have the power to approve of the establishment of large industries. States are also in a position to compete for foreign direct investment, with automatic approval of such investment assured in most areas. All these developments represent considerable decentralization of economic decision making.

Since a major part of current investment in the economy is by the private sector, the Central Planning Commission's control over investment has been drastically reduced. State government investments in sectors such as education, health, power, roads, and irrigation are (in most cases) only nominally under the scrutiny of the Central Planning Commission. These are areas in which a major part of public sector investment will take place in the future, all mainly in the sphere of the states.

One can conclude that liberalization in India has not only led to a much more efficient economic system but has strengthened federalism. The state governments now enjoy powers that, in the spirit of the Constitution, they were meant to enjoy, but which the central government, in order to implement centralized planning, had previously prevented them from using.

Toward a Common Market

In the field of taxation, the states had used the powers given to them by the Constitution, unhindered by central government intervention, except for prohibition of levying sales tax on sales at two stages, prior to export, and limitation of the rate of sales tax on "goods declared to be of special importance in inter-state trade." Tax provisions of the Constitution were not really designed to create and sustain an efficient productive system within a common market. To cite an example, the cascading type of sales tax that was levied in European countries in the inter–world war years and old taxes surviving from the Mughal era like Octroi (tax on the entry of goods into a local area) were assigned to the states that used them. The founders had clearly stipulated that states could not tax interstate sales; however, the central government endowed itself with that power through a Constitutional amendment and levied a central sales tax on interstate sales, whose rate was raised from time to time to raise additional resources. These cost-increasing and distortionary taxes could be levied because the resulting inefficiencies were protected by import controls and high taxation of imports. To counteract the higher costs resulting from inefficient taxes, exports were subsidized in several ways that led to further distortions. Liberalization and globalization have meant that, in order to maintain competitiveness, the states have had to be persuaded to switch to economically efficient taxes, such as state value-added tax. Thus, liberalization, which made possible the enhancement of the area of powers that could be wielded by the states, has at the same time led to pressure for restraining them from actions that would adversely affect growth and national welfare. But the restraints that are being imposed would also mean that each state would be protected from the adverse effects of "wrong" tax policies of other states.

Raja J. Chelliah

BIBLIOGRAPHY

Chelliah, R. J., et al. *Trends and Issues in Indian Federal Finance.* New Delhi: Allied Publishers, 1981.

Datta, Abhijit. *Union-State Relations.* New Delhi: Indian Institute of Public Administration, 1984.

Rao, M. G., and T. Sen. *Fiscal Federalism in India: Theory and Practice.* New Delhi: Macmillan Publishers, 1996.

Rao, M. G., and N. Singh. *Political Economy of Indian Federalism.* Oxford University Press, 2004.

Sharma, J. N. *Union and the States: A Study in Fiscal Federalism.* New Delhi: Sterling Publishers, 1974.

Vithal, B. P. R., and M. N. Shastri. *Fiscal Federalism in India.* New Delhi: Oxford University Press, 2001.

ECONOMIC REFORMS OF 1991

The immediate factor that triggered India's economic reforms of 1991 was a severe balance of payments crisis that occurred in the same year. The first signs of India's balance of payments crisis became evident in late 1990, when foreign exchange reserves began to fall. With the onset of the Gulf War, world oil prices starting increasing, and remittances from Indian workers in the Gulf region fell sharply as many of these workers left the region. From a level of U.S.$3.11 billion at the end of August 1990, foreign exchange reserves dwindled to $896 million in January 1991. The rapid loss of reserves prompted the Indian government to initially tighten restrictions on the importation of goods. However, it was increasingly clear by the beginning of 1991 that the import compression, by limiting the imports of capital and intermediate goods, was restricting the rate of economic growth and of

Mobile Phone Use in Agra, near the Taj Mahal. The 1991 reforms have freed Indian entrepreneurs from the shackles of bureaucratic controls, and the business class has responded to the new opportunities by significantly increasing its investments in productive capital. AKHIL BAKSHI / FOTOMEDIA.

exports. Furthermore, it was evident that the payments crisis was no longer primarily due to the trade deficit, but was driven by adverse movements in the capital account, in particular the drying up of commercial loans and a net outflow of deposits held in Indian banks by nonresident Indians, reflecting a loss of confidence in the government's ability to manage the balance of payments situation. The new government of Prime Minister P. V. Narasimha Rao, who assumed office in June 1991, moved swiftly to deal with the situation. It implemented a macroeconomic stabilization program on an urgent basis, along with a comprehensive and far-reaching overhaul of the policies governing India's and industrial sectors.

Rationale

The decision to embark on the reforms following the crisis of 1991 was primarily motivated by the beliefs of former finance minister Manmohan Singh (prime minister

FIGURE 1

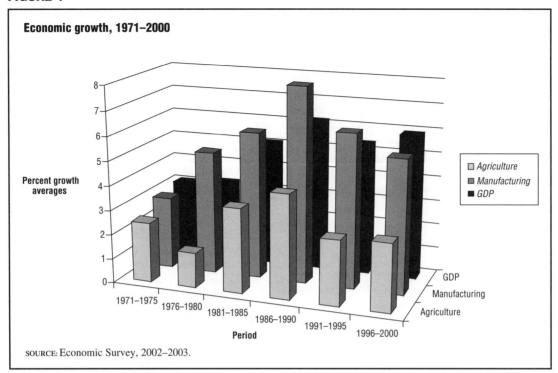

Economic growth, 1971–2000

SOURCE: Economic Survey, 2002–2003.

since 2005) that the roots of the financial crisis were structural in nature and lay in the import-substituting industrialization strategy followed by India's governments since 1947. The main elements of this strategy were inward-looking trade and foreign investment policies, along with extensive bureaucratic controls over production, investment, and trade, and a substantial public sector presence in the economy, going beyond the conventional confines of public utilities and infrastructure.

The trade regime was highly restrictive, as nearly all imports were subject to discretionary import licensing or were channeled by government monopoly trading organizations. The only exceptions were commodities listed in the open general license (OGL) category. Capital goods were divided into a restricted category and the OGL category. While import licenses were required for restricted capital goods, those in the OGL could be imported without a license, subject to several conditions. The most important of these were that the importing firm had to be the "actual user" of the equipment and could not sell the latter for five years without the permission of the licensing authorities.

Regarding industrial policy, the two key components of the regulatory framework were the Industries Development and Regulation Act of 1951 and the Industrial Policy Resolution of 1956. The first piece of legislation

introduced the system of licensing for private industry. The licensing system governed almost all aspects of firm behavior in the industrial sector, controlling not only entry into an industry and expansion of capacity, but also technology, output mix, capacity location, and import content. The principal aim of this act was to channel investments in the industrial sector in "socially desirable directions."

The system of controls was reinforced in the 1970s with the introduction of the Monopolies and Restrictive Trade Practices (MRTP) Act in 1970 and the Foreign Exchange Regulation Act (FERA) in 1973. The MRTP Act stipulated that all large firms (those with a capital base of over 20 million rupees) were permitted to enter only selected industries, and that too on a case-by-case basis. In addition to industrial licensing, all investment proposals by these firms required separate approvals from the government. The FERA provided the regulatory framework for commercial and manufacturing activities of branches of foreign companies in India and Indian joint-stock companies with a foreign equity holding of over 40 percent.

The industrial licensing system, in conjunction with the import licensing regime, led to the elimination of the possibility of competition, both foreign and domestic, in any meaningful sense of the term. As it became

FIGURE 2

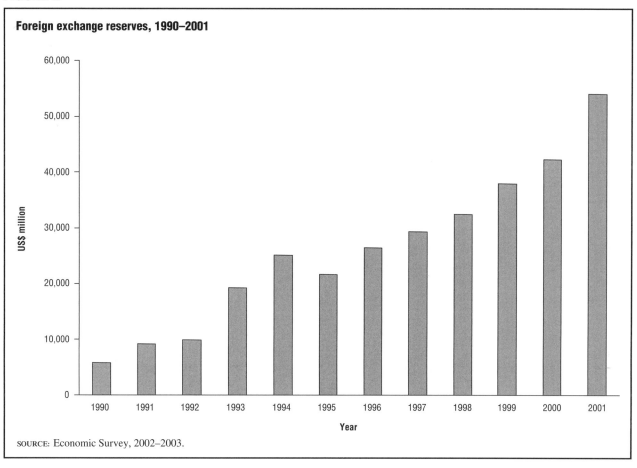

Foreign exchange reserves, 1990–2001

SOURCE: Economic Survey, 2002–2003.

increasingly complex over time, it led to a wasteful misallocation of investible resources among alternative industries and also accentuated the underutilization of resources within these industries, thus contributing to high levels of inefficiency in the industrial sector. As J. Bhagwati (1993) noted, "the industrial-cum-licensing system . . . had degenerated into a series of arbitrary, indeed inherently arbitrary, decisions where, for instance, one activity would be chosen over another simply because the administering bureaucrats were so empowered, and indeed obligated, to choose."

The 1991 Reforms

The economic reform program specifically targeted the highly restrictive trade and industrial policies. Quotas on the imports of most machinery and equipment and manufactured intermediate goods were removed. A large part of the import licensing system was replaced by tradable import entitlements linked to export earnings. Furthermore, the "actual user" criterion for the imports of capital and intermediate goods was removed. There was also a significant cut in tariff rates, with the peak tariff

rate reduced from 300 percent to 150 percent and the peak duty on capital goods cut to 80 percent. The industrial licensing system was abolished altogether, except for a select list of environmentally sensitive industries. Sections of the MRTP Act that restricted growth or merger of large business houses were eliminated. The list of industries reserved for the public sector was reduced from seventeen to six, and private investment was actively solicited in the infrastructural sector. Foreign ownership restrictions were liberalized, and foreign direct investment was actively encouraged, particularly in the infrastructural sector.

The Indian Economy in the Post-Reform Period

Since the 1990s, the Indian economy has grown at a rate of 5–6 percent per annum, far exceeding the "Hindu rate of economic growth" observed for much of the previous decades since independence. Much of the increase in economic growth can be attributed to the strong performance of the manufacturing sector, in contrast to the 1970s, when the manufacturing sector's performance was dismal (see Figure 1). A significant positive feature of economic performance in the 1990s has been control of the inflation rate, which has fallen to less than 3 percent, significantly below the historical average of around 5 percent. The performance regarding inflation is particularly noteworthy given that, in the context of the Indian economy, the control of inflation is considered to be among the most effective antipoverty measures.

Another positive development in the 1990s was the large increase in foreign exchange reserves over the decade (see Figure 2). In 2001 foreign exchange reserves stood at U.S.$54,106,000,000, a fiftyfold increase to its level at the height of the 1991 economic crisis. The buildup of foreign exchange reserves reflects the sharp decline in the current account deficit as well as the large net capital inflows during the 1990s. The improvement in the balance of payments can be mainly attributed to the large inward remittances through legal channels, as nonresident Indians took advantage of a market-determined exchange rate that was steadily depreciating.

The wide-ranging trade and industrial policy reforms have clearly had a positive effect on India's engagement with the world economy. The openness of the economy— defined as exports plus imports as a ratio of gross domestic product (GDP)—had nearly doubled in less than a decade, and the openness ratio stood at 23 percent in 2000, a significant achievement for an economy that had remained closed to international trade for much of its post-independence period.

The 1991 reforms freed Indian entrepreneurs from the shackles of bureaucratic controls and from a policy regime that encouraged unproductive rent-seeking activities at the cost of activities aimed at increasing productivity and output. The Indian business class responded to the new opportunities provided by the reforms by significantly increasing their investments in productive capital. The surge in private investment observed in the aftermath of the reforms, if continued, promises sustained economic prosperity for India and for its many citizens.

Kunal Sen

See also **Economy since the 1991 Economic Reforms; Liberalization, Political Economy of; Saving and Investment Trends since 1950**

BIBLIOGRAPHY

Agrawal, P., S. V. Gokarn, V. Mishra, K. S. Parikh, and K. Sen. *Economic Restructuring in East Asia and India: Perspectives on Policy Reform.* London: Macmillan, 1995.

Bhagwati, J. *India in Transition: Freeing the Economy.* Oxford: Oxford University Press, 1993.

Bhagwati, J. N., and T. N. Srinivasan. *Foreign Trade Regimes and Economic Development.* New York: National Bureau of Economic Research, 1975.

Joshi, V., and I. M. D. Little. *India's Economic Reforms, 1991–2001.* Oxford: Clarendon Press, 1996.

ECONOMY SINCE THE 1991 ECONOMIC REFORMS

The 1990s saw far-reaching changes in India's economic policy. A severe balance of payments crisis at the beginning of the decade triggered wide-ranging reforms in economic policy during the early 1990s. These reforms brought about a swift turnaround in India's external sector and catalyzed an unprecedented spurt in economic growth during the five years from 1992–1993 to 1996–1997, coincident with the "Eighth Plan" period. Unfortunately, the program of policy reforms lost momentum after 1995, and the early partial success with fiscal consolidation was reversed after 1996. Coupled with some deterioration in the international economic environment in the final years of the decade, these factors contributed to a clear deterioration in growth for the ensuing six years.

Crisis and Reforms (1991–1992)

The deep-seated roots of the 1991 crisis in fiscal laxity, growing reliance on external borrowing, a weakening financial sector and heavy-handed regulation of trade and industry are well known. The proximate trigger of the 1991 crisis was the Gulf War in the second half of 1990–1991, which jacked up international oil prices (and India's oil import bill) and reduced remittance inflows from the Gulf. Unstable coalition politics of 1990–1991 compounded the economic problems and hastened a full-fledged balance of payment crisis. Foreign exchange reserves fell below U.S.$1 billion in early 1991, short-term external debt rose steeply, and exports declined. Despite imposition of severe restrictions on imports, a default on payments seemed imminent by mid-1991, when the new Congress Party government took office. This government, with Manmohan Singh as finance minister, acted quickly to stabilize the macroeconomic situation and initiate long overdue structural reforms.

The systemic nature of the 1991 reforms may be gauged from the fact that within a few months, the following steps had been taken: virtual abolition of industrial licensing; rupee devaluation by 20 percent; the complex import licensing replaced by a system of tradable import entitlements earned through exports (later replaced by a dual, and then market-determined exchange rate); phased reduction of customs duties; fiscal deficit cut by 2 percent of gross domestic product (GDP); foreign investment opened up; banking reforms launched; capital market reforms initiated; initial disinvestment of public enterprises announced; and major tax reforms outlined.

The Economy Rebounds (1992–1997)

The reforms led to a swift restoration of health in India's external sector. Export growth soared to 20 percent in 1993–1994 and the two years thereafter. Inward remittances by nonresident Indians quadrupled from U.S.$2 billion in 1990–1991 to $8 billion in 1994–1995, and rose further to exceed $12 billion in 1996–1997. The current account deficit in the balance of payments never again exceeded 2 percent of GDP and averaged only about 1 percent for ten years after 1990–1991. Foreign investment soared from a negligible $100 million in 1990–1991 to over $6 billion in 1996–1997. Foreign exchange reserves climbed steeply from the precarious levels of 1991 to over $25 billion by the end of 1994–1995. The debt service ratio was halved over the decade. The critical ratio of short-term foreign debt to foreign exchange reserves (proven critical again in the Asian crisis of 1997–1998) plummeted down from the stratospheric heights (380 percent) of 1991 to a very safe 20 percent by March 1995.

The reforms of the early 1990s (with emphasis on deregulation and market orientation) and partial success with fiscal consolidation also ushered in a strong revival of investment and growth. Aggregate investment rose from 22.6 percent of GDP in 1991–1992 to nearly 27 percent in 1995–1996. GDP growth, which had dropped to hardly 1 percent in the crisis year of 1991–1992, recovered swiftly and averaged an unprecedented 6.7 percent in the five years from 1992 to 1997. Per capita GDP grew by almost 5 percent a year, compared to just over 1 percent in the three decades from 1951 to 1980. Growth was broad based, with all major sectors recording better performance than in the 1980s and far better than the outcomes in the thirty years from 1951 to 1980 (see Table 1). Among the factors propelling this growth acceleration were: the productivity gains from deregulation of trade, industry, and finance; the reform-assisted surge in exports; the investment boom of 1993–1996; the partial success with fiscal consolidation; the improvement in terms of trade for agriculture; and the buoyant world economy.

Growth Slows (1997–2002)

The year 1997 was a watershed, which signaled the end of the economic party. In particular, three events occurred within a six-month period to disrupt the momentum of growth. In March, the instability inherent in coalition governments became manifest in the political crisis that ended the Deve Gowda United Front government and ushered in the Inder Gujral United Front government. In July, the Thai financial crisis raised the curtain on the Asian crisis saga, which dominated the international economic arena for the next eighteen

months. Finally, in September, the Gujral government announced its decisions on the Fifth Pay Commission report (regarding government pay scales), decisions that were to prove costly for both the fiscal and economic health of the country.

As the table shows, the rate of average GDP growth dropped to 5.5 percent in the "Ninth Plan" period, 1997–2002. Particularly disquieting were the sharp declines in growth of agriculture and industry. Indeed, the drop in GDP growth would have been much steeper but for the extraordinary buoyancy of the services sector, which averaged growth of 8 percent during these five years. This rapid growth in services was much faster than in industry, a pattern that is quite different from India's past experience and that raises issues of future sustainability. Only a very small part of this services growth can be attributed to the remarkable dynamism in the relatively new sectors of information technology and business process outsourcing. Growth was rapid but from a very small base. By 2002 these new subsectors accounted for perhaps 2 percent of GDP, as compared to over 50 percent of GDP contributed by services as a whole.

Both macroeconomic and structural factors contributed to the growth slowdown. On the fiscal front, there was a significant deterioration in the consolidated deficit of central and state governments, about half of which was directly due to government pay increases following the Fifth Pay Commission. This deficit, which had declined from 9.4 percent of GDP in 1990–1991 to 6.4 percent in 1996–1997, rose steadily in subsequent years to around 10 percent by the end of the decade. Revenue deficits (government dissaving) also worsened by over 3 percent of GDP and fully explained the sharp decline in public saving and aggregate saving. The fall in savings was reflected in similar declines in aggregate investment.

From India's perspective, the international economic environment also weakened after 1997. The Asian crisis of 1997–1998 hurt exports and private capital inflows. The problems were compounded by the economic sanctions, which followed the nuclear tests in May 1998. In the next two years, the surge in international oil prices (much of it eventually passed on to Indian energy users) exerted negative effects. Finally, from the last quarter of 2000, the global economic slowdown took its toll of India's economic performance. The growth of exports slowed to below 10 percent per year in the period from 1996 to 2000.

Other, more structural factors also influenced the deceleration in economic growth. They included the petering out of productivity gains from economic

TABLE 1

Percentage growth of GDP and major sectors					
	1951/1952– 1980/1981	1981/1982– 1990/1991	1992/1993– 1996/1997	1997/1998– 2001/2002	2002/2003	2003/2004[1]
GDP	3.6	5.6	6.7	5.5	4.0	8.5
Agriculture	2.5	3.6	4.7	1.9	−7.0	9.6
Industry	5.3	7.1	7.6	4.5	6.6	6.6
Services	4.5	6.7	7.6	8.1	7.9	9.1

(1) Provisional estimate.

SOURCE: Central Statistical Organization, Government of India.

reforms, which clearly slowed after 1995. Although reforms continued throughout the decade, they never regained the breadth and depth of those of the early 1990s. Key reforms in the financial sector, infrastructure, labor laws, trade and industrial policy, and privatization remained unfinished or undone. Despite good intentions, the bottlenecks in infrastructure became worse over time, especially in power, railways, and water supply, reflecting slow progress in reforms of pricing, ownership, and the regulatory framework. The low quality and quantity of investment in rural infrastructure, moreover, combined with distorted pricing of some key agricultural inputs and outputs to dampen the growth of agriculture. The continuing decline in governance and financial discipline in (especially, but by no means exclusively) the populous states of the Gangetic Plain constrained growth prospects for over 30 percent of India's population.

The postreforms period saw a significant decline in poverty headcount ratios. The percentage of people below a minimally defined poverty line fell from 36 percent in 1993–1994 to 26 percent in 1999–2000. However, over the same period, total employment growth was sluggish, just over 1 percent a year. This is partly attributable to a decline in the labor force participation rate and partly to various policy distortions (including rigid labor laws), which discourage a more labor-intensive pattern of development. Regarding the spatial distribution of income expansion, the continued slow growth of the populous states of Bihar, Uttar Pradesh, Madhya Pradesh, and Orissa in the 1990s has contributed to increasing regional inequalities and raised serious concerns.

Recent Trends and Outlook

Since 2003 there has been renewed optimism about the growth prospects of the Indian economy. The "Tenth Plan," published in early 2003, projected an overall growth of 8 percent for the period from 2002 to 2007. A boom in software exports and remittances (together with reduced import needs of a somewhat sluggish industrial sector) has swelled the country's foreign exchange reserves to unexpectedly high levels (exceeding U.S.$100 billion), dispelling the old fears of a "foreign exchange constraint." The demographic outlook of a rapidly growing labor force and falling dependency ratios hold promise of rapid economic growth. GDP growth in 2003–2004 actually exceeded 8 percent, lending credence to the Tenth Plan projections.

In actual fact, the medium-term growth outlook for India is less bullish. The 8.5 percent growth in 2003–2004 followed slow economic expansion of 4 percent in the preceding year. Much of the economic dynamism of 2003–2004 reflected an exceptional rebound in agriculture from a drought-affected decline of 7 percent in 2002–2003 to a strong 9.6 percent recovery, thanks to the best monsoon in over twenty years. Growth requires investment. India's investment-GDP ratio in recent years remained stuck in the 23 to 24 percent range, not enough to generate sustained growth at 7 to 8 percent. East Asian experience suggests the need for investment levels of 30 percent or higher. A major constraint on India's investment performance has been the high levels of negative saving (revenue deficits) of government budgets, which have offset a strong private savings record. Although the reforms of the 1990s achieved a significant opening up of the Indian economy to external trade and investment, the country's integration with the world economy remains limited, with merchandise exports accounting for only 0.8 percent of the world exports and foreign direct investment inflows for hardly 0.5 percent of the global total. Despite recent initiatives, infrastructure constraints remain severe, especially with respect to electric power, roads, ports, airports, and urban services. The low (2 percent) growth of agriculture reflects serious problems with the organization of support services, low investments, and inappropriate pricing policies. As for the "demographic dividend," the constraints lie on the side of labor

Upscale Shopping Mall in Gurgaon, Delhi's Modern Township. After the economic rebounds of the first half of the 1990s and the ensuing slowdown, a new optimism has returned to India, with a rapidly growing labor force and falling dependency ratios holding the promise of economic growth. AKHIL BAKSHI / FOTOMEDIA.

demand, which remains seriously inhibited by policy impediments such as labor laws.

Sustained economic growth at 7 to 8 percent is possible, but only if serious policy reforms are undertaken to reduce government deficits, improve infrastructure, revamp agriculture, enhance labor market flexibility, and accelerate integration with the international economy. Until then, India's economy is more likely to average growth in the range of 6 percent, which is good but not commensurate with the country's compelling needs for job creation and poverty alleviation.

Shankar Acharya

See also **Banking Sector Reform since 1991; Economic Reforms of 1991; Trade Liberalization since 1991**

BIBLIOGRAPHY

Acharya, Shankar. "Macroeconomic Management in the Nineties." *Economic and Political Weekly* (20 April 2002): 1515–1538.

————. "Managing India's External Economic Challenges in the 1990s." In *Macroeconomics and Monetary Policy*, edited by Montek S. Ahluwalia, Y. V. Reddy, and S. S. Tarapore. New Delhi: Oxford University Press, 2002.

Ahluwalia, Montek S. "India's Economic Reforms: An Appraisal." In *India in the Era of Economic Reforms*, edited by Jeffrey Sachs and Nirupam Bajpai. New Delhi: Oxford University Press, 2000.

Chopra, A., et al. "India: Economic Reform and Growth." IMF Occasional Paper 134. Washington, D.C.: International Monetary Fund, 1995.

Joshi, Vijay, and I. M. D. Little. *India's Economic Reforms, 1991–2001*. New Delhi: Oxford University Press, 1996.

EDUCATIONAL INSTITUTIONS AND PHILOSOPHIES, TRADITIONAL AND MODERN

"Education" comes from the Latin *ex* (out of) and *ducere* (to lead, to guide); hence, to lead out of ignorance into knowledge, out of inability into competence. The desired knowledge and competence, however, will be shaped by historical circumstance and by cultural and social conditions. Education reflects the cultural self-understanding of a society and in turn helps both to determine it and to transmit it across countless generations. In India, with its long history and cultural diversity spanning many languages and religions, a comprehensive account of its educational character would require several volumes. The emphasis here, in this brief discussion, will be philosophical, highlighting the cultural and conceptual contexts of India's various educational systems and the values and ideals they attempt to embody. It is obvious that such rigorous selectivity results in some lacunae, for example, the long period of Muslim rule stretching from around the tenth to the eighteenth century. Muslim influence on Hindu culture has undoubtedly been considerable, but its impact on general, as opposed to sectarian educational patterns and policies, is less salient.

The Traditional Period

This period, for the purposes of this entry, extends from the early Vedic period to the coming of the British in the eighteenth century. It is dominated in the early period by the influence of classical Hinduism and Buddhism. The roots of the ancient Indian pattern of education may be traced to the earliest Vedic works, the four Vedas collectively known as Saṃhitās, the Brāhmaṇas, the Āraṇyakas, and the Upanishads. The purport of the hymns and chants that comprise the Vedas was largely to achieve cosmic harmony (ṛta) and the human prosperity it was believed to bring. This cosmic order was sought initially through sacrifices offered to the gods. Increasingly, the sacrifice itself came to carry the powers that had formerly been attributed to the gods, and much effort was expended on coming up with the most efficacious sacrificial rituals. Concurrently with this emphasis on the sacrifice, there was a contemplative turn away from ritualism to philosophical reflections about the nature of reality and the place of humans within it. Now it is knowledge itself that is seen as salvific, and it sets up a pattern of education in which sages reveal the nature of ultimate reality to select students in search of sacred knowledge. That is the etymological connotation of the term "upanishads," signifying a secret or esoteric knowledge that was largely confined to Brahmans. The rest of society, stratified along class lines, was provided the education appropriate to a particular class—the art of warfare in the case of Kshatriyas and agriculture, commerce, arts, and crafts in the case of Vaishyas. The Shudras who performed menial work were, however, deprived of education. The most detailed account of codes and laws, according to the *caturvarnāshrama* (four varnas) scheme, is provided in the *Manusmṛti* written by Manu, the lawmaker whose classification of social strata is said to have mirrored the makings of the world.

Buddhist influence was responsible for expanding the Vedic scheme of education beyond the caste restrictions imposed by the latter. Part of the appeal of Buddhist institutions of learning, both in India and abroad, was their ecumenical, inclusive character. The Buddhist approach includes both monasteries concerned with the training of monks and "universities," like Nalanda, involved in more secular education and systematic instruction in grammar, medicine, philosophy, and arts and crafts.

Outside the religious framework, kings and princes were educated in the arts and sciences related to government: politics (*daṇḍa-nīti*), economics (*vārttā*), philosophy (*ānvīkṣiki*), and historical traditions (*itihāa*). Here the authoritative source was Kautilya's *Artha Shāstra*, often compared to Niccolò Machiavelli's *The Prince* for its worldly outlook and political scheming.

Principles, values, and goals. Those types of education, though involving different groups, shared at least two characteristics. Religion broadly conceived provided a frame of reference, though to different degrees. Even the Kshatriya prince featured in the *Artha Shāstra* was made to study *trayī* (the Vedas and their commentraries), while for Vedic students education was predominantly religious. Secondly, all ancient Indian education emphasized the role of the teacher, who in the Vedic scheme assumed the mantle of the guru (spiritual preceptor), or the *ācārya* (authoritative teacher), revered and served by his student (*shishya*).

The goal for the Vedic student might be termed "transcendent," that is, transcending the mundane interests and attractions of life to attain direct experience of Brahman and in the ideal case to reestablish union with it. The institution of *brahmacarya* (chastity) enjoined on the student served many purposes; on the one hand, it pulled him away from the lures of the world, and on the other, conserved and sublimated the vital force (*prāna*) for union with the divine. The spiritual character of his education was also marked by the *upanayana*, or initiatory rite, which he had to undergo before being formally accepted by his teacher and beginning his instruction. This solemn ceremony typically took three days, when as expounded in the Atharva Veda, the teacher held the student within him and gave birth to a *dvija*, or twice-born student. The first birth from his parents was physical, but the second birth was spiritual. The close bond with the guru was cemented by the student living with the teacher so as to imbibe his inner spirit and in that way facilitate the attainment of *vidyā* or the highest knowledge leading to *mukti* (liberation).

The goal of Buddhist education, by contrast, was less transcendent and "vertical" and more immanent and "horizontal," in accord with the humanistic character of Buddhism. Within the Buddhist scheme, there were two types of institutions, the monasteries concerned with the training of monks and general universities imparting a more secular education. The goals of the two institutions varied accordingly. The monks were required to follow Buddhist teachings in a strict manner, begging for their food and keeping to the monastic disciplines, so as to bring about an inner renunciation or emptiness (*sunyatā*) and to awaken universal compassion. The students at the universities, on the other hand, while being instructed in the Buddhist teachings were trained to apply them in the world, as, for example, in the field of medicine, as mentioned in a canonical Pali work, *Mahāvagga*.

The goals of princely education were more secular. Mention was made earlier of the *Artha Shāstra*, a work concerned with the imperatives of royal or imperial power. Even though Kautilya describes the work as a species of *rāja-nīti*, the ethics of government, there was far more Machiavellianism in it, designed to make the king an absolute monarch and the state he ruled absolutely dominant.

Agencies and institutions. Ancient Indian educational institutions tended to be located in forests rather than in towns or cities, in an atmosphere of quiet and of natural beauty conducive to mental and spiritual concentration. The Āraṇyakas, or forest books, constitute a significant category of Sanskrit sacred literature. Radha Kumud Mookerji, the eminent Indian historian, says "India's civilization through the ages has been very largely the product of her woods and forests. It started as a rural and not as an urban civilization," and he goes on to cite Rabindranath Tagore: "a most wonderful thing we notice in India is that here the forest, not the town, is the fountain-head of all its civilization" (Mookerji, pp. 640–641).

The home of the teacher served often as the school in the *guru-shisya* relationship that constituted the most important educational pattern of the Vedic system. The intimate bond that thus tied a student to his teacher was familial and sacred. After the *upanayana* ceremony that marked the formal acceptance of student by teacher, a student was expected to live in his master's house and serve his needs, while the teacher was expected to be of high moral character and to teach as much by his life as by his explicit instruction. The Upanishads make frequent reference to pupils bringing firewood to their guru's house, signaling their readiness to serve their teacher and also their desire to keep alive the flame of their own devotion and concentration (*tapas*). These homes of learning, known as *āshramas*, served as places of rest and spiritual focus, removed as they were from the din and bustle of the city.

However, as population and human needs increased and as the division of labor to meet those needs grew more complex, education moved from these sylvan settings into the cities. The period from around 200 B.C. to the rise of the Guptas in the fourth and fifth centuries A.D. saw the emergence of many great urban centers of learning. The Jatakas (folk tales from the lives of the Buddha) provide us with detailed accounts of Takṣashila, capital of the Gandhara kingdom in West Punjab, one of the first such centers where students flocked from all parts of the country, as they did also later to Benares (Varanasi). But without question the most famous such center was the Buddhist monastery Nalanda in Magadha (present-day Bihar). We owe the most meticulous accounts of the eminence of Nalanda, which drew students from all over India and beyond, to two seventh-century Chinese Buddhists pilgrims, Hsieun Tsang and I-Tsing. According to their reports, the curriculum included not only the works of all the eighteen Buddhist schools but also the Vedas, logic, grammar, medicine, metaphysics, arts and crafts, and a great deal more. Knowledge was thus systematized, and methods for imparting it were devised in ancient India long before universities were established in Europe.

The Modern Period

This period spans the interval between Lord Macaulay's Minute on Education of February 1835 to modern India, reflecting the tensions between traditions and modernity. Macaulay's Minute was introduced to the British company's education committee planning the course and general direction of education in British India. On one side were ranged the "Orientalists," who favored the support of Arabic and Sanskrit and the knowledge opened up through these languages. On the other side were the "Anglicists," who championed the cause of learning English and western textbooks. This debate was much more than a quarrel about the desired medium of instruction. Macaulay with his statement that "a single shelf of a good European library was worth the whole native literature of India and Arabia," came down firmly on the Anglicist side. His intention was to produce a cadre of Indians who could help the British run the empire by mastering modern Western knowledge. He considered India's education archaic and moribund. Macaulay's ideas carried the company and Parliament, and with the introduction of modern English instruction, Indian education was brought into the Western world.

Traditional Hindu culture, largely hierarchical, was averse to change, caste-based, status-oriented, religious in character, and generally accepted authority in the form of scriptures, teachers, or family or community elders. Modern Western culture, by contrast, was on the whole egalitarian, meritocratic, cosmopolitan in outlook, democratic in spirit, secular, reason-based, and oriented toward change and material advancement. It would be no exaggeration to say that the tensions between tradition and modernity brought into prominence by Macaulay are still unresolved today, with significant repercussions for the course of Indian education.

An example from the field of philosophy might illustrate the point. While there was a vibrant philosophical climate until around the time of the Mughals in the sixteenth century, Indian philosophy in the modern period has by and large languished. This is not at all to say that there have not been outstanding thinkers in this time frame because there certainly have been a few. It is rather to claim that these few have been somewhat isolated figures whose work has not on the whole generated the schools of thought or the vigorous debate between them that characterized earlier periods. Contemporary Indian philosophers trained largely in a Western idiom are not able to draw creatively on ancient traditions. Part of the problem is linguistic: the ability to plumb the depths of the tradition requires a deep and sophisticated knowledge of Sanskrit and Pali in order to appreciate the subtleties of traditional philosophical argument, and not many contemporary Indian philosophers possess the requisite linguistic and philological skills. In the limited time at their disposal, young scholars prefer to focus on Western philosophy where the academic prestige lies. On the other hand, there are still great Sanskrit scholars whose mode of expression and style of argument is not the modern one, and so one finds two groups of scholars, the traditional *pandit*s and the modern Western-trained philosophers, who ideally should communicate with each other but who unfortunately do not. As a result, a subject that was once the wellspring and foundation of the culture has today fallen on hard times.

This tension between tradition and modernity has generated two responses. On the one side are revivalists, who want to return to a supposedly pure Hinduism and a purportedly golden age of the past. In a globalized and modern world such a simple return to the past is unviable. On the other side are those who tend to equate modernization with Westernization and turn their backs on tradition. This inevitably results in rootlessness and alienation. By far the most creative Indian educational thinkers have been those who have attempted both in their thought in general and in their educational philosophy in particular to effect a creative dialogue between past and present. It is instructive to consider two of them, Mahatma Gandhi and Rabindranath Tagore, before examining the actual situation prevailing in Indian education by way of considering the values and goals at play in education today.

Principles, values, and goals. Both Gandhi and Tagore were sympathetic to and deeply appreciative of India's philosophical and spiritual traditions, though they drew on different parts of them in crafting their views on education. Gandhi was attracted to the moral and didactic parts of the tradition and to the Bhagavad Gītā in particular. Tagore by contrast was drawn more to the speculative and metaphysical richness of the Vedas and the Upanishads and developed an aesthetic philosophy of *ānandā* (joy). These temperamental and philosophical differences were reflected in their respective philosophies of education. While they agreed that education should have a social orientation and be situated in close proximity to nature, and while they also agreed that education should be holistic and integrative, encompassing the head, the heart, and the hands, they disagreed about the main goal of education. For Gandhi the chief purpose of education was moral and social; the focus should be on the building of character within a framework of service to the community. To that end he insisted that intellectual instruction be imparted through a craft and that manual labor be coordinated with academic pursuits. For Tagore, this was too restrictive a goal: for him the main purpose of education was to develop the creative potential of a student and through that creativity to achieve a unity with nature and with his fellow humans. "Deliverance is not for me in renunciation. I feel the embrace of freedom in a thousand bonds of delight" (*Collected Poems*, p. 34).

Whatever their differences, Tagore and Gandhi were idealistic thinkers seeing the purpose of education as disciplining and elevating the spirit and as the balanced development of intellect, imagination, and will. Of the two, it was Mahatma Gandhi who had greater influence on actual educational policies. After many years of preparation, he came up with a plan that became known as the Wardha Scheme of Basic National Education, whose salient features were free compulsory education, instruction in one's mother tongue, handicrafts as an essential instrument of learning, self-supporting education, and training in nonviolence. The plan was tried for a few years but met with fundamental criticism, namely that it concentrated on primary education to the detriment of secondary and higher education and that it was largely village-based and too decentralized to allow for much operational coherence or development in towns and cities where employment opportunities attracted a swelling population.

After independence and Gandhi's death, the direction of India's educational planning was much more pragmatic. The Constitution of India declared India a secular, socialist, and democratic republic, and much of the educational thinking swayed by Prime Minister Jawaharlal Nehru's vision of India as a modern developing industrial nation moved in directions quite different from those of Gandhi's plan. Five national goals were highlighted to guide the course of education: the promotion of democracy; secularism, given the multireligious character of the country; the elimination of poverty through economic and technological development; the creation of a socialistic pattern of society; and national integration. To that end some of the prominent features of the educational planning of the 1950s and 1960s were universal, compulsory, and free education for children up to the age of fourteen, a stress on the education of illiterate adults, an emphasis on science and technology, enlarged and equalized opportunities for Dalits and other "backward" sections of the population, and finally an emphasis on vocational training in technical skills. In general, education was linked closely and directly to the economic growth of the country. As J. P. Naik, member-secretary of India's Education Commission, in the mid-1960s put it: "The main justification for the larger outlay on educational reconstruction . . . is the hypothesis that education is the most important single factor that leads to economic growth . . . [based on] the development of science and technology" (p. 35).

Modern Indian education is thus seen in terms of economic growth and material advancement rather than the acquisition of timeless spiritual knowledge. In its reliance on science and experimental reason, it calls into question traditional emphasis on authority. In its stress on equality of opportunity, it negates the old caste-based system of privilege. In its valorizing of productivity, it moves firmly in the direction of a meritocratic and egalitarian rather than a hierarchical order.

Twentieth-Century Primary School for Children in Rural Haryana. In spite of the egalitarian goals that the Indian educational system set for itself soon after independence, the gap between the urban middle class and the rural poor has increased precipitously, with the imbalance only furthering endemic poverty and illiteracy in some regions of the nation. AMAR TALWAR / FOTOMEDIA.

It is thus no exaggeration to say that India suffers from what the English scientist C. P. Snow once called the problem of two cultures. Snow was referring to the opposition between scientific and humanistic cultures, which to some extent troubles modern India as well. But there is a deeper gulf that is yet to be satisfactorily bridged: the gulf between two different mind-sets and outlooks, the traditional and the modern.

Agencies and institutions. Emphasis on technological development and economic growth in post-independence India has almost reversed the traditional and Gandhian emphasis on rural education. India's major cities have all embraced universities, institutes of science and technology, and centers for advanced studies, many of them highly regarded. These institutions, especially the technical ones, have produced a cadre of engineers and computer scientists who both in terms of quality and quantity are world-renowned. The success of the Silicon Valley in California, of German software production, and of firms like Infosys and Wipro in India is based to a large extent on the excellence and technical skill of a pool of computer personnel produced by Indian technical institutes. At the other end of the scale, however, basic education for the poor has been largely stagnant, so that problems of illiteracy and endemic poverty still remain for the most part unsolved. This imbalance has created what India's preeminent sociologist, the late M. N. Srinivas, called the dual cultures of independent India, the urban middle class and the rural poor. The country's professional classes are drawn largely from the former, which comprises chiefly the high and middle castes and the top strata of minority groups. Those living in villages, except for the middle and large landowners and a few successful traders and artisans, constitute the rural poor. In spite of the egalitarian goals that national education set itself soon after independence, the gap between these two groups has increased precipitously.

India's urban middle class and its intellectuals have thus for the most part adopted a modern Western mindset. This creates a reaction on the part of chauvinist and revivalist groups rendered queasy by what they view as deracination, and consequently raises shrill invocations of a "pristine," mythic Hindu past. This is at times a political ploy to win mass allegiance or votes. The deeper Hindu values and ideals championed by Gandhi and Tagore, among others, are largely unheeded. At the other end of the scale, the rural poor, illiterate and uneducated, remain at the mercy of large- and middle-scale landowners in whose economic interests they work,.

These dualities highlight at least four problems that Indian education continues to face: the increasing politicization of Indian schools and universities which compromises freedom of thought and inquiry; the lack of creative integration of tradition and modernity; an increasing religious polarization, especially in the form of Hindu-Muslim tensions, which calls into question the goals of national integration and a secular society invoked by the Constitution; and finally, the daunting inequalities between rich and poor and between higher and lower castes. Indian education still faces a formidable set of challenges as it attempts to meet the demands of a steadily growing population in a globalized world.

Joseph Prabhu

See also **Artha Shāstra; Indian Institutes of Technology (IITs); Information and Other Technology Development**

BIBLIOGRAPHY

Kabir, Humayun. *Education in New India*. London: Allen & Unwin, 1956.

Mookerji, Radha Kumud. "Ancient Indian Education." In *The Cultural Heritage of India*, vol. II. Kolkata: Ramakrishna Mission Institute of Culture, 1962.

Munshi, K. M., ed. *The History and Culture of the Indian Peoples*. 11 vols. Mumbai: Bharatiya Vidya Bhavan, 1951–1969.

Naik, J. P. *Educational Planning in India*. Mumbai: Allied Publishers, 1965.

Shills, Edward. *The Intellectual between Tradition and Modernity: The Indian Situation*. The Hague: Mouton, 1961.

Srinivas, M. N. "The Dual Cultures of Independent India." In *Collected Essays*. New Delhi: Oxford University Press, 2002.

Tagore, Rabindranath. *Collected Poems and Plays of Rabindranath Tagore*. London: Allen & Unwin, 1958.

ELEPHANTA The island of Elephanta, located 6.8 miles (11 kilometers) off the coast of Mumbai, is well known for a large cave temple dedicated to Shiva. Six minor excavations are also located on the slopes of this island, which owes its name to the Portuguese who, in the sixteenth century, found a large sculpted elephant near the southern harbor. The caves were carved in the sixth century A.D., and it is disputed whether they were sponsored by Kalachuri rulers or by members of a late Maurya dynasty controlling the Konkan at the time. However, as suggested by Walter Spink, significant coin finds at Elephanta seem to link closely the Kalachuri king Krisnaraja, who was a supporter of the Pashupata sect, to the patronage of the main Shaiva cave on the western hillside.

The main cave has a rectangular ground plan with openings on the north, west, and east sides. The north entrance has a two-pillared portico, while the eastern access opens to a court and the western one onto an unfinished space. The interior hall, carved 139 feet (42.5 meters) deep into the basaltic rock, is filled with four rows of pillars with fluted cushion capitals (16.4 feet, or 5 meters high) and displays an unusual layout with two main foci of worship: a square lingam sanctum placed next to the western opening, aligned with the eastern entrance; and a colossal relief depicting three faces of Shiva, carved at the center of the south wall and lined up with the northern entrance. This atypical plan has long puzzled scholars, who have tried to interpret the cave's function and iconographical program, which consists of a number of large sculpted narrative panels placed next to the accesses and on the south wall. On either sides of the north entrance portico appear two slightly damaged reliefs depicting Shiva as Nataraja (Dance King) and as Lord of the Yogis. These two well-known guises nicely counterbalance each other, as they emphasize the static and dynamic powers of Shiva, the god's inner energy and

Large Carving of Elephanta Caves. Tourist contemplating the imposing figure of Shiva inside the Elephanta caves. CHRIS LISLE/CORBIS.

its outer manifestation. Inside the main hall, on the north wall bracketing the entrance, there are two reliefs, one representing Shiva impaling the demon Andhaka, and the other showing Rāvaṇa lifting Mount Kailas. These two scenes both focus on Shiva's role as conqueror of demons and perhaps, much like the two panels in the north portico, seem to function as a pair. Across the pillared hall on the south wall, facing these reliefs, are representations of the god Shiva with his consort Pārvatī: next to the west entrance is the marriage of Shiva and Pārvatī (Kalyanasundara); and next to the east entrance, Shiva and Pārvatī are gambling at dice (Umamahesvara). In these two family depictions, filled with heavenly figures, Shiva continues to be the absolute focus of the scene, as he is much larger in scale.

Across the north entrance, in a recess of the south wall, is the central relief depicting three colossal heads of Shiva (18 feet, or 5.5 meters tall) guarded by two attendants. The iconography of this high relief, generally identified as representing Sadashiva, or "eternal" Shiva, has been object of great discussion. The frontal face depicts a serene aspect of the god, the left profile portrays the angry form of Shiva, and the right one focuses on his feminine appearance. The setting and design of the image implies the existence of a fourth, nonvisible face in the back, and some scholars have proposed that a fifth face, looking upward, should be imagined as completing the icon. The size, position, and quality of the image, as well as its alignment on the north-south axis of the cave, suggest that the patrons placed enormous relevance on this relief, which emphasizes the essence of the god Shiva rather than his actions. Two large-scale panels flank the central Sadashiva: Shiva bearing Gaṅgā (Gangadhara) appears on its right, and the androgynous form of Shiva (Ardhanarishvara) on its left. It is worth noting that these two images, which underline the all-encompassing nature of the god Shiva, beyond duality and distinctions, work as perfect complements to the central icon of Sadashiva. All the reliefs in this cave seem to be the product of a single vision and are related in style and composition. They display great affinity with late Guptan regional idioms from areas adjacent to the Konkan, in particular with the sculpture from Ajanta in inner Maharashtra, and Shamalaji in Gujarat.

The other focus of the great cave at Elephanta is the perfectly square sanctum placed at the western end of the east-west axis. The shrine contains a lingam on a high square base (*yoni*), and has four entrances aligned with the cardinal directions, protected by imposing *dvarapala*s, or door guardians. A similar organization of space and placement of sanctum can be found at Ellora in the Dumar Lena cave (cave 29). At Elephanta, the relationships between the sanctum and the colossal image of Sadashiva on the south wall remain unclear—it is almost as if two different, independent layouts overlap in the same space. The presence of multiple entrances to the pillared hall confirms that the cave at some point in its history had two foci of worship, but it is uncertain whether this was part of the original plan. Recent interpretations maintain that some idiosyncratic features of this cave might be explained with its possible affiliation with the esoteric Shaiva sect of the Pashupatas.

Two subsidiary caves are part of the main cave complex: the larger is next to the east entrance overlooking the east court, and has a small porch leading into a square chamber, with a central lingam shrine that can be circumambulated. The porch is decorated on the left by a large-scale relief of Kārttikeya that appears visually linked to the Shaiva panels inside the main cave hall, and by a poorly preserved depiction of the seven mother goddesses (Saptamatrikas). In the unfinished west court, a small *liṅga* shrine faces the entrance to the cave and is bracketed by damaged reliefs of Shiva Nataraja and Shiva as Lord of the Yogis, the latter very different in style from the other carvings at the site.

Pia Brancaccio

See also **Shiva and Shaivism**

BIBLIOGRAPHY

A recent and accurate overview of the site appears in George Michell, *Elephanta* (Mumbai: India Book House PVT LTD, 2002). For more in-depth analysis, see: W. O'Flaherty, G. Michell, and C. Berkson, *Elephanta, The Cave of Shiva* (Princeton, N.J.: Princeton University Press, 1983); C. Collins, *The Iconography and Ritual of Siva at Elephanta* (Albany: State University of New York, 1988); W. Spink, "The Great Cave at Elephanta: A Study of Sources," in *Essays on Gupta Culture*, edited by B. Smith (Delhi: Motilal Banarsidass, 1983). A "classical" interpretation of the main cave appears in S. Kramrisch, "The Great Cave Temple of Shiva on the Island of Elephanta" in *The Presence of Siva* (Delhi: Oxford University Press, 1981).

ELLENBOROUGH, EARL OF (1790–1871), governor-general of India (1842–1844).

Edward Law, the earl of Ellenborough, served on the Board of Control of Indian Affairs (1828–1830, 1834–1835, 1841) where he advocated the transfer of the government of India to the Crown and took an interest in Central Asian affairs. He advocated a cautious Indian policy except where Britain's long-term imperial interests were directly threatened. His term as governor-general would, however, be no more quiescent than that of his predecessor, Lord Auckland.

Ellenborough hoped to repair some of the damage done by the loss of the "Army of Indus" in the First Afghan War. At his direction, British Indian forces returned to Kabul, sacked the city, then departed, allowing the return to power of Dost Mohammad, the Afghan amir that the war had been ostensibly fought to unseat. Ellenborough greeted the returning "victorious" troops with sumptuous celebrations and parades designed to revive flagging British prestige.

Ellenborough then completed the other major order of business left unfinished by Auckland: the seizure of Sind. Ellenborough dismissed local warnings that the amirs' sovereignty was protected by iron-clad treaties and that they were amendable to British interests. Unfortunately for the amirs, their domains stood between British territory and the southern strategic gateway to India, the Bolan Pass. They also straddled the River Indus. British leaders had long sought to control the northwestern approaches to India and, declaring that the rivalry "of European manufacturers is fast excluding our productions from the markets of Europe," had identified the

Indus one of the most likely "new vents for the produce of our industry" (prime minister Lord Palmerston, quoted in Webster, pp. 750–751). Ellenborough shared these strategic and commercial views. He also knew that the seizure of Sind would secure British control over the Parsi-dominated Malwa opium trade, thus stabilizing the price of Bengal opium and adding to India's revenues. Accordingly, Ellenborough gave Sir Charles Napier, an able and ambitious general, leeway to provoke the amirs into rebellion, thereby justifying the annexation of the region, which was brutally accomplished in 1843.

Ellenborough then aggressively dealt with a crisis in the domains of the late Maratha leader Daulat Rao Scindhia of Gwalior, which were then roiled by an internal succession dispute that held the potential of creating a linkage between Scindhia's disaffected forty-thousand-man army and the Sikhs, who could together threaten nearby Agra and key lines of British communications in the north. Having already ignored and violated a series of treaties with the amirs of Sind, Ellenborough now punctiliously evoked long-dead provisions of an 1804 treaty with Scindhia to justify intervening in the succession dispute. Scindhia's forces were crushed, and a young Maratha puppet was placed on the state's throne under a council of regency supervised by a British Resident.

Ellenborough then contemplated moving against the Sikhs, but the Court of Directors, alarmed by the cost of Ellenborough's militarism, exercised their constitutional right of recall, summoning him home in 1844. The British government was more generous, granting him an earldom for his work in ending the Afghan conflict. He was later reappointed as president of the Board of Control. He continued to take an active interest in Indian affairs until he was forced to resign from that post in 1858 for impulsively allowing the publication of a private letter critical of Lord Charles Canning's settlement of the War of 1857.

Marc Jason Gilbert

See also **Anglo-Afghan Wars: War One (1838–1842); Auckland, Lord; British East India Company Raj**

BIBLIOGRAPHY

Huttenback, Robert A. *British Relations with Sind, 1799–1834: An Anatomy of Imperialism.* Berkeley: University of California Press, 1962.
Imlah, Albert Henry. *Lord Ellenborough: A Biography of Edward Law, Governor General of India.* Cambridge, Mass.: Harvard University Press, 1939.
Webster, Charles. *The Foreign Policy of Palmerston, 1830–1831.* London: G. Bell and Sons, 1951.
Wong, J. Y. "British Annexation of Sind in 1843: An Economic Perspective." *Modern Asian Studies* 31 (1997), part 2: 225–244.

ELLORA (ELURA) The Ellora caves are located in the heart of Maharashtra, near the town of Aurangabad, about 62 miles (100 kilometers) from the site of Ajanta. A modern Hindu shrine in the vicinity of the rock-hewn site is also renowned for being one of the twelve sacred *tirtha*s, or pilgrimage centers associated with the Shiva *linga*. The thirty-four caves, carved onto the steep face of a hill, can be divided into three main groups: Hindu, Buddhist, and Jain. The earliest caves at Ellora, mostly unfinished, appear to be the Hindu ones, clustered around and upstream of a waterfall at the center of the rock-hewn site. Caves 27 and 28, according to Walter Spink, were the first to be excavated, as they make reference to architectural features occurring at Ajanta. Caves 20, 21, 26, and 29, also known as Dhumar Lena, are grandiose in conception and appear to be architecturally and stylistically related to Elephanta and other sixth-century excavations in the Konkan. Caves 17 and 19 follow, showing a complete local assimilation of features common at other rock-hewn sites in the Konkan and inner Maharashtra. The last of the early excavations linked to the sphere of Kalachuri influence in the region is cave 14, also known as *Ravana ka khai* (Demon Ravana's cave), judging from its location and innovative iconography. All of these early Hindu units are dedicated to Shiva, as the presence of reliefs depicting the god and his associates, as well as *linga* shrines, seem to indicate.

The most grandiose Hindu rock-cut temple of the subcontinent was completed at Ellora during the eighth century A.D. Cave 16, better known as Kailash, consists of a temple structure excavated in the round out of the Deccan trap, emerging like a freestanding structure from the hill out of which it was dug. This 197 foot long (60-meter) and 98 foot (30-meter) deep temple was carved mostly during the time of the Rashtrakuta king Krishna I (r. 757–783). Dedicated to Shiva, this monolithic structure evoking the god's Himalayan dwelling materializes almost like a self-generated (*svayambhu*) structure within the domain of the Rashtrakutas to serve their political ambitions and help legitimize their power in the Deccan. The body of the Kailash temple consists of three independent parts, linked together by small bridges: an entrance pavilion, followed by a shrine hosting an image of Nandi (the "bull vehicle" of Shiva), and finally the actual temple. The southern style, or Dravida temple, cruciform in plan, consists of a pillared hall decorated with wall paintings (now mostly lost), and a sanctum enclosing a Shiva *linga* surmounted by a *shikhara* (tower) on the outside. The outer walls of the Kailash, once also painted, are embellished with images portraying Hindu mythological scenes and deities carved deep into niches framed by pillars. Worth noting is the Rāvaṇa scene, rendered with great intensity; the three-dimensional figure of the demon powerfully emerges from the living rock.

Rock Panel at Ellora Complex. Portion of sculpted back wall, cave 15 (also called Dashavatara) at the Ellora complex. Depicts the Gangadhara Shiva in the act of releasing Ganga (the river of heaven) from a lock of his hair. Dates to period of Rashtrakuta rule, c. eighth century A.D. ADITYA ARYA.

All around the base of the temple are sculptures of elephants, almost as if supporting the weight of the entire structure. The Kailash is placed at the center of a rectangular court with multistoried porticoes that house subsidiary shrines and large images of deities. While no inscriptions are immediately associated with this cave, a copper plate inscription from the region mentions this amazing structure as rivaling heavenly abodes. To the same phase of Rashtrakuta patronage can be ascribed the neighboring cave 15, carved high on the cliff, also known as Dashavatara, as well as caves 25 and 22, nestled among the earliest Hindu caves at the site.

The Buddhist caves (2 to 12), located toward the southern end of the cliff, can be roughly dated to the seventh century A.D., an intermediate phase between Kalachuri and Rashtrakuta Hindu patronage at the site. Images of buddhas, *bodhisattva*s, female and other esoteric deities are arranged in each cave, following precise iconographical schemes that suggest the diffusion of early tantric beliefs at Ellora. Geri Malandra has argued that each cave should be understood as a *mandala* (cosmic diagram), thus implying the existence of a programmatic vision for the structures that merges imagery and design. However, most of the Buddhist caves appear to be unfinished.

The most imposing Buddhist excavations at Ellora are caves 10, 11, and 12. Cave 10, or Vishvakarma cave, consists of an apsidal hall (*caitya* hall) containing a rock-cut stupa (dome-shaped monument) measuring over 16 feet (5 meters) in diameter. On the stupa, facing the entrance to the hall, is carved an image of a seated Buddha, flanked by attendants, in a guise reminiscent of Ajanta caves 19 and 26. The elaborate ornamentation of the rock-hewn facade of this cave appears to be a development of earlier *caitya* hall types, with a central horseshoe-shaped window. The cave opens onto a large court with a pillared corridor along the sides. Caves 11 and 12 are unfinished multistoried excavations, apparently conceived to be pillared halls with central chambers hosting a seated Buddha image. Noteworthy is the third floor of cave 12, a grandiose pillared hall with cells opening on either side in which are carved different types of seated buddhas. A row of seated female deities is sculpted on the back wall of this cave, flanking the entrance to the main Buddha sanctum. It is worth remarking that none of the Buddhist caves was intended to be a monastic residence.

The five Jain caves (30–34), all unfinished, sit isolated on the northern spur of Ellora hill and represent the last phase of patronage at the site. Some excavations appear very complex and elaborate. Cave 30 (also known as Chota [Little] Kailash) imitates on a smaller scale the monolithic structure of the Hindu Kailash cave. The two-storied Indra Sabha cave (32) and the Jagannatha Sabha cave (33) appear rather irregular in plan and are filled with images of Tirthankaras (Ford-crossers) and other Jain subsidiary gods and goddesses.

Pia Brancaccio

See also **Ajanta; Buddhism in Ancient India; Elephanta; Maharashtra**

BIBLIOGRAPHY

The most detailed description of the caves appears in the authoritative volume *The Cave Temples of India* by James Fergusson and James Burgess (1880; reprint, Delhi: Oriental Books, 1969). For more interpretative studies see: W. Spink, "Ellora's Earliest Phase," in the *Bulletin of the American Academy of Benares* 1 (1966); G. Malandra, *Unfolding a Mandala* (Albany: State University of New York Press, 1993); and C. Berkson, *Ellora: Concept and Style* (New Delhi: Abhinav, 1992).

ELPHINSTONE, MOUNTSTUART *(1779–1859),*
governor of Bombay (1819–1827). One of the shrewdest
administrators of the British East India Company,
Mountstuart Elphinstone "settled" the vast region of Maharashtra after defeating the Brahman *peshwa* of Pune in 1818.
His father, Baron Elphinstone, was governor of Edinburgh
Castle, where Mountstuart attended school. Appointed to
the East India Company's Bengal Service, he landed in Calcutta at the age of seventeen, and six years later was made
assistant to the company's Resident in Pune.

Fascinated by classical Greek and Roman history,
Elphinstone proved himself singularly adept at governance,
using both sticks and carrots in his daily dealings with the
last *peshwa* of Pune, Baji Rao II, whom he viewed as
"intriguing, lying, and corrupt," but believed could be
"restrained by fear" from becoming "treacherous." Baji,
however, tragically underestimated his young British
master, mistaking Resident (Mountstuart was promoted
in 1810) Elphinstone's soft-spoken advice on how best to
govern his "Land of Marathas" for weakness. One fateful
day in June 1818, Baji watched his "mighty" Maratha force
outside Pune, at Kirkee, crushed by the much smaller, yet
better-armed company of British Sepoys under Elphinstone's command, marking the dawn of British para-
mountcy over western India. Baji was pensioned off and
shipped north with his courtiers to Bithur castle. Elphinstone remained in charge of settling Pune, before moving
on to govern Bombay, ruling a region larger than all of
England, Scotland, and Wales before he turned forty.

Wisely using non-Brahman Maharashtrian Indians to
govern the territory he settled, Elphinstone was careful
to do nothing to rouse the fury of the Brahmans who
continued to live in the region, preserving the sanctity of
their Hindu temples, allowing them to remain tax-free,
continuing to subsidize religious schools as well as other
charitable societies. The company confiscated lands of
the largest "nobles" (sirdars), who had supported the
*peshwa*s, but most other landowners were granted
amnesty as long as they vowed loyalty to the "Great"
(*Bahadur*) Company's Raj. Peasants soon learned that,
though British collectors of their land revenues
demanded no less than the *peshwa*'s servants had, once
taxes were paid they would be left in peace, no repeated
demands made by princely robbers or petty pilferers,
who had in the past returned to demand more grain or
gold. Before Elphinstone left Pune, it was said that even
an old woman could walk across that city at night with
gold on her cane, without fear of robbers or molesters.

The same was true of the work Elphinstone did as
governor of Bombay, drafting a new Code of Laws, laying the foundation of an excellent educational system,
one so widely appreciated by its populace that when he

retired from that job the city's foremost institution of
higher learning was renamed Elphinstone College. After
leaving India, Elphinstone was repeatedly invited to
return as governor-general by the company's Board of
Control, but he declined that honor, preferring to travel
through Italy, writing his useful papers and later his
History of India (1841) at his home in Surrey.

Stanley Wolpert

See also **British Crown Raj; Maharashtra**

BIBLIOGRAPHY

Ballhatchet, Kenneth. *Social Policy and Social Change in West-*
ern India, 1817–1830. London and New York: Oxford
University Press, 1957.
Elphinstone, Mountstuart. *Territories Conquered from the*
Paishwa: A Report. 1822. Reprint, Delhi: Orient Publica-
tions, 1973.
Furber, Holden. *John Company at Work: A Study of European*
Expansion in India in the Late Eighteenth Century. Cam-
bridge, Mass.: Harvard University Press, 1948.
Roberts, Paul E. *India under Wellesley.* London: G. Bell and
Sons, 1929.
Wolpert, Stanley A. *Tilak and Gokhale: Revolution and Reform*
in the Making of Modern India. Berkeley and Los Angeles:
University of California Press, 1962.

EMPLOYMENT STRUCTURE Given the paucity
of dependable statistical evidence, the employment structure in India can be described only for a period beginning
in 1881 to the present, from data based on the decennial
population census until 1960, and the National Sample
Survey (NSS) thereafter. Though the methodology used
in these sources is different, the trends in employment
and its pattern are broadly comparable.

The Nineteenth Century

For India, most of the nineteenth century, at least up to
the 1870s, was a period of economic decline. Exploitative
features of British colonial rule, including the introduction
of burdensome land revenues and tariffs, first by the
British East India Company Raj, then directly by the
Crown, were primarily to blame. More positive features
appeared in the first quarter of the century as law and
order improved, and economic infrastructure and modern
communications were developed. Between 1860 and 1900,
land revenue collection rose by just 25 percent, while the
value of agricultural output (largely due to a rise in prices)
increased by about 116 percent. National income estimates for the period after 1870 suggest that output kept
pace with population, which grew by about 1 percent per
annum. On the basis of the population census, the share of
India's primary sector (agricultural) workforce rose from

approximately 60–65 percent to 70 percent in 1881; that of the secondary sector (industrial) declined from about 15–20 percent to 11 percent, and that in the services sector remained virtually unchanged. The increased relative and absolute size of the primary sector reflected not only a movement away from declining handicrafts within the manufacturing sector, but also increased acreage brought under cultivation, which may have increased agricultural output, though not necessarily output per acre. The industrial output was estimated to have declined.

The Period from 1881 to 1950

Between 1881 and 1911, the share of labor force in agriculture, including allied activities such as forestry, rose slightly, from 72.4 to 74.5 percent, and that of the labor force in manufacturing declined from 10.6 to 9.1 percent. The employment picture did not perceptibly change in the next forty years. The share of employment in the agricultural sector remained almost constant at 75 percent, rising from 74.8 percent in 1911 to 75.7 percent in 1951. On the other hand, the share of employment in the manufacturing sector and the services sector during the same period declined slightly. In the former case, the fall was from 12.2 percent to 11.9 percent, while in the latter case it was from 13 percent to 12.4 percent. Stagnation in employment in the manufacturing sector and the decline in employment in the other two sectors took place despite the rise in net domestic product. It should be noted that the data in 1951 pertain to undivided India (which included Pakistan and Bangladesh). However, the comparison is appropriate, as the figures for 1911 are also for undivided British India.

The statistics relating to employment for the country as a whole fail to reflect the regional picture of employment. While a large part of central India had the same pattern of employment as India as a whole, two groups of states showed different patterns. In the first group, consisting of Kerala, Maharashtra, Madras, and West Bengal, there was a marked shift in the workforce away from agriculture and toward manufacturing. In the second group, consisting of Rajasthan, Orissa, and Punjab, while there was a notable rise in the share of agriculture in the workforce, the share of manufacturing fell sharply. The difference in the employment pattern in these two groups of states was attributable to the varying access of these states to transportation facilities such as internal waterways (as in the case of Kerala), seaports (as in the case of Maharashtra, Madras, and West Bengal), and the railway network.

The Second Half of the Twentieth Century

Trends in employment for the latter half of the twentieth century may be more accurately described for the period from 1961 to 1999–2000, as the 1961 census adopted the concept of participation in productive work more inclusively than did the 1951 census, using income rather than work as the criterion for being in the labor force. The share of agricultural employment during the period from 1961 to 1999–2000 declined from 75.9 percent to 60.4 percent, while the corresponding shares in industrial and service employment sectors increased from 11.6 to 17.3 percent and 12.4 to 22.3 percent, respectively. In sharp contrast to the period from 1881 to 1950, there was a more decisive structural shift in the workforce away from agricultural employment to the fast growing industrial and service employment. The growth in total employment and a major change in its structure were induced by the acceleration in the aggregate and per capita national product. Thus, the gross domestic product at factor cost grew by about 3.4 percent between 1951 and 1980–1981, by 5.75 percent in the 1980s, and then by 6 percent in the 1990s.

J. Krishnamurty

See also **Agricultural Labor and Wages since 1950; Demographic Trends since 1757**

BIBLIOGRAPHY

Krishnamurty, J. "The Growth of Agricultural Labour in India." *Indian Economic and Social History Review* 9, no. 3 (1972).
———. "Changing Concepts of Work in the Indian Censuses, 1901–1961." *Indian Economic and Social History Review* 6, no. 3 (September 1977).

ENERGY POLITICS AND POLICY India is the world's sixth-largest energy consumer and the world's third-largest producer of coal. China is the second-largest energy consumer, after the United States. China's production and consumption of coal, its dominant fuel, is the highest in the world. Oil demand and imports have been rising rapidly, making China the world's second-largest petroleum consumer in 2003, surpassing Japan. The average projected economic growth rates of 7–8 percent in India and 9–10 percent in China will increase the demand for world energy enormously in the decades to come.

Two major events of 1974—oil pricing shocks and India's atomic test—highlighted some of the linkages of energy, security, and development policies in India. Heavy dependence on oil imports at the time from the Persian Gulf states, Libya, and the Soviet Union had implications for Indian diplomatic, economic, and military policies. Apart from the obvious need to maintain cordial relations with these states to keep oil flowing on affordable commercial terms, India had to step up exports to the oil-supplying

Nehru with Homi Bhabha. Nehru (left) conferring with Homi Bhabha, the principal architect of atomic energy in India. Although the pursuit of a nuclear program initially subjected India to international sanctions that adversely affected its general economy, today's scientists and economic planners contend that expanded nuclear power is the only viable long-term solution to the nation's massive energy needs. PRESS INFORMATION BUREAU / FOTOMEDIA.

countries to prevent a foreign exchange crisis that would have crippled the Indian development program. There was also a military dimension to the international oil crisis. The oil-exporting states of the Middle East were some of the largest buyers of technologically advanced weapons systems from the industrialized countries of the West, which were able to reverse the cost of their oil imports through arms sales. The proximity of these Organization of Petroleum Exporting Countries (OPEC) arms importers to the subcontinent, and the overt or latent military links of states such as Saudi Arabia, Libya, and the shah's Iran with Pakistan carried strategic implications for India. Special purchases of oil and military equipment from the Soviet Union at the time also accentuated India's economic and military dependence on Moscow.

The passing of the international energy crisis by the mid-1980s brought greater economic prosperity to India, both because of successful efforts to tap domestic oil resources, especially in the offshore Bombay High oil fields on the western coast, and because of the decline

and stabilization of international oil prices. Since socialism ended and marketization began in 1991, the Indian economy has grown at a healthy average rate of almost 7 percent per annum. There was a short phase when Indian oil imports from commercial goods exports to Iraq were dislocated following the 1992 Gulf War and the imposition of economic sanctions on Baghdad. But even this problem was overcome through higher oil imports from Saudi Arabia and the Gulf sheikdoms to offset Iraqi oil imports. Memories of the energy crisis faded at the beginning of the twenty-first century.

India has three conventional sources of commercial and industrial energy: oil, coal, and hydroelectric power. Oil of various kinds and oil products are used primarily in the transportation, petrochemical, and household sectors of the economy. The other two energy sources—coal-fired thermal and hydroelectric power—provide some 70 and 25 percent, respectively, of electricity generation in India. India holds some 7 percent of the total estimated world coal reserves, and domestic coal production meets more than half of its total energy needs. Coal is still used marginally in locomotives in some sectors of the Indian railway network. In the rural economy, where about 70 percent of the Indian population lives, there is still considerable use of firewood and agricultural and animal waste. The extensive use of dried cow dung as fuel in the rural areas has led to the establishment of several biogas plants there. The government of India has also been exploring the potential use of geothermal, tidal, and solar power.

India has relatively low oil and gas resources, with oil reserves estimated at 5.9 billion barrels (0.5 percent of global reserves), with total proven, probable, and possible reserves of close to 11 billion barrels. The majority of India's oil reserves are located in Mumbai's offshore fields and onshore at Assam. Due to stagnating domestic crude production, India imported approximately 70 percent of its oil in 2001, much of it from the Middle East (65 percent). This dependence is growing rapidly. The *World Energy Outlook*, published by the International Energy Agency, projects that India's dependence on oil imports will grow to 90 percent by the year 2020.

India is seeking oil import diversification from outside the Gulf. India's investment in overseas oilfields is projected to reach $3 billion in a few years. Of particular interest is Africa, especially Sudan, where India has invested $750 million in oil, and Nigeria, with which India reached a deal in November 2004 enabling it to purchase about 44 million barrels of crude oil per year on a long-term basis. Russia, Vietnam, and Myanmar are also potential suppliers to the Indian oil market. India has entered the international competition in the Caspian Basin, seeking special rights and privileges with Tajikstan, Azerbaijan, Kazakhstan, and Iran.

In 2002 India's electric generation capacity was a total of 120 gigawatts (GW), which included 90 GW thermal, 26 GW hydro, and 3 GW nuclear. In the same year its power plants generated 547 billion kilowatt-hours of electricity, of which 84 percent was conventional thermal, 12 percent hydro, and 3 percent nuclear.

Coal reserves in India are substantial, projected to last another eighty to one hundred years at compound rates of consumption. Despite such large proven reserves, the productivity of operations under the government-owned corporation Coal India Limited and its subdivisions is low when compared with Western standards. The average output per man-shift (each day or night shift that miners work) for Coal India is 0.8 metric ton in underground mines, considerably lower than the range of about 2.5 to 4 metric tons in western Europe, and 8 to 12 in the United States, Australia, and South Africa. Indian productivity, however, compares favorably with China, where it is 0.5 metric ton.

The problem with coal utilization is the location of coal reserves: West Bengal, Bihar, Orissa, and Madhya Pradesh. Political conditions in the first two states have been particularly volatile over the decades, and labor strikes and general political unrest have been extensive. The location of coal resources in the northeastern sector of India requires that it be transported and distributed throughout the country by railway. This makes it vulnerable to disruption or interruption if the powerful labor union, the All-India Railwaymen's Federation, with a membership of between 2 million and 3 million employees, were to go on a nationwide strike. This would not only bring all railway passenger and goods traffic to a halt, it would also paralyze coal-fired thermal plants and thereby industrial activity throughout India. The seriousness of this internal security threat was probably best exemplified by the crisis of 1974, when the All-India Railwaymen's Federation successfully launched a nationwide strike of its over 2 million members. With most power plants carrying less than two weeks of coal supplies, power had to be severely rationed in major industrial cities that were dependent on electricity from coal-fired thermal plants. Apart from this potential problem, there is the additional criticism that coal mining is hazardous to the health of the miners, and that its utilization causes considerable pollution of the atmosphere.

Assessing the total potential of hydroelectric power resources in India is difficult because the flows of Indian rivers vary widely, ranging from thousands of cusecs (cubic feet per second) in the monsoon season to a few cusecs in the dry season. Consequently, estimates of hydroelectric potential in India usually amount to identifying specific targets in each river basin where the potential for hydroelectric power generation is both technically feasible and economically viable. In 1978 the Indian government estimated the potential annual energy generation from hydroelectric plants to be about 400 tetrawatt-hours (tWh). However, the installed hydroelectric generating capacity at that time was only 40 tWh, or just 10 percent of estimated potential, a share that changed little during the next two decades. This meant that a 90 percent potential for clean and renewable hydroelectric power was being wasted annually because of the failure to harness India's rivers. Part of the problem has been the social opposition to large dam building for irrigation and hydroelectric power, as the construction of large dams is perceived to cause environmental damage and would also uproot several hundred thousand villagers from their traditional homes. This opposition eventually killed the huge Narmada Dam project in the mid-1990s, despite World Bank approval and offer of a loan. The Narmada project involved the building of thirty major dams and several hundred smaller dams. On the other hand, China has decided to go through with its highly controversial massive Three Gorges Dam project on the Chang (Yangtze) River. Critics have alleged that the Three Gorges Dam project could lead to another major Chinese disaster like the "Great Leap Forward" of the 1950s, but on a much larger scale.

Although there are limitations and liabilities in developing coal-fired thermal and hydroelectric power and oil as sources of energy in India, these will continue to generate the bulk of electricity in India for several decades to come. But the growth in thermal and hydroelectric generating capacity is not expected to keep pace with industrial and urban demand. Projected energy needs beyond the year 2000 suggest serious shortfalls of up to 20 percent. The crucial gap cannot be filled by increasing oil production, since domestic oil reserves are too limited to meet industrial demand and, in any case, are being depleted rapidly. Almost all of the future oil imports are expected to be absorbed by the petrochemical, household, and transportation sectors of the economy. The concentrated geographic location of coal in the northeastern India and the vulnerability of transporting coal throughout India suggest that coal cannot be guaranteed for the generation of electricity in the major industrial cities. Indian planners and politicians perceive nuclear power as crucial to India's energy needs.

Nuclear energy constitutes less than 3 percent of its total electricity generation. However, the dual-use nature of the peaceful technology also provides India with nuclear weapons capabilities. Unlike Israel and Pakistan, and earlier South Africa under its apartheid regime—all three of which sought a dedicated path toward a nuclear weapons capability—India's nuclear weapons program is mainly an offshoot of its nuclear energy program and

TABLE 1

1995 comparative per capita consumption of electricity (in kilowatt-hours, kWh)

Bangladesh	84	United Kingdom	5,843
Kenya	139	Germany	6,513
India	314	France	7,126
Pakistan	416	Japan	7,281
China	719	United States	12,308
Mexico	1,486	Sweden	16,534
Brazil	1,783	Canada	17,347
Italy	4,588		

SOURCE: Compiled from *India Means Business: Investment Opportunities in Infrastructure,* Ministry of External Affairs, Investment Promotion and Publicity Division, Government of India, 1997.

next twenty-five years and beyond. If I do not make the case now and point out . . . the urgency of accepting its inevitability, I will have done a great disservice" (Pachauri).

There remains the question, however, whether nuclear-generated electricity is commercially viable and affordable compared to the conventional sources of energy. The pro-nuclear power lobby in India suggests that this source of energy may have a cost advantage over coal-fired thermal plants. This has been disputed in Germany and Britain, countries that are now cutting back on their nuclear power programs. However, France, Japan, and South Korea are convinced that nuclear power is a critical source of electricity. As noted earlier, France obtains 78 percent of its electricity from nuclear power. Japan has embarked on a major program of establishing nuclear power plants.

Power remains in the public sector and was not privatized following the marketization and privatization measures of the 1991 economic reforms. Government-run energy corporations include: Oil and Natural Gas Corporation, Oil India Limited, and Indian Oil Corporation in the petroleum sector; Gas Authority of India Limited in the natural gas sector; and Coal India Limited in the coal sector. Government electric power corporations include National Thermal Power Corporation, National Hydroelectric Power Corporation, and various state electricity boards. Major oil terminals are located at the ports of Mumbai, Cochin, Haldia, Kandla, Chennai, and Vizagapatnam.

In 2004 the capacity of the major oil refineries in India were as follows: Reliance-Jamnagar, 540,000 bbl/d (barrels per day); Koyali-Gujarat, 185,100 bbl/d; Mangalore, 180,000 bbl/d; Mathura-Uttar Pradesh, 156,000 bbl/d; Mahul-Bombay (Bharat Petroleum), 120,000 bbl/d; Madras, 130,660 bbl/d; and Mahul-Bombay (Hindustan Petroleum), 111,700 bbl/d.

Since independence in 1947, India's electricity generation capacity has grown by more than sixty times. In 1947 India generated 1,362 milliwatts (mW) of electricity. In 1997 this capacity reached 83,288 mW. Energy projections in India beyond the year 2000 suggest serious shortfalls of about 11 percent, rising to a high of 19 percent during peak periods. Demand for electricity is expected to rise at a rate of 8 percent per annum over the next decade, this despite the fact that overall generating capacity increased from 287 billion units (BU) in 1991–1992 to 420 BU in 1997–1998, and to 502 BU in 1999–2000. With the economic reforms since 1991 generating a growth rate of about 7 percent, the main obstacle to more rapid growth in India is its poor

uses the plutonium extracted from the waste fuel. From an economic development standpoint, India has rationalized the necessity of a nuclear energy program to fill shortfalls in its overall electricity needs. Especially given the costs of mining and transporting coal throughout India from its location in the northeast-central regions, and considering that the great rivers of India cannot all be harnessed appropriately for hydroelectric power to service the major cities of India, a case is made for nuclear energy. Elsewhere in the world, especially in France, Japan, South Korea, Taiwan, and many of the European Union countries, nuclear energy is viewed as essential for meeting increasing energy demands and for reducing reliance on the oil of the Middle East. Oil supply and prices are subject to manipulation by OPEC, and coal mining and coal-fired power plants are considered health hazards. However, the pursuit of a nuclear weapons program subjected India to international economic sanctions that not only affected the general economy, but also hindered technological advances in its nuclear energy program. Many of the sanctions have now been lifted, but technical sanctions remain for India's nuclear energy and space programs. Both India's energy potential and its economy have been affected.

Indian nuclear scientists and economic planners are convinced that nuclear power is the only long-term solution to India's energy needs. The following statement in 1980 by Raja Ramana, director of the Indian Atomic Energy Commission, is reflective of the views of many members of the nuclear scientific community in India: "Looking at it [the future of nuclear energy] with the experience of the past and the terrifying energy problems of the future, I can think of no other source of energy that has been discovered to date except nuclear energy, which can solve the energy problems of this country during the infrastructure of roads, water supply, telecommunications, and especially power.

Raju G. C. Thomas

See also **Economic Reforms of 1991; Infrastructure Development and Government Policy since 1950; Nuclear Programs and Policies**

BIBLIOGRAPHY

Federation of Indian Chambers of Commerce and Industry. *India Economic Profile*. New Delhi: Federation of Indian Chambers of Commerce and Industry, 1998.
Institute for the Analysis of Global Security. "Energy Security." Available at <http://www.iags.org/n0121043.htm>
Pachauri, Rajendra K., ed. *Energy Policy for India*. New Delhi: Macmillan, 1980.
Thomas, Raju G. C. "India's Energy Policy and Nuclear Weapons Program." In *Nuclear India in the Twenty-first Century*, edited by Damodar SarDesai and Raju G. C. Thomas. New York: Palgrave-Macmillan, 2002.
Thomas, Raju G. C., and Bennett Ramberg, eds. *Energy and Security in the Industrializing World*. Lexington: University Press of Kentucky, 1990.

ENVIRONMENTAL CONSCIOUSNESS SINCE 1800

Reports in the early 2000's that the Sariska wildlife reserve in northern India had lost all its remaining tigers is indicative of the deepening crisis into which India's wildlife and its environment have fallen. Vanishing wildlife, depleted forests, and polluted air and water are grave ecological concerns in India. The survival of the majestic tiger—king of the jungle and the top of its food chain—is not just a battle to save an individual species but rather an entire ecosystem and a web of life that sustains human life and livelihoods as well.

Concern for humankind and its environment in India dates back several centuries, when such coexistence was widely practiced among India's tribes and indigenous communities. Tribal peoples, or *adivasi*s, inhabiting the vast forests of the Chhotanagpur and Danakaranya regions in central and peninsular India and Garhwal and other parts of the Himalayas carefully nurtured their forests, as their existence depended on these resources. They usually faced little interference from local chiefs and landlords, who little valued forests, other than to practice *shikar*s, or trophy hunts. British rule, however, dramatically altered these relationships and greatly increased forest exploitation.

India's Forests

The British at first showed total indifference to forests. The only threat to forests came from agricultural expansion, which was actively sought to generate revenue for the government. However, the growing timber needs of the colonial rulers for shipbuilding and other purposes soon hastened forest exploitation. The first reservation of teak was established by the British along the western Indian Malabar coast in 1806 to conveniently supply teak for ships built in dockyards in Goa and other coastal locations. Pressure on forests greatly increased with the arrival of the railways in India in the latter part of the century. Forests were recklessly cut to provide for railway sleepers and, before coal mines became operational, as fuel for locomotives.

Such was the demand for timber that the governor-general in 1862 called for the establishment of a department that could ensure a sustained availability of the enormous timber requirements for railway sleepers. As a result, the first imperial forest department was set up in 1864. The Indian Forest Act of 1865 was the first official attempt at asserting state monopoly rights over forest resources and at curtailing the traditional rights of local communities. The 1865 act, to a large extent, dictated all successive forest legislation in British and post-independence India. The provisions of the 1878 Forest Act, for instance, empowered the state to usurp all "valuable" tracts of forest, needed especially for railway purposes, and to retain enough flexibility over the utilization of the remaining forests. The customary use of forest timber by villagers was henceforth considered not a "right" but a "privilege" exercised solely at the discretion of local rulers.

The next assault on India's forests came during the two world wars, when the British found it expedient to plunder the country's forests to service the huge war demand. Approximately 1.7 million cubic feet of timber (mostly teak) were exported annually from 1914 through 1919 to meet the demands of the British military in Egypt and the Middle East. The impact of World War II was even more severe, when a special Timber Directorate was set up in Delhi to channel supplies of forest produce from India's provinces. As a result of the growing military and mercantile demands of the colonialists, social and ecological needs were increasingly overlooked.

Forest management in the post-independence era has not been much different. India's 1952 Forest Policy is striking in its assertion of the state's monopoly right over forests in order to safeguard the "national interest." The policy states that "the country as a whole is not to be deprived of a national asset by the mere accident of a village being situated close to a forest." While on one hand the rights of local communities to forest resources were severely curtailed, overexploitation of forests to supply the high demands of forest industries, especially pulp and paper, grew even further. The forest department argued that the low productivity of Indian forests was due to the government's "uneconomic" and "conservation oriented" approach and called for replacing the existing natural forests with high-yielding industrially useful trees. The National Commission on Agriculture went even further, outlining a strategy for industrial forestry in 1961. A new program of social forestry was also launched to encourage local communities to raise their own forests, usually on degraded wastelands, to satisfy subsistence needs for fuel and fodder, but the program failed.

Emphasis on industrial forestry extended beyond timber when several commercially attractive minor forest products such as *tendu* leaf (used in making local cigarettes), *sal* seed, and *mahua* flower were nationalized. Sale and marketing of these products was handed over to private contractors, not only depriving tribals of their livelihoods but encouraging corruption and misuse of the resource at the hands of middlemen. The resulting alienation of tribals, particularly in central India, has given rise to local protests, sometimes turning to violent conflicts. The recently established states of Jharkhand (meaning "forest land") and Uttaranchal have their roots in secessionist struggles over natural resource rights.

The rapid decimation of the country's wildlife and forests has led the Indian government to enact new legislation: the Wildlife (Protection) Act of 1972 aimed at protecting wildlife in strictly controlled national parks and sanctuaries, and the Forest (Conservation) Act of 1980 contained strict provisions for preventing the diversion of forest land. However, it is the National Forest Policy of 1988 that is credited with being the watershed in forest governance. The new forest policy aims to achieve ecological balance through conservation of biological diversity, soil and water management, and reforestation, while at the same time meeting the subsistence needs of rural and tribal populations. Reversing the earlier stance, the demands of forest industries are now secondary to these social objectives.

Encouraged by the new policy, a new program of joint forest management has been initiated in various parts of the country. The program aims at involving local communities in the management of state forest lands in return for regulated use of forest resources. Villagers are grouped in forest protection committees (named differently in different states) and work with local forest guards to protect specific forest areas. Community management, based on self-agreed rules and responsibilities, has helped curb misuse and corruption and has ensured a steady flow of forest benefits for participating communities. Although the program is viewed as a growing success, it operates on the basis of individual state resolutions (and often the goodwill of local forest officials), and local communities do not enjoy secure access to state forest resources.

Environmental Problems in the Modern Indian State

While deforestation has been a growing concern, India's environmental problems today span a much wider spectrum and are closely tied to its rapid pace of industrialization and urbanization in recent years. Problems of water and air pollution were first recognized when the government enacted the Water (Prevention and Control of Pollution) Act in 1974 and the Air (Prevention and Control of Pollution) Act in 1981. The 1984 Bhopal gas disaster—in which a toxic leak from the city's Union Carbide chemical plant resulted in the deaths of more than three thousand people—significantly raised environmental awareness and activism in India. It also caused the formulation of the Environment (Protection) Act and the establishment of the Ministry of Environment and Forests (MoEF) as an independent federal department in 1985. The MoEF is tasked with the overall responsibility of administering and enforcing environmental laws and policies.

Despite a greater commitment by the Indian government to protect public health and the environment, policies geared to develop the country's economy have taken precedence in recent years. Market reforms launched in the early 1990s have significantly raised economic growth but have also resulted in a huge cost to the environment. According to the World Bank, environmental damage from unclean air and water and natural resource depletion was valued at U.S.$9.5 billion, or 4.5 percent of the country's gross domestic product in 1992. A high proportion of these costs are attributed to premature mortality from exposure to indoor air pollution (from burning firewood in poorly ventilated kitchens) and the consumption of unclean water.

Growth in energy consumption in the power, industrial, and transportation sectors has resulted in rising emissions of greenhouse gases—the main contributor to climate change—and other pollutants harmful for human health. While per capita emissions are still small, these are growing rapidly, and India already ranks fifth in the world in aggregate greenhouse gas emissions. Given the country's reliance on low-quality coal—77 percent of electricity in India is produced from coal—and its soaring demand for electricity, carbon emissions are likely to grow exponentially. A stumbling block is artificially low electricity prices that have favored a few interest groups at the expense of those who really deserve its benefits. A commercially viable electricity sector could improve the quality of the electricity supply, improving access especially for rural households who otherwise would have to depend on dirty biomass fuels.

Vehicular air pollution in India's large metropolitan cities is already a serious human health hazard. Airborne particulate matter in New Delhi, the nation's capital, has been recorded at five times the World Health Organization limit. The problem is not due to the absence of sound environmental legislation, but rather a lack of proper enforcement at the local level. Lack of official response led the Supreme Court of India to take matters into its own hands by ruling in 1998 that all buses in Delhi must be run on compressed natural gas, a cleaner fuel. But this has not solved problems for other parts of the country, where buses still use diesel, a far dirtier fuel, although its quality has improved due to government action in recent years. A particular problem, however, concerns the price advantage that diesel enjoys over gasoline, which encourages its rampant use.

Availability of adequate freshwater is important for human consumption, growing crops, industrial use, and for sustaining all other life. But freshwater availability has been declining, both in terms of its quantity and quality in India. Water availability per capita reduced from 5,400 cubic meters in 1950 to 2,400 cubic meters in 1991, and several regions in the country are today water stressed. Following the "Green Revolution" of the 1970s, water demand for modern irrigation greatly increased. Overexploitation of groundwater for irrigation has depleted groundwater aquifers and has resulted in land salinization, particularly in intensively cultivated northern parts of India. In other regions, where agriculture is rain-fed, people traditionally took to harvesting scarce rainwater by building ponds and other water retention structures. Several such structures are in use even today in Rajasthan and several parts of southern India, testimony to indigenous knowledge, though concerns have been voiced about their maintenance in recent years.

An equally serious issue concerns water pollution, both inland and along the vast Indian coastline. The most shocking instance is the pollution of the Ganges, the ancient holy river that flows through thickly populated plains of northern India. Municipal and industrial wastes have been allowed to be freely dumped in the river, rendering it unfit for safe human use. The government responded by launching the Ganga Action Plan in 1987, a multipronged project involving wastewater treatment, urban renewal, riverfront development, and public education to make the river pollution-free. Since then, three other rivers have been covered under similar projects. The Ministry of Environment and Forests has also undertaken the preservation of the country's coastline by regulating urban development and controlling pollution along the coast.

While India's environment faces several challenges, there are also reasons for hope. The significance of the environment is recognized in the country's Constitution. The various environmental laws and regulations have not been sufficiently implemented in the past, but the government is now taking its mandate for the environment

more seriously. India is also an active participant in international environmental discussions, having ratified almost all United Nations conventions and treaties on the environment. With a vibrant civil society and a centuries-old tradition of coexistence with the environment, India has a good opportunity to tackle its environmental problems. How well it can balance its environment with the imperative for economic growth and development remains to be seen.

Damanjit Singh

See also **Agricultural Growth and Diversification since 1991; Ethnic Conflict**

BIBLIOGRAPHY

Brandon, C., K. Hommann, and N. Kishor. "The Cost of Inaction: Valuing the Economy-Wide Cost of Environmental Degradation in India." Washington, D.C.: World Bank, 1995.
Gadgil, M., and R. Guha. *Ecology and Equity: The Use and Abuse of Nature in Contemporary India.* London and New York: Routledge, 1995.
Government of India. "Indian Forest Policy 1988." Available at <http://www.envfor.nic>
Guha, R. "Forestry in British and Post-British India: A Historical Analysis." *Economic and Political Weekly* (October 1983).
United Nations Environment Programme and The Energy and Resource Institute. *India: State of the Environment, 2001.* Nairobi and New Delhi: UNEP, 2001.

EPIC ERA. *See* **Mahābhārata; Rāmāyaṇa.**

ETHNIC CONFLICT A defining force in India's modern history and politics, ethnic conflict was the principal cause behind the creation of India and Pakistan as independent nation-states. It has made and unmade governments, led to wars, and precipitated domestic strife in many parts of India. Ethnicity has also been an incubator of Indian democracy. Without ethnic mobilization—made possible because of segmented social diversity—democracy would not have expanded as rapidly as it did in India. The stability of post-independence India has depended largely on the balance between the demands of ethnic communities and the need to build a unified nation-state. While India is recognized as an independent nation-state, its borders remain in dispute, and its ethnic communities spill across into neighboring states. Even when boundaries are well defined, as between India and Sri Lanka, ethnic overlap tends to blur international boundaries, causing conflict.

Indian ethnic communities live on a scale of graded linguistic and cultural differences. Rajasthani, an Indo-Aryan language spoken mainly in the North Indian state

Police in Action after Assam Killings in Nellie. Police take a Tiwa tribe member into custody after the Assam massacre. In February 1983, in one of several "sons of the soil" uprisings, the Tiwa massacred hundreds of migrant Bangladeshis in the border state of Assam. Tensions continue to run deep in the area, with the native Assamese accusing India's central government, particularly the Congress Party, of ignoring its plight—the loss of jobs and land to the newcomers. INDIA TODAY.

of Rajasthan, changes every hundred miles whether one travels north or south, east or west. It absorbs local culture, words, and phrases as it gains distance from the original point and moves toward an area of the next proximate language. The Indian state of Bengal, parts of Assam, and Bihar, as well as what is today the nation of Bangladesh, share scores of dialects derived from Bengali. India's ethno-linguistic communities are for the most part concentrated in compact areas or regions. Thus Bengali is the dominant language in Bengal state, as is Marathi in Maharashtra and Gujarati in Gujarat, although many other linguistic communities reside in those states. This concentration, however, enables an aspiring ethnic community to demand political recognition in forms that range from provincial autonomy to national separation, although demands for separation have mostly been made by ethnic communities living on the borders of India. Officially, India's government recognizes fifteen regional state languages within its twenty-eight federal states and seven union territories.

There is no agreement among scholars about the distinctions between the languages and dialects of India. Linguistic scholars have suggested that there are 325 distinctive languages in India and thousands of dialects. To this linguistic diversity, we have to add several separate religions, as well as divisions of caste and locality. Each criterion divides Indian society differently. Together, all form the complex and layered identity of a modern Indian. The idea of ethnic identity then amalgamates linguistic, religious, and cultural attributes. Each ethnic composite possesses a geographic space, a distinctive history, and a singular perspective on its place within modern India. Some ethnic groups see themselves as targets of discrimination, while others are content with the autonomy and power they have managed to gain for themselves. Since religious and tribal manifestations of ethnic identities are discussed elsewhere in this encyclopedia, this article will focus on the broad cultural constructs that define ethnic identities. The objective here is to provide an overarching frame for understanding the causes of ethnic conflicts. It should be stressed that the story of India's ethnic politics is one of success as well as large failures; some ethnic communities have therefore chosen to integrate, while others have sought separation.

Historical Background

Scholars of ethnicity and nationalism disagree about how to define ethnic identity. Some view ethnic identities as primordial, given and immutable; others believe they are instrumental and are evoked in the service of other social and political objectives. To understand ethnic identity in the Indian context, however, one must view them as constructed identities, buffeted and shaped by historic and sociopolitical events.

Several historical events have shaped ethnic evolution. The rise and fall of empires, the Mughal and then the British, led to the crystallization of ethnic consciousness in several regions of the Indian subcontinent. Before the British arrived on the scene, India was ruled by several large and small kingdoms, each multiethnic and multi-religious but with one or two linguistic groups that had gained dominance because of size and royal patronage. The British absorbed these kingdoms into their empire by 1857, but for the most part ignored the ways in which local communities defined themselves. British policies nevertheless had a profound impact on ethnic self-definition. The British believed that India had not existed as a historical country, and that the British themselves had fashioned it out of a welter of regions and kingdoms. The British would build an overarching state while tolerating social and cultural diversity within their empire. But the British disregarded ethnic overlap when drawing of the borders of their Indian empire. The partition of ethnically united Bengal in 1905 was clearly a British administrative and political convenience. British policies—like the introduction of a census and the recruitment into their colonial army along ethnic ("martial race") and religious lines—reinforced ethnic consciousness. The British colonialists based army recruitment on their belief that certain ethnic groups made better soldiers than others. The Punjabi-speaking Sikhs and the Marathas who spoke Marathi were viewed as hardy and soldierly; the Bengalis were regarded as soft and artistic, better suited to British civil service. These perceptions became part of ethnic folklore and endured beyond the British period into the political life of independent India.

The rise of India's nationalist movement and the way in which it came to be organized was another determining factor in the shaping of ethnic identity. It was, however, Mahatma Gandhi and the Congress Party that systematically wedded ethnicity to Indian nationalism. Congress delineated its provincial organization not along the imperial map of the Raj, but along the lines of ethnic and linguistic distinctions. The nationalist era taught ethnic communities the value of mass mobilization against a central government. It is then not surprising that for independent India, management of "ethnic nationalism" and its incorporation into pan-Indian nationalism has been the single most important problem since 1947.

The Nature of Ethnic Conflict

Why have some ethnic groups in India long sought integration, while others have demanded separation? Several characteristics of ethnic demography and political economy can be offered as explanations. First, there is a correlation, though not a perfect fit, between ethnic "homeland" and ethnic identity. Possessing many of the features of a "nation," ethnic communities seek cultural and political autonomy. This characteristic compelled Prime Minister Jawaharlal Nehru to agree in 1955 to a linguistic reorganization of the Indian federation, creating linguistically discrete provinces. Ethnicity thus became the principle on which India would henceforth create new or merge existing state-provinces. Since then, India has added many new states to its union through internal reorganization. The creation of three new states in 2000, carved out of Uttar Pradesh (Uttaranchal), Bihar (Jharkhand), and Madhya Pradesh (Chhattisgarh), are instances of the most recent efforts at appeasing ethnic demands. The extent of autonomy granted to state-provinces—on which the Constitution is ambivalent at best—has been a persistent source of domestic tension. Frequently, the success of one ethnic group has triggered demands for parallel recognition by other ethnic groups within the same state-province. The Sikh demand for a separate state triggered counterdemands by Punjabi Hindus and resulted in the creation of the state of Harayana, carved out of Punjab in 1966. The creation of Nagaland in 1963 triggered demands for separate provincial states all over the Northeast region, and led to the division of Assam into seven new states in 1972. Ethnic tensions are aggravated by the perception that the central leaders favor one ethnic group over another.

Ethnic groups can be divided into those forming the core and those residing on the geographical periphery of India. The former are part of the Indian heartland, the latter frequently share kinship and identity with fellow ethnics across the borders. Overlapping ethnic nationalities include the Indian Kashmiris and the Kashmiris across the Line of Control in Pakistan; the Tamils in India's state of Tamil Nadu and the Tamils in the north and east of Sri Lanka; the Bengalis in west Bengal and those in what is now Bangladesh; the Nagas on both sides of the India-Myanmar border; and the Nepalis on both sides of Indo-Nepal border. Frequently, ethnic communities on the border are poorly integrated into the Indian union. Pakistan would not have been able to foment insurgency in Kashmir had the Kashmiris been fully content to remain within the Indian Union. As most popular movements are prone to do, ethnic conflicts have a rhythm; they rise and fall. Ethnic communities are known to move from autonomy to separatist militancy, and then back to autonomy. The separatist movement in Punjab followed this rhythm between the 1970s and the 1990s.

Democratic expansion and economic growth have also contributed to ethnic tensions. Relatively better economic opportunities have led to mass migration from Bangladesh into India, particularly into the bordering state of Assam. The native Assamese have mobilized in protest against the new migrants and have accused the central government of deliberately ignoring their loss of jobs, overcrowding, and political shifts unfavorable to the native Assamese. Assamese leaders charge that India's central government, largely dominated by the Congress Party, sought the migrant vote and therefore ignored the Assamese demands. These suspicions led to several "sons of the soil" movements in Assam since the 1970s.

Economic growth since 1947 has affected different ethnic groups differently. Some have gained while others have been slower to benefit. The sense of relative deprivation among rival ethnic groups has frequently led to violence. The separatist movement among the Sikhs in Punjab was nurtured by the perception that the government in New Delhi did not give Sikhs all that they deserved, and that their state of Punjab had been cheated out of its fair share of industrial investment for development. Economic nationalism constitutes an important element in the Naga and Assamese separatist movements. The Nagas claim they do not belong in India, while the Assamese charge that India's central government has exploited Assam of its oil and other rich resources without making corresponding investments. Economic grievances are often combined with charges of mistreatment. Sikh anger flared up when Sikhs were searched and mistreated by the Harayana police during the Asiad games in 1983. By 1984 Punjab was in the grip of a violent insurgency. The Jharkhand Tribal movement and violence in Manipur and Assam also underline the importance of these grievances in the rise of ethnic protests.

Ethnic conflicts also arise because they are grist to the political mill of electoral campaigns. Political leaders appeal to pride, historic achievements, and current injustices—real and imagined—to win elections, to deny the same to opponents, and to gain office, position, and power. Indian politicians have become extremely adept at mobilizing ethnic mass support for all manner of political and personal objectives. The threat of mass disaffection, whipped up by ethnic leaders, works effectively against a central government unwilling to accede to ethnic demands. Ethnic leaders who command a large following in a particular province are not unlike feudal lords commanding loyalty from their "captive" fiefdoms based on myths of common origin, language, and religion. This is evidenced by the existence of a large number of regional and provincial political parties, which regularly win elections and form governments in India. A few examples are: the Akali Dal in Punjab, Telugu Desam in Andhra, Dravida Munnetra Kazagham (DMK) and All-Indian Dravida Munnetra Kazagham (AIDMK) in Tamil Nadu, and the Assam Gano Parishad in Assam. Similarly, ethnic leaders such as Lalo Prasad Yadav in Bihar, Chandrababu Naidu in Andhra, Jayalalita in Tamil Nadu, and Prafulla Mohanta in Assam have prevailed because of their appeals to fellow ethnics. Mindful of the political advantage of ethnicity, political parties nominate individuals who enjoy high standing in their ethnic constituencies.

Excessive centralization and heavy-handed rule by central governments are usually behind the powerful surges of ethnic protests. A closer examination, however, suggests that centralization alone is rarely the sole reason for ethnic disaffection. More often than not, demographic pressures, as in Assam, a change in the distribution of power within an ethnic community, as in Punjab, or political competition among leaders and parties, witnessed almost everywhere else in India, can change the position of an ethnic group within India's polity, leading to conflict.

While fears of fragmentation propelled India's National Congress leaders to adopt a largely unitary Constitution in 1950, the pulls of electorates mobilized along ethnic lines have since forced India to cede greater autonomy to linguistic regions and ethnic communities. Ethnic communities have in turn regularly organized under the banners of ethnic parties. From 1950 to the mid-1970s, India enjoyed a period marked mostly by ethnic cooperation, but from about 1975 that spirit of compromise had all but vanished. From 1980 to 1990, India was jolted by violent ethnic conflicts, several serious enough to revive fears of disintegration. Since 1990, however, with economic reforms and the growth of prosperity, the balance has again tilted in favor of unity and accommodation.

The Management of Ethnic Conflict

During the last years of the British Raj and in the tragic year after partition in 1947, Hindu-Muslim-Sikh violence claimed the lives of more than a million people, and Indian leaders became extremely wary of separatist demands. The Constitution was therefore designed to balance the overriding need for unification against demands for autonomy. India was to be a secular federal democracy with a strong central government that had vast powers over its federal units, especially in the event of local or national emergency. India's Constitution did not define the criteria by which India's federal units were to be created. Originally, however, the federation was to be divided on the basis of administrative efficiency.

The first reaction to the administrative federation began in South India's Telugu-speaking Andhra with the demand for a linguistically defined Andhra province in 1952. Other large and numerically dominant ethno-linguistic groups soon followed, and by 1954, ethnic agitation had spread far and wide. In 1956 Prime Minister Jawaharlal Nehru's government finally agreed to reorganize the Indian federation along ethno-linguistic lines. Problems remained, however, in areas that could not be neatly divided into separable ethnic spaces, such as the provinces of Bombay and Punjab. Northern Bombay, with its Gujarati majority, emerged as Gujarat in 1958; the rest of that province, with Bombay as its capital, became Maharashtra state, with a Maratha-speaking majority. The stories of ethnic conflict in Kashmir, Assam, Tamil Nadu, Darjeeling (Nepalis demanding Gorkhaland), Nagaland, Mizoram, and Manipur are too long and complex to be told here. We may, however, examine a couple to understand how various conditions combined together to create ethnic conflict. The province of Punjab consisted of Sikhs and Hindus, who both spoke Punjabi but worshiped at separate temples. This religious distinctiveness was exploited by ethnic leaders in each community. The Nehru government refused the demand for a separate Sikh Punjabi Suba (province) on the grounds that in secular India, religion could not be the basis for federal division. The Shiromani Akali Dal Party, which represented Sikhs demanding autonomy, subsequently abandoned the religious argument and claimed an autonomous Punjab state on the basis of language alone. In 1965 Indira Gandhi, the third prime minister of India, proposed the creation of three new states out of India's existing Punjab: Harayana, Punjab, and Himachal Pradesh. The national Parliament, in which the Congress Party commanded a majority, promptly obliged. In the new Punjab, the Sikhs were a majority, but that numerical advantage did not translate into political dominance, which the Akali Dal leaders most coveted, since a substantial segment of the Sikh community continued to vote for the Congress Party. The Congress Party's dominance in Punjab was based on putting together a winning alliance between Punjab's Hindus and Sikhs, including the poor, lower caste farmers, and urban Sikhs. However, by the late 1970s, the political economy of Punjab had changed dramatically. A whole new class of peasant proprietors had emerged to take power in the Akali Dal. Economic changes brought Congress's dominance to an end in Punjab, but Congress was unwilling to surrender Punjab to its rival, the Akali Dal.

The tensions between the two parties mounted to dangerous levels of violence. The Akalis led demonstrations and strikes, and passed their famous Anandpur Sahib Resolution of 1973, which demanded that Punjab be given autonomous jurisdiction over all subjects except foreign policy, defense, and currency. Changes in government at the center in 1977 temporarily defused the tensions, but they resurfaced in 1979, when the Congress Party and Indira Gandhi were reelected. The forces that had paralyzed Punjab previously—intensifying party competition, religious extremism, and tensions between the central government and the province—soon plunged the province into violence. This time the struggle revolved around Jairnal Singh Bhindranwale, an obscure Sikh preacher pushed into the limelight by Delhi's Congress leaders with the purpose of splitting the Akali Dal. Bhindranwale soon gained enough Sikh support to abandon his erstwhile Congress sponsors, demanding the creation of Khalistan (Land of the Pure), a separate Sikh state where Sikhs could live without fear of Hindu dominance. The armed confrontation between Delhi's government and Amritsar's Sikh insurgents led to several tragic events: the assault on the Golden Temple, the holiest of all Sikh shrines, in June 1984; the death of Bhindranwale and his followers as well as many troops; and the subsequent assassination of Prime Minister Indira Gandhi by two of her own Sikh bodyguards on 31 October 1984. Rajiv Gandhi, Indira's older son, succeeded his mother as prime minister, then signed an agreement with Sikh Sant Harchand Singh Longowal, the Akali leader who had been marginalized by the militants. But Longowal was assassinated within months of the agreement, and Punjab was again plunged into prolonged militancy. It was not until 1992 that elections could be held in Punjab, and gradually normal political activity returned peace to Punjab. The erosion of the Congress Party's dominance in Delhi, however, accounted for that turn of events, as the new ruling coalition, led by the Bharatiya Janata Party (BJP), incorporated Punjab's Akali Dal into its fold.

Ethnic conflicts in Kashmir and the Northeast region can be traced to many of the same factors: arbitrary centralization of power in Congress's quest for dominance; denial of political autonomy; and the rise of nativist, ethnic, and religious tensions in response to intensifying competition for economic and political opportunities. All were a result of modernization, uneven economic growth, and party competition. There are nevertheless important differences among them. Assam and the Northeast were poorly integrated, first into the British Raj, and later into independent India, and were populated by many hill tribes that had a distinctive culture from that of the plains of Assam. The first tribes to break with Assam and to demand autonomy were the Nagas.

Once the Nagas were given a state, others with equally distinctive cultures and languages could no longer be denied. Between 1972 and 1987, the original province of Assam was divided into seven separate federal states. These measures brought temporary respite from ethnic violence in the Northeast region.

In the Northeast, as well as in Kashmir, there is an added element that has aggravated tensions and increased conflict: interference by neighboring states into what India regarded as its domestic affairs. Pakistan had tried repeatedly in the first four decades to infiltrate and rouse Kashmiri masses against India, but such efforts were not well received on the Indian side of the cease-fire line (now called the Line of Control). This situation changed after 1989, when the National Conference government of Farooq Abdullah collapsed and Kashmir was plunged deeper into turmoil and violence. Militant Kashmiris found ready help in terms of arms and money, training, and safe sanctuaries across the line in Pakistan and returned to attack Indian army troops in Kashmir. The nature of the struggle in Kashmir in the 1990s has, however, changed with the rise of militant Islamic fundamentalism in Afghanistan and Pakistan. The conflict in Kashmir is no longer just about Kashmiri independence or autonomy; it is caught up in the wider struggle between Islamic fundamentalists and the governments of Pakistan and India.

Naga separatism was similarly supported first by China. But such support is not in every instance provided by hostile governments. There are regional bazaars in arms where aspiring groups can purchase lethal weapons. Smuggling in drug, gold, arms, and contraband goods is yet another source of money to finance violent activities. In some instances it is difficult to draw the line between crime and an ethnic "cause." This is evident in the evolution of the United Front for Liberation of Assam (ULFA). By 1986 ULFA had established contacts with agents of Pakistan's Inter Services Intelligence (ISI), as well as with militants from the National Socialist Council of Nagaland (NSCN) and the Kachin Independence Army (KIA). With roughly only an estimated 3,000 armed militants, ULFA created terror in the state, disrupting communications, hitting various economic targets, kidnapping prominent businessmen, and killing government officials. Its activities escalated, reaching unprecedented heights in 1990. As the former government of Assam lost control, the state was brought under President's rule from Delhi in November 1990, and ULFA was banned. Ethnic violence, from Kashmir and Punjab in the north and west, to Darjeeling in the east and Tamil Nadu in the south, has made it difficult to distinguish between political motivations and criminal purpose in any corner of troubled India.

The emergence of coalition governments and the demise of Congress Party dominance, and the relationship between ethnic nationalism and pan-Indian nationalism, have undergone a sea change. Coalition governments at the center brought direct and immediate access to national power and patronage for ethnic leaders and their cohorts. In fact, there are growing concerns in India's media and press over the perceived weakness of the central government and its inability to withstand local pressures and policy compromises that benefit only politically stronger regional leadership. Ethnic leaders have used newly found powers to make and break governments at the center. In 1999 the BJP government collapsed when Tamil Nadu's leader, Jayalalita, pulled her AIDMK Party from the ruling coalition. There are new tensions in Nagaland and Manipur as well as Assam. Violence has claimed thousands of lives in Kashmir, while Hindu-Muslim riots in Gujarat and Mumbai have become fairly routine. This suggests that, while power sharing between India's various nationalities is critical for internal peace, that alone will not eliminate ethnic conflict. An increasingly important condition for social harmony is justice and governance. In India today, poor governance and the maldistribution of resources and employment opportunities have become potent causes of ethnic disaffection.

Maya Chadda

See also **Amritsar; Assam; Bengal; Bihar; Congress Party; Ethnic Peace Accords; Gujarat; Insurgency and Terrorism; Kashmir; Manipur; Mizoram; Nagas and Nagaland; Northeast States, The; Paramilitary Forces and Internal Security; Sikh Institutions and Parties**

BIBLIOGRAPHY

Basu, Amrita, and Atul Kohli, eds. *Community Conflict and State in India.* New Delhi: Oxford University Press, 1998.

Brass, Paul. *Ethnicity and Nationalism: Theory and Comparison.* New Delhi: Sage, 1991.

Chadda, Maya. *Ethnicity Security and Separatism in India.* New York: Columbia Univeristy Press, 1997.

———. *Building Democracy in South Asia: India, Pakistan and Nepal.* Boulder, Colo.: Lynne Rienner, 2000.

De Silva, K. M., and S. W. R. de A. Samarasinghe, eds. *Peace Accords and Ethnic Conflict.* New York: Pinter, 1993.

Ganguly, Sumit. *The Crisis in Kashmir: Portents of War, Hopes of Peace.* Cambridge, U.K.: Cambridge University Press, 1997.

Hazarika, Sanjoy. *Strangers of the Mist: Tales of War and Peace from India's Northeast.* New Delhi: Viking, 1994.

Kapur, Rajiv. *Sikh Separatism: The Politics of Faith.* London: Allen & Unwin, 1986.

Mitra, Subrata, and Alison Lewis, eds. *Subnational Movements in South Asia.* Boulder, Colo.: Westview Press, 1996.

Phadnis, Urmila. *Ethnicity and Nation-Building in South Asia.* New Delhi: Sage, 1989.

Subba, Thanka B. *Ethnicity, State and Development: A Case Study of Gorkhaland Movement in Darjeeling.* New Delhi: Har Anand, 1992.

Taras, Raymond, and Rajat Ganguly. *Understanding Ethnic Conflict: The International Dimension.* New York: Longman, 2002.

ETHNIC PEACE ACCORDS In the post-independence period, resolution of ethnic conflicts, as a part of a nation-building strategy, has been a daunting task of Indian leadership. Out of nine major ethnic conflicts faced by the country over a period of five decades, six were secessionist and three pertained to autonomy. The secessionist movements occurred in the states of Punjab, Tamil Nadu, Assam, Nagaland, Mizoram, and Manipur; the autonomy demand was made by the Bodos (Assam), Gorkhas (West Bengal), and Tripuris (Tripura). The underlying causes of these conflicts were rooted in the manifold grievances of the ethnic groups. For some, forcible territorial integration in the wake of decolonization has been the main issue. Some others have feared cultural assimilation engineered by the dominant groups in their region. The denial of equal socioeconomic and political rights has remained another reason, and some groups have felt powerless in the face of the hegemonic tendency of the central government. In all conflicts, either the perceived or real grievances of the ethnic groups and the nature of the state's response determined the conflict goals. Every conflict turned violent, though the intensity varied. While the Punjab conflict witnessed collective violence against the Sikhs in 1984, as many as five conflicts in Nagaland, Mizoram, Assam, and Punjab attained the dimension of an internal war—a situation marked by continuous and prolonged military engagement between the insurgents and government security forces.

Yet violence has been an important factor in peace processes, and India has used coercion in pursuit of peacemaking, with mixed results. All the nine major peace accords were reached in six conflicts; in three other conflicts—in Tamil Nadu, Assam, and Manipur—there have been no political negotiations. Three conflicts involving the Tripuris, Bodos, and Mizos have thus had two peace accords each. The government has always preferred to negotiate first with the moderate leaders; only after the failure of those talks would the government negotiate with the militant leadership. Two conflicts (involving the Mizos and Gorkhas) have so far ended in political settlement; it is likely that the Bodo conflict will be added to this list if the violent opposition to the 2003 peace accord is neutralized. Conflicts in Punjab and Tamil Nadu have ended in military suppression or coercion by the government, although, in the case of Punjab, it signed a peace accord with the moderate Sikh

leadership. The remaining four ethnic movements (in Tripura, Assam, Manipur, and Nagaland) are continuing. Concerning the Tripura conflict, the Delhi central government signed two failed peace accords; both the Assamese and Manipuri conflicts have not thus far seen a peace process; and protracted negotiations are underway to end the conflict in Nagaland.

Failed Accords

Six out of nine ethnic peace accords have failed. The first such accord was signed on 11 November 1975 between five representatives of a breakaway Naga group (the Revolutionary Government of Nagaland) and Nagaland governor L. P. Singh. Constant military pressure by the Indian forces and growing dissidence facilitated this accord. Popularly known as the Shillong Accord, it did not intend to redress the Nagas' grievances but to end the conflict by seeking the rebels' surrender, the precondition for reaching a final negotiated political settlement. The operative clauses of the accord stated that the representatives of the underground organizations accepted the Indian Constitution and agreed to surrender their arms—details of which were worked out under a supplementary agreement on 5 January 1976. It set a twenty-day deadline for the arms surrender and created peace camps for housing the surrendered militants. Subsequently, a large number of detainees were released. The accord did not restore peace, because only a small section of the Naga leadership participated in the talks. Most Nagas considered the agreement an unequal deal, which the government had negotiated from a position of military strength. The antiaccord forces consolidated themselves under two new militant factions of the Nationalist Socialist Council of Nagaland. Thus, since the 1970s, India's government has faced formidable opposition forces while trying to negotiate peace.

The Mizo Accord came second in the series of failed peace accords. Signed on 18 February 1976, between India's government and Mizo National Front (MNF) chief Laldenga, it was similar to the Shillong Accord. It secured the MNF leadership's acknowledgment of Mizoram as an integral part of India as well as their desire to find a political solution within the framework of the Indian Constitution. However, there was no mention of the specific solution the government was willing to offer. The MNF agreed to ensure an end to the violence by its military wing—the Mizo National Army (MNA)—and to collect the underground cadres with their arms, placing them in camps run with government help. On its part, the government was to declare a suspension of military operations, but only after the rebels stopped their activities. As expected, the accord stimulated internal bickering in the MNF, whose members refused to surrender

Naga Leaders. Thingaleng Muivah (left) with Isaac Chisi Swu prepare to meet then Prime Minister Atal Bihari Vajpayee on Indian soil after three decades in exile. Officials hope the talks will pave the way for a peaceful settlement of an insurgency that has haunted northeast India since independence in 1947. INDIA TODAY.

any arms. Laldenga was isolated in the organization and found his support failing in the Mizo Hills. At the same time, he was under pressure from the government to implement the accord. In 1978 violence erupted, and the government responded with full military operations.

The Punjab Accord, signed on 24 July 1985, was different in two ways. First, it was entered into with the moderate Sikh leadership while the militants were actively involved in armed campaigns. Prime Minister Rajiv Gandhi himself was a signatory. The Akali Dal leader, H. S. Longowal, represented the Sikhs. Second, it tried to address some of the political grievances of the Sikhs. Its main thrust was to satisfy their territorial aspirations, as well as their desire for autonomy. It was agreed that Chandigarh, the shared capital of Punjab and Haryana, would be given to Punjab. In return, Punjab would transfer some of its Hindi-speaking areas to Haryana. Regarding the autonomy demand, the government was to refer

that issue to the Sarkaria Commission, set up to make recommendations on center-state relations. The accord also stipulated that the river water dispute between Punjab and Haryana would be referred to a tribunal headed by a Supreme Court judge. While the government considered the accord a sincere attempt at reconciliation with the Sikh community, the agreement evoked protests from many militant Sikh leaders, who bitterly opposed the Akali Dal's cooperation with the Indian government. Intense violence ensued, including the assassination of Longowal by Khalistani Sikhs on 20 August 1985, during his election campaign. Soon after, the accord itself expired, as the government embarked on a comprehensive counterinsurgency strategy to crush the Khalistani militants.

Two accords (in 1988 and 1993) to end the conflict in Tripura met similar fates. The trilateral accord of August 1988 involving the central and state governments and Tripura's Tribal National Volunteers. The militant organization agreed to end all underground activities; the Indian government promised to extend resettlement facilities, increase tribal representation in the legislature through reservations, to protect tribal interests in land alienation, and to develop agricultural and irrigation facilities in tribal areas. The failure of the accord may be attributed not only to opposition within the militant movement, leading to the rise of splinter groups to carry on the fight, but also to political differences between the central and state governments over its implementation. It took about five more years for the government to coerce, through sustained military operations, another group—the Tripura Tribal Force—to negotiate an accord. Interestingly, the 1993 accord incorporated most of the provisions of the earlier accord. Additionally, it provided some safeguards to protect Tripura tribal culture. As soon as that accord was signed, however, another group of disgruntled leaders began a new armed movement, which continues to shatter Tripura's "peace" as a low-intensity conflict.

The movement for Bodoland presented a similar picture until 2003. The first accord signed between the Assam government and moderate Bodo leadership in February 1993 did not work. Though the accord provided limited autonomy to the Bodos under an autonomous council covering some two thousand villages and twenty-five tea gardens, a section of them remained dissatisfied because of the exclusion of areas lying on the southern bank of the Brahmaputra River, as well as rejection of their demand for a full-fledged state within the Indian union. Dissident militant groups—the Bodo Security Force (BSF) and the Bodo Liberation Tigers (BLT)—took advantage of the general discontent to continue their armed struggle amid heavy military pressure from Indian security forces.

Successful Accords

Two accords have been successful; a third is likely to be the 2003 Bodo Accord. The Mizo, Bodo, and Gorkha leaders have accepted negotiated peace settlements only after they found military engagements futile. The strategy in the Mizoram conflict was to use military pressure to bring the MNF to the negotiating table, so the central government held peace parleys even after the breakdown of the 1976 accord. The talks became protracted due to the intransigence of the MNF, but the government capitalized on the military weakness of the MNA to reach a deal. Once the local population and religious leaders threw their weight behind the peace process, the MNF chief was forced to sign the Mizo Accord in 1986. A step forward from the 1976 accord, it separated the political solution from the immediate surrender of arms. However, the MNF

agreed to bring out, within the agreed time limit, all underground personnel, along with their arms and ammunition. The government offered political concessions, such as conferment of statehood on Mizoram and constitutional guarantees for the religious and social practices of the Mizos. An enhanced allocation of central resources was assured as a special case. The accord generated positive responses from Mizo tribal society. The MNF joined the political mainstream; enduring peace returned to Mizoram—now the most peaceful state in northeast India.

The same can be said about the Gorkhaland Accord of August 1988. The central government, which had been a signatory in the Mizo Accord, in this case merely mediated the accord between the state of West Bengal and the Gorkha National Liberation Front (GNLF). What made the accord possible was the compromise the GNLF made, under military pressure, regarding its original goal: it was prepared to give up its demand for a separate Gorkha state (within the Indian Union) and instead accepted the formation of a Hill Council in the Darjeeling district. Though peace returned to the district, the accord did not fully satisfy all leaders of the GNLF, whose desire for statehood is still articulated, though nonviolently.

The latest peace accord pertains to the Bodo conflict. This is the second accord to be reached on the same conflict within a ten-year period. While the 1993 accord was signed between the state government of Assam and the moderate Bodo leaders in the presence of a representative of the central government, the February 2003 accord was a trilateral one, directly involving as signatories the central and state governments and the BLT, which had been formed in opposition to the 1993 accord. The 2003 accord has created an autonomous self-governing body, the Bodoland Territorial Council (BTC), within the state of Assam. The council's jurisdiction is spread over 3,082 villages; additional villages can also be included if all three signatories agree. The BTC enjoys protection under the Sixth Schedule of the Indian Constitution. In addition, there are guarantees of accelerated infrastructure development in Bodoland; the fulfillment of the economic, educational, and linguistic aspirations of the Bodos; and the preservation of their land rights and ethnic identity. The BSF, which reemerged as the National Democratic Front of Bodoland (NDFB), has opposed the accord, whose success in restoring peace depends upon either defeating the NDFB or coercing it to join the political mainstream.

As in many other countries, secessionist conflicts in India are more intractable than lesser conflicts. The only secessionist conflict to end in negotiated settlement has been the Mizo conflict, because in that case the MNF leadership has compromised, under heavy military pressure, on its original separatist goal.

Ponmoni Sahadevan

See also **Ethnic Conflict; Insurgency and Terrorism; Paramilitary Forces and Internal Security; Tribal Politics**

BIBLIOGRAPHY

Bhattacharjee, Chandana. *Ethnicity and Autonomy Movement: Case of Bodo-Kacharis of Assam*. New Delhi: Vikas, 1996.

Bhaumik, Subir. *Insurgent Crossfire: North-east India*. New Delhi: Lancer, 1996.

Kapur, Rajiv A. *Sikh Separatism: The Politics of Faith*. London: Allen and Unwin, 1986.

Phadnis, Urmila. *Ethnicity and Nation-Building in South Asia*. New Delhi: Sage, 1989.

Subba, Thanka B. *Ethnicity, State, and Development: A Case Study of Gorkhaland Movement in Darjeeling*. New Delhi: Har-Anand, 1992.

Verghese, B. G. *India's Northeast Resurgent: Ethnicity, Insurgency, Governance, Development*. New Delhi: Konark, 1996.

EUROPEAN UNION, RELATIONS WITH

India and the European Union (EU) have shared historical links, political institutions, and a liberal ethos. India's independence and the initiation of the efforts to achieve regional cooperation in Europe both began shortly after World War II. India was among the first countries to recognize the then six-member European Economic Community (EEC), a precursor of the EU. Since then, India has enjoyed many areas of convergence with the EU, ranging from social and cultural relations to economic and political matters. Still, there are many problematic areas of divergence on which both parties will have to work diligently to ensure future cooperation.

Overview of Relations

The table below reflects the slow progression in EU-India relations. After an initial period of stabilization and cautious foreign relations, India established formal diplomatic relations with the EEC in 1963. Besides historical ties, the values of democracy and pluralism were significant promoters of this relationship. With India's policy of nonalignment, this relationship was peripheral during the cold war. Prime Minister Indira Gandhi fully realized the potential significance of economic, cultural, and political cooperation with Western Europe. She was successful in evolving bilateral relations with France and former West Germany, but these agreements were country specific and could not reach the wider European community.

The first major economic assistance came in 1970 when the EU contributed 147 million euros to the Operation Flood Programme for dairy development in India. In 1973, India and the EEC signed their first Agreement on Commercial Cooperation. In 1971, India was included in the Generalized System of Preferences (GSP) program of the EEC. Another Agreement for Five-Year Economic and Commercial Cooperation was signed in 1981. The evolution of the European Community as a political organization thus led to the establishment of closer political and trade relations with India. It was agreed formally to institute an India-EEC Political Dialogue with the establishment of the EEC delegation in New Delhi in 1983. Despite of all these developments, the bilateral relationship remained limited to certain economic areas.

The end of the cold war era placed both India and the EEC in a new environment without ideological barriers. The EEC was formally transformed into the European Community (EC) under the Treaty of European Union (EU), which took effect on 1 November 1993, leading to deeper political and economic integration of the European nations. The EU also moved toward the adoption of a common currency and common foreign and security policies. In 1991 India also started implementing its economic deregulation and liberalization program, emerging as a major economic player in the global market, with a huge potential for investment. As a giant in information technology (IT), India provided additional impetus for the improvement of bilateral relations based on complementary interests.

India's first comprehensive agreement with the EU came into force in August 1994, with the signing of their Cooperation Agreement between the European Community and the Republic of India on Partnership and Development. That agreement covered issues that included respect for human rights and democratic principles; development and diversification of trade and investment; cooperation on technical, economic, and cultural matters; sustainable social progress and poverty alleviation; and support for environmental protection and sustainable development. Concrete steps toward these objectives were clearly stated in a communication approved by the council of the commission on EU-India Enhanced Partnership in 1996. The same year, India's Trade and Investment Forum was held in Brussels, jointly chaired by EC vice president Manual Marin and Indian minister of commerce B. B. Ramaiah. Indian minister for external affairs Jaswant Singh's visit to Brussels in 1999 was another landmark in strengthening relations. Meanwhile, India-EU political dialogue was elevated to the Foreign Ministerial level and institutionalized through the Troika mechanism, comprising of the current EU presidency, the succeeding president and the previous president. The EU-Troika started holding annual talks with India on major bilateral and

LANDMARKS IN INDIA–EU RELATIONS

Year	Event
1963	India establishes diplomatic relations with the European Economic Community (EEC).
1971	EEC includes India in the countries of general tariff preferences under the Generalized System of Preferences (GSP) program.
1981	India and the EEC sign a five-year Commercial and Economic Cooperation agreement (16 November).
1983	EEC delegation in India established in New Delhi.
1988	EC–India Joint Commission Meeting held (March).
1992	Indian and European businesspeople launch a joint initiative, Joint Business Forum (October).
1993	EC and India sign Joint Political Statement, simultaneously, with the Cooperation Agreement on Partnership and Development (20 December), effective from 1 August 1994.
1994	Setting up of Technology Information Center (TIC) in New Delhi.
1996	Commission adopts the communication on EU–India Enhanced Partnership (26 June), approved by the council on 6 December. EU–India Economic Cross-Cultural program is launched (26 November).
1999	European Parliament endorses the commission's Communication on "EU–India Enhanced Partnership" (12 March).
2000	The first EU–India summit is held in Lisbon (28 June); the joint declaration emphasizes a strategic partnership to cover economy, trade, security, and democracy.
2001	The second EU–India summit is held in New Delhi (23 November). A joint communiqué issued after the summit focuses on an Agenda for Action for developing the full potential for bilateral partnership and addresses issues pertaining to global challenges. A Declaration against Terrorism, the EU–India Vision Statement on Information Technology, and the EU-India Agreement on Science and Technology are the highlights.
2002	The European Commission presents Country Strategy Paper 2002–2006 for India, which aims to chart out the course for development and economic cooperation between India and the EU. The third EU–India summit is held in Copenhagen to review the progress in bilateral relations (10 October).
2003	EU Troika meets Indian foreign ministers in Athens (11 January). EU Trade Commissioner Pascal Lamy visits India on 13–14 March to discuss bilateral trade issues as well as the World Trade Organization's negotiations under the Doha Development Agenda with the Indian leaders. EU Cultural Weeks 2003 organized in New Delhi, Bangalore, Chennai, Kolkata, Mumbai, and Chandigarh (22 November–4 December). The fourth EU–India Summit was held in New Delhi, India, on 29 November. Pluralism, democracy, the multipolar world and reconstruction of Afghanistan and Iraq also became the important points of discussion in the summit.
2004	EU Trade Commissioner Pascal Lamy visits India on 19 January to enhance trade ties with the EU and to boost the WTO negotiations under the Doha Development Agenda. EU Commissioner for External Relations Chris Patten visits India on 16 February for a series of EU Ministerial Troika(1) meetings. The troika is led by the Irish minister of foreign affairs, Brian Cowen, accompanied by the Dutch minister for foreign affairs, Dr. Bernard R. Bot. Commission communication on "EU–India Strategic Partnership" of June 2004. The fifth summit between the EU and India was held in the Hague, the Netherlands, on 8 November. The focus of this summit was rich and diversified cultural traditions and the Action Plan for Strategic Partnership.

The list was compiled with the help of *Milestones in EU–India Relations,* available at <http://www.delind.cec.eu.int/en/political_dialogue/milestones.htm> and bilateral documents available at the site of Ministry of External Affairs, India, <http://meaindia.nic.in>

international issues. European commissioner for trade Pascal Lamy visited Mumbai and New Delhi in 2000, which led to the first EU-India summit that year.

That summit was held in Lisbon on 28 June 2000, and wide-ranging issues of political, economic, developmental, and environmental significance were discussed. The Joint Summit Declaration further ensured such summit meetings of foreign ministers every year to examine all impediments to trade and investment in India, with a view to removing them. The second summit convened in New Delhi on 23 November 2001, focusing on strategic and international issues. Its Agenda for Action was a joint statement on international terrorism, with both sides agreeing to help one another in facing the current international situation, with specific reference to Afghanistan and Pakistan. Initiatives on the economic front were striking. Some of the economic landmarks included a joint statement regarding trade and investment, the signing of an agreement on scientific and technological cooperation, and the adoption of a statement on information technology. The third EU-India summit met in Copenhagen on 10 October 2002, reviewing the challenges and possible responses in areas of regional and global peace, the integration of developing countries into the global economy, and issues related to civil society, including poverty alleviation, health care, and education.

EU Trade Commissioner Pascal Lamy played a very significant role in normalizing the bilateral trade issues when he visited India on 13–14 March 2003. The fourth EU-India summit was held in New Delhi, India, on 29 November 2003. Besides pluralism, democracy, and the multipolar world, both sides have reiterated their commitments toward strengthening the role of the United Nations (UN) in the maintenance of international peace and security, the common fight against terrorism and transborder crimes, and the UN Convention on Climate Change. In the changed global context, intense cooperation to promote peace, stability, and reconstruction of Afghanistan and Iraq also became the important points of discussion in the summit.

The fifth summit between the EU and India was held in the Hague, the Netherlands, on 8 November 2004. The focus of this summit was rich and diversified cultural traditions enjoyed by both sides. There was an agreement to work toward the elaboration of a specific chapter on cultural cooperation within the EU-India Action Plan for Strategic Partnership. Successful conclusion of the Customs Co-operation, progress in the negotiations on Maritime Agreement and strategic dialogue on the Information Society was reviewed. The EU-India Action Plan for Strategic Partnership was also drawn in this summit, focusing on the regional and international dimensions of fight against terrorism.

Areas of Convergence

Sociocultural cooperation. The vast English-speaking and technologically skilled population of India, along with the interest of European scholars in studies pertaining to Indian society and culture, forms the basis of sociocultural ties between India and the EU. After their first summit at Lisbon, a think-tank network and an India-EU Round Table were established to discuss social and civil issues. The first EU-India think-tank seminar declared that the EU and India share common goals in the battle against poverty and the welfare of marginalized sections of society. An EU-India Economic Cross Cultural Programme (ECCP) was initiated, with the overall objective of strengthening and enhancing civil society links and cross-cultural cooperation through dialogue between European and Indian media and cultural organizations and by supporting educational and cultural activities. The European Union Film Festival held in New Delhi (6–13 October) and Kolkata (19–25 October) 2000, on the theme of "The City," and the parallel conference on "Cities of Tomorrow" demonstrated mutual concerns over urban planning and sustainable development. Jawaharlal Nehru University's European Studies Programme, with an EC support of 590,000 euros (approximately 30 million rupees), an EC contribution of 200 million euros to the Indian universal elementary education program, and attempts by scholars and the media to change stereotypical depictions of an underdeveloped India in the European media all pointed to the emergence of closer social and cultural ties.

Political and strategic concerns. At the political and strategic level, India and the EU have shared values of democracy, pluralism, commitment to multilateralism, the reformation of international organizations, and a common concern over terrorism and the protection of human rights. According to the EU-India Joint Statement on Political Dialogue adopted in 1994, both sides are committed to defending democracy, human rights, and a peaceful, stable, and just international order in accordance with the UN Charter. In the Declaration against International Terrorism made on 23 November 2001, India and the EU reiterated their commitment to cooperation against international terrorism.

Science and technology. India's inability to realize its goal of complete self-reliance, and the failure of the EU to match the United States and Japan in science and technology during the last half century, provided a foundation for bilateral cooperation in that field. The Agreement for Scientific and Technological Cooperation adopted by the EU council on 25 June 2002 was based on the principle of mutual benefit and reciprocal opportunities. This agreement will enable both India and the EU to share experience and utilize each other's technology for poverty eradication, food security, and environmental sustainability. The conferment of observer status to India at the Council of the European Organization for Nuclear Research (CERN) was a sign of cordial and confident bilateral relations. Information and Communication Technology (ICT) has been another mutually beneficial area of cooperation between the EU and India, both jointly agreeing to establish the Software Service Support and Education Center at Banglore to promote India-EU joint ventures in information technology. The Joint EU-India Vision Statement on Development of the Information Society adopted on 23 November 2001 led to the establishment of the EU-India Working Group on the Information Society, which will work toward enhancing human capacity development, knowledge creation and sharing, and training in related fields.

Trade and economy. At the first bilateral summit, low levels of trade and the need for joint efforts to increase its potential were stressed. A joint initiative was adopted, in which four sectors were specified for potential investment: food processing, engineering, telecommunications, and IT. India exports textiles, jewelry, leather goods, chemicals, and agricultural products to the EU, while India imports chemicals, engineering goods, metal products, and transportation equipment from the EU. After the process of liberalization, and thanks to multilateral trading under the auspices of the World Trade Organization (WTO), EU-India trade increased from 9,975 million euros in 1991 to 25,032 million euros in 2001, a phenomenal growth of 150 percent. By 2003 the EU accounted for a quarter of India's imports and exports and was the largest source of foreign direct investment.

Areas of Divergence

WTO. Though the WTO has brought about greater trade at the multilateral level, the historical legacy of development process has made the WTO negotiations as a point of confrontation for both the sides. As a developed market the EU is seeking greater tariff reduction and more trade facilitation while representing the interests of developing countries. India always supported tariff reduction and inclusion of larger issues within the WTO ambit only after the phased elimination of support subsidies to the farmers of the developed countries. These differences were evident in the Fifth Ministerial Conferences of the WTO at Cancun and later negotiations.

Nuclear nonproliferation. After India's nuclear tests in 1998, nuclear nonproliferation has been an issue of contention between India and the EU. The joint communiqué of the second EU-India summit reiterated "unequivocal commitment to the ultimate goal of complete elimination of nuclear weapons." However, India has a principled stand against any discriminatory approach to nuclear nonproliferation. The EU as a whole had reacted sharply and bitterly against India's nuclear tests and expects unconditional acceptance of the Comprehensive Test Ban Treaty, which India has refused to accept. After five years of tests, it is still not clear whether India and the EU will be able to accommodate and adjust to each other's positions on this issue.

International power relations. India and the EU have their own realistic interests and perceptions of international power relations, and their consequent behavioral differences have affected their relations. Principally, India has always perceived the EU as the shadow of the United States, while India is perceived by the EU as a strategic ally of Russia. India has, moreover, consistently opposed undemocratic practices in governing international institutions, primarily the UN, the International Monetary Fund, and the WTO. The EU is not ready to forgo the superiority built up by its members in creating these institutions. On the question of its own bilateral relations with Pakistan, India has consistently opposed the EU's policy of collaborating with military rulers in the international war against terrorism.

India has genuine concerns over the violence abetted by Pakistan in Jammu and Kashmir, the reformation of the UN and the WTO, and the regional protectionist policies of the EU in agriculture and textile sectors. At the same time, the perception of India as a strategic and business partner is still largely negative within the EU. India is considered a country with administrative impediments and unethical, nontransparent practices in trade-related matters. At the political level, India is known as a country with uncertain and inconsistent policies due to enormous domestic pressures and constraints. India will have to speed up its internal reforms in social and economic matters, while building a positive image as democratic and commercially vibrant country. It will have to review its policy of focusing only on the EU's larger countries, like France, Germany, and the United Kingdom, while ignoring smaller countries of enormous trade potential, like Belgium, the Netherlands, and Italy. More importantly, both sides will have to transcend the historical legacy of colonialism and the inherent conflicts between developed and developing countries, and they will have to strengthen communications and institutional mechanisms to address their mutual disagreements and concerns.

Prafulla Ketkar

BIBLIOGRAPHY

"EC Country Strategy Paper, India." Available at <http://europa.eu.int/comm/external_relations/india/csp/02_06en.pdf>
"EU-India Enhanced Partnership." COM (96) 275. Brussels: Commission of the European Communities, 26 June 1996.

"India's Foreign Policy: Western Europe." Available at <http://www.indianembassy.org/policy/Foreign_Policy/weuro.htm>

"Milestones in EU-India Relations." Available at <http://www/delind.cec.eu.int/en/political_dialogue/milestones.htm>

SECONDARY SOURCES

Bhattacharya, Swapan K. "European Union's Trade with Asia and India: Prospects in the New Millennium." Paper presented at the international seminar on "The European Union in a Changing World," School of International Relations, Jawaharlal Nehru University, New Delhi, 6–7 September 2001.

Chaturvedi, Sachin. "India, the European Union and Geographical Indications (GI): Covergence of Interests and Challenges Ahead." Paper presented at the international seminar on "India, the European Union, and the WTO," organized by Centre des Sciences Humaines, EC Delegation, Fundacao, Oriente, JNU European Union Studies Project, and Konrad Adenauer Foundation, at Jawaharlal Nehru University, New Delhi, 16–17 October 2002.

Jain, Rajendra K. "India and the European Union." In *India, Germany and European Union: Partners in Progress and Prosperity*, edited by Naushad Anwar Sulaiman. Delhi: Kalinga Publication, 2002.

Katyal, K. K. "Strong Case for Enhancing India-EU Relations." *Hindu*, 26 November 2001.

Ram, A. N. "India and the European Union." *World Focus* 21, no. 5 (May 2000): 9–12.

Singh, Jasjit. "India, Europe and Non-Proliferation: Pokhran II and After." *Strategic Analysis* 22, no. 8 (November 1998): 1111–1122.

EXTERNAL DEBT POLICY, 1952–1990 India chronically suffered from a shortage of resources necessary to finance a rising rate of investment required to yield a growing rate of income growth. India's planned program of economic development began in 1952, with its First Five-Year Plan. Being a low-income country, its savings were inadequate to finance investment. Its difficulties were compounded because India needed foreign exchange to supplement its domestic savings to pay for the import of goods, essential for sustaining the rising investment rate. The growth of the domestic savings rate since the 1950s was impressive, but it was not sufficient to fully support the investment required to sustain rapid growth. Foreign resources were not easily forthcoming, as India's exports were far below its import requirements, thereby impelling it to seek foreign assistance. The balance of payments difficulties and the resultant increase in foreign indebtedness that India faced were, therefore, not a temporary phenomenon but inevitable throughout the process of development, with its calculated strategy to keep the rate of investment consistently above the rate of saving.

During the First Plan, 1951–1956, external assistance served two functions: it would make available adequate supplies of foreign exchange to finance imports; and it would supplement the investment resources the country could raise on its own. The balance of payments did not present problems during the First Plan period. Foreign saving as a proportion of total investment turned out to be 4.6 percent, while the external debt to gross domestic product (GDP) ratio averaged 2.05 percent during the period.

The Second Plan, 1956–1961, which put greater emphasis on industrialization, entailed a larger amount of foreign exchange. Of the estimated current account deficit of 11 billion rupees during 1956–1961, 8 billion rupees was assumed to be met by external assistance. The plan, however, ran into unexpected balance of payments difficulties from the very start, and had to be reappraised in 1958, signaling a turning point in India's external position. Stringent restrictions were imposed on less essential imports, and its own foreign exchange reserves were drawn down to the largest extent of 6 billion rupees during the Second Plan period. In addition, external assistance of the order of 8.72 billion rupees was provided in the public as well as private sectors, besides commodity imports of 5.34 billion rupees under the commodity assistance program and borrowings from the International Monetary Fund (IMF) of 55 billion rupees. The external debt/GDP ratio increased to 8.06 percent during the Second Plan period.

The Third Plan, 1961–1966, reflected some rethinking in India's external financing strategy, highlighting self-sustaining growth as a major goal. While it envisaged that normal capital flows would continue, it set out the contours of the concept of self-reliance. The main elements of this concept were import substitution, with the expansion of capital goods and infrastructure industries on a scale that would enable the country to produce domestically the bulk of capital goods and machinery as well as consumer goods, and a well-defined export strategy. It therefore called for the maximum rate of investment and a change in its structure so as to secure an increase in national income of over 5 percent per annum. Accordingly, gross external assistance of 32 billion rupees was allowed for the Third Plan period, with the assistance net of repayments and liabilities arising from Public Law 480 (PL 480) imports and loans to the private sector being around 22 billion rupees. The Third Plan projection, however, went awry, partly because of its unrealistic nature and misconceived domestic and macroeconomic and foreign exchange policies, and partly because of the Indo-Pakistani hostilities that broke out in 1965.

The same policy was continued during the Fourth Plan (1969–1974), more or less, with additional emphasis on doing away with concessional imports of food grains under the commodity assistance program by 1971. The goal was to reduce net foreign aid to one-half the Third Plan level. External debt to GDP ratio was 13.6 percent during the Fourth Plan.

The Fifth Plan (1974–1979) strategy was based on massive exports growth and on containing imports. By the time the plan was adopted, however, the scenario had changed. Owing to a hike in oil prices and a sharp increase in the import prices of certain other important commodities, like fertilizers and food grains, the size of external assistance was pushed up to over 58 billion rupees from the original estimate of about 24 billion rupees. External debt to GDP ratio averaged 13.4 percent during this plan period.

The Sixth Plan (1980–1985) also saw a major change in the pattern of foreign borrowings, which until the end of the 1970s had contained a bulk of concessional foreign assistance. First, nonconcessional flows accounted for a growing proportion of official borrowings. Second, direct borrowings by financial institutions and the private sector grew substantially, unlike in the previous period of planned development. These factors, combined with outstanding borrowings from the IMF and nonresident Indian (NRI) deposits (transfer of funds by Indians living outside India) raised substantially the average cost of foreign debt, and consequently the external debt to GDP ratio spurted up to 15.5 percent. The situation did not improve during the Seventh Plan period (1985–1990). An increase in imports from hard currency areas; diversion of a substantial part of India's exports to Eastern European, Soviet-dominated countries with nonconvertible currencies; and a shift to high cost commercial debt sharply increased India's hard currency external debt.

The current account deficit of 29 percent during this period, which was widening rapidly, was financed by way of external assistance from multilateral and bilateral donors, 24 percent by commercial borrowings, 23 percent through nonresident deposits under the Foreign Currency Non Resident Account plan and Non Resident External Rupee Account, about 13 percent from other capital transactions, and the remaining by a draw-down of foreign currency reserves. External debt to GDP ratio as a result doubled to 30 percent, with foreign savings as a proportion of investment reaching 11.2 percent.

India was the fourth-largest debtor (after Brazil, Mexico, and Indonesia) among developing countries at the end of March 1991. India's total outstanding external debt, including the use of IMF credit and short-term credit, stood at U.S.$71.6 billion at the end of March 1991, steadily increasing from about $8.9 billion in 1971. In terms of the share of total outstanding debt in GNP at

29.2 percent, it was lower than that of Mexico (36.9 percent) and Indonesia (66.4 percent) but higher than Brazil's 28.8 percent. The vulnerability of the Indian economy by the end of 1990 was reflected in large debt service payments on its huge stock of external debt. India's debt service ratio in 1991, at 30.6 percent, was nearly equal to Brazil's 30.8 percent and Mexico's 30.9 percent and was higher than the average of 27.6 per cent for the moderately indebted low income countries group.

India's Approach to External Debt Policy

Until the beginning of the Fifth Plan, there was almost total reliance on official, especially multilateral flows, mainly on concessional terms and recourse to IMF facilities to meet extraordinary situations such as the drought of the 1960s and the oil shocks of the early and late 1970s. Thus, until the 1980s, external financing was confined to external assistance, mostly on concessional terms. The plan strategy was interventionist and biased against exports. This was an era of perpetual foreign exchange shortage, and foreign resources to a developing country like India, where reliance continued to be on external borrowings, was not easily forthcoming. The policy was to approach the developed countries and the World Bank group with an accent on soft terms of interest and other conditions governing loan repayment. In terms of multilateral financing, the relationship with the World Bank and its soft loan window, the International Development Association (IDA), evolved since the beginning of planning. Until 1979 IDA loans formed between 70 to 80 percent of loans from the World Bank group. These loans were at highly concessional rates and for very long maturities. Between 1980 and 1990, the World Bank loan component increased to about 50 percent of the total loans from the World Bank group, of which India was the largest debtor. Since 1958 the World Bank organized the Aid-to-India consortium, consisting of the World Bank group and thirteen other countries (Austria, Belgium, Canada, Denmark, the former West Germany, France, Italy, Japan, the Netherlands, Norway, Sweden, the United Kingdom, and the United States). The consortium was formed to coordinate aid and establish priorities among the major sources of foreign assistance. Consortium aid was bilateral government-to-government, and the loans from the World Bank group were loans given for specific projects.

The trends in external debt reflected the evolution of external debt policy during the plan periods. Until the end of the 1960s, the composition of India's external debt was characterized by the predominance of long-term public and publicly guaranteed debt. Bilateral debt comprised about 75 percent of the total debt, while multilateral debt accounted for about 20 percent. The 1970s saw a shift in the composition of the official debt with the share of bilateral debt progressively reduced to about 50 percent. There was a shift from the official debt toward borrowings from private sources during the 1980s. The composition of official debt itself changed, with the share of bilateral debt decreasing sharply. As a consequence of the above two developments, the terms of borrowing, including maturity, interest rate, and the grace period, turned harder. Short-term debt increased during the latter half of the 1980s. Commercial borrowings accelerated, particularly during the latter half of the 1980s. This increased the cost of debt and reduced the average maturities of the debt portfolio. "Scarce" foreign exchange was also sought through a number of nonresident deposit plans, which offered higher rates of interest relative to prevailing international rates and, in addition, exchange guarantees. This change in strategy proved to be unsustainable toward the end of the 1980s, and in 1990, when the Gulf oil crisis erupted, the government was unable to roll over the short-term debt and commercial borrowings, which coincided with withdrawal of "hot" NRI deposits, which had initially flown in to take advantage of arbitrage in interest rates. India went into a crisis in August 1991 and resorted to use of IMF resources. Since 1991, its debt policy also changed, with de-emphasis on debt-creating flows and greater focus on nondebt creating investment flows, that is, equity. Even among debt flows, limits were imposed on commercial borrowings and within more stringent limits on short-term debt. The high interest and exchange-guaranteed nonresident deposits were dismantled. The current NRI deposits offer interest rates around prevailing international rates, and the exchange rate risk is being borne by the depositor.

Since the mid-1990s, India has surpassed the era of chronic foreign exchange shortages. India now has a strong economy, which attracts foreign capital—short- and long-term, equity and debt funds—under market determined conditions.

A. Prasad

See also **Capital Market; Economic Reforms of 1991; Foreign Resources Inflow since 1991**

BIBLIOGRAPHY

Government of India. *Five Year Plan Documents*. Delhi: GOI, 1951–1990.
Kapur, Munish. "India's External Sector since Independence: From Inwardness to Openness." Reserve Bank of India Occasional Papers, vol. 18, nos. 2–3, June and September 1997.

FAMILY LAW AND CULTURAL PLURALISM

India's family laws, also called personal or customary laws, govern features of family life such as marriage, separation, divorce and its consequences, maintenance for children and other dependents, inheritance, adoption, and guardianship. Independent India retained many aspects of the plural family law system of the British colonial period as a means of cultural accommodation within its multicultural society, especially concerning the accommodation of Muslims. Different family laws govern India's major religious groups—Hindus, Muslims, Christians, Parsis, and Jews—as well as many tribal peoples. Hindu family law also governs those who follow religions of South Asian origin, such as Sikhism and Jainism.

Indian legal pluralism is in tension with the secular commitments of the Indian state, and with the constitutional aim to promote gender equality as the various family law systems uphold unequal gender relations. India's political elite attempted to resolve these tensions in the first decade after independence, through the partial homogenization and reform of Hindu law, the introduction of optional marriage laws in a Special Marriage Act and a constitutional commitment to introduce a uniform civil code to govern all Indians. These policy choices restricted the state's social engineering, however, to Hindu law. They appeared likely to limit efforts to promote gender equality through legal change, particularly through changes in the laws governing the religious minorities as such changes were supposedly left to the initiative of unspecified representatives of these groups, who in practice were often conservative religious and political elites. The price of Indian legal pluralism reflects the problems seen in most multicultural arrangements, in which laws justified in terms of enabling cultural pluralism do not necessarily reflect group norms or practices. The scope for legal change is limited even if citizens demand changes in gender-biased group laws.

Complete legal pluralism involves the application of distinct laws to different cultural groups in all areas of social life, adjudication by distinctive community courts, and a lack of reference to common principles (such as those recognized by international human rights law or national constitutions) in making and implementing law. Where religious groups are the social units to which distinctive laws apply, religious leaders, religious scholars, and priests are the main or sole agents of lawmaking and adjudication. Legal pluralism is only partial in India in many respects. The laws governing Indians are uniform, other than those concerning family life. Indian judiciaries, largely trained in Western legal traditions, are the main agents of adjudication in all disputes brought to state courts. Aside from the state's judiciary, different religious and cultural groups have their own community leaders who act as adjudicative agents, the community institutions involved in adjudication include Hindu caste associations, Muslim prayer groups (*jamaat*s), and local Christian churches and Parsi temples. Individual religious figures, caste leaders, and popularly recognized informal judges also adjudicate family disputes.

The complex nature of Indian legal pluralism provides some room for changes in family law, even while impeding rapid transformation. Over the last generation, Parliament changed the provisions governing all Indians for the prohibition of dowry, and for maintenance payments to indigent women upon separation or divorce. It made divorce easier for Hindus and Christians, including on grounds of mutual consent. Some state legislatures gave daughters the right to demand the partition of ancestral property so that they could access their shares, equal to those of sons, that the law assures them.

Prompted by the growth of public interest litigation, especially since the "National Emergency" of the mid-1970s, the judiciary initiated more changes in family law by interpreting some statutes and features of nonstatutory law in the light of the fundamental rights guaranteed by the Indian constitution. The judiciary changed family law more often than legislatures did, and sometimes prompted subsequent legislative change. This was true, for instance, of the changes introduced in the grounds on which Hindus and Christians could seek divorce, and in the alimony rights of Muslim women.

A Comparison of Hindu and Muslim Law

Many aspects of Indian family law are misunderstood. It is widely believed that the legislative reform of Hindu law in the 1950s made it secular and more conducive to gender equality, more so than the family laws of other groups, particularly Muslims. Many claim that the secularization and homogenization of family law is the only route to greater gender equality.

After the Hindu law reforms of the 1950s, statutes governed more areas of Hindu law than Muslim law. But, religious texts and beliefs influenced these reforms, for instance, the introduction of divorce rights. In addition, these reforms weakened the rights of some women, for instance, the rights of widows to shares in their former husbands' property if they chose to remarry. They further weakened the divorce rights of some Hindu women, who previously could get divorces more easily based on the recognized customs of their castes, and the property rights of others that were governed by matrilineal inheritance laws earlier.

While legislation of the 1950s partly homogenized the major features of Hindu law, the Shariat Act of 1937 had the same effect earlier on Muslim law. It made "Muslim law" applicable to most areas of family life among Indian Muslims (while leaving the content of Muslim law unspecified), and in the process overrode the customs of some Muslim subgroups that had enjoyed legal recognition until then. Partial homogenization was effected in ways that increased the rights of Muslim women more often than it did the rights of Hindu women. This was true, for instance, of the inheritance rights of Muslim women. Daughters gained rights to half the shares that sons enjoyed in their parents' property, in contrast with previously having no rights to inherit parental property. Although no statutes specified these rights, they were recognized in Islam's founding texts as well as in later Islamic jurisprudence, and the Indian judiciary followed these prescriptions in adjudication.

Muslim law is far less codified than Hindu law. Only three short statutes pertain to Muslim law in India: two that outline the divorce and alimony rights of women, and the Shariat Act, which in effect leaves the content of Indian Muslim law to the judiciary's discretion. In contrast, four elaborate acts define the major features of Hindu law. Judges refer far more often to religious sources in adjudicating cases involving Muslims than those involving Hindus.

While Muslim law is less codified and more closely linked to religious sources than Hindu law, the rights of Muslim women are superior to those of Hindu women in some respects. This is true of a daughter's inheritance rights. Hindu daughters have rights to share equally with sons in intestate succession to their parents' self-earned property, in contrast with Muslim daughters, who have rights to only half the shares that Muslim sons enjoy. However, the succession rights of Hindu daughters are restricted to intestate cases, that is, cases in which the parent did not leave a will. Hindu parents are free to will self-earned property as they wish, typically leaving all or most of such property to their sons, or perhaps other male kin. Male coparcenaries, moreover, control ancestral Hindu property in much of India, and daughters do not have any right to demand the partition of such property so that they may control their shares. (They gained this right since the mid-1980s only in five states.) This gives Hindu women little effective access to most forms of family property.

Muslim daughters have the right to half the shares left to sons in all forms of parental property. Muslim parents cannot deny their daughters rights to inherit shares in their property by willing self-earned property to male kin alone, or by effectively presenting more of the property they own as being of ancestral origin. While many do so, their daughters can effectively challenge such disinheritance in the courts. Hindu daughters have no legal recourse under such circumstances in much of India.

Muslim women had fewer rights in other respects than did Hindu women at different points. For instance, until recently, most Indian courts recognized the unconditional right of Muslim men to unilaterally divorce their wives, without giving Muslim women similar rights. In contrast, statutory Hindu law allows divorce based only on mutual consent, or if a spouse is found guilty of a "fault" such as cruelty, desertion, or adultery. From 1973 onward, indigent Hindu women had the right to alimony until their remarriage or death. Many courts did not recognize the right of divorced Muslim women to maintenance from their ex-husbands beyond a three-month period after divorce. The courts allow Muslim men to marry up to four wives (while not permitting polyandry), while Hindu law bans bigamy. The ban on Hindu bigamy is, however, not very effective, as the courts set high standards to recognize the validity of bigamous Hindu marriages. Public debate has highlighted the ways in which Muslim women have fewer rights than Hindu women, though not vice versa, reflecting the recent growth of Hindu nationalism, the widespread vision of Muslims as marginal to Indian citizenry, and the limited understanding of Muslim law.

The limited codification of Muslim law gave judges greater autonomy to initiate legal change, and the judiciary used this autonomy to address some of the gender inequalities in Muslim law over the last generation. The Supreme Court (India's apex court) recognized the alimony rights of Muslim women and placed conditions for the validity of unilateral Muslim male divorce in two landmark judgments in 2001 and 2002. It decreed earlier that bigamy was a ground on which Muslim women could claim divorce, without criminalizing Muslim bigamy. As the apex court defines the law for the lower courts, these judgments made the alimony rights of Muslim women the same as those of non-Muslim women. They also meant that there was similar room for unilateral male divorce among Hindus and Muslims. While Hindu law does not explicitly recognize unilateral divorce, it permits divorce if a couple did not live together for a year after a decree of judicial separation or restitution of conjugal rights, a provision used by many Hindu men but very few Hindu women.

Feasible Routes to Change

Recent judicial reforms in Muslim law indicate some routes available for changes in Indian family law that would give women greater rights. Judges introduced these reforms with reference to early and more recent Islamic religious and jurisprudential traditions, statutory Muslim law, and features of the Indian constitution (the fundamental rights to life, equality, and dignity). Their reference to constitutional principles did not lead them toward the secularization or homogenization of family law, yet enabled greater gender equality. Other judicial and legislative changes in Hindu and Christian law followed this pattern. For instance, divorce was made possible for Christian women on grounds other than adultery, because Protestants had long accepted divorce on such grounds, and even Catholic Church leaders came to support the right of Christian women to seek divorce under conditions of spousal cruelty or desertion. The recent legal changes effected convergence in some features of the different Indian family laws, and were restricted to some of the gender inequalities in family law.

While more Hindus (especially Hindu nationalists) demand a uniform civil code (UCC), consensus has not yet emerged about the content of a UCC. Many Hindus are likely to resist a UCC that favors much greater gender equality, and others to resist a UCC that draws from the different existing family laws and associated cultural traditions. If change in family law occurs within a framework of legal pluralism, this is partly because of the changing patterns of mobilization regarding family law policy. The introduction of a UCC was a major demand of women's organizations and other civic associations aiming to promote gender justice until the 1980s. This goal seemed increasingly unrealistic, however, with the passage of time. Hindu nationalists particularly embraced the demand for a UCC after the Congress Party government, under Rajiv Gandhi, appeared to give in to conservative Muslim pressure to overturn in 1986 earlier judicial reforms that gave Muslim women permanent alimony rights (the Shah Bano case). Many women's organizations shifted their focus, from demanding a UCC to promoting gender-equalizing reform within the context of legal pluralism, because of their desire to avoid an association with the Hindu nationalists.

While some key legislators engaged in making family law have belonged to parties that demand a UCC, their legislative initiatives have been for piecemeal changes that do not clearly move family law toward homogenization. Along with resistance from the religious minorities and the tribal peoples to a UCC, and resistance among many individuals in all religious and ethnic groups to the promotion of gender equality, the recent orientations of the major policy-making agents suggest the likelihood of gradual, halting gender-equalizing change, within the context of legal pluralism, in the foreseeable future.

Narendra Subramanian

See also **Development Politics; Gender and Human Rights**

BIBLIOGRAPHY

Agarwal, Bina. *A Field of One's Own: Gender and Land Rights in South Asia.* Cambridge, U.K. and New York: Cambridge University Press, 1994.

Agnes, Flavia. *Law and Gender Inequality: The Politics of Women's Rights in India.* New Delhi and New York: Oxford University Press, 1999.

Basu, Srimati. *She Comes to Take Her Rights: Indian Women, Property and Propriety.* Albany: State University of New York Press, 1999.

Derrett, J. D. M. *Religion, Law and the State in India.* New York: Free Press, 1968.

Larson, Gerald, ed. *Religion and Personal Law in Secular India: A Call to Judgment.* Bloomington: Indiana University Press, 2001.

Mansfield, John H. "The Personal Laws or a Uniform Civil Code?" In *Religion and Law in Independent India,* edited by Robert D. Baird. New Delhi: Manohar, 1993.

Menski, Werner F. *Modern Indian Family Law.* Richmond, U.K.: Curzon Press, 2001.

———. *Hindu Law: Beyond Tradition and Modernity.* New Delhi and New York: Oxford University Press, 2003.

Mukhopadhyay, Maitrayee. *Legally Dispossessed: Gender, Identity, and the Process of Law.* Mumbai: Stree Press, 1998.

Parashar, Archana. *Women and Family Law Reform in India.* New Delhi: Sage Publications, 1992.

FAMINES Famines, defined as large-scale episodes of acute starvation, were a frequent occurrence in South Asia until the mid-twentieth century. In 1770 nearly a third of the population of Bengal died due to a famine. Around 1877 about 4 million lives were lost, mainly in Bombay and Madras presidencies. In 1896–1897, more than 5 million perished, and in 1943, more than a million died in Bengal's famine. The incidence of mass starvation leading to death diminished substantially in the post–World War II period. Devastations of such magnitude had long-term demographic, economic, social, and political consequences, raising two questions: Were famines in this region a product of natural disasters or the result of human agency? Why did famines disappear after 1943?

Although famines have a long history in the region, some of the best-documented episodes of famine in India occurred after British rule began. The 1769–1770 famine in Bengal occurred five years after British takeover of taxation rights in the province. That famine reportedly followed two years of erratic rainfall, but was clearly worsened by the ruthless efficiency of the new regime in collecting land taxes, and by a smallpox epidemic. The 1812–1813 famine in western India, which particularly affected the Kathiawar region, came in the wake of several years of crop losses attributed to attacks by locusts and rats. The legendary Guntur famine of 1832–1833 followed crop failure as well as excessive and uncertain levels of taxation on peasants. In at least three episodes in nineteenth-century western India—in 1819–1820 in Broach, 1820–1822 in Sind, and 1853 in Thana and Colaba—famines were caused by monsoon flooding and resultant crop loss. The 1865–1867 famine in coastal Orissa followed several seasons of erratic rainfall, but was worsened by the persistent refusal of the local administration to import food. In the last quarter of the nineteenth century, major famines causing in excess of a million deaths occurred three times: 1876–1878, 1896–1897, and 1899–1900. In each case, there was a crop failure of unusual intensity in the Deccan plateau, possibly the most famine-prone region in India.

In the twentieth century, major famines were fewer. In 1907–1908, an extensive crop failure and epidemic threat was effectively tackled by state relief machinery. Food procurement for World War II, combined with a crop failure, caused perhaps the harshest famine of the twentieth century, the 1943 Bengal famine.

Causes: Food Availability and Entitlement

A section of the colonial bureaucracy believed that famines were expressions of a Malthusian imbalance between resources and population in the region, the impact of which colonial relief efforts helped mitigate. Whatever the merits of that view, an element of high risk was indeed intrinsic to the resource endowment of the region. The greater part of the Indian subcontinent combines three months of monsoon rains with extreme aridity the rest of the year, which dries up much of the surface water. The rains make growing one crop relatively easy, but growing another crop is dependent upon irrigation systems that need to harvest groundwater or to transport water from long distances and are, therefore, relatively expensive. The dependence on a natural supply of water increased the risk of crop failure, and single-cropping reduced security against the failure of the monsoon crop. El Niño–type disturbances of the tropical oceanic atmospheric systems could make rainfall more unpredictable. Sudden and large-scale scarcities of food, therefore, were potentially part of the cycle of India's agricultural production.

Nationalist critics of British colonialism in India believed the scale of mortality during the nineteenth-century famines resulted from imperial economic policies. The argument consisted of two parts, an assertion that the intensity of famines increased in the nineteenth century, and a belief that British trade and taxation policies were primarily responsible. Land taxes were believed to be too high. Food exports were believed to increase food shortages for the local population, while nonfood crop exports encouraged farmers to give up food production. Both factors raised food prices. The colonial administration answered these charges by arguing that in fact foreign trade stabilized prices, since exports increased in times of low prices, and fell in times of high prices. Recent research on this question has found support for the thesis that foreign trade did stabilize food availability and prices.

While both these perspectives identified mass starvation with absolute scarcity of food, more recently the relationship between food availability and starvation has been recast in the more general "entitlement" approach advanced by Amartya Sen. In this view, access to food depends on an individual's entitlement to food by means of direct production, market purchase, or gifts and transfers. It is possible to consider scenarios in which food supplies are adequate, but certain groups face large declines in market-based or transfer-based entitlements to food. Famines can be caused by the inability to buy food or a collapse of transfers, even as food availability does not fall. The Bengal famine of 1943, and perhaps several other "war famines" in India, seem to illustrate this view.

Food for Work Program, Rajasthan. Since the 1960s, India has developed a number of comprehensive programs to address the poverty and famine resulting from severe drought. In this 1986 photo, women in hard-hit Rajasthan queue up for supplies as part of a rural Food for Work program. AMAR TALWAR / FOTOMEDIA.

Consequences

Consistent with the predictions of the entitlement approach, the effect of famines varied according to livelihood, gender, and social status. Further, famines affected both livelihood and demographic patterns, and through these effects could delay a return to normal conditions even as the proximate cause of the famine disappeared.

Crop failures affected artisans and wage workers in the rural areas much harder than the peasants. The latter usually had some stocks of food. But laborers were unable to obtain food as soon as food prices increased, because money wages were poorly indexed. The association between food prices and famine mortality, therefore, was a strong one. The effect of food prices on the incidence of rural poverty persisted in the late twentieth century, even as famines or starvation deaths became less frequent. Artisan incomes too declined during famines, for households stopped buying anything other than food with the onset of a famine. The 1876 famine drove large numbers of rural laborers and hand-loom weavers of

South India to enlist for emigration to British tropical colonies abroad. The 1896 and 1899 famines again encouraged permanent migration. Famines also affected land transfers between the poor and the richer peasants, but these effects are not well researched.

The two late nineteenth-century famines (1876–1878 and 1896–1898) had severe impacts on population growth rates. For example, almost the entire expected natural increment in population in Madras and Bombay presidencies between 1871 and 1881 was carried off by the excess mortality from 1876 to 1878. In both these episodes, the first few months after a harvest failure saw a rise in food prices, followed by a decrease in conceptions due to famine amenorrhea, and a rise in deaths. Deaths were more common among men, who left home in search of work, among children and the elderly, and among the lower castes. Short-distance migration increased during a famine, and caused severe health crises. Almost always, crop failure drove people to change diets and forage for food in the forests and commons. In the first few months of starvation, more fodders and seeds were consumed, and livestock mortality therefore increased. Toward the end of a famine, epidemic diseases claimed lives. Sustained malnutrition reduced biological resistance to smallpox, plague, cholera, pneumonia, and diarrhea, and left the population susceptible to malarial death. Ironically, the spread of malaria was sometimes attributed to waterlogging due to the construction of irrigation canals as part of famine relief measures. These demographic conditions, together with the shortage of livestock and seeds, made any return to normal cultivation difficult even as the rains came back. After a famine ended, the mean age at marriage for women declined somewhat, marital fertility and birth rates tended to rise above average, and death rates fell below average.

Famines also created social stresses. Food riots, burglaries and raids, mob violence, and the sale of children increased, causing a rush of convicts into the prisons. Ironically, prisons were the only places where food was easily available.

Famine Policy

In the early nineteenth century, the British East India Company left famine relief largely to the native princes. The very real prospect of famines had encouraged the construction of state granaries in pre-colonial India, which were used for relief purposes. Common measures to prevent the occurrence of famines included the building of irrigation tanks and canals. On a more limited scale, private and temple charity were also at work. However, both the granaries and the private systems were localized, whereas the incidence of starvation was widely dispersed.

In the second and the third quarters of the nineteenth century, a discourse emerged in administrative circles on the need for building irrigation works and for the restoration of disused tanks as insurance against future famines. However, a clear policy in this regard did not take shape until 1880–1881. There was resistance within the administration to expenditure on irrigation, which, it was felt, brought uncertain returns. State agency in relief, it was sometimes argued, interfered with the agency of the market in bringing food to the needy. The ferocity of the 1876 famine, brought home by a series of influential books and articles in English, reduced such resistance.

Between 1876 and 1896, a state relief infrastructure was put in place in British India. The main elements of the policy were relief camps, where starving persons could receive food in exchange for labor at public works projects, such as the construction of railways or irrigation canals. A Famine Insurance Fund was started in 1881, out of which relief-related expenditures were to be funded. The relief camp was not unknown in 1876, but its effectiveness during that episode was in serious dispute. Its scale was limited, the labor requirement was rarely enforced due to a shortage of supervisors, and entry was based on the degree of distress, which was hard to define and subject to abuse. By the end of the century, however, the relief camp was a well-established institution in Madras and Bombay presidencies, and could mobilize thousands of laborers for construction works. The Famine Commission of 1881 outlined the relief policy, and the provincial Famine Codes wrote detailed instructions for local administrations to follow. If the relief camps were efficient in mobilizing labor, they were not very effective in averting large-scale mortality. Many seekers of relief, such as the artisans, could not offer the kind of labor the camps wanted and paid for. Some did not want to eat the same food as others due to caste prejudices. Women often avoided the camps. The Famine Codes became progressively lengthier to accommodate this heterogeneity.

With the exception of the 1943 "war famine" in Bengal, famines causing large mortality more or less disappeared in twentieth-century India. The state relief system functioned much better. The spread of irrigation and multiple cropping stabilized food availability. In the interwar period, internal markets were efficient in carrying food from excess supply to shortage regions. Easier migration contributed to this process. The railway network, in facilitating these movements of goods and labor, had a mitigating impact. Along with market efficiency, there was a change in political attitudes. Free markets in food came to an end at about the time of World War II. The government during the war and subsequent governments in independent India controlled food trade. Exercise of state power in the former case led to a famine. Exercise of state power in the latter period prevented any recurrence.

Serious and large-scale erosion of access to food did recur in India briefly in 1966–1967, but had no significant impact on mortality. Starvation deaths, though rarer, continue to occur in parts of the arid zones poorly served by irrigation and transportation. While large-scale starvation deaths became less frequent in post-independence India, malnutrition has persisted.

Tirthankar Roy

See also **Economic Development, Importance of Institutions in and Social Aspects of; Poverty and Inequality**

BIBLIOGRAPHY

Dyson, T. "The Demography of South Asian Famines." *Population Studies* 45, no. 1 (1991): 5–25, and 45, no. 2: 279–297.

McAlpin, M. B. *Subject to Famine: Food Crises and Economic Change in Western India, 1860–1920.* Princeton, N.J.: Princeton University Press, 1983.

Report of the Indian Famine Commission. Part III: Famine Histories. London: Indian Famine Commission, 1885.

Sen, A. K. *Poverty and Famines: An Essay on Entitlement and Deprivation*. Oxford: Clarendon Press, 1981.

Visaria, L., and P. Visaria. "Population (1757–1947)." In *The Cambridge Economic History of India*, vol. 2: *c.1757–c.1970*, edited by Dharma Kumar. Cambridge, U.K.: Cambridge University Press, 1983.

FEDERALISM AND CENTER-STATE RELATIONS

The achievements of Indian federalism are quite astounding and counterintuitive. Despite the multiplicity of social and ethnic divisions, federal institutions have survived. In the 1940s and 1950s, language was a divisive issue, but since the implementation of linguistic states, language movements have been domesticated and multilinguism and bilinguism can be found in most regions of the country. Secessionist movements in Punjab and in the Northeast region have evolved into movements of regional autonomy, seeking recompense from the central government rather than independence. Despite fiscal stresses and strains, central revenue capacity continues to hold in India; tax revolts of the kind witnessed in Russia or Brazil are unheard of. A majority of India's regional units have well-developed democratic systems with regular elections, party competition, and regional parties. Regionalization of the polity has proceeded in tandem with democratization, so that new regional forces representing hitherto unprivileged sections of society—for example, the Bahujan Samaj Party—have acquired strong roots in some states such as Uttar Pradesh, and new parties—Lok Shakti in Karnataka, for example—have arisen to challenge the monopoly of political power enjoyed by existing political formations. Most citizens' strong regional identities coexist with their pan-Indian identities; in India there is no zero-sum relation between national and regional identities. Did federalism play a major role in these transformations? Federalism is ultimately a formal institution insofar as it refers to a set of constitutional provisions, but in the Indian case, its ethnic and socioeconomic roots give it a substantive and societal basis not necessarily found in other federations. Also, in the 1990s, federalism has become livelier and more dynamic, embedded within larger political and economic changes currently underway in India.

Ideas about Regional Autonomy, Central Power, and Federalism

Federalism in India is not merely a set of institutions, but a set of evolving ideas and practices about how the balance of central and local power should be organized, and subnational movements perceived. At the center of the discourse around regional autonomy and central authority are the notions of state stability, the political unity of India's boundaries, and the concept of the Indian nation.

During the formation of India's Constitution, debates concerning relations between the central government and the provinces were contentious and extensive. India's Constituent Assembly debated whether to institutionalize a strong center or strong states, and what procedures were to govern the relations among them. The nature of pre-independence religious conflicts organized across territory (Punjab, Kashmir, and Bengal) and partition played major roles in generating and shaping ideas about the federal Constitution in India.

One dominant theme of India's Constituent Assembly was whether giving power to regional units would threaten the unity of India, and whether the principle of cultural autonomy and self-determination was contradictory to "national unity." Some argued that India needed to embody "one corporate nation, a homogenous nation," while others suggested that cultural autonomy and national unity could be made consistent with each other. B. R. Ambedkar, the leader of the Dalit community and the chairman of the Drafting Committee of the Constituent Assembly, argued that while he was an advocate of a "strong united Centre," in the present circumstances, "it would not be prudent, it would not be wise," since the problem was "how to make the heterogeneous mass we have today" make a decision "in common."

In December 1946 the Objectives Resolution moved by Prime Minister Jawaharlal Nehru affirmed that the Constitution of an "undivided country" would allow the regional units to "retain the status of autonomous units" in a substantial manner. Immediately after Viceroy Lord Mountbatten announced his partition plan on 3 June 1947, the Constituent Assembly decided in favor of writing a Constitution with provisions for a strong center. Earlier, the term "Federation of India" had been used, but it was replaced by the term "the Union of India." This terminology was meant to clarify that the federation was not the result of an agreement by the states to join the Union; therefore, no states had the right to secede from the Union.

After independence, concepts of national integration and "unity in diversity" continued to animate discussions of federalism. Unfortunately, the issue of regional demands was understood as one that challenged the government and national unity. Thus, the central government sought to discipline such demands as well as make them discursively unacceptable. So, regional autonomy movements—in Kashmir, Assam, or Punjab—were framed by the government as challenges to the integrity of the state, and the enhancement of central government authority was seen in a zero-sum relationship to regional autonomy. In the 1980s, this created enormous strains in managing center-state relations. Since then, the language of terrorism has been inserted into the discourse, and India has instituted many terrorism-related laws, such as the Terrorist and Disruptive Activities Act and the Prevention of Terrorism Act. Thus, the discursive economy of state power was and continues to be negative toward regional movements, although the state has negotiated much more effectively with intransigents and "terrorists" in recent times.

Formal Institutions of Indian Federalism

India's federalism, similar to that of Canada and Germany, and in contrast to that of the United States, is framed within a parliamentary system. The Constitution of India is the foundational text that lays out the structure of center-state relations. In addition, certain juridical and legislative initiatives have created institutions that mediate center-state relations.

India's Constitution has been described as "quasi-federal," in that it frames many centralist features within a federal framework. The primary articles (Seventh Schedule of the Constitution) demarcate authority between the states and the center: a Union List, a State List, and a Concurrent List. While most key subjects such as defense and national infrastructure are controlled by the Union government, many important subjects are controlled by the states: law and order, agriculture, and health. Residual powers remain with the central government.

This center-state allocation of powers was dominated by a highly centralist provision—Article 356, referred to as President's Rule—that allows the national cabinet to disband a state legislature under certain conditions. A related constitutional provision that seeks to ensure central control is the role played by the governor, the appointed head of each regional government. In the 1970s and 1980s, the role of the governors became controversial as central rulers used their services to discipline states ruled by the political opponents of the Congress Party.

It is notable that in the 1990s, the provision of President's Rule has been challenged, and after a crucial judicial ruling, its institutional force to meddle in the democratic rights of states has declined substantially. In the S. R. Bommai judgment in 1994, the Supreme Court ruled against the misuse of Article 356. The unanimous judgment by the nine-judge constitutional bench, delivered on 11 March 1994, further held that any proclamation under Article 356 would be subject to judicial review,

thereby giving the federal compact a new institutional force. This, combined with the changes in India's party system, has given some leeway to the president to refuse to impose President's Rule. President K. R. Narayanan in October 1997 returned the Union cabinet's recommendation to impose President's Rule in Uttar Pradesh. Again, in 1998, Narayanan refused to support such a recommendation for Bihar. Thus, with changes in India's party system and the political context of federalism, the power of the provision of President's Rule to constrain the autonomy of states has been significantly attenuated.

One interesting centralist feature of the Indian Constitution that has nevertheless operated to accommodate regional demands and substate movements can be found in Articles 2, 3, and 4, according to which the national Parliament has extensive powers to reorganize the boundaries of states. These provisions "enable Parliament by law to admit a new state, increase, diminish the area of any state or alter the boundaries or name of any state." Seemingly a centralist provision, this has allowed a rare flexibility at the heart of Indian federalism so that central institutions can respond to pressure to create new states. In 1955, after the Linguistic Commission gave its recommendation, the provision was used for the first time to create language-based states. Since then, this provision has been used many times, most recently in 2000 to create three new states of Chhatisgarh, Uttaranchal, and Jharkhand, reconstituting Madhya Pradesh, Uttar Pradesh, and Bihar, respectively. The formation of the new states did arouse some concern that there would be an intensification of demands for the creation of additional states in other parts of the country: Telengana in Andhra Pradesh and Vidarbha in Maharashtra have already staked their claims. Yet, these assessments have lost the power to challenge the basis of central power in India. This means that movements are able to address their demands of regional expression without challenging the integrity of the nation-state; thus, a centralist feature has acquired important decentralizing consequences, making Indian federalism stable. Another distinctive set of institutional features of Indian federalism is a set of asymmetric rules regarding some states, called "Special Category" states. Article 370 gave provincial autonomy to Jammu and Kashmir, and other provisions regulated the affairs of the Northeast states. Each of these provisions has given stability to India's federal institutions.

In addition to such constitutionally mandated rules, some institutions were created in response to demands and pressures from regional elements. In 1983, for example, the Sarkaria Commission was set up to study federal relations in India. The Sarkaria Commission invited responses by all regional governments and opposition parties. It concluded that India's center-state relations suffered from "administrative over-centralization" and offered moderate changes in India's institutional design. This commission became both a signpost of troubled center-state relations as well as the central government's desire to address some of those problems by a comprehensive assessment. Yet, most of its recommendations (except two) were not implemented.

Cyclical Movements from Centralization to Decentralization

Despite these centralist features, the Indian experience of federalism has moved from strong centralization imperatives to decentralizing ones, and the balance between national and local power has shifted over time. From 1947 to 1964 the central and national institutions held sway, although regional actors and subnational institutions were not trampled over, but rather aggregated in a different combination with central institutions. The dominance of the inheritor of the national movement—the Congress Party—and its ability to integrate and represent provincial interests was crucial to this integration. The relationship between national and local leadership was a mutually dependent one. In developmental terms, the state with its national plans and "rational" allocation across different regional units created a national market and a national development agenda, howsoever imperfect. From 1964 to 1969 the regional impulses held sway, as transitional instability after the death of Nehru and an economic crisis at the state level (food crisis) allowed regional elites—largely strong Congress state leaders—to lay claims on shaping the policies of the national government and the national Congress Party. Thus, tendencies toward localization, factionalization, and ruralization dominated the period between 1964 and 1971.

Yet, Indira Gandhi reasserted executive and personal authority, reorganized the Congress Party, and re-articulated the developmental vision of the central government toward populist policies. She was able to craft a new national majority coalition that, at face value, undermined the power of regional powerbrokers. Thus, from 1971 to 1977, centralization tendencies again seemed dominant in India's polity. After a brief decentralizing interlude, when the Janata government was in power (1977–1980), with Indira Gandhi's return to power, the power of the central government and the Congress Party again seemed dominant. The prime minister intervened violently to control the resurgent Khalistan movement in Punjab and tried to undermine the regional party—the National Conference—in Jammu and Kashmir. Yet many of these centralist attempts backfired and made reconciling regional autonomy with expanding central power imperative. In the 1980s her centralization attempts were

of a different quality, linked with regional concerns and interests more systematically than before; trampling over regional interests was proving more difficult than before in the face of regional resurgence. Thus, the pendulum swings between centralization and decentralization in India's polity were not equally balanced; the center of gravity had begun to shift to localization and decentralization. In a similar vein, the process of consolidating central power always remains tenuous and begins to disintegrate soon after such attempts. In the 1990s, the trend certainly shifted much more toward decentralization or "decentering" (Echeverri-Gent). Changes in India's party system contributed to this shift; it clearly seems that the regionalization imperative in India's policy and political economy has become a stable feature.

The Changing Party System and Federalization

The 1990s witnessed unprecedented changes in the party system: the era of one-party dominance (1947–1989) seems to be over; instead a competitive multiparty system seems here to stay. What is interesting is that the dominance of the Congress Party has not been replaced by another national party (the Bharatiya Janata Party, or BJP, for example) or multiple national parties, but rather by the rise of coalitional politics and the national importance of regional or single-state parties. In 2004, even when the Congress Party returned to power, it did so in a coalitional arrangement. India is undergoing a process of federalization or regionalization of its party system. This process of federalization encompasses multiple dimensions. First, as is apparent from the Table 1, the simple physical presence of regional parties has increased in the national Parliament.

Regional parties have become important in national government formation. Both national parties—BJP and the Congress Party—need the support of regional parties and alliances with regional parties to form a government (this is also apparent after the 2004 elections). Third, national parties have themselves acquired regional personas. This is true of the BJP and the Communist Party of India (Marxist) as well as most other national parties. The Congress Party, a national party par excellence, too has had to accommodate to regional pressures in Maharashtra, Tamil Nadu, Uttar Pradesh, and West Bengal, where regional formations such as Nationalist Congress Party, Tamil Manila Congress, and Trinamool Congress have weakened its base and national scope.

This emergent reality must be understood as mutually self-enforcing: party system change at the national level (the displacement of Congress party dominance) has evolved in a dialectical relationship with the regionalization of India's polity. While both have independent sources

TABLE 1

Percentage share of regional parties' seats and votes in the Parliament in the 1990s

Parties	Lower house election year							
	1991		1996		1998		1999	
	Seats	Votes	Seats	Votes	Seats	Votes	Seats	Votes
Congress	42.7	36.5	25.8	28.8	26.0	25.8	21.0	28.3
BJP	22.0	20.1	29.6	20.3	33.4	25.6	33.5	23.8
Other national (multi-state) parties	20.9	24.7	18.8	20.0	11.8	6.6	13.3	14.1
Subtotal of national parties	85.6	81.3	74.2	69.1	71.2	58.0	67	66.2
Regional (single state) parties	6.9	9.3	20.4	17.7	26.3	26.4	26.8	23.5

Notes: These figures do not total 100 percent, as many small parties and independents are not included.
Regional and single state parties: Telugu Desam, Samajwadi Party, Shiv Sena, DMK, AIADMK, Biju Janata Dal, National Congress Party, Trinamool Congress, Rashtriya Janata Dal, PMK, Indian National Lok Dal, J& K National Conference, MDMK, and RSP.
Other national (multistate) parties:
1991: JD (Janata Dal), JP (Janata Party), LKDB (Lok Dal-Bahugana), CPM, CPI, and ICSS (Indian Congress Socialists)
1996: CPM, CPI, Samata, Janata Dal, AIIC (Tiwari), and Janata Party
1998: CPM, CPI, Samata, Janata Dal, and BSP
1999: CPM, CPI, Janata Dal (U), and BSP

SOURCE: Author's calculations from Butler, David, Ashok Lahiri, and Prannoy Roy, *India Decides: Elections 1952–1995*, New Delhi: Books and Things, 1995; election commission web site available at <http://eci.gov.in>; and Rao, G. V. L. Narasimha, and K. Balakrishnan, *Indian Elections: The Nineties*, New Delhi: Har-Anand Publications, 1999.

and origins, they have begun to acquire a mutually reinforcing effect in the late 1990s. Regionalization has speeded up the process of party system change, while the opening up of the national governmental system in the form of coalition governments has allowed important spaces to regional parties, who deploy their national roles and participation to regional ends; this accelerates the process of regionalization even more.

Identity Politics in India's Regions

Indian federal relations have seen an abundance of ethnic and secessionist movements at the subnational level. In the 1940s, the Dravidian movement arose in South India seeking a separate Dravidian state; since then, Punjab, Kashmir, and the Northeast states (Assam, Manipur, and Nagaland) all have witnessed strong quasi-separatist movements organized around territory, identity, and ethnicity. Many have transformed into regional parties that seek to govern their states (Tamil Nadu, Ghorkaland in West Bengal, and Jharkhand, among many others) by articulating a regional cultural identity; others have continued to be violent and confrontational (Manipur, Kashmir). Most analysts have explained these movements separately.

Economic explanations fail to explain the persistence of regional movements in states such as Punjab and

Assam: while one state has the highest per capita income in India, the other has been one of the most backward states in the country. The level of development (in Punjab) did not prevent confrontational and mobilization movements against the central government; the economic deprivation of Assam and its exploitation by the central government and by economic elites within the state did play a role in enhancing the sense of relative frustration that sparked the rise of an anti-Bengali subnationalist movement. In the late 1980s the United Liberation Front of Assam described India's relationship with Assam as "colonial" and demanded that multinational companies and Indian-owned companies do more for the development of the state. Yet, the Khalistan movement in Punjab arose soon after the "Green Revolution" in a prosperous state. Thus, the rise and persistence of subnationalist movements across different regions needs better explanations and answers.

First, while cultural roots must be incorporated in any analysis, identities in India are not given or ascriptive, but rather can be created and mobilized by political entrepreneurs. Thus, the role of parties and politicians in shaping and activating identities can be important. These instrumental political actors, consciously or unwittingly, not only articulate regional aspirations, but also create or make available new social spaces for "the reproduction of subnational meanings and political projects" (Baruah 1997, p. 511). Second, understanding the role of society or what is fashionably called "civil society" may be necessary. Yet, analysis of civil society must not be seen as opposed to the role of party and ethnic entrepreneurs. The relationship between party (political organizations) and society may be the key to understanding the nature of and the changing prospects of ethnic regionalist movements. In Tamil Nadu, DMK (Dravida Munnetra Kazhagam) and its various inheritor parties played a major role in shaping Tamil identity over time. Similarly, in Assam, two organizations, the Asom Sahitya Sabha (the Assam Literary Society) and the All Assam Students Union, proved to be crucial. Moreover, the rise of subnationalism is not unrelated to economic processes: urbanization, expansion of communications, literacy, educational institutions, and industrialization. This has been true in Assam, Jammu and Kashmir, and Punjab. It is the process of modernization that activated feelings of relative deprivation and frustration among the mobile population of these regions. It is not a coincidence that students played a major role in both Assam's and Kashmir's movements. Despite the interactive effects of economic change on cultural identities, economic change has had an independent logic in shaping center-state relations.

Economic Change and Federalism in India

The fiscal structure of the Indian Constitution is quite centralized, as the central government collects most of the taxes and then distributes them to the regional states through the finance commissions that are constituted once every five years for that purpose. The revenue sources of the provinces are limited and inelastic, although the states have been politically constrained not to tap agricultural taxes, further limiting their revenue base. Despite a fiscally centralist Constitution, rapid changes in federal economic relations urge attention to ways in which the economic liberalization process has affected federalism and vice versa.

Federalism and subnational governments have played a major role in shaping the nature of economic liberalization underway in India. First, federalism made economic reform politically sustainable by displacing opposition to reform at the state level. The "energies of economic interests" were dispersed in twenty-six states, leading to fragmentation of opposition along regional lines. This is true for both business interests and labor unions, whose actions, opposition, or protests tend to get "quarantined" within states. Second, federalism encouraged new supporters of reform to emerge from India's

regions. As subnational governments renewed their efforts to reregulate the central policy of liberalization, they created new coalitions, new interests, and new incentives in favor of reform. Many chief ministers themselves became aggressive supporters of economic reform (for example, Andhra Pradesh's Chandrababu Naidu, Tamil Nadu's J. Jayalalitha, and Digvijay Singh of Madhya Pradesh). Regional capitalists or capitalists concentrated in one region of the country began to support liberalization more forcefully than national-level capitalists. This is true of the software capitalists (Infosys, Wipro, and others) based in Karnataka. Interestingly, reform of subnational governance mechanisms was stimulated by these processes.

Simultaneously, economic liberalization further accelerated the process of federalization, prompting "a change in federal relations from intergovernmental cooperation towards interjurisdictional competition among the states" (Saez, p. 135). Basically, competition unleashed by economic liberalization took an interstate form insofar as states began to compete with each other to offer concessions to global and national business actors. While this dynamic had some negative consequences in undermining regional states' revenue capacities, it ensured some scope for market competition and the disruption of monopoly power of national business classes as well as the national bureaucracy. Both regional business classes and the regional bureaucrats were more supportive of reform than the national civil servants and national business interests.

Thus, economic liberalization has begun to affect the nature of center-state relations quite substantially. New supporters of reform—regional elites—seek participation in the national government and national politics as a means of getting crucial benefits from the liberalization process. The national area continues to be an important site for their interaction with national resource-rich institutions, as well as access to global actors, such as the World Bank, and global capital. Second, economic reform has unleashed a fiscal crisis that has crucial center-state components. The central government has withdrawn from some of its functions by displacing its public goods responsibilities to the regional states; this creates strong hunger for resources and revenues at the regional level. At the same time, federal transfers to the regions are declining; this implies that the asymmetry between revenues and expenditures at the regional level continues to grow. Fiscal deficits of states in India grew quite substantially in the 1990s, constituting almost 40 percent of the total fiscal deficit. This phenomenon has been stimulated by the ongoing economic reform in India. Further, a "race to the bottom" effect is evident after the onset of economic liberalization, as regional elites shed their public expenditure responsibilities. Thus, the provision of health, education, and irrigation infrastructure, the responsibility of states in a federal system, suffers much more in federal India than it would in a unitary system undergoing liberalization.

Aseema Sinha

See also **Political System: Constitution; State Formation**

BIBLIOGRAPHY

Baruah, Sanjib. "Politics of Subnationalism: Society versus State in Assam." In *State and Politics in India*, edited by Partha Chatterjee. Delhi: Oxford University Press, 1997.

———. *India against Itself: Assam and the Politics of Nationality*. Philadelphia: University of Pennsylvania Press, 1999.

Brass, Paul R. "Pluralism, Regionalism and Decentralizing Tendencies in Contemporary Indian Politics." In *Ethnicity and Nationalism: Theory and Comparison*, edited by Paul Brass. New Delhi: Sage, 1991.

———. "National Power and Local Politics in India: A Twenty-Year Perspective." In *State and Politics in India*, edited by Partha Chatterjee. Delhi: Oxford University Press, 1997.

Butler, David, Ashok Lahiri, and Prannoy Roy. *India Decides: Elections 1952–1995*. New Delhi: Books and Things, 1995.

Echeverri-Gent, John. "India's Decentered Polity." In *India Briefing, 2002*, edited by Alyssa Ayres and Philip Oldenburg. Armonk, N.Y.: M. E. Sharpe, 2002.

Franda, Marcus F. *West Bengal and the Federalizing Process in India*. Princeton, N.J.: Princeton University Press, 1968.

Ganguly, Sumit. *The Crisis in Kashmir: Portents of War, Hopes of Peace*. Washington, D.C.: Woodrow Wilson Center Press; Cambridge, U.K. and New York: Cambridge University Press, 1997.

Jenkins, Rob. *Democratic Politics and Economic Reform in India*. Cambridge, U.K.: Cambridge University Press, 1999.

Saez, Lawrence. *Federalism without a Centre: The Impact of Political and Economic Reform on India's Federal System*. New Delhi: Sage, 2002.

Saha, Anindya. "The Indian Party System, 1989–1999." *Seminar* 480 (August 1999): 24–34.

Sinha, Aseema. "From State to Market via the State Governments: Horizontal Competition after 1991 in India." Paper presented at the annual meeting of the Association of Asian Studies, Boston, April 1999.

Subramanian, Narendra. *Ethnicity and Populist Mobilization: Political Parties, Citizens and Democracy in South Asia*. Delhi: Oxford University Press, 1999.

Wallace, Paul, ed. *Region and Nation in India*. New Delhi: Oxford and IBH Publishing, 1985.

FEMALE INFANTICIDE. *See* **Gender and Human Rights.**

FEMALE SEXUAL POWER. *See* **Devī.**

FEMINISM AND INDIAN NATIONALISTS

The platform of women's rights was central to the nineteenth-century social reform movement, which crystallized both nationalist aspirations and feminist responses to patriarchy. In the twentieth-century nationalist upsurge, Indian women mobilized against colonial rule. When independence was granted in 1947, they achieved important rights.

Colonial Constructions of Gender

Women's rights were first advocated in India by men of the elite, whose missionary teachers compared the modern post-Enlightenment developments of the West with India's apparently moribund society burdened by archaic caste and gender hierarchies. Filtering their understanding of these new Western ideologies through the humanistic lens of ancient Hindu scriptures like the Upanishads, men of the literate castes concluded that India had declined from a "golden age" free of caste and misogyny, which were medieval accretions. Like their British colonial rulers, the reformers denounced female illiteracy and high caste customs like prepuberty marriages, *sati* (widows' immolation on their husbands' funeral pyres), polygamy, widow abuse, and enforced widow celibacy. They also cast a critical eye on female domestic seclusion in the *zenānā* (women's quarters) and the *purdah* (veil), a custom prevalent among Muslims and Hindus.

Elite class men reinforced the rhetoric of Britain's civilizing mission by accepting the colonial critique of Indian society. Early official surveys on the absence of high caste women in schools appeared to prove that Indian women were completely subjugated and submerged in ignorance. Feminist scholars argue that customs like *sati* became more common during the wars for colonial hegemony over India. Women of the literate classes, however, were often taught informally at home, and village women often chose religious mendicant vagrancy over a brutal domestic life. Influenced by Victorian views, literate Indian men undertook to improve the condition of elite caste women, while underestimating the potential of working-class women.

Male Reformers' and Women's Rights

The earliest Bengali reformer was Ram Mohan Roy (1772–1833), who denounced polygamy and *sati* through his Amitya Sabha (Friendship Association) in 1815, and the Brahmo Samaj (Society of Brahma) in 1828. A similar *bhadralok* (elite class) humanist was Ishwarchandra Vidyasagar, who petitioned to legalize widow remarriage in Bengal in the 1850s; Vishnusastri Pandit, D. K. Karve, and Viresalingam Pantulu started widows' remarriage associations in Bombay and Madras in the 1870s and 1880s. The Prārthana Samaj (Prayer Society) in 1867 and the Vedic Hindu revivalist Ārya Samāj (1875) also promoted women's education and criticized misogynistic marriage customs as detrimental to female health. In 1896, Justice M. G. Ranade and his wife Ramabai started the Ladies Social Conference, a secular forum within the Indian National Congress. In 1884 B. M. Malabari's tract on child brides and abused widows horrified Victorian England. In 1891 colonial legislators enacted the Scoble Bill, raising the age (of married girls) for consensual sex from ten to twelve in India. Liberal Hindus like Raghunatha Rao, M. G. Ranade, and Gopal Krishna Gokhale supported such legal reforms, unlike Bal Gangadhar Tilak who opposed colonial intervention in Hindu customs.

Feminist Writers and Activists

Several nineteenth-century women writers refuted the charge of female intellectual inferiority and denounced child marriage, widow abuse, dowry, and *purdah* in vernacular and English literature, while founding schools. The pioneer was Pandita Ramabai Saraswati (1858–1922), a Sanskrit scholar who married out of her caste and who became a vociferous feminist after her husband and family died in a famine. She began the first Indian feminist organization, Ārya Mahilā Sabhā (Association of Aryan Women) in 1881. Male reformers appreciated her call to the colonial government to create schools for women doctors and teachers. To pay for her studies in England, she wrote *Stree Dharma Niti* (Women's religious ethics) in Marathi in 1881. After much soul-searching, she converted to Christianity in 1884, and she wrote *The High Caste Hindu Women* (1888) in English to finance her nonsectarian widows' home, Sharada Sadan. Conservative Hindus like Bal Gangadhar Tilak accused her of proselytizing their daughters, whom they withdrew from the school. Clearly, feminists had to toe the line or be punished by male nationalists.

In 1882 Tarabai Shinde wrote *Stri Purush Tulana* (A comparison of men and women) in Marathi, accusing men of lust and duplicity and of falsely portraying women as seductresses. In 1891 Sarat Kumari Chaudhurani exposed the neglect of girls in her Bengali work, *Adorer na Anadorer?* (Loved or unloved?). The Muslim Rokeya Sakhawat Hossain advocated gender equality in Bengali, while her English novel, *Sultana's Dream* (1905), describes a topsy-turvy world of male seclusion in *mardana*s resembling women's *zenānā*s. Savitribai Phule (1831–1897), a dutiful Hindu wife, described her radical work of educating the lowest castes. Some others were loyal Indian wives but ardent Christians, like Kripabai Sattianadhan (1862–1894), who laid the blame for women's plight squarely on Hinduism in her English novel, *Kamala: The Story of a Hindu Life* (1894). Less

famous women criticized patriarchy in journals like *Mathar Manoranjani* in Tamil in the 1890s, *Sadhana* in Bengali in the 1890, *Stree Darpan* in Hindi in 1909, *Khatoon* in Urdu, and *Stree Bodh* in Gujarati.

Motherland and Mothers of the Nation

Nationalism intensified after Bankim Chatterji's 1883 poem "Bande Mataram" (Hail to the motherland) was set to music by Rabindranath Tagore (Thakur) and became the anthem of Indian nationalism. The paradigm of divine motherhood for the nation helped raise the status of its domestic mothers. After the 1905 Partition of Bengal, women joined men in boycotting and burning English goods. Young men in Maharashtra and Punjab, as well as Bengal, appeared ready to become martyrs for the motherland; "New Party" Congress activists, led by Bipin Chandra Pal and Tilak, advocated radical revolution. While some men felt threatened by women emancipated from domestic servitude, humanist authors Rabindranath Tagore (1861–1941), C. Subramania Bharati (1882–1924), and A. Madhaviah (1872–1925) praised women's education in their prose and poetry.

Women awakened to their dual identities as feminists and nationalists in this era. Sarladevi Ghoshal Chaudharani (1872–1946), a feminist Hindu revivalist, started her journal *Bharati* in 1895 and the Bharat Stree Mahamandal (Great Society of Indian Women) in 1910 at Allahabad. At an international women's suffrage meeting in 1910 in Budapest, Kumudini Mitra advocated violent revolution to win gender rights. Women like Bina Das (b. 1911) and Santi Ghose (b. 1916) attempted to kill British officials. Communist women often subordinated feminism to the class struggle, while nationalists argued that freedom would guarantee women's rights.

Elite women believed that women's rights were central to national revival through legal means, and they began feminist associations across India to improve their conditions. Mahatma Gandhi's exhortations to men to emulate female moral superiority helped to empower women. Perceiving themselves as selfless mothers of the nation, they heeded his call to aid its poor women. When he launched his *satyagraha* ("hold fast to the truth") campaigns of nonviolent resistance in India after 1917, many women joined, energized by his fervor.

Feminist Associations

The primary goals of most women's associations were to improve women's literacy and health by abolishing child marriage, enforced widowhood, and *purdah*. Imitating Ramabai's Ārya Mahila Samāj, elite women formed similar sectarian and local organizations. In 1886,

Swarnakumari Debi (1856–1932), Rabindranath Tagore's sister, started Sakhi Samiti (Women's Friendship League) to spread knowledge among women and widows. In 1900 in Bombay, Parsi women founded the Stri Zarothoshti Mandal (Parsi Women's Organization). Other welfare groups included the Young Women's Christian Association and, in 1915, the Anjuman-e-Khawatin-e-Islam (Association for Muslim Women). Viresalingam Pantulu and his wife Rajya Lakshmi founded the Andhra Mahila Sabha (Andhra Women's Club) in 1910 for girls' education and widow remarriage.

Between 1902 and 1912, Indians established many girls' schools based on the Indo-centric curriculum advocated by Annie Besant in 1904, and girls' school enrollment rose substantially. In Madras in 1906, elite Indian and European women started the nonsectarian Tamil Māthar Sangam (Tamil Women's Organization), which met in Kanchipuram in 1907 and 1914. In 1908 its women activists delivered papers at an all-India Ladies' Congress (*parishad*), from which the secular Women's Indian Association (WIA) drew its initial members, on 8 May 1917 in Adyār, Madras. Impressed by the Tamil Māthar Sangam, the Irish suffragist Margaret Cousins proposed an all-Indian organization in 1915. The WIA was India's first major multiethnic feminist organization. Its initial success was partly due to its effective use of the framework of the Theosophical Society whose head, Annie Besant, was chosen as the first WIA President. Cousins became the WIA's first honorary secretary, a role shared with Dorothy Jinarajadasa, the Irish wife of a Sri Lankan Theosophist. As the "daughters of India," they pledged to guide the nation, serve the poor, promote women's education, abolish child marriage, raise the age of sexual consent to sixteen for women, and win female suffrage and the right to elected office. The WIA was the first organization to connect women's social and sexual subjugation with patriarchy, poverty, and political disenfranchisement.

On 18 December 1917, Sarojini Naidu (1879–1949) headed a WIA delegation to Secretary of State Edwin Montagu. They requested female suffrage on a par with men in expanded provincial legislatures after the 1919 Government of India Act. Although the franchise commission in London did not immediately sanction their request, WIA feminists won an appeal supported by C. Sankaran Nair, the Indian member of the commission, and Indians in the legislative councils. Provincial legislatures were instructed individually to decide upon female suffrage, so that a few women voted in Madras in 1921, in Bombay in 1922, and in other provinces after 1930. In 1927 Muthulakshmi Reddi was elected to the Madras Legislative Assembly as India's first woman legislator.

Portrait of Sarojini Naidu Pioneer suffragette Sarojini Naidu. She was among fourteen women included in the Constituent Assembly, the body charged with drafting an independent India's constitution in December 1946. FOTOMEDIA ARCHIVE.

Two other important organizations were the National Council of Women in India (NCWI), founded in 1925, and the All India Women's Conference for Educational Reform (AIWC), founded in 1927. The NCWI was headed by Mehribai Tata, the wife of a prominent Parsi industrialist. Despite its commitment to women's issues, the NCWI's dependence on the British colonial government, patronization of the poor, and conservative attitudes precluded its popularity. The AIWC began with a secular agenda on women's education and marriage reform in Poona in 1927, led by the Rani of Sangli, the Begam of Bhopal, and the Maharani Chinmabai Saheb of Baroda. However, there were ideological and class differences over how to effect social changes amongst women in *purdah*. The AIWC has become less elitist and still functions.

After 1920 the WIA and AIWC published their own journals, providing information on legislative bills, such as the one to abolish the dedication of *dēvadāsi* dancers to temples, where they were reduced to prostitution. The system was legally abolished in 1928 due to the eloquence of Muthulakshmi Reddi. The WIA also campaigned against *purdah* and for the 1930 Sarda Act, raising the minimum age of marriage for girls to fourteen. The AIWC campaigned to raise school enrollment of girls, and literacy rates rose over the next decades; it was also instrumental in revamping family laws on divorce and property rights.

Women and Independence

If early reformers had argued that women were the weaker sex, Mahatma Gandhi emphasized their nobility and self-sacrifice, and his cotton-spinning program was influenced by women. His appeal to elite class women to purify the nation and to aid their disadvantaged sisters was answered by donations of jewelry, the wearing of homespun cloth (*khadi*), and the picketing of shops that sold foreign goods and liquor. However, he initially resisted allowing women to join his 1930 Salt March to Dandi, but Sarojini Naidu, Kamaladevi Chattopadhyaya (1903–1990), and Khurshed Naoroji (1894–1966) persuaded him to change his mind. Thousands of women from across India were jailed for "stealing" salt from India's beaches. Aruna Asaf Ali (1906–1996), Durgabai Deshmukh (1909–1981), and Rajkumari Amrit Kaur (1889–1964) were in the front ranks of "salt thieves." The formation of the women's wing of the Indian National Congress in 1942, led by Kamaladevi Chattopadhyaya, facilitated women's mobilization in the Quit India movement.

Jawaharlal Nehru staunchly supported universal suffrage and women's rights. In recognition of their contributions, fourteen women were included in the Constituent Assembly to draft independent India's constitution in December 1946. These pioneers were Ammu Swaminathan, Kamala Chowdhuri, Begam Aizaz Rasul, Sarojini Naidu, Hansa Mehta, Sucheta Kripalani, Dakhsayani Velayudhan, Durgabai Deshmukh, Vijayalakshmi Pandit, Begam Jahanara Shah Nawaz, Begam Ikramullah, and Lila Roy. Besides the 1940 Hindu Marriage Validating Act, which removed the caste bar in marriage, post-independence acts favorable to women include the 1955 Hindu Marriage Act, which allowed divorce, and the 1956 Hindu Succession Act, which removed gender disparities in inheritance.

Progressive and conservative grassroots women's organizations have consolidated in postmodern India. Women now organize strikes and *morcha*s (protests) against inflation, discriminatory labor practices, and economic marginalization. They have denounced ministerial interference over female inheritance, as in the Shah Bano case; the resurgence of *sati* in Rajasthan, in the Roop Kanwar case; dowry deaths related to consumerism; and

commercial destruction of trees and the environment, as in the Chipko movement. Others strive to improve women's literacy and health; yet these rights must be carefully and consistently guarded against resurgent erosion.

Sita Anantha Raman

See also **Devī; Women and Political Power; Women's Education**

BIBLIOGRAPHY

Bharati, C. Subramania. *Chandrikaiyin Kadai* (Chandrika's story). 1925. Madras: Sangam Books, 1982.
Chatterji, Bankim Chandra. *Anandamath.* 1882. Translated by Basanta Koomar Roy. Delhi: Orient, 1992.
Deshmukh, Durgabai. *Stone that Speaketh: The Story of the Andhra Mahila Sabha,* vol. 1. Hyderabad: Andhra Mahila Sabha, 1980.
Gandhi, Mohandas K. *Women's Role in Society,* edited by R. K. Prabhu. Ahmedabad: Navjivan Trust, 1959.

SECONDARY SOURCES

Basu, Aparna, and Bharati Ray. *Women's Struggle: A History of the All India Women's Conference, 1927–2002.* Delhi: Manohar, 2003.
Chatterjee, Partha. "The Nationalist Resolution of the Woman Question." In *Recasting Women: Essays in Colonial History,* edited by Kumkum Sangari and Sudesh Vaid. Delhi: Kali for Women, 1989.
Forbes, Geraldine. "The Indian Women's Movement: A Struggle for Women's Rights or National Liberation?" In *The Extended Family: Women and Political Participation in India and Pakistan.* Delhi: Chanakya, 1981.
———. *Women in Modern India.* Cambridge, U.K.: Cambridge University Press, 1996.
Kaur, Manmohan. *Role of Women in the Freedom Movement, 1857–1947.* Delhi: Sterling Publishers, 1968.
Kosambi, Meera. *At the Intersection of Gender Reform and Religious Belief.* RCWS Gender Series. Mumbai: SNDT Women's University, 1993.
Kumar, Radha. *The History of Doing: An Illustrated Account of Movements for Women's Rights and Feminism in India, 1800–1990.* Delhi: Kali for Women, 1997.
Lateef, Shahida. "The Indian Women's Movement and National Development: An Overview." In *The Extended Family: Women and Political Participation in India and Pakistan.* Delhi: Chanakya, 1981.
Raman, Sita Anantha Raman. *Getting Girls to School: Social Reform in the Tamil Districts, 1870–1930.* Kolkata: Sree, 1996.
———. "Crossing Cultural Boundaries: Indian Matriarchs and Sisters in Service." *Journal of Third World Studies* 18, no. 2 (Fall 2001): 131–147.
Sharma, Radha Krishna. *Nationalism, Social Reform, and Indian Women.* Patna: Janaki Prakashan, 1981.
Talwar, Vir Bharat. "Women's Journals in Hindi, 1910–20." In *Recasting Women: Essays in Colonial History,* edited by Kumkum Sangari and Sudesh Vaid. Delhi: Kali for Women, 1989.

Tharu, Susie, and K. Lalitha. *Women Writing in India 600 B.C. to the Early Twentieth Century.* New York: Feminist Press, 1991.

Wolpert, Stanley. *Tilak and Gokhale.* Berkeley and Los Angeles: University of California Press, 1962.

FEUDALISM The word "feudalism" inevitably brings to mind a number of images: an aristocratic class of landed warrior-nobles constantly at war among themselves, a preponderantly agrarian economy serviced by an impoverished peasantry, and a religious establishment emphasizing values of hierarchy and submission to authority. While the images may have a pronounced European connotation, they may not be entirely out of place in India, and historians, both European and Indian, have for some time debated whether there could be an "Indian feudalism." The problem, however, is first and foremost one of definitions, for it would seem that there can be as many conceptions of feudalism as there are historians working on the subject. Indeed, in European writing alone, the term has had an exceedingly complex history over the last three hundred years. Two general features, however, seem to unite most concepts of feudalism. First, feudalism is deemed the great political or social order that preceded the rise of the absolutist or colonial state, which, arguably, in turn gave birth to key features of recognizably modern societies and economies. Second, representations of feudalism have rarely been simply neutral descriptions. Many early writings on feudalism were written with a strong reformist agenda, and were part of the liberal project of defeating the political order of the *ancien régime.* Later, concepts of feudalism or semifeudalism have been regularly invoked in Marxist political thought as part of their own accounts of the rise of bourgeois society.

The first systematic argument for the existence of feudalism in India was forwarded by Lieutenant Colonel James Tod, who served the British East India Company at the turn of the nineteenth century and first published what would become a famous work on western India, *Annals and Antiquities of Rajasthan* in 1829–1832. Inspired by Henry Hallam's recently published *History of the Middle Ages,* Tod argued that the Rajputs of India had a system of "pure feuds" analogous to those of medieval Europe. For Tod, this was the case because the Rajputs, being of "Scythian" racial stock, were descended from the same Central Asian peoples who formed the forebears of the tribes in early Europe. The feudal compact that emerged in both places was based on obligations between vassal and sovereign secured through bonds of kinship or personal loyalty. The claims by Rajput kings to have descended from either the sun or the moon created a factional political system, in which disputes were resolved through feuds. Though a strong king might reduce such internecine warfare, it remained a systemic feature of Rajput society. Tod admitted that the Rajputs, as he encountered them, had been subjected to an exterior despotic force from North India, and he counterposed Rajput feudalism to the centralized rule of powers like the Marathas and the Mughals. Tod believed that if the Rajputs could be restored to their original prosperity, they would not only pose no threat to British interests (with their own divisive tendencies keeping them in check), but that they would also prove potential allies against any Russian encroachment on Britain's valuable possessions in India.

Tod's idea of Rajput feudalism was largely overtaken and displaced by other theories among British historians in colonial India, but some of its features tended to become absorbed into a more generalized notion of ancient and medieval Hindu polities as atomistic, divisive, and entropic, which often mixed uneasily with notions of Oriental despotism. Soon, this image itself became associated with a putative "medieval" period emerging among historians in both imperialist and nationalist circles. According to Vincent Smith's famous history of early India, the great ancient imperial experiments of the Mauryans and the Guptas collapsed by the seventh century, giving way to a medley of petty states engaged in unceasing internecine warfare. Smith's stance was that this was the natural state of affairs among Indian princes unless they were checked by some superior authority like the British. Nationalist historians mapped representations of feudalized political chaos onto the idea of the fall of the golden age and medieval decline, often using political chaos as an explanation for "national weakness" before invading Islamic armies.

Though such notions of a vague political feudalism have persisted in some historical circles, they have been largely overtaken by a more systematic treatment of feudalism from an entirely different angle since the 1950s, when scholars of Marxist persuasion sought to come to terms with pre-colonial Indian society. The classification of societies through the "mode of production" concept had been an integral feature of Marxist historical thought from its inception. Its impetus came from Marx himself, who in order to develop a better understanding of the rise of capitalism, proposed a sequence of modes of production in Europe, beginning with primitive communism, which evolved sequentially into the "slave" and "feudal" modes of production and finally into a capitalist mode of production. What made each mode of production unique was its peculiar combination of forces of production (tools, materials, and labor processes) and relations of production (the ownership of productive forces), and following from this, the particular means by which a ruling class extracted surplus from the laboring class. Feudalism, from this point of view, could be characterized on the one hand as an agrarian society composed of small-scale peasant producers who met their own subsistence needs with a labor force based on the family, and on the other as a society in which a class of landed lords extracted surplus from these peasants through rent. Feudal rent was deemed "noneconomic" because it was not settled through the dynamics of the market forces, but instead on the superior force possessed by the land-owing class with its coercive, lordly prerogatives. This class was a military aristocracy whose ranks were divided into great lords and free vassals who entered into feudal "compacts," whereby a piece of landed property (fief) was held by the vassal from the lord in return for military service or counsel. In contrast to the life of the aristocracy was the unfree condition of peasants or "serfs," who had no property rights (save that of use), were restricted in movement, and were obliged to surrender the product of their labor over and above what was needed for the reproduction of the peasant household.

Marxist Interpretations

How India measured up to this portrayal is a vexed and complex topic. Marxist thinking on India's pre-colonial society may be traced to Karl Marx himself, who wrote several pieces on British imperialism in India from the 1850s. Drawing on diverse sources, Marx argued that Indian society, as elsewhere in Asia, differed substantially from that of Europe. Here Marx drew on thinking from the seventeenth and eighteenth centuries that, written against the backdrop of European absolutist states, saw Asiatic governments as despotic in nature. Other sources included Henry Maine's theory of the self-sufficient, isolated village community in India and the general notion, championed by G. W. F. Hegel and others, that Asian societies were static and unchanging. On these bases, Marx concluded that India and other Asiatic societies could not be placed in the developmental continuum of European society (slave or feudal) and instead developed the controversial concept of the "Asiatic mode of production." The key features of the Asiatic mode of production included the absence of private property resulting from the king's absolute ownership of all land, state control of irrigation and public works, and the decentralized and communal nature of production at the village level. The absence of private property, combined with despotic (as opposed to feudal) rule, prevented India from developing the dynamic forces that led to social development, a process which was only brought about through the external force of colonialism. Despite its obvious moorings in the Orientalist perception of the East, the Asiatic mode of production suggested by Marx and Friedrich Engels represented an important and often neglected contribution to further social analysis—the attempt to account for the specificity of societies outside Europe. The concept, however, was largely abandoned during the period of the Third International (1919–1943), the congress of different communist parties across the globe, and during the anti-imperialist movements of the 1930s by communist intellectuals, who instead sought to understand Asiatic societies in terms of the unilinear development from primitive communism to capitalism.

It is against this background, and the additional context of a robust nationalist historiography, that a number of Indian Marxist historians in the 1950s and 1960s reassessed early Indian society in terms of Marxist categories. A vast amount of new information on precolonial Indian society had come to light in the hundred years since Marx's first articles on the subject, and much of this evidence contradicted the premises of the Asiatic mode of production. It suggested in the first instance that while the village remained to some extent an independent economic unit, it possessed a far greater degree of economic differentiation than Marx had assumed. Also, Marx's idea that all of the surplus product of the village went entirely into the hands of the state was incorrect. There was, in fact, a whole class of hereditary claimants to shares in rent: courtiers, military retainers, provincial lords, and religious institutions in earlier times, and in later times Mughal *zamindar*s (landowners). Such claims further indicate the presence of what Marx had thought was absent in India, the private ownership of land-shares. The situation of the classes that held these shares, placed between the king and the peasants, suggests an arrangement generally akin to feudal land ownership. Most importantly, it is clear that political and economic structures, land ownership, and trade and commodity production underwent change over time in pre-colonial India, contradicting the presumed stasis of Asiatic society before the coming of European imperialism.

Indian Feudalism

Marxist historians subsequently developed the theory of "Indian feudalism" to explain the social formation emerging with the Guptas in the fourth century and extending down to the establishment of the Turkish power in Delhi during the thirteenth century. Marxist historians of later medieval India have been more reticent in applying the category of feudalism to the great Muslim empires of northern India. For the earlier period, the pioneering study of D. D. Kosambi suggested two phases of development: an initial phase of "feudalism from above," in which kings alienated land rights to subordinates, functionaries, and religious institutions; and a later phase of "feudalism from below," in which a class of landed intermediaries emerged at the village level. Kosambi's observations were supplemented by the more detailed and comprehensive works of R. S. Sharma and others in the 1960s. Sharma began with the point that the alienation of tax revenues in the land grants from the Gupta period was accompanied by the surrender of administrative and judicial powers, resulting in the parcelization of sovereignty and the decentralization of state power. While most of the extant land grants preserved on permanent materials (copper plate or stone) were made to religious institutions, evidence suggests that royal functionaries and servants were also remunerated in land revenues. Numerous officials and military retainers from the sixth century appear to take titles that imply land ownership (*bhogika*, *bhogapati*). Part of the argument here has also rested on wider economic factors. There is a well-documented contraction of the larger urban centers, a decline in trade networks and petty commodity production, and an apparent paucity of coinage in North India during post-Gupta times. In such an increasingly ruralized economy, payment for services, whether religious or secular, was necessarily in land revenue rather than cash.

The royal charters and records, which by the sixth century begin to include genealogical introductions in high poetic style, do seem to suggest considerable evidence for the growth of "lord-vassal" relationships among ruling elites, though no single feudal compact can be attested in the legal literature of the period. The famous Allahabad pillar inscription of the Gupta king Samudragupta (ruled c. 330–380) mentions that subordinate kings were expected not only to pay tribute and offer themselves for military assistance, but were to provide daughters (in marriage), and attend court to pay physical obeisance to the Gupta monarch. The emphasis on personal submission and courtly hierarchy was highly pronounced in political life, from the proliferation of increasingly calibrated titles (*sāmanta*, *mahāsamanta*, *mandalesvara*, *mahāmandalesvara*) for ranks of subordinates, to elaborate gestural, verbal, and sumptuary protocols (like the bearing of insignia and possession of five musical instruments in public procession), which were enacted between men of different rank at court. Literary and genealogical records also suggest the existence of a loose code of warrior ethics that emphasized a fierce but honorable heroism as well as a compassionate irenism. The latter tendency may have been the influence of religious elites (Brahmans and monks) who regularly attended or served at the more important aristocratic households. Religious institutions, however, tended to reinforce rather than undermine feudal social relations, and the symmetry between religious and political ideologies in this period is notable. Hindu temples, for example, were much like palaces in their spatial arrangement—the

central god of the temple was surrounded by subordinate forms and divinities in a carefully calibrated fashion to reflect perceived rank and hierarchy. The major religious ideology of the period, *bhakti*, or devoted participation in the majesty of god, conceived of lordship as an encompassing yet hierarchical mastery that mirrored the nested rights which obtained between lords and their inferiors in the secular realm. Religious and courtly texts in fact present a single dispositional and affective vocabulary to encode relations between lords and subordinates across both religious and political realms: the subordinate honored his lord with loyalty (*bhakti*) and service (*pūjā*, *sevā*), and the lord in turn exhibited his grace (*anugraha*) through the bestowal of favor (*prasāda*). In fact, religious and political realms were largely continuous, leading some scholars to argue for a great "chain of being" in medieval India.

How the political order was constituted is somewhat uncertain, as some vassals seem to have originally been independent lords of minor royal status who entered service through conquest and subordination, while others seem to have been courtiers or functionaries who were granted lands by the king as favors. These two categories often merged over time. Because of the difficulty in interpreting the meaning of many terms for hereditary administrators and vassals left in the inscriptional record, and because of their regional variation, it is difficult to indicate the precise stages and structures of feudal organization. Yet by the sixth century it is clear that there were a large number of hereditary intermediaries between the royal authority and the producing classes. This situation was compounded by a tendency of subinfeudation, as the alienation of revenues in land grants often (and sometimes necessarily) conferred upon donees the right to have the land cultivated by other groups, leading to a hierarchy of shares and rights on the land. The consequences of this "feudalization" for peasants were serious. First, the system of land grants tended to transfer the communal rights of village cultivators to donees, who in turn often conferred shares to tenants, petty officials, and other "great men of the village" who enriched themselves from the threshing floor at the expense of the direct producer. The proliferation of intermediaries thus placed a continual burden on the actual cultivator, as the increase in rents and imposts drained all but the bare minimum of produce necessary for the reproduction of the peasant household. Sharma and others have additionally pointed out the existence of corvée or forced labor-rent (*vishti*) as well as legal restrictions on the movement of the peasantry (villages were granted with their inhabitants, and donees could restrain them) as indications of their serflike status.

Historians of Indian feudalism recognized deficiencies in the evidence, differences on a number of points with the European model, and significant variations in regional development within the subcontinent itself. While the system of land grants was well-established in central India and Maharashtra, for example, it seems to have been significantly weaker in the Punjab, where very few land records have survived from medieval times. The explanation (not altogether satisfactory) for this state of affairs has been the existence of a more robust money economy in the region under the Hindu Shahi dynasty. It was generally held that the feudal system that evolved from Gupta times was effectively disrupted in the thirteenth and fourteenth centuries by the establishment of the Delhi Sultanate, which saw the centralization of political power, the relegation of the feudal class to petty landlords, and a new invigoration of trade and commodity circulation.

Challenges and Debate

By the late 1970s a number of dissenters to the theory of Indian feudalism had emerged from within the ranks of Marxist historians in India, and they were joined by scholars of various disciplines from outside the Marxist tradition working on such topics as monetary history, urbanization, and "state formation" in early India. The challenges to the feudalist thesis were twofold. The first was evidentiary. There were long-standing critiques by epigraphists that the evidence of the land charters could not support the existence of vassalage, but only of religious "landlordism" at best. The theory of a demonetized economy was challenged as resting on weak methodology, and it was suggested that North India, during the period between A.D. 600 and 1000, had just as many coins in circulation as in earlier times. Similarly, the thesis of widespread urban decay had to be counterbalanced by the fact that while archaeology seemed to demonstrate that the great cities of early historic India did witness a marked contraction in size, the period also saw considerable urban growth, as new regional capitals and smaller urban settlements emerged throughout many regions in the subcontinent. The other challenges to the feudalist position were theoretical. It was pointed out that the evolution of feudal structures was attributed entirely to state action instead of class relations, as in Europe. The notion of a subject peasantry was also challenged. These arguments combined with a number of other critiques, which suggested that the entire theory of Indian feudalism had borrowed too heavily from European precedents, and had a tendency to force the Indian evidence into ready-made European historical case studies rather than using Marxist theoretical tools to deal with the Indian evidence. Such criticisms for the most part were not intended to dismiss entirely the relevance of the feudalism concept or Marxist approaches as such, but to underscore the inability of such model-based methods to account for the specificity of the Indian situation. Needless to say, these critiques and alternatives elicited a vigorous debate, which featured in the pages of history journals sporadically for nearly two decades. The discussions have led to the question of whether there can be variants of feudalism, and if so, what degree of variation in any particular instantiation might risk rendering the concept so inclusive as to lose any discriminatory meaning.

The debates took place in the context of new, often non-Marxist, theories of state formation and long *durée* development in early India. An important contribution of one of these latter approaches, which has been called "integrative" or "processual," has been the emphasis on reading the evidence of the period as "productive"—mostly in criticizing the thesis of political fragmentation and urban decay—that is, inquiring into what grew up in medieval India rather than what fell apart. Such an approach, perhaps ironically, has considerable potential for re-orienting and invigorating any theory of Indian feudalism that has yet to be realized. As it stands, it is perhaps an open question as to whether the theory of Indian feudalism is in disrepute. But any trip to parts of the Indian countryside even today, where the rural poor endure conditions of abject poverty and staggering inhumanity at the hands of landed interests, in part as the result of age-old social relationships at the village level, surely vindicates the fundamental concerns of Marxist scholarship in India, whatever the fate of "Indian feudalism."

Daud Ali

See also **Guptan Empire**

BIBLIOGRAPHY

Bailey, Anne, and Josep Llobera, eds. *The Asiatic Mode of Production: Science and Politics.* London: Routledge and Kegan Paul, 1981.

Chattopadhyaya, B. D. *The Making of Early Medieval India.* Delhi: Oxford University Press, 1994.

Deyell, John. *Living without Silver: The Monetary History of Early Medieval North India.* Delhi: Oxford University Press, 1990.

Habib, Irfan. *The Agrarian System of Mughal India, 1556–1707.* 2nd ed. Delhi: Oxford University Press, 1999.

Jha, D. N. *The Feudal Order: State, Society and Ideology in Early Medieval India.* Delhi: Manohar, 2000.

Kosambi, D. D. *An Introduction to the Study of Indian History.* Mumbai: People's Publishing House, 1956.

Mukhia, Harbans, ed. *The Feudalism Debate.* Delhi: Manohar, 1999.

Sahu, Bhairabi Prasad, ed. *Land System and Rural Society in Early India.* Delhi: Manohar, 1997.

Sharma, Ram Sharan. *Indian Feudalism: c. 300–1300.* 2nd ed. Delhi: Macmillan, 1980.

Tod, James. *Annals and Antiquities of Rajasthan, or the Central and Western Rajpoot States of India*. 1829–1832. Reprint, London: George Routledge and Sons, 1914.

Yadava, B. N. S. *Society and Culture in Northern India in the Twelfth Century*. Allahabad: Central Book Depot, 1973.

FILMĪGĪT *Filmīgīt* (English "film" + Hindi *gīt*, "song") refers to the music (particularly the songs) of popular South Asian movies. Many films have five or six major musical items; each song and its elaborate choreography acts as commentary on the drama. The songs are often as important as the story and the actors, and producers sometimes prerelease selected items in order to determine whether or not to release a film. A song's success ensures a film's release. Although each linguistic region has a film industry, the most important center is Bombay (Mumbai), which carries the moniker "Bollywood."

The diverse audience within India, as well as other parts of the world, and the increasingly cosmopolitan attitudes of India's middle class demand an exceptionally eclectic musical approach. The composers and music producers for popular film incorporate a variety of different regional genres, idioms, and instruments, as well as Western ideas. A film might incorporate a small orchestra, sitars, temple bells, electric guitars, synthesizers, and folk drums (such as the *dholak*); it may borrow from classical Indian and European compositions or imitate Latin American and East Asian musical styles. One result is a kind of pan-Indian musical style that has had a normalizing effect on South Asian communities around the world.

Many songs follow the verse-chorus format of popular religious and folk songs, usually with an instrumental introduction and an interlude. One regional style of folk song and dance genre that composers have used extensively in Indian film is that of Panjabi *bhāngrā*. Whether the film is set in northwest or south India, Bollywood music producers often insert *bhāngrā* rhythms and dance movements. Indeed, *filmī bhāngrā*, with the addition of Western bass and drums and an electronic mixing, has gained an appreciative young audience in Britain.

Vocal melody dominates *filmīgīt*, and a select group of playback singers (most notably Lata Mangeshkar) are in demand to perform these songs. In a fiction well known to film fans, screen actors mouth the words of recordings made by the playback singers. The separation of roles has allowed some singers to be active for decades as new sets of fresh young actors add their dramatic gestures as part of their interpretation.

Filmīgīt melodies have characteristic Indian vocal ornamentation and Indian and Western scale patterns often accompanied by chords that, while resembling Western harmonic practice, are distinctly South Asian.

Gordon Thompson

See also **Film Industry; Music**

BIBLIOGRAPHY

Arnold, Alison. "Popular Film Song in India: A Case of Mass-Market Musical Eclecticism." *Popular Music* 7, no. 2 (1988): 177–188.

FILM INDUSTRY In the years leading up to the 1990s, Bollywood was a glamorous cottage industry, churning out hundreds of films annually for a domestic market whose population was poised to edge over the one billion mark by the end of the millennium. Because the films were in Hindustani, a variant of the Hindi language, approximately 40 percent of the population, especially in the northern regions, became cinema fans. Whether they crowded the new multiplex theaters in the cities or huddled in the rural villages in front of makeshift screens fashioned from little more than a sheet stretched between two trees, they alone determined which film became a hit, not through a single viewing but by revisiting the same film dozens of times. The industry knew how to play to its audience and rarely strayed from convention. The films were structurally the same, the formula aptly described, somewhat tongue in cheek, by novelist Ashok Banker: "What else can you expect from a genre that requires every film to have a young good-looking romantic lead couple, half a dozen or more lengthy songs lip-synced by actors to playback singers, costume changes every five minutes and an utter disregard for most film narrative conventions?"

Nevertheless, in terms of production, the industry thrived. In 1991 Bollywood released a record 215 films. The market, however, remained relatively insular, with exports shipped mainly to the Gulf states. That changed in 1995 with *Dilwale Dulhania Le Jayenge*, a huge hit in the United Kingdom and the United States that launched a trend. Producers suddenly realized that scattered around the world was a vast nonresident Indian audience, estimated at 20 million in more than a dozen countries, all hungry to see the latest Bollywood films. To satisfy demand, and to attract an even wider audience, producers began releasing both contemporary and classic Hindi, and a few Tamil, films on DVD, with subtitles in English and wide-screen presentation. As a result, in 1995 the steadily increasing popularity of Bollywood films in emerging markets sparked an annual growth rate of 15 percent, three times that of India's 5 percent gross

Bollywood Movie Poster. Advertisement for the 2000 film *Kaho Naa . . . Pyaar Hai* (Say this is love) that captured the imagination of the Bollywood-watching world. A huge hit on the subcontinent and blockbuster phenomenon with the Indian diaspora, it also made its lead, Hrithik Roshan (shown here), an international celebrity. FOTOMEDIA ARCHIVE.

domestic product growth. In a good year, a Bollywood hit could earn revenues of 25 percent or more, and by 2000 Bollywood's global annual revenues were estimated at $1.3 billion.

Overall, film revenues increased sixfold between 1991 and 1999. Whereas *Saudagar*, released in 1991, generated total revenues of a reported 43.6 million rupees, Subhash Ghai's *Taal*, released nine years later, raked in 266.9 million rupees. As revenues rose substantially during that period, so did the cost of filmmaking. By the end of the decade, the cost of a major Bollywood production featuring the top stars was budgeted at between 150 and 200 million rupees. The leading actors commanded a lion's share of the film's budget, their fees ranging between 15 million and 30 million rupees, depending on their star status. In 1993, for example, Sanjay Dutt demanded and

got 4 million rupees for a film, when only two years earlier he had signed up to make an R. K. Nayyar film for a mere 50,000 rupees. Similarly, a screen heroine like Madhuri Dixit in 1993 was getting 2 million rupees a film. By 2000 a superstar like Shah Rukh Khan was charging up to 30 million rupees per film, while a costar of Dixit's stature could expect between 10 million and 12.5 million rupees.

The top Bollywood stars signed contracts to act in three to four films simultaneously, which considerably slowed production on individual films, sometimes by up to six months. Once the films were released, the producers of course expected a payday. Domestic rights sold to the various distributors made up the bulk of a film's revenue, which hovered around 80 percent, while overseas rights drew close to 12 percent. Music rights, which brought in between 4 to 5 percent of a film's earnings, were also a major revenue generator. Music companies like Saregama, TIPS, Sony Music, and Venus competed fiercely to acquire the music rights of the latest films, since film music accounted for 70 percent and new film music for 48 percent of India's total music sales. Yet, even with a stellar cast, only 20 percent of the 160-odd Hindi films released in a year were commercially successful, and approximately eight of them were viable hits.

With the steady rise of revenues, the film industry attracted parallel criminal enterprises. As early as 1991, the same year the industry released its record number of films, Bollywood estimated it was losing as much as 10 million rupees a day to video piracy. By 2001 India estimated its trade losses due to piracy at $70 million. Throughout that ten-year span, pirated films were available in India's major cities well before the film's local theatrical release. Although India had its own copyright laws, enforcement was lax and haphazard. Raiding small-scale pirates was commonplace, but the larger pirates remained elusive, either because of official protection, or because they set up smaller "fall guy" operations to avoid capture. If arrested, their prosecutions were hampered. Such was the case of two factories in the state of Haryana and the state of Rajasthan known to be manufacturing a significant number of the pirated VCDs. The facilities were raided, but because of slow, cumbersome, and costly criminal procedures weighted against the legitimate copyright owners at every step, they soon reopened and were back in operation.

By the end of 2001, the Bollywood film industry had 608 criminal cases pending in the courts, only four of which resulted in conviction. The first conviction was in January 1997, when a Bangalore court sentenced a video pirate to three years hard labor in a case that dated from 1993. The second conviction came in May 1997, when a New Delhi magistrate sentenced a cable operator (the first to be convicted for cable piracy) to six months hard labor and ordered him to pay a fine of 5,000 rupees, which at the time amounted to approximately $103. In early 1999, the third conviction, following a raid conducted in 1986, resulted in a sentence of one year in prison and a fine of approximately $118. The fourth case, the first of its kind brought against a video pirate under the new 1995 Indian Copyright Act, was decided in December 1998. Some of these cases, however, were reversed on appeal.

If piracy had been financially damaging to the film industry, the infiltration of the Indian mafia was insidious. Yet the symbiosis between Bollywood and the Indian criminal underworld was nothing new. More than thirty years ago, crime boss Haji Mastan was so enraptured with an aspiring Bollywood actress that he began producing films with her in the starring roles. Decades later, Abu Salem, one of the more prominent gangland figures, even named his sons after his favorite on-screen heroes. Suketu Mehta, who wrote the critically acclaimed *Mission Kashmir*, explained the connection for this romance between film and crime: "The Hindi filmmakers are fascinated by the lives of the gangsters, and draw upon them for material. The gangsters, from the shooter on the ground to the don-in-exile at the top, watch Hindi movies keenly, and model themselves—their dialogue, the way they carry themselves—on their screen equivalents."

The romance ended there. Evading the jurisdiction of the Indian police by operating from Karachi in neighboring Pakistan, as well as from Nairobi, Dubai, and even New Jersey, and conducting their criminal activities by cell phone, the crime bosses lured financially strapped filmmakers into loan-sharking schemes, where the payoffs were exorbitant regardless of the film's box-office performance. They also used overseas concerts as money-laundering fronts, with the stars agreeing to appear as headliners in order to avoid starring in mafia-funded films.

An insight into just how deeply the crime bosses had insinuated themselves into the Bollywood film industry came to light when Sanjay Dutt was arrested on charges of dealing with the mafia following the Mumbai communal riots of 1993. During his trial, a taped phone conversation surfaced that allegedly featured Dutt ingratiating himself with mafia crime boss Chhota Shakeel. The tape was later introduced as evidence in a separate trial when film producer Bharat Shah was facing charges of conspiring with underworld figures to murder Bollywood superstars Hrithik Roshan, Aamir Khan, and Shah Rukh Khan.

Stars were not the only ones targeted. Producer Mukesh Duggal was shot and killed in Mumbai in June 1997. Two months later, allegedly on orders from Abu Salem, producer Gulsham Kumar was shot dead outside a Mumbai temple. In December of that year, producer Manmohan Shetty survived an attempt on his life. In 2000 director Rajiv Rai also escaped a kidnapping/murder attempt and moved to London. A year later, director Rakesh Roshan survived an assassination attempt outside his Mumbai office because he reportedly refused to sell the overseas rights of his *Kaho Na . . . Pyaar Hai* to gangsters. And in late 2001 the Indian police revealed a mafia plot to kill actor Aamir Khan and director Ashutosh Gowariker after they had spurned extortion attempts following the success of *Lagaan*.

Toward the close of the decade, an estimated 40 percent of the film industry's finances came from organized crime. To loosen the underworld's grip on the film community and to stem the wave of attacks on its celebrities, the Indian government in 1998 granted Bollywood industry status. Two years later the official mechanisms were in place, which allowed filmmakers to obtain loans and other forms of aid from financial institutions as well as to secure insurance for delays and losses. Still, some remained skeptical. "The industry is often guilty of tax evasion, and big people in it lead a lifestyle far beyond their declared incomes," the *Hindu* newspaper declared in its editorial pages. "Unless these cobwebs are cleared, the cinema here will continue to be plagued by failure and unsurmountable hardship."

But Bollywood made efforts to clean up its act. By 2002 there were at least half a dozen public offerings for film-related companies, although they all traded at less than half their opening price. Meanwhile, such Indian corporate titans as the $8 billion Tata Group and the $13 billion Reliance Industries were seriously considering venturing into film production. Bankers, too, saw Bollywood in a different light. In 2001 the Industrial Development Bank of India became the first to lend $13.5 million to fourteen Bollywood productions. Similarly, Insight Productions and iDream Productions, each an offshoot of local investment banks, were confident they could turn a profit by imposing hard-nosed business methods on what had long been a chaotic industry. Consequently, police authorities estimated that by 2002 only 10 percent of Bollywood's films were backed by mob financing.

Official governmental recognition also conferred cultural legitimacy. Ever since the premiere screening of the first Hindi, albeit silent, full-length feature film *Raja Harishchandra* in 1913 at Mumbai Coronation Cinematograph theater, Bollywood had been India's orphan industry. According to writer Vijay Mishra, "The Cinematograph Acts of 1918 and 1919 and the establishment of the

Indian Cinematograph Committee of Inquiry in 1927 were informed by an emphatic definition of cinema as pure entertainment without any social (and even artistic) significance. These assumptions about cinema made their way into postcolonial India's Cinematograph (Amendment) Act of 1973, too." Only recently has Mumbai cinema begun to receive attention as an object of serious critical scholarship from Mishra and others.

Meanwhile, the debate over how Bollywood acquired its name raged on. Theories abounded, but Madhava Prasad believed she may have settled the issue. In a 1932 issue of *American Cinematographer*, she found an article by Wilford E. Deming, an American engineer who claims that "under my supervision was produced India's first sound and talking picture." In the article, he mentions a telegram he received as he was leaving India following his assignment: "Tollywood sends best wishes happy new year to Lubill film doing wonderfully records broken." He went on to explain that "our Calcutta studio was located in the suburb of Tollygunge . . . Tolly being a proper name and Gunge meaning locality. After studying the advantages of Hollygunge we decided on Tollywood. There being two studios at present in that locality, and several more projected, the name seems appropriate." Thus, Prasad concluded, "it was Hollywood itself, in a manner of speaking, that, with the confidence that comes from global supremacy, renamed a concentration of production facilities to make it look like its own baby."

Nowadays, Americans are familiar with Bollywood, more by its influence than by its product. Director Baz Luhrmann candidly admitted his *Moulin Rouge!* was inspired by Bollywood's cinematic extravaganzas. Andrew Lloyd Webber's musical *Bombay Dreams*, replete with Bollywood overtones, headed for Broadway following a successful run in London's West End. In 2002 Hyperion Pictures announced it was going into production on the musical comedy *Marigold*, which represented the first full-fledged joint venture between Hollywood and Bollywood. That Western artists were borrowing from Bollywood remains significant. The last decade of the twentieth century marked the milestone when Bollywood came into its own as a vibrant industry, accorded respect and globally appreciated as a cultural phenomenon in its own right.

Michel W. Potts

BIBLIOGRAPHY

Banker, Ashok. *Bollywood*. London: Pocket Essentials Film, 2001.
"Married to the Mob: Bollywood's Mafia Underbelly." Available at <http://www.Bollywhat.com>
"Misty Frames." *Hindu* 1 November 2000.

Mishra, Vijay. *Bollywood Cinema: Temples of Desire*. New York: Routledge, 2002.

FINANCE COMMISSION One of the distinguishing institutions of India's federal polity, the Finance Commission provides a constitutional mechanism for the transfer of resources from the national to subnational governments in a fair and judicious manner. India's Constitution vests powers to levy most of the major revenue-yielding taxes, including income tax and general excise duties, with the central government. The only mass-based tax assigned to the states is the sales tax. On the other hand, many functions that require large expenditures, including police, public health, and sanitation, are assigned to the states, creating a serious gap in the fiscal system, with roughly 55 percent of aggregate expenditures undertaken at the state level, while only about 35 percent of aggregate revenues are raised by the states. All of India's states need transfers, but the most backward states need the greatest assistance from the central government to enable them to provide even minimal public services.

Article 280 of India's Constitution mandates the president to appoint an independent Finance Commission at least once every five years to recommend to the president: the proper distribution of taxes collected by the central government, that are to be shared between the central government and the states and their allocation among the states; and the principles that should govern "grants-in-aid" to states in need of assistance, which the Parliament is authorized to make under Article 275. Since 2000, revenues from all central taxes constitute a divisible pool. The president may also refer "any other matter" to the commission for its recommendations "in the interests of sound finance." Since 1993, following constitutional recognition of a "third tier" of government in the country, namely village and district *panchayat*s and urban municipalities, the Finance Commission has been required to recommend measures to help state governments supplement the resources of the local bodies. The commission is also advised to keep in mind the revenue needs of both the central government and the states in meeting their essential expenditures. In recent years the commission has also been asked to review "the state of finances of the Union and the states" and suggest ways "to restore budgetary balance and maintain macroeconomic stability." Every commission is normally required to make recommendations to cover a five-year period.

Since independence there have been twelve Finance Commissions. Recommendations of the commission are accepted by Parliament without modification, with rare

TABLE 1

Criteria and relative weights for determining *inter se* shares of states in union taxes: Tenth and Eleventh Finance Commissions

Criterion	Tenth Finance Commission	Eleventh Finance Commission
1. Population	20.0	10.0
2. Income–distance(1)	60.0	62.5
3. Area	5.0	7.5
4. Index of infrastructure	5.0	7.5
5. Tax effort(2)	10.0	5.0
6. Fiscal discipline(2)	—	7.5

(1) This reflects the difference in the per capita income of a given state from that of the highest income state or that of a group of states with the highest per capita income.

(2) As measured by formulas spelled out in the respective commission's reports.

SOURCE: Courtesy of author.

exceptions, regarded almost as an impartial "award." Apart from taking note of the legitimate revenue needs of both levels of government, two cardinal commission principles have been to treat all states on a uniform basis, and to use the transfer mechanism to reduce interstate inequalities. "Upgradation grants" have been a regular feature of the transfers. Grants are also recommended for relief in the event of natural calamities. Commission transfers, comprising tax share and grants-in-aid, have generally been unconditional, the former being regarded almost as an "entitlement" of the states.

The states have persistently complained that transfers have not been adequate, though transfers to states as a proportion of central government revenues have risen from less than 25 percent in the 1950s to around 35 percent by 2002. Nevertheless, the states find it increasingly difficult to meet their expenditure out of the revenues made available to them.

Transfers have played a significant role in reducing revenue disparities among the states, per capita revenue of low-income states from their own sources usually being less than one-third that of the higher-income states. Per capita current expenditure of poorer states is nearly two-thirds that of the richer states. Even so, interstate disparities in revenue capacity have increased over the years, and federal transfers have not fully offset the fiscal disabilities of the poorer states.

A factor undermining fiscal discipline among the states has been the manner in which commission grants are determined. After laying down the formula for tax devolution, the commission assesses the budgetary position of each state by projecting its revenue and expenditure. Although the projections are made on reasonable

assumptions regarding the likely growth of the states' revenue and expenditure, in reality "history" dominates the estimates, tending to breed fiscal laxity among the states. The Tenth and Eleventh Finance Commissions have tried to rectify this deficiency by introducing weights for "tax effort" and "fiscal discipline" in their tax devolution formula as shown in Table 1.

Debt relief measures recommended by the recent commissions are also linked to criteria designed to induce better fiscal management. How far such devices help inculcate fiscal discipline remains to be seen. Attaching strings to statutory transfers also raises questions about the central government's infringement of the states' fiscal autonomy.

Not all the blame for the ills of the transfer system can be attributed to the commission, however. Contrary to the constitutional scheme, a substantial portion of transfers has been routed through other channels. About one-third of the revenue transfers to the states has been dispensed by the Planning Commission, a body created to draw up and implement the five-year plan. Some funds are transferred by central ministries at their own discretion. Such multiplicity of channels with overlapping jurisdictions has blurred the overall efficiency the transfers.

Despite its perverse effects, the gap filling approach continues to cast its shadow over the commission's transfer scheme. The Ninth Commission attempted to introduce normative principles in deciding the transfers. The Eleventh also tried to anchor the transfers to objective norms. But their attempts did not go very far.

Even a fully normative transfer scheme may not succeed in inculcating fiscal discipline among the states without a credible commitment to a "no-bail-out policy" on the part of the central government. Debt relief granted by the commission periodically has not much helped to improve matters.

There is thus urgent need for reforms of the transfer system if the Finance Commission is to play the constitutional role more effectively.

Amaresh Bagchi

BIBLIOGRAPHY

Bagchi, Amaresh. "Fifty Years of Fiscal Federalism in India." Kale Memorial Lecture, Gokhale Institute of Politics and Economics, Pune, 2001.

Bird, Richard M., and F. Vaillancourt. *Fiscal Decentralization in Developing Countries.* Cambridge, U.K.: Cambridge University Press, 1998.

Godbole, Madhav. "Finance Commissions in a Cul-de-Sac." *Economic and Political Weekly* 36, no. 1 (6–12 January 2001): 29–34.

Rao, M. Govinda, and Tapas K. Sen. *Fiscal Federalism in India: Theory and Practice.* New Delhi: Macmillan, 1996.

Vithal, B. P. R., and M. L. Sastry. *Fiscal Federalism in India.* New Delhi: Oxford University Press, 2001.

FISCAL SYSTEM AND POLICY FROM 1858 TO 1947

The fiscal system of British India has figured prominently in debates on the political origins of underdevelopment. The question often asked is: Did India's political status compromise the government's capacity to make investments?

Federal Structure

Two features persistently influenced the fiscal system of British India: the federal structure, and susceptibility to external shocks. Before British Crown rule began in 1858, the finances of the three major presidencies—Bombay, Bengal, and Madras—were nearly autonomous. The basic structure of federal finance was established in the first twenty years of British rule. Under the new arrangement, customs, salt tax, opium tax, and railway income were the main revenues raised and used exclusively by the central government. Receipts of provincial administrative departments, such as law and justice or education, went only to the provinces. Land revenue and excise taxes were shared. Only the central government could borrow. As for expenditure, the central government was responsible for defense, while the provinces were left in charge of local administration, education, and public health.

This structure caused persistent friction between the central government and the provinces. The provinces believed they had control over sources of income that were too few and too limited. The Government of India Acts of 1919 and 1935 and the legislative assemblies that were created after 1920 restructured federal finance and exposed it to organized pressures from elected representatives. Major changes were introduced: the divided heads of revenue were abolished, land revenue was given over to the provinces, and the central government took the income tax. The central budget now had to be balanced by contributions for the provinces, which increased contention. These changes did not alleviate provincial grievances over their minimal sources of revenue, while they remained responsible for expanding expenditures for a growing population. The 1935 Act, however, went somewhat further in giving a larger share of revenue to the provinces.

One outcome of this system of divided sources of revenue was the growing inequality between the provinces in per capita tax burden and expenditure. Bengal, with its "permanent settlement," raised less revenue than its land was worth and thus spent less. Bombay and Madras raised more land revenue and spent more.

Instability

Under normal conditions, the government balanced its budget, that is, balanced current revenue and expenditure. In the pre–World War I period, government investment was financed out of public saving, but increasingly thereafter it had to be financed by borrowing. The equilibrium was often upset by famines, wars, and depressions. The wars fought by the British East India Company, the uprising of 1857, and the famines of 1876 and 1896 each imposed a burden of growing debt. Until the war, the main source of borrowing was London. Usually these debts were paid back from current revenues, but military expenditure during World War I created a crisis. It not only forced the government to borrow, but also forced it to turn to Indian sources of funding since London was no longer an easy money market. Another debt crisis appeared at the time of the Great Depression, when the creditworthiness of the Indian government came into question for the first time in history.

World War II again found India in serious deficit. The government spent larger sums and proportions of the budget than ever before on defense, for its own troops and also on behalf of Great Britain's war expenses. Taxes and borrowing proved insufficient to cover the deficit. But this time there was a central bank and substantial monetary autonomy. Consequently, the money supply increased to finance the deficit as never before. The supply of essential goods, including food grains, on the other hand, was being diverted to support the war effort. The net effect was massive inflation, with disastrous consequences for India's rural poor. The last days of the war saw government controls imposed on supplies of essential commodities. This was the precursor of the public distribution system, with which independent India has become familiar. The end of the war also saw the liquidation of India's accumulated foreign debt. Given Britain's sterling debt to India throughout the war, India began its independence with an ample credit balance in sterling.

Revenue and Expenditure

There were two major types of governmental expenditure in British India: expenditure in India and expenditure abroad. The two most important expenditures abroad were pensions paid in sterling to retired British employees and the interest on public debt raised in London. The government could finance its expenditure by three means. The first was current revenues, 70 to 80 percent of which were raised in taxes. The second was borrowings from abroad, and the third borrowings at home.

In the nineteenth century, the most important tax was the land tax. In 1858, it accounted for as much as 50 percent of total revenues. Next in importance were the opium and salt taxes. The government had a monopoly on the production of opium, and a near monopoly on the production of salt. Together, these two taxes accounted for 24 percent of all revenues in 1858. The income tax and customs and excise taxes together yielded no more than 12 percent of revenue. Clearly, the tax structure was both income-inelastic and regressive. Over the next sixty years, the pattern changed: the share of the land tax decreased to about 20 percent of all revenue in the 1920s, opium and salt taxes dwindled, and income tax, customs and excise expanded their combined share to over 50 percent.

The land tax as a proportion of the value of agricultural production declined from possibly 10 percent of net output in the mid-nineteenth century to less than 5 percent in the 1930s. At the same time, financial stringency forced the government to experiment with more elastic sources of revenue, such as customs and income tax. Until the interwar period, pressures from British exporters were too strong for comprehensive revenue tariffs to be introduced. The pressure eased, and counter-pressures grew stronger. Income tax again became the scene of a battle, though a more subdued one. The government was unable to impose that tax on self-employed people. The groups that could be more easily targeted and assessed were those closest to the government, including prominent landlords, government employees, and owners of modern industry, many of whom were Europeans. Though some of these groups stoutly resisted being taxed, their resistance weakened over time.

For most of this period tax revenue as a proportion of the national income remained small and almost static at about 5 to 7 percent. Shifts in the composition of tax revenues made little difference to the government's spending power, even as the economy grew, leaving it ever more dependent on borrowing.

The main items on the expenditure side were defense, civil administration, and debt service. Each of these items was politically controversial. The Indian army was not only costly to maintain, it was repeatedly drawn into serving Britain's imperial interests outside India. The cost of imported administrative personnel was frequently excessive, and debt service was imposed by the poverty and dependence of the state itself.

Drain

The most controversial item of all was the "Home Charges," or the government's payments abroad for "services" received. These payments were called by Indian nationalists an imperial "drain" or "tribute," seen as intolerably wasteful. The "drain theory" became an explanation for the political roots of India's poverty and underdevelopment. There was some truth, and some exaggeration, in the drain theory. The truth was that British government employees serving in India were indeed often overpaid. The exaggeration was that measures of drain tended to lump all factor payments together, whereas a lot of these payments were for technical services that had no substitutes in India. The broadest measure of drain (Home Charges or net factor payments abroad as a ratio of national income) was about 1.5 to 2 percent in 1901. The real drain was considerably smaller, and therefore quantitatively insignificant. Further, the drain theory assumed that the amount potentially saved on this account would have been available for investment, which was not necessarily the case.

Investment and Growth

Gross investment as a proportion of expenditure declined from 24 percent in the period from 1898 to 1913 (annual average) to 16 percent in the 1930s. Net investment was smaller still and falling faster. The three main areas of investment were railways, irrigation, and roads and buildings. The railways' share in gross investment fell from 51 percent in the period from 1898 to 1913 to 27 percent in the period from 1930 to 1938. Irrigation accounted for about 11 to 16 percent throughout. The share of roads and buildings increased from 31 to 46 percent. In the prewar period, public investment was mainly financed from public savings. But in the interwar period, the percentage dropped sharply.

Unquestionably, the primary objective of this fiscal system was governance and not development, on which it had a mixed effect. Did it actually contribute to underdevelopment? The question remains.

Tirthankar Roy

See also **Balance of Payments; Money and Credit, 1858–1947; Trade Policy, 1800–1947**

BIBLIOGRAPHY

Kumar, Dharma. "Fiscal System." In *The Cambridge Economic History of India*, vol. 2, *c. 1757–1970*, edited by Dharma Kumar. Cambridge, U.K.: Cambridge University Press, 1983.
Roy, Tirthankar. *The Economic History of India, 1857–1947.* Delhi and New York: Oxford University Press, 2000.

FISCAL SYSTEM AND POLICY SINCE 1952

India is a federal democratic republic with a multilevel parliamentary system of government. The Constitution of India mandates, since 1993, three levels of government (central, state, and local) with specification of the powers and functions of each tier, through lists set out in schedules seven, eleven, and twelve. India's fiscal policy, emanating ultimately from the cabinet, must be approved by the Parliament and by the legislative assemblies of the states.

Article 112 of the Constitution requires the government to lay before both houses of Parliament—the Lok Sabha (the lower "house of the people") and the Rajya Sabha (the upper "council of states")—an annual financial statement every year. The statement sets out estimates of expenditures separately for sums required to meet expenditures charged on the Consolidated Fund of India, including: the emoluments and allowances of the president and other expenditures of his or her office; debt charges for which the government of India is liable; salaries, allowances, and pensions of the judges of the Supreme Court; and expenditures declared by the Constitution or the Parliament to be so charged. Estimates of such expenditures are not open to voting in Parliament and can only be discussed. Estimates of all other expenditures must be presented in the form of demands for grants to the Lok Sabha for approval. Once the demands are approved, a bill has to be introduced for appropriation of moneys required to meet the grants for expenditures.

India's fiscal year begins on 1 April and ends on 31 March. The proposals for expenditures, taxes, and borrowings set out in the budget for the year commencing in the following April are presented to Parliament on the last working day of February every year. Parliament can be approached with proposals for supplementary, additional, or excess grants when the sums already authorized prove insufficient or when need arises for supplementary or additional expenditures on some new service not previously contemplated. Along with detailed accounts of the receipts and expenditures of the government for the year to come, budget documents contain information on receipts and expenditures for the year about to end as well as the preceding year, constituting a rich source of data on India's public finances.

The budgets are accompanied by statements by the finance minister reviewing the performance of the economy and announcing the intent of the government on various matters affecting the economy and the life of the people. The budget session of Parliament constitutes an important public event in India and is preceded and followed by intense lobbying and by discussions in the press and among the public, testifying to the vibrancy of India's democracy. Similar procedures are followed in the states, with the difference being that the state budgets are usually presented in their respective legislative assemblies after the Union budget has been unveiled.

The expenditures contained in the budget proposals for a given year on approval by the legislature are meant to be appropriated in the year in question; any excess requires *ex post* approval, while shortfalls are not allowed to be carried over to the subsequent year. In order to ensure that the expenditures incurred in a year are within the limits approved by Parliament (in the case of the Union), a detailed verification and scrutiny of the expenditures incurred is undertaken after the year's end by the comptroller and auditor general of India, an authority mandated in the Constitution with statutory protection. The audit reports of the comptroller are submitted to the president, who then causes them to be laid before each house of Parliament (Article 151). The comptroller is also required to audit the accounts of the states; the state audit reports are submitted to the governor of each state, who thereafter transmits them to the state assemblies. There are also parliamentary committees to undertake the verification and scrutiny of government expenditures and accounts, including the Estimates Committee, the Public Accounts Committee, and the Committee on Public Undertakings, and there are standing committees for every ministry.

Taken together, the budget process thus provides a comprehensive fiscal system to ensure that the finances of government are run according to the wishes of the people, articulated in Parliament by their representatives. Public funds should be used efficiently, irregularities duly detected, accountability enforced, and corrective measures taken. Government budgets are debated openly before they are adopted by Parliament. Their implementation also comes under close scrutiny, and yet the actual operation of the system is marked by shortcomings that have tended to undermine fiscal discipline and efficiency.

The scrutiny of expenditures at the parliamentary stage is not as thorough or detailed as one might expect, partly because the accounts are not always transparent. Factors that make the budget nontransparent include: the multiplicity of budget heads for classification, such as "developmental" and "nondevelopmental" and "plan" and "nonplan." Parliamentary scrutiny is also often perfunctory, inasmuch as large chunks of expenditure are "guillotined" in Parliament, without any discussion, for lack of time. Moreover, as the budgets are framed only for one year, supplementary budgets are routinely presented to Parliament and the state assemblies, as there is a tendency to underestimate expenditure in the original budget.

Until recently there was no legal constraint on the central government to borrow either from the Reserve

Bank of India (RBI) or from the market. As a result, deficits in government budgets that were not covered by borrowing from the market or from abroad were met ultimately by borrowing from the RBI through short-term borrowing instruments called "Treasury bills." Since 1997, by virtue of an understanding entered into with the RBI, recourse to Treasury bills by the Union government has been discontinued. Cash flow problems are met through ways and means advances from the RBI. Similar provisions exist for the states. However, this budgetary constraint is often evaded through off-budget borrowing (e.g., borrowing through state-owned enterprises guaranteed by the government). Parliament has recently taken measures to restrain the tendency to finance deficits with improvident borrowing, passing in 2003 the Fiscal Responsibility and Budget Management Act to compel the Union government to reduce its deficits to stipulated levels. The law also requires the government to place before Parliament statements setting out its medium-term fiscal policy, fiscal policy strategy, and macroeconomic framework.

Fiscal Policy: The First Three Decades

When India attained independence in 1947, the role of government was minimal, rarely extending beyond the maintenance of law and order and the provision of relief after calamities like droughts, floods, and famines. Some public works were undertaken from time to time, but their scale was limited. The proportion of gross domestic product (GDP) going into public spending was barely 9 percent. Current revenues (tax and nontax) were more than adequate to meet current expenditures. The gap between revenue and expenditures—the fiscal deficit—was less than 1 percent.

After independence, government activity expanded rapidly, driven by initiatives taken by India's leaders to promote economic development and the general welfare of the people. The aggregate expenditure of government (central and states combined) rose to over 15 percent of GDP in the first ten years and kept growing, reaching 22 percent in the 1970s. Capital expenditures increased from 1.7 percent to nearly 7 percent. Though the government resorted to borrowing for financing capital expenditures, the fiscal deficit remained moderate, no more than 4 or 5 percent of GDP. Current expenditures were financed entirely by current receipts; in fact the revenue budgets generated some surplus, which, though small, could be used for capital spending.

Given the objectives set for fiscal policy by India's policy makers, such expansion of government was to be expected. The strategy of planning that the government of India adopted for development envisaged a leading role for the public sector in lifting the country out of abject poverty and satisfying the legitimate aspirations of the people. At the same time, emphasis was on "democratic planning," allowing a large role to the private sector as well. The primary responsibility for raising the level of saving and investment in the economy—which was crucial for initiating development—was, however, assigned to the public sector. Since this was to be achieved within the framework of a mixed economy, it was recognized that fiscal policy, along with monetary and credit policy, would play a critical role. The other major objectives of planning, for which fiscal policy instruments were to be relied upon, were: to bring about a progressive reduction in inequalities and regional disparities; and to influence the level and direction of economic activity. These objectives were reiterated in successive plans, with varying emphasis.

Additional instruments, "quasi-fiscal" in nature, were also employed to serve the objectives of the plans. To secure the flow of private investment into priority areas, a regime of licensing and control was imposed, empowering the central government to exercise control over all substantial investments in the private sector. Further, large segments of the economy were brought directly into the public sector through nationalization. Control was exercised over the flow of investment into the private sector with the creation of development finance institutions in the public sector and nationalization of major commercial banks in 1969. Control was then exercised over the production, distribution, and pricing of several commodities, like sugar and steel, and a fraction of their output was preempted through "levy" at below market prices, mainly by invoking the Essential Commodities Act of 1956. Even so, fiscal policy continued to play a vital role in running the economy and was used extensively to subserve the objectives of the plans. The results, however, did not always meet expectations.

On the positive side, in less than ten years, the level of capital formation in India's economy rose from 10 percent of GDP to over 16 percent, and further to 23 percent at the end of the next two decades. Gross domestic saving increased from less than 10 percent of GDP to nearly 13 percent in the early 1960s and to over 20 percent during the 1970s. Even at fairly high levels of investment during the 1970s, the resource gap of the Indian economy (that is, current account deficit) remained mostly below 1 percent of GDP. Although the bulk of savings originated in the private sector, the public sector also made a significant contribution, forming in some years over 20 percent of the total. But that was far from adequate to meet the requirements of the public sector. Nearly 40 to 50 percent of investment in the economy took place in the public sector, and that required intersectoral resource transfers on a large scale. Fiscal policy was used to play a supportive role in this endeavor.

The fiscal system also provided support for investment in physical capital (plant and machinery, in particular) through liberal capital allowances in income tax. Also, there was tax holidays for new industrial undertakings in the early years. In view of their employment potential, concessional treatment was accorded to small-scale industries in both direct and indirect taxes. Along with quantitative restrictions on imports, customs tariffs were used to protect domestic industries and to help implement the policy of import substitution. Other objectives pursued through the tax system included environmental protection and encouraging the use of certain inputs in specified lines of production.

Equity too figured prominently among the objectives of public policy pursued with the help of fiscal instruments. Personal income and wealth were taxed at steeply progressive rates. Then there were estate duties on wealth passing on death and gift taxes on gifts made *inter vivos*. Indirect taxes were used in a big way to favor the poor by distinguishing between essentials and luxuries. Several public services were provided free or at prices well below cost, particularly power and irrigation water. Exports were liberally subsidized.

Whether or to what extent progressive taxation helped the cause of redistribution or regional equity is not clear. There is some evidence that estate duty and gift taxes served to restrain the concentration in the distribution of wealth. However, confiscatory income and wealth taxes were believed to have spawned a huge "black economy." A study carried out in the late 1980s revealed that around 40 to 50 percent of taxable incomes were probably concealed from tax authorities. Attempts to mitigate the ill effects of high rates of income and wealth taxes through exemptions and concessions weakened the potency of the taxes as instruments of redistribution, opening up loopholes and undermining the revenue potency of India's tax system. In any case, agricultural incomes remained outside the purview of central income tax by virtue of the constitutional plan of tax assignment. The weight of direct taxes in the country's tax structure declined from 37 percent at the time of independence to about 14 percent in the 1980s. Regional disparities too did not come down significantly, though they did not worsen.

The revenue productivity of indirect taxes suffered because of a plethora of exemptions and concessions. The revenue lost in this process was sought to be made up through high, multiple rates and by levying taxes on virtually all countries at all stages of production and sale, with excise levied by the central government and sales tax by the states, rendering the tax system complex, non-transparent, and distortionary. By virtue of an amendment to the Constitution in 1956, interstate sales were brought under taxation through parliamentary legislation (the Central Sales Tax Act). The states of origin were entrusted to administer the tax and retain the revenue. The tax structure that emerged as a result, rather than fostering an efficient, self-reliant economy, constituted a major source of distortion and inefficiency. Neither equity nor resource allocation was well served.

Regarding stabilization, the main concern of fiscal policy in macromanagement was keeping inflationary pressures in check, rather than acting as a stabilizer or stimulator of the economy. Fiscal policy, working in tandem with monetary policy, was remarkably successful in maintaining macrostability and keeping inflationary pressures in check, barring a few episodes of double digit inflation in the 1970s. Unlike many developing countries, India did not experience hyperinflation. Nor did it suffer the convulsions that rocked many economies during the oil shocks of the 1970s. In fact, for nearly three decades after independence, government finances were in reasonable balance.

The 1980s and Beyond

Things took a turn for the worse in the 1980s. The deterioration began in 1979–1980, as the central government's revenue budget for the first time went into the red and the consolidated fiscal deficit rose beyond 6 percent of GDP. Consolidated fiscal deficit crossed 10 percent in 1986–1987, and the average for 1985–1990 measured 9 percent. As a fallout of those deficits, the ratio of government debt to GDP went up to nearly 62 percent in 1990–1991, compared to 46 percent in 1980–1981.

The persistence of large fiscal deficits, together with a chronic imbalance in the external sector, led to a full-blown economic crisis in 1991. The crisis, triggered by the Gulf War, was marked by inflation of nearly 14 percent and a severe balance of payments problem. Foreign exchange reserves dwindled to a level sufficient for import cover of less than one month. The crisis compelled policy makers to undertake some radical reforms to stabilize the economy and launch a program of structural adjustment to correct the chronic imbalances and inefficiencies that had brought the economy to crisis. With liberalization as its keynote, India's economy was opened up; quotas were removed, industrial licensing was all but eliminated, and the financial sector was unshackled. Fiscal consolidation figured prominently in the reform program.

While the immediate task of reform was to reduce the fiscal deficit to manageable levels by compressing expenditure, the aim was to see that government finances were restored to health on a sustainable footing. Fiscal restructuring was undertaken with reforms on several fronts: reforms of the tax system to minimize inefficiencies while enhancing revenue productivity; reform of public expenditure management; and restructuring of the public sector. Institutional changes were also made to secure better coordination of monetary and fiscal policies.

Tax reform. Radical reforms were undertaken in both direct and indirect taxes to reduce heavy dependence on foreign trade taxes, turning more to taxes on income and domestic trade while minimizing their distortionary effects. The reforms that were initiated in 1991–1992 continued through the 1990s and are still in progress.

The strategy was to have a small number of broad-based taxes with moderate rates and few exemptions or concessions. The maximum marginal rates of personal income tax were brought down from 60 to 30 percent, and corporate income tax to around 35 to 40 percent, from 65 to 70 percent in 1980–1981. Presumptive taxation sought to widen the base, bringing selected services under taxation. Customs duties were reduced progressively from a peak of 150 percent to 25 percent. Rates of major ad valorem excise duties were compressed, and a three-rate structure of 8, 16, and 24 percent was introduced.

Expenditure management. Measures were taken to cut down and check the growth of government expenditure and to change its composition. These measures included: zero-based budgeting for ongoing programs, review of staff requirements of government departments and agencies, and the introduction of a voluntary retirement program. Subsidies were brought under scrutiny and reduced through cost recovery. An Expenditure Reforms Commission was appointed to identify specific areas for action. To contain the growth of pension payments, a partly funded contributory pension plan has been instituted for central government employees.

Public sector restructuring. A major thrust of the reforms was aimed at restructuring the public sector by reducing its size and budgetary support. The aim was to downsize government by withdrawing from activities where the private sector could do better or equally well. The reforms also sought to establish better coordination between monetary and fiscal policies. The government of India entered into an agreement with the RBI to discontinue the issue of Treasury bills, which meant automatic monetization of deficits, relying instead on ways and means advances to meet temporary cash requirements. Large-scale preemption of bank deposits for subscribing government bonds through requirements of statutory

liquidity ratio was reduced by cutting down the ratio to 25 percent from nearly 40 percent. Measures were taken by the RBI to widen and deepen the government security markets.

Reforms at state level. Initially, the reforms were primarily the concern of the central government. The second half of the 1990s witnessed moves toward reform at the state level as well, with greater efforts made for revenue mobilization, expenditure compression, and downsizing of government through restructuring of the public sector. Prodded by the central government and realizing the need to reform archaic and inefficient sales tax systems and avoid tax competition among themselves, the states joined together to move toward a harmonized system of value-added tax in place of sales taxes. The process is, however, still to be completed. On the nontax side, state governments moved to reduce subsidies by raising user charges for public services. In public sector restructuring, the focus has been on reforms of the power sector, as the losses of the state electricity boards have been a major drag on state budgets. The central government sought to induce the states with various incentives to undertake reforms essential to the success of the reforms as a whole.

Outcomes and Outlook

The measures initiated toward fiscal correction in the wake of the crisis of 1991 produced some tangible results. The consolidated fiscal deficit of the central government and the states came down from 9.3 percent of GDP in 1990–1991 to 6.9 percent in 1991–1992, then to 6.3 percent in 1996–1997. The ratio of government debt to GDP also registered a decline of 3.7 percent by 1995–1996. The improvement, however, proved short-lived. The fiscal deficit started moving up again in 1996–1997, crossing the 9 percent mark in 1999–2000, and was estimated to be over 10 percent in 2002–2003. Primary deficit, after coming down from 4.9 per cent in 1990–1991 to 1.1 percent in 1996–1997, moved up again, measuring 3.8 percent in 2001–2002.

The debt-GDP ratio also moved up, standing in March 2003 at 75.5 percent. While this overstates the extent of the government's liabilities, in that a part of it (around 10 percent) is debt owed to the RBI, it does not provide a complete picture of the government's debt obligations, as it does not reflect the liabilities likely to arise from off-budget borrowings, such as guarantees extended by the government to borrowings of public sector undertakings and unfunded pension liabilities. As of March 2002, outstanding government guarantees measured 11.5 percent of GDP. A particularly worrying feature of the fiscal scene in the closing years of the 1990s was the growth of revenue deficits, that is, the deficits in the revenue or current budget. In 2002–2003 revenue deficit accounted for over two-thirds of the consolidated fiscal deficit, compared to two-fifths before the reforms.

At current levels, India's fiscal deficits are among the highest in the world and are a cause for serious concern. Given the buildup of foreign exchange reserves, capital controls, flexible exchange rates, and widespread ownership of banks, the economy may not be vulnerable to the kind of crisis that overtook the country in 1991. There are no symptoms of crisis associated with fiscal imbalance of this magnitude. However, it is generally agreed that these deficits, particularly the revenue deficits arising from growth of the government's consumption expenditure, need to be brought down.

Even after a decade of reforms, though the economy is much stronger than before, India's fiscal situation has yet to stabilize. While there is no case for adhering to rigid budget-balancing rules all the time—budgets must adjust to the emerging situation in a constructive way—some basic rules of the game, like raising the revenue ratio in a nondistortionary fashion to meet current expenditures and a hard budget constraint, are yet to gain general adherence.

In a way, the inability of the Indian government to sustain the fiscal consolidation that began in the early 1990s is traceable to the weaknesses of a periodically elected federal democracy. Profligate promises made to the electorate by some of the leading political parties, like the promise of free power to farmers in the 2004 general elections, would seem to corroborate this prognosis. Reflecting a recognition of this reality, prescriptions for fiscal discipline now rely more on institutions such as "rules," insulated from politics, which focus on the task of addressing structural imbalances, leaving the task of contracyclical action to automatic stabilizers. The Fiscal Responsibility and Budget Management Act, passed by India's Parliament in 2003, set out a road map for eliminating revenue deficits in the central budget by 2008, and progressively reducing fiscal deficits with targets set annually. Several moves have been initiated to achieve greater transparency budget. Besides, the transfer mechanism, with built-in incentives for prudent fiscal behavior, is being used increasingly to inculcate fiscal discipline among the states. Whether all these remedies succeed in curing the malady of India's chronic fiscal deficits, however, only the future will reveal.

Amaresh Bagchi

See also **Economic Reforms of 1991; Economy since the 1991 Economic Reforms; Subsidies in the Federal Budget; Taxation Policy since 1991 Economic Reforms**

BIBLIOGRAPHY

Acharya, Shankar, et al. *Aspects of the Black Economy in India.* New Delhi: National Institute of Public Finance and Policy, 1986.
Anand Mukesh, Amaresh Bagchi, and Tapas Sen. "Fiscal Discipline at the State Level: Perverse Incentives and Paths to Reform." In *Fiscal Policies and Sustainable Growth in India*, edited by Edgardo Favaro and Ashok Lahiri. Delhi and New York: Oxford University Press, 2004.
Bagchi, Amaresh, and Pulin Nayak. "A Survey of Public Finance and the Planning Process: The Indian Experience." In *Tax Policy and Planning*, edited by Amaresh Bagchi and Nicholas Stern. Delhi and New York: Oxford University Press, 1994.
Bagchi, Amaresh, and S. P. Chaudhury. *Operation of Estate Duty and Gift Tax in India: A Review.* Mimeograph. New Delhi: National Institute of Public Finance and Policy, 1983.
Hausmann, Ricardo, and Catriona Purfield. "The Challenge of Fiscal Adjustment in a Democracy: The Case of India." Paper presented at NIPFP/IMF Conference on Fiscal Policy in India, 16–17 January 2004, New Delhi.
Lahiri, Ashok, and R. Kannan. "India's Fiscal Deficits and Their Sustainability in Perspective." In *Fiscal Policies and Sustainable Growth in India*, edited by Edgardo Favaro and Ashok Lahiri. Delhi and New York: Oxford University Press, 2004.
Pinto, Brian, and Farah Zahir. "Why Fiscal Adjustment Now." *Economic and Political Weekly* 39, no. 10 (6 March 2004): 1039–1048.
Rajaraman, Indira. "Fiscal Developments and Outlook in India." Paper presented at NIPFP/IMF Conference on Fiscal Policy in India, 16–17 January 2004, New Delhi.
Rakshit, Mihir. "On Correcting Fiscal Imbalances in the Indian Economy: Some Perspectives." *Money and Finance* (July–September 2000): 19–56.
Rao, M. Govinda. "State Finances in India: Issues and Challenges." *Economic and Political Weekly* 37, no. 31 (3 August 2002): 3261–3271.
Reserve Bank of India. *Handbook of Statistic on Indian Economy.* Mumbai: RBI, 2002–2003.
———. *Annual Report, 2002–2003.* Mumbai: RBI, 2003.
———. *Report on Currency and Finance, 2001–2002.* Mumbai: RBI, 2003.
———. *State Finances: A Study of Budgets of 2003–2004.* Mumbai: RBI, 2004.
Srivastava, D. K. "Budget Processes and Expenditure Management in India." In *Fiscal Policy, Public Policy, and Governance*, edited by Parthasarathi Shome. New Delhi: National Institute of Public Finance and Policy, 1997.

FITCH, RALPH *(1550–1611), English merchant.* Ralph Fitch, the first English merchant to reach India, wrote home to London from Portuguese Goa, where he had been taken prisoner by the Venetians from his captured ship *Tiger.* "Here be Moors and Gentiles," Fitch reported. "They worship a cow and esteem much of the cow's dung to paint the walls of their houses. They will kill nothing, not so much as a louse. . . . They eat no flesh, but live by roots and rice and milk. And when the husband dieth his wife is burned with him if she be alive" (letter of 1853, in Locke). Fitch thus reported such exotic Hindu customs as *sati* and cow worship, but he also wrote of how fabulously rich many Goan merchants were, and how palatial and sumptuously furnished were their homes.

Fitch escaped from captivity in 1584, venturing north to great Mughal emperor Akbar's capital, Fatehpur Sikri, which at the time had twice the population of London, as did the other great Mughal capital, Agra. His letters home now praised the fabled jewels many Indians wore on their elegant silks and satins, and spoke of the rich profusion of spices, which England desperately needed to preserve its meats and mull its ale. Enterprising Fitch went on to Varanasi, where he observed Hindus bathing from its *ghats* and the cremation of bodies on the bank of the busy Ganges; he then sailed farther east to Bihar's capital, Patna, where he met many wealthy merchants from Bengal and Burma. He left India in 1586 to sail off to Malaya, starting home from Southeast Asia in 1591.

Fitch's firsthand accounts of fabled India and its amazingly rich variety of peoples and produce helped whet the appetites of London merchants, who eagerly sought to sail east in the next century, when England's East India Company vessels first headed for the Indian Ocean, determined to break the Catholic Portuguese monopoly of the spice trade and run their blockade, as would the equally bold Protestant Dutch sea captains from Antwerp and Amsterdam. Haarlem-born Jan Huygen van Linschoten had arrived in Goa as secretary to its archbishop just two years before Ralph Fitch was brought there as a prisoner, and Linschoten returned home a year after Fitch did, carrying priceless secret Portuguese navigation maps in his baggage, allowing Dutch vessels to cross the Indian Ocean without being blown to its bottom by monsoon winds. The Dutch quickly established themselves in force on the Spice Islands they coveted, massacring English merchant "allies" there at Amboina in 1623. The English company then fell back to buy spices along India's Malabar coast, and at the great Mughal port of Surat, seeking silks and saltpeter from the rich province of Bengal, all of which they first learned about in reports by Ralph Fitch.

Stanley Wolpert

See also **British East India Company Raj; Goa; Portuguese in India**

BIBLIOGRAPHY

Chaudhuri, K. N. *The Trading World of Asia and the East India Company, 1660–1760.* Cambridge, U.K. and New York: Cambridge University Press, 1978.

Furber, Holden. *John Company at Work.* Cambridge, Mass.: Harvard University Press, 1948.

Locke, J. C. *The First Englishmen in India: Letters and Narratives of Sundry Elizabethans.* London: G. Routledge, 1930.

FIVE-YEAR PLANS. *See* **Economic Development, Importance of Institutions in and Social Aspects of.**

FOLK ART In the vast panorama of India's sociocultural diversity, creative expressions are closely linked to diurnal rhythms, fertility cults, and protective rituals. Traditional ways of life as well as professions shape the form of creative expression. Women as the nurturers of the household have played the dominant role in performing rituals; many folk expressions arose from these traditions, thus evolving a parallel creative expression to the classical arts. In addition, there are professional groups that cater to the ritual needs of different communities. These professionals intervene between the physical and mythical world, involved not only in rites of passage but also serving as healers and as propitiators of the gods and the spirits that populate the inner hidden world. Many folk expressions are multifaceted, combining the creation of objects for worship with ritual mudras, song, dance, and performance, and well-known schools of folk art have evolved from these traditions.

Folk art from the earliest times included works created by women for ritual purpose, such as wall and floor paintings, hand-molded gods and goddesses, and offerings to sacred shrines to propitiate their gods. Art objects created by women for the family and for exchange as gifts cementing social relationships, also serve as an expression of their dreams, their longings, and their anguish. Traditional craftspeople, of course, also produce art for ritual use by the people of a village community or by shamans, who are not only the priests and genealogists of different communities, but who visually create and narrate the tales of deified heroes, as well as those of the progenitors of craft guilds. Pilgrim centers also became important centers for folk art.

Different communities have distinctive styles of artistic expression. In Gujarat's Kutch, a single village may contain several different groups, such as Ahirs, Rabaries, Lohanas, and Bhatias, each creating art objects in a distinctive style. The same is true of most rural communities, the unique ethos of each reflected in its artistic motifs, which are connected to ancient tribal or caste origins.

Painting on Floors, Walls, and Paper

In most Hindu households, a woman's daily morning task is the creation of floor decorations, known as *alpona*,

The ritual paintings of Mithila, North Bihar, Madhya Pradesh, and Warli have long been recognized and acknowledged as sensitive expressions of a folk art tradition. Mithila, a poverty-stricken area, had an extraordinary tradition of painting on mud walls. The most elaborate was the Kobar Ghar, paintings for the nuptial chamber, which were created to bless the inner room where the young couple would be together for the first time. The ritual focal point was a tree form of lotuses, often with a female head on the top, known as the *kamalban*, alongside of which was painted bamboo. These motifs were not only associated with fertility but were also subtle delineations of the sexual organs. Paintings of sacred Hindu couples—Rāma and Sītā, Shiva and Pārvatī—brought the blessings of the eternally united gods. The Brahman and Kayasta styles of painting were quite distinct. Older women painted from memory directly onto the mud walls, while others relied upon aide-mémoires kept on paper. Brahman women's work often exhibited a great spontaneity, while Kayasta women's paintings were usually linear and more controlled. Interesting ancient folk stylizations of a veiled woman with one eye and of floating animals and birds are sometimes mistakenly interpreted by Western viewers as the influence of the European modernists Paul Klee and Joan Miró.

Painting moved from village walls to paper, thanks to the encouragement of government departments, to add income to impoverished village families. Many women artists, including Jagdama Devi, Sita Devi, Mahasundari Devi, and later, Ganga Devi, emerged as highly creative and successful popular artists.

Another art form, the paintings of the Warli, a tribal group of Maharashtra in western India, also emerged from the walls of village huts. Originally, men were prohibited from painting, but the emergence of a lucrative art market broke this prohibition. One of the finest Warli painters, Jivya Soma Mashe, is a male folk artist who has won many awards.

The Navarātras, the nine nights devoted to the worship of the mother goddess, which require strict fasting, were also the occasion for creating images of the goddess, painting or preparing mud figures in relief on the walls. These were then immersed in a local pond or river with great ceremony. From this ancient ritual evolved a popular modern tradition, the elaborate creation of Goddess Durga images, in Bengal.

These traditions are also associated with the seventy-two *vrata*s, rituals of fasting and praying performed by women, which are the early beginnings of narrative folk painting. The paintings continue to be used to tell the stories associated with each *vrata*. *Hoi*, for example, is created

Detail of Krishna from Wall inside One of Orchha's Palaces. Orchha is a medieval city in central India (now in Madhya Pradesh) founded in 1531. Its crumbling palaces, pavilions, and gates are testmony to a rich feudal lifestyle that encouraged the patronage of art and craft forms, including Lipai, the mud-based process used to create this mural. CHRISTINE PEMBERTON / FOTOMEDIA.

aripana, and *kolam*. These auspicious patterns are meant not only to welcome visitors and to propitiate the household gods, but also to provide food for unseen creatures, or spirits. In South India each dot of the *kolam*, created with dots of pure rice flour, is believed to feed three ants. Each design, every motif has a symbolic significance; some of the stylized patterns can be found as well in the tattoo designs created by wandering tattoo artists.

In different seasons, for festivals and rites of passage, each house is painted, and that too is traditionally women's art. Among the women in Saurashtra and Kutch, Gujarat, the Meos of Haryana, and the Jats and Harijans of Punjab, dung- or mud-work walls, encrusted with mirrors, decorate the interiors of the village huts, creating a shimmering inner landscape.

for the protection of children and *karvachaut* for the protection of a husband. The women recite the stories painted on the walls, a tradition that is still practiced. In urban areas, however, lithographic prints have taken the place of the wall paintings, curtailing women's creativity.

The women of Kumaon, in the mountainous areas of Uttar Pradesh, create images of Lord Shiva and his family, which are worshiped by the household during Mahashivaratri, and then left outside on the ledge of the house. The collection of these images placed on the house ledges evokes an art gallery.

Other Art Forms

Indian women create a vast range of artistic products, using recycled or common materials that often hold no intrinsic value; yet their labor and artistic expression transform these materials into works of great value. The finest pieces may be the sculptural forms created from golden grass in North Bihar, made by the women of the household for a young bride as gifts to be taken to her new home. Grass elephants, peacocks, statuesque men, and boxes are made to simulate the dowry gifts of the wealthy landlords of the area. Wastepaper and rags are pulverized to create papier-mâché figures of men, women, animals, and large grain containers, further enlivened by painting, as gifts and for decorating the home. Elaborate palm leaf, bamboo, and straw baskets are created as gifts. The women of Chettinad in Tamil Nadu make exquisite baskets from dyed palm leaf that are as fine as any embroidered cloth and that also serve as wedding gifts.

Textiles. Throughout India, new clothes are never made for a newborn child; instead, a patched wrapper is created from rags, often collected from different individuals who have led long and happy lives. These patches are stitched together with great care for the newborn baby. The rag wrappers, known as *kantha, sujani, gudree,* and *dharkhee,* are representative of the spirit of Chind-deo, the "Lord of Tatters," and Chinddevi, the "Goddess of Tatters"; not only are they protective clothes, they also symbolize a child's purity, connecting him with the final stage of life, *sanyas,* when a person gives up all attachments to family and hearth.

Woven *durries* of Punjab and Haryana, created by the Jat community, are made only for the household, and as gifts for their children or relatives, as an act of bonding. Pictorial scenes from folk epics such as Heer Ranja or from local ballads are created, often interspersed with lines from folk songs or a form of poetry, for example, *Bagha wich aiyee bahar koil kuk uthi* (The spring flowered and the nightingale began to sing).

Scrolls. A number of folk artists created painted ritual cloths, which were used by the shamans of different communities for celebrating deified heroes. These scroll paintings are of ancient origin and are mentioned in ancient texts. The Pabuji ka Phadh, Ramdeoji-ka Phardh are painted by Brahmans of Shapura, Rajasthan, and are used by the Bhopas, the priests of the local communities, to celebrate the lives of the heroes, thus earning merit for the community. The creation of wall paintings, known as Pithoda, by the shamans of the Rathwa tribe is an important household ritual through which the legend of Pithoda is related.

The painters, or *patuas,* of the painted scrolls (*pata*) of Bengal are often those who relate the stories as they move from village to village. The Ghazi Pat, which is now found only in Bangladesh, was painted by a Brahman but used by Muslim performers, who sang, danced, and told the story, which is an interesting syncretism of Muslim and Hindu beliefs. The Hindu *patuas* of West Bengal were painters and wandering minstrels who unrolled their long scrolls scene by scene as they sang the story. Jadu *pats,* magical scrolls, were created by the Jadu *patuas* for the tribal Santhals, of the Santhal and Pargana districts of Bihar, as well as among the Santhals of Bengal. They claimed that creating the image of the ancestor would help them find their way to the other world. The Chitrakuthis of Paithan in the Deccan were famous for their extraordinary paintings, which they used to relate religious legends.

Scrolls painted in Andhra of the Markandaya Purāṇa were created specially for the Padmasalis, a weavers' community. The painters also created clay figures of the main characters, which were used along with the scrolls to tell the story of Bhavana Rishi, their progenitor.

Centers of the folk art tradition. Places of pilgrimage became important centers for the creation of ritual objects as well as mementos for pilgrims to carry back to their homes. Important schools of art emerged from this tradition. Kalighat paintings achieved fame because of the large number of pilgrims who visited the temple. Local *patuas,* as well as painters who had lost their courtly patrons, thus found other outlets for their talent. They began to paint pictures of gods and goddesses, as well as local scenes and narratives. European influence was seen in the use of watercolor in place of gouache, and in the use of bold lines for creating figures. These paintings were not only bought by Europeans, but were also appreciated by the Bengali elite, who had been exposed to contemporary art in Europe. Jamini Roy, a contemporary painter inspired by Kalighat painting, became world renowned. Kalighat painters continued their tradition by painting on clay plaques, which were used to decorate family shrines as well as the home.

The *pata-chitra* painting of Orissa was practiced by local painters, whose primary duty had been and continues to be the painting of the deities Lord Jagannath, Balram, and Subhadra of the Jagannath Temple of Puri. They created replicas of the images for the pilgrims, both in wood and on a canvas created from cloth and a paste made of vegetal materials. They painted Subhadra, scenes from the Gītā Govinda, and depictions of a number of deities for sale to pilgrims. They also painted the *ganjifa*, local playing cards, a tradition maintained in many parts of India. Raghurajpur village on the outskirts of Puri has a number of such well-known painters.

Tanjore, an important pilgrimage center in Tamil Nadu, developed a range of paintings depicting Lord Krishna as a child and as a lover surrounded by the *gopi*s, lovelorn women devotees of Vrindavan, as well as paintings of other gods. The paintings were painted on treated wood, using gold and silver, and were even encrusted with stones and jewels. Tanjore also became known for its glass paintings.

The Bhats, a priestly caste of the lower castes of Rajasthan, were string puppeteers who carved and dressed their puppets, performing throughout North India. According to their oral tradition, they played in the Mughal court and evolved their art at the court under a Persian master puppeteer, though there is also a reference to the string and shadow puppetry of Central Asia. Rajasthani puppeteers may have been responsible for the spread of string puppets throughout India. Orissa had a tradition of string puppets, painted in the *pata-chitra* style, while Bengal had a tradition of rod puppets as well as string puppets. Leather shadow puppets were found in South India in Karnataka, Andhra, and Kerala. Kerala shadow puppets, made of buffalo hide, were distinctive and echoed the classical style as represented in the bronze and wooden sculptures. Beautifully carved wooden dancing puppets with articulated body movements and eye movements are used in temple processions in Tamil Nadu.

The *dhokra*, or *cire-perdue* (lost wax) technique of metal casting of Bastar in Madhya Pradesh, Bihar, and Orissa was created by itinerant metalsmiths known as Kasars, Malhars, and Mals. Originally they moved from place to place, living on the fringe of the village, and were often treated as vagrants. They would buy broken brass pots and melt them to create their pieces. The base was made out of clay, and the figure was shaped from strings of wax. Thus spiral patterns appeared on the finished pieces. They created images worshiped by the tribal people, as well as ritual objects and jewelry worn by the men, women, and shamans. Each of the center's had a distinctive style of work. Over the years, Bastar and West Bengal further developed the art as a form of creative expression. Jaidev Baghel of Bastar has emerged as an artist whose work is exhibited in galleries in India and abroad.

Karnataka also has centers where the *ciré-perdu* method is used for casting anklets, belts worn by the traditional shamans, who perform the rituals of exorcism, by the worship of the Bhoota figures, as well as performance of ritual dance and plays in Kerala associated with the Theyyam and worship of Bhadrakali.

Some of the richest forms of creative expression are to be found in Kerala in the celebration of temple festivals and the enactment of rituals for ancestor worship and healing. One of the most powerful performances is the creation of large floor paintings of the powerful goddess, Bhadrakali, from which the goddess is believed to appear. Her painted face, headdress, and costume create a world of fantasy in which, accompanied by loud drumming, the battle between good and evil is enacted. The *theyyam*, or ritual performance, patronized by landed gentry, brings into play the creation of mythical characters with the use of palm leaves, straw, paint, and facial as well as body masks, enhancing the viewers' entry into a mythical world.

Recognition and acclaim. A new class of folk artists has emerged as a result of their recognition and promotion by well-known artists, art historians, and art institutes. A number of artists began the study and advocacy of the work of folk and tribal artists: Shankho Choudary, a sculptor, initiated his students at the Baroda Fine Arts Faculty in the 1950s into an appreciation of folk arts; and J. Swaminathan, the well-known painter, promoted the cause of folk and tribal artists, presenting a policy paper to the Governing Council of the Lalit Kala Akademi (the institution for contemporary art), stating that it should give equal status to folk and tribal artists. As director of the Kala Bhawan in Bhopal, Swaminathan ran workshops jointly for contemporary and folk artists. He also held exhibitions at which the work of folk and tribal artists was hung alongside the work of contemporary artists. Haku Shah, a sensitive contemporary artist, was responsible for encouraging the talent of many folk artists, such as Saroja Bai and Ganesh, whose works were featured in international exhibitions and now are preserved in a number of museums. Balan Nambiar, a sculptor and enamel artist from Kerala, made a detailed study of folk expression in Kerala State. The photographs taken by the well-known artist Jyoti Bhat were responsible for the discovery of Sona Bai, whose work in clay created a unique environment.

An exhibition organized by Dr. Jyotindra Jain, called "Other Masters: Five Contemporary Folk and Tribal Artists of India," at the National Crafts Museum in New Delhi brought the works of Sona Bai, Jivya Soma Mashe, Ganga Devi, Jangardh Sing Shyam, and of the great Manipuri potter Nilomani Devi into the public eye. Though Jain's catalog of the exhibition, as well as his book on Ganga Devi, focused public attention on the enduring creative work of Indian folk artists, great numbers of them will no doubt continue to work in anonymity.

Jasleen Dhamija

See also **Bandhani; Paithani; Papermaking; Patola; Textiles**

BIBLIOGRAPHY

Appaswamy, Jaya. *Glass Paintings*. New Delhi: Lalit Kala Akademi, 1970.

Archana, Shastri. *The Language of Symbols: A Project on South Indian Ritual Decorations of a Semi-permanent Nature*. Chennai Crafts Council of India, 1984.

Archer, Mildred. *Indian Miniatures and Folk Paintings*. London: Arts Council of Great Britain, 1967.

———. *Indian Popular Painting in the India Office Library*. London: H. M. Stationery Office, 1977.

Archer, W. G. *Kalighat Paintings: A Catalogue*. London: Victoria and Albert Museum, 1971.

Barucha, Rostam. *Rajasthan, an Oral History: Conversations with Komal Kothari*. New Delhi and New York: Penguin, 2003.

Dhamija, Jasleen "Embroideries." *Marg* 23 (no. 2): 1964.

———. *Indian Folk Arts and Crafts*. New Delhi: National Book Trust, 1970.

———. *Women and Handicrafts: Myth and Reality*. New York: Seeds, 1981.

———. *Crafts of Gujarat*. Ahmedabad: Mapin, 1985.

Elwin, Vernier. *The Tribal Art of Middle India*. Mumbai: Oxford University Press, 1951.

Jain, Jyotindra. *Folk Art and Culture of Gujarat*. Ahmedabad: Shreyas Folk Museum of Gujarat, 1980.

———. *Painted Myths of Creation: Art and Ritual of an Indian Tribe*. New Delhi: Lalit Kala Akademi, 1984.

———. *Ganga Devi: Tradition and Expression in Mithila Painting*. Ahmedabad: Mapin, 1997.

———. *Other Masters: Five Contemporary Folk and Tribal Artists of India*. New Delhi: Crafts Museum, 1998.

———. *Kalighat Painting: Images from a Changing World*. Ahmedabad: Mapin, 1999.

Kosambi, D. D. *An Introduction to the Study of Indian History*. New Delhi: Popular Prakashan, 1967.

Kothari, Komal. "The Shrine: An Expression of Social Needs." In *Gods of the Byways: Wayside Shrines of Rajasthan, Madhya Pradesh & Gujarat*. Oxford: Museum of Modern Art, 1982.

———. "Epics of Rajasthan." *Journal of the National Centre for the Performing Arts* 13, no. 3 (September 1984): 1–19.

———. "Performer Gods & Heroes in the Oral Epics of Rajasthan," In *Oral Epics in India*, edited by Stuart H. Blackburn and Peter J. Claus. Berkeley: University of California Press, 1989.

Kramrisch, Stella. *Unknown India: Ritual Arts in Tribe and Village*. Philadelphia: Philadelphia Museum of Art, 1980.

Mookerjee, Ajitcoomar. *Folk Art of Bengal*. Kolkata: University of Calcutta, 1939.

Ramanujan, A. K. *The Collected Escays of A. K. Ramanujan*. New Delhi and New York: Oxford University Press, 1999.

Reeves, Ruth. *Ciré-Perdue Casting in India*. New Delhi: Crafts Museum, 1962.

Welch, Stuart. *A Flower from Every Meadow: Indian Paintings from American Collections*. New York: Asia Society, 1973.

FOLK DANCE Dance plays an important role in celebrating South Asian life-cycle events and calendrical rituals, as well as religious beliefs, and appears to have done so for millennia. Every Indian language and social group has its own words for dance, emphasizing the local and unique over the national and common. Indeed, no single word can commonly translate the idea of dance, and no single encyclopedia entry could hope to discuss every dance form, classical or folk. Moreover, dance provides numerous examples of the codification of "folk" tradition into classical praxis. When aristocrats brought regional dances into their courts (as with *kathak*) and when temples standardized village dance dramas (as with *kathakali*), they helped link cosmopolitan and rural India. Thus, dance illustrates a continuum between the folk and the classical in South Asian performance traditions. Dancers in "folk" traditions may spend many hours perfecting their choreography with the assistance of teachers, learning patterns and techniques passed down from previous generations. However, these dance contexts can also spawn improvised and spontaneous gestures that can take on choreographic lives of their own.

In many cases, folk dance seems to begin as stylized gestures illustrating either daily routine or episodes of religious stories. If, for example, during devotional singing an individual stands up and demonstrates how a character in the song walked or behaved, then the careful execution of those movements becomes dance. When, in the context of music, individuals reenact daily chores such as carrying a water pot on the head, or illustrate their ability to handle weapons such as swords, the careful execution of those movements becomes dance. And, when these actions are isolated, abstracted, and socialized, dance is a consequence. Sometimes, children's games are the source of dances. For example, in the *hikat* of Jammu and Kashmir (and found widely in similar forms throughout South Asia), pairs of dancers cross and extend their arms, clasping their partner's wrists, leaning backward and spinning in time with the music. The dance ends when one of the dancers becomes too dizzy or the rate becomes too fast. Notably, the dance teaches a participant to rely on a partner—whose counterbalance keeps you from falling during the dance and who will hold you if you fall. In an agrarian society where success and survival are linked with mutual dependence, the lesson is not frivolous.

Regional genres, such as Gujarati *garbā*, can function both in the contexts of life-cycle events (such as

Gujarati Folk Dancer. On 21 September 2003, in Ahmedabad, a Gujarati folk dancer, in swirling traditional attire, rehearsing for the upcoming Hindu festival of Navarātri. Navarātri is the longest Hindu festival, lasting for nine consecutive nights. AMIT DAVE/REUTERS/CORBIS.

weddings) and calendrical rituals associated with religious festivals (such as Navarātrī, in which it is the preferred form of worship for mother goddesses). However, at the core of this musico-choreographic form is a celebration of fertility, both etymologically (*garbā* derives from *garbhā*, "womb") and symbolically. For example, one of the most common central points of this circular and repetitive dance is a perforated earthen pot (*garbhā dīpā*), which represents life within the womb. Other representations in this tradition can be a pot of water with a coconut stopper or a basket of seedlings. Women gather in the evening during Navarātrī (nine nights of autumnal celebration) wearing long embroidered skirts with inset mirrors, short blouses similarly decorated, and long scarves. As they dance in a circle, they bend, clap, and repeat the pattern, while singing songs praising the mother goddesses and asking for their blessings. The twirling dancers, with the light of the *garbhā dīpā* reflecting

off their skirts, illustrate the reality of dance, not as entertainment, but as a cathartic experience that, combined with fasting, brings the goddess into their midst as a fellow dancer. The genre also has gendered versions: *garbo* (masculine) for women and *garbī* (feminine) for men. (*Garbā* is the plural form.) Regional variants include Punjabi *giddhā*, performed at festivals or in connection with wheat, both during sowing and harvesting. This dance can also mark the arrival of rain or of a new baby and has a rich musical tradition.

A variation of this dance style is *kummi* of Tamil Nadu, Andhra Pradesh, and Kerala, the songs of which sometimes describe everyday tasks such as chores, while others are dedicated to specific gods. Women perform *kummi* as a counterpart to men's dances, and it can take multiple forms, even within the same region. In Tamil Nadu, for example, the *kummi* is both a "flower dance," extolling the beauty of flowers, and a "housewife's dance," to name just two of many. The dance is also performed during Dīvālī, when cattle (the animals considered sacred to Shiva and Krishna) are decorated and led in a procession accompanied by music and dance. New rice is cooked and girls dance—stepping, jumping, pirouetting, and clapping to form circles.

In northwestern India, a *rāsa* or *rāso* can be a legend set in verse and sung about kings or warriors (such as the *Prithvirāj Rāso*), suggesting that perhaps the widespread dance of the similar name might have begun as an enactment of scenes in these stories. These dances share movements and perhaps origins with dances that have distinctly military associations, such as the *katthak* of the Pathans. In this case, male dancers perform a series of stylized military motions with swords and shields, complete with feints, turns, and pivots. Similarly, in eastern India, men perform versions of the *chau* dance-drama, particularly the *puruliā chau* of West Bengal and Bihar, in the spring. This last version includes mock reenactments of fights between the principal characters, in which dancers strike their "weapons" against each other in a stylized battle. *Serāikela chau* in Bihar also uses stylized martial movement, but today prominently includes rural and rustic themes. *Chau* dancers also wear masks in most (but not all) traditions and depict episodes from the Mahābhārata and the Rāmāyaṇa, as well as other religious stories. Another martial and religious themed dance is the *parāsa* (after *parāsu*, "battle ax") dance of Sirmur in Himachal Pradesh, where male dancers wield clubs and reenact the story of Parashu-Rāma (an incarnation of Vishnu) defeating Renuka.

Stick dances occur in various forms throughout India and celebrate deities, agriculture, marriage, and life-cycle events and, while they may vary in specific features and functions, the fundamental elements remain the same. The defining characteristics are the use of two sticks and, like *garbā*, choreographic patterns of one or more counterrevolving concentric circles (or sometimes, two parallel lines). *Rāsa* stick dances share the characteristic of dancer pairings; dancers beat their own sticks together and with those of other dancers in time with the music. Stories of Krishna are often themes in stick dances, though some regions, such as Travancore and Cape Comorin, pay homage to other deities, such as Shiva and St. Francis Xavier. Stick dances can be found throughout India and commonly have connections with agriculture, the dance movements often reflecting this association as dancers pat the earth, imitating the sowing of seeds. Some social groups use stick dances to celebrate life-cycle events. For example, Rajasthani Bhils perform a version of *rāsa* called *jhoriā* (referring to the pair of wooden sticks) at weddings. Performances of *rāsa* in northern India typically occur on festivals such as Vasant Pancamī, Navarātra, and Sharada Purnima, which celebrate harvests. But while *rāsa* commonly has links with agricultural cycles, individual societies ultimately dictate the content of the dance. The *rāsa*s of some communities, such as those found in Manipur, are less related to agriculture, while in many of Saurashtra's villages, *dandiā rāsa* ("stick" *rāsa*) dances are nearly synonymous with harvests. Communities throughout Gujarat, Saurashtra, and Maharashtra perform dances of this type, maintaining the fundamental traits of *rāsa*, while imprinting the movements with regional stylistic features.

Variations of the *rāsa* exist even within regions. Some dances replace sticks with stylized swords, others remove vocals and dance only to the accompaniment of drums, and the sticks vary in size and style. *Rās līlā* in Manipur is generally elaborate and thematic, with different varieties such as *basant rāsa* ("spring" *rāsa*, depicting the amorous quarrels of Rādhā and Krishna), *kunj rāsa* (the love of Rādhā and Krishna), *mahā rāsa* (the separation of Krishna and Rādhā), *divā rāsa* ("daytime" *rāsa*), *nitya rāsa* ("everyday" rasa), *nātnā rāsa* (Krishna playing with the milkmaids), and others. Some of these are in the form of a circle (such as the *mahā rāsa* and the *nātnā rāsa*), while others are more dramatic representations. In Sirmur of the Himalayan region, *rāsa* performances occur during the Maghi or Bisu festivals and, unlike the dance in Graj and Manipur, use many instruments and focus less on deities and more on stories of mortal love. One variation, the *rās līlā*, found particularly in Uttar Pradesh, reenacts Krishna legends in various celebrations, and some local variants have sophisticated patterns of foot stamping and flowing arm movements. In the Punjab, *jhummar* seems to be a variation on *bhangrā* (see below), but is performed by women with sticks during festivals like Navarātra.

Again, women move in circles, often pirouetting (as in other Indian circle dances) and striking pairs of sticks together and against those of other dancers.

In Kerala and Karnataka, another variation on *rāsa* is the *kōlāttam*, a ribbon and braid dance that originally was a fertility dance, but which has also come to symbolize the triumph of the goddess Mohini over the demon Basmasura. Although the dance has developed agricultural associations throughout the decades, the *kōlāttam*'s popularity has spread to homes, schools, and cities, making the dance primarily social today. Some communities, however, still maintain the earlier principles of the *kōlāttam*. In Tamil Nadu, for example, girls perform the *kōlāttam* by moving around the circle or square and hitting sticks high and low as they bend from side to side. Opposing dancers hit sticks as they dance around the circle, moving forward and backward, leaping onto and away from their toes. *Kōlāttam* can also focus on religious, philosophical, or musical ideas through song, and may celebrate deities such as Rāma.

Dances celebrate many occasions in the Punjab, but by far the best-known Punjabi dance is *bhangrā*, originally performed by farmers after a harvest but now widely performed by men in public contexts. Again, this dance is gendered. Women sometimes perform *bhangrā*, but only in private contexts, such as in the home or with family. However, when men perform *bhangrā*, they commonly engage in intensely kinesthetic movement meant to illustrate the physical prowess of the dancers. They may even engage in gymnastics and activities such as human pyramids. The jumps, spins, bends, and other exaggerated movements in time with the drumming are usually accompanied by the dancers holding their arms above their heads, often snapping their fingers, with the head either slightly downturned or bent back, suggesting a kind of self-absorption. *Bhangrā* became one of the most popular dance forms in twentieth-century popular Indian films and, because of this identity, *bhangrā* and its variations have spread internationally, especially in British club settings. Today, *bhangrā*-like dances can be seen in wedding processions in Bengal, Gujarat, Himachal Pradesh, and Kerala.

Some folk dances have become the subject of elaborate urban and suburban competitions that attract thousands of people. *Bhangrā*, *garbā*, and *dandiā rāsa* are the choreographic fields upon which dance clubs and teams compete; they are judged not only on the intricacy and execution of the dances, but also for their costumes and stage props. One part of the strategy for a successful performance in these competitions is to evoke historical or regional variations. *Bhangrā* dancers might swing a farmer's stave (*lāthī*) as part of their choreography, attempting to evoke an authenticity to their dance (the presumption being that a rural performance would be more "authentic" than an urban or suburban performance), but also demonstrating the virility of the men dancing (the *lathi* being a formidable weapon in the right hands). In *garbā* competitions, women and girls will often dance with pots on their heads, sometimes with lamps burning inside, and, in the most elaborate situations, some performers may dance with a *mandapikā* (lamp tree). *Dandīā rāsa* competitions may have the most elaborate choreographies. The essential dance pattern itself is already complex: an inner circle moves counterclockwise, an outer circle moves clockwise, and dancers are paired with a different partner after each set of gestures and one partial rotation of each of the circles. The gestures can be simple (the commonest consisting of about eight strikes against your partner's sticks and your own) or much more elaborate (e.g., dancers twirl before, during, and after the strikes, perhaps also kneeling and striking the floor). Dance teams can come from such diverse sources as neighborhood associations and police academies. Universities in Gujarati-speaking western India commonly have *dandīā rāsa* clubs. All will purchase or create elaborate costumes that attempt to be both colorful and authentic, sometimes to the point of being too flamboyant and only romantically authentic.

A contributing factor to the codification of folk dance in India has been the central government, whose annual Independence Day celebrations in Delhi have regularly featured troupes of dancers from the different states. Performed in a large stadium, only those dances that involve the most people in the brightest costumes, making the grandest gestures, have an impact. The intimacy and contextual importance of the local art form is lost.

Gordon Thompson
Kasha Rybczyk
Shelley Smith

See also **Dance Forms**

BIBLIOGRAPHY

Thompson, Gordon. "Music and Values in Gujarati-speaking Western India." Ph.D. diss., University of California at Los Angeles, 1987.
Vatsyayan, Kapila. *Traditions of Indian Folk Dance*. New Delhi: Indian Book Company, 1976.

FOOD SECURITY Defined as a condition in which all people have physical and economic access to sufficient, safe, and nutritious food to meet their dietary needs and preferences, food security is considered by the United Nations a basic human right. The current world food system normally functions efficiently, at least in an economic sense, though not a moral one. It provides at reasonable prices adequate food of their choice to those who can afford to pay for it.

Thus food security is a problem of the poor, in poor countries. The hungry of the world are hungry because they are poor. They are poor because they own too few resources of land, capital, or skills. Poverty can also be a most vicious circle, since from lack of food the poor may not be physically or mentally productive enough to earn adequate income, thus perpetuating their poverty. Hunger is primarily a problem of poverty, not of food production. If all the world's poor were given sufficient income, more food would be demanded and produced. But if more food were produced because farmers were given higher prices, the poor, whose incomes would not have changed, would remain hungry.

Food security for a country is also a matter of underdevelopment. A poor country deficient in food production is vulnerable to transient influences that reduce domestic production or increase world market prices, as it cannot import the food it needs. While it is conceivable—for example, in some nuclear winter scenarios—that global food production could fall so much below the demand that even rich nations would not find enough food, such supply shortages are very unlikely. The technological food production potential of the world, even without exotic technologies, is so great that the inability to produce food at any cost is not likely to threaten the food security of wealthy nations.

What constitutes "adequate" food intake is still a matter of contention among nutritionists. The general approach is to consider the basal metabolic rate, the number of calories that a person needs while lying down but wide awake, and take some multiple of that as the norm for adequate caloric intake. Metabolic rates vary, of course, across similar individuals (in height, weight, gender) and also across time for a given individual. Individuals learn to live with fewer (or more) calories over time. Yet, no matter how one measures hunger and poverty, one finds that hundreds of millions of persons suffer from hunger and poverty in the world and in India.

In addition to the millions who suffer from persistent hunger, many others who normally get enough to eat live precariously on the margin of subsistence. They are vulnerable to all manner of external influences, which can easily reduce their food consumption and bring them into the ranks of the hungry. A major threat to the already inadequate food consumption of the poor is from any temporary drop in real income. The real income of the poor can also fall because food prices rise.

When India's monsoon rains fail, the poor not only lose employment but food prices rise as well. Even when the rains fail in a remote, prosperous country, the price of food for the poor may increase. The rich country would then either export less food grains or import more grains, and the world market prices of food grains would go up. A country's booming domestic economy could aggravate the hunger of the poor if their incomes do not rise as rapidly as do increases in food prices. Apart from such sudden drops in real income, a creeping loss may occur if employment opportunities do not keep pace with the growth in the labor force.

Both persistent hunger and transient hunger, the extreme form of which is famine, have underlined the fact that to deal with chronic hunger is to deal with poverty and underdevelopment. Amartya Sen (1981) and Jean Drèze and Sen (1989) have extensively examined how to deal with the extreme case of transient hunger, namely, famine. Famines have led to large-scale deaths since World War II in some countries but not in India. The question is why some governments fail to take effective action in time to prevent mass deaths due to famine. Drèze and Sen stress the role that freedom of the press and media plays in mobilizing timely and effective action against famine.

The State of Food Security in India

India's national level of food security is reflected in the availability of food, whose net availability at the aggregate level in per capita terms has been maintained at reasonable levels and has been increasing over the years, though since 1997 it has been coming down a bit for two reasons. Diversification due to better quality food (milk, edible oils, etc.) has reduced demand for grains; and high levels of minimum support prices for wheat and rice set by the government reduced the demand and increased output and led to net accretion of nearly 40 million tons of buffer stocks from 1997 to 2001.

Domestic production of food grains, dependent to a large extent on India's rains, fluctuates from year to year. The government thus holds buffer stocks of food grains to ensure that availability does not suffer. The size of the buffer stock should be adequate to fill the gap of any fall in production caused by a sequence of poor monsoons, keeping prices at reasonable levels.

The state of food insecurity at the individual level is reflected in the number of persons who do not get adequate food to eat and who show signs of malnutrition. The poverty line in India is defined as the level of consumer expenditure at which people in rural areas will consume 2,400 calories per person per day and those in urban areas 2,100 calories per person per day. Based on household consumption surveys carried out by the National Sample Survey Organization the estimated number of persons below the poverty line has been coming down. Transient hunger, however, can throw almost 10 percent of India's rural population into poverty from one year to the next.

Government programs, such as buffer stock policy, to provide food security have not been very effective. Another indicator of food insecurity is the level of malnutrition in India. In 1997–1998 the percentage of stunted children (height-for-age) was 57.1 percent among the rural poor and 49.6 percent in urban areas, very high proportions indeed.

Policies for Food Security

Once adequate food is available at the national level, providing food security to all is to provide adequate real income to all. The government has followed a variety of policies to do so. Poverty removal has been the main objective of all of India's five-year plans and all political parties. The policies have included transfers of food, such as public distribution of food at subsidized prices through ration shops, Midday Meal programs, Mother and Child Nutrition programs, and income-enhancing programs, such as employment guarantee plans, Food for Work, and other employment programs, and many other antipoverty programs, described briefly below.

Public distribution. Under the public distribution system, selected items of mass consumption, such as wheat, rice, other cereals, sugar, oil, and kerosene, are provided at subsidized prices to ration card holders in limited quantities. People are free to buy additional quantities in the open market. Ration cards are now issued to everyone. This program is now considered one of the government's most significant antipoverty initiatives. In 2004, under the Targeted Public Distribution System, each family below the poverty line is entitled to a quota of 22 pounds (10 kg) of food grains at subsidized prices (about 50% of cost). Families above the poverty line received a lower subsidy (90% of cost). However, the large difference between the issue price to the poor and the open market price provided incentives for diversion of considerable amounts of grain into the open market, and such leakage, coupled with exclusion errors in targeting, implied that very little subsidy reached the poor. The objective of providing adequate food to all has not as yet been realized.

Antyodaya Anna Yojana. This program was introduced in early 2001 for the poorest of the poor, as identified by *gram panchayat*s (village leaders) and *gram sabha*s (village councils). Antyodaya households are entitled to 77 pounds (35 kg) of grain a month at highly subsidized prices (Rs. 2 per kg for wheat, and Rs. 3 per kg for rice). A survey of destitution in five states indicates that the program is doing well. The selection of Antyodaya households appears to be quite fair. In some areas, however, the survey found that many households had been deprived of their entitlements by ration shop dealers. The program covers only about 5 percent of the rural population. If these limitations are overcome, the Antodaya program holds much promise.

Food security through ICDS. Malnutrition among children and women is severe in India. Integrated Child Development Services (ICDS), perhaps the largest of all food supplementation programs in the world, was initiated in 1975 to: improve the health and nutrition of children in the 0–6 year age group by providing supplementary food; to provide early stimulation and education to preschool children; to provide pregnant and lactating women with food supplements; and to enhance mothers' abilities to provide proper child care through health and nutrition education.

A World Bank and Government of India review in 1997 found that ICDS services were much in demand, but there are problems in delivery, quality, and coordination. The program might perhaps be improving food security at the household level, but has failed to effectively address the issues of prevention, undernourished child/mother detection, and management.

Food security through midday meals to schoolchildren. The provision of free midday meals to schoolchildren encourages enrollment and retention, in addition to providing food security to children. School feeding programs often double enrollment within a year and can produce a 40 percent improvement in academic performance in just two years, the World Food Program has found in its study of a number of states in India.

The program, first introduced in the southern state of Tamil Nadu in 1956, has proved remarkably successful in improving school enrollment in that state. With modest cost, the benefit has been dramatic, increasing school enrollment in the state: in primary schools, up 31 percent, from 5.04 million in 1985–1986 to 6.59 million in 2002–2003; in middle schools, dropouts decreased from 24 to 13.85 percent during the same period. Apart from boosting school attendance and child nutrition, midday meals have an important social value. As children learn to sit together and share meals, there may be an erosion of caste prejudices; the gender gap may also be reduced as female school attendance increases.

The Supreme Court of India in November 2001 directed all of India's "State Governments/Union Territories to implement the Mid-Day Meal Scheme" in every government and government-assisted primary school, offering every child a midday meal of no fewer than 300 calories and 8–12 grams of protein each day of school, for at least 200 days.

Food security through employment programs. The best-known employment program is Maharashtra's Employment Guarantee Scheme (EGS), started on 26 January 1979, guaranteeing employment to all adults eighteen years and above who are willing to do unskilled manual work. The act bestows a right to work on every adult person residing in rural areas of Maharashtra. Only the needy offer themselves for work, and the supply of employment has to adjust to demand, so that fluctuations over seasons and over years are automatically taken into consideration. It is also self liquidating. When economic growth provides opportunities for better paying jobs, people would automatically stop coming for work in EGS programs. Though EGS has not eliminated rural poverty in Maharashtra, there is some evidence of decline in the depth of poverty there. Another important benefit of EGS is that by providing an alternative opportunity for employment to rural workers, it increases their bargaining power and increases rural wages.

The many programs to provide food security have surely made some impact and have been extremely important as short-term measures. However, perhaps the best long-term measure for food security is economic development that provides enough income for all Indians to buy as much food as they need.

Kirit Parikh

See also **Economic Development, Importance of Institutions in and Social Aspects of; Famines; Poverty and Inequality; Subsidies in the Federal Budget**

BIBLIOGRAPHY

Bigman, D., and P. V. Srinivasan. "Geographical Targeting of Poverty Alleviation Programs: Methodology and Applications in Rural India." Mimeograph, Indira Gandhi Institute of Development Research, Mumbai, 2001.

Bigman, D., S. Dercon, D. Guillaume, and M. Lambotte. "Community Targeting for Poverty Reduction in Burkina Faso." *World Bank Economic Review* 14, no. 1 (2000): 167–193.

Chelliah, R. J., and R. Sudarshan. *Income Poverty and Beyond: Human Development in India.* New Delhi: Social Science Press, 1998.

Cornia, G. A., and F. Stewart. "Two Errors of Targeting." In *Public Spending and the Poor: Theory and Evidence*, edited by

D. van de Walle and K. Nead. Baltimore: Johns Hopkins University Press, 1995.

Dev, S. M. "India's (Maharashtra) Employment Guarantee Scheme: Lessons from Long Experience." In *Employment for Poverty Reduction and Food Security*, edited by J. von Braun. Washington, D.C.: IFPRI, 1995.

Dev, S. M., M. H. Suryanarayana, and K. S. Parikh. "Rural Poverty in India: Incidence, Issues and Policies." *Asian Development Review* 10, no. 1 (1992): 35–66.

Dev, S. M., and Jos Mooi. "Patterns in Social Sector Expenditure: Pre- and Post-reform Period." In *India Development Report 2004*, edited by Kirit Parikh and R. Radhakrishna. New Delhi: Oxford University Press, 2004.

Drèze, J., and A. Sen. *Hunger and Public Action*. Oxford: Clarendon Press, 1989.

———. *India: Economic Development and Social Opportunity*. New Delhi: Oxford University Press, 1998.

Dubey, A., and S. Gangopadhyay. *Counting the Poor: Where Are the Poor in India?* Sarvekshana Analytical Report no. 1. New Delhi: Department of Statistics, Government of India, 1998.

Ghosh, J., A. Sen, and C. P. Chandrasekhar. "Using Foodstocks Productively." *Economic and Political Weekly* 31, no. 21 (1996).

Government of India. *Report on Food Security*. New Delhi: Expenditure Reforms Commission, Government of India, 2000.

Hirway, I., and P. Terhal. *Towards Employment Guarantee in India*. New Delhi: Sage Publications, 1994.

———. *Towards Employment Guarantee in India: Indian and International Experiences in Public Works Programme*. New Delhi: Sage Publications, 1997.

Jha, S., and P. V. Srinivasan. "On Targeting Food Subsidies." In *Reforming India's Social Sectors: Strategies and Prospects*, edited by K. S. Prabhu. New Delhi: Sage Publications, 2001.

———. *On Improving the Effectiveness of PDS in Achieving Food Security*. Mimeograph, Indira Gandhi Institute of Development Research, Mumbai, 2002.

Lal, D. "Economic Reforms and Poverty Alleviation." In *India's Economic Reforms and Development*, edited by I. J. Ahluwalia and I. M. D. Little. New Delhi: Oxford University Press, 1997.

Parikh, K. S. "Food Security: Individual and National." In *India's Economic Reforms and Development: Essays in Honour of Manmohan Singh*, edited by I. J. Ahluwalia and I. M. D. Little. New Delhi: Oxford University Press, 1997.

Parikh, K. S., ed. *India Development Report, 1997*. New Delhi: Oxford University Press, 1997.

———. *India Development Report, 1999–2000*. New Delhi: Oxford University Press, 2000.

Parikh, K. S., and R. Radhakrishna, eds. *India Development Report, 2002*. New Delhi: Oxford University Press, 2002.

Sen, A. K. *Poverty and Famines*. Oxford: Clarendon Press, 1981.

FOREIGN RESOURCES INFLOW SINCE 1991

The period from 1990 to 1992 can be regarded as a watershed in the historical profile of external capital flows to India. Prior to that period, external assistance constituted up to 80 percent of net capital flows. Foreign direct investment (FDI) was repressed by an inward-looking regime guided by a socialistic view of India's economic development. Portfolio investment was virtually nonexistent. In the 1980s, shortfalls began to be experienced, as external financing needs expanded in response to an increase in growth. A modest recourse to international financial markets by Indian corporates—mainly public sector enterprises—in the second half of the 1980s was accompanied by a reliance on high-cost deposits by nonresident Indians. The Iraqi invasion of Kuwait in August 1990 would alter this canvas dramatically.

The war in the Persian Gulf precipitated a combination of shocks into an unprecedented balance of payments crisis. Crude oil import costs surged threefold, even as evacuation of expatriates from the war zone and the loss of key export markets in the Gulf region dealt crippling blows. The almost coincident disintegration of the Soviet Union disrupted a fifth of India's exports and a steady source of strategic imports. To add to the acute situation, the application of prudential norms under the Basel Capital Accord of 1987 led to the restriction of lending by international banks to developing countries, including India. Suddenly there was a collapse of capital flows. Credit ratings were downgraded, and this triggered a flight of nonresident deposits and even a moderation in bilateral and multilateral aid. By July 1991 the foreign exchange reserves had run down to a level of less than a week's imports and, for the first time in its history, India approached the brink of default on external obligations.

Stabilization

The response to the crisis was equally spectacular. An orthodox International Monetary Fund (IMF)–style stabilization program was put in place, supported by IMF funding and exceptional finance from donors. Unconventional measures included the sale/pledge of monetary gold, a two-stage devaluation of 18–19 percent, immunity from taxes for inward remittances from nonresident Indians and their investments in India Development Bonds, issued to beat the subinvestment grade credit ratings. By November 1991 came the turnaround. The crisis passed, and with it went the paradigm that had driven India's previous economic development. As stability returned, structural reforms were put in place, including a measured liberalization of the capital account.

Two compulsions weighed upon policy authorities in the choice of a gradualist approach over a "big bang." First was the sheer magnitude of the reform effort—an economy of continental dimensions, housing 15 percent of the world's population. Second, there was the unenviable task of implementing stabilization and structural reforms simultaneously on a crisis-ravaged economy. In addition, the reforms were an article of faith with the international community, and time was running out.

Considerable time was spent in setting up the preconditions for the liberalization of the capital account. Over the years 1991, 1992 and 1993, fiscal compression and tight monetary policy were put in place. Industry and foreign trade were virtually deregulated from licensing, tariffs were lowered sharply, and a dual exchange rate regime was instituted to prepare the evolutionary foreign exchange market for a greater role in determining exchanges rates (earlier the exchange rate was administered by the Reserve Bank of India [RBI] under a trade-weighted peg). FDI, highly restricted hitherto on account of ownership considerations, was allowed into all key areas of Indian industry at international rates of taxation and with free repatriability. Portfolio investment by foreign institutional investors was allowed into Indian stock exchanges under similar considerations. Indian companies were permitted to make both debt (convertible bonds) and equity (global depository receipts) issuances in international stock exchanges. The process of liberalizing exchange control was set in motion, leading up to current account convertibility and India's acceptance of the obligations of Article VIII of the IMF's Articles of Agreement from 1994. At the same time, the brief but traumatic brush with debt default during the crisis laid the foundations of a strategy for external debt management. External commercial borrowings were routed through an approval procedure emphasizing maturity, cost, and end-use, within an overall exposure ceiling. Short-term debt was monitored under a subceiling.

The operating framework of monetary policy was undergoing a silent transformation, as if in anticipation of the deluge of capital flows to follow. Nonresident deposit accounts carrying exchange guarantees from the RBI and instruments of automatic monetization of the fiscal deficit were phased out in a planned manner. There was a progressive shift to indirect instruments of monetary control, and statutory preemptions were lowered to minimum levels prescribed in relevant legislation.

Surges in Capital Flows

Shortly after the progression from dual exchange rates to a unified, market-determined exchange rate system in March 1993, India faced its first encounter with surges in capital flows. Beginning in August 1993 and extending well into 1995, waves of foreign investment inflows dominated the balance of payments, accounting for almost half of net capital flows in 1993–1995. FDI rose from near-negligible levels in 1990–1991 to exceed U.S.$1.3 billion in 1994–1995 (fiscal year). Leading the flood, however, were portfolio investment flows: foreign institutional investors in Indian stock markets, offerings of global depository receipts (GDRs) paper in overseas equity markets, convertible bonds raised abroad by Indian companies, and Indian offshore funds. In each of these years, portfolio investment flows averaged U.S.$3.5 billion. After a hiatus of almost four years, India renewed access to short-term trade credits toward the close of 1994–1995.

The visitations of private capital flows were clearly a response to the strengthening macroeconomic fundamentals. The economy grew by over 7 percent from 1993 to 1996, well above trend. A robust expansion of both merchandise and invisible exports easily accommodated the surge in import demand in response to the liberalization in trade and industrial policies. Despite sizable repayments of bilateral and multilateral aid, repurchases from the IMF, and net outflows under the discontinued nonresident deposit accounts with exchange guarantees, there occurred a hitherto unprecedented buildup of the foreign exchange reserves to a level of over U.S.$25 billion in March 1995, equal to about ten months of imports. In turn, this posed challenges to the conduct of monetary policy. A combination of policy responses—sterilization, external liberalization, retention of funds abroad—could not head off upward pressures on inflation, which rose above 10 percent in 1993–1995. A social resistance to inflation in double digits, entrenched in the Indian polity, manifested itself tellingly in a withdrawal of confidence in the government of the day. A fractured political mandate decisively ended the office of the "original reformers" in 1996 for a period that would last until 2004.

By early 1995, the capital flows ebbed and the downside of the roller-coaster experience with mobile capital flows was about to begin. Persistent surplus conditions in the foreign exchange market throughout 1993–1995 had been assuaged through passive interventions (purchases) by the RBI. Consequently, the nominal exchange rate of the rupee remained fixed over a period when the U.S. dollar was going through a pronounced appreciation against major currencies. Inflation differentials between India and the rest of the world were widening sharply, and the policy authorities themselves indicated discomfort with the building appreciation in the real exchange rate. Burgeoning imports had been comfortably financed all along, but when the capital flows ebbed, signs of incipient pressure became evident by August 1995. A spurt in the demand for domestic bank credit pushed up domestic interest rates, feeding an upward drift in the forward premium. Downward pressures on the exchange rate intensified in October, and India had its first taste of a currency attack. Expectations of a free fall of the rupee ran rife, disrupting the tranquil market conditions. The RBI engaged in exchange market interventions (sales), but this had the effect of withdrawing domestic liquidity and causing short-term interest rates to soar. Accordingly, interventions were soon backed up with money market support and an easing of reserve requirement stipulations on deposits with banks.

Capital flows remained, by and large, impervious to the currency turmoil. Net inflows under nonresident deposits actually increased in 1995–1996 over the preceding year. There was a welcome spurt in inflows of foreign direct investment, which exceeded U.S.$2 billion for the first time. The United States emerged as the largest investor. Engineering and electrical equipment were the preferred industries. Portfolio investment flows, on the other hand, were adversely affected by the disorderly conditions in the domestic financial markets and the restrictions imposed by the authorities on the introduction of funds from GDRs, which remained in force until November 1995. There was a slump in issuances of GDRs in overseas stock exchanges. Low equity prices in domestic stock exchanges combined with the unsettled market conditions to dampen investment by foreign institutional investors. In the first quarter of 1996, however, sentiment improved as the currency attack dissipated and the authorities undertook a series of confidence-building measures, including a rollback of the interest rate increases and a tightening of exchange control undertaken to deal with the "bandwagon" effects that had driven financial markets. Indian companies launched about U.S.$0.5 billion of GDRs in the quarter and foreign institutional investment surged, with perceptions of overcorrection in the equity and foreign exchange markets. The medium- and long-term debt flows—bilateral and multilateral aid and external commercial borrowings—continued to be dominated by large repayments. Access to short-term trade credit was extremely modest. For the first time since 1993, net capital flows fell short of the external financing requirement set by a higher current account deficit. This necessitated a draw down of the foreign exchange reserves on the order of U.S.$1.2 billion.

The currency attack in the second half of 1995–1996 (fiscal year) turned out to be only a temporary disruption in India's tryst with private capital flows. The inflows resumed strongly in the following year. Net inflows under nonresident deposits recorded a threefold increase, marking the return of confidence. The largest inflows were into rupee deposits under the nonrepatriable scheme. FDI maintained its uptrend, benefiting from enhancement in equity holding limits and an expansion of the industries for which approval was automatic. The sluggish domestic capital markets and policy relaxations prompted a large number of GDR issuances. Portfolio investment by foreign institutional investors was maintained, as overheated international capital markets propelled a diversification of portfolio flows in favor of emerging markets. Debt consolidation was pursued apace with substantial amortization of external aid and commercial borrowings, including the "bullet" redemption of the India Development Bonds issued at the height of the crisis of 1990–1992. Expanding energy requirements resulted in higher short-term trade credits in order to finance imports of petroleum products.

Asian Crisis

The fiscal year 1996–1997 was a turning point of sorts, presaging the cataclysmic Asian crisis that would reverberate across the world. International trade slowed down, and shifts in consumption patterns in mature economies provided early indications of the synchronized global slowdown that would dominate the second half of the 1990s. India's merchandise exports and industrial production were adversely affected. The demand for bank credit remained damped by the tightening of monetary policy during the currency turbulence of the preceding year. As the growth of the economy moderated from the scorching pace set in the period 1993–1995, non-Petroleum, Oil, and Lubricants imports slowed down sharply. Indian industry entered a period of painful restructuring and organizational change, as corrections to the massive capacity expansion in the first flush of liberalization had to be made in a more realistic assessment of demand.

Buoyant capital flows were interrupted in the first half of the fiscal year 1997–1998 by exchange market turbulence generated by the floating of the Thai baht. Sporadic speculative attacks led to a slackening of investment by foreign institutional investors in Indian stocks and even outflows in the period from November 1997 to February 1998. GDRs dropped sharply and were mainly in the form of disinvestment by public sector entities. The rekindled appetite for external commercial borrowings in the first half of the year was choked off in the second half by a sharp rise in the forward premium as monetary policy braced itself to defend against the crisis spreading across Asia. Corporate entities that had raised funds preferred to hold them abroad. Net inflows into nonresident deposits halved over the year, reflecting the generalized sense of uncertainty as well as the imposition of incremental reserve requirements; in fact, net outflows occurred in the period of exchange market volatility. FDI flows were untroubled by the surrounding chaos and exceeded U.S.$3 billion. FDI was allowed into financial services. Mauritius emerged as the most important source of FDI inflows into India as transnational corporations sought exemptions from Indian taxes by exploiting treaties for avoidance of double taxation.

India emerged relatively unscathed from the Asian crisis. Foreign exchange reserves were built up by U.S.$3 billion, and the nominal exchange rate held its own in an environment of domino effects among Asian currencies. In the following year, however, Asian financial markets experienced heightened turbulence and contagion spread to Russia and Brazil amidst fears of the competitive devaluation of currencies. A global slowdown, which began in mid-1997, deepened in 1998, and world trade underwent a substantial contraction. The spectacular increase in private capital flows to developing countries, including India, in the first half of the 1990s collapsed. The domestic financial markets were buffeted by bouts of instability during May–September 1998. The stormy international environment was worsened by sanctions on India imposed by industrial countries in response to nuclear testing. Monetary policy measures were deployed in conjunction with the issue of Resurgent India Bonds (RIBs) of U.S.$4.2 billion for nonresident Indians. Other types of external commercial borrowings and issuances of GDRs registered a sharp decline. Net outflows were recorded by foreign institutional investors, and even FDI was distinctly lower than in the fiscal year 1997–1998. By contrast, net inflows into nonresident deposits rose significantly, impervious to the generalized global uncertainty, and revealed a definite home bias. Net capital inflows taken together were lower by more than U.S.$1 billion. Ultimately, it was the RIBs that shored up the balance of payments in an extremely testing year, enabling a buildup of reserves to a level of U.S.$31.4 billion by March 1999.

Stability returned to international financial markets in early 1999 to mark the close of an eventful decade. The global economy staged a V-shaped recovery. The resumption of growth was particularly strong in the crisis-hit economies of Asia, shaped by successful macroeconomic adjustment and strict financial policies. Net private capital flows to developing countries resumed modestly but were dominated by substantial repayments of bank lending. Hardening crude oil prices emerged as the major risk to an improved global outlook. In India, a broad-based firming of industrial activity ensured that trend growth of over 6 percent was maintained, despite the shadow cast by border tensions in May 1999. The RBI resumed a graduated liberalization of capital flows. Foreign corporate entities and high net worth individuals were allowed to invest in Indian stock markets through foreign institutional investors. All sectors of the economy, except for a short negative list, were opened to

FDI on an automatic basis. The policy regime for external commercial borrowings was substantially liberalized with the approval procedures largely moved out of the Ministry of Finance to the RBI. End-use stipulations were relaxed, except for real estate and equity investments in light of the experience gained in the Asian crisis. Outward FDI was encouraged, and Indian companies engaged in knowledge-based activities (information technology [IT], biotech, and entertainment) were allowed enhanced capabilities for the acquisition of companies abroad. Policies for the import of bullion were also liberalized, with banks and financial institutions allowed to freely import gold and silver.

Net capital flows returned to pre-1998 levels on the back of a renewal of portfolio investment by foreign institutional investors, resilient flows to nonresident deposits, and a larger recourse of Indian entities to international equity markets. For the first time, American depository receipts (ADRs) entered the portfolio of capital flows to India. FDI continued to be sluggish, despite a greater focus domestically on the speedy implementation of FDI proposals and the opening up of the insurance sector. The debt flows in the form of external aid and commercial borrowings continued to remain muted, reflecting lackluster domestic investment demand. For the fourth year in a row, there was an accretion to the reserves of over U.S.$ 6 billion in 1999–2000. By June 2000, all liabilities to the IMF incurred in the crisis of 1990–1991 were repaid.

Global Slowdown

The advent of the new millennium began another phase in India's experience with capital flows. A deepening of the global slowdown from mid-2000 to late 2003 was accompanied by large sell-offs in international equity markets, the bursting of the IT bubble, and a receding of private capital flows to emerging markets as risk aversion increased in the aftermath of the currency crises in Turkey and Argentina. Repayments of bank loans continued to be sizable. Beginning with a significant reduction in fiscal year 2000–2001, India's current account deficit turned into a surplus in 2001–2002 after two decades. Surpluses persisted in the ensuing years, powered essentially by the strength of remittances from Indians residing abroad. By 2003 India became the highest recipient of such inward remittances, accounting for 14 percent of global flows. Merchandise exports regained lost momentum, particularly since 2002–2003. The generalized aversion to emerging markets was reflected in a sharp decline in trade credits, syndicated loans, and other types of commercial borrowings in 2000–2001, as well as a fall in investment by foreign institutional investors and FDI over the previous year. Net inflows into nonresident deposits, however, continued their uptrend, reflecting the confidence of non-resident Indians in the Indian economy. Indeed, the invulnerability of nonresident deposits to the vicissitudes of the international financial environment turned out to be a source of strength to India through an extremely difficult decade. The shortfall in various types of external financing in 2000–2001 was bridged by the launching of the India Millennium Deposits of U.S.$5.5 billion, again targeting nonresident Indians.

Fortuitously, this shortfall would prove to be a transient experience, as capital flows became stronger in 2001–2002 and 2002–2003, led initially by FDI and nonresident deposits but dominated in 2002–2003 by large inflows in the form of banking capital as exchange rate movements and interest rate differentials made rupee assets highly attractive. In 2003 and 2004, a massive surge in investments by foreign institutional investors was the most striking feature of capital flows to India, supported by the buoyancy of nonresident deposit inflows and continuing inflows of banking capital. By May 2004, India held the sixth-largest stock of foreign exchange reserves in the world, a far cry from the low point of July 1991. Beginning in 2002, India became a lender to the IMF. The level of the reserves currently exceeds the stock of India's gross external debt.

Capital flows weathered subinvestment grade credit ratings, the general aversion to emerging markets, adversities peculiar to India such as sanctions, terrorist attacks, a terrible drought, and soaring crude oil prices to endorse the underlying strength and resilience of the Indian economy in the decade of the 1990s. In fact, throughout 2004, even after undertaking large prepayments of external debt and bullet repayment of RIBs, policy authorities were actively engaged in strategies to temper the massive influx of capital. Efforts to counter the expansionary impact of the inflows on monetary conditions threatened to deplete the stock of monetary instruments and innovative strategies have had to be combined with orthodox measures of monetary policy to deal with the inflows.

Since the turn of the twenty-first century, there has been a perceptible acceleration in the speed of capital account liberalization. New economy industries—IT, e-commerce, telecommunication, financial services, mass rapid transport, airports, urban infrastructure, even defense—have been opened to foreign direct investment, along with a removal of quantitative restrictions such as dividend balancing through exports imposed on FDI in consumer goods industries. Overseas business acquisitions through ADRs/GDRs have been significantly enhanced, up to several times the size of export earnings, and outward FDI is now allowed up to 200 percent of the net worth of the domestic investor. All approval procedures relating to external commercial borrowings have been delegated to the RBI for proposals beyond U.S.$500 million. Below that amount, approvals are not required.

Since the opening up in 1991, India's experience with capital flows has been marked by episodes of surges and short-lived reversals. The policy regime has emphasized stability and gradualism and a shying away from the more dramatic attempts at liberalization in neighboring Asia. A hierarchy of capital flows has emerged but not entirely in consonance with policy preferences. Inflows into nonresident deposits have turned out to be the most durable flows, in spite of measures to slow them down as part of the overall approach to contending with capital flows. Special bond issues for nonresident Indians have filled in exceptional financing gaps in periods of stress. FDI has, in general, not lived up to policy expectations, held down primarily by implementation gaps in the process of turning proposals into actual inflows. Investment by foreign institutional investors and raising of ADRs/GDRs/FCCBs (foreign currency convertible bonds) have exhibited volatility and sensitivity to shifts in market conditions. Foreign investment, both direct and portfolio, is now entrenched in India's capital account, with a share of more than 50 percent of net capital flows. The reliance on debt flows has declined substantially. While the policy for external commercial borrowings has been modulated in tune with the needs of the economy and the compulsions of prudent external debt management, the appetite of Indian corporate entities has been muted by the slowing down of investment demand since the second half of the 1990s. The reliance on external aid that characterized the period up to the 1980s has dissipated completely. Active efforts are underway to prepay bilateral and multilateral donors and seek, in a redefinition of self-reliance, freedom from aid.

Michael Debabrata Patra

See also **Commodity Markets; Debt Markets; Economic Reforms of 1991; Economy since the 1991 Economic Reforms; Information and Other Technology Development; International Monetary Fund (IMF), Relations with; Money and Foreign Exchange Markets**

BIBLIOGRAPHY

Patra, Michael Debabrata, and S. Pattanaik. "Exchange Rate Pass through and the trade Balance: The Indian Experience." *Reserve Bank of India Occasional Papers*, December 1994.
Patra, Michael Debabrata, and S. Pattanaik. "Exchange Rate Management in India: An Empirical Evaluation." *Reserve Bank of India Occasional Papers*, September 1998.

Rangarajan, C. "Recent Exchange Rate Arrangements: Causes and Consequences." *Reserve Bank of India Bulletin*, September 1991.
Reserve Bank of India. *Annual Reports*, 1990–1991 to 2003–2004.

FORSTER, E. M. *(1879–1970), author of* **A Passage to India.** Edward Morgan (E. M.) Forster was a Cambridge don, and author of the renowned Anglo-Indian novel, *A Passage to India*, published in 1924. Forster's passionate affair with India started in 1906, when he tutored Syed Ross Masood at Oxford. He fell in love with the handsome aristocratic Indian Muslim, and at his invitation left England on his first sea voyage to India in 1912. Forster briefly stayed with Masood and his family in Bankipore, a town he found "horrible beyond words." He also spent time on that first passage with his British Civil Service friend, Rupert Smith, in Allahabad. Smith took Forster to Buddhist Bodh Gayā and the Barabar ("marabar") Caves, which they visited by elephant, as would his fictional protagonist, Dr. Aziz. On his way out of India, Forster stopped in the central Indian state of Chhatarpur, where he met the maharaja of Dewas, who invited him to serve as his private secretary. After World War I, Forster returned to Dewas for six months in 1921, his diary account of which was later published, in 1953, as Forster's only other book about India, *The Hill of Devi*. Forster began writing his *Passage to India* in 1913, after returning home from his first trip. He borrowed the title from Walt Whitman's poem of the same name:

Not you alone proud truths of the world,
Nor you alone ye facts of modern science,
But myths and fables of old, Asia's, Africa's . . .
Passage to India!
The races, neighbors, to marry . . .
The oceans to be cross'd, the distant brought near.

"When I began the book," Forster wrote his friend Masood, "I thought of it as a little bridge of sympathy between East and West." By the time he finished, however, he realized how "unexplainable" a "muddle" British India was, how impossible it seemed for even the most passionately empathetic men of England and India to live in harmony as loving friends. In the novel, British magistrate Ronny Heaslop's mother, Mrs. Moore, is probably the character whose liberal, loving philosophy of life most closely reflected that of Forster, though Schoolmaster Fielding also reflected at least part of the author's brilliant mind. Fielding's unorthodox ecumenical preference for the friendship of "natives" like Dr. Aziz to the company of stuffy and pompous British officers like Ronny or Collector Turton at the British Club branded him an "outcaste" if not a "traitor" to his "own" race. Yet even

Fielding fails at the end of this remarkable book to convince Aziz that they at least can truly be friends, though "It's what I want. It's what you want."

But in 1924, India was still locked under the steel-frame imperial grip of the British Raj, so their "horses didn't want it—they swerved apart; the earth didn't want it, sending up rocks through which riders must pass single file; the temples, the tank, the jail, the palace, the birds, the carrion, the Guest House, that came into view . . . didn't want it, they said in their hundred voices, 'No, not yet,' and the sky said, 'No, not there.'" Twenty-three years later, when India emerged independent of British rule, men like Forster and Masood, or Fielding and Aziz, were free to pursue their relationships as equals, no longer fearing or resenting each other as masters and servants.

Stanley Wolpert

See also **British Crown Raj; British Impact**

BIBLIOGRAPHY
Forster, E. M. *A Passage to India*. New York: Harcourt, Brace & World, 1924.
———. *The Hill of Devi*. New York: Harcourt, Brace, Jovanovich, 1953.
Furbank, P. N. *E. M. Forster: A Life*. New York: Harcourt, Brace, Jovanovich, 1978.
King, Francis. *E. M. Forster and His World*. New York: Charles Scribner's Sons, 1978.

FRENCH EAST INDIA COMPANY The French East India Company (La Compagnie Française des Indes Orientales), was founded as a monopoly by royal edict of Louis XIV in 1664 at the strong urging of his finance minister Jean-Baptiste Colbert. The king was its largest investor, and the crown effectively controlled the company. After an inauspiciously disastrous beginning, it eventually became moderately successful and profitable but was always undercapitalized and dependent on loans, often from the treasury.

The establishment of the French East India Company was part of Colbert's ambitious mission to revamp France's economy. Its founding implied the removal of the monopoly from the Compagnie de l'Orient started by Cardinal Richelieu in 1642. Richelieu's company had become entangled in the colonization of Madagascar, which it saw as a necessary way station on the sea-lanes to India. As a consequence, it was unable to meet the demand for fine Indian silks and cotton goods, and a substantial market share had been taken by "foreign businesses." Colbert, a mercantilist, wished to slow, if not

Jean-Baptiste Colbert's Efforts (1664–1683). Colbert's efforts to regulate and expand France's economy in the seventeenth century, the formation of the French East India Company having been his brainchild, were soon threatened by the extravagances of the monarchy. ARCHIVO ICONOGRAFICO, S.A./CORBIS.

prevent, the steady export of wealth required to pay for the trade balance. At the time, it is estimated that the French market was purchasing 30 percent of the textiles and spices imported by other joint stock companies, chiefly the English and Dutch East India Companies.

Colbert's company was granted a fifty-year monopoly of trade east of the Cape of Good Hope, given charge of the colonization of Madagascar, two adjacent isles (Réunion and Mauritius), and trading centers in India, Sri Lanka, and Indonesia. Unfortunately, the initial reaction of French merchants was tepid; of the 15 million livres envisaged, just over eight million livres (three million from the king) were raised. Colbert's company was nearly always undercapitalized and often had to borrow money to operate from season to season.

Personnel were a second problem, solved by recruiting among the Dutch. The Dutch were hardy mariners and skilled shipwrights. Dutchmen had been crews on Portuguese vessels when that country had a monopoly on the spice trade. Once Dutch crews learned how to navigate to the Moluccas, they went into business for themselves. By 1664 there were experienced Dutch captains and sailors to be had. A third obstacle was the lack of adequate vessels, so Colbert established a port and shipyard named, appropriately enough, Lorient, on the Atlantic coast.

The first decades of the Compagnie Française des Indes Orientales were checkered. The company faced stiff competition from the Dutch East India Company, which harassed the French merchant marine and occasionally confiscated cargoes. Support from French merchants was never enthusiastic for they were subject to strict royal control. Furthermore, the company's administration deteriorated after the deaths of Colbert in 1683 and his son, the marquis de Seignelay, in 1690. The initial voyages were so commercially disastrous that Colbert had to resort to lies to hide the magnitude of the losses in order to raise more capital.

Affairs in India were better, however. François Martin, left behind after a French defeat by the Dutch and the *qutbshah* (king) of Golconda in San Thomé, founded Pondicherry in 1674. Pondicherry became the center of French India, lying about 85 miles (137 km) south on the Coromandal coast from the English East India Company's trading center at Fort St. George (Madras, now Chennai). Even though port facilities were inconvenient, the commercial viability of Pondicherry was based on the availability of silk and cotton textiles, calicoes and muslins, produced by nearby village cottage industries. The profitable commercial activity caught the jealous attention of the Dutch East India Company, which drove out the French in 1693. The Compagnie Française des Indes Orientales, facing deficits due to failed adventures in Madagascar and Thailand, was helpless. After a sojourn in France, where he was received cordially by king and company, Martin was named governor of Pondicherry for the third time and as director of all French factories in Surat, Chandarnagar, Calicut, Dhaka, Patna, Qasimbazar, Balasore, and Jogdia. He remained in Pondicherry, the Indian capital of the French East India Company, until his death in 1706.

With the Treaty of Utrecht in 1713, the Dutch East India Company withdrew to Indonesia, leaving England and France the only rivals in India, much as their rivalry was to dominate European affairs for the next hundred years.

When the fifty-year monopoly of the Compagnie Française des Indes Orientales expired the next year, a ten-year extension was granted to the by-then moribund company. Shortly afterward, Louis XIV died, and the duke of Orleans succeeded as regent. In 1717 the regent granted monopoly trade rights in the Caribbean, Canada, and Louisiana to a publicly traded French West India Company, La Compagnie Française des Indes Occidentales, founded by John Law, a Scottish financier. Two years later, Law persuaded the regent to meld the dormant East India and the nascent West India companies, and the conglomerate was titled simply the Company of the Indies (La Compagnie des Indes).

The new company's public stock offering was a brilliant success, briefly doubling and redoubling in value. It immediately purchased the tobacco monopoly, which was a steady source of revenue, allowing it to pay its promised dividends even as the stock was becoming grossly overinflated. The bubble burst, and by the summer of 1720, panic set in. There was a run on the Royal Bank, and the company's shares plunged. The company offered to accept all its shares at face value in return for a perpetual monopoly (its ten-year extension was due to expire in 1725), and it was restyled the Perpetual Company of the Indies (La Compagnie perpétuelle des Indes).

The crash tarnished the reputation of the Perpetual Company, however, which had to be restructured in 1723 into a private regulated monopoly, but one in which the king and regent still had substantial investments. However, the Perpetual Company was successful for several decades, becoming a serious rival to the English East India Company, and was responsible for the major French impact on India. After the Seven Years' War, the Perpetual Company declined steadily, and was completely moribund by the French Revolution.

J. Andrew Greig

See also **French Impact**

BIBLIOGRAPHY

Bouche, Denise, and Pierre Pluchon. *Histoire de la Colonisation Française.* 2 vols. Paris: Fayard, 1991.

Furber, Holden. *Rival Empires of Trade in the Orient, 1600–1800.* Minneapolis: University of Minnesota Press, 1976.

Malleson, George. *History of the French in India.* Delhi: Renaissance Publishing, 1984.

Weber, Henry. *La Compagnie Française des Indes (1604–1875).* Paris: Libraire Nouvelle de Droit et de Jurisprudence, 1904.

FRENCH IMPACT France's most influential and successful period in India coincided almost completely with the reign of Louis XV (1723–1774). After the death of Louis XIV in 1715, the French East India Company created by Jean-Baptiste Colbert was replaced by a reconstructed French company of the Indies (Compagnie Française des Indes). The reason had to do with the moribund state of the company of Colbert, and the agents of this change were the regent, the duke of Orléans, and his financial adviser and controller general, John Law. This new company was far more profitable than its predecessor, and it reached its apex of power and influence in India during the governor-generalship of Joseph François Dupleix. At one point, it was a major threat to the British East India Company's commercial empire and seemed to be in position to drive its rival from the subcontinent. At its height, the French were perhaps the wealthiest and most powerful Europeans in India. However, largely due to repeated wars for supremacy fought between France and England in Europe, North America, and India, the French Company of the Indies lost its primacy and then its vigor during the Seven Years' War. It lasted until the French Revolution, but as a shell of the company that Dupleix had left behind at the time of his recall in 1754. The tactics and strategy adopted by Dupleix to accomplish this primacy formed the paradigm for what came to be called the "Nabob Game" when adopted by his rival and imitator, Robert Clive. French control and influence continued in Pondicherry, even now a French-speaking enclave on the Coromandal coast.

In 1714 the monopoly of the French East India Company (La Compagnie Française des Indes Orientales) founded by Jean-Baptiste Colbert expired. At the time of Louis XIV's death the next year, the company too seemed to be terminally ill. Its prospects were dim; the War of the Spanish Succession had cut profits, it was heavily in debt, its capital was undersubscribed, and disputes among the directors had sapped their energy and made it harder to obtain credit. In the previous three years the company had been leasing its trading privileges to merchants from St. Malo, the main competitor to the company's own port facilities in Lorient, its only revenues. Before dying, Louis XIV had granted the moribund company a ten-year extension with the expectation that the additional time would allow it to turn around or at least provide for its orderly liquidation.

Louis XIV also left behind an empty Royal Treasury. In this difficult environment, the duke of Orleans, regent (1717–1723), turned to a package of financial initiatives to stimulate the French economy. They were proposed by a Scotsman, John Law, who had seen the success of the Bank of England (flourished 1694) in increasing the money supply through the issuance of bank notes and the subsequent creation of financial enterprises that increased the value of those bank notes through guaranteed bonds and transferable stocks.

Street Sign in Pondicherry. Surviving French and Tamil street sign in Pondicherry, seat of the eighteenth-century La Compagnie perpétuelle des Indes (Perpetual Company of the Indies). In their astute analysis of Indian politics and exploitation of divided factions, the French set the course of subsequent British expansion on the Indian subcontinent. FRANCOIS GAUTIER / FOTOMEDIA.

John Law's major proposals led to the creation of a Bank of France (La Banque Gènèrale) empowered to issue paper bank notes and to the merger of trade monopolies in both the West Indies and East India into one French company chartered by the regent. In 1717 the regent had granted Law monopoly trade rights in the Caribbean, Canada, and Louisiana to a publicly traded French West India Company, La Compagnie Française des Indes Occidentales. Its merger in 1719 with La Compagnie Française des Indes Orientales resulted in an entity named, simply, Company of the Indies (La Compagnie des Indes). It was formed over the objections of both the French company's directors and the merchants of St. Malo, and litigation continued until 1751.

The sale of stock in the conglomerate precipitated an inrush of capital and unprecedented speculative fever. Prices doubled and redoubled, but within months, the market crashed in a scenario reminiscent of the "South Seas Bubble" in contemporaneous England. A rush on the Bank of France soon exposed the fact that there was not enough specie on hand to cover all the paper bank notes. To salvage the situation, Law, on behalf of the Company of the Indies, offered to accept all shares at face value in return for a perpetual monopoly (its ten-year extension was due to expire in 1724). It was consequently renamed the Perpetual Company of the Indies (La Compagnie perpétuelle des Indes), the name it retained until its demise.

Its credit seriously tarnished, the Perpetual Company of the Indies cut all ties with Law and was exhaustively reorganized into a private monopoly in which the king and regent kept substantial investments, but with a board of directors appointed by the king and closer royal oversight by the controller-general. The initial influx of capital had enabled Law's company to begin to put essential infrastructure into place, commissioning ships, buying cargoes, engaging crews, and otherwise preparing for voyages to India. Law had wisely purchased the tobacco monopoly, which assured a steady income, in return for an extension in perpetuity of the monopoly then slated to expire in 1724, and that provided for a steady and reliable annual income.

In addition to the tobacco monopoly, the major assets of the Perpetual Company were its trade monopolies with Asia and the West Indies. Commerce from the West Indies was generally disappointing, with only the slave trade showing profits. In India the major assets were trading colonies. French establishments, some no more than a warehouse, were located in Surat, Chandarnagar, Calicut, Dhaka, Patna, Qasimbazar, Balasore, and Jogdia, but Pondicherry on the Coromandal coast in India was the most vital of them all. Even though its port facilities were insufficient, its commercial viability was based on the ready availability of the silk and cotton textiles, for example, calico and muslin, produced by nearby cottage industries.

In order to grow its assets, the Perpetual Company expanded and improved its trading colonies. A settlement in Mahé was established, as was a secure and reliable way station on the Île de France (present-day Mauritius), replacing the never-successful stopover in Madagascar. During the 1730s under the leadership of Dupleix, Chandarnagar, close to Calcutta, was turned into a viable and habitable center of trade. East Indiamen of the Perpetual Company had, therefore, a choice of ports with which to engage in country trade. Country trade referred to a trading voyage between ports east of Africa to anywhere in Asia, but most often within India.

Agents for all East India companies engaged in country trade to supplement their meager salaries. Fortunes could be made in this private commerce, but by engaging in it, they played a dual role, purchasing goods as agents for their companies as well as on their own behalf. Due to a lack of effective controls, agents could make enormous fortunes at the expense of their company's profits. The hint that these fortunes were obtained by defrauding their employers underlay the pejorative use of the term "nabob" to refer to such agents.

The Perpetual Company of the Indies was also profiting from a decrease in competition. The Dutch East India Company, the chief bane of Colbert's company, withdrew to Indonesia after the Treaty of Utrecht in 1713. So the Perpetual Company of the Indies was in competition only with the British East India Company. By around 1740, French trade equaled half that of the English and might well have surpassed it, except that the British Company was heavily invested in tea, a commodity popular in England.

A third reason the restructured company's trade grew so dramatically was that it had three activist and extraordinarily capable governors-general in India: Pierre Christophe Lenoir, Pierre Benoist Dumas, and Joseph François Dupleix. They were ably supported by directors in Paris who valued Indian experience; both Lenoir and Dumas became directors upon their return. De Godeheau de Zaimont, the director who replaced Dupleix in 1754, had worked in India years before. Dupleix was a supernumerary director, whose proxy attended regular meetings in Paris.

As already mentioned, Dupleix was the governor of Chandarnagar responsible for developing that trading colony's value to the company. The administration of Dupleix as governor-general in Pondicherry (1742–1754) coincided with the height of French influence, wealth, and power, and so he is rightfully regarded as the greatest of France's governors-general and is often considered the inventor of the Nabob Game. Dupleix's version of the Nabob Game is perhaps the greatest contribution of the French in India.

Dumas and Dupleix, perhaps more than any other Europeans, analyzed the political situation in India and saw how to use it to French advantage. With the death of the last of the Great Mughals, Aurangzeb, in 1707, the vast territories he had spent his life conquering began to break up, leaving the potential for chaos. By the 1720s, any potentate with a title and armed forces, such as a *mānsabdār*, could gain control of a region and claim to rule. All that was required was taking control of its resources, assuming its governance, albeit without openly rebelling against the center, and actively using for their own ends whatever share of imperial authority they could grab. The Mughal successors to Aurangzeb were weak and offered little or no resistance to these secessions. Some of the first to go, and certainly the most notable, were the *nawāb* of Oudh (present-day Ayodhya) and the nizam of Hyderabad. Although their revenues and titles had been granted them by the Mughal emperor, once they removed themselves to their territories they began increasingly to rule as if sovereigns. They assumed the right to appoint revenue officials and collect land taxes, to select their successors, pursue independent diplomatic and military activity, and mint coins locally. For Muslim rulers, the final break was marked when their name was recited during Friday prayers.

By the 1730s, the Perpetual Company of the Indies was also pursuing the benefits of having titles and land revenues granted by Mughal authority, but with autonomy at least equal to the local governors, or *nawāb*s. For instance, in 1736, during the administration of Dumas, the Perpetual Company of the Indies was given the title of *nawāb* and the rank of *mānsabdār* over five thousand cavalry by the Mughal emperor. Dupleix, stationed at the time in Bengal, closer to the Mughal court, was instrumental in this initiative. He was also in regular correspondence with the *nawāb* of Oudh. Dumas in

Pondicherry would have been in diplomatic contact with the nizam of Hyderabad. Clearly, the Perpetual Company had established independent diplomacy with important elements of the Mughal administration of the country. Because Dumas insisted that the title of *nawāb* and rank of *mānsabdār* belong to the company, a corporate entity, and not to him, he anticipated the question of succession. Additionally, the company obtained the right to mint silver rupees in Pondicherry, saving several percent in minting costs. When combined with the grants given of the right to collect revenues in villages in the vicinity of Pondicherry, the Perpetual Company had become, for many intents and purposes, a sovereign entity in India, although it remained a commercial concern in France.

From both political and commercial points of view, assuming Mughal titles and ranks were brilliant moves that became central to the Nabob Game. Not only were demands on the company coffers reduced, a new revenue stream in local currency was introduced to the books. Company control of villages could also be used for encouraging the production of piece goods in cottage industries. A further benefit was the legitimization of armed force—an attractive prospect to a wealthy trade center in times plagued by plundering warlords.

Upon Dumas's retirement to France, where he took a seat on the board of directors, his successor, Dupleix, was faced with a new challenge: armed rivalry with the English in South India. During the private war between the English and French companies (1744–1748) that echoed the War of Austrian Succession (1740–1748), Dupleix captured Madras (Chennai) with the help of a fleet under the command of Mahé de la Bourdonnais. It was restored to English control under the terms of the Treaty of Aix-la-Chapelle, but by then, both companies had became ever more deeply involved in India's local power struggles, allying with or battling, at different times, the Marathas, the nizam of Hyderabad, and the *nawāb* of Arcot.

Unfortunately, time was not on the side of the French East India Company. It had lost a significant part of its merchant marine to the British navy during the war. English forces under the command of an energetic Englishman, Robert Clive, reversed Dupleix's initial victories on the ground in India. It is said that Clive had studied Dupleix well and used his methods boldly. As French losses mounted, Dupleix's policies were perceived back in Paris to be too expensive, and so the directors of the company recalled him in 1754. He died there in 1763, disgraced, disappointed, in debt, and embroiled in lawsuits.

During the Seven Years' War (1756–1763) between France and England, the French were repeatedly defeated in India. Pondicherry was captured in 1761 (and returned to the French). British ascendancy could no longer be challenged after British East India Company victories against the Mughals in Bengal, again with Clive in command, and the decline of the Perpetual Company of the Indies as an economic and political force in the wake of the Seven Years' War. In 1769 the Perpetual Company of the Indies lost its monopoly and thenceforth merely languished until the French Revolution, when it was finally overthrown along with the rest of the old regime.

The impact of the French in India was primarily as European trading pioneers. The Perpetual Company of the Indies formed by John Law during the Regency recovered from early disaster and collapse, only to prosper for three decades because of the energy of its governors-general, notably Pierre Benoist Dumas and most especially Joseph François Dupleix. Their contribution to the history of India, if it can be termed as such, was to correctly analyze and exploit the internal political situation on the subcontinent for the commercial interests of the Perpetual Company. In doing so, they, and particularly Dupleix, set the course of European expansion on the subcontinent that was followed by the British East India Company.

J. Andrew Greig

See also **British East India Company Raj; Clive, Robert; Dupleix, Joseph François; Nabob Game**

BIBLIOGRAPHY

Bouche, Denise, and Pierre Pluchon. *Histoire de la Colonisation Française.* 2 vols. Paris: Fayard, 1991.
Furber, Holden. *Rival Empires of Trade in the Orient, 1600–1800.* Minneapolis: University of Minnesota Press, 1976.
Malleson, George. *History of the French in India.* Delhi: Renaissance Publishing, 1984.
Weber, Henry. *La Compagnie Française des Indes (1604–1875).* Paris: Libraire Nouvelle de Droit et de Jurisprudence, 1904.

FUNDAMENTAL RIGHTS India's constitutional framework, developed between 1947 and 1950, adapted the British Government of India Act of 1935 to the needs of the new Indian state. India's Constitution is essentially a Western constitution. The parliamentary system was a legacy of Britain; the federal system was adapted from the Canadian Constitution; the financial relationship between the central and state governments came from Australia; the concept of social policy objectives and directives embodied in the preamble came from Ireland; and the chapter on Fundamental Rights was drawn from the U.S. Constitution's Bill of Rights. Yet despite its Western structure, the style and process were essentially Indian, and the interpretation of fundamental rights in India has been different from that of the Western democracies. In the West, these rights are considered the inherent rights of the individual. In India, they tend to be perceived as derived from the state. The state grants them, and the state can take them away through constitutional procedures.

India's democratic Constitution places the well-being of society and the security of the state above the fundamental rights of the individual. Thus, in India, fundamental rights are not always guaranteed when they conflict with the interests of society and the preservation of the state. Democracy and fundamental rights may be suspended if warranted by external wars and internal conflicts, although the Constitution requires that such actions must be endorsed by Parliament every six months, up to a maximum of eighteen months. The determination of whether the suspension of democracy is warranted or not is to be made by Parliament. This essentially means that if the party holding the reins of government carries a two-thirds majority in Parliament, it may assume authoritarian powers through constitutional means.

The "Emergency" Articles

India's Constitution identifies three types of emergencies that may justify the suspension of fundamental rights. The first is a "National Security Emergency" (Article 352), under which the president, acting on the advice of the prime minister, may proclaim a state of emergency if the "security of India, or any part of its territory is threatened by war, external aggression or armed rebellion." When Article 352 is invoked, Articles 353 and 354 then go into operation. They allow the central government to suspend the federal provisions of the Constitution, thereby giving it direct control over the states and over all revenue. In effect, the central government may impose a unitary system of government. The second is a "Constitutional Emergency in the States" (Article 356) under which the president, acting on the advice of the governor of a state and the prime minister, may proclaim a state of emergency in that state if he is satisfied that the normal process of government cannot be carried out in accordance with the Constitution. The third type of emergency identified by the constitution is a "Financial Emergency" (Article 360), which may be declared by the president, acting on the the advice of the prime minister, if the financial or monetary stability or the credit of the country is threatened.

All of the above proclamations must be approved by Parliament. Article 352, on external threats to national security, was invoked by the Congress Party government of Indira Gandhi during the yearlong Bangladesh sepa-

ratist movement in 1971, which culminated in the war with Pakistan in December of that year. The same article was invoked, in the name of threats to internal security, by the Indira Gandhi government when it declared a state of "National Emergency" throughout the country between June 1975 and March 1977. Article 356, "Emergency in the States," has been invoked on different occasions in various Indian states, including Kerala, Assam, Punjab, and Kashmir. Article 360, "Financial Emergency," has never been used, although drastic economic measures, such as the banning of all industrial strikes, were adopted during the National Emergency between 1975 and 1977.

The government of India under various prime ministers, from Jawaharlal Nehru to P. V. Narasimha Rao, have resorted to Article 356, "Emergency in the States." This article has frequently been invoked when the ruling government of a state was no longer able to muster the required parliamentary majority in the state legislature. This has led to "President's Rule," in which the state government is taken over directly by the central government until new elections can be held and a new state government put in place. More controversial, however, has been the resort to Article 356 in some Indian states where the state government is unable to cope with the crisis, irrespective of whether a parliamentary majority is retained by the state-based political party. This has been problematic in states such as Nagaland, Punjab, and Kashmir, where separatist movements, which have included armed insurgencies and acts of terrorism, have occurred. Similarly, widespread religious, linguistic, or ethnic rioting in a state has also led to the suspension of the state government, as has occurred in Assam. However, the suspension of the democratic process under conditions of internal security and instability has been ad hoc, regional, and temporary. After the crisis is over, the democratic process is restored.

The provisions of the Emergency Articles 352 and 356 are supplemented by the provisions of two other articles—Articles 358 and 359—which enable the president, acting on the advice of the prime minister, to suspend fundamental rights and protection clauses as guaranteed under Articles 13 to 32 of India's Constitution. Such suspensions must also be approved by Parliament within six months. The suspension of the rights and protection clauses, especially Article 19, which embodies the "Seven Freedoms," is accompanied by the right of the central government to resort to preventive detention, that is, to arrest and detain persons to prevent them from indulging in acts, as yet uncommitted, that may be detrimental to national security and to the maintenance of law and order. Under the subtitle "Right to Freedom," Article 19 of India's Constitution states: "Protection of certain rights regarding freedom of speech, etc. (1) All citizens shall have the right (a) to freedom of speech and expression; (b) to assemble peaceably and without arms; (c) to form associations of unions; (d) to move freely throughout the territory of India; (e) to reside and settle in any part of the territory of India; (f) to acquire, hold and dispose of territory; and (g) to practise any profession, or to carry on any occupation, trade or business." However, once the emergency is declared and approved by Parliament, the Constitution empowers the government to prevent citizens from appealing to the courts for the protection of their fundamental rights. Not even Article 32, which incorporates the "right to constitutional remedies" and the "writ of habeas corpus," can overcome central government powers, made possible under Articles 352 to 360, that relate to national emergency.

The imperial-type powers lodged in India's Constitution are a legacy of British rule, which, ironically, also provided India with the basic structure of a democratic system. The Indian president's ability to proclaim a state of emergency when the country's security is threatened was a power held by the British viceroy under the Government of India Act of 1935. The British had exercised these emergency powers between 1940 and 1945, when they were at war with Germany and Japan and simultaneously had to deal with the Indian struggle for independence and with Hindu-Muslim violence. Such viceregal powers were reinforced by the British through the Defence of India Act of 1939; under its terms the British Indian government could resort to "preventive" detention of those who were deemed threats to internal law and order for political reasons, even though they were not charged with committing illegal acts. The nature of these problems has not changed fundamentally since India obtained independence in 1947, nor have the far-reaching powers that were assumed by the newly independent Indian government.

Legislative Measures

During the 1962 Sino-Indian War, the Defence of India Rules (DIR) were introduced, which included the practice of "preventive detention." Communists in India who were felt to be a threat to the nation were detained without showing cause. During the 1965 Indo-Pakistan war, many Muslims were detained on the suspicion that they might resort to sabotage. All were immediately released on the cessation of hostilities. The DIR remained in force until 1968, six years after the 1962 Sino-Indian War and three years after the 1965 Indo-Pakistani War had ended. During the 1971 Indo-Pakistani crisis, the Maintenance of Internal Security Act was introduced, which provided far-reaching powers to detain citizens who might be a threat to the state. The provisions of this act were used to justify the detention of several opposition

leaders in attempts to curb the violence in areas of ethnic strife, especially in the border regions.

Following the declaration of the "National Emergency" in June 1975 by Prime Minister Indira Gandhi and the passage of the 42nd Amendment in 1976, the fundamental rights embodied in the constitution were suspended, and the practice of preventive detention was expanded. This was the infamous legislation that introduced the mechanics of an authoritarian state in India. When the actions were challenged, the Supreme Court of India reversed its earlier judgments that fundamental rights were inherent and inviolable by the state, and favored the legislative powers of the state (provided proper procedures were followed) over the rights of the individual. It argued that fundamental rights were rights granted by the state to its citizens and could be suspended if national security and the survival of the state so warranted.

After Indira Gandhi's Congress Party lost to the Janata Party in 1977, the 42nd Amendment was abrogated by the 44th Amendment in 1978. The conditions for declaring an emergency were made much more stringent, and limitations were placed on the suspension of democratic rights. However, during the violent Sikh separatist movement in the 1980s, new legislation was introduced, including the 1980 National Security Act under Prime Minister Indira Gandhi, and the 1987 Terrorist and Disruptive Activities Preventive Act (TADA) under Prime Minister Rajiv Gandhi. Legislation that eroded the democratic process continued under the Congress government of Rajiv Gandhi. Under TADA, suspected terrorists could be detained for up to one year without trial, and court hearings and the testimony of witnesses could be conducted in secret.

The continuing deterioration of law and order in the 1980s led to the passage of the 59th Amendment in March 1988. The amendment nullified parts of the 44th Amendment by permitting the suspension of Article 21 in Punjab during an "Emergency," and sought to further amend Article 352—the National Emergency Article—of the Indian Constitution. The 42nd Amendment had substituted the words "internal disturbance" (a vague and loose show of cause) for the words "armed rebellion" (a more stringent show of cause). The 44th Amendment restored the original words, so that the justification for an internal emergency would only take place in the case of an "armed rebellion." However, the more restrictive term "armed rebellion" did not seem to apply to the intensifying Sikh terrorist campaign in Punjab. Although it did not call for the return of the milder term "internal disturbance" in order to invoke the far-reaching Article 352, the Rajiv Gandhi government felt that something less than the term "armed rebellion" had to be adopted in order to invoke the National Emergency clause of the Constitution. The 59th Amendment sought to apply the National Emergency provisions only to Punjab, but fears of misuse was expressed by several opposition members of both the Lok Sabha (the "House of the People," Parliament's lower house) and the Rajya Sabha (the "Council of States," Parliament's upper house).

Subsequently, the power to detain suspected terrorists without trial was further strengthened for the two regions where separatist violence was strongest, Punjab and Kashmir. This legislation was provided through the Armed Forces (Punjab and Chandigargh) Special Powers Act in the 1980s, the Jammu and Kashmir Public Safety Act in the 1990s, and the Armed Forces (Jammu and Kashmir) Special Powers Act in the 1990s. The Muslim revolt in Kashmir was accompanied by an increase in the frequency and magnitude of Hindu-Muslim violence in northern India, especially in the states of Gujarat, Uttar Pradesh, Bihar, and Maharashtra.

Allegations have been perennial in India that TADA has been widely misused throughout the country to address basic criminal and law and order cases that had little to do with terrorism. The act was considered to be a violation of the rule of law in a democracy. Periodic efforts have been made by members of the ruling and opposition parties to revoke TADA since its passage in 1987. But the Congress Party government's Home Minister, S. B. Chavan, declared in 1994 that TADA would not be repealed. He acknowledged that there had been widespread misuse of an act that had been intended to deal with terrorists, but stated that the chief ministers of the states had been warned not to misuse TADA. The government was endorsed by the Constitution Bench of the Supreme Court in September 1994 in the Sanjay Dutt case when it declared that "there is no reason, in law, to doubt its constitutionality or alter its proper construction" (*Pioneer*, New Delhi, 6 and 9 September 1994). In a fifty-eight-page judgment, the five members of the Constitution Bench, headed by Justice A. M. Ahmedi, affirmed the state's right to make special provisions for the prevention of, and for coping with, terrorist activities.

These powers continued to be used to deal with secessionist-related insurgencies and terrorism in Kashmir, Assam, and the tribal Northeast region. In the aftermath of the terrorist attack on the World Trade Center on 11 September 2001, and the terrorist attack on India's Parliament on 13 December 2001, a long-debated legislative proposal labeled the Prevention of Terrorist Ordinance was passed, which abridged the rights of the individual, legalizing detention on suspicion alone. The legislation resembles the Patriot Act in the United States passed later that year.

In sum, when the security and stability of the country are threatened, one set of articles permits the central government of India to qualify and suspend the democratic freedoms provided under another set of articles that supposedly guarantees those freedoms. India's democratic constitution in effect provides easy recourse for its own overthrow through constitutional means on the grounds of national security. No doubt, the suspension of the democratic constitution is intended to be temporary. But there is no guarantee that a prime minister who resorts to drastic constitutional methods will restore democracy. The liberal constitutional provisions in India are a would-be tyrant's dream. So far no prime minister has grossly misused the privilege, although Prime Minister Indira Gandhi came close to doing so between 1975 and 1977. In the end, even she restored democracy after twenty-two months of "Emergency" rule that had been declared in the interests of national security. After the passage of the 59th Amendment in March 1988—which sought to apply the national emergency provisions only to insurgency and terrorism in Punjab—several opposition members argued that the bill would be utilized eventually in other parts of India and thus would amount to a "declaration of war on the people" (*Times of India*, 24 March 1988).

Raju G. C. Thomas

See also **Assam; Gandhi, Indira; Gandhi, Rajiv; Government of India Act of 1935; Jammu and Kashmir; Punjab**

BIBLIOGRAPHY

Austin, Granville. *The Indian Constitution: Cornerstone of a Nation.* New York: Oxford University Press, 1999.
Grover, V. *The Constitution of India.* New Delhi: Deep and Deep, 2001.
Hardgrave, Robert, and Stanley Kochanek. *India: Government and Politics in a Developing Nation.* 3rd ed. New York: Harcourt Brace Jovanovich, 1980.
Hart, Henry, ed. *Indira Gandhi's India.* Boulder, Colo.: Westview Press, 1976.
Jaswal, Nishta. *Role of the Supreme Court with Regard to the Right to Life and Personal Liberty.* New Delhi: Ashish Publishing House, 1990.
Mehta, M. *Constitution of India and Amendment Acts.* New Delhi: Deep and Deep, 1990.
Park, Richard L., and Bruce Bueno de Mesquito. *India's Political System.* 2nd ed. New York: Prentice-Hall, 1979.
Pylee, M. V. *Introduction to the Constitution of India.* Columbia, Mo.: South Asia Books, 1995.
Thomas, Raju G. C. *Indian Security Policy.* Princeton, N.J.: Princeton University Press, 1986.
———. *Democracy, Security, and Development in India.* New York: St. Martin's Press, 1996.

GALBRAITH, JOHN KENNETH (1908–), economist, ambassador to India (1961–1963).

John Kenneth Galbraith served as a highly effective ambassador of the United States to India from 1961 to 1963. One of President John F. Kennedy's closest friends and advisers, Galbraith quickly became Prime Minister Jawaharlal Nehru's good friend as well, expediting India's economic and educational development by serving as a personal link between India's first prime minister and America's young president. Forty years after his invaluable ambassadorial tour ended, India awarded ninety-year-old Galbraith its highest foreign official honor, Bharat Vibhushan.

Born in Ontario, Canada, on 15 October 1908, Galbraith received his doctoral degree in economics at the age of twenty-six from the University of California at Berkeley. For the next eight years he taught at Harvard and Princeton, becoming a U.S. citizen in 1937. From 1941 to 1943 Galbraith worked as assistant and deputy administrator in Washington's Office of Price Administration, while also serving on the editorial board of *Fortune*. He was appointed director of the U.S. Strategic Bombing Survey in 1945, carefully assessing the overall impact of heavy "saturation" bombing on German cities, finding it far less effective than had been commonly believed in Washington. After World War II, Galbraith was appointed director of the Office of Economic Security, charged with the important job of developing sound economic policies for occupied Germany and Japan. Thanks to his humanitarian planning, both defeated nations were soon back on their feet, avoiding any tragic repetition of the harsh post–World War I economic depression, wrought by vengeance, which paved the way for Adolf Hitler's rapid rise out of the ashes of a bankrupt Weimar Republic.

Professor Galbraith returned to teaching at Harvard in 1949, the year he published his *Beyond the Marshall Plan*. *The Great Crash* was published six years later, and only three years after that his most famous work, *The Affluent Society*, which so wisely called for less wasteful emphasis on the production of luxury goods and far greater expenditure on public services to help America's impoverished unemployed and homeless claim their fair

John Kenneth Galbraith. Galbraith as photographed with Jackie Kennedy (whose late husband he had served) at an exhibition of Northern Indian painting, Asia House, NYC, 22 September 1965. Almost forty years after his ambassadorial tour had ended, India awarded Galbraith its highest diplomatic honor, Bharat Vibhushan. BETTMANN/CORBIS.

share of America's dream. Professor Galbraith's stunningly prolific pen turned out more than twenty-five books, including his splendid diary of the years of his diplomatic work in India, *Ambassador's Journal*, published in 1969. As renowned for his wit as his singular wisdom, Galbraith concisely called India's polity "a functioning anarchy," perhaps the most famous succinct summary of any global government.

Distinguished Professor Galbraith held the Paul M. Warburg Chair in Economics at Harvard until his retirement at age seventy-five in 1983. He served as national chairman of Americans for Democratic Action from 1967 to 1969, and in 1972 he was president of the American Economic Association. He has received no fewer than forty-five honorary degrees from universities the world over, including Harvard, Oxford, Moscow State University, the University of Paris, and the University of Toronto.

At the age of ninety-five, Galbraith published *The Economics of Innocent Fraud*. He has never stopped writing, advising Democratic presidents of the United States for more than six decades, from Franklin D. Roosevelt to John F. Kennedy and Bill Clinton. Galbraith was twice honored with America's highest civilian award for public service, the Medal of Freedom, first by President Harry S. Truman in 1946, next by President Clinton in 2000. Few economists and even fewer diplomats and public servants have had as pervasively salubrious an impact on the lives of countless millions of people as has John Kenneth Galbraith.

Stanley Wolpert

See also **Nehru, Jawaharlal; United States, Relations with**

BIBLIOGRAPHY

Galbraith, John Kenneth. *Beyond the Marshall Plan.* Washington, D.C.: National Planning Association, 1949.
———. *American Capitalism: The Concept of Countervailing Power.* Boston: Houghton Mifflin, 1952.
———. *The Great Crash, 1929.* Boston: Houghton Mifflin, 1955.
———. *The Affluent Society.* Boston: Houghton Mifflin, 1958.
———. *The New Industrial State.* Boston: Houghton Mifflin, 1967.
———. *Ambassador's Journal: A Personal Account of the Kennedy Years.* Boston: Houghton Mifflin, 1969.
———. *Economics and the Public Purpose.* Boston: Houghton Mifflin, 1973.
———. *The Age of Uncertainty.* Boston: Houghton Mifflin, 1977.
———. *Annals of an Abiding Liberal.* Boston: Houghton Mifflin, 1979.
———. *A Journey through Economic Time: A Firsthand View.* Boston: Houghton Mifflin, 1994.
———. *The Good Society: The Humane Agenda.* Boston: Houghton Mifflin, 1996.
———. *The Economics of Innocent Fraud: Truth for Our Time.* Boston: Houghton Mifflin, 2004.

GAMA, VASCO DA *(c. 1460–1524), Portuguese explorer.* Portuguese sea captain Vasco da Gama discovered the Cape of Good Hope route to India in May 1498, relying on the expertise of local seamen, both Indian and Arab, to sail across the ocean they knew so well. Crucial to da Gama's crossing of the Indian Ocean to Calicut was the assistance given by Arab navigator Ahmad ibn-Madjid, who knew the secrets of the treacherous monsoon. Ibn-Madjid's help allowed Vasco da Gama to become the first European to reach India by sea.

Vasco had left Lisbon on 8 July 1497 with four ships, reaching Mozambique on 2 March, Malindi on 14 April, anchoring 12 miles (19 km) off Calicut on 18 May 1498. The first encounter of Europeans with India was fraught with misunderstandings on both sides. Vasco da Gama and his men, mistaken for Muslims, were at first warmly received by the Hindu ruler, the *samuri* (*zamorin* in Portuguese records) of Calicut. Vasco and his crew, on the other hand, thought that the Malabar ruler and his subjects were Christians. The Portuguese worshiped in a Hindu temple, which they assumed was a chapel dedicated to the Virgin Mary. At the instigation of the powerful local Muslim merchants, the *samuri*'s attitude toward Vasco da Gama and his men quickly changed. The *samuri* found Vasco's goods to be of "inferior quality" and the Portuguese sailors' refusal to pay the traditional customs duties on their purchases only intensified local dislike of the arrogant visitors.

Da Gama left on 5 October 1498 without the trade treaty he sought, but with precious cargo, which brought Portugal a hefty profit of sixty times its investment after meeting the expenses of the entire voyage. The human costs of the first voyage, however, were very high. Of the 170 Portuguese sailors, only 55 survived, most dying of scurvy. In Lisbon, Vasco da Gama received a tumultuous public welcome, rewarded by King Manuel I with presents, cash, an annual pension, and the exalted rank of "admiral of the Indian Ocean."

On his second voyage to India, in 1502, Vasco da Gama was brutal beyond belief. He seized a ship headed for Mecca, and after confiscating the goods, burned it with hundreds of Muslim pilgrims—men, women and children—on board. He extracted treaties of "friendship and trade" from the rulers of Cannanore and Cochin by terrorizing the rulers and their subjects, bombarding the coast, killing scores of innocent, unarmed fishermen, and selling many others into slavery.

Vasco da Gama was sent for the third time to India in 1524, with the title of viceroy, to cleanse the Portuguese administration there. Within two months of his arrival, however, he died. Fourteen years later, in keeping with his will, his body was taken to Portugal and interred on his estate at Vidigueira. For Portugal, he remains its greatest hero.

D. R. SarDesai

See also **Portuguese in India**

BIBLIOGRAPHY

Gama, Vasco da. *A Journal of the First Voyage of Vasco da Gama, 1497–1498*, translated and edited by E. G. Ravenstein. London: Hakluyt Society, 1898.

Hart, Henry Hersch. *Sea Road to the Indies: An Account of the Voyages and Exploits of the Portuguese Navigators, Together with the Life and Times of Dom Vasco da Gama*. London: Hodge, 1952.

Madan, D. K. *Life and Letters of Vasco da Gama*. New Delhi: Laurie Books, 1998.

Subrahmanyam, Sanjay. *The Career and Legend of Vasco da Gama*. Cambridge, U.K.: Cambridge University Press, 1998.

GANDHARAN ART AND ARCHITECTURE

Gandhara is the ancient name given to the region that today surrounds the city of Peshawar in northern Pakistan. Between the early second century B.C. and the eighth century A.D., active trade with the Mediterranean, South Asia, and China made this a multiethnic, wealthy area, and provided an economic foundation for the creation of many Buddhist centers. The word "Gandharan" is also used to describe sculptural finds from a series of culturally related areas beyond the Peshawar plains, such as the Swat valley, the Buner and Taxila regions, eastern Afghanistan, and even parts of Kashmir. This larger area has come to be described as Greater Gandhara.

Alexander the Great conquered Gandhara in the mid-fourth century B.C. Following his death, his generals divided the empire, initiating a period of Indo-Greek kingdoms known primarily through scattered numismatic evidence. The archaeological remains of the city of Ai Khanoum indicate that for a time a Hellenistic colony existed in Afghanistan. In the third century B.C., the North Indian Mauryan king Ashoka issued several edicts stressing nonviolence (*ahimsa*) and duty (*dharma*); these were carved on boulders in northern Pakistan and Afghanistan. This is generally understood as the beginning of Buddhism in the region, even though the inscriptions do not explicitly refer to this religion. During the following two hundred years, different Central Asian groups, including the Parthians and Scythians, repeatedly invaded Greater Gandhara before the Kushans (initially known as the Yüeh-chih) began to move toward Afghanistan from the western Chinese borderlands. Kushan rule culminated under the kings Kanishka I and Huvishka in the second century A.D., by which time this dynasty had established a united and stable kingdom extending beyond the Hindu Kush and across northern India.

Gandharan architecture and its associated figurative sculpture offer a glimpse of the religious life of this region and a paradigmatic model for the study of the larger South Asian Buddhist tradition. The first Greater Gandharan Buddhist sites were probably established early in the second century B.C., Butkara I in the Swat valley and the Dharmarajika complex in Taxila. These early centers share many characteristics with contemporary Buddhist sites in India, including large hemispherical stupas (solid mounds housing relics of the Buddha). The dating of these first sites is debated; some scholars believe they were founded in the third century B.C. during the Mauryan dynasty, but enough numismatic evidence survives to place them with confidence in the second century B.C. Archaeological excavations of the city of Sirkap in Taxila provide valuable information for this poorly understood period, as this center was already established prior to Alexander's invasion and was occupied by various groups in succession until the time of the great Kushans. John Marshall's excavation of this city and the surrounding Buddhist sites of Taxila provided masonry evidence for determining a sequence for the architecture. Finds from Sirkap show that a broad range of Near Eastern and Mediterranean gods were popular, and they attest to the sophisticated and eclectic tastes of the multicultural elite. Of particular interest are the many classical foreign luxury objects that came from the West along a complex system of trade routes. Our understanding of this trade system is also based on an excavated hoard of trade goods, found at the site of Begram in Afghanistan, which includes Mediterranean objects as well as those from China and South Asia.

Early Gandharan Tradition

Although the origins of the Gandharan Buddhist tradition are obscure, it is clear that this new religion became popular in the late first and early second centuries A.D. Under the Kushans, many Buddhist sites were founded, notably Takht-i-bahi, Jamal Garhi, and Thareli in the Peshawar basin; Mohra Moradu, Jaulian, and Kalawan in Taxila; and the Swat sites of Saidu, Panr,

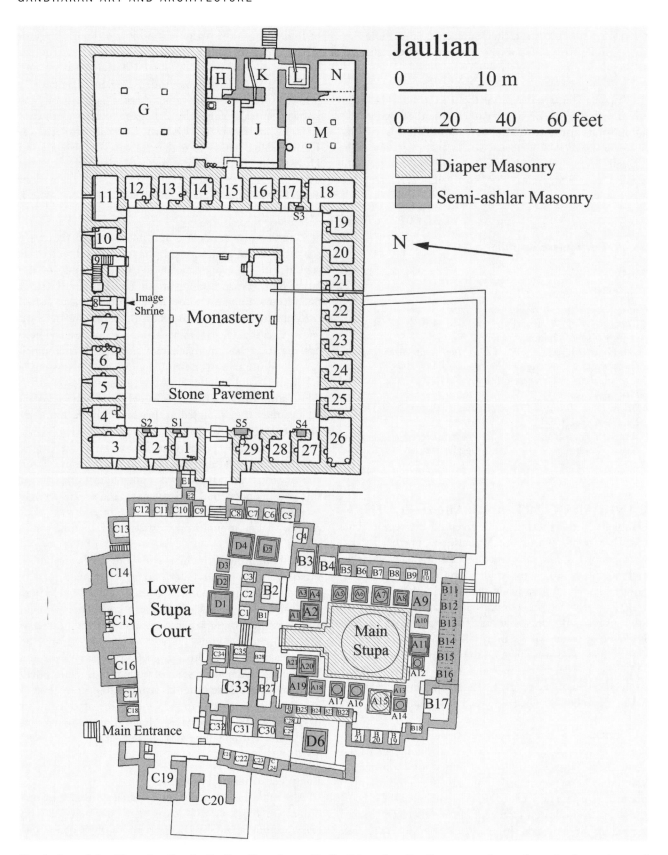

Rendering of the Floorplan for the Jaulian Complex at Taxila. Like other Gandharan sacred areas from the first and second centuries A.D., it included a main stupa (or shrine) and a quadrangular monastery. Over time, subsidiary stupas were added, another widespread architectural practice. Such shrines possibly displayed relics of the Buddha. PUBLIC DOMAIN.

and Butkara III. By this time both the layout of the sites and the embellishing sculpture were quite different from their North Indian counterparts, and a true Gandharan idiom can be recognized. A typical Gandharan sacred area of this period was founded with the fabrication of a main stupa and a quadrangular monastery, as can be seen at the Taxila site of Jaulian. A sacred area could not exist by itself; it relied on the care provided by a resident monastic community, and all the religious complexes in Gandhara invariably included one or more monasteries. Commonly, these took the form of multistoried structures, like the one at Jaulian, where monastic cells were organized around an open courtyard, with attached rooms for cooking, storage, and other such uses. When steep, mountainous terrain precluded the construction of quadrangular monasteries, the monks lived in groups of smaller multistoried structures (3–4 rooms per story). The main stupa was believed to contain powerful relics of the Buddha and was the primary devotional focus for both lay and monastic devotees. Surrounding the main stupa at the Jaulian site are heterogeneous subsidiary stupas that were added over time; Gregory Schopen has suggested that these small stupas contained the cremated remains of the monastic dead. The practice of erecting shrines that housed small stupas within the sacred area was widespread; in some instances, such shrines probably also were used to display relics of the Buddha.

Significant numbers of schist narrative sculptures that recount the Buddha's life were found in conjunction with an apparent surge in building activity in the second century A.D. Typically, these panels ringed small stupas and were read in conjunction with the ritual act of circumambulation (*pradaksina*). These reliefs placed great emphasis on the historic personage of the Buddha (Shakyamuni); sequential reliefs depict his miraculous birth, childhood, great departure, role as teacher of the Buddhist *dharma*, and performer of miracles, as well as his death and cremation and the ultimate distribution of his relics. The narrative illustrated in these sculptures appears to relate closely to early texts such as the Lalitavistara and the Abhiniskramana Sūtra. In some instances, the early narrative sculpture shows remarkable stylistic affinities to northern Indian sites such as Bharhut, especially those produced at early Swat sites like Butkara I, Saidu, or Marjanai. It is clear that in the earliest periods of Gandharan activity, the Buddhist traditions of northern India were vitally important to this provincial Buddhist community; this probably also explains the emphasis given to the above-mentioned texts.

The vast majority of narrative imagery produced in Greater Gandhara (c. 2nd century A.D.), however, shows clear affinities to Western Classical styles. It is important to remember that in the Greater Gandharan region by

Relief Found in the Village of Mohammed Nari (in the Peshawar Basin). Here, the Buddha preaches from his lotus throne, flanked by standing *bodhisattva*s. Historic Buddhas line the base, and the top portion depicts the Great One about to depart on his wordly travels. The relief (yet to be definitively identified by art historians) marks a moment of transition in Gandharan art, with its mix of early narrative and later iconic elements. PUBLIC DOMAIN.

this time, Mediterranean Classical architectural features, such as Corinthian pillars, had been popular for nearly four hundred years. Early scholars attributed to the Hellenistic Greek contact the emergence in Gandhara of anthropomorphic images of the Buddha in the narrative and iconic images. This assumption led these scholars to date much of Gandhara's sculptural production to the first centuries B.C., and they suggested that this contact with the Greeks was the source for the anthropomorphic Buddha found throughout South Asia. Today it is clear that the exchange of styles occurred later, with the Roman Empire, leaving the origin of the Buddha image an open question. Gandharan sculptors appear to have selectively appropriated and recontextualized classical forms. For example, the Bodhisattva from Mekhasanda wears northern Indian garments and jewelry suited to a prince, but the drapery follows classical conventions and the body is quite naturalistic in style. The face, however, is more in line with the North Indian tradition of representing the Bodhisattva as an idealized being.

The emergence of iconic images marked a transition in Buddhist practice; they replaced the narrative panels that had been so popular in Gandhara during the second century (narrative imagery was also common in other parts of South Asia in this early period). Some scholars have seen this as an indication of the doctrinal shift from Nikāya (early) Buddhism to Mahayana (later, "Great Vehicle") Buddhism, but this has recently been called into question. In Gandhara the main stupa remained the central object of veneration, even as monumental imagery and depictions with complex iconography became popular. The identification of some of these complex panels has been much debated, as the Nikāya-Mahayana affiliation of the Gandharan Buddhist tradition rests in part on this interpretation. Alfred Foucher saw them as related to the early narrative and interpreted them as components of the life of the Buddha, specifically when he performed miracles at the city of Saravasti. More recently, other scholars have suggested that the panels represent Buddhist "pure lands" (heavens with living Buddhas) and thus are clearly Mahayana scenes. In a relief found in the village of Mohammed Nari, the Buddha sits on a lotus throne and preaches; he is flanked by standing *bodhisattva*s (pure land characteristics). The historic Buddhas, however, adorned the base, and at the top the Buddha is shown, prior to his enlightenment, in the palace and embarking on his great departure. The identification of the relief remains open, but it is clear that this representation marks a moment of transition, because a mix of early narrative and later iconic elements are present.

Later Gandharan Sites

Between the third and fifth centuries A.D., the patronage of Buddhist sites dramatically increased; old sites were expanded and many new centers were founded. This increase in patronage must have been economic, not dynastic; the Kushan empire was fading at this time, and only a vague idea of the political landscape can be formed on the basis of coin finds of the late Kushans, Kushano-Sassanians, Sassanians, and Kidarites. Relic monuments such as stupas and stupa shrines were augmented with free-standing Buddha and *bodhisattva* images placed in chapels that enclosed the sacred area. It was at this time that Jaulian's main stupa court was encircled by image shrines that would have housed life-sized Buddha and *bodhisattva* images. Schist remained an important sculptural medium between the third and fifth centuries A.D., but during this time sculptors began to produce images in stucco, probably because it was faster and cheaper. The tremendous wealth of patronage during this period

is attested by the number of images found in the sacred areas, as can be seen in an 1890s photo of sculpture recovered from the site of Loriyan Tangai. By the fourth and fifth centuries A.D., iconic images became monumental in size, a trend that apparently culminated at the late sixth-century site of Bamiyan, in Afghanistan, where a Buddha image more than 174 feet (53 m) meters tall was cut into a rock face. At this time, small image shrines with complex iconography began to appear in the monasteries, apparently for the private devotional needs of the monks. At many sites, pious donations of small stupas and image shrines filled the public sacred area around the main stupa. This proliferation necessitated the expansion or creation of additional sacred areas to accommodate donations; at Jaulian this was the lower sacred area, where three monumental image shrines were fabricated.

Between the fifth and seventh centuries A.D., Chinese Buddhist pilgrims began to visit Greater Gandhara to see famous relics, like the alms bowl or skull bone of the Buddha. These visitors included Fahsien (A.D. 401) and Xuanzang (A.D. 630), who both documented their trips. Their accounts reveal much about the late Gandharan Buddhist tradition and suggest a dramatic fifth-century decline in Buddhist patronage in the Peshawar basin (ancient Gandhara). The archaeological evidence supports these written records, for very few coins datable after the fifth century have been found in Gandharan sacred areas, and new construction seems to have stopped abruptly at most sites. The main stupas found at Bhamala and Shah-ji-ki-dheri are notable exceptions. Sparse numismatic evidence indicates that only a few isolated Buddhist centers, especially those in the Swat valley, remained active until the eighth century. In Afghanistan, it appears, Buddhism continued to flourish during this late period at sites like Hadda and Bamiyan.

Kurt Behrendt

See also **Alexander the Great; Buddhism in Ancient India**

BIBLIOGRAPHY

Behrendt, K. *The Buddhist Architecture of Gandhara*. Leiden: E. J. Brill, 2004.

Errington, E. "Numismatic Evidence for Dating the Buddhist Remains of Gandhara." In *Silk Road Art and Archaeology: Papers in Honour of Francine Tissot*, edited by E. Errington and O. Bopearchchi. London: Strathmore Publishing, 1999–2000.

Faccenna, D. *Butkara I (Swāt, Pakistan), 1956–1962*. 5 vols. Rome: IsMEO, 1980.

Foucher, A. *L'art Gréco-Bouddhique du Gandhâra: Étude sur les origines de l'influence classique dans l'art Bouddhique de l'Inde et de l'Extrême-Orient*. 2 vols. Paris: E. Leroux, 1905.

Kuwayama, S. "The Buddha's Bowl in Gandhara and Relevant Problems." In *South Asian Archaeology 1987*, edited by M. Taddei. Rome: IsMEO, 1990.

Marshall, J. *Taxila: An Illustrated Account of Archaeological Excavations Carried out at Taxila under the Orders of the Government of India between the Years 1913 and 1934.* 3 vols. Cambridge, U.K.: Cambridge University Press, 1951.

Rhi, J. "Gandharan Images of the Srāvastī Miracle: An Iconographic Reassessment." Ph.D. diss., University of California, Berkeley, 1991.

Rosenfield, J. *The Dynastic Arts of the Kushans.* Berkeley and Los Angeles: University of California Press, 1967.

Schopen, G. "Burial 'Ad Sanctos' and the Physical Presence of the Buddha in Early Indian Buddhism: A Study in the Archaeology of Religions." *Religion* 17 (1987): 193–225.

Taddei, M. "Oral Narrative, Visual Narrative, Literary Narrative in Ancient Buddhist India." In *India, Tibet, China: Genesis and Aspects of Traditional Narrative*, edited by A. Cadonna. Florence: L. S. Olschki, 1999.

Zwalf, W. *A Catalogue of the Gandhara Sculpture in the British Museum.* 2 vols. London: British Museum Press, 1996.

GANDHI, INDIRA *(1917–1984), prime minister of India (1966–1977 and 1980–1984).* Prime Minister Jawaharlal Nehru's only child, Indira Gandhi was elected to succeed him as prime minister, just two years after his death. Born in Allahabad in the palatial mansion of her grandfather, Motilal Nehru, Indira was reared in lonely luxury. Her mother, Kamala, soon after Indu's birth, was incurably afflicted with tuberculosis. Indira seemed so frail a child that her "Auntie Nan," Vijaya Lakshmi Pandit, the first woman to preside over the United Nations General Assembly, feared that "Indu-Boy" (as Nehru fondly called his daughter) might somehow have caught her mother's illness. Indira would emerge more powerful, however, than any man in Nehru's Cabinet.

Education and Marriage

Indira learned her best lessons in history and politics from her brilliant father. During several of the long years Nehru spent behind British bars, he wrote weekly letters to his daughter, offering her "glimpses of world history." She had another remarkable teacher as well, Bengal's *Guru-Dev* (Divine Teacher) Rabindranath Tagore, to whose private college *Shanti-niketan* (campus of peace) she went for little more than one year, obliged then to accompany her mother to the Swiss sanatorium in which she died. Nehru was released from prison to visit his wife and daughter in Europe and went to Moscow for the tenth anniversary of the birth of the Soviet Union. Both Nehru and Indira were to remain ardent Socialists for the rest of their lives. Indo-Soviet friendship became a powerful pillar of Prime Minister Gandhi's foreign policy. V. K. Krishna Menon, Nehru's alter ego in London, became Indira's close friend and adviser. Her future husband, Parsi Feroze Gandhi, long devoted to her sick mother, accompanied Indira in her travels around Europe just prior to and during the first few years of World War II. Nehru strongly opposed the marriage, but Indira prevailed, marrying the husband she chose in March 1942.

Political Power

Indira's son Rajiv, heir to her premier power, was born on 20 August 1944. Her second son, Sanjay, born three years later, died in a stunt plane crash in Delhi three years before his mother. Indira's own passion for power was long hidden behind her seeming disinterest in office, but as Nehru's official "hostess" and constant traveling companion during his decade and a half as prime minister, she learned all that was required to be chosen by her Congress Party colleagues as India's first female prime minister in 1966. Her first half decade at the top proved so successful that Indira Gandhi was virtually worshiped by millions of Indians and Bangladeshis as an incarnation of the "Mother Goddess" Durgā. She led India to victory over Pakistan in the Bangladesh War, when Dhaka surrendered in mid-December 1971. "Madam" Gandhi had signed a twenty-year Indo-Soviet Treaty of Friendship that June, which provided India with heavy Russian tanks and artillery for its campaign across Bangladesh, as well as potential "nuclear support" if India were ever threatened with a U.S. attack. The independence of Bangladesh, after a quarter century as East Pakistan, diminished what remained of Pakistan by more than half its population, also stripping Islamabad of most of the hard currency earned from the export of Bengali jute. Indira Gandhi thus towered over South Asia as its most powerful premier, hailed by her own people as "Mother India," admired by Bangladeshis as their nation's "Liberator," feared by Pakistan's fallen General Yahya Khan and by his humiliated successor, Zulfikar Ali Bhutto.

Decline and Fall

Though Indira reigned supreme in foreign affairs, domestically she faced increasingly difficult problems and mounting political opposition. Global inflation of crude oil prices hit India's economy harder than it would have in times of peace. Unemployment rose sharply and strikes wracked Bihar and Bombay soon after the war had ended in so stunning a victory. Railroad workers and miners joined in slowing down, if not closing, crucial sectors of India's urban economy. Former Congress colleagues of Nehru called upon his daughter to either take appropriate action in helping heal open wounds or "step down." Bombay's Congress leader, Morarji Desai—who had run unsuccessfully against Indira for Nehru's mantle,

Indira Gandhi with Her Two Sons. Photographed in 1967 in the garden of their home, then Prime Minister Indira Gandhi with her two sons, Sanjay (left) and Rajiv (right). It was commonly assumed that Sanjay would enter politics, but he perished in an airplane crash in 1981. Rajiv became prime minister after his mother's assassination in 1984, but he too died the victim of an assassin's bullet–in 1991 while mounting a campaign to once again hold India's highest office. HULTON-DEUTSCH COLLECTION.

later joining her as finance minister in her Cabinet—resigned after she ignored his advice. Now he led a popular Janata (People's) Party opposition movement, together with Bihar's Jaya Prakash (J. P.) Narayan, Nehru's oldest Socialist comrade-in-arms, aimed at forcing Indira to resign or suffer ignominious national electoral defeat.

In May 1974, faced with mounting internal opposition, Indira Gandhi triggered India's first underground nuclear explosions—warnings both to Pakistan's bellicose new premier Bhutto, as well as to Morarji and J. P., of just how powerful "Mother India" was. But Janata Party opposition only grew louder, and in June 1975, Allahabad's High Court Justice Jag Mohan Lal Sinha found Prime Minister Gandhi guilty of two counts of electoral malpractice, each carrying mandatory penalties of resignation and abstention from elective office for six years. Rather than step down, however, Gandhi had her president declare a "National Emergency," giving her dictatorial

powers, imprisoning her opposition, including Morarji and J. P., banning every opposition party, shutting off power to Delhi's news presses, and canceling elections. India remained under her autocratic power in darkness and fear for a year and a half, from 26 June 1975 until 18 January 1977. Indira Gandhi's "Emergency Raj" was the most shameful and tragic period in more than half a century of India's independent rule.

The Janata Party's victory in national elections of April 1977 appeared to end Gandhi's political career. Yet constant squabbling among the aged leaders of that coalition only proved them impotent to solve any of India's most pressing problems, reopening doors of power to "Madam Gandhi," who returned in January 1980, on a popular wave of electoral support. Gandhi was faced in her last four years with growing opposition from Punjab's Sikh community. Militant Sikhs demanded an independent nation-state of Khalistan (Land of the Pure). Gandhi tried to counter Punjab's most popular Sikh leaders with younger candidates of Sanjay's choice, whom she thought they could "control." By early summer of 1984, however, it seemed clear to her that "Sant" Bhindranwale, who seized control of Amritsar's Golden Temple, was no "Saint" at all, but a fanatical extremist determined to lead a Sikh revolt against India. In June she unleashed the army, whose Operation Bluestar left Bhindranwale and all his followers inside the temple compound dead, claiming the lives of one hundred Indian troops and later of Indira Gandhi herself, who was gunned down in her Delhi garden by two of her own trusted Sikh guards on 31 October 1984.

Stanley Wolpert

See also **Bangladesh; Bhutto, Zulfikar Ali; Gandhi, Rajiv; Nehru, Jawaharlal; Nehru, Motilal**

BIBLIOGRAPHY

Abbas, K. A. *Indira Gandhi: Return of the Red Rose.* Mumbai: Popular Prakashan, 1966.

Bhatia, Krishna. *Indira: A Biography of Prime Minister Gandhi.* London: Angus & Wilson, 1974.

Frank, Katherine. *Indira: The Life of Indira Nehru Gandhi.* London: HarperCollins, 2001.

Gandhi, Indira. *My Truth.* Delhi: Was, 1981.

Gupte, Pranay. *Mother India.* New York: Scribner's, 1992.

Jayakar, Pupul. *Indira Gandhi.* New Delhi: Penguin, 1992.

Malhotra, Inder. *Indira Gandhi.* London: Hodder & Stoughton, 1989.

Mehta, Ved. *A Family Affair.* Oxford: Oxford University Press, 1982.

Mohan, Anand. *Indira Gandhi.* New York: Hawthorn, 1967.

Nayar, Kuldip. *The Judgment: The Inside Story of the Emergency in India.* Delhi: Vikas, 1977.

Sahgal, Nayantara. *Indira Gandhi: Her Road to Power.* New York: Frederick Ungar, 1982.

Thakur, Janardan. *Indira Gandhi and Her Power Game.* Delhi: Vikas, 1977.

Vasudev, Uma. *Two Faces of Indira Gandhi.* Delhi: Vikas, 1977.

Wolpert, Stanley. *Nehru: A Tryst with Destiny.* New York: Oxford University Press, 1996.

GANDHI, MAHATMA M. K. *(1869–1948), political and spiritual leader, father of nonviolent resistance in India to British rule* Mahatma (Great Soul) Mohandas Karamchand Gandhi was India's greatest political leader and social reformer. His global legacy has touched the hearts of more people than any Indian since the Buddha. Born in what is now India's Gujarat State on 2 October 1869, Mohandas was the youngest child of Karamchand and Putlibai Gandhi. His father, Karamchand, chief minister of the princely state of Porbandar, was wealthy and influential. Gandhi's devout mother was a Vaishnava Hindu and also a devotee of Jainism and fasting, the practice of which her brilliant son was to convert into a political weapon. Young Mohan's marriage was arranged by his parents when he was only eleven or twelve to his Hindu Modh Vania child bride, Kasturba ("Ba") Makanji, who remained his wife for life, mothering their four sons, Harilal (b. 1888), Manilal (b. 1892), Ramdas (b. 1896), and Devdas (b. 1900).

Early Years in London

Mohan was restless and eager to travel beyond the provincial borders of his father's state, which he did soon after his father died. Nursing and Āyurvedic medicine fascinated Gandhi all his life. He nursed and massaged his dying father during his last illness, delivered his son Devdas, and prescribed remedies for all his followers and disciples, ministering warm enemas and hot bath holistic cures for everything from head to stomach- and backaches. The remedy he trusted most of all was prayer, daily calling out Rāma's name, which was the last word he uttered at the moment of his assassination. The Sanskrit inscription of Mahatma Gandhi's dying cry, "He Ram!" is carved on the onyx stone memorializing the "Step of Peace"—Shanti Ghat—at which his remains were cremated on the bank of the River Yamuna in Delhi.

Despite the strict Hindu prohibition of Gandhi's caste (*jati*) elders against his venturing out upon the ocean's "dark waters," and his devout mother's pleas, eighteen-year-old Mohan steamed from Bombay to Southampton in the fall of 1888, eager to "see and know" London, the world's greatest city, teeming capital of Empress Victoria's Crown Raj. He ventured there to study law, however, not medicine, for his elder brother, who supported him, felt certain that as a British barrister, Mohan would much better serve the Gandhi family's needs and ambitions.

Soon after landing in London, Gandhi's mind focused more on questions of religious philosophy than either law or politics. His mother had exacted three vows from her beloved son. He solemnly promised her to abstain from meat, wine, and women while abroad. Much of Gandhi's first cold and lonely month in London, therefore, was spent in long walks, searching for a vegetarian restaurant. After finding one, he befriended British Quakers and some English clergy there, who, much the same as Hindus and Jains, believed it sinful to eat any part of soul-endowed animals. He soon joined London's Vegetarian Society, and there he met members of London's Theosophical Society, two of whom invited him to join them in studying the Bhagavad Gītā, one of Hinduism's most important ancient works of religious philosophy. Gandhi later reinterpreted the fierce battle that followed the Gītā as an allegory of humankind's struggle on the field of "soul" (*atman*), rather than as the Epic Mahābhārata's blood-drenched Aryan conflict for control

Mahatma M. K. Gandhi. April 5, 1930: The indomitable Gandhi on his famous Salt March. BETTMANN/CORBIS.

of India on the "field of Kuru" (Kuru-kshetra), north of Delhi.

Gandhi met Theosophy's Russian founder, Madame Blavatsky, in London, as well as her charismatic disciple, Annie Besant, who later moved to Madras (Chennai) as president of the Theosophical Society there, becoming the only English woman ever elected to preside over the Indian National Congress. Besant tried very hard to convert Gandhi to Theosophy, but he remained as impervious to her pleas as he would to those of many Christian ministers. Throughout his life, Gandhi remained true to the Hindu faith of his birth, though he studied every religion and read aloud from many scriptures other than the Gītā at his evening prayer meetings. All "true" religions, Gandhi insisted, adhered to the same universal moral principles, "truth" (*sat* or *satya*) and "nonviolence" (*ahimsa*). He equated those two ancient Hindu ideals to "God."

For his first years in London, Gandhi was too busy mastering culinary "Experiments with Truth" (as he would title his autobiography) and English common law

to focus his Yogic meditation on transforming those twin moral aspects of God into a force powerful enough to shake the world's mightiest empire. Inner Temple barrister Gandhi left London and sailed home to Bombay (Mumbai) on 12 June 1891. His mother died while he was abroad, but he had remained faithful to her vows. His elder brother now expected his barrister sibling to be of great value in all his business dealings with British officials and in British courts of law. Scrupulously sensitive and truthful, Gandhi could neither plead falsely in any court nor speak less than the truth to anyone. He could find no acceptable work in India, so he took on a case in South Africa, though it paid little and obliged him to leave his young family again, sailing from Bombay this time for what he believed would be just one year.

The Impact of South Africa

Gandhi's two decades in South Africa transformed him from an ineffectual British barrister into a uniquely brilliant and powerful Mahatma. He went to South

Africa to represent a wealthy Gujarati Muslim merchant in a family dispute, but experienced such humiliating racial prejudice there as to make him resolve to lead a mass struggle against it for almost twenty years. In South Africa, Gandhi endured harsh months behind bars, emerging as the Indian community's foremost defender of human rights in Natal and the Transvaal as well as in the Union of South Africa. Gandhi's expulsion from a first-class railway coach, despite his elegant barrister's dress and the expensive ticket he purchased, and his exclusion from many clean hotel rooms—merely because of the shade of his skin and Indian birth—made him resolve soon after his first year in South Africa to abandon his barrister's top hat and tails in favor of the peasant garb worn by indentured Tamil laborers.

In South Africa, Gandhi found his political voice. As spokesman for the Indian community against Britain's Colonial Office autocrats and Boer bullies, Gandhi fought to remove the invidious poll tax charged to every Indian. On the eve of his final departure from South Africa in 1914, Gandhi reached what he had believed to be a firm agreement with General Jan Smuts to remove that tax, but soon after he left it was reintroduced. Political activism, however, was only one of many changes South Africa wrought in Gandhi's life. He established a highly successful legal practice in Johannesburg, keeping no fewer than four Indian clerks busy from dawn to dusk, attracting brilliant full-time British idealists to his side, including several talented young women as well as men. Gandhi's fearless honesty and passionate criticism of every injustice and all human prejudice proved so charismatic that wherever he went to speak or lingered to live, men and women of every faith, color, and class rallied to his side and supported his principled causes.

Gandhian Socialism

Young Gandhi experimented in communal as well as familial and personal reforms. He established his first ashram (rural community) in Durban, inspired by John Ruskin's and Robert Owen's handicrafts and Utopian ideals. Gandhi was also influenced by his careful reading of the Bible at this time, as of the Gītā, and of John Bunyan's *Pilgrim's Progress* and Leo Tolstoy's *The Kingdom of God Is within You*. His ashram was named Tolstoy Farm.

"The Uplift of All"—Sarvodaya—was the ultimate goal of Gandhi's rural community movement, which brought together individuals from many lands, all devoted to rural communal living, sharing in every fruit of the soil they tilled as well as in every hardship they jointly endured. Gandhian "socialism" resembled that of early Christian orders and later Utopian socialist communities. He insisted that every member of his ashram

take solemn vows of truth and nonviolence and abstain entirely from sex as well as from alcohol, meat eating, and luxuries of any kind. He taught each of his disciples the divinity of truth and nonviolence, which he also called "love," and the virtues of daily prayer, hand labor, and rural self-sufficiency.

In 1906 Gandhi launched his first nonviolent noncooperation movement in Johannesburg, against the British colonial government's Asiatic Ordinance Bill, which would have required every Indian to register and to be fingerprinted. He called that "Black Act" criminal, and vowed "cheerfully" to welcome imprisonment rather than comply. Gandhi's passionate yogic embrace of suffering had now begun, vowing from this time to abstain from sexual relations with his wife, eliminating "passion-inducing" foods from his diet, cutting back on sleep as well as curtailing his daily nourishment before sunset to goat's curd, fruits, and nuts. He hardened himself, toughening his body to prepare for police brutality or isolation in prison cells. He named his new method of revolutionary noncooperation *satyagraha*—a Sanskrit compound meaning "hold fast to the truth." Mahatma Gandhi spoke now of an "inner voice" directing him, which he called the voice of "God that was Truth." He warned his followers of dark dangers confronting them, flogging, long prison terms, even death. He urged them to pray and be fearless. India's first prime minister, Jawaharlal Nehru, later defined Gandhi's greatest message to his nation as "Forget fear!"

Gandhi's Nonviolence

Nonviolence (*ahimsa*), one of India's most ancient religious beliefs, emerged long before the dawn of the Christian era, an ethical ideal of early Buddhism and Jainism. Gandhi insisted that *ahimsa* was Hinduism's "highest religious law" (*paramo Dharma*). He equated it to "God" and "truth," also redefining it in positive terms as "love." The powers of truth and love were so great, Gandhi argued, that united they could "move the world." Such was the force he focused against British imperialism in its final four decades of the first half of the twentieth century. Gandhi purified himself by praying to Rāma, and he armed himself with India's most ancient yogic weapons: suffering (*tapas*), fasting, and breath (*atman*) control before launching any revolutionary movement. He never defended himself with physical weapons of any kind, nor did he hate his opponents, teaching his followers to love those who sought to harm or arrest them.

Home to India

Soon after the start of World War I, Gandhi returned to India, joining Gopal Krishna Gokhale at his Servants of India Society in Pune. Moderate Anglophile Gokhale had presided over India's National Congress in 1905, inspiring Gandhi to join the Congress. He was hailed by Gandhi as "my political guru" (divine teacher). Gandhi also admired Pune's revolutionary Hindu nationalist leader, Lokamanya (Beloved of the People) Bal Gangadhar Tilak, launching his first nationwide *satyagraha* the day Tilak died, 1 August 1920. By then, Gandhi had established his first Indian ashram at Sabarmati, on the outskirts of Gujarat's capital, Ahmedabad. Gandhi was most ably assisted in several provincial *satyagraha* movements by a fellow Gujarati, Sardar Vallabhbhai Patel, who remained his political lieutenant. Patel appealed to Gandhi to join his struggle on behalf of Gujarat's famine-wracked peasants in the spring of 1918, after which the Sardar became a devout disciple of the Mahatma. The failure of India's annual monsoon rains conspired with British wartime shipping of India's meager grain reserves to troops on the Western Front to bring famine to Gujarat's Kheda district.

At the start of his Kheda *satyagraha*, Gandhi inspired thousands of his peasant followers with his stories of the noble virtues of ancient India's great civilization, contrasting it to the "Satanic civilization" of the West, whose worst recent crime was World War I. Still he felt ambivalent about war, attempting to help the British Raj recruit Gujarati peasants for its army a month after his Kheda *satyagraha* ended in only partial victory. Peasants were shocked that he, "a votary of *ahimsa*," would urge them to join the British army! His failure as a "recruiting sergeant" led to Gandhji's worst breakdown, which "nearly ruined my constitution," as he confessed on the eve of the Allied victory that relieved him, "at death's door." The aftermath of armistice proved even more disillusioning to India and to Gandhi than had the long years of war.

Post–World War I Politics

British fears of "sedition" and "terrorist" violence brought the immediate extension of harsh martial defense of India "Black Acts" in the wake of the War. "I can no longer render peaceful obedience to . . . such devilish legislation," Gandhi responded. Like most Indian nationalists, Gandhi had expected freedom (*swaraj*) as India's reward for its loyal wartime support of the Raj, providing almost a million troops to the West and millions more in sterling, as well as countless tons of wheat, steel, and shipping. The Punjab had recruited most of India's valiant troops, Sikhs and Muslims, who fought bravely in France and Mesopotamia, only to return home to brutal British repression and racial discrimination rather than the freedom they had anticipated. On 30 March 1919, police opened fire on a crowd in Delhi, killing several protesters, which led Gandhi to proclaim 6 April 1919 a day of protest and national prayer.

Massacre in Jallianwala Bagh

One week later, on 13 April 1919, in Punjab's Amritsar, whose Golden Temple is the most sacred center of the Sikh faith, British Gurkha and Baluchi troops were ordered by the British brigadier to open fire, without warning, at point-blank range on thousands of unarmed peasants gathered inside an almost totally enclosed nearby garden, Jallianwala Bagh. Four hundred innocents were shot dead, another 1,200 left wounded inside that garden, now India's premier shrine to the nationalist struggle's martyrs to freedom. Mahatma Gandhi was arrested and sent back to Bombay when he tried to enter Punjab, that entire province being locked under the most brutal martial repression. Crawling orders were posted over several of Amritsar's narrow lanes for all Indians residing there, whippings lashed onto the naked backs of those daring to disobey.

Jallianwala Bagh alienated millions of previously loyal supporters and admirers of the British Raj. Wealthy Anglophile lawyers like Motilal Nehru, father of India's first prime minister, became converts to Mahatma Gandhi's revolutionary leadership and methods. Gandhi called upon all Indians to boycott British titles and law courts, as well as imported British manufactured cloth, consigning the latter to "freedom pyres." He urged Indians to spin their own cotton and weave their own cloth, assuring his followers that the "music" of millions of spinning wheels would be the anthem of India's freedom, destined to liberate Mother India's children from thralldom to imperial oppressors. He made a monthly minimal amount of hand-spun cotton (*khadi*) the dues of membership in India's National Congress. "There is no deliverance without sacrifice and self-control," Mahatma Gandhi instructed his followers. "Is the country ready?" he asked. Were the Hindu majority in Congress ready to embrace their Muslim neighbors as "brothers"?

"Hindu-Muslim Unity," Gandhi taught, was a primary pillar of Indian independence. Without unity, multicultural India would fall apart. His vision and warnings proved prophetic. His appeal reached the Muslim masses, whose hatred of British rule was intensified by Britain's postwar annexation of the Turkish caliph's (*khilafat's*) North African domain, after having so often denied any territorial ambitions during the war. The Khilafat Movement, led by Shaukat and Mohammed Ali, was hailed by Gandhi as his own "cause," embracing the Ali brothers as his "brothers," leading many Hindus to question the wisdom of their Mahatma's political strategy in embracing that pan-Islamic movement. Tens of thousands of Indian Muslims abandoned homes in India to march north to Afghanistan in support of a caliph ("deputy" of God), whose soldiers erected barbed wire at his borders to stop them. Moderate Muslim leaders of

India's National Congress, like Barrister Mohammad Ali Jinnah, also disapproved of Gandhi's revolutionary appeals to India's Muslim masses, as well as to illiterate Hindu peasants to "boycott" all British goods and institutions, fearing he would only provoke violence. Mahatma Gandhi listened to his "inner voice," however, as he launched nationwide *satyagraha*.

Leader and Guru of the Indian National Congress

From 1920 until 1945, whether in prison or on silent retreat in his last Central Indian ashram, Seva-Gram (village of service), or on one of his many "walking pilgrimages" (*pada yatras*), "Great Soul" Gandhi was hailed by his Congress Working Committee followers as virtually divine, even after he resigned from the Congress, whose Constitution he had rewritten and democratized. For Mahatma Gandhi was never primarily a political leader, sickened by the corruption, falsehood, and jealous in-fighting of politics, turning away from it to his cotton spinning, rural uplift work, and the struggle against "untouchability," which he viewed as the darkest sin of Hinduism, and to his holistic health cures, including Brahmacharya.

After the Nagpur Congress in December 1920, when Gandhi won the clear support of an overwhelming majority of new delegates to launch his multiple-boycott noncooperation movement nationwide, he lost the backing of many influential moderate leaders, most important of whom was Jinnah, who later led his Muslim League in demanding a separate Muslim nation-state of Pakistan.

Chauri Chaura Tragedy

When Gandhi launched nationwide *satyagraha*, he optimistically promised his Congress followers freedom (*swaraj*) from the British Raj in one year. Long before that, however, he learned of the murders by immolation of twenty-one Indian police, forced to burn inside their wooden station house by a mob of *satyagrahis* in Chauri Chaura. "I have committed a Himalayan blunder!" Mahatma Gandhi cried, calling a halt to *satyagraha*. For the first requirement and virtue of any *satyagrahi* was *ahimsa*. The remorseful Mahatma abandoned all political action and retired to the peaceful calm of his rural ashram, spinning cotton on his hand loom, weaving it into cloth "of our own country" (*sva-deshi*), remaining silent one day every week, periodically fasting. "All of us should be in mourning" for Chauri Chaura, Gandhi said. Jawaharlal Nehru, when he learned in his prison cell of Gandhi's decision to call off India's revolution, wrote "We were angry." Just when national resistance had started to build and to gain momentum, Nehru felt that,

thanks to Gandhi's scruples, it "wilted away." But Gandhi believed that means and ends were inextricably related, and that only nonviolent means could result in good ends. Soon after the British realized how unpopular Gandhi had become, they arrested him. When he almost died of appendicitis in 1924, however, he was released for surgery, after which he returned to rural and religious reform work

Struggles against Untouchability

"Untouchability is a blot upon humanity and therefore upon Hinduism," Gandhi argued, leading several important struggles against that Hindu "caste" crime, which treated some 10 percent of India's Hindu population as "polluted outcastes," denying them admission to temples or the use of village wells, treating them as creatures lower than animals. Gandhi risked his own life fighting this "age-long prejudice," arousing the ire of many orthodox Brahmans, who viewed him as a "traitor" to his faith. In 1932, when British prime minister J. Ramsay MacDonald classified "untouchables" as "separate" from "upper caste Hindus," awarding them a separate bloc of electoral seats on enlarged councils, as the British had earlier done with India's Muslims, Gandhi launched a fast-unto-death, determined to sacrifice his life rather than allow "perfidious Albion" further to divide and thus longer to rule over India's "enslaved" population. He thus brilliantly united his religious and political powers, magnifying the force of each, forcing the Raj withdraw its "Communal Award," rather than to risk allowing a Mahatma to die protesting it. Untouchable leaders, like Dr. B. R. Ambedkar, however, who had lobbied at London's Round Table Conferences for those separate electorate seats, angrily resented Gandhi's intervention, considering him no better than the most reactionary of Brahmans. But Gandhi continued his long struggle to abolish untouchability, renaming Hindu "outcastes" *Harijans* (children of God), insisting that at least one of them should always live in his ashram, treating them as his own "children."

Breaking the Salt Tax Monopoly

Gandhi's most famous *satyagraha* began on 12 March 1930, when he led a band of faithful disciples on his 240-mile antisalt tax march south from Sabarmati ashram to Dandi beach. The British Raj long enforced its monopoly on the sale of salt throughout India, annual tax revenue from which was second only to that collected from land. "Next to air and water," Gandhi told his long-suffering nation, salt was the "greatest necessity of life . . . the only condiment of the poor . . . by taxing which the State can reach even the starving millions." That invidious salt tax was 2,400 percent of its sale price, yet salt could be picked up free on every beach along India's some 2,000-mile (3,400 km) littoral. That was exactly what Gandhi did on 6 April, when he reached Dandi beach, cheered by Sarojini Naidu as India's "Deliverer!" Millions of Indians rushed down to the sea to break the British monopoly, "stealing" lumps of sea salt and using them instead of buying tax-stamped inflated packages. Before year's end, every jail cell in India was filled with more than 60,000 salt *satyagrahi*s. Gandhi never contested any jail sentence, welcoming each return to his prison "temple" (*mandir*) cell. During most of his years behind bars, he prayed while spinning cotton.

Quit India Movement

Gandhi never lost faith in *ahimsa*, rejecting every British demand that he should support Britain and its Allies in World War II. In the final decades of his life, he rejected the concept of "just war," insisting that all mass violence was evil. Some of his closest British Christian friends abandoned him when, shortly after the beginning of World War II, Gandhi launched his individual *satyagraha*, sending his most devout disciple, Vinoba Bhave, out publicly to break British martial law. The British Raj waited, however, before arresting Gandhi himself, reluctant to rouse mass Indian opposition while Japan was fast approaching India's eastern border. Early in August 1942, the Congress Working Committee appealed to Gandhi to come to Bombay to lead them again in one final mass *satyagraha* to end the Raj. Gandhi agreed, resolved to demand that every British soldier and civilian immediately "Quit India." "Do or die!" was the mantra he coined for this *satyagraha*, but the night before he was ready to launch it, he was driven away in the dark, incarcerated behind British bars until the war's end.

Last Years and Assassination

Mahatma Gandhi was deeply depressed by postwar conflicts in India, primarily between Hindus and Muslims, who fought over the imminent division of British India's loaves and fishes, as the few remaining days of the Raj dwindled. Britain's newly elected Labour Government, led by Prime Minister Clement Attlee, found its Indian "jewel" more a liability than an asset. Of all the leaders of India's National Congress and the Muslim League, Gandhi alone refused to accept young Viceroy Lord Mountbatten's hasty plan to partition South Asia into a "moth-eaten" Pakistan and a much diminished India. Partition would be the "vivisection of Mother India," Gandhi cried. But when Mountbatten announced his partition plan early in June 1947, he set the date for all British troops to be withdrawn from South Asia at the midnight birth of independent India on 15 August 1947. That was also when multicultural

Bengal and the Punjab were slashed in half—the latter "Land of Five Rivers" through its Sikh population's heart—triggering the most tragic flight of over 10 million terrified Hindus, Muslims, and Sikhs who awoke to find themselves on the wrong side of unguarded, ineptly drawn borders, leaving a million innocents to die in the following months.

At his evening prayer meetings in New Delhi, Mahatma Gandhi cried out against the tragic plight of old Delhi's Muslims, violently driven from their ancestral homes, robbed, beaten, or murdered by Sikh and Hindu mobs maddened by reports of Muslim rapes and murders of Hindus and Sikhs in Pakistan's Punjab and North-West Frontier province. "What brutalities are going on!" Gandhi cried. "People are trying to see that there is no Hindu left in Pakistan and no Muslim in Hindustan."

He decried as well the Indo-Pak War in Kashmir, which started in October 1947 and was destined to continue, with interludes of seeming calm, for more than half a century. "Today my wings are clipped," Gandhi groaned as he watched fighting escalate in Kashmir's Vale. "If I could grow my wings again, I would fly to Pakistan." When asked by his disciples why he did not urge his political heirs (Nehru and Patel) to Congress power in New Delhi to end the war, Gandhi replied. "No one listens to me . . . if I could have my way of nonviolence . . . we would not send our army." But "I have no say with my people today." A month before his assassination, Gandhi offered himself as "arbitrator" of the conflict that still plagues India's relations with Pakistan and has cost over 50,000 lives, as well as billions of dollars. "I shall advise Pakistan and India to sit together and decide the matter," the wise Mahatma suggested, but he was never called upon by Nehru to assist India in resolving the conflict over Jammu and Kashmir state. "Today mine is a cry in the wilderness," Gandhi said.

On Friday, 30 January 1948, Mahatma Gandhi was shot dead by a hate-crazed Hindu Brahman, Naturam Godse, who called India's saintly father a "traitor," and a "lackey" of Pakistan. "The light has gone out of our lives," Nehru mourned after Gandhi died. "Conflicts must be ended in the face of this great disaster." Neither the conflict between India and Pakistan over the State of Jammu and Kashmir, nor lesser conflicts among Hindus and Muslims, whether in Gujarat or Ayodhya, have been resolved as yet. "In our age of moral decay," Albert Einstein wrote, memorializing Mahatma Gandhi, "he was the only statesman who represented that higher conception of human relations in the political sphere to which we must aspire with all our power."

Stanley Wolpert

See also **Gokhale, Gopal Krishna; Nehru, Jawaharlal; Pakistan and India; Patel, Sardar Vallabhbhai; Satyagraha; Tilak, Bal Gangadhar**

BIBLIOGRAPHY

Ashe, Geoffrey. *Gandhi.* New York: Stein & Day, 1968.
Brown, Judith M. *Prisoner of Hope.* New Haven, Conn.: Yale University Press, 1989.
Erikson, Erik H. *Gandhi's Truth: On the Origins of Militant Nonviolence.* New York: Norton, 1969.
Gandhi, M. K. *An Autobiography: The Story of My Experiments with Truth,* translated by Mahadev Desai. Boston: Beacon Press, 1957.
Gandhi, Rajmohan, *The Good Boatman: A Portrait of Gandhi.* New Delhi: Viking, 1995.
Payne, Robert. *The Life and Death of Mahatma Gandhi.* New York: Dutton, 1969.
Tendulkar, D. G. *Mahatma: Life of Mohandas Karamchand Gandhi.* 8 vols. Delhi: Publications Division, Ministry of Information & Broadcasting, Government of India, 1954.
Wolpert, Stanley. *Gandhi's Passion: The Life and Legacy of Mahatma Gandhi.* New York: Oxford University Press, 2001.

GANDHI, RAJIV (1944–1991), prime minister of India (1984–1989).

Born in 1944, Rajiv Gandhi was the eldest son of Indira Gandhi, daughter of the first Indian prime minister, Jawaharlal Nehru. Rajiv's father, Feroze Gandhi, was a Parsi, a Gujarati-speaking Zoroastrian, who was briefly elected to India's Lok Sabha (lower house of Parliament).

Like his grandfather, Jawaharlal Nehru, Rajiv studied at Cambridge University, but he failed to complete his engineering degree there. While at Cambridge, he met Sonia Maino, the daughter of an Italian industrialist, who was studying English at a local college. They married, and Rajiv Gandhi became a pilot for Air India, resisting a political career until he was finally persuaded to run for office by his mother, Prime Minister Indira Gandhi, after the accidental death in 1980 of Rajiv's younger brother, Sanjay. Until then, Sanjay Gandhi was being groomed to succeed her as prime minister. Rajiv was elected to Parliament in 1981 from the rural constituency of Amethi in Uttar Pradesh. Following the assassination of Prime Minister Indira Gandhi in 1984, the Congress Party persuaded Rajiv Gandhi to succeed his mother as head of the Congress Party and as prime minister of India.

Forty years old at the time, Rajiv Gandhi led his Congress Party to victory and was welcomed as prime minister on a wave of sympathy for his assassinated mother and widespread admiration for his youthful dynamism and modern outlook. His politics as prime minister was not divisive or controversial, nor very striking or groundbreaking, compared to that of his mother and his grandfather. His tenure was notable for promoting high technology in India, though without much impact on reducing poverty.

In the foreign arena, he continued his mother's close ties with the United States, and in particular, promoted the close personal ties that she had established with President Ronald Reagan. Closer to home, his fateful foreign policy mistake was India's intervention in Sri Lanka, which was locked in a devastating civil war between the Sinhalese government and the rebellious Tamil areas of the north seeking an independent Tamil Ealam (nation). In an agreement with President Julius Jayawardene, the Sri Lankan president, Rajiv committed several divisions of the Indian Peace Keeping Force (IPKF) to the Colombo government to help it disarm and pacify the Tamil militants. Having gone to "disarm" the rebellious Liberation Tigers of Tamil Ealam (LTTE) and bring about peace, the IPKF ended up fighting the LTTE, and was withdrawn ten years later with no peace in sight.

Scandals and allegations of corruption during his tenure plagued Rajiv Gandhi, especially one that revolved around claims that he had received "kickbacks" from Bofors, a Swedish company that made the long-range guns purchased by India's defense ministry. The Congress Party suffered electoral defeat in 1989 and was succeeded by a coalition led by the Janata Dal party under Vishwanath Pratap Singh as prime minister. This coalition government proved shaky, however, and Rajiv started campaigning again in 1991, when new elections were called. While campaigning outside Madras (now Chennai) in South India, a female LTTE suicide bomber detonated a bomb, killing Rajiv Gandhi and eighteen others.

Raju G. C. Thomas

See also **Gandhi, Indira; Gandhi, Sonia; Nehru, Jawaharlal**

BIBLIOGRAPHY

Aggarwala, Adish C. *Rajiv Gandhi: An Assessment.* New Delhi: Amish Publications, 1993.
Bhattacharjee, Arun. *Rajiv Gandhi: Life and Message of India's Second Slain Prime Minister.* Kolkata: Ashish Publishing House, 1992.
Gandhi, Sonia. *Rajiv Gandhi's World View.* New Delhi: Vikas Publishing, 1991.
Healy, Kathleen. *Rajiv Gandhi: The Years of Power.* New Delhi: Vikas Publishing, 1989.
Merchant, Minaz. *Rajiv Gandhi: The End of a Dream.* New Delhi: Viking, 1991.

GANDHI, SONIA (1946–), Congress Party leader, widow of Rajiv Gandhi.

Sonia Gandhi, the widow of former prime minister Rajiv Gandhi, who was assassinated in 1991, entered politics in 1998 after being persuaded by the Congress Party to lead the organization during that year's general elections. She was elected to Parliament in 1999 from Jawaharlal Nehru's Rai Bareilly constituency, adjacent to Rajiv Gandhi's rural constituency in Amethi, Uttar Pradesh. Rajiv and Sonia Gandhi's son, Harvard-educated Rahul Gandhi, now holds this Parliamentary seat. The Congress Party lost to the Bharatiya Janata Party (BJP)–led coalition in the 1998 elections, and then again in 1999, following the collapse of the BJP coalition in a successful vote of no-confidence. In the April 2004 general elections, riding on the Gandhi name and visibility, she led the Congress Party and its allies back into office. Her victory generated strong passions among extreme Hindu nationalists because of her foreign origins and Christian faith. Concerns about causing deep political divisions in India, and fears of assassination, as in the cases of her husband and her mother-in-law, Indira Gandhi, prompted her not to assume the office of prime minister.

Sonia Maino Gandhi was born in 1946 in the small Italian town of Orbassano, near Turin. Her father was a building contractor, and she was raised as a traditional Roman Catholic. She met Rajiv Gandhi in England, where she had gone to study English at a school in Cambridgeshire, while he was studying engineering at Cambridge University. Sonia and Rajiv were married in 1968. They returned to New Delhi and moved into the residence of Rajiv's mother, Indira Gandhi, who was then prime minister of India. Thereafter, she adapted to the Indian way of life to become part of the Nehru-Gandhi political family, learning Hindi, wearing saris, and adjusting to Indian culture and cuisine. Their daughter, Priyanka, was born in 1970, and their son, Rahul, in 1972.

Sonia Gandhi refused to accept the office of prime minister following her successful 2004 election campaign, wisely remaining president of the Congress Party. She chose the former finance minister under the earlier Congress government, Dr. Manmohan Singh, an Oxford-educated economist, to assume the position of prime minister. He became India's first Sikh prime minister. Sonia Gandhi remained the political power behind the prime minister shaping key Congress government policies.

Raju G. C. Thomas

See also **Gandhi, Indira; Gandhi, Rajiv; Singh, Manmohan**

BIBLIOGRAPHY

Bakshi, S. R., et al. *Sonia Gandhi: The President of the AICC.* New Delhi: South Asia Books, 1998.
Gandhi, Sonia. *Two Alone.* New Delhi: Penguin Books, 2004.
Rupa, Chatterjee. *Sonia Mystique.* New Delhi: Virgo Publications, 2000.
Sanghvi, Vijay. *Congress Resurgence under Sonia Gandhi.* New Delhi: Kalpaz Publications, 2004.

GANDHINAGAR The capital of Gujarat, Gandhinagar ("city of Gandhi") is named after Mohandas Karamchand Gandhi, the native son of Gujarat revered worldwide as the Mahatma, the "Great Soul." Gujarat, called the melting pot of India and treasure trove of architectural styles, derives its name from *Gujjara-ratta*, the form it takes in Prakrit, the ancient Indic dialect. Its Sanskrit name, Gurjjara-rastra, literally means the "country of the Gurjjaras." The Gurjjaras were a Central Asian tribe, believed to have entered India along with the Huns in the mid-fifth century, when the imperial control of the Guptas was in decline. The region the Gurjjaras settled was called Gujarat by the tenth century, when Mulraj Solanki, the founder of the Hindu Chalukyan dynasty, established his capital at Anhilwara Patan. Anhilwara in time came to be replaced by Ahmedabad, which was selected by Muzaffar Khan as his sultanate's capital in 1412. In time, the city came to rival Manchester, U.K., in textiles. Bombay (present-day Mumbai) became the capital of the region when the British placed Gujarat under their Bombay presidency, and it was not until 1960, after the unilingual (Gujarati) state of Gujarat had been created from bilingual Bombay, that Gandhinagar, about 15 miles (24 km) north of Ahmedabad on the right bank of the Sabarmati River, was selected as the site of the capital city for the new state.

The selection of the site for the new capital was not without controversy. Princely Baroda (present-day Vadodara) and industrial Ahmedabad both wanted the honor of being named the capital city. But Baroda was ruled out because of its princely status, which was deemed incongruent with the democratic properties of independent India. Moreover, Fatesinghrao Gaekwad, the ruler of Baroda, was of Maharashtrian origins, which was not viewed favorably in Gandhi's Gujarat. Ahmedabad was ruled out because of its overcrowded character, even though the mill owners, led by Ambalal Sarabhai and Kasturbhai Lalbhai, lobbied very hard to shift the capital to Ahmedabad.

Gandhinagar became a battleground for the competing ideals that had surfaced during the building of Chandigarh and Bhubaneswar. The mill owners of neighboring Ahmedabad, backed by Indian architect and planner Balakrishna Doshi, wanted the American architect Louis Kahn to build Gandhinagar as a worthy rival to Le Corbusier's Chandigarh. There was, however, tremendous political pressure to make Gandhinagar a

Policeman Stands Guard at Swaminarayan Hindu Temple in Gandhinagar. On 24 September 2002, several gunmen entered the imposing Akshardham Temple in Gandhinagar and indiscriminately opened fire on Hindu worshipers, killing 32 people (including 11 children) and wounding another 100. Four days later, a policeman stands guard at the site, where thousands have gathered to pray for the victims. The captured gunmen were later identified as Muslim extremists with links to Pakistan. REUTERS/CORBIS.

purely Indian enterprise, partly because the state of Gujarat was the birthplace of Mahatma Gandhi. Even though, in the end, negotiations with Kahn broke down over payment in U.S. dollars, he exercised some influence in the construction of Gandhinagar from Ahmedabad, where he was building the Indian Institute of Management campus. The Gujarat government also considered the option of creating a consortium of private Indian architects, including Doshi, Charles Correa, Achyut Kanvinde, Hasmukh Patel, and others; but in the end the government recruited American-trained Hargobind K. Mewada, who had apprenticed with Le Corbusier in Chandigarh, to complete the project. The development of Gandhinagar, like its older cousins Chandigarh and Bhubaneswar, was in part an educational experiment and social welfare project, as well as a venture in professional city planning and architecture.

Ravi Kalia

See also **Gandhi, Mahatma M. K.; Gujarat; Urbanism**

BIBLIOGRAPHY

Kalia, Ravi. *Gandhinagar: Building National Identity in Postcolonial India*. Columbia: University of South Carolina Press; New Delhi: Oxford University Press, 2004.

GAṆESHA In Hinduism, no other god is as often invoked as Gaṇesha, or Gaṇapati, "lord of the *gaṇas*," or Shiva's dwarf attendants, Gajānana, "he with the elephant's head." Predominantly the god of good luck, Gaṇesha is worshiped at the start of any important enterprise. Son of Shiva and Pārvatī, he is, however, not their natural offspring. His real origin lies in India's far distant past; even the compilers of the Purāṇas and other ancient writers have lost all track of it.

There are many different accounts of Gaṇesha's birth. According to the Shiva Purāṇa, Pārvatī fashioned a handsome boy out of the unguents and other applications she had used in her bath, and asked him to guard the entrance to her apartment against strangers. When

Painting of Gaṇesha. In the desert city of Jaisalmer, in the region of Rajasthan, painting of the elephant-headed Gaṇesha, the Hindu god of good fortune. His image often adorns doorways or building walls, as here. ROMAN SOUMAR/CORBIS.

Shiva, her husband, arrived, the boy barred him, not knowing Shiva to be his father. Shiva, not knowing the boy's identity, decapitated him in anger. To placate the disconsolate Pārvatī, Shiva quickly brought the child back to life by placing the head of the first living thing he could find on the boy's body.

As the god's birth is narrated in the Skanda Purāṇa Pārvatī was amusing herself by forming a figure out of the remains of her bath; she could make only the torso with the remains. Later, her elder son Skanda finished the task by adding the head of an elephant to the incomplete body.

In the Varāha Purāṇa, it is Shiva himself who gave his handsome young son an elephant's head, a portly form, and serpents for the sacred thread. The story in the Brahmavaivarta Purāṇa is that the malevolent planet Shani (Saturn) bore a curse: the head of anyone at whom he looked would fall off. Not knowing this, Pārvatī made him gaze at her newborn son, whose head fell off at once; it was later replaced by that of the king of the elephants.

References and Iconography

References to Gaṇesha, Gajānana, Vināyaka, and Gaṇapati can be traced back to the Vedic period. The name Vināyaka occurs already in the Gṛihasūtras, books of rules for worship by householders. As many as six Vināyakas are named, who are malevolent—or at least mischievous—beings. Under their influence, men and women are afflicted by many misfortunes. In slightly later texts, the six Vināyakas coalesce into one, but by then he has come to be associated with Ambika, or "Mother," that is, Pārvatī. He is her son, and he can be pacified when offerings are made to him.

Vināyaka, Gaṇesha, and Gajānana all fit into the type of *yaksha*s, the fickle-minded, temperamental beings of early mythology. Indeed, what may be perhaps a prototype of Gaṇesha comes from Amaravati in South India. There, on a fragmentary beam of a stupa railing, a corpulent *gana* with an elephant's head is pulling a thick cord.

A portly form and an elephant's head are of course the god's most distinctive characteristics. Among the attributes of Ganesha images are a bowl of *modaka* sweets, his own broken tusk, an ax, and a radish in his hands; his mouse mount; and his sacred thread of a cobra. He has many colors—red, white, turmeric-yellow, and even black—but the predominant colors are various hues at the red end of the spectrum, which are described imaginatively as molten gold, rising sun, and vermilion.

Not only does Ganesha have the head of an elephant, he may have two of them, or three, four, five, or even six. These forms, however, are extremely rare, with the exception of the five-headed form. Sometimes, instead of five heads, there are five images of Ganesha, or *pañcaganesha*.

It is obvious that a god with such universal appeal would be represented in many ways. Images of the god for worship in the household and in his temples portray him as having two, four, or more arms, occasionally numbering up to as many as twenty. He may be seated, standing, or dancing; alone, with his consorts, or in the company of his parents and his brother Skanda-Kartikeya. As a god presiding over good luck, Ganesha may be represented together with his other "partner gods," Kubera and Lakshmī.

One of the earliest images of Ganesha is in a cave at Udayagiri in central India, of the early fifth century. He has only two arms; the right hand is broken, but the left hand holds a bowl of his favorite sweets, with the trunk curving to partake of the contents. Ganesha's penis is erect. This is a trait of some Shaiva images, suggesting the retention of the semen, and continence—paradoxical though it may seem. And though Ganesha indeed was influenced by the Tantric cult, in an image of so early a date, not too much should be inferred; perhaps it is only evidence of the god's impish nature and origin.

The posture of sitting at ease seems to come naturally to this portly deity, with one thick leg folded on the seat and the other folded at the knee and resting also on the seat. It is as such that Ganesha has come down to us from the fifth-century Pārvatī temple at Nachna in entral India. One hand of this two-armed god holds the sweet bowl, while the other holds a large radish, another of his favored foods. A string of pearls with many loops serves as his coronet, and a cobra playfully forms the sacred thread.

In the Deccan, in the sixth century, representations of Ganesha were created at Elephanta, Aiholi, and Badami. In the great cave at Elephanta near Mumbai (Bombay), for example, a two-armed Ganesha is participating in his own way in his father's dance, his trunk curving in delight. In the Ravalphadi cave at Aiholi and in cave 1 at Badami in Karnataka as well, the sparsely and simply clad adolescent god witnesses the cosmic dance of Shiva, the bowl of sweets in one hand, as ever. In North India, a charming panel from the brick temple at Bhitargaon shows a spirited tussle between Ganesha and Skanda over a bowl of *modaka* sweets.

When Ganesha is endowed with more than two arms, they are most often four, but there are sometimes six or eight, and occasionally even up to twenty. When he has four hands, among the most frequent attributes are the elephant goad, the battle-ax, the noose, the single tusk, and the bowl of sweets. There is also a very beautiful six-armed Ganesha, dancing and listening to the sound of his own bell-ornaments, from Kannauj in North India.

Ganesha also figures in panels of the Saptamatrkas, or the Seven Divine Mothers, where he guards one flank of the row of the Mothers, with Shiva or Virabhadra guarding the other. There are also more esoteric forms of Ganesha, his many forms and uses described in the Tantras.

Ganesha's wives are Siddhi ("Success") and Buddhi ("Wisdom"), who are the god Brahmā's daughters. For while Ganesha is on the one hand the facilitator of all enterprises, he at the same time also presides over the higher functions of the mind. Ganesha has profound wisdom and a prodigious memory—it was he who undertook the task of writing down the epic Mahābhārata, verse by verse, as soon as the sage Vyasa composed it. In all cases, the notions of wisdom, knowledge, success, accomplishment, and well-being are present.

Worship of Ganesha

There are a number of days that are sacred to Ganesha but the most important is the Ganesha Caturthi, the fourth day in the bright fortnight in the Hindu month of Bhadrapada (August–September). In Maharashtra in particular, nine places came to be known as being sacred to the elephant-faced god. They are Morgaon, Theurgaon, Sidhtek, Varad, Murud, Ganagapur, Lenyadri, Ranjangaon, and Ojhar.

The worship of Ganesha spread beyond the present boundaries of India. His sculptures have been found in Afghanistan. Ganesha also entered the Buddhist Mahayana pantheon of Tibet, Japan, and countries of Southeast Asia.

As discussed above, the authors of the Purānas asked how Ganesha came to have an elephant's head on a human body, and came up with many mythical explanations. But perhaps the correct question to pose is: how did an elephant come to have a man's body?

All these mythological stories have the distinctive appearance of being retrospective; they attempt to explain the god's unusual form by invoking some other previous mythological happenings. Is it possible that they are approaching the question of the human body and elephant head from the wrong end, trying to explain the origin of the elephant's head on the human body? In other words, is it possible that it is the elephant—such as the Amaravati *yaksha*—that is the original god, so to speak, and that therefore we are to explain rather how a human body came to be associated with it, and not the other way around.

Kirit Mankodi

See also **Elephanta; Shiva and Shaivism**

BIBLIOGRAPHY

Brown, Robert L., ed. *Ganesh: Studies of an Asian God.* Albany: State University of New York Press, 1991.

Coomaraswamy, Ananda K. *Yaksas.* Delhi: Munshiram Manoharlal, 1980.

Courtright, Paul B. *Ganesa: Lord of Obstacles, Lord of Beginnings.* New York: Oxford University Press, 1985.

Krishan, Yuvaraj. *Ganesa: Unravelling an Enigma.* Delhi: Motilal Banarsidass, 1999.

Martin-Dubost, Paul. *Ganesa, the Enchanter of the Three Worlds.* Mumbai: Project for Indian Cultural Studies, 1995.

Pal, Pratapadiya, ed. *Ganesh the Benevolent.* Mumbai: Marg, 1995.

GANGES. *See* **Geography.**

GAT-TORĀ Gat-Torā (*gat*, Hindustani, "form" or "movement of the body in dance" + *torā*, Hindustani, "an ornament for the wrists") is instrumental music in North Indian classical music, particularly for the sitar and sarod, in which a composition alternates with improvisations. Masit Khan, who lived in the late eighteenth and early nineteenth centuries, popularized this form of performance, and one of the most important of these composition patterns bears his name. *Gat*, as a reference to a way of walking, also refers to a kind of drum composition for tabla and a category of dance movements.

In sitar and sarod performance traditions, *gat* refers specifically to a kind of precomposed melody and to the entire measured section of the performance (as contrasted with the unmetered *ālāp* section) that such precomposed melodies commence. A *gat* presents the *rāga* (underlying melody) in a composed melodic form and often illustrates the qualities of the *tāla* (underlying time cycle).

*Gat*s are commonly composed of one or more sections, each of which will be in its own specific register.

GAT-TORĀ (MELODIC SOLOIST WITH TABLA)	
vilambit lay	appearance of *gat*
	often begins with a drum solo (*peshkār*)
	features long solos, often with elaborate *tihā'ī*s
madhya lay	increasingly virtuosic solos
drut lay	short fast *tān*s
	fewer tabla solos
atidrut lay	metered *jhāla*
	dramatic devices such as *sawāl-jawāb, tār paran/sāth sangat*
	may conclude with an elaborate *cakradār paran* played in unison

The most important of these sections is the *sthā'ī* (Sanskrit, "steady") and is usually limited to the lower and middle registers (*purvāng*). Complementing the *sthā'ī* is the *antarā* (Sanskrit, "contrast") which serves as a counter theme and usually explores the middle and upper registers (*uttarāng*).

Most commonly, the beginning of the *sthā'ī* (the *mukhrā* [Hindustani, "face"]) emphasizes beat one (*sam*) of the *tala* in such a distinctive way that musicians often repeat only this part of the *gat*, especially when they get to the final and fastest portions of the performance.

Two standardized rhythmic patterns for *gat* are common. In *Masitkhānī gat* (*gat* in the style of Masit Khan) the *mukhrā* begins on beat 12 in slow or medium-tempo *Tīntāl* and cadences on the *sam* in a tripartite rhythm. *Rāzākhānī gat* (*gat* in the style of the Raza Khan family, notably of Ali Raza) and other fast-tempo *gat*s tend to be less regular than *Masitkhānī*. This more specific use of the word *gat* as a composition refers to a rhythmic pattern of plectrum strokes (usually mnemonically represented by the syllables *dā* and *rā*). These *gat*s also imply melodic shape so that, over all, the term has a matrixlike quality encompassing metric, rhythmic, pitch, and kinesthetic organization.

The notion of *torā* encompasses the elaborations that contrast with the recurring *gat*. Explorations of the *rāga*, *tāla*, and the limits of the performer's technique occur in the *torā*'s that come between statements of *gat*. These improvisations (sometimes known as *tān* [extension]) usually exhibit the virtuosity of the performer. In the broader structural context of performance, the *gat* marks the point at which the drummer enters and, in alternation with the improvisatory *torā*s (especially in some performance traditions), where the drummer solos. Vice versa, when the melodic soloist is improvising or playing precomposed elaborations, the drummer maintains the time with a *thekā* representing the *tāla*.

After the melodic soloist has finished with his or her solo variations and improvisations, performances sometimes feature various kinds of interaction between performers, commonly the soloist and the drummer. Perhaps the most notable of these is the *sawāl-jawāb* (Hindustani, "question-answer"), a telescoping responsorial format. Sometimes this occurs between two instrumental soloists, one of whom states a musical line in one musical medium while the other repeats it, translating the musical line into the characteristic shape of his or her medium. The most common version of *sawāl-jawāb* is between a melodic instrumental soloist and a drummer.

Gordon Thompson

BIBLIOGRAPHY

Miner, Allyn. *Sitar and Sarod in the Eighteenth and Nineteenth Centuries*. Delhi: Motilal Banarsidass Publishers, 1997.

GENDER AND HUMAN RIGHTS

The rights of women are an inalienable, integral, and indivisible part of universal human rights. At the beginning of the twenty-first century, women perform an estimated 60 percent of the world's total work but receive only 10 percent of the world's income and own a mere 1 percent of the world's land. They constitute nearly 60 percent of world's poor. Recent attempts at structural adjustments and economic liberalization have led to further marginalization of women and an increasing feminization of poverty, particularly in the developing countries. India is no exception to these trends.

The traditional Indian social structure is heavily tilted in favor of men, giving them authority and prestige while confining women primarily to domestic roles. Even if women work outside the home, most of them have no control over their own earnings. Even in the case of highly educated and professionally qualified women, a dowry is still provided at the time of marriage. That is why in many communities, the birth of a female child is still treated as a curse and a financial liability. In some regions sex detection tests and female infanticide are widely practiced, disturbing India's male-female ratio adversely over the last few decades.

India still does not have a uniform civil code. Personal and family laws discriminate not only between men and women but also between one woman and another. A Hindu woman is not entitled to a share in joint family property. Under Muslim law, a male child is entitled to double the share of a female child. A Parsi girl is discriminated against in matters of inheritance in case she decides to marry out of the community. Most Indian girls are treated as *paraya dhana* (somebody else's property) in their parental homes and as outsiders by their new families after marriage. Very few women have the courage to raise their voice against such discrimination, and most women remain unequal, dispossessed, and disadvantaged throughout their lives.

Under ancient Indian concepts, culture, and ethos, women were honored with the status of *devī*s or goddesses, yet in practice were denied human rights and basic freedoms. After independence in 1947 some steps were taken to bridge gender-based disparity legally. For instance, the Constitution of India gave Indian women civic and political freedoms equal to those of men. Whereas Article 14 guarantees "equality before law" and "equal protection before law," Article 15 prohibits discrimination on grounds of religion, race, caste, or gender.

The Indian government has also passed various legislation—including the Hindu Marriage Act, the Hindu Succession Act, the Dowry Prohibition Act, the Immoral Traffic Prevention Act, Medical Termination of Pregnancy Act, Indecent Representation of Women Prevention Act, and the *Sati* Prevention Act—to safeguard the dignity, control of sexuality, and reproductive rights of women. Many judicial verdicts have also favored the rights of women in order to raise their status. However, the constitutional and legal provisions appear to be too radical in view of prevailing sociocultural realities, which frequently create a resistance to the special protection and acceleratory measures that were designed to enable women in India to achieve their just and equal position in society. The majority of women in India act as custodians of family well-being and in general are neither aware of their legal rights nor anxious to assert themselves against established norms and practices. Traditional values and behavioral norms, which have evolved over thousands of years, inhibit women from asserting themselves as individuals, except in a very limited context.

The success of several thousand Indian women who, after independence, used courage, financial means, and family support to break sociocultural barriers does not imply the emancipation of Indian women or the enjoyment of human rights by Indian women in general. Most Indian women are still waiting for equality, and many are

Women on a Pilgrimage to Obtain Water for Their Households in Kutch, Gujarat. Although India's Constitution gurarantees women civil and political rights equal to those of men, traditional values and behavioral norms, evolving over thousands of years, have coalesced with lack of education and poverty to prevent many women from succeeding as individuals. AMAR TALWAR / FOTOMEDIA.

forced to live what may be considered subhuman lives. Working women have to face additional problems, owing to conflicts in their educational values and age-old socialization practice. Inequality affects not only the mental health and physical well-being of India's women, but also the well-being of their families and society at large.

As such, it is in the interest of humankind to protect women's rights as human rights. Addressing the World Congress of Women at Moscow in June 1987, Mikhail Gorbachev observed "The status of women is a barometer of the democratism of any state and an indicator of how human rights are respected in it." Fortunately, India has a rich tradition of vociferous women's movements and nongovernmental organizations sensitive to women's issues. The National Human Rights Commission and the National Commission for Women have been striving to promote and preserve women's rights as human rights in India. Both are statutory bodies. The National Human Rights Commission was established in 1993, with the power to investigate and recommend policy changes, punishment, and compensation in cases of human rights abuse (though it is prohibited by statute from directly investigating allegations of human rights abuses by the army and paramilitary forces). The National Commission for Women was constituted in 1992 to facilitate the redress of grievances and accelerate the socioeconomic development of women.

Both the government and nongovernmental organizations rely on active and positive support from the media to portray images consistent with the acknowledgment of girls and women as individuals capable of relating to other persons on the basis of mutual respect. Education is also playing an increasingly vital role in the mainstreaming and sensitization of a gender perspective of human rights in India, transforming notions of "men" and "women" into a broader view of humankind.

Asha Gupta

See also **Family Law and Cultural Pluralism; Human Rights; Women and Political Power; Women's Education**

BIBLIOGRAPHY

Agarwal, Bina. "The Idea of Gender Equality: From Legislative Vision to Everyday Family Practices." In *India: Another Millennium?*, edited by Romila Thapar. New Delhi: Viking, 2000.

Saksena, Anu. *Gender and Human Rights: Status of Women Workers in India*. Delhi: Shipra Publications, 2004.

GENERAL (NATIONAL) ELECTIONS

India's first "general election," as national elections are called in India, was held in 1952, following the adoption of India's independent democratic Constitution in 1950. The first election was a monumental event. A nationwide election based on adult franchise on such a scale had never been undertaken before. It required the recruitment of armies of election officers, thousands of ballot boxes, and hundreds of polling stations. Given the fact that some 80 percent of the adult voting population was illiterate at that time, parties and candidates were identified by pictures and symbols. There were some unusual and unexpected problems, such as a marauding tiger preventing some voters from getting to their poll booth, and paper rupees being stuffed in some ballot boxes by people who thought they were donation boxes. Overall, the first election ran smoothly. Since then, elections in India have been held regularly in accordance with constitutional requirements. By the end of 2004, fourteen general elections had been held: in 1952, 1957, 1962, 1967, 1971, 1977, 1980, 1984, 1989, 1991, 1996, 1998, 1999, and 2004.

Elections to the lower house of Parliament, known as the Lok Sabha (House of the People), are based on adult franchise and a direct vote. There are 545 seats in the Lok Sabha, of which all but two are subject to direct election. Those two seats are nominated by the president of India, on the advice of the prime minister, to include special minorities who may not otherwise be represented. National electoral constituencies are formed in accordance with population, giving more populous states more seats. Members of Parliament's upper house, the Rajya Sabha (Council of States) are elected indirectly by elected members of the Vidhan Sabhas (state legislatures), and through nominations by the president of India on the advice of the prime minister.

India's ruling government may call for the dissolution of Parliament and for new general elections to the Lok Sabha at any time after it takes office. However, the government cannot remain in power for more than five years

Congress Party Supporters. Their banner asserts, "Only the Congress Party can offer us a stable government," giving voice to the popular concern over the instability of various coalition or minority governments in India after 1989. INDIA TODAY.

and must call for new elections by the end of its fifth year in office. The Lok Sabha is then dissolved, and new national elections must take place. The ruling government may also fall if a majority of the members of Parliament pass a vote of "no confidence." This happened at the national level only once, in 1998, although state governments have frequently been dissolved by such votes, with members of the ruling state governments defecting to the opposition by walking across to the opposition benches. An antidefection law was adopted in 1985 as the 52nd Amendment to India's Constitution.

General Elections during the Nehru-Gandhi Dynasty, 1952–1977, 1979–1989

Between 1952 and 1989, the Congress Party under the "Nehru Dynasty" (prime ministers Jawaharlal Nehru, Indira Gandhi, and Rajiv Gandhi) dominated Indian elections, winning clear majorities in all national elections.

After Nehru's death in May 1964, the Congress Party government was briefly headed by Prime Minister Lal Bahadur Shastri, until his own sudden death in January 1966, the only time before the death of Rajiv Gandhi in 1991 that a non-Nehru family member formally led a Congress government.

Following India's defeat of Pakistani forces in East Pakistan in December 1971 in the war for an independent Bangladesh, Indira Gandhi led her party to an overwhelming victory against the divided opposition parties, gaining more than a two-thirds majority in the Lok Sabha. Her declaration of the "National Emergency" in June 1975 generated a strong reaction against her. In the March 1977 elections, Gandhi's Congress Party was defeated by a quickly forged coalition of parties called the Janata Party (People's Party), led by former Congress Party leader and finance minister Morarji Desai. Indira Gandhi's Congress won only 153 seats, 34.5 percent of the votes. The Janata Party was composed mainly of breakaway Congress Party groups, socialists, and members of the right-wing Hindu nationalist Jana Sangh. Infighting and factionalism among that motley group brought down the Janata government in 1980.

In the 1980 elections, the Congress Party, led by Gandhi, won 351 of the 539 seats contested in the 545-seat Lok Sabha. Following Gandhi's assassination in 1984, her son Rajiv Gandhi led the Congress Party to an overwhelming victory, securing 396 Lok Sabha seats, an unprecedented 49 percent of the votes. In the 1989 elections, the Congress Party won only 193 of the 525 seats contested.

The main opposition parties to the Congress Party were the earlier reincarnations of the Bharatiya Janata Party (BJP), namely, the Bharatiya Jan Sangh (until 1971) and the Bharatiya Lok Dal (until 1977); the Communist Party of India ; the breakaway Communist Party of India Marxist; the Swatantra Party; the Praja Socialist Party; and the Samyukta Socialist Party.

The Post-1989 Era of Coalition Politics and Governments

The defeat of Rajiv Gandhi's Congress Party in 1989 ushered in a decade of coalition and minority governments. The first of these, a coalition government called the National Front under Prime Minister V. P. Singh of the Janata Party (1989–1991), was followed by a minority Congress Party government under Prime Minister P. V. Narasimha Rao (1991–1996), and then by two short-lived minority United Front coalition governments under prime ministers H. K. Deve Gowda and I. K. Gujral (1996–January 1998). With no party obtaining a simple majority in the March 1998 elections, a coalition

government led by the BJP, under Prime Minister Atal Bihari Vajpayee, took office. A year later, in April 1999, the Vajpayee government fell, losing a vote of no confidence in Parliament by a single vote. The loss was caused when the All-India Anna Dravida Munnetra Kazhagam (AIADMK) party of Tamil Nadu, led by Jayalalitha Jayaraman, defected from the coalition. These weak and unstable governments contrasted sharply to the period from 1947 to 1989, when the Congress Party ruled with a clear majority of seats, except for a brief interval between 1977 and 1979. However, even during Congress Party majority rule, the party received less than 50 percent of the total votes, varying between 34.5 and 48.1 percent.

In the March 1998 elections, the Hindu nationalist BJP and its allies secured 252 seats in the 545-seat Lok Sabha, of which 179 were secured by the BJP. The Congress Party and its allies received 167 seats, including 141 by the Congress Party itself. The United Front secured 97 seats. Minor parties and nominations filled the remaining seats. Since 1998, the ability of BJP- or Congress Party–led coalitions to remain in power for the full five-year term has appeared tenuous. For example, after the BJP-led coalition took office in 1998, Tamil Nadu's AIADMK, led by Jayalalitha Jayaraman, continued to escalate its demands for cabinet posts and other privileges. The AIADMK won only 18 seats in parliament in 1998, compared to the BJP's 178, but its membership in the coalition was crucial for the BJP, giving Jayalalitha's AIADMK a disproportionate number of political offices and power.

Regional parties have assumed important roles in making or breaking the BJP- and Congress Party–led coalitions during this period. These include the Akali Dal, the Sikh party of Punjab; the Telugu Desam Party of Andhra Pradesh; the Dravida Munnetra Kazhagam (DMK) and AIADMK of Tamil Nadu; the National Conference of Jammu and Kashmir; the Asom Gana Parishad of Assam; and the Bahujan Samaj Party (BSP) of North India, a party of the Dalits (former "untouchable" castes).

Reversal of Fortunes: 1999 and 2004 General Elections

National elections were called by the ruling BJP coalition government in the spring of 2004, India's fourteenth general election since 1952. As in the previous elections in 1989, 1991, 1995, 1998, and 1999, no single party was able to claim a majority in the 2004 elections. This time, however, the coalition of parties led by the Congress Party and its leader, Sonia Gandhi, defeated the ruling coalition led by the BJP under Prime Minister Vajpayee.

The main allies of the Congress in the 2004 elections were the breakaway nationalist Congress Party, the AIADMK of Tamil Nadu, the Rashtriya Janata Dal, the Republican Party of India (primarily a Dalit party), the Kerala Congress, and the Muslim League of Kerala. Elected members from the Communist Party of India and and the Communist Party of India Marxist, classified under other parties, supported the Congress coalition in Parliament to keep it in power without being a formal part of the coalition. The main allies of the BJP were the Shiv Sena, the DMK, the Telugu Desam of Andhra Pradesh, the Akali Dal of Punjab, the Indian National Lok Dal, the Biju Lok Dal, the Samata Party, and the Lok Shakti.

The Congress Party, identified with Sonia Gandhi, is the political heir of the original Indian National Congress (INC), founded in 1888, which led India to independence. After the death of Nehru in 1964, and especially after his daughter Indira Gandhi took over as prime minister in 1966, factions within the Congress Party broke away to form separate parties. The split began with a rift between Prime Minister Indira Gandhi and the finance minister Morarji Desai, leading to two Congress parties, Congress (I) and Congress (O). Breakaway new Congress parties were, however, unable to claim the legacy of the original INC, which continued to be held by the Nehru-Gandhi family and its loyal supporters.

In 2004, Sonia Gandhi's INC contested 417 seats in the 545-seat Lok Sabha, winning 145 seats. The Congress coalition as a whole won 220 of the 428 seats that were subject to elections. The BJP, led by former prime minister A. B. Vajpayee, contested 334 seats and won 138. The BJP coalition as a whole won 185 seats. Independents and smaller parties won 137 seats.

In comparison, in the previous 1999 general elections, the BJP and its allies had won a majority of 298 seats, compared to 135 seats won by Congress and its allies. Independents and smaller parties won 137 seats in 1999. The 2004 general election was thus a surprising turnaround from the 1999 general election.

Reasons for the success of Congress and its left-wing supporting parties in 2004 have been attributed to the greater attention it paid to the rural poor compared to the BJP, which trumpeted the success of its high tech revolution that largely benefited a rising Indian middle class, variously estimated at between 15 and 30 percent of the population. The Nehru-Gandhi mystique and the popular image of Sonia Gandhi among the masses, a white woman in a white sari and a red *tilak* on her forehead, along with the campaign conducted by her children, Rahul Gandhi and Priyanka Gandhi Vadra, played an important role in the success of the Congress coalition. The defeat of the BJP has also been attributed to its promotion of a hardline Hindu nationalist ideology, which alienated the religious minorities of India (20 percent of the population), especially Muslims and Christians. The Akali Dal, the minority Sikh party of Punjab, was allied with the BJP. Additionally, the BJP's high caste Hindu image and its alliance with the more extreme Shiv Sena and its nonparty affiliates, the Vishwa Hindu Parishad and the Rashtriya Swayamsevak Sangh (RSS), alienated much of the Dalit populace. The Dalits, the former "untouchable castes" also known as the Scheduled Castes, may constitute as much as 25 percent of the population, and have remained outside the caste-based Hindu fold, from which they have been excluded for two millennia.

Until the electoral campaign of early 1998, the BJP and other more radical Hindu parties, especially the Shiv Sena, argued for the rejection of the secular ideals of Nehru's Congress Party, which are also espoused by most other Indian parties, including the Janata Dal, the Samajwadi Party, the two main factions of the Communist Party, and the regional parties in the south (the Tamil Maanila Congress and the two factions of the DMK of Tamil Nadu, and the Telugu Desam of Andhra Pradesh). The secularism of all of these parties have now come to represent the equality of all religions in practice, rather than the Western concept of the separation of church and state. On the other hand, the Hindu nationalists represented in the BJP—the Shiv Sena, the RSS (an unarmed paramilitary Hindu nationalist affiliate of the BJP), the Bajrang Dal, and another nonparty organization called the Vishwa Hindu Parishad (VHP)—wish to establish India as a Hindu state under the political banner of "Hindutva." The more benign version of the relatively more moderate BJP's Hindutva would be a broad Hindu Weltanschauung, of which other religious groups would also be a part. The VHP and RSS, and the more extreme elements of the BJP and the Shiv Sena, however, have talked of marginalizing or even Hinduizing all of India's minorities.

In early 1998, with the BJP on the threshold of gaining even more seats in the Lok Sahba and possibly forming the next government itself, the party moved even more toward the secular ideology of the other parties. Indeed, the BJP's main leader and designated shadow prime minister, Vajpayee, publicly declared in January 1998 that a BJP government would retain India's secular Constitution and would continue to implement the secular policies of previous governments. Such reassurances were further reinforced by statements from L. K. Advani, who subsequently became the home minister and deputy prime minister in the BJP government.

Even the more radical Hindu party, the Shiv Sena, called for reconciliation between Hindus and Muslims. As a symbol of this new move, the ultranationalist Hindu leader of the Shiv Sena, Bal Thackeray, went further by calling for the erection of a Hindu-Muslim monument at Ayodhya, where the fifteenth-century mosque of the Mughal emperor Babur had been demolished by Hindu mobs in December 1992, triggering widespread Hindu-Muslim rioting and killing. In making this ideological shift, the BJP and its main ally, the Shiv Sena, were able to draw some Congress Party members to their fold, as well as members from other secular regional parties. There are at least two reasons for this ideological shift on the part of the BJP and the Shiv Sena. Unlike the earlier Hindu Mahasabha (banned after one of its members assassinated Mahatma Gandhi), and its successor, the Jana Sangha, from which the BJP originated, the BJP has learned that an avowedly Hindu nationalist platform causes fear and adverse reactions among India's Muslim minority of 120 million, as well as among the other 50 million Christian and Sikh minorities. Secessionist violence in Kashmir, Punjab, and the Christian tribal states of the northeastern region could also be aggravated.

Additionally, the emphasis on Hindu nationalism in Hindi-speaking North India has not generated support from the Dravidian states in the South—Tamil Nadu, Andhra Pradesh, Karnataka, and Kerala—which constitute about 20 percent of India's population. More importantly, the image of Hindu nationalism represented by upper caste Hindus has alienated the Dalits and the other "backward castes" (the lower caste Shudras), who constitute together about 70 percent of the Hindu population (about 55 percent of the Indian population). Without support from these groups, the BJP would have difficulty obtaining an electoral majority in the Lok Sabha—the main reason they were a marginal party for decades until the 1990s. Democracy in India has, in fact, reversed the power of the Hindu caste hierarchy, with Brahmans carrying the least number of electoral votes, less than 5 percent.

Raju G. C. Thomas

See also **Advani, Lal Krishna; Ayodhya; Bharatiya Janata Party (BJP); Congress Party; Gandhi, Indira; Gandhi, Rajiv; Gandhi, Sonia; Hindu Nationalist Parties; Hindutva and Politics; Shiv Sena; Vajpayee, Atal Bihari; Vishwa Hindu Parishad (VHP)**

BIBLIOGRAPHY

Baxter, Craig, Yogendra K. Malik, Charles H. Kennedy, and Robert C. Oberst. *Government and Politics in South Asia.* 5th ed. Boulder, Colo.: Westview Press, 2002.

Chibber, Pradeep K. *Democracy without Associations: Transformations of the Party System and Social Cleavages in India.* Ann Arbor: University of Michigan Press, 1999.

Frankel, Francine R., et al., eds. *Transforming India: Social Dynamics of Democracy.* Delhi: Oxford University Press, 1999.

Hardgrave, Robert, and Stanley A. Kochanek. *India: Government and Politics in a Developing Nation.* 6th ed. Orlando, Fla.: Harcourt College Publishers, 2000.

"Indian Elections, 2004." Available at <http://www.indian-elections.com>

Kohli, Atul. *Democracy and Discontent: India's Growing Crisis of Government.* Cambridge, U.K.: Cambridge University Press, 1990.

Singh, V. B., and Shankar Bose. *Elections in India: Data Handbook on Lok Sabha Elections, 1952–1985.* New Delhi: Sage, 1986.

Sisson, Richard, and Ramashray Roy, eds. *Diversity and Dominance in Indian Politics.* 2 vols. New Delhi: Sage, 1990.

Thomas, Raju G. C. *India Files.* London: Jane's Information Country Reports, 1996–2001.

GEOGRAPHY Although the spatial connotations of the name "India" have varied substantially over time, this article will consider the components of the region included within the British Indian empire just prior to its partition in 1947, that is, the present republics of India, Pakistan, and Bangladesh, plus the small neighboring states of Ceylon (now Sri Lanka), the republic of the Maldives, and the former British protectorates of Nepal and Bhutan. Excluded from this purview will be Burma (now Myanmar), all or parts of which were included within the Indian empire between 1824 and 1937, and Afghanistan, a British quasi-protectorate from 1880 to 1919. The total area being considered comes to just over 2 million square miles (5.12 million sq. km). In latitude, the region extends from roughly 37° 5′ north, near the meeting point of the borders of Afghanistan, China, and the disputed state of Kashmir, south to 8° 3′ north, at Kanyakumari (Cape Comorin), the southern extremity of the Indian mainland, or 0° 40′ south at the southernmost Maldivian atoll. The region's longitudinal extent is from 60° 24′ east, at the westernmost point of the Pakistani province of Baluchistan, to 91° 27′ east near the point of convergence of the borders of the Indian state of Arunachal Pradesh, China, and Myanmar.

In respect to both physical and human geography, the area we shall be considering is exceedingly varied, more so than the whole of Europe. In this essay we shall limit our discussion to a consideration of its landforms and their associated land uses, other aspects of physical geography, economic geography, and settlement patterns. For discussions of historical, political and social geography, including such important topics as administrative structure, religion, language and caste, readers should refer to appropriate articles elsewhere in this work.

Terrain Regions and Associated Land Use

The region is conventionally divided into three main physical divisions: the northern mountain wall, the Indo-Gangetic Plain, and the so-called peninsular massif, including Sri Lanka and several island groups in the Indian Ocean. The northern mountain wall extends from the shores of the Arabian Sea northeastward through much of Pakistan to that country's northern border with Afghanistan; then in a southeasterly and easterly direction through northern India, Nepal, and Bhutan, along or in close proximity to the border of China; and finally, roughly southwestward along the border between India and Bangladesh on the west and Myanmar on the east, to the Bay of Bengal. Thus, it forms a barrier that largely isolates the region from the rest of Eurasia, giving rise to the concept of a distinct Indian subcontinent. This isolation gives the region a distinct climatic regime, as well as distinctive fauna and flora, and has served throughout history to limit interaction between its inhabitants and those of neighboring lands.

The northern mountain wall.
The northern mountain wall consists of numerous mountain ranges of relatively recent geological origin and also includes several distinctive intermontane vales. The principal mountain range, the greater Himalayas, forms a great arc, roughly 1,500 miles (2,400 km) long, occupying the central portion of the border region. A number of its peaks exceed 25,000 feet (7,750 m). Among these, on Nepal's border with the Xizang (Tibetan) Autonomous Region of China, is Mount Everest, the world's highest summit, at 29,028 feet (8,848 m). Several ranges run parallel to and south of the greater Himalayas. These include the lesser Himalayas and the much lower Siwaliks, fronting on the Indo-Gangetic Plain. Toward their western limit in Kashmir, the Himalayas are roughly paralleled also by several ranges to their north. The most prominent of these, running along the border with the Xinjiang Uygur (Sinkiang) Autonomous Region of China, is the Karakoram Range, whose tallest peak, K2 (Mt. Godwin Austin) is among a cluster of closely grouped summits rivaling those of the Himalayas in elevation. In both the Karakorams and the Himalayas, glaciers are prominent. Those of the former range are the largest in the world outside the polar regions. The principal vales within the Himalayan system are those of Kashmir and Nepal, each exceedingly fertile and constituting the hearth of a distinctive and enduring culture. Natural vegetation and land use within the Himalayan region varies greatly. Deforestation is a major ecological problem. The density of the forest cover tends to decrease from east to west; windward slopes are much more heavily wooded than leeward slopes; and altitude exercises a major climatic control analogous to the influence of latitude at lower elevations. Terraced agriculture is common at elevations up to 8,000 feet (2,400 m), and pastoral activity occurs at many levels.

The mountains extending along Pakistan's boundary with Afghanistan and covering much the greater part of the province of Baluchistan are arrayed in numerous discontinuous chains. Wildly jagged and mainly barren in aspect, they include relatively few peaks in excess of 10,000 feet (3,000 m). Among the more prominent ranges (proceeding from north to south) are the Safed-i-Koh, the Sulaimans, the Kirthar Range, and, along the Arabian Sea coast, the Makran Range. Between the ranges, especially in the southwest, are numerous arid depressions, while cutting through the mountains farther north are several fabled passes, most notably the Khyber, Kurram, and Bolan, through which streams of invaders from Central Asia intermittently made their way into the subcontinent. Agriculture in this region is scant and dependent on several forms of irrigation, including *karez*, ingenious gravity-controlled tunnel systems. Pastoral activities also engage much of the largely tribal and nomadic population, many of whom—when political conditions permit—travel hundreds of miles between summer and winter pasturelands in Afghanistan and Pakistan.

The ranges forming the eastern segment of the northern mountain wall also consist of numerous discontinuous chains, few of which are much more than a hundred miles in length. Summits range from more than 15,000 feet (4,500 m) in the north to less than 5,000 feet in the south. While less jagged than the mountains of the west, their dense vegetative cover, torrential streams, endemic diseases, and, in former times, head-hunting inhabitants severely inhibited passage through the frontier region. The area forms the home of a host of tribal groups, who still mainly practice shifting slash-and-burn agriculture, supplemented by hunting, fishing, and gathering. Increasingly, however, these groups are turning toward more sedentary forms of cultivation.

The Indo-Gangetic Plain.
Immediately south of the northern mountain wall lies the Indo-Gangetic Plain, the world's largest continuous expanse of alluvial (river-deposited) soil. This plain extends with no perceptible break from the Arabian Sea to the Bay of Bengal. In the west it is watered by the Indus and its five main tributaries, the Chenab, Jhelum, Ravi, Beas, and Sutlej (from west to east). These rivers all drain into Pakistan from areas held by India (largely from the disputed state of Jammu and Kashmir). When the 1947 partition interposed an

international boundary within the Indus drainage basin, a major problem arose over water allocation. This issue was largely resolved, however, by the 1960 Indus Waters Treaty, whereby all the water of the three western rivers was allocated to Pakistan, while that of the Ravi, Sutlej, and Beas went to India. To make this division work, it was necessary to build new canals within Pakistan to link the western to the eastern rivers, thereby establishing the world's greatest integrated irrigation system.

Most of the Indian portion of the plain is watered by the Ganges (Ganga) and its tributaries, chief among which are the Yamuna, a right-bank tributary, and (from west to east) the Ghaghara, Gandak, and Kosi, all left-bank tributaries. These all emanate from the Himalayas and have relatively even year-round flows, whereas the Chambal, Ken, and Son rivers, flowing out of the peninsular massif, have very uneven regimes with maximum flows during the summer (wet monsoon) season. In the far east, the plain extends along the course of the mighty Brahmaputra, the flow of which far exceeds that of the Ganges. The Ganges and Brahmaputra systems converge in what is now Bangladesh to form an enormous delta, which is exceedingly prone to devastating floods from high river levels and surges of ocean water from tropical cyclones in the Bay of Bengal.

With maximum elevations lower than a thousand feet (300 m) above sea level, the average slope of the plain is less than one foot per mile. The inhabitants of the plain, especially in its upper reaches, distinguish between terraces of old alluvium (*bhangar*) and riverine tracts of new alluvium (*khadar*), often several tens of feet lower. The *khadar* tracts are more prone to flooding in the summer high-water season and tend to be more fertile than the *bhangar*; but, as modern canal irrigation is located mainly on the latter, the initial advantage enjoyed by the *khadar* has largely been reversed. Additionally, much irrigation comes from deep, mechanized tube wells tapping the vast reserves of groundwater found throughout the plain.

Virtually all of the Indo-Gangetic Plain is intensively cultivated. Over much of Bangladesh, rural population densities exceed 2,000 per square mile (roughly 800 per sq. km), higher than in any other predominantly rural region of the world, while densities of more than a thousand per square mile are found in many other plains localities. The plain thus supports nearly two-fifths the total population of India, more than four-fifths that of Pakistan, almost all that of Bangladesh, and roughly half that of the subcontinent as a whole. Two, or even three, crops per year are possible in well-watered regions. Little remains of the original vegetative cover, but villagers maintain groves of trees for fruit, shade, and firewood.

Straddling the Indo-Pakistani border is the Thar Desert, most of which, from a topographic perspective, may be considered an extension of the Indo-Gangetic Plain, despite the protrusion through the largely wind-deposited soils of numerous starkly dramatic hilly outliers of the peninsular massif. The area supports a mixed agricultural and pastoral economy and somehow sustains population densities that would be unimaginable in comparable environments in other parts of the world.

The peninsular massif. The peninsular massif, an area of great geological antiquity, is a remnant of the vast former southern continent of Gondwanaland. It comprises a portion of the Indo-Australian tectonic plate, the northern flank of which (now covered by the alluvium of the Indo-Gangetic Plain) collided with and subsided below the northern Eurasian plate to force the rising of the Himalayas and adjoining mountain ranges. The massif includes a highly variegated assemblage of plateaus, worn-down mountain ranges, escarpments, interior basins, and riverine plains, as well as a relatively narrow west coastal plain and a somewhat wider coastal plain to the east.

In its northern reaches, between the east-west trending Vindhya Range (actually a south-facing escarpment), the drainage of the massif is mainly to the northeast. Just south of the Vindhyas lie the west flowing Narmada and Tapti Rivers. Further south, virtually all rivers of any consequence—including (from north to south) the Godavari, Krishna, Tunghabhadra, Penner, and Kaveri—flow eastward from crests close to the Arabian Sea to the Bay of Bengal. Prominent among the highlands of the massif are the Western Ghats, a long, imposing, west-facing, fault-line escarpment terminating southward in the Nilgiri Hills. Just south of the Nilgiris lies the Palghat, the principal pass between the east and west coastal plains and, in the far south, the Palni and Cardamom Hills. These southern hill ranges contain summits surpassing 8,000 feet (2,400 m), the highest in peninsular India. Elsewhere, few elevations reach even half that altitude. The so-called Eastern Ghats (a toponymic invention of British geographers) are actually a discontinuous series of highlands more or less parallel to the coast of the Bay of Bengal. The northeastern portion of the massif, an area known as the Chhota Nagpur, is a complex hill and plateau region that is still largely forested and the home of numerous tribal peoples. As it happens also to be a highly mineralized region, containing the best and most abundant coal and iron ore resources in India, it is now undergoing rapid industrialization and has become an area of substantial immigration. Forming the northwest edge of the massif, bordering the Thar Desert, are the Aravalli Mountains, on whose craggy summits are situated many of India's most striking hill forts. Though now militarily useless, they provide a source of substantial tourist revenue.

Vegetative cover, soils, and agricultural land use in the peninsular massif are no less varied than the terrain. Forested tracts are, for the most part, small and largely degraded as a result of repeated clearing, often by fire, for agriculture and other purposes. Although soils are generally poor in interior locations, those derived from the basaltic rocks underlying a large western tract known as the Deccan Lava Plateau are relatively rich. So, too, are the alluvial soils along the courses of the major rivers and the largely deltaic soils of the two coastal plains. The intensity of agriculture and the resultant rural population densities depend mainly on soil fertility and rainfall, though irrigation by canals, tube wells, and tanks also plays a major role in determining agricultural productivity. The southern highlands are major areas of plantation agriculture.

The physical geography and land use of Sri Lanka largely mimic the patterns found in the southern peninsular portion of India. To the west of Sri Lanka lie the Maldives, a group of tropical atolls now comprising an independent republic. The Laccadive Islands, a union territory of India, form a similar island group to their north. Finally, in the Bay of Bengal, closer to Myanmar than to the Indian mainland, are the little developed, largely tribal Andaman and Nicobar Islands, which also comprise an Indian union territory.

Climate

No less than terrain, climate profoundly impacts the livelihood and lifestyles of the peoples of the region. Its dominant aspect, the monsoon regime, is more pronounced here than in any other part of the world. The temperature, wind, moisture, and rainfall patterns associated with this regime combine to produce three seasons: a hot, dry season from about March to mid-June; a hot, wet season from about mid-June to the end of September; and a relatively cool, dry season from early October to February. These are modal conditions; the actual duration of the three periods will vary not only from one part of the region to another, but also from year to year.

From March to mid-June, the temperature difference between the Indian Ocean and the more rapidly heating subcontinent becomes increasingly great, and a system of low atmospheric pressure becomes well established over the latter region. Increasingly steady landward winds bring considerable humidity, but little rain, to most of the region, creating a dusty period of steadily increasing discomfort and physiological stress.

Around late June the jet stream, a fast-moving current of air flowing eastward at altitudes of 25,000 to 35,000 feet (7,625 m–10,675 m), typically shifts from a position just south of the Himalayas to a path several hundred miles farther north, beyond the Tibetan Plateau. This shift usually occurs within a short time span and generates a rapid inflow of moisture-laden air, usually accompanied by torrential downpours. This phenomenon, known as the "burst of the monsoon," marks the onset of the so-called wet or southwest monsoon season. Despite its simplified directional name, the general flow of monsoon air is actually in two branches, one blowing eastward from the Arabian Sea across the west coast of India, and another northward from the Bay of Bengal. Monsoon rains are then produced in several ways, all involving the rising of air and its resultant cooling below the dew point, the temperature at which atmospheric saturation occurs: (a) when air streams are forced upward by intervening highlands such as the Western Ghats or the Himalayas, (b) when fronts form due to the confluence of the two main air streams, and (c) when the diurnal heating of the atmosphere causes sufficient upward convectional flow. Conversely, where monsoon winds cross highland barriers and descend their leeward slopes, the air masses heat up and increase their moisture-bearing capacity. This results in relatively dry "rain-shadow" conditions. The dry belt just east of the Western Ghats is the most prominent area exemplifying this phenomenon.

In the cool, dry season, that of the so-called northeast monsoon, the prevailing wind pattern is essentially reversed. As the Eurasian land mass cools, atmospheric pressures over the much warmer Indian Ocean become lower than those on the continent, and the flow of dry air is mainly from the northeast and from land to sea. Additionally, the desiccating effect is enhanced because of the descending flow of air from the Tibetan Plateau and the subcontinent's northern mountain rim onto the relatively low-lying terrain to the south.

Over most of the subcontinent, some two-thirds to four-fifths of the total rainfall is registered in the wet season. Total annual precipitation varies from around 450 inches (over 11 m) at Cherrapunji in the Khasi Hills (Shillong Plateau), lying directly in the path of the eastern branch of the monsoon in northeast India, to as little as 5 inches in the heart of the Thar Desert. But on the plains of India and Bangladesh, rainfall exceeds 100 inches (roughly 2.5 m) in only a few small areas.

Coastal areas experience monsoon rains as much as two months earlier than do deep interior locations and the length and intensity of their monsoon season is commensurately greater. Apart from this broad generalization, details of the pattern of rainfall vary greatly in relation to local topography, in respect to both elevation and the orientation of highlands and coasts relative to the paths of prevailing winds. Southeastern India and eastern Sri Lanka, for example, are exceptional in experiencing maximum rainfall during the period from October to December, because the initially dry winds of the northeast monsoon pick up moisture as they cross the Bay of Bengal and then lose it as they blow across these areas. Another area departing from the general seasonal regime is a belt along the southern flank of the northern mountain wall, which experiences the tail-end effects of winter storm systems moving eastward from the Mediterranean Basin.

The monsoons play a pivotal role in agriculture. Their substantial year-to-year variability in terms of timing and total precipitation makes for considerable uncertainty in crop yield. As a rule, the greater the average precipitation, the more dependable the rainfall, but few areas are totally free from the prospect of drought. Devastating tropical cyclones, which are most common along the northern shores of the Bay of Bengal, constitute yet another major climatic hazard.

Temperatures over most of the region generally peak in late May or early June, just prior to the cooling downpours of the southwest monsoon. A secondary maximum is often experienced in September or October, when precipitation wanes. In the northwest, where total annual rainfall is low, July is usually the warmest month. Temperature ranges tend to increase with distance from the coast and also with latitude. The difference between the mean temperature of the coolest and warmest months in Sri Lanka or near the southern tip of India, for example, fluctuates by no more than a few degrees around the annual mean of 80°F (27°C). In marked contrast to these marine conditions is the continental regime of Punjab. In Lahore, for example, the mean daily high temperature in late June is 104°F (40°C), while the mean daily low in January is only 39°F (4°C). Freezing temperatures, however, are rare on the northern plains and are virtually unknown on the peninsular massif. Temperatures are moderated substantially in highland locations, with many mountain towns, especially in the Himalayas, serving as "hill stations," where those who can afford to do so may escape the scorching heat of the plains.

Natural Vegetation and Fauna

Over the ages, some four-fifths of the forests that once blanketed the greater part of the region have been removed to make way for agriculture and for other uses. As in the past, however, the remaining natural vegetation reflects the distribution of rainfall. Areas of high precipitation (over 80 or so inches, or roughly 2 m) are marked by tropical, broad-leaved evergreen forests, a larger proportion of which survive than in forests in drier areas that are easier to clear. With increasingly dry conditions, one encounters scattered stands of mixed forests, partially

evergreen and partially deciduous. Forests in nonmountainous areas with less than 40 inches (101 cm) of rainfall are entirely deciduous. Still drier climates are characterized successively by open scrub, or *jangal*, then grassland, and ultimately scrubby desert vegetation. Coniferous forests are confined to the northern mountain rim. Many of the region's 17,000 or so flowering species are found only in the subcontinent.

The subcontinent, along with most of Southeast Asia, forms a major part of the highly diverse Oriental or Indian zoogeographic province. Among its characteristic primates are the rhesus monkey and Hanuman langur. Its carnivores include tigers, leopards, and lions (confined to the Gir Forest in the Kathiawar Peninsula), mongooses, jackals, and foxes. Wild herds of elephants survive in several protected areas, as does the Indian rhinoceros. Other mega-fauna include several species of deer and wild bison. Among the more than 1,200 species of birds are herons, storks, ibis, flamingos, and cranes. Reptiles include crocodiles, gavials and cobras, pythons, and nearly 400 other species of snakes, many of which are poisonous. The variety of fish, insects, and other forms of animal life is exceedingly great.

Economic Geography and Settlement Pattern

Agriculture, forestry, and fishing. Despite sweeping economic changes since independence, agriculture, including animal husbandry, remains the predominant occupation in almost all parts of South Asia, accounting for about three-fourths of the labor force in Nepal, two-thirds in Bangladesh, three-fifths in India, half in Pakistan, and one-third in Sri Lanka. In all those countries its impress on the landscape is pervasive and profound. The scale of most operations, however, is quite small (except in parts of Pakistan and several plantation areas). Moreover, as per capita returns from agriculture are much less than in other sectors of the economy, the proportions of the gross national product derived from that sector are less than one-fourth the total in all of the countries named, except Nepal. The forms of agriculture and the combinations of crops and livestock vary enormously throughout the region, depending on climate, irrigation, soil type, proximity to urban markets and ports, culture and other factors. Staple crops, especially grains, account for a substantial majority of the total area sown. Other staples include a wide variety of pulses, such as gram (chickpeas), lentils, and peanuts. Potatoes are a major crop in the Himalayan region and, because of improved storage facilities, have become increasingly important on the Gangetic Plain as well.

Over most of the subcontinent, farmers recognize two growing seasons: the *kharif* season, in which crops mature over the wet monsoon months, and the *rabi* season, in which crops mature more slowly during the cool season and are harvested after the initial summer rains, or earlier if irrigation permits. In very wet areas, including parts of Bangladesh and Assam, three crops per year may be possible. Rice is almost always the principal staple crop where there is sufficient rainfall, in that it yields more calories per unit area than any other grain. Annual rainfall of 80 or more inches of rain will permit the cultivation of two crops of rice. With 40 to 80 inches (101–202 cm), farmers will typically seek to produce a summer crop of rice and a winter crop of wheat, pulses, or vegetables. Somewhat drier areas will grow mainly wheat, almost always as a *rabi* crop, with gram or vegetables in the *kharif* season. Generally, 15 to 20 inches (38–50 cm) of rain will suffice for a single crop of wheat. Where soils are poor, however, sorghum (*jawar*) and various millets (*bajra, ragi*, etc.) are likely to take the place of wheat. Maize is grown mainly in hilly and mountainous areas, especially in the northern mountain regions. Intertillage of grains, other than rice, with pulses is common.

Livestock occupy a very important place in the region's agriculture. Cattle (largely of the distinctive zebu breed) and buffalo are numerous and are utilized as draft animals, for milking, as providers of leather, and as sources of fertilizer. Goats and sheep are also multipurpose animals. Camels, horses, and donkeys serve mainly as beasts of burden, as do yaks and *dzo* (yak-cattle hybrids) at high elevations in the Himalayas. Per capita consumption of meat, however, is quite low. Other sources of animal protein include milk (production of which has increased enormously in recent decades), eggs, and fish. Fish are derived from both marine and freshwater sources and, increasingly, from aquaculture in flooded rice paddies.

Many areas of the subcontinent specialize in the cultivation of nonstaple crops. The foremost of these is cotton, the chief cash crop in much of both Indian and Pakistani Punjab, much of the interior of Maharashtra, and parts of Gujarat. Jute is a major fiber crop in much of Bangladesh and parts of West Bengal, Bihar, and Assam. Sugar is very widely cultivated in small quantities, and forms a major specialty crop over much of western Uttar Pradesh, Indian and Pakistani Punjab, and the leeward slopes of the Western Ghats. Tobacco is especially important in the delta regions of Andhra Pradesh.

Tree crops, which vary greatly throughout the region, include mangoes, oranges, and other citrus species. Coconuts, which provide food, vegetable oil, fiber, fuel, and building material, are of particular importance in the Indian state of Kerala and in Sri Lanka. Other useful palm species include the palmyra (sugar palm), areca (betel palm), and dates. Kashmir and other mountain regions are sources of apples and other temperate fruits.

Plantation cultivation is restricted to only a few relatively small areas. Unlike most agriculture in South Asia, it involves large-scale, highly capitalized corporate enterprises and employs large gangs of mainly immigrant labor. The chief plantation crop, by far, is tea. Neatly manicured tea plantations cover much of the highlands of Sri Lanka, which has surpassed India as the world's leading tea exporter. They also occupy similar terrain in the Indian states of Kerala and Tamil Nadu and are important along the lower flanks of mountains in West Bengal and Assam, as well as in northern Bangladesh. Coffee is grown in Sri Lanka, Kerala, and Karnataka, at elevations lower than those favored for tea, and rubber plantations are found at still lower elevations in Sri Lanka and Kerala.

Commercial and subsistence forestry are practiced in many scattered localities, mainly where rugged terrain makes cultivation impracticable. Among the many timber species, teak (sometimes grown on plantations) and sal are most prominent, while highly priced sandalwood and rosewood are also important. Pines and other conifers are extensively cut for timber in the western Himalayan region. Bamboo and a great variety of wild species are gathered as building materials and for fuel and other purposes.

Nonagricultural rural activities. Throughout recorded history, agriculture has been supplemented by a wide range of ancillary activities that, in the context of regional socioeconomic systems, have been carried out largely by members of occupationally specialized castes, such as weavers, potters, carpenters, well diggers, leather workers, traders, and so on. Muslims and followers of other faiths in rural India were also integrated within this hereditary system, in which services rendered were compensated by payments in grain or other goods, rather than by cash. Over the past century or more, with the increasing commercialization of agriculture and the supplanting of craft-made goods by the products of modern factories, this system has been greatly eroded and in some areas has virtually ceased to exist. Nevertheless, many traditional occupations continue to be pursued, often precariously, by particular castes, though increasingly within a market-based nexus.

A characteristic feature of rural India is the periodic market (*hat*) to which households resort to obtain goods that are typically not available in most villages: spices, cooking oils, brassware, bangles, saris, textiles, tools, and so forth. Most such markets occur on a particular day of the week and are served largely by itinerant merchants, craft specialists, and local hawkers of agricultural produce.

There are also larger, more widely scattered seasonal markets, often associated with the observance of religious festivals (*melas*), at which a broader range of goods and services may be procured. Entertainers, astrologers, medical practitioners and, nowadays, government-sponsored purveyors of useful information (e.g., on family planning) are prominent actors at such venues. Apart from the periodic markets, there are thousands of small market towns (*mandis*), combining both wholesale and retail functions for the surrounding countryside. Their importance has grown greatly with the commercialization of agriculture in recent decades; and many such towns are also centers for the provision an expanding array of administrative, educational and medical services.

Rural settlement pattern. In contrast to the United States, almost all cultivators in the region reside in agglomerated settlements that vary in size from hamlets of only a dozen or so households to large villages with 5,000 or more inhabitants. A substantial majority, however, live in villages ranging in population from 500 to 2,500. Most villages are of an irregular shape, growing outward, with no predetermined plan, from an initial nuclear locality. Within almost all villages there is a high degree of residential segregation by both religion and caste. In general, households of the higher castes and those of the caste that initially settled the village will occupy the central portion of the village, while lower castes and (in India) Muslim groups will occupy peripheral locations. The degree of segregation of the low-ranking castes, especially those formerly held to be untouchable, may be such as to consign them to separate tributary hamlets, which may be as much as a half-mile distant from the main village settlement.

Within the village, lanes and alleys between houses are typically narrow and winding, often terminating in dead ends. Most houses are built mainly of dried mud mixed with straw and smoothed on the exterior with a cow dung and mud paste; but those of more affluent households are typically made of brick or, in some regions, even of stone. In northeastern India and Bangladesh, bamboo and various types of reeds may replace mud as a construction material. Wood is sparingly used, largely for roofing beams and doorframes. Roofs are generally flat in relatively dry areas and peaked in wetter areas, with increasingly steep slopes in areas of greater precipitation. Houses of poor families typically have roofs of mud or straw (made from the stalks of rice and other grains, or from reeds), whereas those of wealthier households will most likely be of sun-baked tile. Detailed study will reveal great regional differences in vernacular forms of domestic architecture. Also varying greatly is the exterior décor of housing and the designs made on the floors of courtyards, the production of which is largely in the hands of women.

Houses typically accommodate both humans and livestock and include spaces for storing provisions for both. Granaries, however, are frequently built as separate, adjacent structures. Living space is generally scanty and furniture and other household furnishings are sparse. Many houses have a small area set aside for family worship.

While some settlements are wholly residential, most contain a variety of structures given over in whole or part to specialized functions: temples, mosques, schools, the offices of the *panchayat* (village council) and/or cooperative, shops, and small handicraft enterprises. Open spaces, facilitating social intercourse, are found mainly at or in close proximity to public buildings, the homes of major land owners, threshing floors, and large, widely shared wells. Village groves are also commonly situated near such wells.

In general, villages tend to be more compact in the north and west of the subcontinent than in the east and south, as well as more inward-oriented. That is, individual houses form parts of high-walled compounds, the inhabitants of which all belong to the same caste or other ethnic group and are likely to be related to one another by birth or marriage. Windows to the street are either altogether lacking or tend to be small and barred, while within the compound houses open onto interior courtyards. This arrangement facilitates the exclusion of women from public view. Toward the south and east, rural settlements tend to be more open. Spaces between houses are greater and the proportion of the population living in exterior hamlets increases.

Some regions display marked variations from the foregoing generalizations, In Tamil Nadu, some adjacent areas, and the Kathiawar Peninsula of Gujarat, for example, villages tend to be laid out on a grid pattern, which is thought by some scholars to provide a link to the supposed Dravidian founders of the ancient Indus civilization. Over most of Bangladesh and coastal Kerala rural dwellers live mainly in isolated households, rather than in village agglomerations; but, given the dense populations of those areas, few households there would be out of shouting distance from their nearest neighbors. In many tribal regions, especially in northeastern India, small hamlets, rather than proper villages, are the norm and houses are laid out on either side of a single village lane. Hamlets are also common in mountainous regions in which it is difficult to find large areas of terrain flat enough for the building of larger settlements.

Mineral resources, mining, hydroelectric power, and industry. India is well endowed with a wide range of mineral resources, whereas the other countries of South Asia are relatively mineral poor. Among India's resources are abundant and widespread reserves of coal, mostly bituminous; widespread, and largely high-grade, iron ore deposits; a wealth of minerals used as ferro-alloys, especially manganese; substantial quantities of bauxite, used in the manufacture of aluminum; modest supplies of copper, lead, zinc, antimony, silver, and gold; a variety of precious and semiprecious gemstones; and an abundance of such ordinary, low-value (per unit of weight) minerals as ceramic clays, refractories (for use in smelting furnaces), limestone, rock phosphate, and building stone. The chief area of concentration of mineral products is the Chhota Nagpur, but many other portions of the peninsular massif contain locales of significant mineral production.

India's coal reserves are among the greatest in the world, though the amount of coking coal, suitable for use in metallurgical industries, is limited. Thermal energy from coal-fired plants is the principal means of meeting the country's energy needs. The most important mines, those of the Jharia-Raniganj Field, near the northeastern edge of the Chhota Nagpur, provide coal of good coking quality. Their location, near major sources of iron ore, has led to a concentration of the iron and steel industry in this region. Uranium is also produced in the Chhota Nagpur and helps sustain the country's five nuclear reactors. Nuclear power, however, accounts for only a small fraction of India's total energy output.

India's most serious energy deficiency is that of petroleum and natural gas. Although production from fields in eastern Assam (the first to be developed), Gujarat, and the "Bombay High" (off the coast of Maharashtra) has grown rapidly, growth in demand has also been rapid. Hence, Indian petroleum production seldom exceeds 30 to 40 percent of its needs. Natural gas supplements petroleum as an energy source to only a modest degree.

Hydroelectric installations are very widespread in India and are largely associated with multipurpose river basin development plans that include irrigation, navigation, and recreation. In all, they provide approximately a sixth of all the electric power consumed in India.

Mineral resources in South Asian countries other than India include modest supplies of petroleum, natural gas, and coal, as well as a variety of minerals needed for chemical industries and construction in Pakistan; some natural gas and a little coal in Bangladesh; and various gemstones in Sri Lanka. Hydroelectricity is well developed in both Pakistan and Sri Lanka, to meet domestic needs, and in Nepal, mainly for export to India, the source of the engineering expertise for their construction. Modern developments notwithstanding, throughout South Asia firewood, cow dung, and other traditional organic sources continue to be major providers of energy in the rural economy.

Beginning with cotton milling in the mid-nineteenth century, the industrial revolution has largely transformed the traditional way of life for a substantial fraction of the population of South Asia and has significantly impacted all but the most remote of areas. Among modern manufacturing enterprises, the most ubiquitous are those related to the processing of agricultural goods and the weaving and processing of textiles. Given the differential availability and costs of the factors of production, other industries are prominent in only one or a few specialized production centers.

Industries that typically locate close to the source of raw materials are those that involve refining and loss of weight in the manufacturing process, for example, rice milling, sugar refining, cotton ginning and spinning, the processing of coir (coconut fiber), cigarette manufacture, the tanning of leather, the preparation and packaging of tea, and the smelting of minerals. Most such simple activities take place in relatively small urban centers or near plantations and mines. More sophisticated manufacturing, such as the weaving of cloth, the manufacture of shoes and wearing apparel, cement and chemical industries, light engineering industries, and so forth gravitate to larger cities. Few among the hundreds of cities in South Asia (i.e., places with populations of 100,000 or more) are without establishments devoted to several of these forms of manufacturing production.

Of particular importance in recent years has been the growth of foreign investment—mainly from the United States, but also from Japan and other developed countries—taking advantage of the abundance of cheap labor in assembling wearing apparel, footwear, small appliances, and so forth, much of which is produced for distribution through mass retail marketing corporations. Special industrial zones, with privileged production conditions and tax benefits for foreign investors, have been created in a number of ports and other cities to stimulate such development. Both Bangladesh and Sri Lanka have been important beneficiaries; in both countries clothing and accessories now account for more than half the total value of exports.

At a more technologically advanced level, metallurgical, heavy engineering, industrial chemical, pharmaceutical, and electronics industries are concentrated either in ports or locations in which bulky resources, such as iron ore and coal, can be combined with minimum transportation costs; or in other large cities (those with a million or more people), where capital and ancillary services (banking, insurance, advertising, etc.) are relatively abundant and where purchasing power is highest. Thus, one finds the manufacture of steel and steel products in Jamshedpur and other cities of the Chhota Nagpur, as well as in several port cities (including Karachi in Pakistan and Chittagong in Bangladesh, which utilize imported scrap metal and/or iron ore); automobile assembly plants in Chennai, Delhi, Pune, and Kolkata; high-tech electronics and aviation industries in Bangalore; pharmaceutical producers and petroleum refineries in Mumbai; ship building in Vishakhapatnam; and so forth. There are very few manufactured goods that India cannot produce. But, because it is not yet fully competitive with more advanced countries, some industries survive only because of high protective tariffs. As India moves increasingly toward a free trade regime and away from government-owned industries, the future of inefficient producers is likely to be bleak.

The global revolution in electronic communication has ushered in two major developments of which India has become a major beneficiary: first, the spectacular growth in the production and exporting of computer software; and subsequently, the outsourcing, mainly by American firms, of consumer services in such fields as banking, insurance, health maintenance industries, and the like. This has resulted in an enormous boom in the training and utilization of relatively cheap, but highly skilled, labor in such cities as Bangalore, Hyderabad, and Chennai. This has had a major favorable impact on India's balance of payment.

The globalization of labor markets has also led to significant flows of South Asian labor, both skilled and unskilled, to developed countries in North America and Europe as well as to the Middle East. Particularly important source areas in respect to the Middle East are Pakistan, Bangladesh, and Kerala. Remittances from overseas have been an important source of capital for both investment and consumption in many parts of South Asia.

A final aspect of globalization that has significantly impacted South Asia and that holds tremendous promise of future change is tourism. The number and variety of sites worthy of a visit defies the imagination: Mughal architectural masterpieces, such as the Taj Mahal, the nearby ruins of Fatehpur Sikri, or the Red Fort of Delhi; the great Hindu, Buddhist, and Jain temples (including cave temple complexes such as those at Ajanta and Ellora) found throughout India; the dramatic fortress cities of Rajasthan; the ruins of such ancient cities as Mohenjo Daro, Harappa, and Taxila in Pakistan; distinct cultural niches such as the Vale of Nepal or Manipur; areas of scenic splendor, such as Kashmir; national parks and other pristine areas reserved for nature study, trekking or serious mountaineering; and tropical beaches such as those of Kovalam, Goa, and the Maldives. Some of these have long been favorites of privileged elite classes, while others became meccas for more penurious globetrotters in

and since the 1960s. Most sites await the development of modern hotels and improved travel facilities to reach their full potential. In relation to their populations, the Maldives, Nepal, and Sri Lanka have reaped the greatest gains from tourism.

Infrastructure. The fact that most of the countries of South Asia could develop to the extent that they have over the past century is attributable to no small degree to changes in their economic infrastructure, begun during the colonial period and, in many respects, accelerated in the period since independence. In the case of Nepal and Bhutan, however, the physical isolation resulting from their mountainous terrain creates a serious and persistent obstacle to development.

The building of railroads was of particular importance. Even before independence, India had the world's third-largest rail system, a major catalyst for subsequent development. While railroad mileage has not been greatly extended in South Asia since independence, the quality and volume of service has continued to expand. Today, Indian railroads log more passenger miles per year than in any other country in the world. Relatively speaking, however, more effort went into the building of roads. Although per capita ownership of automobiles remains very low by world standards, few areas are now out of reach of bus service, and the transportation of goods by truck has greatly multiplied. Few villages cannot be reached by road, at least during the dry season. While the rail system remains a government monopoly throughout South Asia, bus systems have become increasingly privatized. In the deltaic terrain of Bangladesh, the complex network of broad rivers greatly hampers overland transport, especially in the rainy season; hence, river traffic, largely in simple "country boats," carries a greater volume of goods than either road or rail. Finally, air services, both nationally and privately owned, are also expanding rapidly throughout South Asia.

Among the colonized areas of the world, India stood out for the quality of its institutions of higher learning. In addition to its indigenous traditions of learning, universities, along Western lines, were established in its major cities as early as 1857 and have proliferated in subsequent generations, especially so in the period since independence. In contrast to this emphasis on higher education, the reduction of illiteracy in South Asia, especially in the countryside and among females, has proceeded slowly. The most notable exceptions are in Sri Lanka and the Indian state of Kerala. Both attach great importance to education at all levels and have achieved virtually universal literacy. In general, Pakistan and Bangladesh lag behind India in their educational attainments, and the reliance of ordinary Pakistanis on education in traditional religious education in *madrassah*, given the paucity of government-sponsored alternatives, presents a significant potential obstacle in the way of economic development and the integration of Pakistan into the modern world.

Finally, one must note the remarkable extension, throughout South Asia, of government services in the form of community development schemes, public health clinics, government-aided cooperatives, and so forth. Nongovernmental organizations, including indigenous self-help programs such as those of the Grameen Bank in Bangladesh and SEWA (Self-Employed Women's Association) in India have also made enormous strides. All of these are engaged in one way or another in improving human capital. Therein may lie the best hope for the future of South Asia.

Urbanization and urban morphology. Despite the fact that South Asia is still among the least urbanized regions of the world, its total number of urban dwellers at the beginning of the twenty-first century was already in excess of 400 million. Of these, roughly 135 million lived in cities of a million or more inhabitants. The proportion of urban dwellers to the total population in 2003 was about 36 percent in Pakistan, 28 percent in India, 25 percent in Sri Lanka, 24 percent in Bangladesh, and only 13 percent in Nepal. Among the region's cities are some of the world's largest and most rapidly growing. The 2001 populations, to the nearest million, of India's largest metropolitan areas (suburbs included) were: Mumbai (Bombay), 16 million; Delhi, 13 million; Kolkata (Calcutta), 13 million; Chennai (Madras), 6 million; Bangalore, 6 million; Hyderabad, 6 million; Ahmedabad, 5 million; and Pune, 4 million. Another twenty-four cities had populations of from 1 million to 3 million each. The leading cities in the remainder of South Asia were: Dhaka, in Bangladesh, 12 million; Karachi and Lahore, in Pakistan, 9 million and 5 million; and seven others, with populations from 1 million to 2 million each.

As with villages, though to not quite the same degree, cities tend to be residentially segregated. Thus, many neighborhoods will be identifiable by their dominant religion, caste, language group (in that many cities have substantial populations of interstate or interprovincial migrants), and/or economic class. Within such neighborhoods, social clubs, places of worship and the purveyors of foods, other goods and services cater largely to the needs and preferences of the socially dominant group.

The spatial arrangement and architecture of cities also reflects the time of construction of particular areas and the functions they are intended to serve. There is, for example, usually a densely crowded old city core, dating from the pre-colonial period. Often walled (though many

city walls have now been dismantled in whole or part), the old city is typically marked by a confusing maze of narrow streets and alleys and is likely to include the mansions of the original urban gentry, the principal places of worship, and traditional markets, often containing streets given over wholly to the vending of particular goods such as grains, sweets, saris, jewelry, and hardware. The burgeoning of urban population has, almost invariably, caused an overflow from the original core area to neighborhoods that are somewhat less crowded and slightly more regular in their layout. To one side of many an old city one often finds an adjacent area or areas known as "civil lines" or the "cantonment." As their designations imply, these were originally built mainly to accommodate the British civilian and military personnel and their families and household servants. Such areas are spaciously and regularly laid out and are marked by colonial-style bungalows, with broad verandas and adjacent gardens. Since the departure of the British, the civil lines and cantonments have been occupied mainly by Indians performing the same functions as those of the former colonial overloads.

In some industrial cities one finds squalid "coolie lines," built by factory owners to accommodate the mill hands, a large proportion of whom are likely to be immigrants from surrounding rural areas. Similar "lines" are found adjacent to many mines, plantations, and railway workshops. Since independence, there has been a proliferation of various types of housing "colonies," located mainly along and beyond the urban periphery. For relatively affluent families, these consist mainly of single-family dwellings, with small surrounding gardens; but more commonly they are comprised of drab multifamily apartment houses, many of which reflect the housing styles of the Soviet Union and Eastern Europe during the Stalinist period.

At an economic level below that of ordinary, regularly employed salaried laborers are masses of slum dwellers who, for the most part, survive from irregular and low-paid work, or who live from begging and other socially undesirable activities. This segment of the population occupies dilapidated tenements or inhabits flimsy, makeshift huts. One must also note that South Asian cities have more than their share of roofless pavement dwellers.

Finally, as in all major cities in an age of economic globalization, the megacities of South Asia are also witnessing the growth of central business districts, with skyscraper office buildings, major banking establishments, a wide range of other commercial services, shopping malls, luxury hotels, restaurants, and so forth. One may safely assume an acceleration of urbanization in the decades ahead and increasing concentration of economic activity and wealth-generation in South Asia's cities, widening income gaps between the economic elite and the masses, greater urban congestion and pollution, increased crime, and mounting challenges to urban governance.

Joseph Schwartzberg

BIBLIOGRAPHY

Ahmed, Aijazuddin, ed. *Social Structure and Regional Development: A Social Geographic Perspective, Essays in Honour of Professor Moonis Raza.* Jaipur and New Delhi: Rawat Publications, 1973.

Ahmed, Aijazuddin, and A. B. Mukerji, eds. *India: Culture, Society and Economy: Essays in Honour of Asok Mitra.* New Delhi: Inter-India Publications, 1985.

Breton, Roland J.-L. *Atlas of the Languages and Ethnic Communities of South Asia.* Walnut Creek, Calif., London, and New Delhi: Altamira Press: 1997.

Crane, Robert I., ed. *Regions and Regionalism in South Asian Studies: An Exploratory Study.* Monograph no. 5, Duke University Monograph and Occasional Paper Series. Raleigh, N.C.: Duke University, 1967.

Johnson, Gordon. *Cultural Atlas of India: India, Pakistan, Nepal, Bhutan, Bangladesh & Sri Lanka.* New York: Facts on File, 1996.

Maloney, Clarence. *Peoples of South Asia.* New York: Holt, Rinehart and Winston, 1974.

Misra, R. P., ed. *Contributions to Indian Geography.* 13 vols. New Delhi: Heritage, 1983–1994.

Mukerjee, Radhakamal. *Man and His Habitation: A Study in Social Ecology.* Mumbai: Popular Prakashan, 1968.

Schwartzberg, Joseph E. *Occupational Structure and Level of Economic Development in India: A Regional Analysis.* New Delhi: Office of the Registrar General, 1969.

Schwartzberg, Joseph E., ed. *A Historical Atlas of South Asia.* New York and Oxford: Oxford University Press, 1992.

A Social and Economic Atlas of India. Delhi and New York: Oxford University Press, 1987.

Sopher, David E., ed. *An Exploration of India: Geographical Perspectives on Society and Culture.* Ithaca, N.Y.: Cornell University Press, 1980.

Spate, O. H. K., and A. T. A. Learmonth. *India and Pakistan: A General and Regional Geography.* 3rd ed. London: Methuen, 1967.

GLOBALIZATION India embraced economic globalization in the wake of its severe balance of payments crisis in 1991. Today, India's economy is largely integrated into the global economy. Overall, the achievements have been positive. The country has been able to move beyond the specter haunting it since independence: the stagnant 3 percent per annum growth, known pejoratively as the "Hindu growth rate." India's economic growth in the ten-year period from 1992–1993 to 2001–2002 averaged slightly over 6 percent a year, making India one of the fastest-growing developing economies in the world.

Over four decades of statism and "export pessimism"—characterized by pervasive government planning and regulation, earning India its once dubious distinction as the most controlled economy in the noncommunist world—have given way to significant industrial and trade liberalization, financial deregulation, improvements to supervisory and regulatory systems, cuts in tariffs, the removal of quantitative restrictions, and policies more conducive to privatization and foreign direct investment. India's traditionally high custom duties were systematically lowered in its budgets from 1991. Maximum tariff rates, which exceeded 300 percent, and the average (import-weighted) tariff rate, which stood at 87 percent in 1990–1991 (the highest in the world), have been lowered.

During the prereform period, with import-substituting industrialization the cornerstone of economic development, the principal instrument of industrial policy was an elaborate industrial licensing framework under the Industries Development and Regulations Act of 1951. The act required a government license for either establishing a new production unit (above a certain defined size), or making substantial expansion to an existing unit. A long (and growing) list of industries, including iron and steel, heavy machinery, oil and petroleum, air transport, mining, and telecommunications, were reserved solely for the public sector, under the intrusive eye of the Monopolies and Restrictive Trade Practices Act of 1970. This heavily protected industrial sector has witnessed the virtual abolition of the industrial licensing system as well as other regulatory impediments. Industrial licensing has been abolished for all but fifteen industries. Similarly, in an attempt to encourage greater private sector participation in the economy, many sectors that had previously been reserved for the public sector have been opened for private investment, including power, telecommunications, mining, ports, transportation, and banking.

Prior to 1991, restrictions on foreign direct investment were so strict that it was reduced to a trickle. After 1991, Indian companies with sound financial positions were permitted to raise capital from abroad by issuing equity in the form of global depository receipts, foreign currency convertible bonds, and other debt instruments. The government also created the Foreign Investment Promotion Board to facilitate one-stop, "fast-track" shopping for foreign investors. Automatic approval has been granted for joint ventures with up to 74 percent foreign equity participation, and 100 percent foreign equity and ownership are permitted in export processing zones and units that are export oriented. These reforms

Corporate Headquarters of Nestlé in New Delhi. The Swiss food giant has been in India for ninety years: With six manufacturing plants, thousands of employees, leading domestic market shares in semiprocessed foods, and double-digit sales growth driven by export revival, it remains a broad-based economic presence in India. AKHIL BAKSHI / FOTOMEDIA.

have not only forced Indian companies to improve the quality of their products, but have also enabled many to restructure their activities through mergers and acquisitions.

Similarly, in the financial sector (especially banking), the Reserve Bank of India has strengthened prudential requirements and introduced a capital risk-asset ratio system as a measure of capital adequacy, thereby raising minimum capital and capital adequacy ratios to conform to international standards. By 1995 the government set the minimum capital adequacy requirements at 8 percent of risk-weighted assets for Indian banks with foreign branches. In 1998 the standard was raised to 9 percent (effective March 2000), with government securities given a 2.5 percent risk weight, to begin reflecting interest-rate risk. By the end of 2000, only about two dozen public sector banks fell short of this standard. Greater competition in the banking sector and improvements in the capital and debt markets have reduced reliance on central bank financing. Banks and financial institutions are now permitted access to capital markets to expand their equity

base, and the passage of the Foreign Exchange and Management Act in 1999 has greatly streamlined foreign exchange regulations.

Cumulatively, these reforms reawakened what John Maynard Keynes called the "latent animal spirits" of India's entrepreneurs, thereby giving a sharp boost to growth. Nowhere has this dynamism been more evident than in the information technology (IT) industry and the service sector. Ten years ago, India's computer industry had sales of U.S.$150 million. In 2001 its exports were over $9.6 billion, 2 percent of India's gross domestic product (GDP). Similarly, the share of IT (mainly software) in total exports increased from 1 percent in 1990 to 18 percent in 2001. IT-enabled services such as back-office operations, remote maintenance, accounting, public call centers, medical transcription, insurance claims, and other bulk processing are rapidly expanding. The city of Hyderabad is now known as Cyberabad, and Indian companies such as Infosys, Wipro, and Satyam may yet become household names around the world. Robust exports of food and capital goods, garments, engineering tools, and refined petroleum products have also contributed much to India's growth in recent years. However, it is India's rapidly expanding services sector (which currently accounts for about 40 percent of India's GDP, 25 percent of employment, and 30 percent of export earnings) that has provided recent growth and stability.

India's foreign exchange reserves have risen steadily, from U.S.$42.3 billion in March 2001, to $54.1 billion at the end of March 2002, to a record level of nearly $72.4 billion in January 2003. In the foreign exchange market, dealers are now allowed to buy and sell foreign exchange for current as well as capital account transactions, and firms earning foreign exchange through exports are allowed to retain a certain proportion of the proceeds to avoid costs of conversion and reconversion. Since the rupee was floated in March 1992, its significant nominal and real devaluation relative to its value prior to 1991 provided a much-needed impetus to trade. The exchange rate of the rupee in terms of the major currencies of the world has remained reasonably stable, notwithstanding occasional fluctuations caused by normal market forces of supply and demand. It is particularly noteworthy that, for the first time, the World Bank has classified India as a "less-indebted country."

Like the proverbial rising tide that eventually lifts all boats, the fruits of economic liberalization have benefited (albeit unevenly) most sectors of society, making a significant dent in the country's stubborn poverty problem. The latest official surveys indicate that poverty levels fell from about 40 percent of the population to roughly 28 percent during the second half of the 1990s. This translates into a net reduction in rural poverty of some 60 million people between 1993–1994 and 1999–2000. In rural India, poverty was down to 27 percent, while urban poverty fell by around 8 percent, from 32 to 24 percent.

The accomplishments of the 1990s are dwarfed only by what remains to be done. One urgent task is to correct the growing regional and state-level economic imbalances, as growth continues to vary sharply among the twenty-eight states and seven union territories that make up the Indian union. Second, constraints associated with infrastructure and regulatory bottlenecks have become increasingly evident. Reforms are badly needed in the area of infrastructure: roads, railways, telecommunications, electric power, air transport, and ports all need radical expansion as well as improvement in the quality of services. Third, economic reforms have generally bypassed the agricultural sector, which accounts for about one-quarter of GDP and provides the livelihood of roughly 70 percent of the population. Initially, agricultural growth

resulted from the expansion of cropped areas; then, since the 1970s, the "Green Revolution," which increased the use of high-yielding varieties of seeds, commercial fertilizer, pesticides, and irrigation, spurred further growth. However, even as the Green Revolution contributed to sharp increases in agricultural production and productivity, its strategy also led to increasing reliance on explicit subsidization of inputs such as nonorganic fertilizer, and implicit subsidization of inputs such as irrigation and power through deliberate underpricing. The central government's fertilizer subsidies amounted to 110 billion rupees (U.S.$2.3 billion), or 0.4 percent of GDP in 2002–2003. The major beneficiaries of this subsidy were the inefficient domestic fertilizer industry and high-income farmers. Fertilizer use, moreover, must be complemented with a regular supply of water. The heavily subsidized electric power enables farmers to draw water from irrigation canals or to pump it from deep wells at relatively little cost. The overuse of urea (nitrogenous fertilizers) and water has greatly aggravated the problem of waterlogging, topsoil depletion, pollution of ground water, and a host of related environmental problems. While it is generally agreed that a phased increase in fertilizer prices and the imposition of user charges for irrigation and electricity would prevent abuse and raise resources to finance investment in rural infrastructure, the powerful rural interests, given their influence and control over large electoral constituencies, have made this task politically difficult. In fact, successive governments have generally skirted the issue, threatening to raise prices and cut subsidies in their budget speeches, only to back down later under political pressure.

Further exacerbating agricultural diversification and productivity are outdated laws and regulations. For example, the government's guaranteed price supports for food grains—crucial in the 1960s and 1970s to give farmers the incentives to produce more food grains—have long outlived their usefulness. Today, price controls are maintained for staples to ensure remunerative prices for farmers. In fact, support prices have long been fixed higher than market prices, encouraging overproduction. The result has been a substantial increase in stocks to unsustainable levels—over 60 million tons in mid-2002, against a norm of around 17 million tons—considered necessary to avert famine and ensure food security. In recent years, the costs of maintaining these stocks have been so prohibitive that it is not uncommon to allow food grains and other commodities to rot in poorly maintained, rat-infested storage facilities. While short-term measures, such as selling excess grain below cost, are usually undertaken, this is not a viable long-term solution. Both the central and state governments have tried to justify the maintenance of high support prices on the grounds that it allows them to subsidize the sale of certain commodities to low-income families through the public distribution system, but it is well known that such distributed grain rarely reaches the needy. The agricultural sector is also shielded through import and export controls, including tariffs and export restrictions. Perhaps the most pernicious are the interstate sales tax, and restrictions on interstate and even interdistrict movement of agricultural commodities. The price support system clearly needs to be better aligned to market demand if farmers are to be encouraged to shift from food grains like wheat and rice to other staples.

Though the financial sector reforms have liberalized Indian firms' ability to raise and hold money offshore as well as foreign investors' ability to invest in India and to repatriate their investments, the government still maintains controls on international capital movements. The 1997 Committee on Capital Account Convertibility (the Tarapore Committee) recognized the gains to capital account convertibility in terms of increased funding for investment and risk diversification, and recommended that India move toward capital convertibility over a three-year period. However, the committee's report, issued just three weeks before the floating of the Thai baht in July 1997 and the onset of the Asian financial crisis, halted the move toward capital account liberalization. India's cautious approach to capital account liberalization helped limit contagion during the Asian crisis by containing short-term debt. The authorities must nevertheless ease capital account liberalization as India's financial system and fiscal policy are strengthened. Compared to China, India's ability to attract foreign investment remains disappointing. During the 1990s, foreign direct investment in India averaged 0.5 percent of GDP, while in China it was 5 percent of GDP.

Although the number of activities reserved for the public sector has been reduced from six to three and the number of sectors reserved for small-scale industry (units whose investment in plant and machinery cannot exceed $250,000) has been reduced from 821 to 799, those numbers are still too high. This "reservation" policy has created protective enclaves within the industrial sector, with an adverse effect on industrial competitiveness and job creation. Accelerating the pace of divestment and privatization of public sector enterprises will help reduce the public sector deficit by raising revenues, increasing the efficiency of resource use, and helping to realign government policy in a way that contributes to faster economic growth.

As the Asian financial crisis clearly demonstrated, a strong and well-regulated financial sector can serve as a critical bulwark against global market turmoil. This not only means having in place prudential and supervisory systems to ensure financial stability; authorities must also take swift corrective actions to deal with weak or insolvent institutions. Despite India's achievements in strengthening prudential and supervisory systems, considerable weaknesses remain. At the core of the problem is the fact that a few government-owned banks (particularly the State Bank of India, the country's largest commercial bank) still account for roughly 80 percent of the banking sector. The vast majority of these banks are chronically undercapitalized and burdened with huge nonperforming loans. Weak banks can put the entire economy under risk during a crisis. While public ownership of banks has created an aura of invulnerability to shocks, it is urgent that the authorities move expeditiously to reduce the high level of nonperforming loans, restructure weak banks, and close insolvent public-sector banks.

Economic globalization demands constant innovation. While India's software industry is one of the fastest-growing sectors in the economy, it is important to note that India may not realize its vast potential unless some important policy changes are made. The software industry's focus is currently on mostly proprietary work for foreign multinationals, which is only a small part of the world's software market. India's cost advantage, because its software professionals are inexpensive, will be eroded as other players (such as China) with similar or lower costs enter the market. Finally, although India has been able to exploit the opportunities economic globalization has provided, the process continues to draw fierce domestic opposition. Thus, making the benefits of economic globalization meaningful to all of its more than 1 billion citizens remains India's major challenge.

Shalendra D. Sharma

See also **Agricultural Growth and Diversification since 1991; Economic Reforms of 1991; Economy since the 1991 Economic Reforms; Foreign Resources Inflow since 1991; Industrial Growth and Diversification; Information and Other Technology Development; Trade Liberalization since 1991**

BIBLIOGRAPHY

Bhagwati, Jagdish. *In Defense of Globalization.* New York: Oxford University Press, 2004.
Brecher, Jeremy, and Tim Costello. *Global Village or Global Pillage.* Boston: South End Press, 1994.
Chua, Amy. *World on Fire: How Exporting Free Market Democracy Breeds Ethnic Hatred and Global Instability.* New York: Doubleday, 2003.
Friedman, Thomas. *The Lexus and the Olive Tree.* New York: Farrar, Straus and Giroux, 2004.

Gray, John. *False Dawn: The Delusions of Global Capitalism.* New York: New Press, 1999.

Greider, William. *One World, Ready or Not: The Manic Logic of Global Capitalism.* New York: Touchstone Press, 1997.

Ohmae, Kenichi. *The End of the Nation State.* New York: Touchstone Press, 1995.

Toussaint, Eric. *Your Money or Your Life: The Tyranny of Global Finance.* London: Pluto Press, 1999.

GOA Located on the South Konkan coast of western India, approximately 250 miles (402 km) south of Mumbai, Goa is bounded by Maharashtra in the north, Karnataka in the east and south, and the Arabian Sea on the west. Before it attained statehood on 30 May 1987, Goa was a union territory. Its area of 1,429 square miles (population 1,343,998; 2001 census) makes it the smallest of the twenty-eight states of the Indian union. In 2003 it was judged the richest state in India by the magazine *India Today*, and had the highest rate of literacy at 82.3 percent. It is one of the most popular tourist destinations for domestic as well as international tourists. Despite intensive exploitation of iron and manganese ore as well as general industrialization since 1961, the state has retained its famed natural beauty, thanks to successive environmentally conscious governments.

A former Portuguese colony for 450 years, acquired by Afonso de Albuquerque in 1510, Goa was made the capital of the Estado da India periodically under a viceroy or a governor-general with authority over all Portuguese possessions from Sofala in East Africa to Macao off China. Goa was also dubbed "Rome of the Orient" because it was the headquarters of the papal ecclesiastical enterprise in the East, where the "incorrupt body" of St. Francis Xavier has been kept since 1553. Goa saw new peaks of prosperity under the Portuguese, at least until 1580, as a substantial slice of the profits from their extensive spice trade poured into the city of Old Goa, enabling the government to build impressive office buildings and churches, mostly following Iberian architectural style. In 1759, compelled by persistent outbreak of plague in Old Goa, the administration was moved to Nova Goa (New Goa), also called Panaji. Before Portuguese rule, Goa formed part of the adjoining kingdoms in Maharashtra and Karnataka. It had earlier formed the southern part of the Mauryan province of Aparanta, later coming under its feudatory chief, the Bhoja family, and still later under the Silaharas, Kadambas, and Chalukyans of Badami. From 1312 to 1370 it came under Delhi's Muslim sultanate. Later, Vijayanagar acquired it and developed it as its principal port of entry for Arabian horses. In 1489 Goa came under the Bahamani kingdom, and after the latter split into five separate entities, under the Adil Shahi rulers of Bijapur.

The Portuguese acquired Goa in two stages: Velhas Conquistas (Old Conquests) consisting of Tiswadi (thirty villages), Bardez, Mormugao, and Salsete, all acquired in the sixteenth century; and the Novas Conquistats (New Conquests), made in the eighteenth century, comprising Pernem, Sanguem, Quepem, Ponda, Sattari, Bicholim, and Canacona. The rigors of the Inquisition in the Old Conquests account for the overwhelming majority there of Catholic converts, while later tolerance is reflected in the overwhelming majority of Hindus and their temples in the New Conquests. By the end of Portuguese rule in 1961, Goa's population was 60.8 percent Hindu and 36.1 percent Catholic; the rest were Muslims, Luso-Indians, and others, with no Portuguese settlers despite their 450 year rule.

Goa's prosperity declined along with the erosion of Portuguese power from the late sixteenth century. Beginning in the nineteenth century, large numbers of Goans, particularly Catholics from poor families, sought employment as butlers in affluent British households, as waiters and cooks in expensive urban restaurants and hill stations, and in diverse jobs on oceangoing vessels. Both Hindus and Catholics migrated for educational and employment opportunities—about 150,000, or over one-fourth of the entire Goan population, to British India, over 100,000 to Mumbai, and several thousand more to Portuguese and British East Africa.

In 1946, on the eve of India's independence, with the discovery of iron and manganese ore, Goa became both fiscally solvent and a source of valuable foreign exchange to Portugal. Even the small portion of foreign exchange made available in Goa was enough to import many luxury items. Goans "could wear a hundred watches on each arm," and smuggling increased across the porous border to the rest of India. With no income tax or sales tax to pay, business in Goa boomed. Despite such sudden economic betterment, the colonial government faced growing opposition, supported by the large numbers of émigrés. The National Congress of Goa, established by Tristao Braganza da Cunha, a Goan Catholic, in 1930, spearheaded the movement for independence. Expecting the Portuguese to leave the moment the British would quit the subcontinent, leaders of the Indian independence movement had paid no attention to Goa, whose population was, according to official Portuguese statistics, 98.7 percent Indian, the rest being transitory Portuguese officials and army personnel. In 1951 Portugal decreed that Goa and all other Portuguese colonies were "overseas provinces" entitled to North Atlantic Treaty Organization's protection. The Indian government's pleas for negotiations with Portugal on the same lines as France with regard to its Indian colonies fell on deaf ears. Instead, further curbs on freedoms were instituted,

Facade of Sé Cathedral. Also known as St. Catherine's Cathedral, witness to the intensely religious history of Goa. Its construction commenced under the Portuguese viceroy Redondo in 1562, but was not finished for another ninety years. With an elaborate Corinthian-style interior, the church is dedicated to the saint on whose feast day the city was recaptured by the Portuguese in 1510. AMAR TALWAR / FOTOMEDIA.

including the strictest censorship. Evading such tight controls instituted by a dictatorial regime, Goans offered *satyagraha*, or nonviolent resistance, courting arrest. Such prominent professionals as Dr. T. B. Cunha, Telo Mascarenhas, Dr. Pundalik Gaitonde, Dr. Rama Hegde, Advocate Gopal Mayekar, and others were sentenced to ten- to fifteen-year prison terms and were deported to Portugal and Angola. Hundreds were detained for indefinite period in Goan jails. Unarmed Indians, including Goans who attempted to cross into Goa as nonviolent Gandhian *satyagrahi*s in 1954 and 1955, were shot down in cold blood. The irresistible force of the spirit of free India was met by the obstinacy of Portuguese premier Antonio de Oliveira Salazar, who refused to acknowledge the "winds of change" sweeping the European empires from Africa and Asia. Failing moral and diplomatic approaches, Prime Minister Jawaharlal Nehru finally turned to a military solution. "Operation Goa," lasting thirty-six hours, began with the bombing and disabling of the only Portuguese frigate, SS *Afonso de Albuquerque*. Indian troops marched in from three directions, taking Goa with hardly any resistance from Portuguese forces, welcomed warmly by the overwhelming majority of Goans on 19 December 1961.

D. R. SarDesai

See also **Albuquerque, Afonso de; Gama, Vasco da; Portuguese in India**

BIBLIOGRAPHY

Bhandari, Romesh. *Goa*. New Delhi: Roli Books, 1999.
Cunha, Tristao B. *Goa's Freedom Struggle*. Mumbai: Antonio de Cruz, 1981.
De Souza, Teotonio R. *Goa through the Ages*. New Delhi: Concept Publishing, 1987.
Gaitonde, P. D. *The Liberation of Goa*. New Delhi: Oxford University Press, 1987.
Priolkar, A. K. *The Goa Inquisition: Being a Quartercentenary Commemoration Study of the Inquisition in India*. Mumbai: Bombay University Press, 1961.
Rao, R. P. *Portuguese Rule in Goa, 1510–1961*. Mumbai: Asia Publishing House, 1963.

Shastri, B. S. *Socio-Economic Aspects of Portuguese Colonialism in Goa, Nineteenth and Twentieth Centuries.* Panaji: University Publishers, 1990.

Shirodkar, P. P. *Goa's Struggle for Freedom.* Delhi: Ajanta Publishers, 1988.

GODDESS IMAGES

India is unique in its multifaceted goddess worship. Unlike the goddess worship of the ancient Western world—which has largely vanished, except in the veneration of the Virgin Mary as a semi-divine figure, or in modern attempts to revive ancient pagan goddess cults—Indian goddess devotion is a vibrant living tradition. For her worshipers the Goddess sums up all the powers of this life and the hope of salvation in the next. Worshipers of Mahadevi (the Great Goddess) seek *bhukti*, meaning the enjoyment of the things of this life, as well as *mukti*, the quest for spiritual liberation in the hereafter. There are many different paths to these two goals, and the complexity of goddess imagery reflects this. Buddhists, Jains, and Hindus honor the Goddess in a variety of roles. She is the source and support of life and the architect of death and destruction. She brings forth life, nurtures creativity, embodies wisdom, destroys the wicked, and takes the dead. Her many images reflect this array of meanings.

Forms of Goddess Images

There are hundreds of forms of the Goddess in India; sometimes she is recognized as immanent in natural phenomena such as Prithvi, or Mother Earth, or the holy river Ganga, or the sacred mountain Nanda Devi, but more often artists create her imagery to fulfill a multitude of social roles and designations. Traditionally, artists followed prescriptive religious and sculptural texts in portraying the image of the Goddess in her various forms. However, this does not mean that subject matter, styles, or media remained static over time, or over the vast geography of the Indian subcontinent. Regional schools, individual artists, patrons, developments in ritual, and diversity of materials all contributed to the rich variety of goddess imagery.

As the origin of life, the Goddess is represented as Lajja Gauri, whose neck sprouts a lotus blossom rather than an identifying head. She is shown with her legs splayed in a birth-giving posture, her two hands holding lotus buds, symbolic of regeneration. As Lajja Gauri, she is beyond the specifics of particular identity and is the nondifferentiated conduit of all life and creativity.

Sri Lakshmī, goddess of wealth and fertility, is worshiped by both Hindus and Jains. Lakshmī is said to have emerged from the churning of the primordial milky

Early Indian Sculpture of Mother Goddess. In India, a rich variety of goddess imagery abounds, Here, third-century B.C. sculpture of Mother Earth, Lajja Gauri. With a barely identifiable head, she is beyond the specifics of a particular identity and is the conduit of all life and creativity. Collection of the National Museum, New Delhi. ANGELO HORNAK/CORBIS.

ocean. She is often depicted emerging from a lotus and lustrated by elephants, representing the wealth of the monsoon rains. These are reminders that the Goddess is intimately connected to the primordial waters, the fertilizing rains, and the nourishing sap of creation. This iconography can be traced throughout the centuries and became the modern ideal in the nineteenth-century Raja Ravi Varma oleolithographs. Ravi Varma's articulation remains the most common representation of Lakshmī in contemporary commercial calendar prints.

As Pārvatī, or Uma, the Goddess is the ideal consort. Her iconography reflects the Indian notions of idyllic beauty, with long limbs, graceful hands, narrow waist, wide hips, and full breasts. During the South Indian Chola period (c. A.D. 850–1279), bronze artists delighted in the loving depiction of these attributes. In these images the Goddess is never cloaked in drapes or veils; her beauties and perfections of fluid form are sensuously revealed as if she were almost nude. However, we must remember that when in worship, the Goddess would have been clothed in silks, jewels, and flower garlands.

The Goddess may also represent the tragic aspects of existence: she sums up decay, destruction, disease, and death. As Kālī or Chamunda, she is the embodiment of all these dark powers of unmaking. As Kālī (the Dark One), she is shown in seventeenth- through nineteenth-century paintings with black skin, disheveled hair, and angular jutting arms and legs. She is often shown dancing in ecstatic violence amid the carnage of battle. As Chamunda, she is represented as a withered hag, with desiccated breasts, protruding ribs, and crazed eyes, maw agape, ready to consume her victims. She frequently wears a garland of severed heads and is ornamented with snakes and scorpions.

The Goddess is sometimes depicted in groups such as the Sapta Matrkas, a collection of seven angry (*ugra*) deities. Their images were usually installed in ancillary shrines located next to Shiva temples. *Yogini*s were groups of goddesses who ruled the occult and violent forces of tantric Hinduism. *Yogini* worship arose in the seventh century; followers were attracted by the promise of magical powers. *Yogini*s were worshiped in groups of 64, or sometimes 42 or 81 images. *Yogini* rites took place in unusual hypaethral temples (open to the sky) situated in remote rural areas. *Yogini* imagery reflects the complexity of identity and ritual; there are bear-, goat-, rabbit-, cow-, elephant-, and snake-headed *yogini*s, as well as more easily identified goddesses such as the Sapta Matrkas, Chamunda, and Kālī, who are also incorporated into the *yogini* groups.

The Power of the Goddess

The Hindu goddess represents *shakti*, the catalyzing energy of the divine. In eighteenth- and nineteenth-century paintings, Kālī is frequently revealed with hair disheveled, tongue lolling, standing astride the corpse of her consort Shiva. Shiva is inert, except for his erect phallus. This is a reminder that without the sexualizing and energizing presence of *shakti*, the divine feminine power, the male gods could not perform their necessary roles for the harmonious balance of the cosmos. Hindus thus say: "*Shakti ke bina, Shiva shava hai,*" which means, "Without Shakti, Shiva is a corpse."

Unlike the Hindu Goddess, the Buddhist Goddess is, in theory, a more passive presence representing salvific wisdom rather than active good works. As Prajnaparamita (Perfected Wisdom), the personification of the Prajnaparamita Sūtra, she is spiritual insight par excellence. She is portrayed as a beautiful young woman, often holding a copy of the Prajnaparamita text as her defining attribute. As Tāra, she is the savioress of Buddhism, and the divine consort of the *bodhisattva* Avalokiteshavara. Tara represents spiritual knowledge, the passive balance

to the male Avalokiteshvara's active compassion. Within Tantrayana Buddhism it is essential that wisdom and compassion unite to form enlightenment. This union is graphically represented in the images of the male and female divinities in sexual embrace.

Why are there so many forms of the divine feminine? The Hindu Goddess embodies all aspects of the psyche, but especially the threshold regions of birth, death, and intuition. She is often the birthing, witnessing, and destroying aspects of religious consciousness. It is the Goddess who usually brings forth new life, nurtures it, and brings about its death and reabsorption into the divine matrix. In Buddhism these aspects of the divine feminine represent a less physical role and instead represent the growth and maturation of gnosis.

Historical Development of Goddess Images

If we look at goddess images strictly from the standpoint of historical development, we can see an almost continuous divine female presence throughout Indian history. Megalithic constructions from Kerala indicate that it is most likely that goddess worship was in force in the Indian subcontinent from prehistory. The numerous terra-cotta figurines from the Indus Valley Civilization (c. 2300–1750 B.C.) are evidence for the ubiquity of the female image in historical antiquity. Because the Indus script has not been adequately deciphered, we cannot know if or how these figures were in worship, but we can surmise from their numbers that they were of significance to the Indus Civilization, and that they probably represent a cult of the Goddess.

Again, with the evidence of numerous terra-cotta figurines, as well as stone rings decorated with nude female forms and vegetative motifs, we can surmise that the Goddess was of continuing religious importance during the Maurya period (323–185 B.C.). Despite the intervening rise of male-dominated Vedic religion, the Maurya period figurines are strikingly similar in style and iconography to the earlier Indus Valley images.

By the first century B.C. we begin to find stone sculptures of *yakshi*s. *Yakshi*s are female nature spirits, goddesses of the earth and vegetation, and particularly trees, whose origins can probably be found in the ancient pre-Vedic goddesses. The *yakshi*s were conduits of fertility, pulling up the invigorating sap of creation from the bowels of the earth. The *yakshi* cult must have been a powerful focus for devotion, for we find *yakshi* imagery at many early Buddhist sites. This indicates that early Buddhism, while focused on a primarily atheistic philosophy, was also sufficiently pragmatic to accommodate itself to the needs of the laity. At Buddhist sites such as Bharhut (c. 100 B.C.) and Sanchi (25–50 B.C.), we find many sculptures of these auspicious divinities closely associated with specifically identifiable trees, such as the mango or the *ashoka*. The *yakshi*'s direct, wide-eyed gaze is touched with a sweet smile; her figure is broad-hipped, full-breasted, with a narrow waist. She is lavishly ornamented with jewels, and her hair is arranged in elaborate braids. She raises an arm above her head to grasp a branch, and a leg is poised to kick the trunk, indicating that it is she who pulls up the sap of creation and brings the trees into flower and fruition.

Some of the earliest Buddhist female images represent Hariti, the goddess of children and smallpox. Hariti represents the ambivalence associated with the divine female: she is the guardian of children, but also ravages children with her fevers. Hariti images from the Kushana period (c. late 1st–3rd centuries A.D.) reflect the syncretic religious atmosphere of the period. In an image from Sahri Bahlol the goddess is portrayed as queenly, with high pearl encrusted diadem; she wears a Greek *chiton*, but has tusklike fangs. In one of her two right hands she holds a wine cup, perhaps an allusion to Dionysian cults present at this time, and in the other she supports one of her five hundred children; in one of her two left hands she holds a trident to ward off evil (an emblem associated with the Hindu god Shiva), and in the other a vase of *purnaghata* shape, indicating the vase of endless prosperity associated with the pregnant belly of Mother Earth.

As Indian religions developed, the identities of goddesses become expanded in texts such as the Devi Mahatmya of the Mārkaṇḍeya Purāṇa (5th–6th centuries A.D.). The story of Durgā slaying Mahisa, the ever transformative buffalo demon, is a favorite theme, appearing in stylized form as early as the second century. In the more elaborate narrative sculptures of the struggle, such as the great seventh-century Pallava period relief at Mamallapuram, the Goddess is shown as the epitome of the continuous fight between good and evil, knowledge and delusion. The artist has depicted her as ever vigilant; her face and posture are graceful, but uncompromising. The battle portrayed is furious, but the Goddess's eventual victory is indicated by her assured pose and the recoiling posture of the demon. The Goddess offers *moksha* (liberation) to her devotees, the narrative battle image promising that just as she will quell the demons representing ego and self-delusion, she can surely guide her worshipers to salvation from their own egotistical desires and self-deceptions.

Identities and images of the Goddess continue to evolve. In 1996 activists of the Hindu right wing condemned the contemporary Muslim Indian painter M. F. Husain for his nude portrayal of Sarasvatī, the goddess of learning. Despite the ubiquity of nude or almost nude goddesses in antiquity, the celebrated artist was assailed for his supposed insult to the dignity of the Goddess. The politico-religious clash brought about a national debate on the meaning and the suitable representation of the Goddess in art, as well as the ownership of image and meaning. This debate, as farcical as some aspects of it were, reiterated to many that images of the Goddess, aesthetically pleasing as many are, were not intended solely as works of art, but as docetic tools to provide the worshiper with the physical means to take *darshan* (the viewing) of the divinity. The constructed image provides a physical nexus for the devotee and the Goddess to see and be seen by each other, and to provide the visual interaction necessary for the incorporation of the divine reality into the mind of the worshiper.

Mary Storm

See also **Indus Valley Civilization; Jain Sculpture; Monuments; Sculpture: Buddhist**

BIBLIOGRAPHY

Banerjea, J. N. *The Development of Hindu Iconography*. 1941. Reprint, Kolkata: University of Calcutta, 1956.

Bhattacharyya, N. N. *Indian Mother Goddess*. Kolkata: Indian Studies Past and Present, 1971.

Coburn, Thomas B. *Encountering the Goddess: A Translation of the Devi-Mahatmya and a Study of Its Interpretation*. Albany: State University of New York Press, 1991.

Coomaraswamy, Ananda. *Yaksas*. Parts I-II. 2nd ed. New Delhi: Munshiram Manoharlal, 1980.

Dehejia, Vidhya. *Yogini Cult and Temples: A Tantric Tradition*. New Delhi: National Museum, 1986.

Dehejia, Vidhya, ed. *Devi: The Great Goddess: Female Divinity in South Asian Art*. Washington, D.C.: Smithsonian Institution, 1999.

Erndl, Kathleen M. *Victory to the Mother: The Hindu Goddess of Northwest India in Myth, Ritual, and Symbol*. New York and Oxford: Oxford University Press, 1993.

Hawley, John Stratton, and Donna Marie Wulff, eds. *Devi: Goddesses of India*. Berkeley: University of California Press, 1996.

Huntington, Susan L., with contributions by John C. Huntington. *The Art of Ancient India*. New York: Weatherhill, 1985.

Kinsley, David. *Hindu Goddesses: Visions of the Divine Feminine in the Hindu Religious Tradition*. Berkeley: University of California Press, 1986.

Kurtz, Stanley. *All the Mothers Are One: Hindu India and the Cultural Reshaping of Psychoanalysis*. New York: Columbia University Press, 1992.

Larson, Gerald James, Pratapaditya Pal, and Rebecca Gowen. *In Her Image: The Great Goddess in Indian Asia and the Madonna in Christian Culture*. Santa Barbara: University of California Press, 1980.

Rhie, Marilyn M., and Robert A. F. Thurman. *Wisdom and Compassion: The Sacred Art of Tibet*. New York: Tibet House, 1996.

Tiwari, J. N. *Goddess Cults in Ancient India*. Delhi: Sundeep Prakashan, 1985.

GOKHALE, GOPAL KRISHNA (*1866–1915*), *Indian educator and politician, president of the Indian National Congress (1905).* Gopal Krishna Gokhale was one of the wisest moderate leaders of India's National Congress, revered by Mahatma Gandhi as "my political guru." Born in Maharashtra's village of Kotaluk, the younger son of a Chitpavan brahman clerk in Kolhapur State's administration, Gopal inherited little money but was brilliant and diligent enough to master English literature and write Victorian-style poetry, as well as poetry in his own language, Marathi. At Pune's Deccan College, Gokhale committed many passages from the works of Edmund Burke, John Stuart Mill, and John Morley to his prodigious memory. He later was to become one of Morley's most highly respected advisers, during Liberal Morley's half decade as secretary of state for India, from 1906 to 1910. He also mastered mathematics, a subject he taught for several years at Pune's New English School, after living for a year in Bombay at Elphinstone College.

One of young India's most enlightened social reformers as well as liberal nationalists, Gokhale supported the first municipal high school for girls, started in Pune, bringing him into sharp conflict with religiously conservative popular Hindu leaders, like Bal Gangadhar Tilak, who argued that a "woman's place was in the house," not in school. Gokhale and Tilak remained poles apart on every issue of social reform and political action. In the "age of consent" controversy, Sir Andrew Scoble's 1891 bill to raise the minimal age of "rape" in India's Penal Code despite a child wife's "consent" from ten to twelve years, won Gokhale's strong support. Tilak led outraged Hindu Brahman opposition to that timid legislative attempt to save the lives of young girls from often lethal attacks on their wedding nights by husbands three or four times their age. Similarly, Tilak and Gokhale stood at opposite sides of barricades raised over Hindu widow remarriage. Since 1829 the burning of Hindu widows as *sati*s (true ones) had been abolished by British Indian Law, and since 1854, Hindu widow remarriage received legislative legitimacy; yet Hindu widows were still expected to reside, unadorned, in rear quarters of Hindu Brahman households. Gokhale, and his sage role model, Justice Mahadev Govind Ranade, led an enlightened vanguard of Hindu reformers who knew that female education and reforms in all spheres were prerequisites to national freedom.

Political Role

Gokhale took an active role in India's National Congress and became the youngest leader ever elected to preside over that premier political body, at its Benares Congress in 1905. Gokhale's eloquence and brilliance in denouncing the "cruel wrong" of Britain's first partition of Bengal did not, unfortunately, suffice to reverse that

Portrait of Gopal Krishna Gokhale. With his message of conciliation and negotiation, rather than violence, Gokhale played a pivotal role in early nationalist actions. He proved to be one of India's most enlightened social reformers as well, boldly supporting, for instance, the first municipal high school for girls in Pune. This stand brought him into sharp conflict with conservative Hindu leaders. K.L. KAMAT/KAMAT'S POTPOURRI.

act of imperial arrogance when Liberal Morley took charge of Whitehall's India Office a year later. But Morley sought and followed Gokhale's advice in many matters relating to his Indian Council Reforms Act of 1909, and before the end of his tenure helped to draft the reunification of Bengal announced by King George on his visit to Delhi in 1911.

Impact on Mahatma Gandhi

Gokhale also supported Gandhi's South African struggle at every meeting of India's Congress. He visited his political heir in South Africa to bolster Gandhi's courageous *satyagraha* there against the discriminatory poll tax levied on all Indians, bringing hope to Gandhi and his followers at crucial times in their fight for equality. When Mahatma Gandhi left South Africa at the start of World War I, it was to return to India to join Gokhale's Servants of India Society in Pune, so eager was he to work for India's rebirth as an independent nation under "Mahatma" Gokhale's tutelage. But just a few weeks later,

Gokhale's heart, long weakened by diabetes, gave out. "He is dead, but his work is not dead," Mahatma Gandhi eulogized his guru, India's greatest moderate nationalist.

Stanley Wolpert

See also **Gandhi, Mahatma M. K.**

BIBLIOGRAPHY

Gandhi, M. K. *Gokhale: My Political Guru.* Ahmedabad: Navajivin Publishing House, 1955.

Shahani, T. K. *Gopal Krishna Gokhale: A Historical Biography.* Mumbai: R. K. Mody, 1929.

Srinivasa Sastri, V. S. *Life of Gopal Krishna Gokhale.* Bangalore: Bangalore Printing and Publishing Co., 1937.

Turnbull, E. L., and H. G. D. Turnbull. *Gopal Krishna Gokhale: A Brief Biography.* Trichur, 1934.

Wolpert, Stanley A. *Tilak and Gokhale: Revolution and Reform in the Making of Modern India.* Berkeley and Los Angeles: University of California Press, 1953 and 1961.

GOLDEN TEMPLE. *See* **Sikhism.**

GOVERNMENT OF INDIA ACT OF 1919

World War I had an all-pervasive impact on India—socially, economically, and politically. A wide range of problems emerged after the war, collectively labeled "dilemmas of dominion" by historian Judith Brown, which irrevocably altered relations between Britain and India. Among India-related issues highlighted by the war were the increasingly contentious internecine struggles among British interest groups regarding the administration of the subcontinent and its long-term future. This pressure was exacerbated by the increasingly urgent and divergent demands on British authorities by articulate and well-organized Indian groups. The exigencies of war and the demands by different Indian groups magnified the need for reform on the constitutional front.

Great Britain had moved circumspectly concerning Indian participation in government, both in India and in London. Statements on Britain's willingness to include Indians in administrative positions in India and to selectively expand Indian participation in government were on record from Victoria's Proclamation of 1858 and various India-related acts in 1858, 1861, and 1892. With the Indian Councils Act of 1909, however, the British believed that they had taken major steps forward in Indian constitutional development by introducing even more elements of representative government in India. The number of nonofficial Indian members elected to the central and provincial legislatures in India was increased. For the first time, legislatures could discuss the government of India's budget. Indians were admitted to the inner sancta of Indian governance—the viceroy's executive council in Calcutta, and the secretary of state's Council of India, in London. Significantly, while the British did not introduce truly responsible government to India (many constraints on legislative power remained in British hands), it did interject into the Indian political scene the "communal" or "separate" electorate for Muslims, which remained an element of all subsequent constitutional legislation in India until its eventual culmination in the partition of the subcontinent in 1947.

The 1909 act did not stem the call for expanded Indian participation in India's governance. The frustration and discontent with the political situation grew unabated into the first years of World War I, and the imperatives for retaining Indian support in a time of crisis—conceding some element of expanded Indian participation in government—led to Secretary of State Edwin S. Montagu's public proclamation of Britain's new goals for India. On 20 August 1917, Montagu announced that the goal of British policy was to establish responsible government in India. He then traveled to India and with the viceroy, Lord Chelmsford, issued a report in 1918 that was essentially given life as the Government of India Act of 1919. Indian response to the proposals was at first guarded, the expectation being that the British would reward India for its enormous human and material contributions to the war efforts. That expectation was short-lived.

While the Montagu-Chelmsford Report was being formulated, Indians received perhaps a more accurate barometer of Britain's intentions through other events: the swift enactment of the Rowlatt Acts in 1919 (to sustain martial law and restrict public activities), shock at Britain's ineffective response to a major influenza outbreak, and the Amritsar Massacre in the spring of 1919. Thus, when the act of 1919 was finally issued, harkening a "new era" in British-Indian relations, its constitutional advances were, from the Indian perspective, limited and cosmetic, and actually widened the fractures in Indian polity.

The act of 1919 did not make any substantive change in the legal relationship between the governments at Whitehall and Delhi, and only moderately reshaped the executive council of the central government in India, expanding it to include three Indian representatives. The most radical change introduced by Great Britain was the introduction of "dyarchy" into provincial administration in India. Under this plan, responsibility for some key areas devolved to the provincial level. Some domains were actually transferred to Indian ministers who were responsible to provincial legislatures through the electorate. Transferred areas included agriculture, public works, education, and local self-government. However, several key elements remained in British hands—irrigation, land revenues, military matters, currency, police, justice, and press controls. Although Indian franchise was expanded by almost 10 percent and the official majority ended in both the provincial and central legislatures, British officials could retain the power to "certify" legislation and retained a de facto veto over Indian legislation.

Indians, already anxious about the sincerity of British reforms in the act of 1919, were disheartened by the retention and expansion of the principle of separate electorates in the act. Not only were separate electorates set aside for Muslims, but other minorities received special consideration, and certain privileged groups had reserved seats in Indian government. The act of 1919 was set in motion against the backdrop of increasing Indian anxiety and disappointment at British behavior, and against the backdrop of Mahatma Gandhi's assumption of leadership in the Indian National Congress and the departure of Mohammad Ali Jinnah on a separate search for Muslim identity in India. Yet, in spite of its limitations, the act of 1919 did introduce direct elections based on a wider franchise than ever before. Additionally, it provided expanded opportunities for Indians in both administratively responsible positions and in the consultative process, however circumscribed. One further, albeit important change was built into the act of 1919. For the first time since its creation in 1858, the salaries of the secretary of state, his staff, and operational expenditures of the India Office were placed on the British estimates rather than funded through Indian revenues. This had a progressive effect of allowing the Treasury and Cabinet increased influence in India Office affairs until its end in 1947.

Arnold P. Kaminsky

See also **British Crown Raj; British India Office, The; Chelmsford, Lord; Montagu, Edwin S.**

BIBLIOGRAPHY

Burke, S. M., and Salimk al-Din Quraish. *The British Raj in India: An Historical Review*. Karachi: Oxford University Press, 1995.

Nehru, Jawaharlal. *Toward Freedom: The Autobiography of Jawaharlal Nehru*. New York: John Day, 1942.

Robb, Peter G. *The Government of India and Reform*. Oxford: Oxford University Press, 1976.

Ryland, Shane. "The Making of the Government of India Act, 1919." Ph.D. diss., Duke University, 1970.

GOVERNMENT OF INDIA ACT OF 1935 This legislative act by the British government of India initiated significant changes in the colonial administration of India and formed the future substructure of the constitutions of the newly independent dominions of India and Pakistan in 1947. The Government of India Act of 1935 must be contextualized by pointing out that the ebb and flow of Indian nationalist politics had during the interwar years become a raging torrent. Against the backdrop of sustained tension, disillusionment, and economic dislocations of the so-called twenty-year truce, the Government of India Act of 1919 and piecemeal British legislation in the 1920s failed to assuage Indian political demands. Indeed, the extension of the communal electorate in 1919, and its further expansion in J. Ramsay MacDonald's Communal Award in 1932, created seemingly unmanageable fissures in the India body politic. As early as 1927, the British government attempted to address growing contentiousness and disorder (from their viewpoint, of course) by sending the Simon Commission (1927) to India to assess the next step in constitutional development for the colony. There were no Indian members of the commission, and it was met everywhere by cries of "Simon, go back." In the wake of this debacle, the Indian National Congress and the Muslim League proposed their own plans for constitutional movement, which simply highlighted the growing divergence of the parties. In rapid succession, the (Motilal) Nehru Report (1928) proposed essentially dominion status for India within the British Empire, followed by a Congress resolution calling for *purna swaraj* (complete independence) in 1929. Mohammad Ali Jinnah and the Muslim League responded immediately with their Fourteen Points, rejecting the logic of Congress representation for all Indians, and the following year, as Congress declared Independence Day (26 January 1930), Muhammad Iqbal, poet laureate of the future Pakistan, raised the call for an independent Muslim state in northwestern India. (In 1933 the name *Pakistan* was coined.)

The tension increased considerably with Mahatma Gandhi's march to the sea in March 1930 and the British government of India's arrest of the entire Congress Working Committee following the ensuing upsurge in civil disobedience. The British government then tried another approach: a Round Table Conference was convened in London. Everyone was there—except Congress, which, as historian Stanley Wolpert notes, "was like trying to stage *Hamlet* without the Prince of Denmark." Little came of the first Round Table Conference, and before a second conference might convene, some resolution of the impasse had to be effected. Viceroy Lord Irwin concluded the Gandhi-Irwin Pact with Mahatma Mohandas K. Gandhi in March 1931. Gandhi agreed to attend the Second Round Table Conference as the sole representative of the Indian National Congress. Further, he agreed to moderate the *svadeshi* movement by excluding the burning of British goods, and he agreed to withdraw

Congress's demands for a public inquiry into police behavior during the civil disobedience movement.

While Muslims, Sikhs, and Dalits ("untouchables") argued for separate representation, Gandhi repeated his position that Congress represented all Indians, and he was especially adamant that untouchables were, in any case, Hindus. Despite his success in broadcasting to America for the first time, and even after achieving some success in the depressed British midlands that had been deeply affected by his boycott efforts at home, the Second Round Table Conference ended unsuccessfully, and Gandhi returned home. Ostensibly because civil disobedience had erupted during his absence, a new governor-general, Lord Willingdon, jailed Gandhi. When J. Ramsay MacDonald's Communal Award was made public in 1932, Gandhi began a fast unto death, which ended only when the leader of the Dalits, B. R. Ambedkar, concluded an agreement with Gandhi to stand select Dalit candidates within the Congress allocation, but not in any separate electorate. Britain moved ahead with a Third Round Table Conference at the end of 1932 and produced an almost universally disdained White Paper in 1933, outlining the gist of what would become the Government of India Act of 1935.

British administrators believed that any forward step in Indian constitutional development had, logically, to include not just the key players in British India, but also representatives of the over five hundred Indian princes whose territory comprised roughly one-third of the subcontinent outside direct British rule. The cycle of noncooperation and civil disobedience movements, the persistence of communal tensions, and British equivocation between repression and reform as the solution to the "Indian problem" had to end. After three conferences and three years of white papers, drafts, and parliamentary maneuvering, the India Act of 1935 was passed.

The act marked a major step toward conferring "dominion status" on India, but it fell short on several counts. Its key provisions extended fiscal autonomy to the provinces, abolished dyarchy at the provincial level, and enabled Indian ministers to hold key portfolios that had hitherto been reserved for the British. However, Indian politicians were quick to note that provincial authorities retained the technical ability to act independently of their largely Indian legislatures in certain cases. The India Act of 1935 also extended dyarchy to the central government of India. Thus, the act allowed increased participation by Indians at the highest levels of government, but it left certain official members "irremovable" by the people of India and responsible only to the British Parliament. Finally, all acts of the central legislature were still subject to the approval or reservation by the governor-general, or in extreme cases, disallowance by the Crown. This last caveat was somewhat anomalous. The provision approximated the conditions of the Colonial Laws Validity Act of 1865 applied by Britain to its dominions. Oddly, that restriction, which had been repealed in the Statute of Westminster in 1931, was here being reasserted in the Indian case.

Another significant feature of the 1935 act was the proposal for a federation of British and princely India. Framers of the act envisioned an elected council of state and a federal assembly. But this part of the act was never effected. It had too many "democratic" features for most princes, and it remained a paper plan. The Joint Select Committee of Parliament that drafted the act was headed by Lord Linlithgow, who was then posted to India as viceroy to oversee its implementation.

Overall, the India Act of 1935 shifted the locus of Indian governance to the subcontinent. More Indians than ever participated in local, regional, and national levels of government. Yet, the act retained key provisions for a British veto of important legislation, and more repulsive, from the standpoint of Congress, was its retention of the Communal Award and separate electorate system. Jawaharlal Nehru, in his condemnation of the India Act of 1935, called it a "new charter of slavery." The Muslim League also opposed the act. Nevertheless, all Indian political parties contested elections when the act (without its federal plan) went into operation in 1937. Those elections initiated the penultimate phase of the Raj, but any chance that the act might evolve into a working plan for a united India was interrupted by the advent of World War II. Nonetheless, in 1947 the Government of India Act of 1935 was accepted by both India and Pakistan, with few amendments, as their provisional constitutions.

Arnold P. Kaminsky

See also **Ambedkar, B. R., and the Buddhist Dalits; British Crown Raj; Gandhi, Mahatma M. K.; Government of India Act of 1919; Iqbal, Muhammad; Linlithgow, Lord; Nehru, Jawaharlal; Princely States**

BIBLIOGRAPHY

Bhagwan, Vishnoo. *Indian Constitutional Development.* 7th rev. ed. Parts I–II. New Delhi: Atma Ram, 1999.

Bose, Sugata, and Ayesha Jalal. *Modern South Asia: History, Culture, and Political Economy.* London: Routledge, 1998.

Bridge, Carl. *Holding India to the Empire: The British Conservative Party and the 1935 Constitution.* New York: Envoy Press, 1986.

Moore, Robin. *The Crisis of Indian Unity, 1917–1940.* Oxford: Clarendon Press, 1974.

GRAMDAN. *See* **Bhave, Vinoba.**

GUJARAT A state in western India, Gujarat in 2001 had a population of 50.6 million and an area of 75,700 square miles (196,000 sq. km). Gujarat is shaped like an amphitheater, encircled by rugged hills, with its plains opening to the sea and the Kathiawar penisula at its center. The semicircle has a radius of about 186 miles (300 km). This setting provided in some periods of history a base for regional powers. Mighty Indian emperors tried to control this rich region and its maritime trade throughout Indian history. Nevertheless, Gujurat has acquired an impressive historical personality of its own.

Ancient History: From the Indus Civilization to the Guptan Empire

Gujarat was an important outpost of the ancient Indus Valley (Harappa) Civilization. Two ports of this civilization are located at the eastern and western side of the Kathiawar penisula: Lothal, which has been excavated long ago, and the much larger Dholavira, where excavations are still in progress. Harappan sites like Oriyo Timbo and Rojdi in the interior of Kathiawar have shed light on the material culture of this time. The grazing of cattle and the growing of millets seem to have been the most important agricultural activities in this area. There is a theory that some of the millets came from Africa and helped to sustain people in the arid parts of Gujarat, where wheat and barley did not grow.

Gujarat participated in the maritime trade of the Indus Civilization. It also attracted European seafarers at the time of the greatest expansion of the Roman empire. *The Periplus of the Erythrean Sea*, written by an anonymous author around A.D. 50, testifies to the importance of Bharuch (Barygaza) as an leading emporium of his time. He mentions that goods from Ujjain were available at Barygaza. He also reports that the Saka rulers of the time insisted that maritime traders would visit Barygaza and not other ports farther down the coast. Cotton textiles were among the major items of trade, and they were taken by Indian traders as far as the ports in the Red Sea. The Gujaratis must have been prominent among those maritime traders, and they must have continued in this trade throughout many centuries. Tome Pires, the Portuguese traveler who met Gujaratis in the ports of Southeast Asia around 1515 was deeply impressed with their business acumen. He even recommended that his countrymen should learn from them. Khambat (Cambay), which he visited, was in his time the most important emporium of Gujarat; it reached out to Aden in the west and to Malacca in the east and depended on these farflung connections.

Kutch Woman in Colorful Attire. Located in northwestern Gujarat, Kutch is a microcosm of India's vibrant cultural diversity, honoring the rich traditions of some eighteen different tribes, cultures, and languages. AMAR TALWAR / FOTOMEDIA.

While Gujarat, with its long coastline and its many ports, was deeply attached to the Indian Ocean, it was also connected to North India by caravan routes to Agra and Delhi, one passing through Palanpur via Mount Abu to the north, the other following the Narmada valley and turning north at Burhanpur. But from the north came invaders as well. The legendary Krishna who came down from Mathura to settle at Dwarka is worshiped in Gujarat to this day. Ashoka had his famous edicts inscribed on the Girnar rock near Junagadh, and in A.D. 150 the Saka ruler Rudradaman I adorned the same rock with a Sanskrit inscription. Skandagupta of the great Gupta dynasty added another Girnnar inscription in 456. When the Huns invaded India around 500, they wiped out the last empire of ancient India, but there is no evidence of their rule in Gujarat. However, the Rajputs and Gurjars, who are supposed to have come with the Huns from Central Asia, then imposed their rule on Gujarat, which became known as Gurjaradesha. The rule of these people was at first rather decentralized. Many little kings established local strongholds. But in due course some larger political units emerged.

Medieval History: Rajputs, Gurjars, and the Sultanate of Gujarat

The local dynasties that ruled medieval Gujarat were the Valabhis (c. 490–770), with their capital near the present city of Bhavnagar, and the Chalukyas or Solankis (c. 942–1242). The Chalukyas established their capital at Patan Anhilvada in the plains at the foot of the hills about 62 miles (100 km) northeast of Ahmedabad. Their king Bhim Dev I (r. 1022–1054) was a powerful ruler, but even he could not prevent the destruction of the great Shiva temple at Somnath by the Afghan invader Mahmud of Ghazni in 1026. This attack remained an episode, and the reign of the greatest king of the Solankis, Siddhraj (1094–1143), was a period of glory for medieval Gujarat.

Gujarat also provided a safe haven for the Parsis who fled their Iranian home about 716 to protect their religious identity from the Muslims. But in due course, Muslim conquerors also reached Gujarat. Under Ala'-ud-Din Muhummad Khalji, the Delhi Sultanate extended its sway to Gujarat, and a Muslim governor was installed at Patan in 1298. But the control of Delhi over Gujarat was always tenuous, and in 1407 the last governor of the Delhi Sultanate, which had fallen prey to the invader Timur, turned into a sultan of Gujarat. His grandson Ahmad I (r. 1411–1442) then founded Ahmedabad in 1411 near the old town of Asawal. The famous architecture of the new capital reflected a beautiful synthesis of Hindu and Muslim art. The greatest sultan of Gujarat was Mahmud I Begada (r. 1458–1511). He consolidated his realm and extended its sway from Jungadh in the west to Champaner in the east. He subdued the Rajput rulers of these two fortified strongholds and made Champaner, approximately 75 miles (120 km) southeast of Ahmedabad, his new capital, from where he could launch further expeditions toward Malwa. The sultans of Gujarat derived most of their wealth from the taxing of maritime trade and were envied by the rulers of North India for that. But until the Mughals established their empire, Gujarat could very well defend itself against covetous invaders.

Gujarat under the Mughals and under the British

Humayun attacked Gujrat and sacked Champaner in 1535. But he soon had to leave Gujarat as his power was threatened in the north. Gujarat was then ruled by a series of weak sultans and ambitious courtiers. It was also threatened from the sea by the rising power of the Portuguese, who managed to entrench themselves at Div. When Akbar turned his attention to Gujarat, his conquest of this rich region was nearly effortless. The nobles of Gujarat surrendered to him. He did not even have to defeat them in a major battle. The only dangerous enemies he had to confront in Gujarat were his own rebellious cousins, the Mirzas, who had established a stronghold in South Gujarat. After he had vanquished them, Gujarat became one of his most precious possessions. Contemporary Europeans actually called Akbar the King of Cambay, because Cambay (Khambat) was the greatest port of his empire before it silted up and was then replaced by Surat.

When the Mughal empire declined, the Marathas established strongholds in Gujarat. Their great king Shivaji sacked Surat in 1664, but he did not establish any permanent territorial rule over Gujarat. This was left to a Maratha general of the eighteenth century who became the Maharaja Gaekwad of Baroda (Vadodara). When the British established their colonial rule in India, they entered into an alliance with the maharaja of Baroda, and his heirs continued to rule a large part of Gujarat until 1947. Under British rule, Gujarat consisted of a patchwork of princely states interspersed with districts under direct British control. In one of these princely states, Porbandar on the coast of Kathiawar, Mohandas Karamchand Gandhi was born in 1869, later emerging as the Mahatma, the greatest son of Gujarat, to lead the Indian freedom movement.

Gujarat in Independent India

After 1947 Gujarat remained part of the giant Bombay presidency, which had been composed by the British out of various incompatible elements. The Maharashtrians were most vocal in claiming their own linguistic state within India, but this also included Bombay (Mumbai), in which Gujarati businessmen controlled almost all economic activities. The government of India was reluctant to permit a reorganization of the Bombay presidency, as they felt that this would endanger national unity. But due to persistent agitation, Gujarat and Maharashtra were finally separated in 1960, and Mumbai and Ahmedabad became the capitals of Maharashtra and Gujarat, respectively. Later, Gujarat established a new capital, Gandhinagar, about 19 miles (30 km) north of Ahmedabad. Initially, the Congress Party, which had been in power in the Bombay presidency, also remained in control of the two new states. But in recent years the Bharatiya Janata Party (BJP) has emerged as a new force, particularly in Gujarat. The new state is in the forefront of Indian economic development, but this has also increased social tensions. Gujarat has a very assertive new middle class, which tends to support the BJP.

The Muslim Massacre of 2002

The most striking event of Gujarat's recent history was the massacre that cost the lives of thousands of

Muslims in the city of Ahmedabad. The Muslim minority amounts to only about 9 percent of the population. However, while in most parts of India the Muslims are poor artisans, workers, and peasants, there have been many rich traders among the Muslims of Gujarat. They participated in maritme trade, and many of them settled overseas. In general, they got along well with the Hindu middle class, but obviously some competition and rivalry have developed in recent times. The event that triggered the massacre in Gujarat was an attack of a Muslim mob on a train carrying Hindu activists who had visited Ayodhya, the site of the mosque destroyed in 1992. The train was stopped at a Muslim settlement near Godhra and several of its cars were burned, causing the death of several dozen women and children.

The revenge that was inflicted on the Muslims of distant Ahmedabad, who had not been involved in this crime, was terrible. There is evidence that it was not spontaneous but was pursued in a systematic manner. The police did not interfere, and the state government remained suspiciously inactive. Even middle-class Hindus participated in the looting of Muslim property. Voices were raised demanding the resignation of Chief Minister Narendra Modi, but he defied all criticism. In the subsequent elections he projected the pride (*gaurav*) of Gujarat and won with a large margin. The national leadership of his party, the BJP, did not censure him. Only after the loss of the national elections in 2004 did the former prime minister, Atal Bihari Vajpayee, admit that the massacre in Gujarat may have contributed to a setback of his party at the national level. It was an irony of fate that this extraordinary outbreak of communal violence happened in Gujarat, whose most famous son, Mahatma Gandhi, had advocated nonviolent conflict resolution. Gandhi also had very good relations with Muslims. He had been sent to South Africa by a Muslim businessman from Gujarat, and he had involved the Muslim traders from Gujarat in his campaign against racial discrimination in South Africa. He had quelled Hindu-Muslim riots in Kolkata (Calcutta) and in Delhi in 1947, and he would have been shocked by the terrible massacre of Muslims in his home state.

Dietmar Rothermund

See also **Ayodhya; Bharatiya Janata Party (BJP); Gandhi, Mahatma M. K.; Guptan Empire; Humayun; Indus Valley Civilization; Muslims**

BIBLIOGRAPHY

Commissariat, M. S. *A History of Gujarat Including a Survey of Its Chief Architectural Monuments and Inscriptions*, vol. I: *From A.D. 1297 to A.D. 1573.* Mumbai: Longmans, Green, 1938.

Kulke, Hermann, and Dietmar Rothermund. *A History of India.* 4th rev. ed. London: Routledge, 2004.

GUJRAL, INDER KUMAR *(1919–), prime minister of India (1997–1998).* Inder Kumar Gujral, political leader and global diplomat, was born in Punjab's Jhelum on 4 December 1919. Young Inder attended Hailey College in Lahore, was elected president of its Student Union, and served as general secretary of the Punjab Student Federation. Inspired by Mahatma Gandhi's *satyagraha* campaigns, he soon joined India's freedom struggle and was jailed by British police, together with his mother, Pushpa, during Gandhi's "Quit India" movement in August 1942. The tragic partition of India in mid-1947 forced the Gujrals to flee their home in what overnight had become Pakistan, settling down in Delhi. Inder volunteered to help care for many desperately impoverished Hindu and Sikh refugees, forced by fear to flee their homes in the aftermath of Punjab's hastily inept partition.

Modeling himself on India's first prime minister, Jawaharlal Nehru, Gujral joined the Indian National Congress Party, devoting himself to vigorous political action and social reform. His refugee camp work in Delhi won him the admiration of those he had helped to find jobs as well as homes, and they elected him to serve as vice-president of New Delhi's municipality, over which he later presided for many years. Nehru remained Inder Gujral's role model both in politics and social activism. Like Nehru, he was inspired by Western humanism and socialist ideals, never losing his passionate faith in democratic India's capacity to create a better future for all its people, regardless of their caste or creed, their ethnicity, or their income. He also has remained a lifelong student of India's history, and, like his poet-wife Shiela, a devotee of poetry, memorizing many of the best works of Persian and Urdu poetry, as well as epic Sanskrit *shloka*s, and poems written in Punjabi, Bengali, and English. "India is a country of vast diversities," Inder Gujral reminded his troubled nation at one of its darkest hours in the summer of 2002—as both India and Pakistan remained at high alert due to threat of nuclear war—"of language, religion, ethnicity and historic experiences, but we have chosen to stay together as one Nation. Gandhi and our freedom struggle gave us our logo . . . 'Unity in Diversity'—not uniformity." He refused to abandon his faith in Indian secularism to any reactionary "Hindu-first" prejudice or battle cry preached by political opponents.

Inder Gujral was first elected to the Lok Sabha (the lower house of India's Parliament) in 1964, retaining his seat until 1976, when he resigned from Indira Gandhi's Cabinet, where he had served as minister of information

Inder Kumar Gujral. Gujral the day he became India's prime minister, 21 April 1997. Though his tenure was brief (not quite a year) and he was unable to negotiate a peaceful end to the conflict in Kashmir, he did launch a number of diplomatic initiatives with India's other South Asian neighbors. BALDEV/CORBIS SYGMA.

and broadcasting and planning. Minister Gujral refused to take orders from Prime Minister Gandhi's younger son, Sanjay, who once tried to dictate which news stories he should approve or reject for publication during the "National Emergency" of 1975–1976. Gujral was again elected to Parliament from 1989 to 1991, and from 1992 to 1998. He then served as minister of external affairs in 1989 and 1990 and in 1996 and 1997, after which he also became India's prime minister, from 21 April 1997 until 19 March 1998, leading a multiparty Janata coalition government in New Delhi. Nehru and Gujral were India's only two prime ministers who served as their own foreign ministers.

Prime Minister Gujral presided over India's festive fiftieth anniversary National Day celebrations in New Delhi's Parliament at midnight on 15 August 1997. Speaking the next morning from the ramparts of Delhi's Red Fort, he reaffirmed India's faith in Gandhian nonviolence and Nehruvian secularism, promising to root out corruption at every level of government, and to resolve "peacefully through bilateral negotiations" differences with India's neighbors, including India's half century of

conflict with Pakistan over the state of Jammu and Kashmir. Though his tenure as prime minister proved all too brief to permit Inder Gujral to negotiate a peaceful end to Kashmir's tragic conflict, he unilaterally launched a number of confidence-building measures with India's other South Asian neighbors, including Nepal and Bangladesh, and his creative policy of "preemptive peace and friendship," known as the Gujral Doctrine, remains his most enduring diplomatic legacy to India's polity and history.

Stanley Wolpert

BIBLIOGRAPHY

Gujral, Inder Kumar. *A Foreign Policy for India.* New Delhi: Government of India, 1998.
Gupte, Pranay. *Mother India: A Political Biography of Indira Gandhi.* New York: Macmillan, 1992.
Naipaul, V. S. *India: A Wounded Civilization.* New York: Knopf, 1977.
Prasad, Bimal, ed. *India's Foreign Policy: Studies in Continuity and Change.* New Delhi: Vikas, 1979.
Singh, Amrik, ed. *The Partition in Retrospect.* New Delhi: National Institute of Punjab Studies, 2000.

ENCYCLOPEDIA OF *India*

Wolpert, Stanley. *Nehru: A Tryst with Destiny.* New York: Oxford University Press, 1996.

———. *Gandhi's Passion: The Life and Legacy of Mahatma Gandhi.* New York: Oxford University Press, 2001.

———. *Shameful Flight: The Last Years of the British Empire in India.* New York: Oxford University Press, 2005.

GUPTAN EMPIRE A powerful imperial polity based in northern and central India between the fourth and sixth centuries A.D., the Guptan empire was often regarded as embodying a classical age of Indian art and literature. The Guptan period witnessed the crystallization of a cultural and political order that would set a pattern for centuries to come. In the third century A.D., the Sassanian empire in west Asia effectively curtailed Kushana power, and in India a number of principalities that formerly owed allegiance to them became independent. The Gupta family seems to have been among these groups, though its origins are obscure. The Guptas may have ruled in the region of Magadha or, more likely, in the western Gangetic Plain. The first important king of the family was Chandragupta I (reigned A.D. 320–335), who married into the well-established and prestigious Licchavi dynasty of northern India. Chandragupta I ruled along the Ganges (Ganga) River from Magadha in the east to Saketa and Prayāga in the west. The famous "Guptan era" used to date inscriptions between the fourth and sixth centuries begins with his accession to throne. His son Samudragupta (reigned A.D. 350–375) seems to have inherited the crown amid controversy. He may not have been the eldest son, and his Allahabad pillar inscription makes much of him being "selected" by his father over others of "equal birth." Contemporary coins mention another Gupta prince named Kacha who was probably a rival. Samudragupta's political capabilities, however, are hardly in doubt. According to the long eulogistic introduction composed by his courtier Harisena on the Allahabad pillar, Samudragupta conquered numerous kings through a performance of a *digvijaya*, or "conquest of the directions." These included: rulers of the northern Gangetic region, who were "violently uprooted"; forest or tribal chiefs in central India, who "were made into servants"; and kings of southern and eastern India, who were "captured and released," that is, defeated but allowed to retain their kingdoms, and who, like other kings of eastern and western India (notably the Shakas and Kushanas), paid homage to Samudragupta. Perhaps more important than the extent of Samudragupta's conquests is the political structure it implied, since in all but the most proximate regions of his empire, he allowed defeated or submissive kings to retain their kingdoms in return for some form of service. These services, which are formally mentioned for the first time in the Allahabad inscription, included, variously, the paying of tribute,

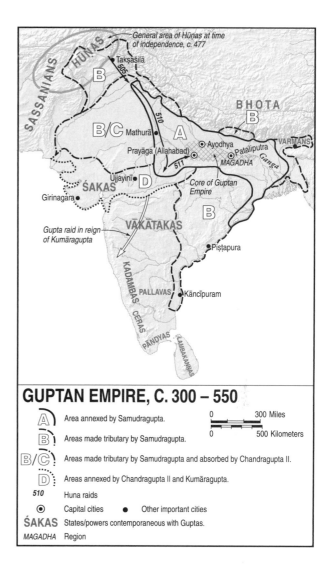

GUPTAN EMPIRE, C. 300 – 550

- (A) Area annexed by Samudragupta.
- (B) Areas made tributary by Samudragupta.
- (B/C) Areas made tributary by Samudragupta and absorbed by Chandragupta II.
- (D) Areas annexed by Chandragupta II and Kumāragupta.
- **510** Huna raids
- ⊙ Capital cities ● Other important cities
- **ŚAKAS** States/powers contemporaneous with Guptas.
- *MAGADHA* Region

0 — 300 Miles
0 — 500 Kilometers

court attendance, the gift of maidens, and the offering of military assistance. While the Guptan monarch took imperial titles like "Great King over Kings" (*mahārājādhirāja*) and "Supreme Lord" (*paramabhattāraka*), subordinate rulers were permitted only more modest titles like "Great King" (*mahārāja*).

Samudragupta was succeeded by his son Chandragupta II (reigned A.D. 375–415) who also seems to have risen to the throne through the elimination of a rival, one Rāmagupta, whose existence is attested by coins and literary sources. A marriage between Chandragupta II's daughter Prabhāvatīguptā and the Vākātaka king Rudrasena II secured the southern borders of the newly founded Guptan settlements in middle India at Udayagiri and Arikana. Chandragupta II's major military campaign was fought against the Shakas in western India, and he took the title Vikramāditya (Sun of Prowess), perhaps to commemorate his success against them.

A notable feature of early Guptan political culture is its attempt to invoke the bygone imperium of the Mauryas. This is suggested not only by the use of the name "Chandragupta," the founder of the Mauryan empire, but also by supplementing Mauryan rock faces and pillars with Guptan royal inscriptions, as well as imitating Mauryan lion capitals. The famous text on statecraft, the *Artha Shāstra*, which was attributed to the minister of the Mauryan king Chandragupta, also seems to have been reworked during the Guptan period by one Visnugupta. The reasons for such an evocation are unclear, for in many ways Gupta imperial culture was also innovative and formative. Imperial terminology and protocols of service, deference, alliance, and war were standardized by the end of the Guptan period and remained largely stable (with some modification) for nearly a millennium. Religiously, the period saw a great consolidation and bid for court patronage of the theistic cults, Shaivism and Vaishnavism. The transition to Sanskrit as a courtly language, which had begun during Kushana and Shaka times, was completed by the fourth century, and from Gupta times, both the practice and patronage of the arts (literature, music, and drama) became the sine qua non of aristocratic and urban existence. Samudragupta, for example, is praised in his inscriptions as proficient at both prose and poetry and is depicted on his coins seated, playing a lyre. The famous Sanskrit poet Kālidāsa, author of a number of poems and dramas, also lived at the court of Samudragupta's son Chandragupta II. Vātsyāyana, author of the treatise on romantic love called the Kāma Sūtra, also probably lived in the Guptan period.

The structure of the Gupta empire was less "centralized" than the Mauryan, and although some officials remained the same, there was an expansion in both palace personnel and lesser, semiautonomous officials. Two characteristics of Guptan polity may be noted. First, landed lords became the essential building blocks of polity, either as subordinate kings who retained patrimonial lands or palace servants who were deeded property and over generations came to wield effective lordship. Second, the importance of such landed lords as political subordinates and royal servants meant that kings employed men who had significant local power bases, and who were often more than ready to assert autonomy in moments of imperial weakness. These processes taken together are thought to herald an epoch of "Indian feudalism."

The latter half of the fifth century saw a slow decline of Guptan fortunes. Chandragupta II was succeeded by Kumāragupta (reigned A.D. 415–454), who fought off a branch of the White Huns, or Hephthalites (known as the Hūnas in Indian sources), from the northwest. Kumāragupta's successors were less fortunate, and due in part to internal problems, Guptan power slowly shrank in the next fifty years, until at the end of the fifth century the Hūnas were able to enter northern India. We find Hūna inscriptions in Arikana, the erstwhile city of the Guptas in central India, dated at the beginning of the sixth century. As Guptan power contracted and finally disappeared entirely in the first half of the next (sixth) century, a number of smaller kingdoms, formerly subordinate to the Guptas, asserted independence. These families most typically adopted Guptan political vocabulary and thus ensured a lasting legacy for the dynasty down to the thirteenth century.

Daud Ali

See also **Artha Shāstra; Kālidāsa**

BIBLIOGRAPHY

Bakker, Hans. *The Vākāṭakas: An Essay in Hindu Iconology.* Groningen: E. Forsten, 1997.
Bhandarkar, D. R. *Inscriptions of the Early Gupta Kings.* Revised edition of *Corpus Inscriptionum Indicarum*, vol. 3, edited by B. Chhabra and G. S. Gai. Delhi: Government Epigraphist for India, 1981.
Gupta, P. L. *The Imperial Guptas.* 2 vols. Varanasi: Vishwavidyalaya Prakashan, 1974–1979.
Jha, D. N. "Land Revenue in the Mauryan and Gupta Periods." In *Economy and Society in Early India*, edited by D. N. Jha. Delhi: Munshiram Manoharlal, 1993.
Maity, S. K. *Economic Life in Northern India in the Gupta Period, c. 300–550.* 2nd ed. Delhi: Motilal Banarsidass, 1970.
The Raghuvamsa of Kālidāsa with the Commentary of Mallinātha. Sanskrit text, edited with an English translation by G. R. Nandargikar. Delhi: Motilal Banarsidass, 1982.
Smith, Bardwell. *Essays on Gupta Culture.* Delhi: Motilal Banarsidass, 1983.

GUPTAN PERIOD ART The Gupta dynasty governed much of northern India for about two hundred years after its founding by Chandragupta I in A.D. 320. During this period, sculpture in stone and terra-cotta rose to high aesthetic levels, and the earliest Hindu stone temples were created. It was a period of not only outstanding artistic accomplishments but also the creation of some of India's most honored poetic compositions, including the plays and poetry of the famed Kālidāsa. We have the testimony of Chinese Buddhist pilgrims who visited India during this time, describing the social, cultural, and political customs and institutions, which were, by our contemporary standards, unusually enlightened. Modern historians have used such exemplary characteristics to propose the Guptan period as a "Golden Age," a time when Indian art and culture reached its apogee, creating a classical standard against which all Indian traditions can be compared. While these claims are not unfounded, it is important to remember that knowledge of the Guptan dynasty and the art of the period was lost early in ancient India, and was only rediscovered by nineteenth-century scholars and antiquarians, who used the Guptan period for various nationalist and political purposes.

The Guptan kings themselves, although they ultimately controlled much of northern India, were not major patrons of sculpture and architecture. There is only one temple site known today that was actually patronized by the Guptas: Bhitari, in modern Uttar Pradesh, which has an inscription by Skandagupta (reigned c. 455–467), the last of the major Guptan kings. The temple remains at Bhitari are brick. Terra-cotta and stone were used to decorate the temples, and small pieces found at the site of what was once a large stone Vishnu image are probably part of the Vishnu sculpture that Skandagupta's inscription mentions he had made.

While the Guptan kings cannot be connected to any temple or sculptural patronage other than Bhitari, they were producers of lavish gold coins whose tiny images, including portraits of the kings, rank among the most accomplished artistic creations of the period. The portraits of the kings show them performing a variety of tasks that are part of the vocabulary of kingship, including sacrificing by placing incense into a censer and playing the lyre to indicate the king's musical and intellectual accomplishments. A coin type of Samudragupta (reigned A.D. 350– 375) shows a horse standing before a sacrificial post (*yūpa*) with the Sanskrit inscription reading: "The king of kings who performed the horse sacrifice wins heaven, having protected the earth." The coin commemorates Samudragupta's performance of the vedic horse sacrifice (*ashvamedha*) that would make him a universal king (*cakravartin*), while on the reverse is an image of the queen holding a flywhisk.

Scholars assume that during the Guptan period many Hindu temples in brick, like the remains of those at Bhitari, were built throughout northern India, particularly in the Gangetic Plain. Only one fairly complete example remains today, however, that at Bhitargaon. The assumption is that the other temples have been over time dismantled and their bricks reused. The only secure evidence for their existence, however, are the various finds of loose terra-cotta reliefs that turn up and must once have decorated brick structures. Many of these terra-cotta reliefs are of the highest quality and are a major artistic accomplishment. The plastic quality of terra-cotta worked well for Guptan artists, who favored a fluid and unencumbered sculptural modeling.

It was also during the Guptan period that Hindu temples began to be made of stone, both temples that were rock-cut caves as well as temples built from stone blocks. Again, these temples are found mostly in relatively

Fifth-Century Stone Sculpture. During the Guptan period, northern India, now returned to native rule, experienced a degree of artistic achievement by which later civilizations continue to be judged. NATIONAL MUSEUM / FOTOMEDIA.

peripheral geographical areas, in an arc of what must have been forested land around the edge of the Gangetic Plain and outside the Guptan heartland, mostly in what is today Madhya Pradesh. These temples and caves are all small and structurally diverse, indicating their early date and novelty. The absence of early stone temples elsewhere in northern India remains unexplained.

The earliest Hindu cave temples are located at Udayagiri near Vidisha in Madhya Pradesh. There are twenty rock-cut caves, all very simple, with a single cell and one doorway with a porch. There are indications that some of the caves had structures built in front as well, probably of wood. Two inscriptions at the site name Chandragupta II who, while not the patron, came to the site to celebrate a battle victory around A.D. 401. Because of the inscription, we can date caves 5 and 6 to around A.D. 400. The facade of cave 6 has a series of images carved in relief. The importance of these dated images cannot be overstated, as it is the first time we have Hindu images set into a context. While Hindu icons date from around the first century B.C., almost all are from Mathura and are loose finds, so that we have little idea how they were originally intended to be organized.

The image series at cave 6, starting from the far left side, begins with the elephant-headed Gaṇesha. Across the front (from the left) is Vishnu, then two door guardians on each side of the door to the cell, then a second Vishnu, and two images of the goddess Durgā as killer of the Buffalo Demon. On the right side are two shallow niches that once housed now very ruined sets of the Seven Mothers (sapta mātṛkās). Finally, flanking the top of the door to the cell are two females, personifications of the sacred rivers, Gaṇgā and Yamunā. The cell itself is today empty, but it would have held a Shiva liṅga. Thus, the little cave has an elaborated and surprisingly complicated iconography that involves Shaivite, Vaishnavite, and Shakta deities, and such imagery as paired door guardians and river goddesses that have remained standard at Hindu temples even today.

One of the most famous and frequently illustrated sculptures from ancient India is that of the Boar avatār of Vishnu (Varāha) carved in high relief in the niche next to cave 6. The figure has a boar head and human body, and is shown in triumph having rescued the earth, here personified as a woman holding onto the Boar's tusk, from the watery flood of the ocean. While the story of the rescue comes from a number of texts, the enormous tableau (the Boar is 12 feet [3.6 m] tall), with detailed and numerous figures carved across the back and sides of the niche, has been interpreted by scholars as having an allegorical meaning related to Chandragupta II's victory in conquering most of northern India for the Guptas. It was under Chandragupta II's reign (c. 375–415) that the Guptas reached the height of their political power, with Chandragupta removing the last of the resisting political powers and consolidating the geography of his kingdom. This included the area around modern Allahabad, where the two rivers, the Ganges and the Yamuna, join together. This is one of the most sacred areas to the Hindus, and these two rivers are depicted on both sides of the Boar niche, coming together to form one river and flowing into the ocean, represented by the wavy lines at the bottom of the relief. This is the ocean from which the earth has been rescued, but it is also a pun on the name of Chandragupta's father, Samudragupta, as Samudra means

"ocean"; the imagery implies that now the Guptas control India from ocean to ocean across northern India.

The earliest Hindu temples built in stone date to slightly later than the Udayagiri cave 6, that is, the first quarter of the fifth century, and like the cave temple consist of a simple cell with a porch. Some of these fifth- and sixth-century temples retain part of what were towered roofs, but none is complete. Scholars are divided on whether some of the earliest temples, such as Sanchi Temple 17, were actually flat-roofed, without a tower, but the tower very quickly became standard on all Hindu temples, as seen on temples today as well.

The Vishnu Temple at Deogarh, of the early sixth century, is one of the best preserved of the Guptan Hindu temples. While the single-cell shrine is small (inside about 9 feet square), it has an exquisitely carved doorway and three large relief panels on each of the other three sides. There are still sections of the tower remaining as well. The shrine is set on a square, raised plinth of earth, enclosed with low stone walls with directional stairs and small, now ruined, shrines at each of the four corners. The three relief panels are each masterpieces of Guptan period relief sculpture. Each panel depicts a form of Vishnu—as the savior of the entrapped elephant, as an ascetic, and as preserver of the universe while lying on the cosmic snake. The concept of the Hindu deity in the temple shrine manifesting himself on the walls of the temple in the four directions and in multiple forms for the worshiper, who circumambulates the outside of the temple in worship, is seen in its nascent form at Deogarh.

Jain and Buddhist Art of the Guptan Period

The Guptan kings were Hindus, but both Jainism and Buddhism were also important religions during the Guptan period, for which art and architecture were produced in great numbers. At many sites, for example at Mathura, all three religions existed together, with art being created in a shared style but depicting different gods and their stories. The focus of Buddhist worship was on the stupa, a relic mound that by the Guptan period was highly elaborated in hundreds of forms, materials, and sizes, and on the Buddha in human or anthropomorphic form. One of the most amazing sites in India is Ajanta, a rock-cut monastic site of some thirty caves that stands as one of the world's inspired artistic accomplishments and dates primarily from the second half of the fifth century.

The histories of Buddhist rock-cut architecture and that of the Hindu caves stand in stark contrast. We have seen the beginning of Hindu rock-cut architecture at Udayagiri with the simple cave 6 of about A.D. 400. By that date, the Buddhists had been making rock-cut caves for over five centuries, and were producing structures of elaborate complexity. The late appearance of Hindu architecture in stone versus that of the Buddhists is due in part to the Hindus' lack of the highly organized monastic structure of the Buddhists, which could plan, finance, and create enormous monastic complexes of stone with involved and extensive narrative reliefs. Hindus at that time worshiped their deities in local shrines, under trees, and in their homes, all of which did not call for temples and large icons.

When and where the anthropomorphic Buddha image was first created continues to be the focus of considerable research and debate. By the first century B.C., small images were being made, but it was the monumental images created at Mathura around A.D. 125 that were to be decisive for the form of the Buddha image in India. By the Guptan period, the Buddha image had a fairly consistent iconography: the robe of a monk, a cranial bump, and certain standard hand gestures. At Mathura, the Guptan-period Buddha retained much of the earlier monumental Buddha style, including the broad shoulders, large arms, and swelling chest. A new type of Buddha image appeared, however, at another site, that of Sarnath, the place near Varanasi on the Ganges River where the Buddha gave his First Sermon. The Sarnath Buddha image appeared in the second half of the fifth century, and was a radical departure from the Mathura type of Buddha image from which it was ultimately derived. Rather than the powerful and masculine Mathura Buddha, the Sarnath images were much slighter in build, with delicate facial features and narrow shoulders, their robes clinging tightly to their bodies without any indication of fabric folds. It is this new style of Buddha image that became popular, influencing images across India and ultimately in China and Southeast Asia as well.

The Vakataka Dynasty

The rock-cut monastery of Ajanta mentioned above, while created during the Guptan period, was not under the control of the Guptan dynasty. Ajanta was in an area controlled by the Vakataka dynasty. Scholars have long categorized the art of Ajanta, and indeed all art in northern India during the fourth to sixth centuries, as "Guptan art." It has only been since the mid-1990s that the full importance of the art done under the Vakatakas, who ruled more or less simultaneously with the Guptas and were at times related to them through marriage, has become clear, due to recent finds and excavations.

The Vakatakas were split into two branches. The eastern branch ruled the territory where Ajanta was built. A western branch, which ruled near modern Nagpur, patronized Hindu temples and art. Excavations and field research at sites such as Mandhal, Ramtek Hill, and Paunar have revealed archaeological and artistic material that is only just now being evaluated, but it is clear that our placement of this material within a Guptan stylistic tradition is not correct. The Hindu sculpture from Mandhal, for example, in its squat heavy forms and unusual iconography, has yet to be integrated into the art historical traditions of India as we know them today. Whether or not the Guptan period can be considered an artistic Golden Age, there remains plentiful material and scholarly rethinking for future art historians.

Robert Brown

See also **Ajanta; Ashvamedha; Guptan Empire; Kālidāsa; Sculpture: Buddhist; Shiva and Shaivism; Vishnu and Avatāras**

BIBLIOGRAPHY

Bakker, Hans T. *The Vakatakas: An Essay in Hindu Iconology*. Groningen: Egbert Forsten, 1997.

Brown, Robert L. "Vakataka Hindu Art." In *The Vakataka Heritage: Indian Culture at the Crossroads*, edited by H. T. Bakker. Groningen: Egbert Forsten, 2004.

Harle, J. C. *Gupta Sculpture: Indian Sculpture of the Fourth to the Sixth Centuries A.D.* Oxford: Oxford University Press, 1974.

Jamkhedkar, A. P. "The Vakataka Area and Gupta Sculpture." In *The Golden Age: Gupta Art—Empire, Province and Influence*, edited by K. Khandalavaha. Mumbai: Marg, 1991.

Jayaswal, Vidula. *Gupta Period: Excavations at Bhitari*. New Delhi: Aryan Books, 2001.

Miller, Barbara Stoler. "A Dynasty of Patrons: The Representation of Gupta Royalty in Coins and Literature." In *The Powers of Art: Patronage in Indian Culture*, edited by Barbara Stoler Miller. Delhi: Oxford University Press, 1992.

Pal, Pratapaditya. *The Ideal Image: The Gupta Sculptural Tradition and Its Influence*. New York: Asia Society, 1978.

Williams, Joanna Gottfried. *The Art of Gupta India: Empire and Province*. Princeton, N.J.: Princeton University Press, 1982.

GURKHAS. *See* **Nepal.**

GURMUKHI. *See* **Languages and Scripts.**

GURU NANAK (1469–1539), *first of the ten Sikh gurus.* Nanak was the first of the ten Sikh gurus (saintly teachers), a line that ended with the death of Guru Gobind Singh in 1708. Nanak belonged to the saintly tradition of folk poets of northern India, like Kabir, who died about twenty years before Nanak was born. The verses of both Nanak and Kabir were included in the Adi Granth, the sacred book of the Sikhs. Nanak believed in the Akal Purakh (Supreme Being) and rejected all outward forms of worship.

Guru Nanak. In November 2003, members of the Sikh community presented a portrait of Guru Nanak to former Prime Minister Atal Bihari Vajpayee (right). Approximately 35 million Sikhs live in India, most in Punjab, their ancestral home. AFP/GETTY IMAGES.

He was born to a Hindu family at Talwandi, a village in the Punjab. In addition to Hindi, he learned Persian and Arabic at school, then worked as an accountant. He married and had two sons, but then he embarked on a long walking trip, attracting followers everywhere. Hindus and Muslims were equally touched by his teachings. He became a legendary figure, and there are many stories about his life, some of which reflect the radicalism of his belief. Once he saw pilgrims bathing in the Ganga (Ganges) throwing water toward the rising sun, believing that it would reach their ancestors. Nanak turned around on hearing this and threw water toward the west. When asked why he did this, he replied that he was watering his fields in the Punjab. The pilgrims made fun of him, but he replied that if the water they were throwing reached their ancestors, his water would surely reach his fields. It is also reported that he visited Mecca, where he fell asleep with his feet pointing toward the Kaaba. A guard woke him, scolding him for pointing his feet toward God. He then requested that the guard move his tired body in any direction where he thought his feet would not point at God.

In his old age, Nanak returned to the Punjab and lived with his family. There he was joined by a very ardent follower named Lehna. Nanak anointed him, renaming him Angad. Guru Angad then became his successor as the second guru of the Sikhs. It was this act of installing a successor that helped to make Nanak the revered founder of the Sikh faith; otherwise, he might have been remembered simply as one of India's saintly poets and religious reformers.

Dietmar Rothermund

BIBLIOGRAPHY

Grewal, J. S. *Guru Nanak in History*. Chandigarh: Publication Bureau of Panjab University, 1969.

McLeod, W. H. *Guru Nanak and the Sikh Religion*. 2nd ed. Delhi: Oxford University Press, 1976.

GURUS. *See* **Sikhism.**

HAQ, A. K. FAZLUL *(1873–1962), Muslim political leader.* Abul Kasim Fazlul Haq (also spelled "Huq") emerged in the first part of the twentieth century as a charismatic Bengali Muslim leader with mass appeal. He was the first important leader who did not come from a landholding family and was not a member of the aristocratic Muslim families who dominated Bengal politics until the partition of India in 1947. He rose on his own merits. He was in favor of intercommunal harmony, and at heart believed in a united Bengal comprising both Hindus and Muslims.

Haq was born to a well-to-do Muslim family in a village in the Barisal district (now in Bangladesh) in 1873. Both his grandfather and father were district-town lawyers—a *muktear* (with knowledge of Persian) and a pleader (with knowledge of English), respectively. Education and a professional career were an integral part of Haq's family heritage.

Haq had a traditional Arabic and Persian education at home. He graduated from the Barisal District School in 1890, and was admitted to Kolkata's prestigious Presidency College. He graduated from the College with triple honors in chemistry, mathematics, and physics in 1894. He was the first Muslim student to earn a master's degree in mathematics and, the following year, a law degree from Calcutta University.

Haq began his career as a teacher and a journalist. He taught for two years at Rajchandra College in Barisal in 1903 and 1904, then became an editor of two Bengali-language journals and a newspaper daily, *Navayuz* (New Age). He joined the government service in 1906 and served in several important mid-level posts in Bengal and Assam until 1912. He decided to move to Kolkata and join the Bar. He served as a junior to the famed judicial luminary Sir Ashutosh Mookherjee, later vice chancellor of Calcutta University. He came in close contact with the prominent nationalist leaders of the time, mostly moderates such as W. C. Bonnerji, Surendranath Banerjea, Ashwini Kumar Dutt, Shamsul Huda, and Abdul Rasul.

Like a few other Muslim leaders in the first quarter of the twentieth century, Haq saw no contradiction between being a member of both the Indian National Congress and the All-India Muslim League, of which he was a founder in Dhaka in 1906. From 1916 to 1921, he was president of the All-India Muslim League. All through his political life, from 1913 until the partition, he was a member of the Bengal legislature. He was instrumental in drafting the Lucknow Pact of 1916, bringing the League and the Congress together on a common platform. He served as the Congress's general secretary in 1918 and 1919. He did not, however, favor Gandhi's noncooperation movement. From 1930 to 1933, he represented Indian Muslims at the Round Table Conference in London.

He broke away from the Muslim League in 1936, as major policy differences between him and Mohammad Ali Jinnah surfaced, proving insurmountable. He formed a new political party, the Krishak Praja Party, in 1937. During the elections of that year, he won handily against the Muslim League leader Nazimuddin in the Bengal legislature. He offered to form a coalition government with the Congress in Bengal. The Congress leadership refused to accept his offer. The League seized the opportunity and agreed to join Haq's coalition. As a partner of the League, Haq was briefly persuaded by its growing separatist strategy. He moved the Pakistan resolution in 1940 in Lahore. A year later, discouraged by the League's extremist rhetoric and action, he resigned from the League, which led to the ministry's fall. In 1946 Haq rejoined the League, only to leave it again after the partition to form the Krishak Shramik Party in 1954. After winning the election in East Pakistan that year with an overwhelming majority, he formed and led the United Front Ministry. With the Muslim League reduced to a shambles in East Pakistan, Haq was named the chief minister. Sheikh Mujibur Rahman joined Haq as an ardent follower. Haq made a nostalgic journey back to Kolkata after forming his cabinet. At a highly charged emotional moment during a public meeting in Kolkata, he spoke about the commonality and unity of the two Bengals. His ministry was dismissed and replaced by Governor's Rule. Tired of politics and disillusioned, A. K. Fazlul Haq died in 1962.

Throughout his personal and political life, Haq negotiated between his rural roots in Bengal among Muslims and Hindus, and the challenges of provincial and national politics. As a result, there were several overlapping layers to his personality that also shaped his politics. He was a Bangla-speaking, hearty and robust, rustic Muslim who loved his land and people; he was also a highly educated, urbane Bhadralok (intelligentsia) who endeared himself to Kolkata's Hindu elites. He was a contrast to the traditional landholding Muslim aristocrats, yet his prominence in his profession and in politics enabled him to marry, not once but three times, into aristocratic North Indian Muslim families. In sum, Haq remained a quintessential Bengali: he is loved and revered in both West Bengal and Bangladesh today as Sher-i-Bangal (The Tiger of Bengal).

Dilip K. Basu

See also **All-India Muslim League; Congress Party; Rahman, Sheikh Mujibur**

BIBLIOGRAPHY

Broomfield, John. *Elite Conflict in a Plural Society*. Berkeley: University of California Press, 1968.
Gordon, Leonard. *Bengal: The Nationalist Movement*. New York: Columbia University Press, 1974.

HARA. *See* **Hinduism (Dharma); Shiva and Shaivism.**

HARAPPA The Indus Civilization was first discovered in the course of exploratory excavations at Harappa by Alexander Cunningham in 1856 and 1872. Major excavations between 1920 and 1934, directed by Rai Bahadur Daya Ram Sahni and Madho Sarup Vats, found that the site had been badly looted of bricks, but important inscribed seals, architecture, figurines, and sculptures were discovered that have contributed greatly to our understanding of Indus culture. Subsequently, numerous excavations were conducted by different officers of the Archaeological Survey of India and, after 1947, by the Pakistan Department of Archaeology and Museums.

Harappa is situated on a low Pleistocene terrace between two major tributaries of the Indus River, the Ravi and the ancient Beas (now the Sutlej). One-third of the ancient site is occupied by the modern city of Harappa, which is still an important regional center for agriculture and craft production. Harappa was connected by trade to Mohenjo-Daro in the south, as well as to distant regions such as Central Asia, the Persian Gulf, and Mesopotamia.

Although this is the type-site for the Harappa culture, most of the popular focus shifted to Mohenjo-Daro, where spectacular architectural remains were well preserved. Nevertheless, Harappa's most important contribution is that it is the only major city that has revealed the full sequence of occupation, beginning from the earliest farming village to the rise and eventual decline of the city. The mounded ruins of ancient Harappa consist of three large walled sectors and several smaller suburbs that cover approximately .6 square miles (150 hectares). The original settlement was probably a single village during the earliest part of the Ravi Phase, around 3500 B.C. As it grew in size, it split into two sections, and by the Kot Diji Phase (2800–2600 B.C.) there is evidence for two distinct mounds that appear to have been surrounded by separate mud-brick perimeter walls. During the Harappa Phase (2600–1900 B.C.), these walled areas were enlarged, and new perimeter walls were built to enclose each sector of the urban center. Gateways at strategic locations in the walls allowed the dominant elites in each sector to control access into and out of their neighborhoods. Economic as well as political competition probably stimulated the continuing expansion of the site during the 700 years of the Harappa Phase. Three periods of settlement growth and expansion can be defined, and these are associated with the construction of new suburbs, changes in seals and writing, new pottery forms, specialized crafts, and changing trade networks.

Excavations in the walled suburb of Mound F have revealed some of the most famous structures at the site, dating from the middle and latter part of the Harappa Phase. Discoveries of a large furnace for firing pottery, a hoard of copper tools, and a hoard of jewelry suggest that prosperous merchants and craftsmen inhabited this part of the site. The so-called granary was built around 2450 to 2200 B.C. on a massive mud-brick foundation over 164 feet (50 m) north-south and 131 feet (40 m) east-west. There is no evidence that this structure was used for storing grain or other commodities. Almost two hundred

Remains of the Granaries of Harappa, Pakistan. The so-called granaries of Harappa, built between 2450 and 2200 B.C. The circular brick platforms were originally thought to have been utilized for husking grain, but recent archaeological reexamination has not uncovered any evidence of this or the use of the entire structure for storing grain. ROGER WOOD / CORBIS.

years later, we see the construction of circular brick platforms that were thought to have been used for husking grain, but re-examination of these circular platforms has not uncovered any evidence of grain or chaff. Another important set of buildings, constructed around the same time as the circular platforms, appear to have been constructed with identical floor plans and orientation as part of a housing project. Although originally referred to as workmen's quarters, these houses are substantial brick structures that could have housed merchants and traders.

During the Late Harappa Phase (1900–1300 B.C.), some areas of the city were overcrowded, possibly as a result of refugees from regions to the east, where the Sarasvati-Ghaggar-Hakra River was beginning to dry up. Harappa is the only excavated Indus site where there is strong evidence demonstrating the gradual transition from the Harappa to the Late Harappa Phase. Continuities in some technologies and art styles and changes in other aspects of technology indicate that the transition was neither abrupt nor the result of replacement by new people. However, in the end there was a major change in religion, and the Harappan extended burials were replaced by pot burials that contained the secondary burial of long bones and skulls. We know from later Vedic texts that the people who came after the Harappans spoke an Indo-Aryan language and practiced a very

different religion. After the Late Harappan period, the region was not abandoned, but the upper levels of the site were destroyed, and fragments of Gupta brick architecture and sculpture dating to around A.D. 320 to 454 are all that remains of what must have been a very large Early Historic city.

Jonathan Mark Kenoyer

See also **Indus Valley Civilization; Mohenjo-Daro**

BIBLIOGRAPHY

Kenoyer, Jonathan Mark. *Ancient Cities of the Indus Valley Civilization.* Karachi: Oxford University Press, 1998.
Meadow, Richard H., and Jonathan Mark Kenoyer. "Excavations at Harappa 1993: The City Walls and Inscribed Materials." In *South Asian Archaeology 1993*, edited by A. Parpola and P. Koskikallio. Helsinki: Suomalainen Tiedeakatemia, 1994.
———. "Excavations at Harappa 1994–1995: New Perspectives on the Indus Script, Craft Activities, and City Organization." In *South Asian Archaeology 1995*, edited by B. Allchin and R. Allchin. New Delhi: Oxford and IBH Publishing, 1997.
Possehl, Gregory L. *The Indus Civilization: A Contemporary Perspective.* Walnut Creek, Calif.: AltaMira Press, 2002.

HARDINGE, LORD *(1858–1944), viceroy of India (1911–1916).* Liberal Lord Charles Hardinge of Penshurst served as viceroy of India from 1911 to 1916. His first major act was to recommend the reunification of Bengal, announced by King George V on 12 December 1911 at his grand Delhi durbar coronation. Not only was provincial Bengal's heartland reunited, but the capital of British India would be removed from Bengal's Calcutta (Kolkata), to be resurrected in New Delhi, on the historic ruin-strewn plains around Old Delhi, where no fewer than nine previous capitals of North India, including that of the Great Mughals, had flourished and fallen. When Viceroy Hardinge entered Old Delhi atop his royal elephant in 1912, he was wounded by a terrorist's bomb, thrown from a high window into his howdah. His wife never fully recovered from the shock, dying soon afterward. One other viceroy, Lord Mayo, had been assassinated by a Pathan prisoner in 1872. Lord Hardinge stoically carried on, however, until the Mespot disaster in World War I prompted his departure from India.

In early August 1914, when Lord Hardinge declared India at war with Germany, he hardly anticipated the all but universal support in response, declarations of loyalty to the British Raj loudly proclaimed by all of India's some six hundred princes, as well as most of its people, Hindu, Muslim, and Sikh alike. Within the first month of war, two British Indian divisions and a cavalry brigade embarked from Karachi's port to Marseille, bolstering the Western Front on the very eve of the fiercest German assault against Ypres; thousands of Indian troops were killed, several heroes among them posthumously honored with Victorian Crosses. Soon after Turkey joined the Central Powers before the end of 1914, Indian troops were shipped to the Persian Gulf, easily capturing Basra as they started up the road toward Baghdad, which they never reached. The "Mespot" (Mesopotamian) disaster that all but destroyed India's army at Kut before they surrendered in April 1916 would soon force Britain's secretary of state for India, Austen Chamberlain, to resign, leading to Viceroy Hardinge's replacement by Horse Guard double Captain Viscount Chelmsford.

Hardinge returned home to rejoin Whitehall's Foreign Office, where his public career had begun in 1906, serving for the remaining years of World War I as permanent undersecretary of state for foreign affairs. He was one of Britain's most brilliant and accomplished diplomats, and one of India's most sympathetic viceroys.

Stanley Wolpert

See also **Bengal; Chelmsford, Lord**

BIBLIOGRAPHY

Ellinwood, DeWitt C., and C. D. Pradhan, eds. *India and World War I*. Delhi: Manohar, 1978.

Hardinge, Charles, Baron Hardinge of Penshurst. *My Indian Years: 1910–1916*. London: J. Murray, 1948.

Lucas, Sir Charles. *The Empire at War*, vol. 5. London: Oxford University Press, 1920.

Wolpert, Stanley. *A New History of India*. 7th ed. New York: Oxford University Press, 2003.

HARI. *See* **Hinduism (Dharma); Vishnu and Avatāras.**

HARSHA *(c. 590–647), ruler of North India (r. 606–647).* King Harsha ruled over much of North India during the first half of the seventh century. The sources for reconstructing Harsha's life include a biography written by the court poet Bāna, a handful of inscriptions issued by Harsha and contemporary rulers, and the travel account of the Chinese monk Hsieun Tsang, who visited Harsha's court toward the end of his reign. Harsha (also known as Shīlāditya) belonged to the Vardhana or Pushyabhūti family of Sthānvīshvara in eastern Punjab. Though their origins are obscure, the Vardhanas seem to have taken royal titles not long after the fall of the Gupta empire at the beginning of the sixth century, when they were subordinate to more powerful houses like the Maukharis of Kanauj. The family's fortunes began to change in the reign of Prabhākara Vardhana (c. 580–606), Harsha's father. This king's military conquests and alliances made him a formidable enough ruler to attract a marriage proposal for his daughter Rājyashrī (Harsha's sister) from the prince Grahavarman, of the powerful Maukhari house. Soon after, Prabhākara Vardhana was taken ill and died suddenly. Though his court biographer, Bāna, portrays Harsha as his father's choice in succession, other sources indicate that his elder brother, Rājya Vardhana, actually inherited the throne. But other events soon changed the course of dynastic politics.

A rival alliance between kings from Malwa and Gauda attacked Kanauj. When news arrived that Grahavarman had been killed and his queen Rājyashrī imprisoned, the young Rājya Vardhana set off to avenge his brother-in-law and release his sister. Though successful in battle, he was treacherously murdered while negotiating with the king of Gauda. According to Bāna, the ministers of the ruined Maukhari court then invited young Harsha to ascend the throne. As inheritor of both his patrimonial lands as well as the more powerful Maukhari kingdom, Harsha was now the most powerful king in North India. He immediately embarked on a conquest of eastern India to avenge the death of his brother and to subdue the Gauda sphere of influence; he then turned his attention to the kingdoms to the west and eventually southward to Mālwa. Harsha's victories did not lead to the accession of lands directly to his empire, but rather to the establishment of a hierarchy of vassals and subordinate kings called *sāmanta*s.

Harsha's empire was among the most famed in Asia, receiving emissaries from the Tang emperor and drawing a number of prominent poets and scholars to his court. He himself was a skilled poet and wrote two palace dramas, *Ratnavalī* and *Priyadarshikā*). The culture of Harsha's age, though still very much like that of the Guptas, reveals a discernible predilection for luxury and the trappings of a "feudal" mannerism. Politically, his long-term goal was the defeat of the powerful Chalukya dynasty in the Deccan, who regarded Harsha as the mere lord of "northern" India. Harsha and the Chalukyan king Pulakeshin II (r. 610–643), accompanied by their *sāmanta*s, met in battle near the Narmada River between 630 and 634, where Pulakeshin seems to have been victorious, dashing Harsha's ambitions of an India-wide empire. Harsha had no successor, and his death is usually seen as the beginning of a period of full-blown feudalism in North India.

Daud Ali

BIBLIOGRAPHY

Devahuti, D. *Harsha: A Political Study*. 3rd ed. Delhi: Oxford University Press, 1998.

The Harsa-Carita of Bana. Translated by E. B. Cowell and F. W. Thomas. Delhi: Motilal Banarsidass, 1968.

Priyadarsika: A Sanskrit Drama by Harsha, King of Northern India in the Seventh Century A.D. Sanskrit text edited and translated by G. K. Nariman, Williams Jackson, and Charles Ogden. New York: AMS Press, 1965.

HARSHA VARDHANA. *See* History and Historiography.

HASTINGS, WARREN (1732–1818), *British East India Company's governor of Bengal (1772–1773), first governor-general of India (1774–1785).*

Warren Hastings was born into a noted English family then in reduced circumstances. An uncle paid for his private education, which revealed his brilliance as a scholar. However, his financial situation was such that in 1750 he had no choice but to accept a clerkship in the East India Company's service in Bengal. Over the next fourteen years, the company overthrew the Indian rulers of Bengal and introduced a corrupt "dual government." During this turbulent era, Hastings served as a councilor in Kassimbazar, as Resident at Murshidabad, and ultimately as a member of the Governor's Council in Calcutta. Hastings denounced the rapacity of his fellow agents and the mistreatment of Bengal's indigenous leaders. Disgusted with his compatriots, he went on leave to Britain in 1764, having established a reputation for courage and resourcefulness, as well as for an unrivaled capacity to place duty over personal interest; he had so little enriched himself at the company's and India's expense that he had to borrow the money to pay for his return voyage to India in 1769, when his prior service earned him appointment as second in charge of the company's Council in Madras.

In 1772 Hastings was appointed governor of Bengal, a title expanded to that of governor-general of India by the Regulating Act of 1773. Of the thirty-two British officers to hold that rank, Hastings is one of the very few whose name still inspires admiration among Indians. This recognition is derived from the efforts Hastings made to bridge the cultures of Britain and India; he had quickly mastered Persian, the language of the Indian courts, spoke both Bengali and Urdu, and had some knowledge of Arabic. He used his period of leave in Britain to press for the establishment of a school for the education of the company's servants in Indian languages and culture and sought the creation of a scholarship in Persian at Oxford. He subsequently encouraged research into Arabic studies as well as Sanskrit and Hindu law, and he founded the Asiatic Society of Bengal. He also supported the translation of the Bhagavad Gītā into English (writing a learned introduction to the text) and lent support to a fellow Persian and Arabic scholar, Sir William Jones, who identified the historic linguistic link between Sanskrit and Latin.

Hastings's affinity for India influenced his administrative policy. Not long after assuming office as governor of Bengal, the company determined that his government should "stand forth as *diwan*," ending whatever remained of the *nawāb* of Bengal's authority; the company itself began collecting the revenues of the province, rather than doing so through Indian officials. Hastings complied, but attempted to retain Indian revenue agents, whose work would be supervised by company managers. This arrangement ultimately pleased neither the company's servants nor Indians, but Hastings strove to blend Indian traditions with Western practices when he later reconstituted Bengal's judicial system. Hastings's revenue reforms and his establishment of a cadre of Collectors and Magistrates, backed by courts of civil and criminal appeal, laid the foundation of modern Indian public administration.

Hastings was also instrumental in the preservation of the company's dominions. In the decade spanning 1774 and 1785, the company faced a series of severe challenges at once imperial and regional. Under the provisions of the Regulating Act of 1773, his authority over the company's other provinces was unclear. A simple majority of Hastings own four-man council could, moreover, vote to overrule his actions, an issue so critical that Hastings was forced to resolve it, in part, by fighting a duel with his most bitter council opponent, Philip Francis.

When conflicting financial as well as political relations between the company, the Mughal emperor Shuja-ud-Dawla, the Marathas, and Afghan freebooters (known as Rohillas) threatened the frontiers of Oudh (Awadh), Hastings did not hesitate to intervene, though the territory in question lay beyond the company's domains. The resulting Rohilla War eliminated the Rohillas, strengthened Oudh, and added a crore (ten million) rupees (over £1,000,000) in tribute to the company's coffers. Though a subsequent Parliamentary Committee investigating the war urged Hastings's recall, the company's directors refused to do so.

Ruthless may be the only word to describe the pressure Hastings brought to bear on the Chait Singh, the raja of Benares, to contribute to the company's coffers in order to help defray the costs of conflicts with the Marathas and Mysore, as well as with the French. Chait Singh, however, had also intrigued with Hastings's enemies on his council. Hastings showed no mercy: Chait Singh was ultimately deposed, a nephew installed in his place, and the raja's annual tribute to the company was raised from 22.5 lakhs, or 2,500,000 rupees (£225,000) to an exorbitant 40 lakhs, or 4 million rupees (£400,000). Hastings employed an equally self-serving interpretation of a previous treaty with the *nawāb* of Oudh to successfully extort funds from the *nawāb*'s mother, the begum of Oudh, which enabled the *nawāb* to pay off his enormous debts to the company.

The First Maratha War from 1775 to 1782 was not of Hastings's making, but he defended the Bombay Council's ill-advised decision to back the young *peshwa* Raghunath Rao, who had turned to them for support against his Maratha rivals. Bombay's early military losses in this cause were later overcome as a result of Hastings's decision to risk sending a brigade of enforcements on a heroic march from Allahabad to Surat in 1779. The performance of these troops and Hastings's skillful diplomacy eventually brought a satisfactory end to the otherwise ill-starred conflict by the Treaty of Salbai in 1782.

Hastings employed the same martial daring and diplomatic skills in dealing with a dangerous alliance of Indian and French forces in the south. The ill-considered policies of the company's servants in Madras had provoked a war with a dangerous coalition of forces led by Hyder Ali Khan of Mysore and the nizam of Hyderabad in 1779. The timing of this conflict was unfortunate, for it coincided with a revolt in Britain's North American colonies, which had evolved into a global war with France and its allies in Europe. France was thus eager to exploit the turbulence in South India. It offered the support of its naval forces in the Bay of Bengal to Haidar Ali and the nizam's forces when they defeated a company army in the Carnatic and occupied its capital, Arcot.

Though then fully occupied by the struggle against the Marathas, Hastings effectively dealt with the deteriorating situation in the south. After suspending the company's governor in Madras and persuading the raja of Berar and Mahadaji Scindhia to break with the enemy alliance, Hastings launched fresh offensive operations in the Carnatic, supported by reinforcements that successfully marched from Bengal to Madras. Hastings's diplomacy and bold military strokes led to the Peace of Mangalore in 1784. This treaty stipulated little more than a mutual cession of conquests, but by the time of its signing, France's chief potential ally and the linchpin of any southern alliance, the nizam of Hyderabad, was firmly in the company's camp.

With the company's territory and revenues secure and with the British government committed to fresh Indian legislation (the Regulating Act of 1784), which he did not support, Hastings resigned his office in 1785. On his return to Britain, he sought only to cultivate his garden in Windsor, but his old enemy Philip Francis joined a host of British

politicians to secure Hastings's impeachment by Parliament in 1787. His trial commenced the following year. Among his accusers were Edmund Burke, Richard B. Sheridan, and Charles James Fox, whose principal charge was Hastings's extortion of funds from the begums of Oudh.

The length of the trial (145 days over seven years—the longest in British history) worked in Hastings favor, as did the dignity with which Hastings managed his defense and the common knowledge that Hastings had derived only a modest fortune from his long service to the company. He was acquitted of all charges in April 1795. The company soon restored his finances, which were decimated by the cost of the trial. The prince regent offered him a peerage in 1806, but the government withheld its assent when Hastings made the revocation of his bill of impeachment a condition of his acceptance. He was, however, greeted with a standing ovation when he attended Parliament to offer testimony during the debate over the renewal of the company's charter in 1813, and he was made a privy councilor the following year.

Marc Jason Gilbert

See also **British East India Company Raj**

BIBLIOGRAPHY

Bernstein, Jeremy. *Dawning of the Raj: The Life and Trials of Warren Hastings.* Chicago: Ivan R. Dee, 2000.
Lyall, Alfred. *Warren Hastings.* 1889. Reprint, Freeport, N.Y.: Books for Libraries, 1970.
Moon, Penderel. *Warren Hastings and British India.* 1947. Reprint, London: Hodder and Stoughton, 1962.

HEALTH CARE At least seven different systems of medicine function in India. Professional skills in some traditional systems are acquired through apprenticeship, and the right to practice is formalized by becoming a registered medical practitioner (RMP) with the relevant board, council, or association. Hence, most Indians move freely from one type of medical science to another. Nevertheless, allopathic (Western) medicine is predominant in the country. It is financed and managed by both public and private sectors. The former is free of charge to the poor, and of nominal cost to all others. It accounts for approximately 18 percent of the overall health spending and 0.9 percent of the Gross Domestic Product (GDP). Responsibilities are shared by local, central (federal), and state governments. The latter provides the services. The central government sustains about 25 percent of public expenses. It focuses on developing and monitoring national standards and regulations, linking states with funding agencies, and sponsoring schemes for implementation by state governments.

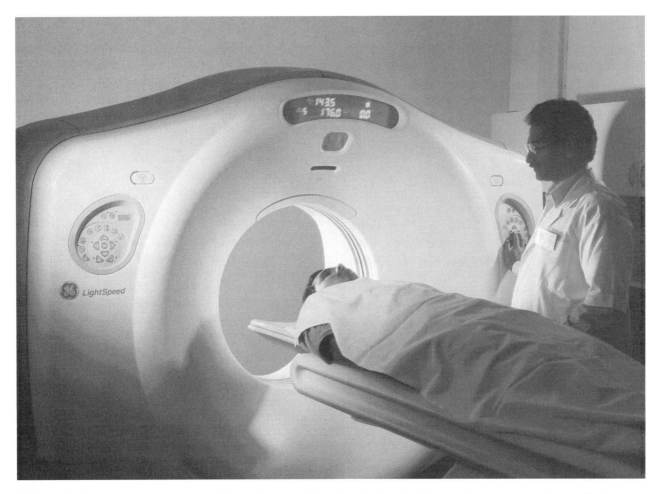

High-Tech Cardiac Assessment at the Fortis Hospital, Chandigarh, Punjab. Though this institute provides world-class care, in partnership with several renowned Western hospitals, such medicine is largely unavailable to most Indians, who remain reliant on India's public health infrastructure—a system plagued by obsolete equipment, overcrowded and run-down facilities, lacking services and health-care professionals. DINESH KHANNA.

Remarkable achievements have been made since independence in 1947. Life expectancy rose from 36.7 to 64.6 years. Eradication of smallpox (1981) and Guinea worm (2000) accompanied steep declines in *kala azar* (black fever), leprosy, malaria, and polio. The number of doctors increased from 61,800 to 503,900, and nurses from 18,054 to 737,000. By 1991 the country had 22,400 primary health centers, 11,200 hospitals, and 27,400 dispensaries. These facilities form a tiered system that funnels complicated cases into urban hospitals while providing routine treatment in the countryside. By the 1990s the country had approximately 10 hospital beds per 10,000 individuals, a threefold growth in ten years, and 128 medical colleges, a 300 percent increase since 1950.

However, the per capita expenditure on public health in India is half that of other comparable countries. Only 23 percent of Indians have safe drinking water because of inadequate spending on related subjects like hygiene and sanitation. Similarly, little is invested in preventing the adulteration of foodstuffs or controlling pollution. Furthermore, the poorest 20 percent of the population have more than double the rates of mortality, malnutrition, and fertility in comparison with the richest quintile. A 1995–1996 national survey also revealed that tobacco intake and alcohol abuse were highest in the lowest quintile. The plight of the estimated 90 million disabled has, likewise, received little attention.

Health-Care Sectors

The government sector. The cornerstone of the government's health-care system, especially in the countryside, where 72 percent of Indians live, is the primary health center (PHC), as based on the recommendations of the Bhore Committee (1946). The following guiding principles of the committee remain the basis of the government's medical organization for the country:

• No individual should lack access to medical care because of inability to pay for it.

- Special emphasis on preventive methods, and on communicable diseases.
- The establishment of a primary health unit (center) per 10,000–20,000 population with 75 beds, 6 doctors, and an equal number of public health nurses.
- Provide one bed per 175 people, one doctor per 1,600, and one nurse per 600 citizens.
- Build 650 bed hospitals at *taluka* (300,000 people) level and a 2,500 bed hospital in each district (3 million population).
- No patent protection for pharmaceutical products.
- Fifteen percent of government expenditure on health care.

Slow economic growth, rapid rise in population, and shifts in government priorities were acknowledged fifteen years later by the Mudaliar Committee. Accordingly, the goals of the Bhore Committee were essentially halved: the ratio of PHCs was decreased to one per 40,000 people; the bed strength reduced to one bed per 1,000; and the ratio of doctors was one per 3,000. The committee also recommended that the central government build one medical college per 5 million people. Bowing to international pressure, process patent protection for up to ten years for pharmaceuticals was instituted. The committee was the first to examine the other systems of medicine in the country, and concluded that it was too early to integrate them. The Jain Committee (1966) concentrated on enhancing maternity facilities, enlarging health insurance coverage, and augmenting resources by increasing fees for services. Social activism was an important feature of the Srivastava Committee (1975). It recommended compulsory service for two years at a PHC for every doctor between the fifth and fifteenth year of a physician's career. It also proposed the creation of a Medical and Health Education Commission. Fifteen years after the Mudaliar Committee, Srivastava suggested selective integration of different health systems.

Decline in public expenditure on health was a major concern for the Indian Council of Medical Research-Indian Council of Social Science Research Joint Panel (1980). Consequently, it advocated that 6 percent of the gross national product be spent on medical services. The National Health Policy (1983) aimed for universal primary health coverage by encouraging greater participation of private practitioners and nongovernmental organizaions (NGOs) with the public sector and the utilization of village-based workers to treat simple ailments. Similarly, the National Population Policy (2000) sought comprehensive reproductive and child health care through the collaboration of the government with NGOs and the private sector. Further decentralization of planning and program implementation was intended by involving community groups and *panchayati raj* institutions. (*Panchayat*s are autonomous village councils with administrative, civic, judicial, and social responsibilities. Over 270,000 elected *panchayat*s are currently operational.)

An important feature of rural health care is the specific "camps" organized by medical colleges, NGOs, and charitable hospitals. Fully self-contained camps are set up for three to five days. Doctors operate on cataracts, fix bones, provide plastic surgery for cleft lip, and so forth. Usually held in winter, when days are short and crisp and working hours long and exhilarating, camps have a festive air about them. In some parts of the country they are a regular feature, and villagers eagerly await their return.

Despite years of planning, the public health infrastructure is modest because of insufficient funding. Hence, hospital equipment is often obsolescent or unusable, buildings dilapidated and overcrowded, and the availability of essential medications, capricious. Furthermore, chronic scarcity in specialties like anesthesiology and radiology results in critical deficiencies in public health services. Nursing care is inadequate, for there is a very low ratio of nursing personnel to doctors and beds. Low staff morale is reflected in poor quality of service and absenteeism. These problems are compounded by inadequate mobilization of private practitioners and NGOs and an excessive focus on sterilization to meet family planning targets.

The private sector. India's reliance on private spending on health is among the highest in the world. Accordingly, primary, secondary, and tertiary care is offered principally through independent practitioners. This sector is largely unregulated and little constrained by medicolegal considerations. For instance, Indians receive three times as many injections (3.4 per year) as Western patients because it is more lucrative for the physician to administer injections than to prescribe oral medicines. About 40 percent of Indians borrow money or sell assets to pay for hospitalization. The private sector accounts for 78 percent of overall expenditure on health and 4.5 percent of GDP.

Civil society. Since the 1980s, increased participation by NGOs and other civil institutions has considerably improved the implementation of national disease control programs. In addition, civil activists and voluntary organizations stimulate awareness and debate on various health issues and take major initiatives in preventive medicine and disaster relief. NGOs are prominent in funding rural camps.

Health insurance. About 15 percent of Indians enjoy some form of health insurance, whether social or private. The latter is small. The largest such insurer, Mediclaim, has a mere 2.5 million subscribers. Social plans such as

Modern-day *sadhu* (ascetic), wearing only beads with his face caked in ash, raises his hand in blessing to the unknown photographer. According to Hindu mythology, his beads, or *rudraksh*, have medicinal powers.
TOBY SINCLAIR/FOTOMEDIA

TOP: In Calcutta, now known as Kolkata, the Victoria Museum. Built at the behest of Lord George Curzon (one of the British Raj's most flamboyant and much derided viceroys) and of marble from the same quarry that had supplied the builders of the Taj Mahal in the seventeenth century. AMIT PASRICHA/FOTOMEDIA

BOTTOM LEFT: Throughout India's numerous and varied states, images of the old and the new constantly converge. TOBY SINCLAIR/FOTOMEDIA

BOTTOM RIGHT: On a crowded city street, the multitude of life that is India. TOBY SINCLAIR/FOTOMEDIA

TOP: At a roadside bazaar in Jaipur, framed images of popular Hindu gods. Thousands of such prints are sold throughout India each year for less than U.S. $1 each. ADITYA PATANKAR/ FOTOMEDIA

BOTTOM LEFT: The rickshaw remains the cheapest mode of transport in India and may be observed just about everywhere, from congested city streets as here to dusty country roads. DINESH KHANNA/FOTOMEDIA

BOTTOM RIGHT: In anticipation of Holi, a shop displays its colorful wares. On the eve of this Hindu festival, an effigy of the demon Holika is set afire to symbolize the triumph of good over evil. The next day, friends and relatives gather, sprinkling each other with colored powder to celebrate. DINESH KHANNA/FOTOMEDIA

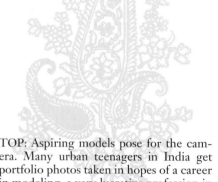

TOP: Aspiring models pose for the camera. Many urban teenagers in India get portfolio photos taken in hopes of a career in modeling, a very lucrative profession in India. AKHIL BAKSHI/FOTOMEDIA

BOTTOM: In Uttar Pradesh, a roadside vendor displays a variety of salted savories. TOBY SINCLAIR/FOTOMEDIA

TOP: Dotted across India's long coastline are many holiday resorts, including a host of posh destinations. In one such setting, these chefs proudly display their handi-work. AMIT PASRICHA/FOTOMEDIA

BOTTOM: In a small town of southern India, local men gather outside a wrestling club. TOBY SINCLAIR/FOTOMEDIA

TOP: There is no limit to the number of different-language dailies one may purchase in India, whose newspaper industry must cater to a literate population of some 600 million people. TOBY SINCLAIR/ FOTOMEDIA

BOTTOM: On the roads of Kerala, a not unusual sight: a commercial vehicle and an elephant riding side by side. AMIT PAS-RICHA/FOTOMEDIA

TOP: A literacy class in Rajasthan. In recent decades, the Indian government, in tandem with non-profits, has sought to educate women in impoverished rural communities, where the rate of female illiteracy remains regrettably high. AMIT PASRICHA/FOTOMEDIA

BOTTOM: A mother and her daughter at an internet cafe in Kolkata. Cyber cafes are used by over half of India's internet users to access the web. JAYANTA SHAW/ REUTERS/CORBIS

TOP: High in the Himalayas (below Dharamsala, home to the Dalai Lama in India), young monks ride with a Tibetan family. AMITA PATANKAR/FOTOMEDIA

BOTTOM: In the city of Varanasi during the festival of Dala-Chatha, which is celebrated a week after Diwali in November, thousands gather on the banks of the Ganges, where all life is said to begin. Hindus believe that immersion in the river's waters, on designated holy days, will cleanse them of their sins. HENRY WILSON/FOTOMEDIA

Employee State Insurance Scheme and Central Government Health Scheme cover another 30 million. Comprehensive health care is also provided to government employees, active or retired, and their dependents. Large companies do the same.

A remarkable success is the ESI Act (Employees' State Insurance) of 1948. ESI is an integrated need-based insurance that provides maternity leave, financial assistance for both temporary and permanent physical disability, vocational rehabilitation, and wages for survivors of workers killed due to employment injury. Factories with at least ten workers and companies with twenty or more employees are covered by the act. By March 2001, there were 238,486 companies in the program. Its hospitals, dispensaries, and other services are efficient and well run. Its beneficiaries are almost 33 million workers and their families. However, the urban and rural poor rely largely on the public health system outlined earlier.

External assistance. South Asia receives the lowest official development assistance per capita in the world, and less than 7 percent of it goes to the health sector. Assistance was largely in family planning, maternity care, and child health. Except for the eradication of malaria and leprosy, other disease control programs received scant consideration. Since 1995, external assistance increased partly in response to the HIV/AIDS pandemic and the rise of other communicable diseases. Another factor was the decision of the International Monetary Fund and World Bank to participate in programs with "a human face." The latter sought collaboration with the International Development Association (IDA) to establish nationwide surveillance of quality controls for foods and drugs.

The World Health Organization (WHO) is the only agency whose funding is outside normal budgetary mechanisms. This flexibility allows WHO to focus on disaster relief, tobacco control, and identification of parameters that increase the responsiveness of health systems to the needs of the poor.

The United Nations (UN) advocates the privilege of good health as one of the fundamental rights of every human being. In India, the UN has largely limited itself to a global fund for the control of communicable diseases.

The G-8 governments (Britain, Canada, France, Germany, Italy, Japan, Russia, and the United States) are assisting with clean water and sanitation projects. The governments also work on mutually satisfactory arrangements for the pharmaceutical industries in India and in the G-8 countries to promote the availability and affordability of lifesaving medicines.

Indian communities abroad are active in donating medicines and equipment, and setting up hospitals and clinics in India. In addition, doctors return to the country to teach, train, and provide specialized services.

India has bilateral health arrangements with a number of countries. USAID supports three major bilateral projects: HIV/AIDS in Tamil Nadu, population control in Uttar Pradesh, and the establishment of the National Institute of Biologicals for the quality assurance of vaccines. Similarly, the Japanese International Cooperation Agency is setting up a children's hospital in Delhi and collaborating on basic research on cholera. Various European and Canadian agencies are active as well.

Key Health Issues in India

Communicable diseases. The resurgence of communicable diseases like malaria and tuberculosis and the emergence of new infections like HIV/AIDS, new strains of cholera, and different forms of viral hepatitis pose serious challenges to India. The following infections greatly impact the country's ecology and economy:

Malaria. Increased insecticide resistance has developed in malarial vectors. The long-term impact of chemical insecticides on the food chain and ecology is a matter of great concern. Meanwhile, the incidence of the more deadly P-Falciparum malaria has risen by about 50 percent.

Tuberculosis. South Asia is home to about 38 percent of tuberculosis patients worldwide. There are 2.5 million new cases and 600,000 deaths annually. There is also a growing threat of coinfection with HIV/AIDS. The financial and human cost is obvious.

HIV/AIDS. Eight million Indians may be infected, but estimates vary widely.

Waterborne diseases. The common waterborne infections—gastroenteritis, cholera, and some forms of hepatitis—contribute to high levels of morbidity in the population. Recent reports of chemical contamination of underground water, especially in West Bengal, may cause significant medical problems in the future.

Disaster relief. Fifty million Indians suffer drought each year. Half as many are flooded annually. In addition, cyclones, earthquakes, and natural and manmade disasters strike millions. In 1980 a Health Sector Emergency Preparedness and Response Program was finally established. Clearly more work remains to be done.

Generic drugs and vaccines. Low-priced indigenously manufactured generic drugs and vaccines are widely available. Both globalization and the Trade Related Intellectual Property Rights System are likely to result in an increased cost of drugs. India's leading role in software development and computer sciences may keep the costs low by triggering innovations in the development, testing, and marketing of new medications. Costs may fall by 50 to 70 percent from the current average of U.S.$250–500 million per development of a new drug, and the lead time from the discovery of a drug to its introduction in the marketplace may decline from twelve years to five. Development of vaccines may be even cheaper, with a shortened lead time. The ongoing Indo–U.S. collaboration in the development of an AIDS vaccine may be the first of many such undertakings.

Geriatric care. Geriatric care is expected to rise substantially as a result of increased life expectancy, breakdown of the extended family, pressures on the nuclear family, and increased urbanization.

Health research. The Indian Council of Medical Research was established in 1911. For more than ninety years, health research in India faced the same two major problems: low spending on research ($300 million in both public and private sectors in 2001); and neglect by international pharmaceutical companies of medical research on therapeutic drugs and vaccines for tropical diseases because of their limited profitability.

Information, education, and communications. Initiatives are needed for the dissemination of the evolving curative guidelines for diseases such as tuberculosis, malaria, leprosy, cataract blindness, as well as for bringing about behavioral changes to prevent HIV/AIDS and other lifestyle diseases.

Lifestyle diseases. Since the 1980s, there is a noticeable increase in mortality through lifestyle diseases such as diabetes, obesity, infirmities associated with cigarette smoking, cancer, and cardiovascular diseases.

Macro- and micro-nutrient deficiencies. The persistence of macro- and micro-nutrient deficiencies, especially among women and children, leads to chronic morbidity. Deficiencies have a multiplier effect, as they result in a higher incidence of low birth weight babies, which in turn causes both mental and physical retardation.

Mental health. Patients are usually confined to mental hospitals, and drug therapy is the rule. Psychotherapy and rehabilitation still have a limited role in the management of these patients. On the other hand, Indian society is generally tolerant of its "eccentrics and lunatics."

Noncommunicable diseases. Over 10 percent of urban Indians have coronary artery disease. Since the 1970s, the average age of the first heart attack in India has decreased by ten years, and about 50 percent of all heart attacks in Indian males occur under the age of 55, with 25 percent under the age of 40. These striking statistics are unheard of in any other population. Similarly, the incidence of strokes and hypertension has increased dramatically during the past thirty years.

Population control. During the twentieth century, India's population increased from 238 million to more than 1 billion despite almost fifty years of attempts at population control; it was the first country in the world (1952) to launch a national program for family planning. However, following excesses committed during the 1975 emergency, the program was not vigorously pursued. Nevertheless, the total fertility rate fell from 6.0 in 1951 to 3.3 in 1997. Consequently, the National Population Policy (2000) reaffirmed the government's commitment to voluntary and informed population control, and set the ambitious target of achieving net replacement levels of population by 2010.

Preventive medicine. In the late 1990s the central government adopted an integrated Non-Communicable Diseases program. It consisted mainly of health education for citizens and the development of protocols for training physicians in preventive medicine.

Trauma. Increase in trauma caused by violence (political, domestic or otherwise), traffic crashes, industrial accidents, or natural calamities is a significant burden on the health-care systems. As elsewhere, women and children bear the brunt of it.

Vaccine-preventable diseases. Infections such as measles, diphtheria, and whooping cough still pose significant risks to children. While efforts to eradicate polio have made tremendous progress in India, there were still 268 cases in 2001.

Traditional Systems of Medicine

In March 1995 the Department of Indian System of Medicine and Homeopathy was established in the Ministry of Health and Family Welfare. It gave belated recognition to traditional systems of Indian medicine that provide at least 40 percent of health care in the country, especially among the poor and in rural areas. By setting up a separate department, the government sought to improve cooperation among the various systems of medicine, and to better regulate the traditional ones.

These systems are generally geared toward the treatment of simple or chronic ailments. The scientific basis of therapy lies in restoration of the balance between the patient, biofactors (nature, ecology), and body humors (secretions). Hence, the systems are holistic and oriented toward lifestyle instead of focusing on specific organs or diseases. Surgical intervention and diagnostic tests are few. Medicines are invariably cheap, derived from natural sources, and have few side effects.

Āyurveda is the largest of the traditional Indian systems of medicine. Its origins lie in two of the four Vedas: the Rig Veda and the Atharva Veda (c. 1400–600 B.C.). About sixty ancient treatises form the corpus of Āyurvedic knowledge. The two most prominent texts are the Caraka Samhita and the Susruta Samhita, ascribed respectively to the eponymous Caraka, a physician, and Susruta, a plastic surgeon. Susruta reputedly trained under the legendary Dhanvantari at Kashi (Varanasi), the traditional center for surgical expertise in India. Dhanvantari is acknowledged as the "father of Indian medicine." Related to Āyurveda are Siddha (a Tamil version) and naturopathy (which relies on diets prescribed in Āyurveda). The practitioner is called *vaidya*, and the profession was formerly hereditary. Modern Āyurveda still emphasizes its eight traditional disciplines of *kayachikitsa* (internal medicine), *salya tantra* (surgery), *salakya* (ear, nose, and throat), *kaumarabhrtya* (pediatrics, obstetrics, and gynecology), *bhutvidya* (psychiatry), *agada tantra* (toxicology), *rasayana tantra* (nutrition, rejuvenation, geriatrics) and *vajikarana* (sexology). The universal and timeless applicability of these subjects is a tribute to the ongoing relevance of this ancient system of medicine. By the twenty-first century there were 98 colleges of Āyurvedic medicine in India.

Three other systems—Unani, homeopathy, and Tibetan medicine—are from non-Indian sources. Unani is Greek in origin, founded on Galenic concepts of good health being dependent on the balance of four humors (blood, phlegm, yellow bile, and black bile). Seventeen colleges operate in India. Its practitioners are known as *hakim*s. Homeopathy originated in Germany. Treatment is based on empiric observations that highly diluted matter often relieves symptoms caused by that very substance in its concentrated form. For instance, repeated small bites by poisonous snakes protect snake charmers from death following a severe bite. Education is imparted by 132 colleges. With more than 182,000 practitioners, homeopathy is the second-largest system in India. Tibetan medicine resembles Āyurveda. It was established in India in 1961 after the Dalai Lama fled from Tibet to India.

Medical Services as an International Industry

India reportedly attracts approximately 100,000 patients from abroad every year, as certain hospitals provide international standards of care at affordable prices. The Apollo group, India's largest chain (38 hospitals) pioneered the concept by establishing state-of-the-art medical facilities in India's metropolitan centers and other large towns like Pune, Kochi, and Ahmedabad. Most hospitals are also linked to good hotels and shopping centers, which cater to the families of patients. By

2003 the Confederation of Indian Industry, sensing commercial opportunities, became actively involved, offering Indian facilities to Britain's beleaguered National Health Service as a low cost, expeditious alternative for British patients.

The prices of Indian health care are quite low. For instance, heart surgery costs U.S.$8,000 in India, compared to $30,000 in the United States; liver transplantation, which is $300,000 in the United States, is $45,000 in India; similarly, orthopedic surgery is generally available for a tenth to a third of its price in the West.

Both the Indian government and the private sector are active in the growing global telemedical services. Telemedicine was initially available in radiology, cardiology, and pathology. Advances in technology have added electronic stethoscopy, ophthalmoscopy, and spirometry.

Rajesh Kadian

See also **Āyurveda; Health Care for Tourists**

BIBLIOGRAPHY

Baru, R. V. *Private Health Care in India: Social Characteristics and Trends.* New Delhi: Sage, 1999.

Kamalamma, G. *Health and Nutritional Status in India.* Columbia, Mo.: South Asia Books, 1996.

Koenig, M. A., and M. E. Khan. *Improving Quality of Care in India's Family Welfare Programme: The Challenge Ahead.* New York: Population Council, 1999.

Mead, O. *HIV/AIDS Treatment and Prevention in India: Costs and Consequences of Policy Options.* Washington, D.C.: World Bank, 2003.

Misra, R., R. Chatterjee, and S. Rao. *India Health Report.* New Delhi: Oxford University Press, 2003.

Patel, K. *Dimensions of States' Education and Public Health Policies.* Lanham, Md.: Rowman & Littlefield, 1978.

Sharma, P. V. *History of Medicine in India.* New Delhi: Indian National Academy of Science, 1992.

Young, I. *Lonely Planet Healthy Travel: Asia and India.* Oakland, Calif.: Lonely Planet, 2000.

HEALTH CARE FOR TOURISTS By the new millennium, there was a substantial increase in travel to India. Further growth is anticipated as the country opens up its economy and develops more tourist facilities. In addition, trips to South Asia by the Indian diaspora are expected to rise. For travel to India, all foreigners, including those from Commonwealth countries, are required to have a valid passport and an appropriate (entry, transit, or tourist) visa obtained abroad from an Indian mission. Tourist visas are generally valid for 120 days from the date of issue. Though directed toward U.S. citizens, a useful precaution prior to departure is to check the travel warnings posted on the U.S. State Department's web site,

<www.travel.state.gov/travel_warnings.html>. The International Society of Travel Medicine's web site, <www.istm.org>, is also useful.

Precautions before Travel

Medical insurance. Most medical insurances do not cover health-related expenses incurred abroad or the cost of medical evacuation from overseas, unless such specific coverage is purchased before travel. This is particularly true of U.S. Medicare and Medicaid. However, most travel agencies and health insurance companies offer plans for medical coverage during foreign trips.

Vaccinations. Four to six weeks should be allowed for certain vaccinations to take full effect. The following vaccinations should be obtained before leaving for India:

1. Hepatitis A, or immune globulin (IG).
2. Hepatitis B, if exposure to blood (for example, health-care workers), sexual contact with the local population, or a stay longer than six months is anticipated. Hepatitis B vaccine is now recommended for all infants and for children who did not receive it as infants.
3. Japanese encephalitis, only if visits to certain rural areas for four weeks or more are planned.
4. Rabies, if exposure to wild or domestic animals through work or recreation is anticipated.
5. Typhoid vaccination is important because *S. typhi* strains in the region are resistant to multiple antibiotics.
6. As needed, booster doses for tetanus, diphtheria, and measles, and a one-time dose of polio for adults. In 1998, 75 percent of all polio cases in the world occurred in India. The incidence has dropped dramatically following the massive vaccination programs carried out in the country since then.

There is no risk for yellow fever in the Indian subcontinent. A certificate of yellow fever vaccination is required for entry into India if the visitor is coming from certain countries in South America or sub-Saharan Africa, where yellow fever is endemic.

Dental care. Dental appointments should be scheduled early enough to allow time for the completion of necessary or outstanding dental work before departure. Decayed teeth and broken fillings should be tended to and teeth cleaned. Consideration should be given to the removal of partially exposed lower wisdom teeth, especially if a long trip is envisaged. The fleshy covering over such teeth creates a food cap that can cause pericoronitis, a potentially serious infection. Similarly, all root canal

treatment should be completed before travel. On the other hand, most Indian cities have well-trained, well-equipped dentists in private practice. The fees are much smaller than in the West.

Medications. All medications should be properly labeled. Copies of prescriptions, especially narcotics, with a letter from the prescribing doctor identifying such medications, could prove helpful should security or customs officials raise questions about them.

First-aid kits. First-aid kits for travelers are commercially available in most developed countries. The cost varies from U.S.$10.00 to ten times as much, as does weight and size. The kit should contain antacids, analgesics, antibacterial ointments, antidiarrheals (as tablets), antihistamines, antiseptics (including towelettes), calamine lotion, bandages (adhesive, butterfly, and elastic), corticosteroid creams (low-dose emollients are most cost effective), cotton-tipped applicators, hypodermic needles (nonluer lock are more versatile), insect repellants, moleskin (for blisters), waterproof adhesive tapes, oral rehydration salts, single-edged razor blades, sharp scissors, sterile small syringes (nonluer lock, 1 and 3 ml), thermometer (digitals are less fragile, but have limitations), tick-remover forceps, and tweezers. Kits should be packed in the checked-in baggage as most contain sharp metallic objects like razor blades and will not be cleared by airport security. An emergency smoke hood can be carried into the cabin.

Air travel and its medical effects. Air travel is the most common means of transportation to India. Deep vein thrombosis (DVT), jet lag, and motion sickness are the most common medical conditions resulting from long-distance jet travel. DVT, "coach class syndrome," is increasingly common and affects all ages. Most airlines therefore provide instructions on in-seat ankle exercises to minimize the risk. Immobility, cramped seating and dehydration further contribute to DVT. Hence, compression stockings, avoidance of alcohol, consumption of plenty of fluids, and regular walks around the cabin are useful in preventing DVT. An alternative to water is a fluid expander like CeraLyte, which prevents jet lag as well.

Jet lag is caused by the alteration in the endogenous rhythms of the body vis-à-vis environmental changes, especially time. Hence a six-hour journey in the same meridian—for instance, travel from North to South America—is much less likely to cause jet lag than the six-hour trip across five time zones. Travel from west to east appears to worsen jet lag more than a trip in the opposite direction. Reduced output of the regulatory hormone, melatonin, is considered an important underlying factor.

Other factors, like the dehydrated cabin air, older age, night flights, and consumption of alcoholic and caffeinated beverages, also contribute to jet lag. The most common symptoms are increased fatigue and irritability, disturbed sleep patterns, and loss of concentration. The incidence and severity of jet lag is reduced by taking melatonin (3–5 mg), a high-fiber diet, and liberal intake of fruit juices and drinks that contain electrolytes, like Gatorade and CeraLyte. Melatonin is available without prescription at pharmacies and health-food stores.

Pacemaker malfunction does not occur in modern pressurized and insulated airplanes. Most long-range aircraft carry defibrillators for resuscitating the stopped heart resulting from acute myocardial infarction (heart attack). Motion sickness is caused by irritation of the middle or inner ear, and/or the brain stem. It is treated by prescription medicines and may be alleviated by getting a seat in the center of the cabin. Avoiding unnecessary head and eye movements (as when watching television or reading) and abstinence from alcohol and caffeinated drinks further reduces its severity and incidence.

The International Commission on Radiation Protection calculated that air crews, after twenty-five years of regular flying, have a risk of radiation-related malignancies of 25.5–26 percent, as compared with a 25 percent risk in the rest of the population. Hence, radiation is a very small hazard. There is also the unlikely possibility of picking up infections, ranging from the common cold to tuberculosis.

At landing, aircraft are usually disinfected using 2.9 percent d-phenothrin spray. Passengers wearing contact lens should keep their eyes closed during disinfection.

Common illnesses. The most common concern is travelers' diarrhea ("Delhi belly"). About 50 percent of travelers are stricken with this illness. It is caused by a variety of different viruses, bacteria, toxins, and parasites. The most frequent etiology is certain strains of the bacteria E. coli. The onset is usually within the first week of arrival in India. The diarrhea is often associated with nausea, vomiting, abdominal cramps, bloating, low-grade fever, urgency, and malaise. Most cases resolve in a few days without treatment. The most commonly prescribed antibiotics are Quinolones, Trimethoprim-Sulfamethoxazole (Bactrim), and Azithromycin (Zithromax). Antidiarrheals, such as Diphenoxylate (Lomotil) and Loperamide (Imodium), may be judiciously used to reduce the frequency of stools and to prevent dehydration. The safe and simple compound Pepto Bismol, a binding agent that neutralizes toxins and solidifies stools, is recommended for both prevention and cure of symptoms. If the diarrhea is bloody,

severe, or accompanied by chills and high fever, medical attention should be immediately sought.

To prevent travelers' diarrhea, it is advisable to avoid consuming foods or beverages from street vendors and other places where unhygienic conditions may be present. In addition, raw or undercooked meat, seafood, and raw fruits and vegetables, unless they can be peeled or thoroughly washed, should be avoided. Furthermore, tap water, ice, unpasteurized milk and dairy products increase the risk of travelers' diarrhea. Safe liquids include bottled beverages, hot tea and coffee, beer, wine, and sealed bottled water.

Other common illnesses are respiratory tract infection or inflammation, and dengue, a flulike illness occasionally complicated by bleeding. Much rarer are exotic infections like filariasis, Japanese encephalitis, leishmaniasis, leptospirosis, and the plague. All these diseases are transmitted by insects. Accordingly, protection against the relevant insect bites is an important precaution while traveling in India.

If visits to the Himalayas are planned, then gradual ascent above 10,000 feet is desirable to allow the body to adjust to high altitudes. At higher elevations the early symptoms of illness are insomnia, headaches, and nausea. Later, high-altitude sickness characterized by shortness of breath and accumulation of fluid in the lungs can develop. In addition, it is prudent to use sunblock rated at least 15 SPF, because the risk of sunburn is greater at high altitudes.

Health maintenance. In addition to washing hands with soap and running water after meals and morning ablutions, the visitor should take the following precautions:

1. Drink only bottled or boiled water, or carbonated (bubbly) drinks in cans or bottles. Avoid tap water, fountain drinks, and ice cubes. If this is not possible, the water can be purified by filtering it through an "absolute 1-micron or less" filter and adding iodine tablets to the filtered water. Both filters and iodine tablets are available from camping supply stores.
2. Consume thoroughly cooked food or fruits and vegetables that can be thoroughly washed or peeled. A useful axiom: boil it, cook it, peel it, wash it thoroughly, or forget it. An exception: sealed "comfort foods" brought into the country by the visitor.
3. Malaria prophylaxis should be undertaken throughout the year, regardless of official guidelines and recommendations. Medications should be taken before, during, and after travel. The commonly

prescribed medicine, Chloroquine, is not effective in the Indian subcontinent. Instead, mefloquine (Lariam), atovaquone/proguanil (Malarone), or doxycycline is recommended. Malarone is used most often as a once daily dose, starting two days before arrival, and continuing through the trip and for seven days after departure from India.

4. Take protection from mosquito and insect bites by:
- Paying special attention to mosquito protection between dusk and dawn, the period when the type of mosquito-bearing malaria is most active.
- Wearing long-sleeved shirts, long pants, and hats.
- Using insect repellents that contain DEET (diethylmethyltoluamide). For adults, a 25 to 35 percent preparation is available. For children, a 10 percent compound is adequate. DEET should not be used for children under two years of age because of the risk of neurological toxicity.
- Applying insect repellent to exposed skin but not putting it on wounds or broken skin.
- Not breathing, swallowing, or getting repellents into the eyes (DEET is toxic if swallowed). If using a spray, apply DEET to the face by spraying it on hands and rubbing the product over the face, avoiding eyes and mouth.
- Unless housing is air-conditioned or well-screened, using a bed net with a mesh size of less than 1.5 millimeters. The net should be impregnated with the insecticide permethrin or deltamethrin. Spray the bed net with one of these insecticides if pre-treated nets are not obtainable.
- Protecting infants by using a carrier draped with mosquito netting with an elastic edge for a tight fit.
- Children under ten years old should not apply insect repellent themselves.
- Using tweezers or forceps for grasping and removing the head of ticks from humans. Most tick-borne illnesses can be prevented by prompt removal of the head of the insect.

5. To prevent fungal and parasitic infections, keep feet clean and dry, and do not go barefoot.

6. Always use latex condoms to reduce the risk of the human immunodeficiency virus (HIV) and other sexually transmitted diseases.

7. Avoid swimming in freshwater lakes and rivers. Salt-water is usually safer.

Medical facilities. Adequate to excellent medical care is available in major population centers, but services are usually limited in rural areas. Pharmacies are present even in small towns and most larger villages. The Indian pharmaceutical industry is the fourth largest in the world, and most of the latest medications are easily obtainable. The cost of a visiting doctor is low (about $2.00) in the countryside. On the other hand, traffic safety and road conditions, especially in the countryside, are a major health hazard as regulations regarding safety of public transportation are lax; maintenance of roads is poor, and availability of roadside assistance, negligible. Consequently, the capital, New Delhi, despite its slow-moving traffic, experiences more than two thousand road deaths annually.

Terrorism and crime. Petty crime, especially theft of personal property, is not uncommon. But violent crime, including rape, is rare. Areas of instability and terrorism, particularly in Jammu and Kashmir and in the northeast of the country, may expose the visitor to unexpected and sporadic violence, civil disturbances, and kidnapping. In any case, most of these regions are restricted for foreign travelers.

Medical tourism. India reportedly attracts approximately 100,000 patients from abroad every year, as certain hospitals provide international standards of care at affordable prices. The Apollo group pioneered the establishment of state-of-the-art medical facilities in India's four largest metropolitan cities and other big towns like Pune, Kochi, and Ahmedabad. The group, India's largest, operates 38 hospitals and has opened information centers in key foreign countries to attract medical tourists. Other well-known hospitals that attract medical tourists include the All India Institute of Medical Sciences in Delhi; Escorts Heart Institute, also in Delhi; the Madras Institute of Orthopedics and Traumatology in Chennai; the Rabindranath Tagore International Institute of Cardiac Sciences in Kolkata; and the Hinduja Hospital, Mumbai. In general, these hospitals have created connections with good hotels and shopping centers to cater to the needs and comforts of the families of patients. In 2003 the Confederation of Indian Industry, sensing commercial opportunities offered by medical tourism, sent a delegation, led by a prominent heart surgeon, to negotiate with Britain's National Health Service to provide low cost and expeditious health care to British patients. The figures for using India as a destination for health care are compelling. For instance, heart surgery costs U.S.$8,000 in India as compared to $30,000 in the United States; liver transplantation is $45,000 in India, in contrast to $300,000 in the United States; similarly, orthopedic surgery is generally available for a tenth to a third of the price. The expense of certain operations is remarkably cheaper; for instance, cataract surgery, at $1,500 in the United States, is performed for $12 in India. The growth of similar facilities in smaller cities is likely, if small hospitals (100 beds and under) are given the same tax exemptions enjoyed by the larger ones. Traditional Indian strengths in Āyurveda, yoga, naturopathy, and other alternative medicines continue to attract an increasing following as well.

Rajesh Kadian

BIBLIOGRAPHY

The following websites are particularly useful for travelers to India:

<http://www.cdc.gov/travel/indianrg.htm>

<http://www.mdtravelhealth.com/destinations/asia/india.html>

<http://www.passporthealthusa.com>

<http://www.traveldoctoronline.net/regions/india.htm>

HIMALAYAS. *See* **Geography.**

HINDI. *See* **Languages and Scripts.**

HINDU ANCESTOR RITUALS Among contemporary world religions, Hinduism has the oldest and most elaborate complex of ancestor rituals. The Rig Veda and Atharva Veda (c. 1200–1000 B.C.) include hymns for both inhumation burial and cremation, with verses indicating construction of a mound or marker of earth or stone, and rituals performed by mourners on behalf of both the living and the deceased. Two or three centuries later, Brāhmaṇa texts describe a *citi* (mound) to be erected on the *shmashāna* (burning and burial ground) as replica of the *agnicayana* Shrauta sacrifice, a cosmic soma ritual that the deceased had performed with a thousand bricks to create an altar of fire and regenerate the world. Such commemoration entitled this elite householder, who had maintained the requisite three ritual fires in his home until he was cremated by them, to enter *svarga* (heaven) with a new *tanu* (body), hopefully to remain immortal. In the course of time, during the first millennium B.C., the Shrauta, Grihya, and Pitrimedha Sūtras detailed a full-fledged cult of ancestors known as *shrāddha* (from *sraddhā* "faith"), a ritual system still in place today, reinforced by post-Vedic texts such as Dharma Shāstras, Purāṇas, and manuals compiled by ritual authorities over many centuries of changing doctrines.

These manuals on death and the nurture of ancestors are concerned first with the disposition of the body in *antyeshṭi*, the "final sacrifice." Second, because the belief that a new body awaited the deceased in heaven no longer prevailed, there had to be ritual construction of a temporary body for the disembodied "spirit" (*preta*) in its brief passage into the status of "ancestor" (*pitri*, literally, "father," whether male or female). Third, after the deceased had become a *pitri*, located in an otherworldly realm of ancestors, a systematic program of rituals was necessary to nurture that ancestor during all stages of advancement toward another rebirth. All of this proceeds from the doctrines of karma and *saṃsāra* that emerged with a new worldview in the early Upanishads. These late Vedic texts distinguish between the *pitriyāna* (path of ancestors), which leads to the moon, an abode from which the departed return to earth and a new existence, and the *devayāna* (path of gods), which goes to the sun without return or rebirth. The moon retains an important cosmic role in ancestor rites today, as do the moral implications regarding the effect of action (karma) upon the fate of the deceased in rebirth (*saṃsāra*).

The first feature of these manuals regarding death and ancestors is disposal of the now useless old body, ordinarily by cremation on the day of death or the following one. Some communities always bury their dead, however, and suicides, victims of accidents, snakebites, or epidemic disease, as well as small children—all the untimely dead—may either be buried or given to a river, the same disposal being true also for certain ascetics and saints.

The second concern of ritual handbooks turns to *shrāddha* and the assembly of an invisible body by means of *piṇḍa*s, balls of cooked rice or barley, offered along with water and sesame for ten successive days (often abbreviated today). Parallel to ten lunar months of human gestation and ten days of a special fire in the birth room after delivery of a child, these rituals create a transitional body, beginning with the head and ending with digestive powers. On the eleventh day a set of sixteen *shrāddha*s may be done to satisfy the deceased for one year. *Sapiṇḍīkaraṇa*, the moment of blending a *piṇḍa* of the deceased with those representing ancestors, is a dramatic twelfth-day event. Presentations of cooking utensils, clothing, a bed, personal items, money, and enough raw food for a year to a priestly surrogate, a Brahman of degraded status due to the pollution of death, is all for the satisfaction of the still-watchful deceased. It is essential that the surrogate and his relatives are seen to eat cooked food meant for the deceased. The same Brahmans will prepare and eat the supply of raw food during the presumed year-long journey of the deceased to the other world. Several Purāṇas describe this emigration to the kingdom of Yama, lord of the dead, as arduous. To cross the dread river Vaitarani the deceased must hold onto the tail of a gracious cow, formerly sacrificed, but in modern times simply rented for a ritual moment.

The third feature of *shrāddha* takes over following the twelfth day (a symbolic year), with the vulnerable *preta* safely transformed by rituals into a secure *pitri*. The danger of a troublesome, dissatisfied ghost has been overcome. Although not all will be so dutiful, kinfolk may now perform offerings (*tarpaṇa*) as one of five daily sacrifices (*mahāyajñas*) and special monthly rites (*māsika*) on new-moon day (*amāvāsyā*). Certainly all will observe the death anniversary (*pratyābdika*). The recently deceased has joined a company of three generations of ancestors, often understood as dwelling in three hierarchical companies of deities, Vasus, Rudras, and Ādityas, located respectively on earth, in midspace, and in heaven. Men are assumed into the lineage of a deceased father, father's father, and father's paternal grandfather. Ritual authorities vary regarding a married woman, with advocates for the maternal lineage of her father or her husband being two alternatives. In any case, three generations of ancestors require gratification in the form of rice, sesame, water, and mantras or *shloka*s in return for favors in health, prosperity, and longevity of descendants. Beyond the three nearest generations are remote ancestors, dwelling with the Vishvedevas (All-gods). They require little in the way of food, only rice that sticks to the fingers after *piṇḍa*s are offered to the closer kin. It could be said that ancestors of the fourth generation and beyond need only minimal sustenance as they dissolve toward rebirth.

Once a year, in a dark lunar fortnight, *pitri*s are invited collectively for Mahālayā in Bhādrapada (August–September) and Pitripaksha in Āshvina (September–October), festivals not unlike All Hallows' Eve (Halloween), the night before All Saints' Day (November 1 in the Christian calendar). The mid-January solstice festival of Saṅkrānti is another time to honor ancestors. A personal or family choice may be to travel to a pilgrimage center on a sacred river—Varanasi on the Ganges, for example, or Nasik on the Godavari, Shrirangam or Thanjavur on the Kaveri—to immerse bone and tooth fragments preserved from ashes of the cremation pyre, if not already dispersed in a local river. Deposition in a sacred river is meritul to the deceased and may determine a more positive status in the next life.

As with other long-standing religions with multiple choices for religious expression, Hinduism displays considerable variation regarding the actual location of a person after death. Doctrines and practices shift, particularly with regard to sectarian, regional and textual differences, and modern life has diluted attention to rituals. Yet there is astonishing consistency in rituals of death and veneration of ancestors over the past twenty-five or more centuries, and Hindus—not only the most ritually dedicated families—are remarkably devoted to and dependent upon the generations who have gone before.

David M. Knipe

See also **Agni; Bhūta; Hinduism (Dharma); Saṃskāra**

BIBLIOGRAPHY

Kane, Pandurang Vaman. *History of Dharmaśāstra*, vol. 4. Poona: Bhandarkar Oriental Research Institute, 1953. Pages 179–551 provide a scattered but indispensable overview of *antyeshṭi* and *shrāddha* in Vedic and Sanskrit texts.

Knipe, David M. "*Sapiṇḍīkaraṇa*: The Hindu Rite of Entry into Heaven." In *Religious Encounters with Death: Insights from the History and Anthropology of Religions*, edited by Frank E. Reynolds and Earle H. Waugh. University Park and London: Pennsylvania State University Press, 1977. Analysis and interpretation based on textual and field studies of the crucial transition from *preta* to *pitri*.

O'Flaherty, Wendy Doniger, ed. *Karma and Rebirth in Classical Indian Traditions*. Berkeley: University of California, 1980. Essays by leading indologists on Vedas, epics, Purāṇas, Dharma Shāstras, philosophical systems, Āyurveda.

Pandey, Raj Bali. *Hindu Saṃskāras*. 2nd ed. Delhi: Motilal Banarsidass, 1969. Chapter 9 outlines *antyeshṭi* for twelve days (later *shrāddhas* not pursued), with reliable attention to texts and rituals but frequently misguided interpretation.

Parry, Jonathan. *Death in Banaras*. Cambridge, U.K.: Cambridge University, 1994. Anthropological field study of contemporary beliefs and practices in the sacred city; good sections on funerary specialists and spirit possession.

Shastri, Dakshina Ranjan. *Origin and Development of the Rituals of AncestorWorship in India*. Kolkata: Bookland, 1963. Extensive survey of all aspects of death and ancestors according to medieval ritual manuals of Hemādri, Raghunandana, and others.

HINDU AND BUDDHIST THOUGHT IN WESTERN PHILOSOPHY

Europe's encounter with the Brahmanical and Buddhist traditions of philosophy in India has been imbued at once by two simultaneous, and contradictory, tendencies. The first has been a fascination with the unique sophistication and profundity of the classical Indian *darshana*s (visions), and the other a relentless search for self-understanding through comparisons and contrasts with South Asian thought. Each tendency has exhibited both awed appreciation of the insights and trajectories of Brahmanical and Buddhist systems as well as self-absorbed reactions and even contemptuous denigration and dismissal under the banner of European philosophical exceptionalism.

For two and a half centuries, these tendencies of the European reception of classical Indian philosophical thought have followed several distinct phases, which are for the most part chronological but which sometimes overlap. The first phase, that of Orientalism and Romanticism, corresponding with the end of the eighteenth and the greater part of the nineteenth centuries, witnesses an ongoing attempt by European thinkers to familiarize themselves with Indian systems and to assess their meaning and significance for European self-understanding. The second phase, which roughly extends from the end of the nineteenth to the middle of the twentieth centuries, displays a growing ambivalence with and widening rejection of Indian thought from "proper" philosophical contemplation and history. The third phase, running from the middle of the twentieth century to the present, has seen a much more hermeneutically sensitive and professional treatment of classical Indian thought and a concerted attempt, significantly on the part of both Indians trained in European thought and Western philosophers, to incorporate Vedic and Buddhist traditions into analytic and continental paradigms.

Orientalism and Romanticism: The Eighteenth and Nineteenth Centuries

Alexander the Great's brief conquest of the Punjab brought early contact between Greco-Roman philosophical traditions, such as Stoicism, and Indian *darshana*s, such as yoga and Theravada Buddhism, as early as the fourth century B.C. However, no positive evidence of extensive contact and interchange between the South Asian and Western intellectual worlds can be traced back farther than the aggressive Jesuit missionary ventures into India in the sixteenth and seventeenth centuries. An increasing number of missionary reports, however, sparked enough interest to prompt Voltaire (1694–1778) to unabashedly proclaim that India, and not Mesopotamia, was the birthplace of both the world's civilizations and its core—and more or less universal—religious doctrines. It was at this moment in the eighteenth century that the new European "science" of Indology was inaugurated, taking root in the direct and indirect translation of Sanskrit literary, religious, and philosophical classics, such as Khalidasa's *Shakuntala*, the Bhagavad Gītā, the Mahābhārata and Rāmāyaṇa, and the Upanishads, by such figures as William Jones (1746–1794), Charles Wilkins (1749–1836), H. Thomas Colebrooke (1765–1837) and A. H. Anquetil Duperron (1731–1805). Common to these pioneers of Indian studies in Great Britain and on the Continent were the convictions that the Sanskrit language was the earliest manifestation of a "common source" of all European languages and an insistence that the study of classical Indian philosophy could enhance and renew the European philosophical tradition.

These convictions were embraced by early nineteenth-century Romantic philosophers, specifically J. G. Herder (1744–1803) and Friedrich Schlegel (1772–1829). While each of their cumulative views on early Hinduism were revised over their decades of study, both enthusiastically proclaimed immersion into ancient India's civilization to their philosophical contemporaries. Though both were committed Christians, they warned against the biased penchant of Europeans to see themselves as the standard of all culture, citing the antiquity and "pure theism" of the Vedic worldview. Their excitement was, however, tempered by skepticism over the removal of theistic associations from idea of *brahman*, which in their views led to a nihilistic mysticism and dangerous moral indifference. This latter was for Herder and Schlegel exemplified by India's caste hierarchy, which, along with pantheism, represented the tragically "degenerate" state into which India's religions had fallen from their "pristine" early truth. Despite these reservations,

both philosophers thought that the oldest forms of Vedic religious symbols and ethical "compassion" could serve as a remedy for what they perceived as the artificial and arid technicalism of Enlightenment post-Kantian Idealism and the mechanization of European society at large, set in motion by the industrial revolution.

Without question the most fascinating contrast of receptions of Indian thought in nineteenth-century European philosophy can be found in G. W. F. Hegel (1770–1831) and Arthur Schopenhauer (1788–1860). Hegel, whose philosophical progressivism depicted Europe, with its new democratic monarchies and "social" consciousness or spirit, as the culmination of both philosophy and civilization, rejected the common Romantic notion of India as some ideal "birthplace" of humanity from whose perfection society had long since strayed. Taking up Schlegel's critique of the "empty substantialism" of the Upanishadic concept of *brahman*, Hegel could discern no possibility for either dialectical development or socioethical advancement on the basis of such an abstract universal notion. While readings late in his life of Colebrooke's essays on the classical schools such as Nyāya, Vaisheshika, Sāṃkhya, and Buddhism convinced him that "genuine philosophical systems" did indeed exist in India, Hegel retained his adherence to the commitment that India's place at the "beginning of history" relegated whatever philosophical truth could be found there to the "poorest" kind, and while, even if philosophy had been born in the East, it reached its maturity and fruition in Europe. India was a place where "substance" never became "subject," where *brahman* never became individuated, and consequently spirit never became social in Indian civilization.

Schopenhauer was openly contemptuous of this philosophical Eurocentrism. Deeply moved early in his career by Duperron's 1801–1802 secondhand translations of the Upanishads and an ever-widening expertise in secondary literature on Buddhism, Schopenhauer framed parts of his own philosophical system around core concepts of Advaita Vedānta and Theravada and Mahayana Buddism. He posited that human consciousness was deluded by its inbuilt Kantian schematization of experience (what he labeled "the veil of *maya*") into the false metaphysical presumption of seeing the world as a collection of heterogeneous individualities rather than the unitary ground of being (what he styled "Will"). Concomitantly, rather than castigating yogic *samyasin*s and Buddhist ascetics as nihilists, as earlier Romantics had, Schopenhauer hailed the "renunciation of Will" and "perspective of *nirvana*" that they attained as making possible true ethical selflessness and compassion. With this stance, Schopenhauer fully embraced the Romantic view of India so sharply challenged by Hegel, celebrating it as the birthplace of "perennial philosophy." Schopenhauer expected the study of India and Asian thought generally to be the greatest boon imaginable to nineteenth-century Europe, promising it an intellectual "Renaissance" comparable to the one prompted by the fifteenth-century rediscovery of classical Greco-Roman thought.

Perhaps predictably, it was Schopenhauer's enthusiasm that immediately spilled over into the field of Indological studies. The late-nineteenth-century Schopenhauerian enthusiast and Indologist Paul Deussen (1845–1919), a former classmate of Friedrich Nietzsche's, became at once the translator of sixty Upanishads, the editor of the first critical edition of Schopenhauer's works, and president of the German Schopenhauer Society. Wholeheartedly dedicated to Sanskrit studies, he was confident that Advaita Vedānta (and particularly Schopenhauer's spin on it) represented the culmination of philosophical truth, far surpassing all systems from "a-psychic and atheistic" Buddhism to modern Enlightenment thought. This confidence led him to write Indian thought into the larger history of world philosophy; half of the six volumes of his *General History of Philosophy* (1894–1917) were devoted to the schools of the Indian tradition as these were categorized through the fifteenth-century Advaita doxography, the *Sarvadarshanasamgraha*.

In the Romantic period then, we find a remarkable fascination with the histories and core concepts of Brahmanical and Buddhist thought. Nonetheless, this fascination seems firmly located within a larger self-reflection that, rather than investigating the treasures of classical Indian philosophical thought for their own sake, always took stock of the latter in view of a self-preoccupied assessment of the current state of philosophical affairs in Europe. Through studying Indian thought, Europe could learn more about its own origins, identity, and destiny.

Rejection and Dismissal: The Late Nineteenth and Early Twentieth Centuries

Friedrich Nietzsche (1844–1900) was the first major Western philosopher since Hegel to cast serious aspersions and skeptical doubt at the value of Indian philosophy for European thought, although for markedly different reasons than Hegel's. Nietzsche learned and accepted most of what he knew of Indian culture and thought from Schopenhauer and his personal friend Deussen, but suspended his early approbation for Schopenhauerian "pessimism" in search of a philosophical formula for the "affirmation" of both individual life and the rational and spiritually independent *Übermensch* of high culture. Ironically, while Nietzsche found one prototype for the *Übermensch* in the Brahmans of Manu's social order, who legitimated their cultural authority through the establishment of caste hierarchy, he found

one of the most formidable threats to the coming *Übermensch* in the onset of a "European Buddhism," which he equated with nihilism. While admiring Gautama Buddha for his unrelenting "honesty" in denying God's existence in the determination to accept life for its inevitable suffering, Nietzsche saw the Buddha's *nirvāna* and the practices that led to its attainment as the ultimate manifestation of "the denial and hatred of life," the "decadence" of fleeing the world in the face of its meaninglessness and terror. Buddhist nihilism was for Nietzsche too "passive," and it represented a spiritual tendency that might appear to a European to be opposed to Christianity, but at its heart is at one with it. Only the "Dionysian spirit" of the *Übermensch*, which embraced life in *amor fati* and dedicated itself to the "Will to Power," could ward off that attitude toward the body and life as valueless, an attitude of which Buddhism was in his eyes the most perfected manifestation.

Despite the enthusiasm of the Romantic sensibility and Deussen's later efforts, several fateful turns led to the relative eclipse of Indian thought in the reflection of Western philosophers for approximately half a century. One factor was the influence of Hegel on late-nineteenth-century historians of philosophy. While the most popular textbooks of the history of philosophy from mid-century all had chapters on Indian thought, the textbooks from the late nineteenth and early twentieth centuries omit it. The Hegelian contention that the dialectic of Being had its origins in Greek thought began to find its way into more and more late-nineteenth and early-twentieth-century histories of philosophy, which led their authors to foregone conclusions that Asian and pre-Thalic Greek thought should be excluded from a historic appreciation of their topic. On the other hand, those historians who did not ascribe to Hegel's vision of a universal history of philosophy were driven by a professionalization, or specialization in historical research, which left the field of Indian studies to the professional Indologist and thus outside the scope of Western intellectual historiography.

These presumptions can be found in the passing mention made of Asian and Indian thought in some of the twentieth century's most prominent European philosophers. Edmund Husserl (1859–1938), the renowned founder of phenomenology, identified the single most characteristic mark of philosophy as its purely theoretical orientation; philosophy arose out of Aristotelian wonder, not from practical concerns, and its possibilities as a pure eidetic "science" were the legacies of Greek thought. For him, no traditions, such as the Indian or Chinese, where intellectual speculation was so closely tied to soteriological dogmas and concerns, could possibly give rise to genuinely philosophical reflection. While Husserl's early student and "path-clearer" for "hermeneutic ontology," Martin Heidegger (1889–1976), drew much inspiration for his later thought from Chinese Daoist and Japanese Buddhist traditions, he was always careful to qualify this fascination with the recognition that Asian thought had its abode in another "house of Being." It was Greek philosophy that "uniquely and univocally" made the fundamental concern of Western thought a search for the Being of things, and as such "Being" could not be imagined to be the "basic concept" of any other tradition, philosophy is for him "Western philosophy—there is no other kind, neither a Chinese nor an Indian philosophy" (1968, 224). Thinking could certainly take "other paths" in other traditions, but not the distinctly European philosophical path. In the end, Western philosophy proper is actually a tradition of which the cultures of the world should, in his eyes, beware in the face of the progressive intellectual colonization by the West, "the Europeanization of the Earth."

The second phase of European philosophical reflection on the Brahmanical and Buddhist traditions then mixes ambivalent rejection with dismissal. Reasons for such dismissal were both historiographic and ideological. Ironically, however, the neglect to regard Indian thought as a genuine philosophical tradition was sparked in this phase by a motivation strangely similar to that which attracted Romantic Europeans of the first phase to either appropriate or take special note of it. This motivation was a preoccupation with the necessity of Europe to isolate the essence and fulfill the mission of its own philosophical tradition, or at least a particular and historically conditioned self-understanding of that tradition.

Reincorporation through the Analytic and Continental Divide

Against this onslaught of skepticism about the worth of Indian thought for Western philosophical reflection, translations and commentaries on the Brahmanical Buddhist traditions, openly advocating a rekindling of cross-cultural philosophical engagement, began to renew interest. Foremost among the early translators were Theodore Stcherbatsky (1886–1942), who interpreted the Buddhist epistemologies of Dignaga and Dharmakirti through Kantian categories, and Erich Frauwallner (1898–1974), whose treatments of scholastic Buddhism and even Vaisheshika insisted that both could, for at least certain periods in their histories, be considered purely theoretical and nonsoteriological systems. Running alongside these more Continental appropriations were receptions of Brahmanical Nyāya logic as fully compatible with the contemporary formalism of symbolic logic, so much so that the former can be paraphrased into the latter, which we find in Stanislaw Schayer (1899–1941), Daniel Ingalls (1916–1999) and Frits Staal (b. 1930).

Perhaps the most exemplary contrast between the analytic and phenomenological appropriations of Indian thought can be found in two contemporary Indian philosophers trained by both native pandits and European professors, Bimal Krishna Matilal (1935–1991) and Jitendranath Mohanty (b. 1924). Former colleagues at the Sanskrit College in Kolkata, both set themselves the task of ensuring that the classical *darshana*s of India receive proper acknowledgment among modern thinkers, though their approaches varied. Matilal began his career as a Sankritist in Kolkata but then studied under Ingalls and W. V. Quine at Harvard. He vigorously defended Hindu Nyāya realism against Vedantic and Buddhist "idealist" objections, giving the ancient debates lucid expositions to English audiences, notably against the backdrop of more contemporary debates in logic and theory of knowledge. More importantly, he demonstrated how, whether in the guise of the worldly Lokayatikas and Vaisheshikas or under the rubric of "mystical" strands of Mahayana Buddhism or Vedānta, philosophy in India was always undertaken with serious examinations of *pramaashastra* (epistemology), logic comparable in its analytical insight to contemporary symbolic logic and considerations of the philosophy of language. Mohanty for his part became an avid student of Immanuel Kant in Göttingen and later of Husserl in Kolkata before turning his attention to the study of Nyāya and Vedānta. His representations of the classical scholastic debates in India schematized them according to more phenomenological themes. Nyāya, Vedanta and Yogacara-Sautrantika Buddhism were played off against one another based on their differing theories of consciousness, truth, and language. Mohanty came to the conclusion that the presence of the Husserlian concept of the "intentionality" of consciousness could be found to enhance the positions of Nyāya and Buddhism in various contexts, while its lack in some Advaita teachings could be taken to compromise the integrity of the latter. Striking in the cases of both Matilal and Mohanty is the extent to which the analytic and phenomenological debates are replayed in their respective presentations of classical Indian thought, but in addition how each of their presentations suggested native Indian rapprochements in this debate. Each brought vastly improved methodological and hermeneutic tools to bear on the explication of Indian philosophers. Neither saw hermeneutic implications to these presentations that should cause overmuch concern, for while it is true, Mohanty concedes, that the Indian and Western philosophical traditions exhibit important differences, their many historical inquiries and debates "overlap" in profoundly significant ways.

The most recent reincorporations of Brahmanical and Buddhist thought into Western philosophy can be found in the works of scholars such as Harold Coward (b. 1936) and David Loy (b. 1947). Reviewing the skeptical traditions of Bhatrhari's Grammar and Mādhyamika Buddhism, these scholars have found parallels between modern Derridian "deconstruction" and antiessentialist tendencies within the Indian tradition. Just as twentieth-century Anglo-European thought seeks to shed the heritage of "Being"-centered metaphysics and the hierarchical, exclusivist, and imperialistic society it has fostered, so too, they suggest, did exemplary figures such as Bhartṛhari, Nagarjuna, and Shankara challenge dualistic and socially corrupting ontologies, along with artificial intellectual boundaries, within their own heritage. Indian thought once again offers a corrective alternative, in a fashion reminiscent, though in a much modified tone, of the Romantics, to the wayward trajectories of Europe's intellectual legacy.

Thus in the contemporary period of reincorporation, we see the many strands of thought in the West converging around the twin themes of deep appreciation for India's philosophical contributions and an abiding desire to make those contributions speak to their own philosophical problematics. Despite all the interpretive and cultural pitfalls against which such "comparative" or "cross-cultural" philosophy is constantly warned by its critics, however, it was under the circumstances perhaps inevitable that over the past two and a half centuries India has been gradually accepted as a major "conversation partner" for European thought.

Douglas L. Berger

See also **Buddhism in Ancient India; Hinduism (Dharma)**

BIBLIOGRAPHY

Clarke, J. J. *Oriental Enlightenment: The Encounter between Asian and Western Thought.* New York: Routledge, 1997.
Coward, Harold. *Derrida and Indian Philosophy.* Albany: State University of New York Press, 1990.
Ganeri, Jonardon. *Indian Logic: A Reader.* Richmond, U.K.: Curzon, 2001.
Gestering, J. I. *German Pessimism and Indian Philosophy: A Hermeneutic Reading.* Delhi: Ajanta, 1986.
Halbfass, Wilhelm. *India and Europe: An Essay in Understanding.* Albany: State University of New York Press, 1988.
Heidegger, Martin. *What Is Called Thinking?* Translated by J. Glenn Gray. New York: Harper & Row, 1968.
Matilal, B. K. *Perception: An Essay on Classical Indian Theories of Knowledge.* Oxford: Clarendon Press, 1986.
Mohanty, J. N. *Reason and Tradition in Indian Thought: An Essay on the Nature of Indian Philosophical Thinking.* Oxford: Clarendon Press, 1992.
———. *Between Two Worlds, East and West: An Autobiography.* New Delhi: Oxford, 2002.
O'Leary, Joseph S. "Heidegger and Indian Philosophy." In *Beyond Orientalism: The Work of Wilhelm Halbfass and Its Impact on Indian and Cross-Cultural Studies,* edited by Eli Franco and Karin Preisendanz. Amsterdam: Pozman Studies, 1997.
Sedler, J. W. *India in the Mind of Germany: Schelling, Schopenhauer and Their Times.* Washington D.C.: University Press of America, 1982.

HINDUISM (DHARMA) The term "Hinduism" is derived from *Hindu,* the Old Persian form of the name of the River Indus (Sanskrit *Sindhu,* hence also *India*). This Iranian, and then Arab, term for all Indians was only slowly accepted as the self-designation of non-Muslim Indians, such as by the Kashmiri Jonarāja (early 15th century). It commonly signifies the indigenous religion(s) of South Asia, now increasingly called by the Epic term Sanātana Dharma (eternal religion). "Hinduism" is a loose agglomerate of many of the interlinking religions and worldviews of South Asia (and Bali); though overlapping with some other religions, it basically includes those that are neither Islamic, Christian, Buddhist, Jain, Parsi, Sikh, or "tribal" (i.e., *ādivāsī,* "aboriginal"; *vanavāsī,* "forest dwellers").

As this negative description indicates, an effectual definition of Hinduism (used here for brevity's sake) is virtually impossible: it is the sum of the traditional beliefs, rituals, customs, and pertinent social structures of South Asia, including the philosophical and theological representation of these beliefs in some two dozen of schools of thought. Less encompassing definitions (especially those deriving Hinduism simply from Vedic origins, do not sufficiently cover the realities on the ground or in the available texts. The Veda is expressively rejected by many Tantric sects, Vīrashaivism, Buddhism, and Jainism. Nor does the fashionable description of Hinduism as a colonial creation apply: Greek and Chinese visitors (c. 450 B.C.–A.D. 600) saw it as different (as "*deva*" worship") from Buddhism and other ascetic religions (gymnosophists); indigenously, Hinduism was often referred to simply as *dharma.*

However, the religions that emerged from early Hinduism, such as Jainism and Buddhism, and later on, Sikh religion, have had shifting boundaries with Hinduism; they were both included as well as excluded. The authoritative fourteenth-century Sarvadarshanasaṃgraha (or the 11th-century Shivaite Somashambhupaddhati) do include them. All these "views" (*darshana*) and religions were influenced by developments that spread from one religion to the other. Nevertheless, some religions, such as Buddhism, are excluded by their own self-understanding and definition. Interestingly, even in recent times, politically active Hinduism (*Hindūtva*) cannot yet give a good definition of itself: "reciting prayers, reading the Gītā, worshiping the image (*mūrti*) of a deity, reciting *oṁ,* planting the *tulsi* plant" should make one a Hindu. Many South Asians would disagree.

Devotee Offering Worldly Gift to the *Shivling*. *Shivling* (also spelled *shivalinga*) is the state of eternity, the symbolic idol of Lord Shiva usually represented in phallic form. AMIT PASRICHA.

Frequently, Hinduism is indeed more of a *weltanschauung* and a way of life than a "religion" in the traditional Western sense. There is no common "creed" or "statement of faith" or "catechism." Instead, people can choose which god(dess) they want to worship (*iṣṭadevatā*), even the impersonal "deity" Brahma or none at all. A common aspect, however, is the (almost) universal acceptance of the idea of rebirth combined with the effects on a next life of actions in this world (karma). Most Hindus also follow a series of rituals from birth to death and beyond (ancestor rituals, *shrāddha*). Another early, still strongly held belief is that of three "obligations" (*ṛṇa*) incurred by birth: those owed to the deities (*deva*), ancestors (*pitṛ*), and the ancient seers (*ṛṣi*). All must be worshiped and fed in various rituals carried out by the family's priests (Brahman *purohita*s). All these customs, rites, and beliefs bind a Hindu individual into the Hindu community, but they also separate Hindus from non-Hindus, with whom there cannot be, for reasons of purity, any interdining and intermarriage.

Nevertheless, Hinduism has not been static at all but has clearly evolved over time. Some aspects of later Hindu folk religion seem to emerge already in the Indus Valley Civilization (2600–1900 B.C.), though in the absence of script, we cannot be sure. The famous Shiva Pashupati probably is nothing but a neolithic hunting god, and bull-killing scenes may not represent Mahiṣāsuramardinī but rather Mediterranean or South Asian bull fights, while the worship of certain trees (pipal/Ashvattha) and snakes seems reasonably certain.

Roots of Hinduism in the Veda

However, the major roots of Hinduism are found in the Veda (roughly, 1500–500 B.C.), composed by newly arrived Indo-Aryan–speaking people in the northwestern subcontinent and later concentrated in the Kuru realm, which saw many foundational changes in religion, texts, social structure, and politics. Vedic religion has mostly male deities of nature (personifications of the sun, fire, wind, heaven; or the feminime Aditi, dawn, and earth), of social organization (Āditya such as the gods "agreement, share, lot," including the demiurge and warrior god Indra), and many vaguely personalized "powers" (*brahman*, fever, revenge, heat, etc.). These, and even more so the rituals (*yajña*) performed in public (soma, etc.) and domestic situations (birth, marriage, death, ancestor worship), along with the recitation of sacred verses and formulas (mantras of the four Vedas), have in part survived to this day. The large literature of the period, orally composed in archaic Sanskrit and perfectly transmitted, is collected in the Vedic Saṃhitās, their Brāhmaṇa/Āraṇyaka commentaries (the fountainhead of much of Hindu thought and sciences), the late Vedic Upanishads, and the Sūtras.

In the Upanishads, the traditional belief in an automatic reincarnation as human beings was joined with the new theory of karma, which had gradually developed in the newly acculturated eastern region of North India. This foundational combination has influenced virtually all later religions and sects of South Asia. Such new developments were discussed at length in the Socratic-style dialogues of the early Upanishads, which advanced a monism identifying the personal soul (*ātman*) with the universal spirit (*brahman*). In the ascetic mood of the period (note the gymnosophists of Herodotus [c. 485–425 B.C.], the birth of Jainism and Buddhism), a shift occurred away from ritualism to a symbolic interpretation and internalization, much of which is based on the correlating and identificatory procedures of the Brāhmaṇa texts. All of this was foundational for later Hinduism: it abounds in the identification of deities with each other (including even that of Vishnu = Buddha, or now of the Devī = Mary of Lourdes), of the deity with the universe (such as Krishna in the Gītā), of the worshiper with the deity or the universal Brahman, and of various concepts, ideas, and practices as being of equal value in attaining the spiritual goal.

Such new ideas were constantly added to existing older forms of Hinduism, often in framelike fashion, surrounding the Vedic core. However, many of the older forms have also continued independently and still coexist today, so that a solemn Vedic ritual can be performed today by a Brahman who may be a worshiper of Vishnu in his public and family religion, and a Tantric in his private rituals. These developments accrued in several stages. The Vedic period was followed, at least in our texts, by that of the Epics, caused by the ever-changing societal and religious conditions. The ever popular and often re-adapted, fairy tale–based Rāmāyaṇa has recently shown its resilience in a year-long television series; the more complex, giant Mahābhārata (collected c. 100 B.C.), too, has local adaptations (Pāṇḍava in the Himalayas; Draupadī in South India; the Newar god Bhīmsen in Nepal; the five Pāṇḍavas in Indonesia, etc.). In the Epics (including the Harivamsha) some Vedic gods survive, but several new ones were added, such as Krishna and Rāma (both were later incorporated into Vishnu), or Shiva, who developed out of Rudra, and the Devī (Lakshmī, Shrī, Kālī, Pārvatī, etc.). Vedic ritual was superseded by *pūjā*

and *stotra* ("praise" of the gods), or even by the recitation of their names or their texts, which was declared worth many Vedic *yajña*s. The famous Bhagavad Gītā, the "song of the Lord (Krishna)," is a late (first century A.D.?) insertion into the Mahābhārata. Krishna's teachings initially stress, in rather sophistic manner, the moral and societal duties (*dharma*) of a Kshatriya to fight (even his relatives), but with "detachment" as to avoid karmic outcomes; the later sections of the text focus on *karmayoga* and *bhakti*, and finally, on some additional topics such as Sāṃkhya philosophy. The lasting impact of this supposedly unitary, but clearly stratified text is due to the fact that it provides several views to choose from individually; people of all stripes quote from this (frequently translated) text, find solace in it, or bolster their views, from moral action and pacifistic *bhakti* to violent chauvinism.

Guptan Hinduism

The post-Vedic epoch overlapped with the period "between the empires" (c. 230 B.C.–A.D. 320) that saw continuous cultural influence by peoples invading from the northwest (Alexandrian and Bactrian Greeks, Hellenistic Parthians, north Iranian Saka, Central Asian Yue-ji/Kushana). In reaction to this and to the challenge of the prominent contemporary Buddhism and Jainism, new forms of Hindu religion developed, syncretistically incorporating both local trends and foreign influences. In classical Hinduism, under the Guptas (from A.D. 320), a conservative synthesis emerged, after five hundred years of ferment, which set the stage for medieval Hinduism. The hallmark of Guptan Hinduism is its stress on old (often Vedic) features, which hides substantial new developments; it is retrospective and "progressive" at the same time.

The most important innovations include: creation and destruction of the world (viewed as illusion) in cyclical time; *pūjā* and temple worship with figures of deities, pilgrimages, planets (based on the still all-important post-Vedic astrology); yoga; deliverance from *saṃsāra* during one's lifetime; vegetarianism; a strict social system (see below); and the deification of kings (as a walking Vishnu), just as the gods are treated like kings. Further, the codification of the standard Hindu gods (Brahmā as creator, Vishnu as preserver, Shiva as destroyer, the Devī, Ganesha, etc.), with their various forms (*avatāra*s), and their beneficial as well as destructive aspects, always simultaneously with the identification of many local deities (a process still visible with Jagannātha in Orissa, Pattinī in Sri Lanka, or Mastā in the Himalayas). All of this was collected in the eighteen great Purāṇas that, like the Epics, have been eternally popular. They project divine and human history against the framework of cyclical time, with the present, evil Kālī age starting on 18 February 3102 B.C., but they also include, as virtual encyclopedias, subjects from art to medicine. Stories from these genres were retold in local languages and by wandering bards, with the help of paintings. This practice has now been supplemented by adaptations in films and on television.

In the late Guptan period, a new element emerged, again directed against formal "Brahmanical" Hinduism, in the form of Tantra and Bhakti. The latter is the fervent worship of a single, selected deity. It emerged from South India (Ālvār poetry, 8th century), which had just been Hinduized, largely replacing the older Dravidian religion. The new religious outlook gradually traveled northward and is encountered in Sanskrit texts such as the Bhāgavata Purāṇa, or in eastern India, in Jayadeva's Gītā Govinda (12th century) where it was strongly propagated by Caitanya (1486–1533). The various well-known sects of Vishnuism and Shaivism (Bhāgavata, Pāñcarātrin, Kashmiri Shaiva, Shāivasiddhāntin, etc.), of Devī or Gaṇesha worship, and many other, sometimes rather transitory, sects have produced a large amount of narrative, poetical, and devotional texts in Sanskrit and later, especially since about A.D. 1000, also in local languages.

Tantric Movement

From the mid-first millennium A.D. onward, the pan-Indian and pan-religious Tantric movement made its appearance as well. It is based on the dichotomy between the male Purusha and female Prakṛti, the origin of all creation. Identification with them (or other deities) can be reached through a combination of meditation and yoga, with inner and outer rituals. In the left-handed (vāma) Tantra, they also are of a sexual nature; this was at first rejected but still persists, especially in Nepal, Bengal, Assam. There is great and still continuing importance of various goddesses (whether of beneficial or destructive forms, such as the nine Durgās or eight Mātṛkās). Tantra forms yet another frame around Vedic, Epic, and classical Hinduism, and it permeates, whether acknowledged or not (and in spite of still prevailing Victorian prudery in sexual matters), much of modern Hinduism, as seen in the reinterpretation of the Mahābhārata by Nīlakaṇṭha (17th century) and in current ideas about the secret spiritual and mundane power of the recitation of (Vedic) mantras (e.g., in transcendental meditation).

Such new religious developments and the representations of local forms of deities and their myths were collected in local Sthala Purāṇas and Māhātmyas, which often show little similarity with the "official" pan-Indian versions of the deities and their mythologies. Many of such data are available only in local brochures sold at temples, important though largely neglected sources. However, folk religion can be Pan-Indian, too; for example, the minor deity Maṇināga is found in Nepal, Orissa,

and Maharashtra (and probably elsewhere). Such data usually slip under the radar of textual scholars or village-based anthropologists. Folk religion can be astonishingly archaic, for example, with still common animal sacrifice and non-vegetarianism. In addition, the study of local art, inscriptions, and manuscript colophons is important. For example, manuscript colophons indicate the spread of Krishna worship in Nepal and Gujarat around 1550 or 1600. Such historical and geographical data of the spread of certain cults have largely been neglected thus far.

Influence of Islam and Christianity

Medieval Hinduism also saw considerable influence of Islam (especially since the 13th century), which resulted, due to long persisting, soft religious boundaries, in the improbable religious overlap of Muslim Sufi saints and their Bhakti-following Hindu compatriots (e.g., Lallā, the Islamic ṛṣi sect in Kashmir, Tulsīdās, Eknāth, Sūrdās), also Kabīr (1440–1518, who equated Allah with Rāma) and the founder of the Sikh religion, Nānak, as well as many leaders of new theistic sects (including Rāmānuja, Madhva, Basava, Nāmdev, Jñāneshvara), some of a militant and chauvinistic nature.

Due to the influence of British colonialism and Christian missionaries (at first only grudgingly admitted by the British), still another form developed, Neo-Hinduism. Reformers such as Dayanand (1827–1883) or Vivekananda (1863–1902) insisted on eliminating certain traditional aspects and adding other features, often inspired by Christian or Western sources. The movement began with social reforms (Brahmo Samaj, 1828) but soon included tendencies of abolishing "idol" worship, access of worship and "priestly" duties by all, and a perceived return to Vedic times and values (Ārya Samāj, 1875). This was followed by important social and nationalistic trends, such as the uplift of the low caste population, propagated by Mahatma Gandhi.

The Hindutva (Hinduness) movement, active since the 1920s and especially since the 1980s, surprisingly adds a large amount of "Abrahamization," such as the reliance on a narrow band of indigenous, foundational texts (Veda, Gītā, Rāmāyaṇa, etc.), general public access to them, sometimes even a catechism. The texts are reinterpreted as containing the seeds of all human culture. This still ongoing rewriting of history underlines the uniqueness and superiority of "Hinduness" and glorifies a golden age, before the "damage done by the Muslims and the British," in short: god Rāma's realm. The aim to regain this Hindu India was propagated by M. S. Golwalkar (1939) and V. N. Savarkar (1923, repr. 1989) with the slogan: "one country, one culture, one religion," which excludes non-Hindus. However, given the derivation of Hindu-tva from a Perso-Arabic term, joined with the Sanskrit suffix -tva (-ness), the word is as composite as modern India itself. The movement has resulted in the emergence of right-wing Hindutva political parties since the 1980s. All of this is reminiscent of the great restoration and glorification project of the Guptas.

Still another frame surrounding medieval Hinduism is that of modern science and technology. Many Indian scientists merely add selected scientific data to their traditional beliefs, and do not perceive any clash; rather, they use the amalgam to defend the ancient glory and superiority of Hindu India. Subhash Kak (1994), for example, "discovers" items such as planetary distances or the speed of light in the Vedas; others, from Dayanand onward, have found steam locomotives, airplanes, rockets, atomic bombs, and laser beams, always *post factum*.

Hinduism thus has always been a living, constantly changing religion, in which new trends developed, in the absence of any central authority or dogma, in reaction to social and political developments, such as Kuru Sanskritization, the reactions against Buddhist and foreign influences (c. 150 B.C.–A.D. 320), or Tantra and Bhakti against the Brahmanical Hinduism of the Gupta/Harṣa period. Recently, new popular deities such as Santoṣi Mā and even an AIDS Ammā have emerged.

At the local, still predominantly village level, many of the formal divisions and characteristics collapse: local folk religion is intermingled with archaic local traditions, previous forms of Hinduism, Buddhism, Jainism, and even Islam. Hindus visit an Islamic Pīr's grave and Muslims go to Hindu festivals, or the Buddhist goddess Harītī is still in *pūjā* in the guise of a Muslim Pīr, protecting against smallpox. Many basic South Asian concepts (such as the power of sight, heat) are found both in Hinduism and local Islam, though under different names. Conversely, constant Sanskritization, ever since the Kuru realm, can be witnessed in the increasing Hinduization of "tribal" religions in the mountains of Nepal or the more secluded areas of central India, and among the lower caste Hindu communities that imitate higher caste, preferably Brahmanical, lifestyle; for example, the low caste goldsmiths of Karnataka have even claimed Brahman status.

Concepts of Life and Class

In light of the many concurrent forms of Hinduism, even in the daily life of one person, what then are its overarching characteristics? The societal aspects cannot be overestimated; indeed, some want to see Hinduism as a social system rather than a religion. In endocentric classifications, three sets of concepts have been claimed to be encompassing: the four aims of life (*puruṣārtha*), the four stages in life (*āshrama*), and the four "classes" (*varṇa*) of Hindu society, which are subdivided into several thousands of castes (*jāti*).

Purusartha. The "aims in life" that can be achieved *seriatim* include *artha* (material success), *kāma* (sexual desire), and *mokṣa* ("release" from the cycle of recurrent rebirth, *saṃsāra*), to which *dharma* is sometimes added. *Dharma* covers everything from customs, incidental and general beliefs, rituals, ṛṇa (duty), organization of society, and procedure in law courts, to the laws that govern nature, the gods, and the universe. It relates to the whole of Hindu culture, not just its religious or societal aspects. This Epic (and medieval) construct offers "feeling at home" in a fixed, ordered universe and society, the rules of which are spelled out at great length in the respective texts (Dharma Sūtra, Manusmṛti, etc.). Many of its societal aspects are summarized by the three Vedic ṛṇas (obligations): one is born with the primordial obligations (not guilt) toward the gods, ancestors, and primordial poets (ṛṣi); they are sometimes extended to include one's teachers. A first summary is found in the Taittirīya and Kaṭha Shikṣā Upanishads: "Speak the truth, behave according to custom (*dharma*), carry out the (ritual) actions, do not neglect your recitations, . . . do not cut off your family line . . . treat your mother, father, teacher, guests like a god."

Ashrama and *Varna.* Much of this obligation involves rituals, which leads to, as Indians complain, a "ritual-ridden" society, governed by the *varṇāshrama* system. The term refers to the four classes (*varṇa*) of society and the four stages (*āshrama*) in life, from childhood to old age, concepts that are socially imprinted early on. After early childhood, the four stages are: *brahmacārya*, "living as a (celibate Veda) student" in the home of a teacher; *gṛhastha*, married life as a "householder"; *vānaprastha*, living as a married "retiree in a (nearby) forest"; *sannyāsa*, living as a (celibate) ascetic who has "completely thrown away" all strictures of society and strives, alone, for his personal emancipation from the cycle of rebirth. None of these stages, which must be attained by appropriate rituals, are prescriptive, though the *gṛhastha* stage is considered normal, since it ensures the required birth of a son who must carry out the ancestor rituals. The system is an early medieval Brahmanical construct; the Veda had only two stages, the *brahmacārin* and the *gṛhastha*; the *sannyāsin* was added during the Maurya period, while the separate *vānaprastha* stage is still more recent.

Similarly, the division of society (Vedic: *shūdrārya*) into *varṇa*s ("colors," the four classes), is already attested in the famous Puruṣa hymn (Rig Veda 10.90, c. 1000 B.C.). The Vedas enumerate the classes as the three *ārya varṇa*s: the Brāhmaṇa (poets/priests); Kshatriya (or *rājanya*, nobility); Vaishya (belonging to the people), who alone are entitled to perform the solemn (*shrauta*) rituals; the fourth, the non-*ārya* Shūdra *varṇa*, originally was one of artisans—who are thus excluded and included at the same time.

Another large group (*pañcama*) outside and below this system has developed, the Dalit (*harijan, pariah, pore,* formerly called the "untouchables"), who can perform only the most menial and degrading work. These five levels represent a corresponding decline in purity.

The *varṇa* system has been overlaid by several thousands of occupational castes (*jāti*), as exemplified in Manu's law book (c. 100 B.C.), representing a conservative Brahmanical reaction to Buddhist/Jain and foreign challenges. One is born both into a *varṇa* and into a caste and can practically change this status—if ever—only with great effort over several generations, by social upward movement, now called Sanskritization. Occupational castes are perhaps first visible in certain Vedic designations, such as the (always impure) *caṇḍāla, vṛṣala,* washermen, most artisans, fishermen, and so on, and appear, around the beginning of the common era, in normative *dharma* texts or early inscriptions (at Mathura). Caste certainly is not just a colonial invention, as some now want to have it. In the never-colonized Nepal, where good historical records exist (unutilized in fashionable "colonial" investigations), there is not just talk of restoring the *varṇa*s—as is always done by new dynasties—but also, around A.D. 1390 , of restoring the thirty-six castes by the Malla kings. In 1851 the Rāṇās went even further in their *Mulukī Ain,* and compiled the strictest caste regulations anywhere, which lasted until 1960. The current caste altercations and "voter bank" politics show the persistence of caste, in spite of its abolishment after Indian independence (and in Nepal, after 1960). It remains endemic in South Asian society, including Muslims, Jews, and Christians.

As the caste of caste indicates, such modern representations, or the anthropological study of contemporaneous village communities, cannot, however, reliably inform about the situation in the past, for which the (roughly datable) texts and the evidence of archaeology and art must be included. Texts are studied by philologists and historians of religion. They cover the past three thousand years, from the Veda to modern temple booklets; however, they do not always indicate the contemporary social importance of certain forms of Hinduism and related religions. Many forms did not make it into the texts (e.g., village religion), or did so only belatedly (Tantra), once the local form was adapted to "standard" (often Brahmanic) Hinduism and represented by Sanskrit texts. All local forms must therefore be studied, not just "privileged" Brahman rituals and texts: folk tales and songs, accounts and observations of traditional festivals and rites, religious dance, theater, processions, pilgrimages, local and folk art, and so on.

Finally, it must be emphasized again that Hinduism has been an ever-changing entity, with many local variations within South Asia, and now also in its diaspora areas, where acculturation is steadily proceeding: new holy places, such as American rivers, are created, but *pūjā* and many life-cycle rituals remain, as does part of the mythology—if often only in Bollywood fashion and as ahistorical comics. Conversely, traditional dance is elevated from a low caste performing art to one aspired to by immigrants' daughters. What, then, will be the future of Hinduism, now followed by some 800 million of the more than 1 billion people of the subcontinent? Will it develop like the indigenous, not centralized religion of another modern Asian country, the Shinto of Japan—with foundational though little known myths, *pūjā*-like rituals performed out of habit ("one never knows what it may be good for"), and with specialized temples (such as for electronics, success in school, etc.)—while religion plays a relatively small role in daily life. Or, will it develop rather like an "Abrahamic" religion, with an increasing focus on selected normative texts and rituals, bolstered by a new-found self-consciousness and pride in an emerging India, and accompanied by increasing interaction with the distant diaspora, who see all things Indian in sharper focus, though in nostalgic and idealistic ways. We can be certain about one thing: "Hinduism" will remain dynamic.

Michael Witzel

See also **Astronomy; Brāhmaṇas; Buddhism in Ancient India; Devī; Jainism; Rāmāyaṇa; Sikhism; Upanishadic Philosophy; Vedic Aryan India**

BIBLIOGRAPHY

Abbott, J. *The Keys of Power.* 1932. Reprint, as *Indian Ritual and Belief: The Keys of Power.* Delhi: Usha, 1984.

Alsdorf, L. *Beiträge zur Geschichte von Vegetarimus und Rinderverehrung in Indien.* Mainz: Akademie der Wissenschaften und Literatur, 1961.

Babb, L. A. *The Divine Hierarchy. Popular Hinduism in Central India.* New York: Columbia University Press 1975.

Brockington, J. *The Sanskrit Epics.* Leiden: E. J. Brill, 1998.

Bühnemann, G. *Pūjā. A Study in Smārta Ritual.* Vienna: Institut für Indologie der Universität Wien, 1988.

Courtright, P. B. *Gaṇesha: Lord of Obstacles, Lord of Beginnings.* New York: Oxford University Press, 1985.

Dalmia, V., and H. von Stietencron, eds. *Representing Hinduism: The Construction of Religious Traditions and National Identity.* New Delhi: Sage Publications, 1995.

Derrett, J. D. *Hindu Law: Past and Present.* Kolkata: A. Mukherjee, 1957.

Dumont, L. *Homo Hierarchicus: The Caste System and Its Implications.* Chicago: University of Chicago Press, 1980.

Eder, M. "Medieval Devotional Traditions: An Annotated Survey of Recent Scholarship." In *Studies on Hinduism,* edited by A. Sharma. Columbia: University of South Carolina Press, 2003.

Farmer, S., J. B. Henderson, and M. Witzel. "Neurobiology, Layered Texts, and Correlative Cosmologies: A Cross-Cultural Framework for Premodern History." *Bulletin of the Museum of Far Eastern Antiquities* 72 (2002): 48–90.

Farmer, S., R. Sproat, and M. Witzel. "The Collapse of the Indus-Script Thesis: The Myth of a Literate Harappan Civilization." *Electronic Journal of Vedic Studies* 11, no. 2 (2004): 19–57.

Fick, R. *The Social Organisation in North-East India in Buddha's Time.* Kolkata: University of Calcutta Press, 1920.

Fuller, C. *The Camphor Flame: Popular Hinduism and Society in India.* Princeton, N.J.: Princeton University Press, 1992.

Golwalkar, M. S. *We, or the Nationhood Redefined.* Nagpur: Bharat Prakashan, 1939.

González Reimann, L. *The Mahābhārata and the Yugas: India's Great Epic Poem and the Hindu System of World Ages.* New York: Peter Lang, 2002.

Goudriaan, T., and S. Gupta. *Hindu Tantric and Śākta Literature.* Wiesbaden, Germany: Harrassowitz, 1981.

Halbfass, W. *Tradition and Reflection: Explorations in Indian Thought.* Albany: State University of New York Press, 1991.

H'fer, A. *The Caste Hierarchy and the State in Nepal: A Study of the Muluki Ain of 1854.* Innsbruck, Austria: Unieversitōtsverlag Wagner, 1979.

Jaffrelot, C. *The Hindu Nationalist Movement and Indian Politics, 1920 to 1990s.* London: C. Hurst, 1996.

Jamison, S., and M. Witzel. "Vedic Hinduism. " In *Studies on Hinduism*, edited by A. Sharma. Columbia: University of South Carolina Press, 2003. Also available at <http://www.people.fas.harvard.edu/~witzel/vedica.pdf>

Ježić, M. "Textual Layers of the of the Bhagavadgītā as Traces of Indian Cultural History." In *Sanskrit and World Culture: Proceedings of the Fourth World Sanskrit Conference*, edited by W. Morgenroth. Berlin: Akademie Verlag, 1986.

Kak, S. *The Astronomical Code of the Rgveda.* New Delhi: Munshiram Manoharlal, 2000.

Kane, P. V. *History of Dharmaśāstra.* Poona: Bhandarkar Oriental Research Institute, 1930–1968.

Levy, R. I., with the collaboration of Kedar Rāj Rājopādhyāya. *Mesocosm: Hinduism and the Organization of a Traditional Newar City in Nepal.* Berkeley: University of California Press, 1990.

Lingat, R. *The Classical Law of India.* Berkeley: University of California Press, 1973.

Marriott, McKim. *India through Hindu Categories.* New Delhi: Sage, 1990.

Michaels, A. *Hinduism. Past and Present.* Princeton, N.J.: Princeton University Press, 2004.

Mishra, V. B. *Religious Beliefs and Practices of North India during the Early Mediaeval Period.* Leiden: E. J. Brill, 1973.

O'Flaherty, W. D., ed. *Karma and Rebirth in Classical Indian Traditions.* Berkeley: University of California Press, 1980.

Olivelle, P. *The Āśrama System: The History and Hermeneutics of a Religious Institution.* New York: Oxford University Press, 1993.

Peterson, I. V. *The Hymns of the Tamil Saints.* Princeton, N.J.: Princeton University Press, 1989.

Rocher, L. *The Purāṇas.* Wiesbaden: Harrassowitz, 1986.

Savarkar, V. N. *Hindūtva.* 1923. Reprint, New Delhi: Bharti Sadan, 1989.

Schimmel, A. *Islam in the Indian Subcontinent.* Leiden: E. J. Brill, 1980.

Srinivas, M. N. *Religion and Society among the Coorgs of South India.* Oxford: Clarendon Press, 1952.

Srinivasan, D. "Unhinging Śiva from the Indus Civilization." *Journal of the Royal Asiatic Society of Great Britain and Ireland* (1984): 77–89.

Stietencron, H. von. "Hinduism: on the Proper Use of a Deceptive Term." In *Hinduism Reconsidered*, edited by G. D. Sontheimer and H. Kulke. New Delhi: Manohar Publications, 1989.

Witzel, M. "The Development of the Vedic Canon and Its Schools: The Social and Political Milieu." In *Inside the Texts, Beyond the Texts: New Approaches to the Study of the Vedas*, edited by M. Witzel. Cambridge, Mass.: Harvard University Press, 1997. Also available at <http://www.fas.harvard.edu/~witzel/canon.pdf>

———. "Early Sanskritization. Origins and Development of the Kuru State." In *Recht, Staat und Verwaltung im klassischen Indien. The State, the Law, and Administration in Classical India*, edited by B. Kölver. Munich: R. Oldenbourg, 1997. Also available at <http://users.primushost.com/~india/ejvs/issues.html>

———. "Macrocosm, Mesocosm, and Microcosm: The Persistent Nature of 'Hindu' Beliefs and Symbolical Forms." *International Journal of Hindu Studies* 1, no. 3 (1998): 501–553.

HINDU MAHASABHA PARTY. *See* **Hindu Nationalism; Hindutva and Politics.**

HINDU NATIONALISM Hindu nationalism, or Hindutva, is centrally concerned with notions of social solidarity. Hindu nationalism has thus focused on questions of identity, and symbols and practices that link people and groups to the larger community. It is also concerned with notions of prestige and India's place in the global order. It is therefore not surprising that India conducted weapons-related nuclear tests during the tenure of Atal Bihari Vajpayee, India's first Hindu nationalist prime minister.

Hindu nationalism was a force throughout most of the twentieth century, embodied especially in the Rashtriya Swayamsevak Sangh (RSS), a group that historically has viewed its mission as the training of a cadre of nationalist activists. Most Hindu nationalists interested in the political process operated under the broad umbrella of the Congress Party until the assassination of Mahatma Gandhi in 1948 by a former member of the RSS. In the wake of Gandhi's assassination, several Hindu nationalist groups were banned and their members prohibited from participating in the Congress Party and its affiliated organizations. The RSS responded by establishing counterpart groups, using full-time workers (*pracharak*s) to organize new affiliates to work with labor, students, teachers, and journalists. Organizations affiliated to the RSS, popularly referred to collectively as the Sangh Parivar, or "family," took some three decades to recover from their public condemnation in the aftermath of Gandhi's assassination. Only since about 1980 have the RSS and its affiliates managed to recover their earlier self-confidence and substantial popular support.

Hindu Nationalists Converge in Ayodhya, Uttar Pradesh.
After the BJP's call for the construction of a temple at a site in
Ayodhya that was home to a sixteenth-century mosque, that
mosque—the Babri Masjid—was destroyed by an irate mob in
1992. Ownership of the religious site has yet to be determined
in the Indian courts. INDIA TODAY.

The most dramatic example of the new prominence of
Hindu nationalism is the emergence of the Bharatiya
Janata Party (BJP), in many ways its political face. The
predecessor party of the BJP, the Jana Sangh, was formed
in 1951 when many Hindu nationalists were excluded
from the Congress. As late as the 1984 elections to the
Lok Sabha, Parliament's lower, popularly elected house,
the BJP remained a party on the margins. In the 1984
elections, it won only 2 of 543 seats, with less than 8 percent of the popular vote. It has steadily increased its share
of seats in almost every subsequent election, expanding to
85 in 1989, 120 in 1991, 161 in 1996, and plateauing at
182 in both 1998 and 1999. The BJP's gains came largely
at the expense of the long dominant Congress Party,
which dropped from more than 400 seats in 1984 to just
114 in the parliamentary polls in 1999, even while the
BJP won a somewhat smaller share of the popular vote—
24 percent to its rival's 28 percent. The BJP, recognizing

that it needed a coalition to win power at the federal
level, built an alliance known as the National Democratic Alliance (NDA) that assumed power after the 1998
national elections. The coalition has proved stable; it
remained intact during the 1999 national elections and
the usually contentious cabinet selection process, and
internally divisive issues have not resulted in any significant defections. During the coalition government
(1999–2004), Prime Minister Atal Bihari Vajpayee,
Deputy Prime Minister Lal Krishna Advani, and a majority of the federal cabinet were members of the BJP; many
of them were members of the RSS. The BJP-led NDA
lost to the Congress Party–led United Progress Alliance
in the mid-2004 parliamentary elections, 187 to 215 seats
(of 543), though there was very little difference between
the popular vote of the two alliances. The NDA alliance
has largely remained together, though there are signs
that the BJP in opposition may adopt elements of its earlier strident Hindu nationalist agenda.

The BJP is just one of several dozen Hindu nationalist organizations that are loosely linked to the "family" of
organizations associated with the RSS. The RSS thinks
of itself as a school that trains men to be the cutting edge
of social change that will revitalize Hindu society. Since
the 1980s, dozens of new affiliated organizations have
been added, specifically to work among a broad array of
social groups, like tribal communities, the urban poor,
and the Hindu ecclesiastical establishment. Perhaps the
most well known—and controversial—of these is the
Vishwa Hindu Parishad (World Hindu Organization;
VHP) because of its aggressive pursuit of the Hindu
nationalist cultural agenda. This organization has had a
testy relationship with Prime Minister Vajpayee.

Tension in the "Family"

The victory of the BJP in taking power as head of the
national governing coalition in 1998 deepened strains
within the RSS family of organizations. These other
organizations insist on maintaining a commitment to
principles no longer entirely possible for the BJP, which
must make compromises to mobilize popular support and
attract coalition allies. The VHP has harshly criticized
the BJP for its agreement to remove the most controversial parts of the Hindu nationalist cultural agenda from
the Common Agenda of the ruling NDA, several of
whose constituents depend on Muslim support. The
BJP's Hindu nationalist critics argue that the party will
never emerge with a majority on its own unless it reverts
to its unalloyed Hindu nationalist roots. They point out
that the fastest growth of the BJP occurred in the 1991
elections, in the wake of strong party support for the traditional Hindu nationalist cultural agenda, especially a
national campaign on behalf of the construction of a

temple dedicated to the god Rāma in Ayodhya, in Uttar Pradesh. The issue became heated and controversial because the construction was proposed on a site that was occupied at the time by a sixteenth-century Mughal mosque known as the Babri Masjid. The Babri Masjid was torn down by a Hindu mob in 1992, and the question of ownership of the site and some surrounding land has been under judicial review. Other controversial issues within the RSS family are the opening of the economy to foreign investment, cooperation with the United States in the global war on terrorism, and the BJP's relatively conciliatory view, within the Sangh Parivar, on the issue of Kashmir.

The BJP faced a dilemma as it prepared for the national elections in 2004; it needed to activate its Hindu nationalist workers while simultaneously trying to expand its vote base and maintain a diverse coalition. The debate focused around a choice of campaign models: the successful Hindutva theme of the Gujarat state elections in December 2002, or issues of good governance, which the party used in subsequent state elections in Himachal Pradesh and Delhi. The BJP lost the latter set of elections, giving voice to criticism from its Hindu nationalist right that the party needed to reassert its traditional vision, in part to activate the RSS cadre, many of whom declined to campaign for the BJP. The party faced a similar apathetic response from many of the RSS cadre in the mid-2004 elections when it also emphasized the issue governance.

Stability

The RSS has traditionally emphasized internal consensus, and tries to maintain a culture of judiciousness, discretion, and prudence within the Sangh Parivar. Traditionally, the RSS achieved this by placing its most talented full-time workers (*pracharaks*) in key positions in the affiliated organizations. These full-time workers created an informal collaborative network that kept differences within manageable limits. Still another tactic was to emphasize issues with broad cultural and symbolic resonance, and to use these issues to paper over differences. Kashmir has long been an issue with resonance beyond the Hindu nationalist community, and is seen more broadly as an Indian national concern. The planned temple at Ayodhya is also an issue with broad Hindu backing and was employed by the BJP in the early 1990s to counter the efforts of the Janata government to mobilize support for job reservations applicable to historically disadvantaged castes. Increasingly, terrorism has also been used to mobilize activists and appeal to a broader audience, and has risen to the level of a major theme in the wake of the 11 September 2001 attacks in the United States. With the attack in December 2001 on the Lok Sabha Parliament building in New Delhi, the RSS and some of its affiliates have begun to express their suspicion of Muslims in terms of the war on terrorism.

Yet, new developments have undermined the efficacy of the RSS's traditional management strategies. Success has bred its own problems. Full-time workers from the RSS no longer control the levers of power in the BJP below the very top; the party has grown in size and complexity and is thus more difficult to discipline, even if the leadership wanted to do so. The party is now too large to permit the revival of the office of organizing secretary, a position that had existed at each level of the party and was staffed by full-time RSS workers who constituted a parallel structure that enforced discipline. The question of reviving this parallel structure has been debated, but has been rejected as impractical. Other groups within the RSS family have also expanded rapidly over the past two decades. They too rely less on full-time RSS workers. In addition, the consensus on key cultural issues has also broken down. All this has undermined the ability of the RSS to maintain its conventional role of mediator.

RSS as Mediator

The RSS has perhaps recognized that conditions call for a new management style. The present head of the RSS, K. S. Sudarshan, who took control in 2000, has a very different style from his predecessors. He lacks their charisma, and is more the chairman of the board of the RSS executive than supreme moral figure of the whole organization and its affiliates. He must spend more time negotiating differences because pronouncements from the leadership no longer carry the same weight. Not only are RSS full-time workers less influential in many of the affiliates, but several of these organizations, including the BJP, now have senior leaders that outrank the RSS top leadership. Prime Minister Vajpayee and his deputy L. K. Advani are senior in age and experience to Sudarshan, who took on his first leadership role in the RSS (as *pracharak*) only in the 1950s, a decade after Vajpayee and Advani. The breakdown in consensus-building shows itself in the deep internal differences over several significant issues, especially the Hindu nationalist drive to construct a temple dedicated to Rāma at Ayodhya, an effort that combines nationalist fervor, religious conviction, and identity politics. Many religious Hindus believe the site is the precise place where Rāma took human form; many Hindu nationalists consider a temple at the site as a symbol of revived national pride.

Ayodhya. The VHP has been the most vocal and uncompromising on the Ayodhya temple issue. In many ways the explicit religious face of the RSS family, the VHP takes a proprietary view of the issue. The violence connected with the campaign to build a temple, however, has aroused debate on the issue within the BJP and has made their coalition partners unwilling to compromise. The VHP nonetheless has continued openly to confront the government, calling for legislation to allow the construction of a Rama temple. The VHP viewed Prime Minister Vajpayee's caution as a betrayal of a key element of the Hindutva agenda, and regularly called for his resignation.

In an attempt to resolve the issue before the 2004 elections, Vajpayee encouraged the Shankaracharya of Kanchi, a senior Hindu ecclesiastical figure, to negotiate a compromise with the All-India Muslim Personal Law Board. The effort resulted in a proposal calling for the construction of a Ram Hindu temple on an undisputed plot adjacent to the site of the destroyed mosque, and the construction of a wall separating the temple from the original mosque property. The VHP, which was excluded from those talks, rejected any effort at compromise. Caught in the middle, the RSS initially opposed the Shankaracharya's proposal, but then decided to support the proposal while still protesting the VHP's exclusion from the negotiating process. The situation then got very complicated, reflecting intense infighting within the Sangh Parivar that ultimately resulted in a revision of the original proposal. The Muslim leadership rejected the revised proposal. The VHP blamed Vajpayee for his involvement in the failed effort, and, supported by the RSS, immediately resumed calls for legislative action to permit the construction of a Ram temple, prompting the prime minister to threaten to resign.

The issue flared again in the wake of a September 2003 government-commissioned archaeological investigation reporting evidence of a Hindu temple beneath and predating the Babri Masjid on the Ayodhya site. The report inspired the VHP to mobilize hundreds of thousands of supporters for a march in the city in mid-October. Vajpayee called on the organizers to keep the rally peaceful. The government of Uttar Pradesh, controlled by an opposition party, arrested the organizers of the march in an attempt to prevent violence. The VHP leadership charged that the Vajpayee was assisting the state government to quash the protest march. The proposed march did not take place, but the VHP promised to take whatever steps are necessary to build the temple.

Swadeshi. The Hindutva critics have adopted a program of economic populism, once largely associated with the Indian left, opposing privatization and foreign investment on the one hand and arguing for economic self-sufficiency on the other. The labor affiliate of the Sangh Parivar, the Bhartiya Mazdoor Sangh, has strongly opposed globalization, and has received support for its stand from the Swadeshi Jagran Manch, whose leaders are close to the RSS, and which has support from a broad array of student, farmer, and workers' groups. The Mazdoor Sangh organized rallies, some with unions and political

groups opposed to the former BJP-dominated coalition government, to protest initiatives permitting the involvement of foreign companies in the life insurance sector and the sale of public enterprises to private interests. This criticism of globalization has a resonance among small-scale business, the traditional core support group of the RSS, which fears being overwhelmed by large modern enterprises, both Indian and foreign. This criticism also finds substantial support among workers in the organized sector of Indian industry; they fear that the rationalization of industry under private management would result in significant unemployment. The Mazdoor Sangh and other groups also argue that foreign investment is a threat to the nation's sovereignty. Prime Minister Vajpayee resisted this guerrilla activity against his government by appealing to still another traditional ingredient in the Hindu nationalist agenda, the building of a "great India." He argued that globalization is necessary for the 8 to 10 percent annual gross domestic product (GDP) growth rate that would make India an international power.

Kashmir. A dramatic example of the breakdown in consensus-building occurred during Jammu and Kashmir assembly elections in October 2002, when the RSS supported non-BJP candidates running on a platform of a "trifurcation" of the state. That plan, which has been on the agenda of the RSS family for decades, would divide Jammu and Kashmir into three separate states along communal/ethnic lines, thus constitutionally separating the Hindu-majority Jammu area from the largely Muslim Kashmir Valley and the largely Buddhist Ladakh. The BJP had not given the proposal serious consideration for two decades, and when the RSS brought forward the idea of splitting Kashmir along communal lines, the Vajpayee government rejected it as a violation of India's traditional commitment to the "one nation" principle. The only other instance in which RSS activists withdrew support from the BJP on a large scale was in the 1984 parliamentary elections, when the Congress Party made blatant appeals to Hindu nationalism. Despite the growing criticism of the BJP within the Sangh Parivar, the Kashmir rebellion is an exception because the RSS leadership continues to try to dampen criticism of what it still considers a friendly government. The rebellion against the BJP in the state of Jammu and Kashmir, however, reveals the deep opposition to the Vajpayee government's conciliatory efforts and also a weakening of the RSS's mediatory role.

Trends

The RSS and the Sangh Parivar spent most of the last half century in political opposition. The role of opponent fit an ideology that has been deeply suspicious of the government since the founding of the RSS in 1925, a suspicion exacerbated after independence by the periodic efforts of Congress Party governments to ban it. When elements of the RSS family were in power, that political power had a destabilizing impact. Never in the history of the RSS has there been such public bickering. Nonetheless, no senior figures have yet defected from the BJP; there has been no serious challenge to Vajpayee's political leadership, and no Hindus have set up a countering political organization. The only political figure in the BJP, other than Vajpayee, who has charismatic appeal is Narendra Modi, the BJP chief minister of Gujarat, who so successfully ran a tough Hindutva campaign in the 2002 state elections in the wake of communal violence there. Modi scored an overwhelming personal victory in the state, and is seen as the champion of the Hindutva agenda by many Hindu nationalists. Unlike Vajpayee, however, he has virtually no appeal outside the party. He is viewed by some BJP allies as a disruptive figure. Modi for his part is probably too much of a disciplined RSS member to rebel. He may also be conscious of the dismal fate of past party rebels. The most likely successor to Vajpayee is his deputy, L. K. Advani. The two have jointly run the party since the 1970s. They may have policy differences, but they are also close allies and Advani assumed control of the party organization after the 2004 loss of power. It is questionable if the RSS can ever again assert the influence it once had. The consequence is likely to be increasingly acrimonious relations between the BJP and other elements of the RSS family. The likely outcome of this is a greater distance between the BJP and them. Another likely consequence is a growing independence among some of the other larger constituents of the Sangh Parivar.

Walter Andersen
Daniel Consolatore

See also **Bharatiya Janata Party (BJP); Hindu Nationalist Parties; Vishwa Hindu Parishad (VHP)**

BIBLIOGRAPHY

Andersen, Walter K., and Shridhar D. Damle. *The Brotherhood in Saffron: The Rashtriya Swayamsevak Sangh and Hindu Revivalism.* New Delhi: Vistaar, 1987.
Hansen, Thomas B., and Christophe Jaffrelot, eds. *The BJP and the Compulsions of Politics in India.* New Delhi and New York: Oxford University Press, 2001.
Jaffrelot, Christophe. *The Hindu Nationalist Movement and Indian Politics: 1925 to the 1990s.* New Delhi: Penguin, 1999.
Ludden, David, ed. *Contesting the Nation: Religion, Community, and the Politics of Democracy in India.* Philadelphia: University of Pennsylvania Press, 1996.

HINDU NATIONALIST PARTIES

HINDU NATIONALIST PARTIES Hindu social and political consciousness in India, articulated by revivalist movements and charismatic reformers, predates the twentieth century. The Hindu Mahasabha (HM), founded in 1915, was an expression of this consciousness. It was also a reaction to the political activism of the Muslim clergy and sought to represent Hindu interests, though within the established Indian National Congress fold, espousing a pan-Indian nationalism, derived from Hindu cultural roots. The indifference of the HM to land reforms allowed it to cooperate with British India's landed Muslim elite, whose principal concern was any threat to their own position as landlords.

In 1925 Dr. Keshav Baliram Hedgewar, a member of the HM, and a group of his associates established the Rashtriya Swayamsevak Sangh (RSS). The RSS was a militant grassroots organization established to defend Hindus in the aftermath of the Khilafat movement to restore the Caliphate and the subsequent communal riots, which had resulted in many deaths and forced conversions to Islam. The RSS began functioning in an atmosphere of growing religious division in the 1920s, as Hindus and Muslims jockeyed to position themselves to succeed the British in India. Significantly, the RSS proudly recorded its intervention in the religious riots that overtook the central Indian city of Nagpur in 1927 as one of its first successful acts on behalf of Hindus.

The RSS disagreed with the political strategy of the Indian National Congress, which remained secular in its political support of Muslims as well as other minorities of India. The RSS gained support from the Hindu Mahasabha's ties with wealthy Hindu elites, but distanced itself from the HM once it was well established. The latter declined in influence, especially after its expulsion from the Congress in the late 1930s, despite being led by Veer Savarkar, a major architect of Hindu-first nationalist politics. It succumbed to greater conservatism after Indian independence, leading to the departure of its leader, Shyama Prasad Mookherji, founder of the Bharatiya Jana Sangh, predecessor of the Bharatiya Janata Party (BJP).

The RSS wanted to actively address what they perceived as the religious, political, socioeconomic, and cultural challenges facing Hinduism, combating a general lack of Hindu awareness by teaching Indians about their ancient Vedic traditions and historic achievements. The RSS claimed to be the inheritors of the hallowed traditions of an earlier generation of religious and social reformers such as Dayananda Saraswati and Swami Vivekananda. Such a narrow conception of multicultural India inevitably meant a rejection of India's Islamic past. The British conquest of Bengal had also been welcomed as liberation from the Mughal imperial yoke.

The subsequent evolution and perceptions of the RSS were colored by the experience of partition, for which they blamed Muslims. RSS loyalists harbored even greater suspicion of Muslims, based on the creation of Pakistan and India's wars with that nation. Ultimately, the RSS appeared motivated by patriotism, inspired by Italian nationalists Giuseppe Mazzini and Giuseppe Garibaldi. Critics, however, have compared the RSS to the nationalist perversion in Nazi Germany.

The RSS asserts that Hindutva (Hindu-first extremist values) is merely the ancient and eternal culture of India, which Muslims must accept if they remain in India. Their insistence that most Indian Muslims had Hindu ancestors fails to resolve the dilemma posed for Muslims by the glorification of Hindu rulers like Maharashtra's hero, Shivaji, who successfully assailed the Mughal rulers. The RSS expresses fervent admiration, however, for Muslim nationalist leaders of India, admiring men like the current Muslim president of India, A. P. J. Abdul Kalam, the father of India's ballistic missile defense program.

The RSS was banned for a year in 1948, after a former RSS Hindu extremist, Nathuram Godse, assassinated Mahatma Gandhi. For several decades following, the RSS remained outside the mainstream of Indian public life, which was dominated by the secular ideals of India's first prime minister, Jawaharlal Nehru. The RSS was viewed with undisguised dismay and hostility by an influential section of India's English-speaking elite. Many among India's Westernized leaders believed that the RSS and its affiliates represented a pernicious variant of fascism, though millions of Hindus in small towns and villages continue to have faith in it.

The RSS demands the imposition of a uniform civil code throughout India to end Muslim personal law. It also demands a national ban on cow slaughter and the termination of the autonomous constitutional status accorded to the Muslim-majority state of Jammu and Kashmir. Critics argue that the implacable hostility of the RSS and its affiliates to religious conversion, especially as a result of the missionary activities of the newer Christian churches, has become a recipe for intimidation and violence.

The RSS is organized as an organic unit of power, the Shakha, which meets daily. By 2004 there were more than 2.5 million members, in over 25,000 Shakhas, throughout India and abroad. The Shakha is responsible for ideological indoctrination ("man-making") and provides the organizational basis for its various activities, running numerous schools and engaging in voluntary social service.

In 1951 the supreme leader of the RSS, Guru Golwalkar, reluctantly agreed to allow members to enter the electoral fray. The Bharatiya Jana Sangh was then formed, succeeded in 1980 by the BJP. The RSS is the parent organization to members of the Sangh Parivar (family of Hindu-first organizations), including the Bharatiya Janata Party (one of the largest parties in Parliament) the Vishwa Hindu Parishad (World Hindu Council), the Bharatiya Mazdoor Sangh (its trade union affiliate), and the Akhil Bharatiya Vidiyarathi Parishad (student union). It remains the largest organization of its type in the world, with the exception of the Communist Party of China. The RSS itself was led by upper caste Hindu Brahmans through much of its history, like virtually all of India's political parties (until the recent rise of political parties composed of and led by Dalits, former "untouchables").

The RSS uncritically imbibed many of the commonplace collectivist economic certitudes of Indian political life until 1991, when economic liberalization and globalization were ushered in by the Congress and were later accepted by the BJP. The intensification of the campaign to build a Ram temple over the destroyed Babri Masjid in Ayodhya, Pakistan's struggles against India, with its violent spillovers for Hindu–Muslim relations, and the dramatic mobilization of India's deprived communities all test the sagacity of the RSS. The question posed by evolving circumstances is whether the RSS is capable of sustaining the wider interests of the Indian society and polity, instead of giving priority to its narrow Hindu-first imperatives.

Gautam Sen

See also **Bharatiya Janata Party (BJP); Hindu Nationalism; Hindutva and Politics; Vishwa Hindu Parishad (VHP)**

BIBLIOGRAPHY

Adeney, Katharine, and Lawrence Saez, eds. *Coalition Politics and Hindu Nationalism.* London: Routledge, 2005.

Banerjee, Partha. *In the Belly of the Beast: The Hindu Supremacist RSS and BJP of India: An Insider's Story.* New Delhi: Ajanta Books International, 1998.

Bannerjee, Sikata. *Warriors in Politics: Hindu Nationalism, Violence and the Shiv Sena in India.* Boulder, Colo.: Westview Press, 1999.

Corbridge, Stuart, and John Hariss. *Reinventing India: Liberalization, Hindu Nationalism and Popular Democracy.* Cambridge, U.K.: Polity Press, 2000.

Eckert, Julia M. *The Charisma of Direct Action: Power, Politics and the Shiv Sena.* New Delhi: Oxford University Press, 2003.

Hansen, Thomas Blom. *The Saffron Wave: Democracy and Hindu Nationalism in Modern India.* Princeton, N.J.: Princeton University Press, 1999.

Jaffrelot, Christophe. *The Hindu Nationalist Movement in India.* New York: Columbia University Press, 1996.

Malik, Yogendra K., and V. B. Singh, *Hindu Nationalists in India: The Rise of the Bharatiya Janata Party.* Boulder, Colo.: Westview Press, 1994.

Pattanaik, D. D. *Hindu Nationalism in India*. New Delhi: Deep & Deep Publications, 1998.

Sharma, Jyotirmay. *Hindutva: Exploring the Idea of Hindu Nationalism*. London: Penguin Global Publishing, 2004.

HINDU TANTRIC DEITIES Although the origins of Tantrism are lost in remote antiquity, it is certain that Tantrism was a pan-Indian movement by the fifth to sixth centuries A.D. It arose in response and in contradistinction to the orthodox Vedic religion of the Brahmans. Heterodox in nature, Tantrism tends toward obscure secret beliefs and rituals. Although it is difficult to date any of the surviving Tantric texts with accuracy, the earliest Hindu text with specific Tantric content is the Devī Māhātmya (A.D. 400–600). Various Tantric sects continued to produce texts throughout the medieval period and beyond.

Tantric rites were designed to avoid the endless cycles of rebirth and to enable practitioners to reach enlightenment (*moksha* or *mukti*) in one lifetime. In addition, Tantric rituals promise earthly enjoyment and domination (*bhukti*). Accomplishing the two goals is an arduous and lengthy process that can only take place under the direction of a guru. Tantrism emphasizes, in varying degrees, key practices involving intricate and complex rituals, mantras (chanting incantations), spells and magic, secret sounds and syllables and hand gestures, magical diagrams called *yantra*s and *mandala*s, deliberately coded language, and restricted practices and initiations in which secret lore is passed to the student. Yogic exercises and meditation are essential components in Tantric rituals, particularly *kundalīnī* yoga, in which creative energy is directed upward in the body along the nerve centers (*chakra*s). From earliest times, Tantric mystics and seers refined the "supramental" process of meditation that allowed them to scrutinize, dissect, and classify the macrocosmic and subatomic universes. Their knowledge came not through the senses but through minute observations of patterns and sequences perceived through intuitive awareness. Cultic rituals include the formation of an elaborate macrocosmic/microcosmic cosmology located within the human body in which the deity is invoked in the heart. Tantra's psycho-experimental techniques led to highly elaborate systems that were given visual expression in abstract symbolic and diagrammatic images (*yantra*s and *mandala*s) that represented the deity and facilitated merging with the deity in order to bring about the shattering of the individual ego and the ultimate experience in which the seeker and deity became one.

The Tantric Goddess

Hindu Tantrism centers on the Great Goddess (Devī, the Shining One) as the supreme deity and Divine Mother. Tantric texts assert that only the Goddess is

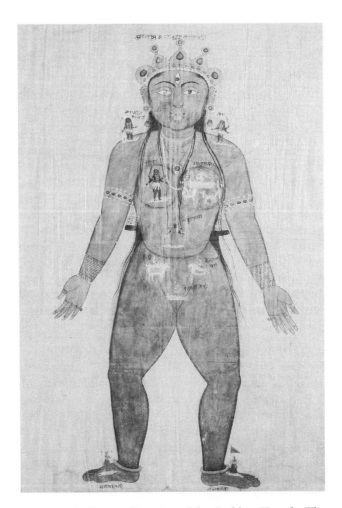

Nineteenth-Century Drawing of the Goddess Kamala. The *Dasa Mahavidyas* (Ten Great Wisdoms) often threaten the accepted social order and challenge their worshipers to reject convention. This nineteenth-century drawing illustrates the tenth such goddess, Kamala (or Kama), who grants power, peace, and prosperity to the material world. NATIONAL MUSEUM / FOTOMEDIA.

capable of granting the dual aims of *mukti* and *bhukti*. The Devī Māhātmya explains that she is eternal, supreme knowledge and the one who grants the boon of final liberation. As the sole and absolute creative force of the universe, she also sometimes is identified as *shakti* (power). Sometimes used as a name for the Goddess herself, *shakti* is the ultimate principle, the source of all; it is the dynamic, manifesting energy of creation, while the male god is the static, unmanifested aspect of reality. Yogis regard *shakti* as the dormant power (*kundalīnī*) in the body that must be awakened in order to rise to the final *chakra* at the top of the head to achieve liberation.

There are countless forms of the Goddess in Hinduism; one text, the Lalitāsahasranāma, provides a list of 1,008 names, but there are, in fact, far too many to obtain an accurate count. They all, however, are emanations or manifestations of Devī. The innumerable manifestations can be grouped into two general categories, the invincible aspect and the benevolent aspect, both of which nurture the practitioner in the quest for spiritual release.

Her invincible forms. Of the invincible manifestations, Durgā, Ambikā, the Saptamātrikās and later Ashtamātrikās, and Kālī are among the most prominent. The beautiful Durgā was born to slaughter the powerful demon Mahishāsura, the symbolic personification of evil and ignorance. So potent was he that the gods were unable to overcome him, thus each was compelled to surrender his individual energy (*shakti*) and contribute it to the collective force that was the Goddess Durgā. She disposed of the demon with ease; decimating the beast symbolizes obliteration of the tenacious human ego, the element that binds the individual to the cycle of reincarnation.

Called on to obliterate the demons, Shumba and Nishumba, the goddess appeared in the world again as Ambikā in order to wage war on the mighty pair and their demonic forces. The battle was so unrelenting and dangerous that the gods, unable to fight themselves, sent aid in the form of the Saptamātrikās, or the Seven Mothers. They are Brahmānī, Māheshvarī, Kaumārī, Vaishnavī, Vārāhī, Indrānī, the relinquished *shakti*s of six major Hindu gods, and Chāmundā, the most virulent energy of the Goddess that issued from Ambikā's forehead. Her best-known name in her dark, violent, and formidable form is Kālī; by virtue of her unparalleled valor in defeating the demon generals, Chanda and Munda, however, she was given the name Chāmundā. The Saptamātrikās always appear in a group and are placed strategically in Shiva temples to indicate a point in the circumambulation of the temple when the seeker and deity may merge. Specifically, the Saptamātrikās embody the seven *chakra*s through which the *kundalīnī* progresses until it is released from the body, at which point the worshiper attains enlightenment. The Saptamātrikās are iconic symbols representing in linear fashion the process of transcendence as it unfolds in the body. Some versions of the myth add an eighth goddess to the group (Astamātrikās). In Nepal, the Astamātrikās became the standard. The Devī Māhātmya identified the eighth as Nārasimhī; various texts give other names.

The invincible Kālī is the manifestation of the goddess often worshiped by Tantric seekers in east India and Nepal. Kālī, the same potent form of the goddess as Chāmundā from the Saptamātrikā group, has been extricated for separate worship. As the final member of the group of seven, she is the deity who presides at the instant of enlightenment. She has a savage power, accompanied by a horrifying howl. She was so intoxicated by her bloody rampage on the battlefield that she could not stop, even when the victory

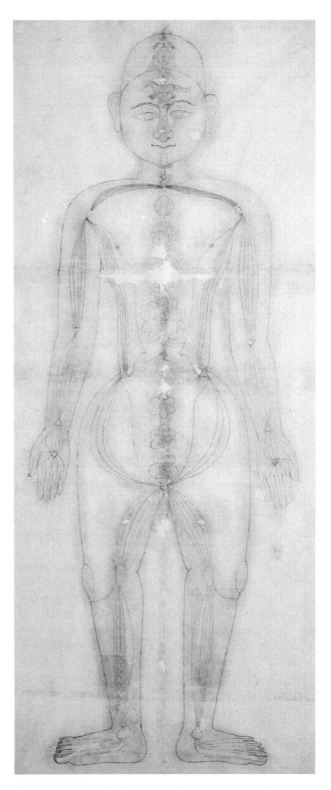

Illustration, c. 1800, Depicting the Spinal Nerve Channels and Centers of the Human Body. In yoga, the *chakras* (centers) denote a point of intersection where the psychic self and the physical self connect; the *nadis* (spinal nerve channels) is the network by which *prana* (the "life force") travels through the *chakras*. NATIONAL MUSEUM / FOTOMEDIA.

was secure. Wildly, she continued killing through a dance that threatened to topple the universe. Finally, her husband Shiva (in this story he represents the passive potential of creation) lay prone in her path. Inadvertently, she stepped on him, realizing at last that she had been out of control. Thus, her appearance is frightening and portrays her dangerous character; she is extremely scrawny, dark skinned, and wears ornaments of severed heads and snakes and an apron of severed hands. She drinks blood, as witnessed by her lolling red tongue and the blood-filled skull cup that she holds. She is the supreme symbol of death and simultaneously new life, that is, a blissfully enlightened life that relinquishes the ego and overcomes all fear of death. While she is celebrated in iconic form for temple worship and festivals, she is represented by her distinctive *yantra* for the initiate engaged in ritual.

The Dasa Mahāvidyās (Ten Great Wisdoms) form a group of ten goddesses whose aim is to stretch one's awareness beyond comfortable standards. Several of them threaten the accepted social order and challenge the worshiper to reject the conventional. Their origin derives from a quarrel between Shiva and Pārvatī. The angry Shiva attempted to leave his wife, who then multiplied herself ten times in order to block all the directions and prevent his escape. Each of the ten Mahāvidyās revealed a new truth to Shiva. Not only was Shiva forced to acknowledge the superiority of the goddess, but he became enlightened as well.

The first Mahāvidyā is Kālī, who represents ultimate destruction. She removes attachments and fears. Tārā, the second, is compassionate. She carries scissors for severing attachments and stands, like Kālī, on the prone body of Shiva. The third, Sodashī, is a beautiful sixteen-year-old girl. She provides inspiration and awareness in the three worlds. Bhuvaneshvarī, the fourth, is the mistress of the phenomenal world. She too is beautiful, unlike the fifth of the group, Bhairavī, who is the Goddess of Decay. Symbolically, she destroys all impediments to clearing the mind and sustaining the yogic state. The sixth is a shocking goddess known as Chinnamastā. She chops off her own head to feed her two daughters. From her neck issue three streams of blood: two pour into the mouths of her offspring and the third flows into the mouth of her own severed head. Her role is to halt the activity of the mind and to remove ignorance. The ugly Dhūmāvatī, as the dark widow, brings destruction, hunger, and thirst. To worship her is to induce a nondual state of consciousness. Bagalāmukhī is a dynamic deity who is invoked to obtain *siddhi*s (supernormal powers). She holds the tongue of a demon to still his evil speech. She paralyzes the tongue so that no evil words are emitted and thus thwarts the accumulation of negative karma. The ninth goddess, Mātangī, symbolizes death and

impurity through her association with the untouchable class. Finally, Kamalā is beautiful, with a golden complexion; she grants gifts of power, peace, and prosperity in the material world.

While the goddesses mentioned here are still actively venerated in Hinduism, worship of the sixty-four *yoginī*s has been abandoned. The *yoginī*s were obscure and esoteric deities that had a following by the ninth century A.D.; they maintained their status in Tantric circles until the fourteenth century. Little can be affirmed, however, about the specifics of their worship because the few texts that survive cloak the esoteric knowledge in coded language. The central figure was Bhairavī, a ferocious form of the Goddess. *Yoginī*s were both benevolent and malevolent and engaged in a dance of destruction. The goal for their devotees was acquisition of *siddhi*s, or supernatural powers, and the acquisition of all sixty-four *siddhi*s led to perfection. There is an obvious but still rather poorly understood relationship of the sixty-four *yoginī*s to the Astamātrikās. Some scholars regard the *yoginī*s as attendants of the goddesses of the eight *chakra*s; thus eight goddesses times eight attendants resulted in a total of sixty-four forms. Others view the *yoginī*s as manifestations of the eight Mātrikās.

Her benevolent forms. The Tantric pantheon of goddesses includes some benevolent aspects. Today in India and Nepal there survives the active worship of the Shaktipīthas, places where pieces of the body of the goddess Satī fell to Earth. An ancient myth records that the insults leveled by the goddess's father Daksha at her husband Shiva caused the goddess to kill herself in protest. In a great state of grief, Shiva picked up her body and raged across the world. Fearing cataclysmic destruction of the universe, the god Vishnu hurled his discus at her corpse, severing it bit by bit. As the body diminished, Shiva came to his senses and mourned quietly. Each place where a portion of the body fell has become a sacred spot. Shrines at the various locations protect odd stones or icons in remembrance of Satī. Within the sacred precinct, a stone representing Shiva as Bhairava attests to the eternal relationship between the goddess and the god. Tantric yogis attracted to the sacred sites had their graves located in close proximity. The Kalighat Temple in Kolkata is a Shaktipītha. The Kamakhya Temple in Gauhati houses the vagina (*yoni*) of Satī.

Another of the benign forms of the Tantric goddess is Lalitā Tripurasundarī of the Shrī Vidyā cult. Shrī Vidyā evolved in South India by the seventh century A.D. and later influenced Kashmir Tantrism. Obscure Tantric practices were refined in Shrī Vidyā to a point at which orthodox Brahmanism and Tantrism merged. Lalitā Tripurasundarī is the supreme deity who embodies all aspects of Devī simultaneously. She is represented in ritual by the Shrī *yantra*, where she resides at the center.

The Tantric God

Shiva is always linked to the Great Goddess, although in Tantrism, he often appears as the fearsome Bhairava. He is worshiped independently in Tantric rites, but more often is paired with the Goddess. The relationship of the Goddess and Bhairava is an extremely complicated one. In Tantrism, he in effect symbolizes the consecrated sacrificer; therefore, the devotee, by ritually identifying with the Godhead, achieves blissful union with the Goddess.

While Tantric rituals must conform to complex criteria, they are in and of themselves valueless unless their inner significance is understood by the practitioner; they are external rites that mirror internal conscious activity. Ultimately, the goal of the ritual is to dissolve vain distinctions between subject and object, internal and external, and to realize undivided oneness. Deities are worshiped to rid the individual of weaknesses and all fetters that prevent liberation. Once the bonds are severed, oneness is then realized through the process called "cosmicization." The process entails a fusion of the collective (the divine) with the individual seeker's consciousness. "Cosmicization" is undertaken through the use of the *yantra* or *mandala*, a diagrammed energy grid that, when combined with proper training and meditation, is the means through which union is achieved. As part of the ritual, the practitioner studies the *yantra* until it is committed to memory (called the absorption concentration). Once the image is perfectly constructed as a mental image, it is regarded as being one thousand times more purified than the original. The potent mind image reenacts the movements of the cosmos and embodies the divine union of opposites. Within the *yantra* are the *trikona*, consisting of upward pointing triangles, representing the God Shiva, and inverted triangles representing the Goddess. The idea is symbolized by the interaction of male and female triangles that eventually become united in the *bindu*, or the nucleus, symbolizing the union of all opposites, zero, infinity, creation and destruction, subject and object. The *yantra* is a dynamic symbol of the cosmos; hence it is represented as an expanding form emanating from the central dimensionless *bindu*, the sacred dwelling place of the deity. Such symbols are not static, but dynamic graphs of the creative process of cosmic evolution and involution.

Katherine Anne Harper

See also **Devī; Goddess Images; Shiva and Shaivism**

BIBLIOGRAPHY

Bhattacharyya, N. N. *History of the Tantric Religion.* New Delhi: Manohar Publishers, 1999.

Brown, C. Mackenzie. *The Triumph of the Goddess.* Albany: State University of New York Press, 1990.

Gupta, Sanjukta, Dirk Jan Hoes, and Teun Goudriaan. *Hindu Tantrism.* Leiden, Netherlands: E. J. Brill, 1979.

Harper, Katherine Anne, and Robert L. Brown. *The Roots of Tantra.* Albany: State University of New York Press, 2002.

HINDUTVA AND POLITICS In 1999 the Bharatiya Janata Party (BJP) formed the central government at the head of a coalition, the National Democratic Alliance (NDA), consisting of twenty-four primarily regional parties. For the BJP, this was the fruition of years of careful groundwork, carried out in conjunction with organizations such as the Rashtriya Swayamsevak Sangh (RSS) and the Vishwa Hindu Parishad (VHP). The BJP had been making advances in the Indian electoral process, but this was the first time it was in a position to form a stable coalition government. While the BJP did not win an outright majority, enabling it to form the government alone, nor beat the Congress Party in the total number of votes garnered, it reaped the benefits of long-term planning and skillful coalition building, as well as the structural and institutional weaknesses that were plaguing the Congress Party. The BJP called for early Lok Sabha (parliamentary) polls in 2004, riding high after successful elections in a number of states. However, in a result that took most observers by surprise, the Congress Party returned to power at the head of a coalition government. The BJP won only nine seats less than the Congress, but the electoral losses of some of its key allies in the polls, coupled with the Congress' ability to form a successful alliance, put the BJP in the opposition.

The BJP represents the political face of India's Hindutva ideology, defined amorphously as Hindu cultural nationalism, or "the essence of being Hindu." Hindutva ideology demands the assertion of India's national identity as a Hindu state, but it defines Hinduism as a cultural construct rather than a religious one. As such, it demands that India's minorities—numbering about 150 million Muslims and several million Christians, among others—reconfigure their beliefs, espousing Hindu values and considering themselves part of an overarching Hindu culture. Such an ideology poses a profound threat to minorities, and to the social cohesion of the nation. The belief that India's authentic culture lies in Hinduism has bred an "antiforeign" outlook, a definition that encompasses both the Muslims and Christians of India. Since the 1980s, the BJP has gone from being a marginal political player, catering to the aspirations of a small upper caste Hindu elite, to a party that enjoys widespread popular recognition and the support of a growing segment of Indians, both at home and among India's wealthy and influential diaspora population.

Bharatiya Janata Party President L. K. Advani. Advani was a forceful proponent of Hindu cultural nationalism, whose first religious caravan (*rath yatra*) sparked widespread controversy, leaving a trail of anti-Muslim violence in its wake. INDIA TODAY.

The Growth of Hindutva Politics

The politics of Hindutva, as represented by India's ruling party, the BJP, cannot be separated from the larger grassroots social movement from which they stem, though the two aspects of the movement clash periodically. The BJP belongs to a family of organizations, known as the Sangh Parivar (or "Sangh Family"), which collectively represent the ideology of Hindutva in its many social and institutional forms. The primary ideological organization within the Parivar is the Vishwa Hindu Parishad (VHP), or World Hindu Council, supported by its youth wing, the Bajrang Dal. The Rashtriya Swayamsevak Sangh (RSS; National Volunteers Society) provides the organizational backbone of the movement, and is paramilitary in nature.

The organizational roots of Hindutva go back to 1914, to the creation of the Hindu Mahasabha, an organization founded to unite the nation against British imperial rule under the banner of Hindu culture. The

Mahasabha's work was bolstered in 1925 by the creation of the RSS by Keshav Hedgewar. Hinduism is a religion that is amorphous in its teachings, open to diverse interpretations and modes of practice, and polytheistic. The Mahasabha saw these values as a weakness, since they provided few means for united mobilization, and therefore were perceived historically as offering little resistance to conquest, either by Muslim conquerors, or by European imperialist powers. The hierarchical social character of Hinduism that privileges its upper castes, coupled with India's complex regional and linguistic diversity, were further barriers to cohesion. The Hindutva movement sought to "re-create" a golden age of Hinduism—a vision best epitomized by the rule of Rāma, a human incarnation of the god Vishnu. The political goal of the Hindutva movement was the creation of a Hindu Rashtra, or nation, modeled on the golden age of Rāma. The ingredients of this golden age, and of a unified Hinduism, however, had to be created, and this has been an ongoing process for the Sangh Parivar.

The antecedents of Hindutva, or the politics of "Hinduness," as both a political and social ideology, date back to the last decades of the nineteenth century and were formulated in reaction to colonial administrative policies. Debates, focused around Hindu revivalism and reformation, dealt with the desire of upper caste Hindus to protect their traditions and values, and to renegotiate their identity in a modern and colonized context. Hindu nationalism reflects the view of high caste reformers and retains strong Brahmanical tendencies.

During the movement for independence, the Hindutva movement mobilized against the Congress Party's secular and pluralist platform. The uniting and mobilization of Muslims against the British government, through the Khilafat movement of 1919, launched with the help of Mahatma Gandhi, fed the insecurities of the Hindutva leaders. Later, the Muslim League's negotiations with the Congress to ensure rights for Muslims further strengthened those insecurities within the Hindutva fold, which from the beginning conceptualized Hinduness in very territorial terms. The Congress decision to accede to the Muslim League's demand for a separate nation of Pakistan and the subsequent creation of Pakistan were seen as betrayals of the principle of a single "united Hindu nation" (Akhand Bharat). The Congress and Mahatma Gandhi were portrayed as pseudo-secularists who were eager to pander to the Muslim minority at the cost of Hindu pride and the Hindu nation. The themes of injured Hindu pride and of victimization, at the hands of Muslims in particular, bred a "majority's minority complex" that has remained powerful within the movement. Mahatma Gandhi was also resented because of his mobilization of the lower castes in Indian society, the empowering of

V. D. Savarkar is one of the principal ideologues of the Hindutva movement. This was his message on the eve of his fifty-ninth birthday, on 25 May 1941. The Hindus should henceforth test all national and international politics and policies through the Hindu point of view alone. . . . Let every Hindu youth who is capable to stand the test, try his best to enter the army, navy and air force or get the training and secure employment in the ammunition factories and in all other branches connected with war crafts. Unforeseen facilities are being thrown open to you. You help no one else more than you help yourselves if you utilize these facilities and opportunities to militarize Hindudom! This done everything else shall follow: if you miss this, nothing else shall avail! This sums up the whole program and the supreme duty of the hour. Hinduize all politics and Militarize Hinduism—and the resurrection of our Hindu nation is bound to follow it as certainly as the Dawn follows the darkest hour of night!

whom was seen as a threat to the upper caste ideological core that was defining the Hindu nation.

While the Hindu Mahasabha and the RSS enjoyed a modicum of popularity in the 1930s and 1940s, the assassination of Mahatma Gandhi at the hands of a Hindu fundamentalist in January 1948, soon after independence, was a turning point for the movement. Gandhi's assassin, Nathuram Godse, was a former Swayamsevak (as members of the RSS are called) and a member of the Hindu Mahasabha. The immediate reason for Gandhi's assassination was his pressure on the Indian government to pay reparations to Pakistan for certain losses during partition, but this was only the last in what Godse saw as a series of betrayals. Gandhi's assassination horrified the public and created a popular uproar against the RSS and the Mahasabha. Nehru and the government clamped down on Hindutva organizations, and while the organizations continued to operate, they fell out of the larger public perception for almost four decades. The VHP was founded in 1964 to further Hindutva's ideological program. The political arm of the Sangh Parivar and the precursor to the BJP, then called the Jana Sangh, was generally a marginal presence in Parliament.

The Devolution of Politics and the Rise of Hindu Majoritarianism

Two related fractures helped to change the political arena from the 1980s onward. The first was the unraveling of the Congress Party's nationwide political hegemony, and the resulting fragmentation of Indian politics. Since the Lok Sabha elections of 1989, no party has won an outright majority in the polls, and a succession of volatile coalition governments has ruled the nation. Regionally based parties have grown in power and prominence, and in the last two national elections, the majority of votes cast were in favor of regional parties.

The end of the Congress monopoly also heralded the end of Nehru's cohesive vision of India as a state united in its diversity, run in a highly centralized manner, and based on a Fabian socialist economic model. Although this opened the political field for regional parties—including the BJP, which remains more regional than national in scope, with most of its support concentrated in North India's "cow belt"—it also left an ideological vacuum, and it was this vacuum that Hindu majoritarian sentiment quickly helped to fill. In order to compete with increasingly vibrant regional parties at the state level, the Congress Party played religious politics and relied on an obliquely defined "populist Hinduism," a strategy that the Parivar emulated with far greater ideological zeal in the northern heartland of India.

The second "fracture" came in 1990, with the central government's decision to implement the Mandal Commission Reforms, an affirmative action program that created reserved seats at universities and in government jobs for the Other Backward Classes (OBCs) of India. This was the first step toward empowering lower caste politics in India, traditionally seen as a Congress "vote bank."

The BJP traditionally received the bulk of its political support from upper caste urban voters. The empowerment of the lower castes created a rift in the Hindu community; with the OBCs constituting over 50 percent of India's Hindus, this was a vote bank the BJP could not afford to lose. Nor could it afford to publicly disagree with the Mandal Commission reforms without further alienating this key demographic. The issue that the Parivar chose to unite Hindu sentiment and buttress its support was that of building a temple to Rāma on the site of a sixteenth-century mosque in Ayodhya, the Babri Masjid, named after India's first Mughal emperor, Babur. The BJP claimed that the mosque stood on the site of Rāma's birth (*Ram janmabhoomi*), and had been built after the destruction of a much older Hindu temple at the site. The goal of building a temple to Rāma at this site has been an integral part of the Sangh Parivar's program of re-creating the history of Ayodhya to substantiate the myths of Rāma, but now an opportunity had presented itself to use the issue in a highly dramatic, politicized way. L. K. Advani embarked on a Rath Yatra (sacred pilgrimage) through North India in a "golden" chariot, much like one in which Rama might have ridden, on an ethno-religious campaign. The Sangh Parivar turned all government efforts to restrain them in their march into a highly effective cult of martyrdom, and gained a wider range of Hindu supporters in the process among the urban and rural lower middle classes, as well as among the unemployed and upper caste students whom the Mandal Commission had disadvantaged. Sangh Parivar workers eventually tore down the mosque in December 1992, unleashing a wave of Hindu-Muslim riots across the nation. The Parivar and the Supreme Court of India have been deadlocked over the fate of the land on which the Babri Masjid stood. The issue, however, has deep emotional resonance for Hindutva to this day.

Balancing Ideology and Politics

Although Hindutva gained ground as an ideology from the 1980s onward, the BJP was unable to form a lasting government at the center until 1999. More importantly, the primary factor enabling the BJP to form the central government after the 1999 elections was structural, not ideological. The regionally based appeal of politics in India today leaves the Congress Party, the BJP's main competitor, at a distinct disadvantage. The Congress Party remains national in scope, and competes directly with regional and caste-based parties in state elections. This makes it difficult for Congress to build coalitions with these parties at the center. The BJP, on the other hand, has an established electoral presence in only a handful of states, and is able to build coalitions with regional parties, who do not feel threatened by it. After the 1999 elections, the BJP was willing to make significant concessions on its ideological platform to build bridges with secular allies, and was able to form a government with twenty-three primarily regional parties, under the leadership of Prime Minister Atal Bihari Vajpayee. Vajpayee's image as a moderate BJP leader, and the emphasis he placed on social and economic issues, helped to keep this coalition together.

While this has been a successful political strategy, it has caused tensions within the Parivar, most notably with the RSS and the VHP. The BJP has had to toe a fine line between alienating its governing coalition and alienating the Parivar by not following its lead on all ideological issues. It depends on both for political power and

legitimacy. This tug of war between two competing needs has led to contradictory statements and policies by the BJP on a range of issues, including the dispute over Kashmir, the Babri Masjid issue, and, most recently, over the Gujarat riots. By following largely centrist policies, the BJP has been able to demonstrate that while the era of coalition politics is there to stay in India, coalitions can be relatively stable.

The increasing participation of regional and caste-based parties has added a new level of vibrancy and enfranchisement to India's democratic fabric, but the new political system also brings with it a host of new problems. Party platforms appeal to narrower needs and concerns, and there is a new degree of political opportunism. This comes at the expense of broader, more long-term national goals, most importantly the need to ensure that India's complex fabric of communities does not lose the ability to live together and share in their common burdens and opportunities. The value of secularism, which is integral to the stability of India, is in danger of being undervalued and ignored under the constraints of making a coalition government function. While the BJP put aside its ideological agenda in the interests of building its broad coalition after the 1999 elections, it remained disturbingly passive on certain key issues, such as the VHP's virulent stance against conversions of Hindus by Christian missionaries. The most serious omission of the government's constitutional duties occurred during the communal violence that broke out in Gujarat in February 2002. Anti-Muslim riots in the state, in retaliation for an attack on Hindu pilgrims returning by train from Ayodhya, remains one of the darkest moments in modern India's history. What sparked the initial attack remains controversial, but what is clear is that the BJP-run state government did little to stop the violence, leading some analysts to conclude that what occurred was a politically supported pogrom against Muslims in the state. Under pressure from the Sangh Parivar, the BJP allowed Narendra Modi to remain chief minister of Gujarat, despite the law and order breakdown in the state. While the BJP's secular allies at the center protested, they remained passive and unwilling to risk their own positions to confront the BJP. In the state elections that followed later that year, the BJP, led once again by Narendra Modi, won with a thumping majority.

The Significance of the Gujarat Elections

The BJP has consistently fared well in Gujarat polls in the early years of the 2000s. Its success was not a major upset, but its landslide proportions in the wake of the riots were a surprise. The impact of the riots was expected to make the Congress Party a stronger contender in the polls. In the months that followed the riots, however, Chief Minister Narendra Modi waged a virulently communal campaign designed to inflame Hindu sentiments and, by association, patriotic zeal. This connection between being a Hindu and being a nationalist is a central tenet of Hindutva ideology, but was used in a uniquely successful way in the Gujarat election. Pulling foreign policy and domestic politics together, Modi was also able to effectively utilize anti-Pakistan and anti-Musharraf rhetoric to garner support in the wake of a terrorist attack that had left people in Gujarat feeling particularly vulnerable. While Hindutva was not the sole or even the determining factor contributing to the BJP's success in Gujarat, it is significant and will continue to play a role at the state and national level, in conjunction with and in reaction to a range of other political drivers.

The passivity of the moderate middle, which does not espouse the Hindu fundamentalism of Hindutva ideology, and the political exigencies of secular parties have created an atmosphere conducive to the growth of extremism. The BJP has been successful in keeping its allies in the NDA just weak enough to remain useful in the coalition but unable to challenge key BJP policies. The fear following the Gujarat elections was that the BJP might be tempted to move from its largely centrist policies to fully embrace in practice the ideological positions of the VHP and a new political strategy that political wags are calling "Moditva" or "Modi-ism." There is also the real fear that the increasing acceptability of religious rhetoric in the political arena is moving the terms of political debate to the right.

Indian politics remain far too complex, however, to respond to so narrow an ideological agenda. Elections in India reflect regional and community-based issues, and this was true of the Gujarat elections, as well as the 2004 Lok Sabha elections. Several factors set the Gujarat elections apart. Gujarat's urban density, degree of industrialization, economic priorities, and the absence of caste politics all played in favor of the BJP. The riots played a key role, and it is noteworthy that they did not spread to any of India's other states. Gujarat's urban centers, particularly Ahmedabad, Baroda, and Godhra, have an unusually bad history of communal violence, and Modi was able to successfully capitalize on anti-Muslim sentiment unleashed by the attack in Godhra that led to the communal riots, as well as on a subsequent terrorist attack by suspected Pakistani militants on the Akshardham temple in Gujarat. Moreover, the BJP landslide was not uniform. In sixty-four constituencies in Gujarat, the BJP and the Congress were neck and neck, and the BJP won by less than 3 percent; in some areas where the margin between the two parties was larger, third parties held the balance of the votes, and strategic alliance building could have delivered a different result.

This is a lesson the Congress Party took to heart in the 2004 general elections, redoubling its efforts to build genuine partnerships with regional parties and successfully sorting out internal dissent and issues of leadership within the party.

But the Gujarat "test case" also highlighted a critical aspect of the Sangh Parivar's work as an effective grassroots social movement. The RSS and the VHP have spent years cultivating a base in Gujarat, through labor unions, social work, building schools, and focusing on backward communities, particularly tribal communities, to draw them away from their traditional Congress support. The different Sangh Parivar organizations have also reached out to the lower castes with reasonable success. If there is a message to be drawn from Gujarat, it is that the full impact of the Hindutva movement will bear fruit through its social organizing, not in the short-term political future of the BJP. Its social organizations occupy a space in civil society that cannot easily be regulated by the state, and these organizations will continue to work for their social revolution with profound consequences for the country.

The victory of the BJP in the Gujarat state elections of 2002 was bolstered by unexpected wins in the Madhya Pradesh, Chattisgarh, and Rajasthan state elections in 2003. The BJP called for early Lok Sabha polls in 2004, expecting to ride this winning streak to another term in office. The BJP's loss in the elections was a result of several factors. Anti-incumbency is strong in Indian politics and certainly played against the BJP. The BJP's "Shining India" campaign, focused on middle class consumerist ideals, had a negative reaction amongst India's millions of rural and urban poor. The election results were also seen as a "Gujarat verdict"—a reaction by the national electorate against overt ideological politics. The BJP also suffered because many of its regional allies suffered losses at the polls, while the Congress' allies fared well.

The larger question underlying the analysis of electoral politics is the future of Hindutva and its implications for India's multireligious population. While in power, the BJP followed a policy of de-linking governance and development from its core ideological issues, and following largely centrist policies. There is a real fear that the BJP will revert to relying on its ideological rhetoric in opposition, where it will not need to balance the needs of political allies or have the responsibilities of governance. Following the elections, there has been a move in the Sangh Parivar to sideline its moderate elements, including Atal Bihari Vajpayee, in favor of more hard line elements who are eager to return to the BJP's "core agenda," which includes a uniform civil code for the Hindus and Muslims of the subcontinent, and the *ramjanmabhoomi* issue.

Looking Ahead

There has been a shift toward, and cohesion of, the religious right in Indian politics in the late 1990s and early 2000s, but that does not trump the dynamics of regionalism and coalition building. The outcome of the national elections still depends on regional factors and the ability of parties to build alliances at the state level.

Regional and caste-based parties thus seem destined to remain the mainstays of Indian politics in the future, and much will depend on the dynamics of particular coalitions, how stable they are, the terms of the debate with the political opposition, and the quality of leaders that political parties produce.

Mandavi Mehta

See also **Bharatiya Janata Party (BJP); Congress Party; Gujarat; Hindu Nationalism; Vishwa Hindu Parishad (VHP)**

BIBLIOGRAPHY

Advani, L. K. *The People Betrayed*. Delhi: Vision Books, 1979.
Andersen, Walter K., and Shridhar D. Damle. *The Brotherhood in Saffron: The Rashtriya Swayamsevak Sangh and Hindu Revivalism*. Boulder, Colo.: Westview Press, 1987.
Basu, Tapan, et al. *Khaki Shorts and Saffron Flags: A Critique of the Hindu Right*. New Delhi: Orient Longman, 1993.
Brass, Paul R. *Caste, Faction, and Party in Indian Politics*. Delhi: Chanakya Publications, 1984.
———. *The Production of Hindu-Muslim Violence in Contemporary India*. Seattle: University of Washington Press, 2003.
Crossman, Brenda, and Ratna Kapur. *Secularism's Last Sigh?: Hindutva and the (Mis)rule of Law*. New Delhi and New York: Oxford University Press, 1999.
Gandhi, Rajmohan. *Revenge and Reconciliation: Understanding South Asian History*. New Delhi and New York: Penguin Books, 1999.
Hansen, Thomas B. *The Saffron Wave: Democracy and Hindu Nationalism in Modern India*. Princeton, N.J.: Princeton University Press, 1999.
Hansen, Thomas B., and Christophe Jaffrelot, eds. *The BJP and the Compulsions of Politics in India*. New Delhi and New York: Oxford University Press, 2001.
Jaffrelot, Christophe. *The Hindu Nationalist Movement in India*. New York: Columbia University Press, 1995.
———. *India's Silent Revolution: The Rise of the Lower Castes in North India*. New York: Columbia University Press, 2003.
Kohli, Ritu. *Political Ideas of M. S. Golwalkar: Hindutva, Nationalism, Secularism*. New Delhi: Deep & Deep Publications, 1993.
Noorani, A. G. *The RSS and the BJP: A Division of Labour*. New Delhi: Left Word Books, 2000.
Savarkar, V. D. *Hindutva*. Poona: S. R. Date; Delhi: World Book Centre, 1942.
Varshney, Ashutosh. *Ethnic Conflict and Civic Life: Hindus and Muslims in India*. New Haven, Conn.: Yale University Press, 2003.

HISTORY AND HISTORIOGRAPHY For over four thousand years, the Indian subcontinent has sustained a brilliant civilization, rivaled in its longevity only by that of China, attracting "conquerors" from every part of the world to its fertile plains and singular riches. From the earliest invading Aryans to its most recent Western colonialists, India has absorbed the elements of other cultures but retained its distinctive identity. India's history is the record of that process of assimilation and transformation over time.

Indus Valley Culture

The roots of India's history lie buried more than four thousand years deep under the fecund soil of the valley of the River Indus, for which India and its great civilization were named by ancient Persian invaders. Over a thousand villages and five major urban sites have been excavated around the Valley of the Indus and its tributary "Five Rivers" (Punjab) that flow into it from the perennially snow-covered Himalayas. Remains of those Indus Valley cities date back to at least 2300 B.C. That technologically sophisticated and artistic Bronze Age of Indian history lasted until about 1700 B.C. Artifacts of Hindu Shiva and Mother-Goddess worship, as well as of ancient yogic practice, have been unearthed in Harappa and Mohenjo-Daro, the two richest Indus sites, and fragments of woven cotton, India's most important handicraft, and of dice and chess, its most ancient popular games, have all been found there, as have the bones of domesticated chickens, India's culinary gift to global appetites.

Aryan Invasions

From about 1500 B.C. seminomadic Indo-European Aryan tribes—the most powerful of which was called Bharata, modern India's Sanskrit name and root of the epic poem Mahābhārata (Great Bharata)—invaded and conquered the Indus Valley. They came over the high Khyber and Bolan passes in the Hindu Khush from the Afghan plateau, galloping down on their horses and in royal chariots, driving herds of cows, which would later be worshiped by Hindus, long after functioning as Aryan currency. Hearty Aryan warriors also brought deadly arrows and hafted axes, but those would not have sufficed to conquer the more advanced cities of Harappa and Mohenjo-Daro had their walls not earlier been breached and their citadels shattered by severe earthquakes, leaving them vulnerable to Aryan cavalry assaults and conquests. Pre-Aryan peoples of the Indus, called Dasas (dark-skinned), were mentioned by Aryan Brahman bards, in their most sacred Rig Veda, as living in "walled cities." *Dasas* later came to mean "slaves," reflecting their fate after they were conquered prior to 1000 B.C., by

ENCYCLOPEDIA OF *India*

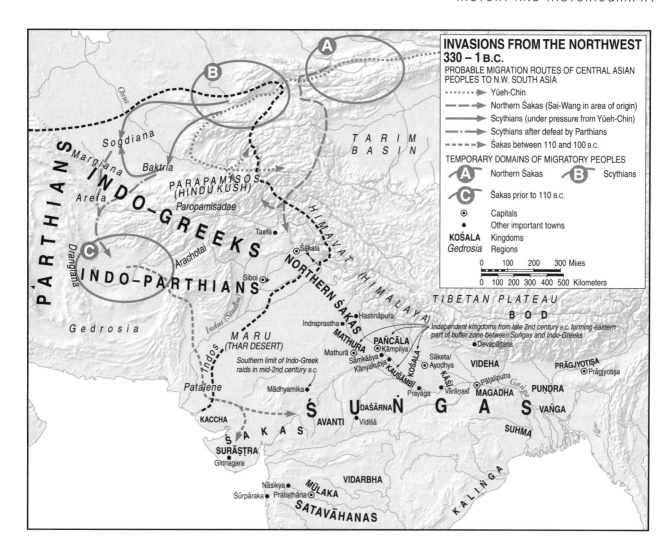

which time tribal Aryans had crossed the Punjab and reached the plateau around Delhi, settling in cities and kingdoms.

The longer epic, Mahābhārata, tells the tale of Aryan tribal cousins in deadly conflict over land near urban Delhi's earliest capital incarnation, Indra-Prastha. The shorter epic, Rāmāyaṇa, tells the story of divine King (Raja) Rāma, reflecting Aryan advances eastward into the forests of the Gangetic Plain around Rama's Kosala capital of Ayodhya, the center of so much Hindu-Muslim tension and conflict over his presumed "birth temple." By 1000 B.C. iron had been discovered in such profusion that it could be peeled off the Barabar Hills of Magadha. The Gangetic thick forests were either burned or cut down, the sedimentary soil turned up for planting by iron plows, and wealthy rajas were arming their soldiers with cheap swords and spears, and erecting capitals of wood with high timber walls and towers over newly planted fields in that richly watered region of North India's powerful, populous plain, modern Uttar Pradesh and Bihar.

Between 800 and 500 B.C. a number of radical new ideas came to light in that Eastern Gangetic heartland of North India, reflecting both orthodox and heterodox rejections of the Vedic Brahmanism taught by Brahman priests, who claimed the privileges of "gods on earth." Princely authors of the orthodox Upanishads (To Sit Down in Front of), also called Vedānta (End of Vedas), philosophic dialogues on the nature of "reality" and ways of controlling it, speculated on how best to understand and escape from the "torture" of rebirth, and attain "release" (moksha) from this world's pain and violence. Optimistic early Aryans had poured libations of clarified butter (ghee) and gold onto ritual fires, carrying the bright sparks of their gifts to Vedic Gods-on-high like Indra and Varuna, believing they would answer all prayers for long life, strong sons, and rich harvests. But skeptical Upanishadic princes asked "Who has ever seen Indra?" losing faith in Brahmanic rituals that cost them herds of fine cattle, bringing scant rewards, daily faced as they were with tigers, snakes, mosquitoes, and savage enemies. They turned inward, swayed perhaps by wise pre-Aryan "yogis" or *muni*s (silent ones), who sat cross-legged and naked in forest clearings, seeking through meditation to control their inner "breath," their "souls" (*ātman*), equating those with a mighty transcendental principle called *Brahman*, originally meaning "sacred utterance."

By the fifth century B.C. heterodox princes, like Siddhartha Gautama (563–483 B.C.) and Mahavira (540–468 B.C.), rejected the authority of the Vedas and their Brahman priests entirely. Gautama, who left his royal palace at the age of thirty, sought wisdom wandering in the forests of Kosala and Magadha for six years, attaining enlightenment in a deer park in Sarnath, near modern Varanasi (Benares). As the Buddha (Enlightened One), he set in motion his Wheel of the Law, preaching the four noble truths of this earliest type of Theravada (Teachings of the Elders) Buddhism. The ultimate Buddhist goal is *nirvāna* (blowing out), much the same "liberation" from life's misery and sorrow as the Hindu goal of *moksha*. Both Buddhism and sage Mahavira's Jainism stressed another important new idea, *ahimsa* (nonviolence), which was later also adopted by Hinduism and, together with cow worship, led to almost universal vegetarianism throughout pre-Muslim India.

Mauryan Imperial Unification

India's first imperial unification came in the wake of Alexander the Great's invasion of Punjab in 326 B.C. Alexander's dream of universal conquest ignited a similarly glorious ambition of North Indian unification in the mind of a "young stripling" who met him on the banks of the River Beas. Chandragupta Maurya was thus inspired to found his Mauryan dynasty in 324 B.C. That first mighty Indian Empire flourished for 140 years. Chandragupta ruled from Pataliputra (modern Patna), his capital on the south bank of Mother Gaṅgā, aided in his empire building by a wise old Brahman minister, Kautilya, author of India's realpolitik "Text on the Science of Material Gain," the *Artha Shāstra*, which may well have inspired Niccolò Machiavelli's *The Prince*. A powerful prince, Kautilya advised, must be "ever wakeful," carefully controlling all of his subjects, including his beautiful "queens" and his mighty "ministers," trusting no one, keeping an army of "spies" as well as soldiers and civil bureaucrats. The "Circle" (*mandala*) system of foreign policy was also first articulated in this text, warning every Indian prince from this time on that his neighboring monarch was always his "enemy," while his neighbor's neighbor was his "friend," and so forth, until in the final circle a "neutral mediator" might at last be found, too remote to have to worry about fighting.

Chandragupta's grandson Ashoka, who reigned from 269 to 232 B.C., was the greatest Mauryan emperor. The first eight years of his reign were no different from his father Bindusara's three violent decades of martial expansion, but after Ashoka's most bloody conquest of tribal Kalinga (modern Orissa), "He of Gentle Visage," as he was called, had a remarkable change of heart, converting to nonviolent Buddhism. Instead of annual imperial hunts, Ashoka undertook "pilgrimages of Religious Law" (*dharma*), planting shade trees along new highways he had constructed, erecting tall sandstone pillars all over India, inscribing them with wise edicts, commending Laws of Nonviolence and Love to his people, rather than hatred and war. Ashoka was hailed as *Chakravartin* (He by Whom the Wheel of the Law is set in Motion), the first universal monarch in history to advocate peace as his primary platform. Between 250 and 240 B.C. Ashoka hosted the Third Great Council of Buddhism, soon after which he withdrew from public life and appears to have died as a Buddhist monk, in 232 B.C. Many claimants followed him, but none proved as wise. The last of the Mauryan monarchs, Brihadratha, was murdered by his Brahman general Pushyamitra Shunga, who founded the Shunga dynasty in 184 B.C. It lasted in much diminished form only until 72 B.C., ruling little more than the old kingdom of Magadha.

Mauryan imperial collapse left the North-West frontier, the classic highroad for India's invaders, unguarded. From 180 B.C. Greco-Bactrians were the first to gallop over those passes, capturing Punjab. King Menander, a Greek converted to Buddhism by a monk named Nagasena, ruled the Indus Valley's "Land of Five Rivers." Another Greek, Heliodorus, erected a stone pillar proclaiming himself a "worshiper" of "Vasudeva," a Hindu god identified with Krishna (Black), one of Vishnu's ten "earthly emanations" (*avatāra*s). From earliest historic times, India has always thus in some measure conquered its "conquerors," luring them with its rich crops, fabled jewels, and artistic beauty, converting them by the warmth, charm, and wisdom of its glorious civilization. The Bactrian bridge erected before the dawn of Christianity between India and the West served as a vital passageway for merchants as well as Buddhist monks, who brought not only their monastic beads and yogic practices to the West, but also the Buddha's wisdom of nonviolence.

Persian Pahlavas and Central Asian Scythian Shakas followed the Bactrians over the same North-West passes, displacing them. They too converted to Buddhism and Hinduism after having settled down in Punjab. The fiercest Central Asian invaders to gallop down from their frozen plateaus to India's fecund plains were Kushans, whose greatest *maharaja* (Great-King) Kanishka ruled over Punjab almost two decades around A.D. 100. Thanks to their metal stirrups, Kushana archers could brace themselves on their saddles, arms and hands free as they galloped to fire their deadly crossbows. They, too, ultimately were converted to nonviolent Buddhism.

While northern invaders thus followed one another for centuries over the Hindu Kush, South India broke free of Pataliputra's hegemony, with competing provincial dynasties carving out independent kingdoms. The great Andhras ruled most of central India from the second century B.C. for nearly four hundred years. Their modern reincarnation is the Telugu Dravidian state of Andhra on the east coast of India's peninsula. Just south of Andhra is India's largest Dravidian-language state, Tamil Nadu, "Land of Tamils." South India's four Dravidian-linguistic states (the other two being Kerala and Karnataka) were probably where the ancient pre-Aryan Indus Valley people originally fled, settling south of central India's Vindhya mountain range, to escape being enslaved by Aryan invaders. Three Tamil kingdoms are mentioned in ancient texts: the Cheras (or Keralas) on the west (Malabar) coast; the Cholas, who became South India's greatest sea power and bronze artists on the east (Coromandel) coast; and the southernmost Pandyas, whose famed "pearls" were coveted by the West when King Solomon was still building his temple. Madurai, the Pandyan capital as early as the second century B.C., remains one of South India's greatest Hindu temple cities, its Meenakshi Temple containing icons of the three most powerful Hindu divinities: Shiva, Vishnu, and Mother Goddess Meenakshi (Devī). The Chola capital, Kanchipuram, home to a much larger walled temple "city," whose giant *gopuram* (towers) are visible for miles in every direction, was captured in the fourth century by a new "robber" dynasty, the Pallavas. These may have originally been Persian Pahlavas, driven south by the Kushanas.

Guptan Reunification

India's second era of imperial unification under the Guptan dynasty was a golden age of classical Hindu glory and power. Chandragupta I was crowned in A.D. 320 at Pataliputra, and assumed the exalted title "Great King of Kings." He doubled his domain by marrying his powerful Lichavi neighbor's daughter, controlling the rich lands to the north and south of North India's Ganges commercial artery. His son Samudra ("Ocean") Gupta reigned from A.D. 335 to 375, conquering Kashmir to his north, and Maharashtra's Deccan to the south, and exacting tribute from the last of the Kushana and Shaka monarchs of Punjab. To celebrate his Napoleonic conquests, Samudra ordered performance of the year-long royal "horse sacrifice" (*ashva-medha*). The pinnacle of Guptan glory, however, was attained in its third reign under Chandragupta II (r. 375–415). Hailed as Vikramaditya

(He Whose Splendor Equals That of the Sun), his court patronized India's greatest authors and artists, including the Shakespeare of Sanskrit drama, Kalidasa, whose beautiful *Shakuntala* is still staged to world acclaim. Hindu temples were erected in growing numbers from this time. Buddhist and Jain caves continued to accommodate many thousands of monks, who adorned their ceilings and walls with stunning frescoes, whose portraits still dazzle visitors with their vivid vitality. Countless Roman coins were shipped East to pay for tons of precious Indian silks and cottons, jewels and spices, ivory and perfumes. Alaric's ransom for Rome in 410 included three thousand pounds of Indian pepper.

Half a century after Chandragupta II died in 415, fierce Central Asian Hsiung-nu "Hunas" (Huns) reached India's Khyber Pass. Toramana first conquered Persia in 484, then took Punjab; his son, Mihirakula, captured Kashmir after 515. North Indian reunification was then briefly achieved under Harsha Vardhana (r. 606–647), who seems to have been a wise and tolerant king, as supportive of Buddhism as Ashoka, yet equally generous to Hindu Brahmans. He ruled his mighty empire from Kanauj, which after his death remained the capital of several later North Indian dynasties.

Most of India reverted, however, to its most common historic pattern of feudal fragmentation, many competing monarchs fighting one another. Political unity has proved the exception rather than the rule of Indian history. Vakatakas of Bundelkhand established their martial grip over the Nagpur-Vidarbha region of Maha-Rashtra, the "Great Country," where Hindu Maratha power would later attain primacy. Hindu Marathas challenged both Mughal Muslim warriors and British East Company Christian merchants alike for hegemony over South Asia. Shivaji Maharaj, father of sixteenth-century Maratha national resurgence, would be crowned at the top of his Deccan "Fortress of the Tiger" as ten thousand Brahmans chanted their Vedic Sanskrit mantras. The Chalukyas of Badami had earlier claimed the Deccan themselves, as did their feudal "Country-Lord" Rashtrakutas in 752. Powerful Rashtrakuta monarchs continued to rule the Deccan until the early tenth century, when another Chalukya dynasty emerged to defeat its old rivals.

The Impact of Islam

After 711 a totally new foreign force, called Islam ("submission" to the will of Allah), born in the desert sands of Saudi Arabia in 622, entered India from the Arabian Sea to conquer the province of Sind, in what is now Pakistan. That wave of Muslim invaders was but the first of a series of Islamic conquests to spread the faith of their Prophet to India, but many more Islamic invasions followed later, most of them over the North-West passes—Turko-Afghans, Persians, and Central Asian Mughals, the last of whom finally conquered virtually all of South Asia by the end of the seventeenth century. Throughout the tenth and eleventh centuries it was Afghan Ghaznavids and Ghors, who plundered the Hindu temple cities of Punjab and Sind on their annual raids against "infidel" Hindus and the naked statues they worshiped, "abominations" to Allah. The great temple city of Somnath, "protected," its people thought, by a jewel-filled magnetized Shiva-lingam, was reduced to rubble, thousands of its inhabitants slaughtered or taken prisoner by Mahmud of Ghazni, who slashed the lingam with his sword, on his last raid in 1025. A legacy of Muslim hatred, never fully erased from the memory of Kathiawar's Hindus, was thereafter inscribed.

Until the thirteenth century Muslims continued to treat India as a land fit only for periodic plunder, a domain at "war," rather than in "submission." However, after 1206—the dawn of the Delhi sultanate, when the first of five Muslim dynasties established dominance over North India—Muslim rule remained an integral part at least of some portion of South Asia, if not its entire length and breadth. The Afghan "Slave" (Mamluk) dynasty lasted less than a century, followed by tougher Turkish Khaljis, who brought the faith of Islam to the Deccan, looting and plundering Devagiri, capital of pastoral Yadavas, worshipers of Krishna. Under Ala'-ud-din Muhammad Khalji (r. 1296–1316), the sultanate reached its peak of power, but his sons were unable to consolidate their father's phenomenal conquests. Turkish Tughluqs ruled for most of the fourteenth century, during which India suffered one of its worst prolonged periods of drought, bringing deadly famine to much of the Deccan, as the sultans in Delhi ignored the plight of dying peasants, impervious to pleas for aid. Farther south, Hindu warriors joined forces to start a "City of Victory" (Vijayanagar), ruled in 1336 by Harihara I (r. 1336–1357), who defeated his neighbors, the Hoysalas, and seven years after taking his throne, controlled most of South India's peninsula. In 1345 rebellion against the Tughluqs spread from Daulatabad, led by Hasan Gangu, who adopted as his reign name Bahman Shah, founding the Deccan's first Muslim kingdom, the Bahmani dynasty.

In 1398 a Central Asian army led by Timur the Lame (Tamerlane) poured over the Khyber, galloping across Punjab to Delhi, which was put to the torch, dragging tens of thousands of Indian slaves back to Samarkand. That dreadful sack of Delhi presaged the demise of the sultanate, though two more dynasties laid claim to its tattered mantle. Turkish Sayyids ruled from 1414 to 1450, displaced by Afghan Lodis, who reigned over North India until 1526. The Lodis were replaced by the mightiest and longest of all South Asia's Muslim dynasties, founded by Central Asia's Mughal (Mongol) Padishah (Emperor) Babur, who skillfully defeated the massive Afghan army that faced him on the field of Panipat on 21 April 1526.

Great Mughals dominated most of India for some two centuries. The dynasty's wisest monarch, Akbar (r. 1556–1605), conquered not only by the power of his Central Asian artillery and crushing elephant corps, but also by the enlightened tolerance with which he won the support of India's Hindu majority by removing the most offensive Islamic taxes demanded by previous Muslim monarchs. Akbar won over several powerful Hindu Rajput monarchs by marrying their daughters, and brought a number of clever Hindu Brahman "land-tax collectors" as well as mighty Rajput princes into his multicultural Mansabdari (administrative "office") system of imperial rule. His heirs were less tolerant, however, than their "Great" (Akbar) progenitor. The mightiest and most bigoted, Aurangzeb (r. 1658–1707), expanded Mughal dominance to its greatest limits over South India, but lost the support of most of his subjects. Hindu Marathas and Rajputs rallied and rose in revolt against Aurangzeb's narrow Muslim intolerance, and a new powerful religious force, Sikhism, earlier founded by Guru Nanak in Punjab, turned from a passive faith of disciples into an "Army" (Khalsa) of "Lions" (Singhs) led by Guru Govind Singh.

Impact of the West

Portuguese Western European sea captains were first lured to India by the rich scent of spices and the prospect of vast profits to be made by venturing around the Cape of Africa in their cannon-bearing caravels, clearing the Indian Ocean of all competing Arab and Venetian merchant vessels. Lisbon grew wealthy from the peppers and cloves of India and the Banda and Molucca Islands of Indonesia, and for most of the sixteenth century, tiny Portugal held a virtual monopoly over the lucrative Indian Ocean trade with its powerful fleet. By the dawn of the seventeenth century, however, Protestant Dutch and English sea captains and merchants pooled their wealth, forming their own East India Companies, arming fleets to challenge and defeat the Catholic Portuguese monopoly. The Dutch were initially stronger than the English, driving them away from the richest Spice Island plantations of Southeast Asia, obliging English merchant ships to fall back on India's Malabar Coast as their second best choice. At Surat they also built their own factory, and ventured to appeal to the "Great Mogor" in Agra for permission to enjoy "quiet trade" with his empire. Other than gold, horses, and watches, however, the West really possessed nothing that Mughal India wanted or needed. India, of course, had so many things the West desired that before very long the bitter complaint of

London's merchants and monarchs was that "India doth drain us of our wealth." The Indian nationalists would later reverse that cry, lamenting the "drain" of "India's wealth by the rapacious West."

French and English merchants, who had established colonial fortress toeholds at neighboring ports along India's eastern Coromandal Coast in the early eighteenth century, battled one another at sea as well as on Indian soil in the wake of Europe's war over Charles's Austrian succession and the subsequent Seven Years' War (1756–1763). The historic revelation of that brief but sharp colonial conflict, between small forces trained by France's brilliant Joseph François Dupleix and British bully Robert Clive on the fragmenting fringe of Mughal power, was that modern European cannon and musket fire sufficed to defeat huge undisciplined armies of South India's nizams and *nawābs*. As Mughal hegemony fragmented into provincial principalities, British company merchant-plunderers like Clive moved into those vacuums of power in Bengal as well as Madras, playing the "Nabob Game" devised by Dupleix, who could have won India for France had he not lost the support of his own company's directors in Versailles. Clever Warren Hastings soon placed his British company's Raj onto a sounder financial base, little more than a decade after Clive's looting of its treasury, and then vigorously integrated the company's remote presidency ports of Bombay and Madras under his own martial and administrative control from Fort William, his Bengal headquarters in Calcutta, capital of the British company's Raj. Britain's Parliament, however, impeached Hastings instead of thanking him, and sent out Lord Cornwallis to restore British confidence in the sound security of their new Indian empire. Landlord Whig that he was, Cornwallis hammered a British "steel-frame" Regulation System down onto the naked body politic of Bengal, knowing nothing of India before he sailed east to secure a new empire for his king and country, to replace the one just lost in North America.

The British Raj

The East India Company and Britain's Parliament jointly ruled distant India from 1773 until 1858. British trained Indian Sepoy armies fought under British officers against Marathas as well as the remnants of Mughal provincial power and periodically invading Afghans from the northwest. In 1761, at Panipat, the mightiest Hindu Maratha army of Pune's Peshwa confronted a flood tide of invading Muslim Afghan cavalry. Both armies so brutally destroyed one another's finest fighters that the much smaller British force, hitherto no match for either contesting indigenous army, was left to claim the remnant of Great Mughal hegemony over South Asia. In 1818 the last of the Peshwa's Maratha force was finally defeated by

the company's Sepoy army. The British Raj thereafter emerged as India's "New Mughal" paramount power, virtually unchallenged by any indigenous competitors until the "Mutiny" of 1857. By the time India's once powerful monarchs, its *padishah*s, maharajas, rajas, nizams, and *nawāb*s, awoke to realize what had become of their vast continental domain—"stolen" from them by a Christian band of British merchants, reducing the greatest of them to suppliants and beggars in their own capitals—it was too late to recapture the powers they had lost. In desperation, an uneasy triple alliance of the last Mughal emperor's Delhi courtiers and garrison, the "mutinied" Sepoy Bengal Muslim troops loyal to their ousted Muslim *nawāb* of Oudh, and Hindu dependents of the pensioner Peshwa of Pune living in a castle outside Cawnpore, sought with insufficient coordination to drive the foreign "usurpers" out of India. But by that time Britain was fully aware of India's unique value to its global prestige and power. The War of 1858 was won by British Crown troops, with the aid of sturdy Sikh soldiers of the Punjab, and Nepalese Gurkhas, who thereafter remained the most trusted "native" recruits to the army of Britain's Crown Raj, which replaced the discredited old company Raj on 2 August 1858.

India's Nationalist Movement

Though British company merchants were initially lured to India for profit or plunder, English missionaries later ventured to the East to "save" souls, remaining to translate their Bibles into Indian languages, opening schools and hospitals, preaching social reform as well as scripture. Still other secular missionaries of Western civilization, Utilitarians and liberal social reformers, swiftly followed as the company secured more territories, drafting civil laws for those "protected" under its Regulation Raj, planning new cities, laying down railroads, putting up telegraph wires, bringing all the blessings, virtue, and barbarism of Great Britain's "civilization" to ancient India's conquered subcontinent. The English language itself proved a potent national unifier of India's new elite who learned it, taking advantage of Britain's "penny-post" that helped to convert India from a divided continent of remote strangers into an inchoate nation-state, unleashing winds of rapid radical change, much too strong for the company's rickety Raj, and ultimately even too powerful for Britain's stronger Crown Raj to withstand.

After 1885, when the Indian National Congress was born in Bombay, brilliant leaders of a "New India" emerged, eager to play some role in administering their own nation, willing at first to work under and in cooperation with British Indian civil servants to rectify all the ills of ailing India's society, to raise their Motherland from depths of poverty to sunny plains of health and happiness. Some Englishmen were wise enough to welcome those overtures, but most of the others were either too fearful or narrow-minded to view Congress's leaders as anything but "terrorists," "anarchists," or "trouble-makers," seeking only to take their jobs away, "useless natives" hoping to run their country without the help of over-burdened white men! Nonetheless, the first two decades of India's Nationalist Movement proved remarkably moderate and cooperative, but after the partition of Bengal in 1905 a new revolutionary wing of the Congress emerged, and cries of "boycott" of British goods and "freedom" (*swaraj*) were raised by leaders of a "New Party," eager to send the British home and to claim all the keys to their "own country" (*swadeshi*).

After World War I, India's Congress was transformed into a mass revolutionary movement under the charismatic leadership of Mahatma (Great-Soul) Mohandas K. Gandhi, who returned home after two decades in South Africa, introducing his *satyagraha* ("Hold Fast to the Truth") movement of nonviolent noncooperation to India. Gandhi's impact was unique, at once mobilizing India's peasant power by the potency of his Hindu religiously based appeal, but alienating many moderate Anglophile Indians, including Muslim-minority leaders like M. A. Jinnah. The Muslim League, which Quaid-i-Azam ("Great Leader") Jinnah transformed into his vehicle leading to the birth of Pakistan, evolved in the last decade of Britain's Crown Raj as a constant counter to Gandhi's and Congress's claim to represent the "Indian nation." South Asia's Muslims, Jinnah insisted, were no mere minority but a "nation" worthy of their own state.

On the eve of their departure from India, after World War II, exhausted Britain agreed, for by that time India's restless Raj had become more of a liability than an asset. British fears of facing a possible civil war in South Asia made them opt for the most hasty, ill-conceived partition of the subcontinent it had taken them more than a century to unify. In mid-August 1947 that "shameful flight" of British troops and withdrawal of any protective cover for unarmed Indians, ordered by vainly impatient Lord Mountbatten, the Raj's last viceroy, triggered a mass migration of over 10 million terrified Hindus, Muslims, and Sikhs of Punjab and Bengal, which left at least a million innocents dead.

Pandit Jawaharlal Nehru, India's first prime minister, welcomed the midnight birth of his nation as "in some measure" the historic fulfillment of Congress's long-deferred "tryst with destiny." Mahatma Gandhi left Delhi on the eve of Nehru's most famous speech, traveling to Calcutta, where he sought valiantly to calm rising tides of communal hatred and violence that threatened to drown all of Bengal and Bihar in a sea of Hindu-Muslim blood. A few months later, rivers of blood did flow through the Punjab, which was divided through the heartland of its Sikh population. Freedom brought with it the first of three wars between India and Pakistan over Kashmir state, draining both newborn nations of so much precious wealth each of them needed for their impoverished peoples. Gandhi returned to Delhi, trying again to heal wounds of ancient hatred that refused to respond even to that wise old Mahatma's messages of "Love" (*ahimsa*) as God. Angry young Hindus shouted at Gandhi whenever he tried to read prayers from the Qur'an at his nightly meetings, or called for an end to the murder of Muslims in Delhi and the stealing of their property. Then he, too, was murdered, early in 1948. "The light has gone out of our lives," Nehru cried that night, but India carried on, and under his dynamic leadership soon emerged as a secular democratic republic.

Stanley Wolpert

See also **Akbar; Aurangzeb; British Crown Raj; British East India Company Raj; British Impact; Buddhism in Ancient India; Clive, Robert; Congress Party; Cornwallis, Lord; Dupleix, Joseph François; French Impact; Gandhi, Mahatma M. K.; Guptan Empire; Harappa; Hastings, Warren; Indus Valley Civilization; Jainism; Jammu and Kashmir; Jinnah, Mohammed Ali; Mohenjo-Daro; Mountbatten, Lord; Muslims; Nehru, Jawaharlal; Portuguese in India; Satyagraha; Sculpture: Mauryan and Shunga**

BIBLIOGRAPHY

Basham, A. L. *The Wonder That Was India.* London: Sidgwick and Jackson, 1954.

Brecher, Michael. *Nehru: A Political Biography.* Westport, Conn.: Greenwood, 1976.

Brown, W. Norman. *The United States and India, Pakistan, Bangladesh.* Cambridge, Mass.: Harvard University Press, 1972.

Embree, Ainslie T., ed. *Sources of Indian Tradition.* New York: Columbia University Press, 1988.

Gandhi, Mahatma. *An Autobiography: The Story of My Experiments with Truth.* Boston: Beacon Press, 1993.

Gordon, Stewart. *The New Cambridge History of India,* vol. II: *The Marathas, 1600–1818.* Cambridge, U.K., and New York: Cambridge University Press, 1993.

Habib, Irfan, ed. *Medieval India.* New Delhi: Oxford University Press, 1992.

Jeffrey, Robin, ed. *People, Princes and Paramount Power.* Delhi: Oxford University Press, 1978.

Jones, Kenneth W. *The New Cambridge History of India,* vol. III: *Socio-religious Reform Movements in India.* Cambridge, U.K., and New York: Cambridge University Press, 1989.

Kenoyer, J. Mark. *Ancient Cities of the Indus Valley Civilization.* Karachi: Oxford University Press, 1998.

Kopf, David. *The Brahmo Samaj and the Shaping of the Modern Indian Mind.* Princeton, N.J.: Princeton University Press, 1979.

Moore, R. J. *Crisis of Indian Unity, 1917–1940.* London: Oxford University Press, 1974.

Nehru, Jawaharlal. *Towards Freedom: An Autobiography.* New York: Day, 1941.

Raychaudhuri, Tapan, and Irfan Habib, eds. *The Cambridge Economic History of India,* vol. I. Cambridge, U.K., and New York: Cambridge University Press, 1982.

Richards, John F. The *New Cambridge History of India,* vol. I: 5: *The Muighal Empire.* Cambridge, U.K., and New York: Cambridge University Press, 1993.

Robinson, Francis. *Separatism among Indian Muslims.* London: Cambridge University Press, 1974.

Spear, T. G. P. *A History of India,* vol. 2. Baltimore: Penguin, 1965.

Thapar, Romila. *A History of India,* vol. 1. Baltimore: Penguin, 1965.

Tharoor, Shashi. *India: From Midnight to Millennium.* New York: HarperCollins, 1998.

Trautmann, Tomas R. *Kautilya and the Arthashastra.* Leiden: Brill, 1971.

Wolpert, Stanley. *India.* Berkeley and Los Angeles: University of California Press, 1991.

———. *A New History of India.* 7th ed. Oxford and New York: Oxford University Press, 2004.

HUMAN DEVELOPMENT INDICATORS

In a broad sense, human development is about freedom. In Amartya Sen's influential work, *Development as Freedom* (1999), five instrumental freedoms are mentioned: economic facilities, political freedoms, social opportunities, transparency guarantees, and protective security. In the subsequent and related rights-based literature, the point is made that development is not only about improvements in outcomes, it is also about processes. However, most standard measures of human development concern economic indicators, sometimes spilling over into socio cum political ones.

The Millennium Development Goals (MDGs), adopted as targets to be attained by developing countries by 2015, are an example. There are eight such goals:

1. eradicate extreme poverty and hunger;
2. achieve universal primary education;
3. promote gender equality and empower women;
4. reduce child mortality;
5. improve maternal health;
6. combat HIV/AIDS, malaria, and other diseases;
7. ensure environmental sustainability;
8. develop a global partnership for development.

Stated thus, these goals are vague; however, targets under these goals make them operationally meaningful and enable one to quantify and measure progress toward the MDGs. There are 18 such targets; this analysis will ignore the 7 targets under Goal 8 (developing a global partnership for development). The targets for the other

TABLE 1

Millennium development goals and targets
Goal 1 — Target 1: Halve, between 1990 and 2015, the proportion of people whose income is less than $1 a day Target 2: Halve, between 1990 and 2015, the proportion of people who suffer from hunger
Goal 2 — Target 3: Ensure that, by 2015, children everywhere, boys and girls alike, will be able to complete a full course of primary schooling
Goal 3 — Target 4: Eliminate gender disparity in primary and secondary education, preferably by 2005, and in all levels of education no later than 2015
Goal 4 — Target 5: Reduce by two-thirds, between 1990 and 2015, the under-five mortality rate
Goal 5 — Target 6: Reduce by three-quarters, between 1990 and 2015, the maternal mortality ratio
Goal 6 — Target 7: Have halted by 2015 and begun to reverse the spread of HIV/AIDS Target 8: Have halted by 2015 and begun to reverse the incidence of malaria and other major diseases
Goal 7 — Target 9: Integrate the principles of sustainable development into country policies and programs and reverse the loss of environmental resources Target 10: Halve, by 2015, the proportion of people without sustainable access to safe drinking water and basic sanitation Target 11: Have achieved by 2020 a significant improvement in the lives of at least 100 million slum dwellers

SOURCE: Courtesy of author.

goals are shown in Table 1. One does notice that targets are a bit more precise up to Goal 5.

UNDP and *Human Development Reports (HDRs)*

The standard source for making cross-country comparisons about human development is the United Nations Development Programme's (UNDP) *Human Development Report (HDR),* which has been used since 1990. These reports predate the acceptance of MDGs as goals or targets in 2000, although subsequent *HDR*s always have a discussion of MDGs. Each *HDR* has a theme, and data on human development and deprivation are provided. For example, the theme of *HDR 2003* was MDGs, and that of *HDR 2004* was cultural liberty. The argument for publishing the *HDR* is obvious. Conventionally, economists have measured development through indicators like per capita income or the percentage of the population below a designated poverty line. But the percentage of the population below a poverty line, known as the poverty ratio or head count ratio, is also based on income or expenditure; and income ought to be an input into the human development process. Instead, development can be more reliably measured by tangible improvements in indicators like health or education attainments.

Having accepted that argument, problems arise. Data must be available, and if cross-country comparisons are to be made, the cross-country data collection must be comparable. That is difficult, even for something as simple as income. Every country has reasonably satisfactory collection systems for aggregate national income, through national income statistics. That can be converted into per capita income by dividing by population. However, that figure will be in national currencies. To use it for cross-country comparisons, there must be conversion into a common currency, such as the U.S. dollar. Should one use official exchange rates for this conversion? That will be misleading, because goods, and certainly services, are often cheaper in developing countries. Therefore, one uses PPP (purchasing power parity) exchange rates. However, to obtain figures on poverty ratios, one needs data on personal income or expenditure distributions, which are not available through national account statistics, but only through surveys. To complicate matters further, some countries have surveys of income, others of expenditure. Nor are surveys held every year. For example, India has reliable large-sample surveys on consumption expenditure, conducted through the National Sample Survey (NSS), once every five years. The last such surveys were held in 1993–1994 and 1999–2000. What does one do for data in the intervening periods? Also, income data through surveys and income data through national accounts never match, and this problem exists for all countries. Such survey-related data problems also crop up for health and education indicators.

Once one has decided on variables and obtained data on the variables, there is the question of constructing an index. This process involves weighting the variables before aggregating them, and subjectivity is involved in almost any selection of weights. It would have been better to leave data on the variables as they are, but the use of indexes is widespread. The *HDR* has five such indexes: HDI (human development index), HPI-1 (human poverty index for developing countries), HPI-2 (human poverty index for selected Organisation for Economic Co-operation and Development countries), GDI (gender-related development index), and GEM (gender empowerment measure). Of these, HPI-2 is not relevant for India.

HDI is the most commonly cited index. It is based on three variables: a long and healthy life (measured by life expectancy at birth); knowledge (measured by adult literacy rate and gross enrollment ratio); and a decent standard of living (measured by per capita gross domestic product in PPP U.S. dollars). The aggregation process is such that the maximum value of HDI is 1 and the minimum value is 0. The higher the HDI value, the better. Depending on the HDI value, countries are divided into three categories: high human development for countries that have an HDI

more than 0.800; medium human development for countries that have an HDI between 0.500 and 0.800; and low human development for countries that have an HDI less than 0.500. With an HDI value of 0.595 (in 2002), India now belongs to the medium human development category, wedged between Namibia and Botswana. In 1975 India's HDI value was 0.411, and it inched up gradually, with India moving to the medium human development category in the 1990s.

Although the latest *HDR* is for 2004, there is a time lag in obtaining data; the data are mostly for 2002. In the three components of HDI, India's life expectancy at birth in 2002 was 63.7 years. The adult literacy rate was 61.3 percent. Censuses are held at ten-year intervals, and the last census was in 2001. The Indian census-based literacy rate is 65.38 percent. The difference between the two figures requires explanation: the 65.38 percent figure is for populations aged seven and above, while the 61.3 percent is for populations aged fifteen and above. India's track record on literacy improved sharply in the 1990s, but there is a serious adult illiteracy problem, which largely explains the difference. India's gross enrollment ratio for primary, secondary, and tertiary schools in 2002 was 55 percent. Finally, India's per capita PPP gross domestic product (GDP) was U.S.$2,670, compared to the official exchange rate per capita income figure of around $500. The improvement in the 1990s occurred largely because of growth and increases in per capita income. The gross enrollment ratio in primary and secondary schools has also improved. For classes (standards) I through VIII (ages 6–14), the gross enrollment ratio is 82.35 percent. What pulls the Indian HDI down is enrollment in tertiary schools (colleges and universities).

Countries are ranked worldwide based on HDI values; as of 2004, India had a rank of 127 out of 177 countries. Attention invariably focuses on ranks, but one must be careful, because the number of countries included in rankings varies from year to year. It is far better to focus on HDI values. There is a correlation between per capita income and HDI values. Given India's per capita income, India's HDI rank should have been ten places higher. Notwithstanding the improvement in the 1990s, India should have done better on human development.

The next index in the *HDR* is HPI-1, based on a long and healthy life (measured by probability at birth of not surviving to age 40), knowledge (measured by the adult illiteracy rate), and a decent standard of living (measured by percentage of population without sustainable access to an improved water source and percentage of children underweight for age). India was ranked 48th out of 94 developing countries in 2004. Of India's children, 15.3 percent will not survive to the age of forty. The adult illiteracy rate (61.3%) has already been mentioned. Sixteen percent of the population does not have sustainable access to an improved water source, and 47 percent of children (under 5) are underweight for their age. The percentage of the population below the poverty line is not used in estimating HPI-1. Internationally, a poverty line of one U.S. dollar per day (sometimes U.S. $2 per day) is used, at PPP and at 1985 prices. At current prices, this is equivalent to around $1.70 a day. The *HDR* tells us that 34.7 percent of India's population is below this poverty line. However, India also has its own national poverty line, corresponding roughly to one U.S. dollar per day. In 1999–2000, 26.1 percent of India's population was below the national poverty line. There is thus some discrepancy between national data and *HDR* data.

The GDI attempts to capture gender disparities. It follows the same methodology as HDI, but factors in male-female differences. India's GDI value in 2004 was 0.572, wedged between Namibia and Botswana and ranked 127th out of 144 countries. There are fewer countries, because gender-disaggregated data are sometimes not available. The GDI rank is more or less the same as the HDI rank (among 144 countries), suggesting that gender discrimination in India is not overwhelmingly more than what the level of human development would suggest. Looking at the individual components of GDI, there are gender-based deprivations in education (literacy and enrollment). And in PPP U.S. dollars, the average male income is $3,820, while the average female income is $1,442. GEM is an indicator of female empowerment, with variables that capture political participation and decision making, economic participation and decision making, and power over economic resources. Requisite data are not available for an Indian GEM or GEM rank to be constructed; 9.3 percent of seats in Parliament are held by women.

National Human Development Report (NHDR)

There is a *Human Development in South Asia* document, published annually by the Islamabad-based Mahbub ul Haq Human Development Centre. It will not be discussed in detail here, because its human development indicators are primarily drawn from *HDR*.

To state the obvious, India is a large and heterogeneous country, and there are significant regional variations. A *National Human Development Report (NHDR)* was published in 2002, providing a wealth of data on human development and deprivation across states and union territories (UTs). Some of this data is reproduced in Table 2. There is more data, especially in terms of rural-urban differences, that is unavailable. The *NHDR* was published when most of the results of the 2001 census were not yet available. Hence, some data are dated, and the developments of the 1990s will not be fully incorporated

until the next *NHDR* is published. That also explains why the HDI figure is available only for larger states. In addition, three states—Bihar, Uttar Pradesh, and Madhya Pradesh—have been bifurcated, leading to the creation of Jharkhand, Uttaranchal, and Chhattisgarh, respectively. Data are not always available for these three new states separately. Data for Bihar, Uttar Pradesh, and Madhya Pradesh are thus for the states before their division. Neither can the HDI and GDI reported in this table be directly compared with the HDI or GDI reported in *HDR*. Although the objective is similar, the methodology is different, so no direct comparisons are possible.

What does this table tell us about human development across India's states and territories? Conventionally, India's "backward" states have been referred to as BIMARU states (BIMARU is an acronym for Bihar, Madhya Pradesh, Rajasthan, and Uttar Pradesh, and there is a pun on the word *bimar*, which means "ill" or "sick" in most Indian languages). Indeed, if we look at the HDI values for 1991 and have a cutoff of 0.350, we find that the states that are below this threshold are Arunachal Pradesh, Assam, Bihar, Madhya Pradesh, Orissa, Rajasthan, and Uttar Pradesh. With the exception of Arunachal Pradesh, the GDI values do not dispute this trend. There is significant deprivation in Assam and Arunachal. However, figures for Madhya Pradesh and Rajasthan are no longer as low as those for Bihar or Uttar Pradesh. Having said that, in addition to the North-East region, the most deprived states clearly are Bihar, Jharkhand, Madhya Pradesh, Chhattisgarh, Rajasthan, Uttar Pradesh, and Orissa. Such identification is also mirrored in the poverty ratio, literacy, and infant mortality figures. A recent report by the World Bank on India's progress regarding the MDGs also focuses on these differences between the states. In general, India seems to be on track for the income poverty and hunger goals, at least on a nationwide basis. India also seems to be on track for the educational goals, except for the elimination of gender disparity. However, India is falling behind on the goals for health.

The "Backward" Districts

Variations exist not only between states, but also within them. State boundaries are administrative ones, and development and deprivation do not necessarily follow such administrative criteria. There has therefore been an attempt to also focus on backward districts, as opposed to backward states alone. In collaboration with UNDP, several states have begun to publish *State Human Development Reports* (*SHDRs*). These are "official" *SHDRs*, as opposed to "unofficial" ones published for some states like Rajasthan and West Bengal. There is also another "unofficial" HDR, published regionally (North, South, West, and East) by the National Council of Applied Eco-

TABLE 2

Human development in India

State/Union Territories	HDI (1991)	HDI (2001)	GDI (1991)	Percent below poverty line (1999–2000)	Literacy (in percent) 2001	Infant mortality rate (per thousand) 1991
Andhra Pradesh	0.377	0.416	0.801	15.77	61.11	55
Arunachal Pradesh	0.328	—	0.776	33.47	54.74	91
Assam	0.348	0.386	0.575	36.09	64.28	92
Bihar	0.308	0.367	0.469	42.60	47.53	75
Goa	0.575	—	0.775	4.40	82.32	51
Gujarat	0.431	0.479	0.714	14.07	66.43	78
Haryana	0.443	0.509	0.714	8.74	68.59	52
Himachal Pradesh	0.469	—	0.858	7.63	75.91	82
Jammu and Kashmir	0.402	—	0.740	3.48	54.46	—
Karnataka	0.412	0.478	0.753	20.04	67.04	74
Kerala	0.591	0.638	0.825	12.72	90.92	42
Madhya Pradesh	0.328	0.394	0.662	37.43	64.08	133
Maharashtra	0.452	0.523	0.793	25.02	77.27	74
Manipur	0.536	—	0.815	28.54	68.87	28
Meghalaya	0.365	—	0.807	33.87	63.31	80
Mizoram	0.548	—	0.770	19.47	88.49	53
Nagaland	0.486	—	0.729	32.67	67.11	51
Orissa	0.345	0.404	0.639	47.15	63.61	125
Punjab	0.475	0.537	0.710	6.16	69.95	74
Rajasthan	0.347	0.424	0.692	15.28	61.03	87
Sikkim	0.425	—	0.647	36.55	69.68	60
Tamil Nadu	0.466	0.531	0.813	21.12	73.47	54
Tripura	0.389	—	0.531	34.44	73.66	82
Uttar Pradesh	0.314	0.388	0.520	31.15	57.36	99
West Bengal	0.404	0.472	0.631	27.02	69.22	62
Andaman and Nicobar Islands	0.574	—	0.857	20.99	81.18	69
Chandigarh	0.674	—	0.764	5.75	81.76	48
Dadra and Nagar Haveli	0.361	—	0.832	17.14	60.03	81
Daman and Diu	0.544	—	0.714	4.44	81.09	56
Delhi	0.624	—	0.690	8.23	81.82	54
Lakshadweep	0.532	—	0.680	15.60	87.52	91
Pondicherry	0.571	—	0.783	21.67	81.59	34
Uttaranchal	—	—	—	—	72.28	—
Jharkhand	—	—	—	—	54.13	—
Chhattisgarh	—	—	—	—	65.12	—

Notes: HDI = Human Development Index; GDI = Gender-related Development Index.

SOURCE: Courtesy of author.

nomic Research. Of the "official" reports, ten states have so far published *SHDR*s: Madhya Pradesh (1995, 1998, and 2002); Karnataka (1999, second *HDR* under preparation); Sikkim (2001); Rajasthan (2002); Maharashtra (2002); Himachal Pradesh (2002); Tamil Nadu (2003); Assam (2003); West Bengal (2004); and Nagaland (2004). Eight *SHDR*s are being finalized: Arunachal Pradesh, Chhattisgarh, Gujarat, Manipur, Orissa, Punjab, and Uttar Pradesh. Nine additional *SHDR*s are under preparation: Andhra Pradesh, Delhi, Goa, Jammu and Kashmir, Karnataka (second *HDR*), Kerala, Mizoram, Tripura, and Uttaranchal. Once all these *SHDR*s are available, one will have a better sense of variations within states.

For instance, the World Bank report identifies eighteen regions, corresponding to the regions used by the NSS, where human development is low: Central Bihar,

Vindhya in Madhya Pradesh, Malwa in Madhya Pradesh, southern Madhya Pradesh, northern Madhya Pradesh, southeastern Rajasthan, Tripura, western Uttar Pradesh, eastern Uttar Pradesh, southern Uttar Pradesh, Jharkhand, northern Bihar, central Madhya Pradesh, southern Orissa, central Uttar Pradesh, southern Uttar Pradesh, southwestern Madhya Pradesh, and southern Rajasthan. District-level data are more difficult to acquire than state-level data. Using district-level data linked to the MDGs, a study by Bibek Debroy and Laveesh Bhandari (2003) identified 69 districts (out of a total of 593 districts) that are the most deprived: 26 in Bihar, 13 in Uttar Pradesh, 10 in Jharkhand, 10 in Orissa, 6 in Madhya Pradesh, 3 in Arunachal, and 1 in Karnataka. Geographically, these are contiguous to another 70-odd districts that are also fairly backward. This list is more or less identical to a list of 170 districts that the government has identified as backward and on which it wishes to focus. There is a listing (schedule) of backward tribes, known as scheduled tribes, and another such schedule of backward castes, known as scheduled castes. "Backwardness" is identified on the basis of agricultural wage rates, agricultural productivity, and share of scheduled tribe and scheduled caste populations. Together, scheduled tribes and scheduled castes account for around 25 percent of the population. Scheduled tribes tend to be concentrated in select geographical areas, while scheduled castes are more evenly spread out.

Government focus means increasing the share of educational expenditure to 6 percent of GDP and that on health to 2 or 3 percent of GDP. The present figures are 3.74 percent for education and 1 percent for health. Simultaneously, through decentralization, accountability, transparency, public/private partnerships, and Right to Information Acts, the efficiency of public expenditure will be improved.

Bibek Debroy

See also **Development Politics; Economic Development, Importance of Institutions in and Social Aspects of; Gender and Human Rights; Scheduled Tribes**

BIBLIOGRAPHY

Debroy, Bibek, and Laveesh Bhandari. *District-Level Deprivation in the New Millennium*. Delhi: Rajiv Gandhi Institute for Contemporary Studies and Konark Publishers, 2003.
Government of India. Planning Commission. *National Human Development Report 2001*. Delhi: GOI, March 2002.
Sen, Amartya K. *Development as Freedom*. New York: Oxford University Press, 1999.
United Nations Development Programme. *Human Development Report 2004: Cultural Liberty in Today's Diverse World*. New York: UNDP, 2004.
———. *Investing in Development: A Practical Plan to Achieve the Millennium Development Goals*. UN Millennium Project, directed by Jeffrey D. Sachs. New York: UNDP, 2005.
World Bank. *Attaining the Millennium Development Goals in India: Role of Public Policy and Service Delivery*. Delhi: Oxford University Press and World Bank, June 2004.

HUMAN RIGHTS The term "human rights," denoting universally applicable moral principles as the rights of all people, was until recently not in common usage in India, either as a language of resistance or as a normative principle in matters of governance. Rights were articulated in the course of the anticolonial struggles as civil liberties and democratic rights. These rights were incorporated in the 1950 Constitution of India as Fundamental Rights which were justiciable in the courts of law, and as the

Directive Principles of State Policy. The latter are seen as indicating the general direction in which the expansion of fundamental rights ought to take place in such areas as socioeconomic equality and justice. In the years after independence, numerous movements emerged against caste and class oppression, and in support of development, civil liberties, and democratic rights for all Indians.

The Legal Framework of People's Rights in India

The Constitution of India and specific laws, along with representative and statutory institutions, provide the framework within which the rights of the Indian people become effective. These rights have helped to engender a process of equality in a society long segmented and stratified by caste, feudal, and class hierarchies. Alongside uniform rights the Constitution also recognizes group-differentiated rights. Religious minorities and weaker sectors of society are guaranteed some special safeguards (e.g., the right to freedom of religion). Similarly, the Directive Principles of State Policy (Part IV of the Constitution) direct India's central and state governments to promote socioeconomic conditions in which legal, political, and cultural rights will become substantial. Article 38, for example, directs the state to commit itself to "the welfare of the people" by promoting a "social order" in which "justice—social, economic and political—shall inform all institutions of national life." To achieve this, the state is urged to "strive to minimise inequalities of income" and to "eliminate inequalities in status, facilities and opportunities." Article 46 likewise instructs the state to "promote with special care the educational and economic interests of the weaker sections of the people and in particular, of the Scheduled Castes and Tribes" and "protect them from social injustice and all forms of exploitation." The Directive Principles thus envisage an active role for the state in providing a range of socially ameliorative rights, including access to adequate means of livelihood, equal pay for equal work, living wages for workers, provision of just and humane conditions of work, and the right to education, public assistance, equal justice, free legal aid, and adequate nutrition and health.

There are specific provisions in the Criminal Procedure Code and the Indian Evidence Act that protect people against arbitrary arrests, detention, torture, and use of force by the police. Specific Acts of Parliament have also sought to give protection to disadvantaged social groups. The Protection of Civil Rights Act of 1955 "penalises the preaching and practice of untouchability in any form and prescribes punishment for enforcing any disability arising from untouchability." Similarly, the Scheduled Castes and Scheduled Tribes (Prevention of Atrocities) Act of 1989 provides for special courts for the trial of offenses against

The Disabled Demonstrate for Their Civil Rights. Though it was believed that certain legal protections would unfold after independence and the formulation of a fully democratric constitution, Indian society continues to be deeply fragmented around issues of caste. INDIA TODAY.

members of Scheduled Castes and Tribes and for the relief and rehabilitation of victims of such offenses. Moreover, special institutions have been created by specific acts of Parliament to protect the needs of disadvantaged groups. These include the National Commission for Scheduled Castes and Scheduled Tribes (The Constitution [65th Amendment] Act, 1990); the National Commission for Women (the National Commission for Women Act, 1990); the National Commission for Minorities (the National Commission for Minorities Act, 1992); and the National Commission for Backward Classes (the National Commission for Backward Classes Act, 1993). The Protection of Human Rights Act of 1993 set up a National Human Rights Commission (NHRC), state human rights commissions in states, and human rights courts for improved protection of human rights. Under this act, "human rights" are defined as rights relating to life, liberty, and equality, and to the dignity of the individual, as guaranteed by the Constitution or embodied in international covenants and enforceable by courts in India.

The Practice of Human Rights: Ambivalences and Divergences

The practice of human rights in India has demonstrated both ambivalences and divergences. The institutional structures of the post-colonial Indian state are embedded in liberal Western principles of freedom and equality of individuals, as well as socialist principles of socioeconomic equality. At the same time, however, the social fabric of India continues to be deeply fragmented and segmented by caste, religion, language, class, and gender. Indian democracy, unfolding within the framework of the Constitution, evinced strong strands of egalitarianism and individual and group freedom. Ironically, however, it also incorporated measures that focused on "securing the state" in ways that eroded personal liberties and freedoms. In a manifestation of this "duality of state structures" in India, its democratic strands thus coexist with authoritarianism. Paradoxically, the Fundamental Rights to Freedom (Articles 19–22) in the Constitution contain provisions for "preventive detention," noting conditions under which these rights can be rendered virtually inoperative. Successive governments made extensive use of these constitutional provisions to enact preventive detention and other extraordinary laws to curb political dissent. Moreover, emergency provisions in the Constitution (Articles 352–360) specify certain conditions of "national emergency," during which parts of the Constitution, in particular those relating to the fundamental rights of citizens, may be suspended.

The Preventive Detention Act of 1950, used against the communists in Telengana, was the first such detention law enacted after the adoption of the Constitution. The Indo-China War of 1962 provided another occasion for the vigorous use of preventive detention. The declaration of emergency due to the war enabled the government to promulgate its Defence of India Ordinance of 1962 and to frame rules under it. The official state of emergency persisted until subsequent wars with Pakistan in 1965 and 1971, and the government continued to detain people under the 1962 act. In 1968 the Unlawful Activities (Prevention) Act was passed, turning many emergency powers under the Defence of India Act into statutory law. Under this act, any organization could be declared illegal, and any individual imprisoned for questioning India's sovereignty over any part of its territory. The Preventive Detention Act, renewed seven times, lapsed in 1969. The states, however, continued to enforce their own preventive detention laws. In 1971 Parliament passed the Maintenance of Internal Security Act (MISA). The Defence of India Act of 1971 introduced some changes in MISA, particularly regarding the period of detention, making it more stringent. Indira Gandhi's "National Emergency" of 1975 suspended the right of access to the courts for the restoration of fundamental freedoms. Under such conditions, MISA assumed formidable powers. Certain amendments were subsequently made by the government, which virtually rewrote the act. The Constitution (39th Amendment) Act placed MISA in the ninth schedule of the Constitution, placing it beyond judicial review. The Constitution (42nd Amendment) Act of 1976 further strengthened the powers of the central government by providing that no law for the prevention of antinational activities could be declared invalid on grounds that it violated the fundamental rights in Part III of the Constitution. In 1977 the Janata Party government repealed MISA. It did not, however, repeal the other extraordinary laws that had been enacted by earlier governments, including the Armed Forces Special Powers Act and the Unlawful Activities (Prevention) Act. Preventive detention laws continued to be enacted by different political parties in power in the states of Madhya Pradesh, Jammu and Kashmir, Bihar, and Orissa. When the Congress Party returned to power, the National Security Act (NSA) of 1980 was enacted, followed in 1985 by the Terrorist and Disruptive Activities (Prevention) Act (TADA) of 1985 and 1987. TADA lapsed in 1995, but in 2002 the coalition government led by the Bharatiya Janata Party pushed through the Prevention of Terrorism Act (POTA) in an extraordinary joint session of Parliament. In December 2004 the new coalition government of the United Progressive Alliance led by the Congress Party of India fulfilled its election promise and repealed POTA. Several provisions of POTA were, however, retained through amendment in the Unlawful Activities Prevention Act, 2004.

Successive Indian governments have deployed extra-constitutional measures, euphemized as "encounters" and "disappearances" to counter insurgencies or class conflicts—for example, against the Naxalites, as the Marxist-Leninist guerrilla organizations are called, against the Khalistan secessionists in Punjab in the 1980s, and against Muslim secessionists in Kashmir since the 1990s. Moreover, the Northeast states of India, in a continuation of British colonial policy, have been viewed as a frontier region, a land to be buttressed and militarily secured. In this view, the specificity of the region as well as differences among the people of the area were overlooked, and the Northeast was construed as a homogenous territorial unit, disturbed and dangerous, control of which was imperative for strategic reasons. Thus movements for self-determination and autonomy in various parts of the region, and struggles grounded in issues of underdevelopment, illegal migrations, questions of identity, and political rights were addressed by the central government with its coercive might in the form of counterinsurgency measures, backed by laws like the Armed Forces (Special Powers) Act of 1958.

Custodial violence is yet another violation of the right to life and liberty of citizens at the hands of the state. Torture, rape, and deaths in custody have been reported in large numbers. While campaigns by civil rights groups and dissemination by newspapers have brought these violations to public notice, the procedure of redemption in these cases, including prosecution and compensation to families of victims, most of whom are poor, remains painfully slow. The NHRC's annual report for the year 2001–2002 cites 165 deaths in police custody and 1,140 deaths in judicial custody.

Another area of human rights violations are crimes perpetrated by dominant sections of the population against marginalized groups. Recent cases of upper caste violence in Haryana, Punjab, and Bihar demonstrate how the fundamental rights of the Constitution are regularly thwarted by the complex hierarchical structures of Indian society. The lynching of Dalits (formerly called "untouchables") by upper caste villagers and members of the Vishwa Hindu Parishad in the Dulina district of

Haryana in October 2002, for example, reveals that the vulnerability of Dalits involved in the leather trade was increased by police threats to implicate them under the Prohibition of Cow Slaughter Act. The shocking pattern of communal violence and murder of Muslims in Gujarat in February 2002 shows a collusion of the state government in acts of brutal violence and its justification by the political leaders of the state.

In all cases of mass violence, as in Gujarat, women suffer directly as victims of rape; they also suffer indirectly when rendered destitute or homeless by displacement, loss of livelihood or the death of wage-earning family members. Another constant problem is sexual harassment at the workplace. Despite guidelines issued by the Supreme Court in 1997 in the Vishakha case, in most places of work there is no attempt to prohibit or punish harassment.

Movements for the Expansion of Rights in India

The concept of rights has progressively widened as a result of popular struggles to include rights not mentioned in India's existing legal-constitutional framework. The right of access to the means of subsistence and control over resources for peasants, the right of indigenous people to their cultural resources, environment, and livelihood, the right to a humane environment and humane development are some of the rights that have emerged as a result of people's movements. The Narmada Bachao Andolan, for example, has sustained a prolonged struggle against the building of the Sardar Sarovar Dam on the River Narmada. The large number of people displaced by its construction has not only raised significant issues pertaining to people's rights, but has also subjected state development projects to greater scrutiny. Similar movements against large dams are seen in other places, including the Tehri region of Uttaranchal. Experiences with development projects and popular struggles have also shown that while these movements have succeeded in raising consciousness about human rights, they have also borne the brunt of state repression. Similar issues of access to resources and claims to a traditional environment and livelihood have been raised in the context of attempts by the state to appropriate forests, which would prevent local people from exercising their claims to the forest and its resources, as in the Chipko movement in what is now the state of Uttaranchal.

It is important to note that a vibrant civil rights movement has developed in India. In a 1982 judgment (*People's Union for Democratic Rights v. Union of India*, AIR 1982 SC 1473), the Supreme Court held that nonpayment of minimum wages to workers amounted to denial of their right to live with basic human dignity, violating Article 21 of the Constitution, which guarantees to every Indian

citizen the fundamental right to life and personal liberty. It is also important to note that the origins of the civil rights movement in India is often traced to the formation of the Indian Civil Liberties Union (ICLU) in Bombay on 24 August 1936 under the initiative of Jawaharlal Nehru, with Rabindranath Tagore as its president, Sarojini Naidu its working president, and other prominent nationalist leaders as members. "The idea of civil liberties," said Nehru in his address to the founding conference of the ICLU, "is to have the right to oppose the government." The ICLU investigated cases of political imprisonment and harassment, police brutalities, bans and restrictions on citizens' and subjects' rights by the British colonial government and by the rulers of the princely states, publishing reports and lodging protests on the basis of its investigations.

After independence in 1947, and with the adoption of a republican constitution, many nationalists' concerns for civil liberties diminished or disappeared. Nationalists who had once vehemently espoused the right to oppose the government now evinced an overriding anxiety over protecting the infant state. Communists involved in peasant movements in the Telengana region of Andhra Pradesh and Tebhaga in West Bengal took the initiative to reorganize the civil rights movement. The Civil Liberties Committee (CLC) was formed in West Bengal in 1948 with the support of renowned intellectuals. It was in this phase that the movement had to face a conceptual dilemma that lingers to this day—the question of political violence. Working on the assumption that state violence was more harmful to civil society than that practiced by revolutionaries, the CLC took the stand that the primary task of the movement was to oppose the authoritarian tendencies of the state and to see that the state did not assume arbitrary powers or move beyond the boundaries set by law.

In 1971 elections the Congress government of Indira Gandhi was reelected, riding high on her populist slogan of "eliminate poverty." The next few years, however, saw the promise of radical change based on economic growth and equitable redistribution slip away. The Congress government faced massive opposition in Bihar, which threatened to assume nationwide proportions, while a similar movement against the imposition of central rule loomed large in Gujarat. Under the Emergency Provisions of the Constitution, Prime Minister Gandhi armed the government with extraordinary powers, proclaiming a "National Emergency," which lasted from June 1975 to 1977. In the pre-Emergency period, the civil rights movement had remained an appendage to one or another regional struggle. While concerns for civil rights were generated in the course of these struggles, these concerns remained at the periphery of those political struggles.

The National Emergency, unlike state repression of struggles in earlier years, caught in its web large numbers of those functioning within the parameters of parliamentary politics, irrespective of their ideological leanings. The Emergency thus shook the urban middle class intelligentsia out of its complacency regarding the durability of the democratic processes. The shared experience of repression generated a sympathetic perception by liberal groups of the more radical groups, while alerting sections of the latter to the importance of constitutional values. This experience shaped the intellectual and political context that led to the emergence of an autonomous civil rights movement. Regional organizations, notably the Andhra Pradesh Civil Liberties Committee, the Association for the Protection of Democratic Rights, the Committee for the Protection of Democratic Rights, the Organisation for the Protection of Democratic Rights, and, at the national level, the People's Union for Civil Liberties and Democratic Rights, all of which were formed either before or during the Emergency, acquired national attention and support.

In addition to civil liberties and democratic rights groups, people's tribunals, human rights commissions, and citizen's initiatives have also investigated specific events. For instance, the Indian People's Human Rights Tribunal, under Justice V. R. Krishna Iyer, was set up by the People's Human Rights Commission on 10 January 1987 in the aftermath of the 1984 massacre of Sikhs in Delhi and in other parts of the country, following the inaction of the government to bring the guilty to justice. The Human Rights Commission consisted of a number of prominent persons, including V. M. Tarkunde, Mrinal Sen, Rajni Kothari, and Romila Thapar. The main objective of the commission was to establish and maintain the Human Rights Tribunal comprising ex-judges of the Supreme Court and the high courts.

In 1993, amid growing domestic concerns over human rights abuses in different parts of the country—particularly the Northeast, Punjab, and Jammu and Kashmir—and international pressures for greater governmental accountability, the Protection of Human Rights Act was finally passed. The act provided for "the constitution of a National Human Rights Commission, State Human Rights Commissions in States and Human Rights Courts for better protection of human rights and for matters connected therewith or incidental thereto." The seminars held at Mumbai, Delhi, Hyderabad, and Kolkata to elicit public opinion on the National Human Rights Commission Bill were, however, strictly official affairs, and very few individuals apart from officials and ministers were invited, giving rise to apprehensions that the NHRC might be yet another attempt to dampen opposition to civil rights violations in India. While various other national commissions, including those on women, minorities, and scheduled castes and tribes, have been made ex-officio members of the commission, the NHRC has been explicitly precluded from taking up cases pending before other commissions, which effectively removes many matters from its purview and limits the scope of its investigations. In its actual working, however, the NHRC has made several significant interventions. It filed a Public Interest Litigation in the Supreme Court, seeking to enforce the rights of the 65,000 Chakma tribals who were being persecuted in Arunachal Pradesh (*National Human Rights Commission v. State of Arunachal Pradesh* Writ Petition [Civil] No. 720 of 1995, SC 295, 1996, 49435.). The NHRC also opposed the Prevention of Terrorism Ordinance and Bill for its ramifications for the promotion and protection of human rights, but with little success. Most recently, it intervened in the Gujarat cases stemming out of the many murders of Muslims in that state in February 2002.

Ujjwal Kumar Singh

See also **Ethnic Conflict; Gandhi, Indira; Gender and Human Rights**

BIBLIOGRAPHY

Anderson, Michael R., and Sumit Guha, eds. *Changing Concepts of Rights and Justice in South Asia.* Kolkata and New York: Oxford University Press, 1998.

Desai, A. R., ed. *Violation of Democratic Rights in India.* Mumbai: Popular Prakashan, 1986.

Expanding Government Lawlessness and Organised Struggles. Mumbai: Popular Prakashan, 1991.

Gopalan, S. *India and Human Rights.* New Delhi: Lok Sabha Secretariat, 1998. Provides details of specific acts of Parliament and constitutional provisions pertaining to human rights.

Kothari, Smitu, and Harsh Sethi, eds. *Rethinking Human Rights.* Delhi: Lokayan, 1991.

Mohanty, Manoranjan, Partha Nath Mukherji, and Olle Tranquist, eds. *People's Rights: Social Movements and the State in the Third World.* New Delhi and Thousand Oaks, Calif.: Sage, 1997.

Prakash, Louis, and R. Vashum, eds. *Extraordinary Laws in India.* New Delhi: Indian Social Science Institute, 2002.

HUMAYUN *(1508–1556), Mughal emperor (1530–1540, 1555–1556).* Born Nasin-ud-din Muhammad in Kabul, Afghanistan, Humayun was the second Mughal emperor of India. In his youth he participated in the Battle of Panipat in 1526 with which his father, Babur, began his conquest of India. Humayun served as governor of Kabul for his father, returning to India shortly before Babur's death. He inherited an empire in name only, appointing his four brothers governors of its provinces, though two of them, Kamran and Askari, combined to deprive him of the Punjab. A Sur Afghan, Sher Shah, leader of the Afghan resistance to the Mughals, controlled Bihar. In 1532 Humayun besieged him at Chunar but did not capture him. Humayun's predicament was worsened by his bouts of lethargy, caused by his increasing addiction to opium, and the threat to his position from his brothers. He invaded Gujarat in 1535, but it was brought under Mughal control only after the death of Bahadur Shah in 1537 at the hands of the Portuguese. That same year, Sher Khan invaded and captured Bengal. Humayun marched east to confront him, but Sher Khan defeated Humayun in battle at Chausa on the Ganges in 1539, assuming the title of Sher Shah, and at Kannauj in 1540, after which Humayun fled for his life, becoming a homeless wanderer in Sind and Rajasthan.

While in Sind in 1542, Humayun's wife gave birth to his son Akbar, the true founder of the Mughal empire. Humayun arrived in Persia in 1544 with a few hundred followers and came under the protection of the Safavid ruler, Shah Tamasp, who gave him support when he converted Shi'ism. With this Persian military assistance Humayun captured Kandahar in 1545, which he had promised to return to Persia, and Kabul in 1553, after three campaigns over an eight-year period against his brother Kamran.

After the death of Sher Shah in May 1545, his son Islam Shah Sur ruled until 1553. After his death, the empire was split into four parts ruled by different relatives, and his young son Firuz was murdered by his maternal uncle. Humayun took advantage of this war and of the growing popular dissatisfaction with Sur rule due to famine, invading India. He captured Lahore in February 1555 and then defeated Sikander Sur, the Afghan ruler of the Punjab, at Sirhind, after which he recovered Delhi and Agra. Once again he was emperor of India. The following year, however, he died after accidentally falling down the stone stairs of his observatory at Purana Qila, which led to the quip, "He stumbled out of life as he had stumbled through it."

Roger D. Long

See also **Akbar; Babur**

BIBLIOGRAPHY

Eraly, Abraham. *The Last Spring: The Lives and Times of the Great Mughals.* New Delhi: Viking, 1997.
Richards, John F. *The Mughal Empire.* Cambridge, U.K.: Cambridge University Press, 1993.

HUME, A. O. *See* **History and Historiography.**

HUNAS. *See* **History and Historiography.**

HYDERABAD Hyderabad State, named for the city long the cosmopolitan capital of kingdoms in India's Deccan plateau, developed autonomy from the Mughal empire in the second half of the eighteenth century and ended only in 1948. India became independent in 1947, and in 1948 Hyderabad State was incorporated into it, acquiring a new national language, Hindi (Hindustani written in Sanskrit script). In 1956 the federal reorganization of Indian states along linguistic lines made Hyderabad city the capital of the Telugu-speaking state of Andhra Pradesh. (The former state's Kannada-speaking districts went to Karnataka and the Marathi-speaking districts, in 1960, to Maharashtra.) The offical state language is Telugu, although English continues to be used for many administrative and educational purposes.

Deccani and Mughal Origins

The state changed orientation over time, pulled by political engagements with powerful neighbors. Nizām al-Mulk, the Mughal nizam, or governor, of the Deccan province in the early eighteenth century, ruled by military force from his capital city of Aurangabad in the western Marathi-speaking region of the Deccan. But the expanding Maratha power in the western Deccan—under Shivaji's successors, the Peshwas—was not the nizam's only regional competitor. The rise of new powers in Mysore and Madras and the increasing activities of the French and English trading companies heightened diplomatic and military competition in southern India. Nizām al-Mulk Asaf Jah I maintained nominal allegiance to the Mughals in Delhi, but he and his successors had established a separate dynasty by the end of the eighteenth century.

Nizām Ali Khan Asaf Jah II, who reigned from 1762 to 1803, stabilized the state. Under him, the capital moved from Aurangabad to Hyderabad, reflecting pressures from the Marathas in the west and from Tipu Sultan in Mysore. Aurangabad and Hyderabad remained, however, almost equally important until the end of the century. Then Hyderabad, an attractive, well-planned administrative city for the Qutb Shahi dynasty in the late sixteenth century, was rebuilt, resettled, and became truly hegemonic.

Hyderabad city began when the Kakatiya Hindu rajas of Warangal established Golconda fort just north of the Musi river by the thirteenth century. In 1364 Golconda passed to the control of the Bahmanis (Shi'a Muslim kings of Iranian ancestry). By 1530 the Bahmani kingdom had split into five Deccani sultanates, with the Qutb Shahi dynasty ruling from Golconda fort. Hyderabad city developed south of the river across from the fort. A bridge was built across the Musi in 1578, but the city's traditional founding date is 1591, when the landmark Char Minar was constructed during the reign of Muhammad Quli Qutb Shah. Popular belief credits Quli Qutb Shah's

The Hyderabad nobility in the eighteenth century was a military one, based on the collection and deployment of resources for warfare. Leading nobles dispensed highly personal patronage. *Vakil*s, or diplomatic agents, were crucial to the patron-client system of the time. Mughal *vakil*s were more prominent in the eighteenth century, followed by those of the Maratha Peshwa, the Peshwa's nominal subordinates, chiefs Scindia and Holkar, and the *nawāb* of Arcot in the late eighteenth century. Securing land revenue and loans from bankers then became important to the state, and the Mughal bureaucracy grew, supporting Hindus and Muslims alike as part of the growing state establishment centered in Hyderabad city. The nizam's household establishment, the Sarf-i-Khas, eventually grew as well, employing many in the city of Hyderabad. Hindus were high-ranking members of the military, revenue, and household administrations, although Muslims were the majority among the nobles of the state.

The culture of both city and state expanded as the Deccani urban culture of the Shi'a Muslim Qutb Shahis—modeled on that of Persia, but with many Telugu-speakers in the ruling class—incorporated the Mughal or Indo-Persian northern court culture and those who brought it. Muharram, the Shi'a commemoration of the martyrdom of Hasan and Husain in 680, continued to be a major public observance. Under the Sunni Muslim nizams, many new men, speakers of Marathi, Kannada, Telugu, and Urdu, entered the ruling class. Other new participants in Deccani politics were the French and British East India companies, contending with each other on Indian soil and giving European military training and arms to Indian soldiers. The nizam eventually lost Machilipatnam, Hyderabad's seaport, to the British East India Company, and the latter, victorious over the French, forced the nizams to sign successive treaties of "subsidiary alliance" in the later eighteenth century. The second largest "native state" in India, Hyderabad remained independent of direct British control, but a British cantonment settled in the hamlet of Secunderabad and a British resident (political representative of the British East India Company and later of the British government) settled in Hyderabad north of the river.

The Influence of British India

With expansion to the north, a second phase of urban development began, the twin cities now being Hyderabad and Secunderabad. The British Residency secured economic concessions for the adjacent Residency Bazaar, attracting many merchants and bankers. A powerful *diwan*, or prime minister, Sir Salar Jung (1853–1883), recruited modern administrators from British India and initiated modernizing projects, such as, in 1874, a railroad linking Hyderabad to Bombay and the British Indian economy.

Street Vendors in Hyderabad. Hyderabad's urban services were good in the mid-twentieth century, but the rising population since then has severely taxed the city's resources. In this 2003 photo, street vendors sell their wares in front of a crumbling colonial edifice. CHRIS LISLE / CORBIS.

founding of the new city to his love for a Hindu dancing girl, Bhagmati, who lived south of the river, and the city was first known as Bhagnagar (after her, or, in other versions, "city of gardens"). After Quli Qutb Shah married her, Bhagmati was renamed Hyder Mahal and the city was renamed Hyderabad. In this first phase, Hyderabad city was closely tied to Golconda fort and its surrounding area, particularly Karwan, where the leading bankers lived.

In 1687 the Mughal emperor Aurangzeb conquered Golconda fort and incorporated the Deccan into his empire. From the 1760s, as the first nizam's successors shifted the capital back to Hyderabad, the great palaces of the nizam and his nobles revitalized the city. Major gates in its walls led to Machilipatnam, the seaport on the eastern coast, and Delhi, the Mughal capital. To the city's south, the establishments of the nizam's military officers formed rural outposts, with weapons stored in their extensive gardens. Other gardens at the city's boundaries housed Hindu temples or Muslim graveyards.

The nizams built a palace near the Residency, and movement from the old walled city to the new Hyderabad accelerated. At the same time, Salar Jung protected the old Mughal administration and its employees in the old city from the new British-patterned administration and its high-ranking employees based in the new city.

As the city sprawled over the boulder-strewn fields and hills along both banks of the Musi River, three historically distinct zones developed in the metropolitan area: old Hyderabad (the walled city dating from the sixteenth century, south of the river); new Hyderabad (north of the river); and Secunderabad (developed from a British cantonment in the early nineteenth century, north of Hussain Sagar Tank or lake). In the nineteenth century, the old walled city fell behind the modernizing new Hyderabad, yet even in the newer city the pace of change was slow. Hyderabad was under a *kotwal* (the Mughal equivalent of a police commissioner, city magistrate, and municipal commissioner) appointed by the nizam until 1869, when a department of municipal and road maintenance was created, which included a municipal commissioner. Hyderabad under the nizams did feature much lower taxes than British India, but this advantage was offset by the delayed development and low level of municipal politics. The 1934 introduction of limited municipal elections, modeled on the 1884 Bombay municipal reforms, came too late to produce experienced local politicians by 1948. Hyderabad city's urban services and general condition in the 1940s were relatively quite good, but the rising population since then has severely taxed the city's resources and services.

Hyderabad State introduced reforms in its judicial and educational systems in the late nineteenth century. In the 1870s, a modern Anglo-Indian legal system replaced the Mughal judicial system, and, in the 1890s, a High Court on the British Indian model was established. The modern educational system began in 1883 and 1884 with vernacular primary and secondary schools in the state's four major languages. These fed into the small and elite English-language Nizam College, affiliated to Madras University in British India in 1886 and 1887. The innovative founding of the Urdu-language Osmania University in 1918 sought to educate more of Hyderabad's youth and equip them for administrative service, using the state's official language and emphasizing its independence from British India. *Purdah*, or the seclusion of women, marked most higher educational institutions until 1948, when it was abolished in Osmania University and elsewhere. The new federal University of Hyderabad was established in the 1980s just outside the city, placing the city firmly on the all-India educational map.

While Hyderabad State fell into the colonial "indirect rule" category during the British period, historians of the princely or native states have found that Hyderabad, the second largest and most populous such state, resisted conforming to patterns typical of other such states. The East India Company had a resident in Hyderabad, but the governor-general and the Madras Council contended over issues within the state, and often the resident and the company were also at odds. For various reasons, Hyderabad had more consistent internal policies and more independence from the resident in the nineteenth century, and Hyderabad's nobility remained dependent upon royal, not British, favor. Difficulties specific to Hyderabad continued in the twentieth century. The seventh and last nizam, Osman Ali Khan, often did not fulfill British wishes or did so for what can easily be seen as his own reasons. Most notably perhaps, in 1917 and 1918, the nizam refused to be associated with those other rulers working toward constitutional arrangements and a Chamber of Princes. Also, again and again the nizam raised the question of "the return of the Berars," referring to the mid-nineteenth century subsidiary alliance treaty ceding that rich province to the British East India Company to support a company-led military force; this issue clearly deflected the nizam's attention from what was going on in the rest of India and led to the state's isolation from the nationalist movement, though it was eventually incorporated into modern India.

Politics in Hyderabad really moved beyond court circles only in the 1930s, when the Indian nationalist movement against British rule finally brought political turmoil into the city. Even in 1947, when India and Pakistan became independent, the nizam thought he could retain his autonomy. He failed to negotiate seriously with India, precipitating the Indian army "Police Action" of 1948, which brought Hyderabad State into the Indian Union. Another rupture came in 1956, when India's reorganization of states along linguistic lines dismembered the old trilinguistic state. Hyderabad city and the Telingana districts were united with the Telugu-speaking districts formerly under British rule and oriented toward Madras city, and Hyderabad became the capital of Andhra Pradesh.

Hyderabad State's history is reflected in its architecture, cuisine, and linguistic and religious diversity. From the fourteenth to the nineteenth centuries in this part of India, successive Muslim-ruled dynasties had promoted Persian as the state language, while the peasants in Hyderabad city's hinterland came from three linguistic backgrounds, Marathi, Telugu, and Kannada (the first an Indo-Aryan language, the latter two Dravidian or South Indian languages). In the city itself, the lingua franca was Urdu or Hindustani, a language developed first in the Deccan under Shi'a Muslim rulers and then in North India under the Mughals. Its structure is derived from the Indo-Aryan or Sanskritic languages of North India; Urdu has many Persian words, and it is written in Perso-Arabic

Chowmohalla Palace, Hyderabad. The palace before its 2002 (recently completed) facelift. Built in 1750 by Nizam Salabat Jung and designed along the lines of the shah's palace in Teheran. INDIA TODAY.

script. Urdu replaced Persian as the official language of Hyderabad State in 1884, and English became important then, too, because of the hegemonic influence of British India and the British-trained Indians recruited to the Hyderabad administration.

Present-Day Hyderabad

Hyderabad State boundaries were dismembered in 1956, but the city continued to have a cosmopolitan population, although the ruling class has shifted its composition over time. It has shifted from mostly Muslim to mostly Hindu, and its languages have changed from Persian and Urdu to Telugu and English. While Hindus are scattered throughout the city, Muslims and Christians are clustered: almost two-thirds of the old city is Muslim; one-fifth of Secunderabad is Christian. Speakers of Telugu are the majority, but sizable numbers of people speak Tamil, Sindi, Gujarati, Marathi, Malayalam, and Kannada, as well as Urdu. The city population has grown steadily since 1881, when it had 367,417 people, to some 5 million at the start of the twenty-first century (save for a 19 percent decline from 1911 to 1921 due to the 1918 plague epidemic). After the formation of Andhra Pradesh, rural to urban migration increased greatly, and extensive industrialization began in the late 1950s. There was some Muslim out-migration, but most immigrants were Hindu Telugu-speakers, some of them replacing departing Muslims in the old city and increasing tensions there. Average population density has been highest in the oldest parts of the walled city, in Secunderabad, and in Hyderabad's economic center just north of the river.

Hyderabad city, arguably more than any city in India, combines features from India's north and south, its Muslim and Hindu peoples, in an urban culture that has always been strikingly cosmopolitan. Hyderabadi cuisine featured Mughal dishes with a Deccani flavor, a touch of tamarind in the lentils, a special rich *biryani*, slow-roasted kebabs, delicious thick-sauced eggplant and green chili dishes (*begara began* and *mirch ka salan*). As in Central Asia and Mughal India, people used to sit on the floor around a *dasturkhana*, or tablecloth, eating with their hands, or, if South Indian, eating from banana leaves spread on the ground or table. South Indian Brahman vegetarian restaurants and Persian tea houses were always there, and spicy coastal Andhra food has come to Hyderabad since 1956.

The defining features of the present city evoke competing versions of the past. Major buildings from the nizam's period, especially those so proudly constructed in the early twentieth century (the High Court, Osmania Hospital, Osmania University, the State Legislature) are still much in evidence. However, the harmonious Mughal design they imposed on the city has been broken by new buildings and monuments as the government of Andhra Pradesh tries to re-create a past reaching back to Buddhism and Hinduism. Andhra's chief minister in the early 1990s, the film star N. T. Rama Rao, installed a huge statue of the Buddha in Hussain Sagar Tank (lake). The new Telugu University has changed the look of the public gardens, its bold, powerful lines suggesting South Indian Hindu temples and contrasting with the earlier, lighter Indo-Saracenic buildings. Along the Tank Bund road from Hyderabad to Secunderabad stand many statues erected by the state government. Almost all are of cultural heroes from coastal Andhra; the last nizam, Osman Ali Khan, and Hyderabad's great nineteenth-century *diwan* (prime minister), Sir Salar Jung, are not included.

The assumption of political power by Andhra's peasant castes has reoriented the city to the eastern coastal districts and to Delhi, India's capital, and the wider world. However, internal differences still reflect the region's history. Development policies favoring the newer urban areas and the coastal regions of the state reflect the still-unsuccessful integration of the former Hyderabadis and the Andhras, and resentment is particularly acute among long-standing residents of the capital city. Hyderabad State ended in 1956, but Hyderabad city still features a Deccani or regional dialect of Urdu, a distinctive cuisine and style of dress, and a leisurely sense of time. The popular culture of earlier days combined Shiʿa Muslim commemorations with Mughal or Indo-Persian court and literary traditions, and this has been overlaid with British Indian culture and Telugu South Indian culture. Hyderabad State's legacy to modern India might be its cosmopolitanism, best exemplified in Hyderabad city, and its political culture that linked people across caste and community lines.

Karen Leonard

BIBLIOGRAPHY

Bawa, Vasant K. *The Nizam between Mughals and British: Hyderabad under Sir Salar Jung.* New Delhi: S. Chand, 1986.

Bilgrami, Syed Hussain, and C. Willmott. *Historical and Descriptive Sketch of the Nizam's Dominions.* 2 vols. Mumbai, 1883.

Briggs, Henry George. *The Nizam: His History and Relations with the British Government.* 2 vols. London: B. Quaritch, 1861.

Fraser, Hastings. *Our Faithful Ally, the Nizam.* 1865. Reprint, Delhi: Modern Publishers, 1985.

Khan, Yusuf Husain. *The First Nizam.* 2nd ed. New York: Asia Publishing House, 1963.

Leonard, Karen. *Social History of an Indian Caste: The Kayasths of Hyderabad.* Berkeley: University of California Press, 1978.

Safrani, Shehbaz H., ed. *Golconda and Hyderabad.* Mumbai: Marg Publishers, 1992.

ILBERT, SIR COURTNEY. *See* **British Crown Raj; Ripon, Lord.**

INDIAN ADMINISTRATIVE SERVICE (IAS). *See* **Political System.**

INDIAN CIVIL SERVICE (ICS), BRITISH. *See* **British Crown Raj.**

INDIAN INSTITUTES OF TECHNOLOGY (IITs) In 1945 the government of India, on the initiative of Sir Ardeshir Dalal, appointed a twenty-two-member committee of industrialists, scientists, and educators, under the chairmanship of N. R. Sarkar, to consider the development of higher technical institutions in India, with the goal of ensuring an adequate supply of technical personnel for India's industrial development. The committee recommended the establishment of at least four "higher technical institutions"—one each in the north, south, east, and west—with the first to be located near Calcutta (Kolkata) and another near Bombay (Mumbai). These institutions were possibly to be modeled after the Massachusetts Institute of Technology (MIT).

In May 1950, Sir J. C. Ghosh, who succeeded Sir C. V. Raman as director of the Indian Institute of Science, Bangalore, was appointed founding director for the first such institute. Named the Indian Institute of Technology (ITT), Kharagpur, it was inaugurated at Kharagpur in West Bengal on 18 August 1951 by Maulana Abul Kalam Azad, minister of education. Prime Minister Jawaharlal Nehru laid the cornerstone on 3 March 1952, and formally opened the institute on 21 April 1956. On the occasion of the convocation of the first graduates of IIT Kharagpur on 15 September 1956, the Indian Parliament passed the Indian Institute of Technology (Kharagpur) Act, declaring it an "Institute of National Importance."

IIT Kharagpur remains the largest of the seven IITs in India. With 19 academic departments, 8 academic centers and schools, and 9 research centers, it offers 22 undergraduate and 63 postgraduate and doctoral programs in almost all branches of engineering and technology. It has the largest technical library in Asia and one of the largest computing facilities in the country.

In 1958 the second Indian Institute of Technology was founded in Bombay, in collaboration with the former Soviet Union. IIT Madras (Chennai) was established in 1959, in collaboration with West Germany, and in 1960, IIT Kanpur was set up in collaboration with a few top American universities, led by MIT. In 1963, IIT Delhi was established by upgrading the College of Engineering and Technology, which had been created in 1961 at Hauz Khas, New Delhi, with British collaboration. The Indian Parliament passed an act in 1961 (which has been amended a few times, most recently in March 2002), known as the Institutes of Technology Act, which declared each IIT an "Institution of National Importance."

In 1995 the sixth IIT was established at Guwahati in Assam, located in a picturesque campus near the Brahmaputra River. Unlike the earlier institutes, IIT Guwahati had no formal collaboration with any other country, since by that time the IIT system was strong enough to assist in its own growth. IIT Guwahati was created as a part of the Assam Accord reached by Prime Minister Rajiv Gandhi with local leaders for the development of the Northeast region of India.

On 21 September 2001, through an ordinance by the president of India, the oldest technical institute of India, the University of Roorkee, was upgraded to an IIT and was renamed the Indian Institute of Technology, Roorkee, in the newly created state of Uttaranchal. The newest IIT of India is therefore also the oldest technical institution, with more than 156 years of service.

The Admission Process

The IITs are known for their rigorous admission process, which attracts high-achieving Indian students. The academic and research programs of these institutes are comparable to those of leading institutions worldwide. Undergraduate admissions are conducted through a joint entrance examination, and postgraduate admissions mainly through the Graduate Aptitude Test in Engineering (GATE). Only about 2 percent of those students who take the screening tests are admitted to the seven IITs. Recently a joint admission test has been initiated for admission to the master of science programs in various sciences and mathematics, and another for admission to the master of business administration programs in the IITs.

At the undergraduate level, a four-year degree program leading to a bachelor of technology (B.Tech.) degree in various branches of engineering at the seven IITs requires that candidates pass a qualifying examination in science and mathematics. IIT Kharagpur and IIT Roorkee also offer a five-year bachelor of architecture (B.Arch.) program. At the graduate level, the admission requirements are a bachelor's degree in engineering (and in some programs a master's degree in science) in addition to passing the GATE, which is a prerequisite for receiving financial assistance from the government. Admission to doctoral (Ph.D.) programs in all IITs are handled at the institute level.

Vision and Development

Each IIT may have its own statement of its vision, mission, and core values, but all share a common theme. These statements are essentially excellence driven, holistic in scope, covering education, research, and outreach, emphasizing national relevance yet global understanding, nurturing academic freedom, creativity, innovation, integrity, and the overall development of their students. Quality in all its endeavors is the hallmark of the IIT system.

IIT Delhi has created a Foundation for Innovation and Technology Transfer, which has established Technology and Business Incubation units to facilitate research ideas and their development into products. IIT Kharagpur and Roorkee have Science and Technology

Entrepreneurship Parks. All other IITs also have institutional mechanisms to promote entrepreneurship and technology transfer. IIT Madras has made notable contributions to technology transfer in the area of communications systems.

The governance of each IIT is essentially comparable. The president of India is the ex-officio visitor of each. The minister of human resource development of the government of India is the ex-officio chairman of the Council of IITs, which deliberates on policy issues common to all IITs. Each IIT has a board of governors, with a part-time honorary chairman and a full-time director appointed by the IIT Council with approval of the visitor. The director is the chairman of the Senate, which is the apex body for all academic policy matters, with each professor of the institute serving as an ex-officio member. There are deans for various academic and administrative functions, as well as faculty boards and research committees. At the lower level, the governance structure may vary at each IIT, as determined by their respective board of governors and Senate. The director of the institute is the principal academic and executive officer, similar to the vice-chancellor or president of a university. The registrar is secretary of the Senate and the Board of Governors.

Engineering Education and the Growth of Technology

Engineering education in India has seen exponential growth since the 1990s, after the All-India Council for Technical Education became a statutory body, empowered by an act of Parliament in 1987 to control the quality of technical education. Over 1,200 degree-awarding engineering colleges exist in various parts of India, admitting some 380,000 students every year. There are, however, regional and discipline imbalances, with an overconcentration of these colleges in certain states and in certain branches of engineering, mostly electronics, computer science, and information technology. There is also an acute shortage of qualified faculty in many engineering colleges.

However, the seven IITs have a capacity of about four thousand students admitted annually, and the quality of their graduates is comparable to the best in the world. There are also eighteen National Institutes of Technology (NITs) in modern India, and several other very good technical universities and institutes. The number of graduate programs in IITs varies from 25 to 55, with over five hundred research students enrolled for doctoral studies.

During more than fifty years of existence, IITs have played a very important role in India's technological development. Their graduates have contributed to government departments, including public works, irrigation, power, railways, highways, and space research, as well as in the private sector for manufacturing and service. Current trends indicate that IIT graduates prefer to join private sector or multinational corporations, with relatively fewer opting for the public sector. About 10 percent of these graduates become entrepreneurs, and 20 percent go abroad for higher studies and research, mostly to the United States. IITs's contributions to research and development laboratories and educational institutions in India is enormous, as nearly 60 percent of those holding doctoral degrees in engineering and technology come from the IIT system, as do nearly 45 percent of those holding master of technology degrees in engineering and technology. In the corporate sector, both nationally and internationally, IIT alumni have made enormous contributions, and have risen to leadership positions at corporations, laboratories, and university departments. Many have reached senior positions in government, technical institutions, and universities as secretaries, directors, and vice-chancellors.

IIT graduates have also contributed to entrepreneurship and technology development in the United States, particularly in the Silicon Valley, working for organizations such as IBM, Microsoft, Intel, Texas Instruments, General Electric, Motorola, Boeing, Ford, General Motors, Bell Labs, and the National Aeronautics and Space Administration. Many of them are senior professors in American universities and technical institutes, or hold top management positions in U.S. corporations. There are an estimated 30,000 IIT graduates contributing to economic development in the United States.

A study of IIT Kharagpur alumni who graduated between 1982 and 1991 found that of 28 percent who went abroad, about 24 percent were in the United States and Canada. About 50 percent of the alumni had taken higher degrees after graduation, half of them in management. About 8 percent of these alumni had reached top positions by 1994, when the survey was conducted.

Prem Vrat

See also **Information and Other Technology Development; Scientists of Indian Origin and Their Contributions**

BIBLIOGRAPHY

The Institutes of Technology Act, 1961. Roorkee: Indian Institute of Technology, 2002.
Pant, Ranjan, and Suvarana Rajguru. *IIT: India's Intellectual Treasures.* Silver Spring, Md.: Indus Media, 2003.
A Walk through History: 50 Years of IIT Kharagpur, Golden Jubilee 1951–2001. Kharagpur: Indian Institute of Technology, 2001.

INDIAN NATIONAL ARMY (INA). *See* **Armed Forces; Bose, Netaji Subhash Chandra.**

INDIA OFFICE AND INDIA OFFICE LIBRARY

The India Office functioned as the home government of Britain's Crown colony in India from 1858 to 1947. It was the natural successor most immediately to the Board of Control (1784–1858) and, in the broadest sense, to the East India Company (1600–1858). Viewed from the outside, the office was often criticized by its own officials as "intolerably cumbrous and dilatory" (Sir Malcolm Seton) and a "marvel of circumlocution" (Lord Kimberley). Indian nationalists since the late nineteenth century considered the office a repository of conservatism and hostility. These images stem partly from a general lack of appreciation of the formal responsibilities of the India Office in the governance of the subcontinent as articulated in the Government of India Act of 1858, and partly from a calculated determination by successive permanent officials in the India Office to cloak the home government in secrecy vis-à-vis both other U.K. institutions of state and the Government of India.

In the early days of the India Office, the India Office staff was a somewhat carefree bunch that attended correspondence business casually and used their mantelpieces for pistol practice. In its first two decades, clerks were castigated as loafers and shirkers who played all day like the fountains in Trafalgar Square—from 10 A.M. to 4 P.M. From the 1880s, the clerks were a much more sober lot, who efficiently processed, evaluated, and cataloged well over a hundred thousand documents a year. The movement of such vast quantities of material necessary for the formulation of policy for India was influenced by several factors, including the physical setup of the India Office (3.5 million cubic feet), logistical procedures, and the performance of subordinate personnel. The flow of paper and the processing of paperwork was the primary responsibility of the permanent undersecretary of state for India, the most formidable of whom was Sir Arthur Godley (later Lord Kilbracken), who managed the position ably for twenty-five years (1883–1909) for ten secretaries of state for India.

Arthur Godley was educated at Rugby and Balliol College, Oxford. He was trained by Benjamin Jowett, who shaped Godley's lifelong high standard of duty, and he spent his political apprenticeship as private secretary to both Lord Granville and William Gladstone. Godley later reminisced that he was "saturated with the Gladstonian tradition of the earnestness of work" (Bassett, p. 225). This passion for administrative efficiency was matched by a carefully cultivated commitment by Godley to not play an active role in politics, and eventually he saw himself more of a "ministerialist," who advised and guided both Liberal and Conservative secretaries of state with whom he worked.

In practice, Godley considered the India Office "very leaky" when he joined it in 1883, and over the next two and a half decades refined the rules and regulations for processing paperwork with precision—from designing cabinet map drawers, to positioning hall porters to move paper along, to negotiating the charwoman's salary, to codifying the division of responsibilities among the permanent staff and committee of the Council of India. Still, he complained of odd, irascible resident clerks such as William Robinson, who, in 1894, "used to roller skate through the corridor of the India Office until prohibited." Godley eventually oversaw the integration of new technology into the office at the end of the nineteenth century, particularly the use of typewriters ("manned," as they were, by "female manipulators") and the telephone.

The essential components of the India Office were the secretary of state, his council (after 1937, advisers), and the permanent correspondence departments. Indian policy was legally conducted by a corporate entity, the Secretary of State in Council, and often required very delicate management by the permanent staff. The Council of India, which was staffed by men who had prior Indian expertise and, after 1909, included several Indian members, had a series of committees that mirrored the permanent departments. Strict rules guided the flow of paperwork from the council and its committees to the correspondence departments to the permanent undersecretary and secretary of state. Balancing this unique projection of Indian ethos into the policy-making arena with the bureaucratic imperatives of the increasingly professional India Office staff was a delicate endeavor and occasionally led to potential legal complications. Godley minimized this internal tension by aligning the correspondence departments and council committees more closely, and by encouraging successive Indian secretaries to use their powers of "persuasion and prestige" to reduce tensions. Godley, and his successors, always reminded India Office personnel that the real source of interference, as he saw it, was, oddly enough, Parliament. Because the India Office establishment was not on the British estimates, deflecting Parliamentary inquiries into India policy seemed an unstated but real priority. The India Office sanitized reports to Parliament in the nineteenth century, maintained its own private printers, and right up through World War II conducted almost daily meetings to vet information to be shared with other ministries and departments of state.

There were modifications to the internal processing of paperwork in the India Office in 1919 and 1923 that corresponded to a great influx of Indian matters referred back to London. The most significant adjustments related to devolving responsibility for some policy matters to departmental secretaries, leaving only serious matters to be sent up to the undersecretaries. Departmental heads could, in fact, now correspond directly with their counterparts in India on many routine matters. Between 1937 and 1940, as a result of the Government of India Act of 1935, a new relationship emerged between the secretary of state for India and his advisers. The Indian secretary now had broader legal powers to deal with secret matters and a less formal imperative to act always as a corporate entity, the Secretary of State in Council. Burmese affairs were slivered off the India Office responsibilities in 1937, although de facto, Burma Office officials worked out of the India Office and overlapped personnel considerably.

On the dissolution of the India Office in August 1947, the official archives of the India Office, Burma Office, East India Company, and the Board of Control, along with smaller groups of records from Haileybury College, the Royal Engineering College at Cooper's Hill, and various overseas agencies administratively linked to India (e.g., Aden, the Gulf, Afghanistan), were transferred to the Commonwealth Relations Office (1947–1966). Thereafter, the India Office Library and Records went to the Commonwealth Office (1966–1968), the Foreign and Commonwealth Office (1968–1982), and finally to the British Library in 1982.

Arnold P. Kaminsky

See also **British Crown Raj**

BIBLIOGRAPHY

Bassett, A. T. *The Life of the Rt. Hon. John Ellis, M.P.* London: Macmillan, 1914.

Husain, Syed Anwar. *Administration of India, 1858–1924.* Delhi: Seema Publications, 1985.

Kaminsky, Arnold P. *The India Office, 1880–1910.* New York: Greenwood Press, 1986.

Moir, Martin. *A General Guide to the India Office Records.* London: British Library, 1988.

Williams, Donovan. *The India Office, 1858–1869.* Hoshiarpur: Vishvesvaranand Vedic Research Institute, 1983.

INDIA'S IMPACT ON WESTERN CIVILIZATION

India's impact on Western civilization has been sporadic and not always easily defined, in contrast to the great influence of Indian religious ideas on Central Asia, Southeast Asia, China, and through China to Japan and Korea, especially in the form of Buddhism. Indian influence in the West can be traced with reasonable certainty from the ancient Mediterranean world of Greece and Rome, through the European Middle Ages, the

Drawing of Englishman Smoking Hookah. Not all representations of Indian culture have been positive, as this drawing possibly created during the era of British colonial rule attests. A humorous image perhaps, but one that reinforces a negative stereotype—bringing to mind the common stereotypes that Indians at home and in the West continue to struggle against. FOTOMEDIA ARCHIVE.

Renaissance, the age of European imperial expansion and decline, to the post-colonial world of the Indian diaspora of modern times.

Greece and Rome (600 B.C.–A.D. 650)

For the ancient Greeks and Romans, India had no definite boundaries, but it was thought of as all the territory beyond Arabia and Persia, the end of the habitable world. The first detailed accounts of what the Greeks knew about India appear in the great history of Herodotus (c. 480–425 B.C.), and these became part of the Western imagination for two thousand years. Some of it was factual, some of it was fantasy. India was thought of as a land of fabulous creatures as well as great wealth, an idea that was to lead Europeans through the centuries to seek to trade with India. Other Greek writers found a striking contrast between the Greek love of freedom and the servility of Indians and Persians, who they lumped together as "Asians."

Fascinating questions about Indian influence on the origins of Greek religion and philosophy arise in relation to the prominence of the idea of reincarnation, so central to

Indian religion, in early thinkers including Plato. This connection, the subject of speculation in recent years, was also mentioned by early writers like Eusebius (c. A.D. 300–359), who relates a story of an Indian visiting Socrates. New information and new influences from India came to the Mediterranean world after Alexander the Great crossed the River Indus in 326 B.C.; his troops returned home from India with tales that were part myth, part fact. Indian religion probably influenced Manichaeism, one of the great heresies of the early Christian church, for Mani, its founder, traveled to India and included the Buddha alongside Jesus among his divine beings. Trade in material goods between India and the Roman world is less speculative than that in ideas, for it finds frequent mention in contemporary Roman writing. Rome imported exotica from India: spices, jewels, fine textiles, ivory, peacocks, elephants, and lions. In return, India wanted only gold from Rome, and the trade balance was very unfavorable to Rome.

The Middle Ages and the Renaissance (500–1500)

India was never unknown to the Western world, but direct communication was rare in the European Middle Ages, with the fantasies and facts of the Greeks and Romans remaining the principal base of knowledge about India. That a few scholars in the Christian West remained aware of the high civilization of India is attested by a seventh-century monk, writing in 662 of the Indians' "subtle discoveries in the science of astronomy . . . of their rational system of mathematics and their method of calculation" (Basham, p. vi). There were persistent stories of a great Christian king somewhere in India, perhaps based on rumors of the ancient Christian church in Kerala. A curious development took place in the late Middle Ages, when the devil, demons, and monsters of the Christian tradition began to be identified with stories of the Indian gods, in all their multitude of forms, animal and human, many-headed and many-limbed. As "much-maligned monsters," Indian deities became a staple of the Western imagination right up to the present time (Mitter, p. 10).

Imperialism and Indian Influence on the West (1500–1947)

When Vasco da Gama reached Calicut on the southwest coast of India in 1498, he was able to report that India lived up to the expectations that Europeans had long held. They "found large cities, large edifices and rivers, and great populations, among whom is carried on all the trade in spices and precious stones" (Lach, p. 96). This was the beginning of European imperialism in India, and the Portuguese established themselves at coastal ports, notably Goa, which became the center of their great Asian sea-based empire. Attempts to evaluate the influence of its Indian possessions on Portugal itself are confused by the

Yoga Instructor Works with a Pupil. To cope with the increasingly stressful demands of their cultures, many Westerners have turned to the centuries-old spiritual teachings and practices of India. IPSHITA BARUA.

motivations for imperial activities, which were different at different times. In the case of Portugal, the motivations seem to have been a seamless mixture of politics, religion, and economics, that is, to strengthen its position in Europe; to win converts to Christianity; and to control as much of the Asian trade as possible.

The dominating motivation of British imperialism in India was economic, and the success of the British in controlling both external trade and land revenue made it possible for Britain to build one of the largest standing armies in the world. British possession of India prevented Russia, or so at least the British believed, from moving southward through Afghan territory into the Arabian Sea and the Indian Ocean. Indian soldiers were used to maintain British power in China and East Africa as well as in Europe and the Middle East in both world wars, and India was the key to the British navy's control of the sea passages to Southeast Asia and China. The Indian taxpayer, not the British, paid for this use of the Indian

army. An argument is sometimes made that the wealth of India helped to fuel Britain's industrial revolution, but while this is dubious, exports of British goods to India certainly helped British trade balances. In the final years of British rule, however, India was of less economic importance, making it easier for the British to leave.

Other areas of Indian influence on both Britain and the West are more intangible but in the long run perhaps more enduring. One of these emerged as Europeans in the nineteenth century discovered the immense wealth of Indian learning in Sanskrit and the other Indian languages. German intellectuals were particularly open to the study of Indian thought and culture. G.W.F. Hegel, while celebrating the antiquity of Indian thought, believed its otherworldliness prevented change and progress, an idea that was taken up by both Karl Marx and Max Weber. The philosopher Arthur Schopenhauer, on the other hand, exalted Indian religions, arguing that intolerance and fanaticism were known only in "the monotheistic religions," Judaism, Christianity, and Islam. In the United States, Indian religious thought found enthusiastic support from Ralph Waldo Emerson and the other Transcendentalists.

It was the character and ideas of Mahatma Gandhi, the most famous of modern Indians, however, more than the great systems of Indian religion and thought, that became for many people in the West the great symbol for the meaning of India. His message of nonviolence had a profound influence on the way that Westerners thought about India's struggle for freedom and independence, and this reaction, particularly in the United States and India, made it more difficult for the British rulers to oppose his demands for Indian freedom. This message was used with telling effect in the 1960s by Martin Luther King Jr., in the struggle by black Americans for equal civil rights in the United States.

Independence and the Indian Diaspora (1947–2017)

The reason for choosing the beginning date—the year when India gained political independence—is obvious enough; the ending date, seventy years later, is often suggested by observers as the time when India will not only be the world's most populous country and its largest democracy, but a political, economic, and military world power. Some of the factors that have contributed to making such influence possible—although all are problematic—can be noted as follows: internal political and economic strategies; shifting international situations; academic studies of Indian history and culture; and the remarkable influence of its migrant people, its "elite diaspora," especially throughout the English-speaking world.

Although Indian culture had influenced Western civilization in a variety of ways since ancient times, remarkable changes that took place after India became independent in 1947 and assumed its place in the comity of sovereign nations; the new Indian nation was widely respected for having achieved not just independence but a mature and stable civil society. Unlike many other newly decolonized nations, India had the seasoned leadership of a political party, the Indian National Congress, which enjoyed widespread support from all levels of society for moderate political and economic strategies for change. There was a general consensus that the future of the nation depended upon commitment to a number of goals, one of which was a commitment to national unity against the tensions of regional, linguistic, and religious differences that had been exacerbated by the partition of the subcontinent into two nations, India and Pakistan. Such tensions continued, but foreign observers were impressed by the success of the authorities in moderating them. Observers were also impressed with the success, against great odds, of the

commitment to a democratic polity that permitted free elections, free speech, and the unfettered operation of rival political parties. The government also impressed foreign observers by its decision to industrialize in order to raise the low standard of living of vast numbers of its people. There was less widespread approval, however, for its decision that this could only be done through a socialist pattern of society, which entailed limitation on foreign investment and governmental control of many aspects of economic life. Many critics, especially in the United States, associated this with India's foreign policy, which was one of attempted neutrality between the two great hostile blocs of the United States and the Soviet Union. There is no question that this policy led to a loss of Indian influence in the West, as dominated by the United States. At the same time, many friendly foreign observers believed that India was following a course that was good for the Indian people. Shifting political international relations, signified by the political disintegration of the Soviet Union in the 1990s, made it possible for India and the United States to move toward more fruitful relations built on the influence India had gained through the years.

Some credit for this influence must go to an important aspect of American academic life: beginning in the 1950s, as part of a movement to broaden the curriculum, universities and colleges began to include the study of Indian cultures and languages. Not only did this increase an appreciation of the richness of Indian culture, it also provided government officials with a new understanding of Indian political life. It was largely among the college-educated that Indian religions found a surprisingly enthusiastic response, not only in converts to such neo-Hindu groups as Hare Krishna but also in a more dispersed receptivity to Hindu spirituality in general, with many Indian gurus finding large followings. Indian classical music became popular for the first time in the West. So did Indian food, with Indian restaurants becoming commonplace.

One of the most striking causes of increased influence of India on the West after 1947 was the migration of large numbers of Indians to the English-speaking world. There had been large-scale migrations of Indians in the nineteenth century, but these were poor laborers, who often went as indentured labor. This new migration came from the educated elites, comprising an "influential diaspora." Many came as graduate students and stayed to occupy prominent places in the professions and business, most famously in information technology. The high point of this particular area of influence came with the sudden growth of "outsourcing," when many U.S. businesses found it more economical to transfer much of their information processing to India. This practice became so extensive that it led to demands, from both British and U.S. governments and workers, for legislative steps to halt the loss of jobs to highly qualified but far less expensive Indian workers, an ironic comment on the growth of Indian influence, precisely in the area of technology long dominated by the West.

Ainslie T. Embree

BIBLIOGRAPHY

Basham, A. L. *The Wonder That Was India*. London: Sidgwick and Jackson, 1963. Standard scholarly work, with many references to India and the West.

Bayly, C. A. *Indian Society and the Making of the British Empire*, vol. 2:1 of *The Cambridge History of India*. Cambridge, U.K.: Cambridge University Press, 1988.

Embree, Ainslie T., and Carol Gluck, eds. *Asia in Western and World History*. Armonk, N.Y.: M. E. Sharpe, 1995. Essays on many aspects of interaction.

Halbfass, Wilhelm. *India and Europe*. Albany: State University of New York Press, 1988. How Indians and Europeans understood each other.

Lach, Donald F. *Asia in the Making of Europe*, vol. 1, bk. 1. Chicago: University of Chicago Press, 1965. Very detailed scholarly work.

Mitter, Partha. *Much Maligned Monster: History of European Reactions to Indian Art*. Oxford: Clarendon Press, 1977.

Pearson, M. N. *The Portuguese in India*, vol. 1:1 of *The Cambridge History of India*. Cambridge, U.K.: Cambridge University Press, 1987.

Singhal, D. P. *India and World Civilization*. 2 vols. East Lansing: Michigan State University Press, 1969. Encyclopedic survey of references.

INDO–AMERICAN RELATIONS. *See* **United States, Relations with.**

INDO–ARYAN. *See* **Languages and Scripts; Vedic Aryan India.**

INDO–PAK WARS: 1948, 1965, AND 1971. *See* **Pakistan and India.**

INDO–SOVIET FRIENDSHIP TREATY. *See* **Russia, Relations with.**

INDO–SRI LANKAN RELATIONS. *See* **Sri Lanka, Relations with.**

INDO–U.S. RELATIONS, CULTURAL CHANGES IN In the opening decade of the twenty-first century, India and the United States found themselves bound together by an expanding web of cultural ties. This development seemed all the more astounding given the history of Indo–U.S. relations, marked more by wary estrangement than warm embrace. Indeed, despite a post–cold war rapprochement, the governments of the two countries continued to find that their interests often diverged. Yet, their peoples have embarked upon a relationship of transcreative synergy across every cultural medium that is profoundly transforming both countries, and that may have significant implications in a rapidly changing geopolitical environment.

The twentieth century has often been called the "American century." The United States grew to global economic and political dominance, ultimately outspending the Soviet Union into oblivion, and thus ending the cold war. The engine of the United States' extraordinary growth during these decades was unmatchable technological innovation. The United States' technological lead was driven in no small part by the brain power of brilliant immigrants, many of whom came from India. The inestimable contributions of thousands of highly trained Indian migrants in every area of American scientific and technological achievement culminated with the information technology revolution most associated with California's Silicon Valley in the 1980s and 1990s.

Yet throughout this period of rapid change, American images of India remained virtually unchanged. The average American thought of India rarely, if at all. Indian high culture barely made a small entry into the rarified world of the urban elite. For the vast majority of Americans, a few forgettable Indian moments consisted of shocking pictures of the desperately poor on the television news, or the orientalized images of maharajahs, palaces, elephants, and tigers from the nostalgic era of the British Raj. Aside from a fleeting moment during the 1960s when the Beatles returned from their pilgrimage to Rishikesh, Indian culture did not penetrate the psyche of the average American. India remained for most Americans a distant, timeless place whose culture's only possible contemporary contribution might be transcendental meditation, useful primarily as a therapeutic escape from the stresses of modern life.

The opening years of the twenty-first century, however, saw a revolutionary transformation of these stereotypical images in the United States. Today, the average American is far more likely to associate India with technological innovation rather than grinding poverty, with hip fashion rather than tigers and elephants, or with the latest movies rather than sitar concerts. India thus has emerged as one of the primary engines of global cultural innovation in the twenty-first century. Its relationship with the United States is no small reason for this incredible metamorphosis. In fact, India's cultural relationship with the United States is changing the very definition of what it means to be American, even as the absorption and reinterpretation of American consumer culture is changing what it means to be Indian.

The biggest factor in the emergence of this new transcreative synergy between India and the United States was undoubtedly the explosive growth of the Indian-American community at the historical moment of the information and communication technologies boom. Cold war imperatives moved the United States to liberalize immigration laws during the 1960s in order to allow a limited number of highly educated and technically skilled immigrants from non-European countries, including India, into the United States. A first wave of Indian physicians, engineers, and scientists came to America during the late 1960s and early 1970s, lured by a standard of living far above anything to which they could aspire at home. Subsequent immigration reforms led to more immigrants; the 2000 census counted more than 1 million persons of Indian descent living in the United States. By 2004, that number had increased to 1.7 million, and was expected to reach over 2 million by 2010 and to double again by 2020, making Indians the fastest-growing immigrant group in the United States.

Indian Americans also became the most prosperous and one of the most highly educated immigrant groups in the country, with a per capita income of $60,093, versus $38,885 for the general population, and with 58 percent holding a bachelor's degree or higher, versus 20 percent for the general population. By 2004, one out of every ten Indian Americans was reported to be a millionaire. Nowhere was the extraordinary success of the Indian American immigrant community more dramatic and more visible than in California's Silicon Valley, where high-tech entrepreneurs from India founded some of the most successful start-up companies of the late twentieth century and created some of the most widely used American products, from Hotmail.com to Corel's WordPerfect.

Meanwhile, two additional phenomena were occurring that would profoundly transform the cultural dynamic between India and the United States. First, the children of the first post-1960s wave of Indian immigrants were entering colleges across the country. In contrast to their technically skilled parents, the second generation, having grown up with a dual cultural heritage, began in increasing numbers to explore careers in the arts, journalism, and the humanities, endeavors that allowed them to express their identity as Indian Americans. The community itself was also changing. As immigration laws expanded to include family members and other categories, the Indian American community became more educationally and economically diverse, with many families living below the poverty line. As the

population grew, "Little India" communities sprang up in every major American urban area, from Devon Street in Chicago, to Jackson Heights, Queens, in New York, to Fremont, California. These enclaves offered all the comforts of "home," from food and clothing to Bollywood movies and Indian film soundtracks. The offspring of Indian and other South Asian immigrant taxi drivers, semiconductor fabricators, and newspaper vendors often "Black-identified," adopting the dress, idioms, and music of African American youth culture. Second-generation Indian Americans began to conjugate the Hindi film songs and Punjabi *bhangra* beats of their parents with the sounds of rap and hip-hop. The 1990s saw an explosion of Indian American DJs, who spliced Hindi film tracks over the pulsing rhythms of both hip-hop and *bhangra*. By the time African American hip-hop star Jay-Z recorded an album with *bhangra*-rap star Punjabi MC, Indo-American fusion pop culture was well on its way into the mainstream.

At the same time, cutting-edge information and communication technologies—often the brain-children of Indian immigrants—were compressing the time it took to bridge what used to be the almost unfathomable distance between North America and India. Along the way, an equally dynamic Indian fusion culture emerging in London was swept into what quickly become a pan-global Indian cultural phenomenon, relayed around the world by an Indian diaspora population of over 20 million. Riding this wave, India burst into the American imagination in the early 2000s as never before. For the first time in its history, the United States, the country that had defined "newness" since its revolutionary beginnings in the eighteenth century, was displaced as the land of the "new" by one of the world's most ancient civilizations, India.

This was due in no small part to the transformation of the "brain drain" model, which had brought the first wave of highly technically skilled Indian workers to the United States, into a "brain circulation" or even a "brain gain" model. Successful Indian immigrant entrepreneurs, physicians, scientists, and engineers began to understand that the very technologies they had helped to invent could provide a ticket home—not to the India they left behind in the 1960s but to an India that their skills could transform into a global center for technological innovation. A steady stream of "America-returned" Indians joined a significant number of highly talented individuals who had never left India, creating high-tech companies such as Asim Premji's Infosys in Bangalore, in Hyderabad, Chennai, and Mumbai. American high-tech companies soon joined the caravan of technology leaders and entrepreneurs on the India trail, with Hewlett-Packard, Intel, General Electric, IBM, Microsoft, and others opening offices in India. Many U.S. companies began to "outsource" highly skilled work, formerly performed at much greater cost in the United States, to India. The NRI, or "non-resident Indian," who had made it in California became a "newly returned Indian" living in a California-style gated community in Bangalore that boasted every amenity one could expect at a posh U.S. address, but at a fraction of the American cost.

Hooked into an American-inspired global consumer culture, with the privatization of Indian television and the advent of satellite broadcast technology and cable, the lifestyle expectations of young urban Indians was irreversibly transformed. The Internet completed the connection, in real time, of young Indians in India with young Indians in the Indian diaspora, adding another dimension to "Cyber-India." The fascination of Indians with the diaspora and the nostalgia of diaspora Indians for an increasingly imaginary Indian homeland spawned a spate of blockbuster movies such as *Kul Ho Na Ho*, starring Bollywood hero and heartthrob Shah Rukh Khan as a newly arrived Indian migrant in New York who falls for one less "fresh off the boat." Young people in Mumbai, Delhi, Bangalore, and Chennai became indistinguishable from their diaspora counterparts. Their tastes had become profoundly internationalized. Thanks to India's liberalized economy and new urban prosperity, international brands of clothing were available in major Indian cities, along with the latest hair styles, makeup trends, club music, and the ubiquitous "mobiles" glued to every ear.

Young Indians went well beyond the passive consumption of global popular culture and international brands. They became active producers of new, hybridized cultural content that landed in the capitals of North America and Europe as the latest craze among non-Indian and Indian diaspora populations alike. Fashion moguls Anand Jon and Sandy Dalal, both based in New York, created their own successful lines of Indian-inspired clothing, while European couture superstars such as Giorgio Armani and Jean-Paul Gauthier began to "cite" Indian colors, textiles, prints, and images in their own work. Composer A. R. Rehman, based in India, became an international sensation, while Bally Sagoo created London-inspired fusion sounds; Norah Jones, the Grammy Award–winning daughter of sitar star Ravi Shankar, created soft jazz croonings that bore no trace of her Indian paternity. English-language Indian literary colossus Salman Rushdie moved to New York, while novelist Chitra Bannerjee Divakaruni and travel writer Pico Iyer remained on the West Coast. Jhumpa Lahiri's debut collection of short stories, *The Interpreter of Maladies*, depicting Indian immigrants caught between India and America, won a Pulitzer Prize for "distinguished fiction by an American author, preferably dealing with American

life." Diaspora Indians became not just Indian stars but, simply, stars.

The Indian American cultural revolution continued at the box office with an explosion of "search for identity" films, from Krutin Patel's *ABCD* to Anurag Mehta's *American Chai* to Nikhil Kamkolkar's *Indian Cowboy*. Ismail Merchant, of the Merchant-Ivory Productions team that produced *A Room with a View* and *Howards End*, continued to turn out films with Indian diaspora themes, such as *The Mystic Masseur*, based on the novel by V. S. Naipaul. New York–based Indian film director Mira Nair achieved the ultimate "crossover" success with her *Monsoon Wedding*, a movie that portrayed the contradictions of contemporary Indians fully engaged in the contradictions of twenty-first-century life, featuring an arranged marriage between a diaspora Indian and an Indian Indian. She went on to produce a sumptuous version of William Thackeray's *Vanity Fair* that featured an Indian musical dance extravaganza right out of the purest Bollywood tradition.

In New York, there was an explosion of Indian American theater, ranging from Aasif Mandvi's side-splitting comedy *Sakina's Restaurant* to the Broadway hit *Bombay Dreams* by musical producer Andrew Lloyd Webber. Contemporary visual artists from India, as well as those working in the United States, including the Gujarati but New York–based painter Natvar Bhavsar and Washington, D.C.–based Anil Revri, sell out shows in trendy galleries such as Sundaram Tagore's gallery in Soho. Their work has a markedly Indian sensibility in terms of color and geometry, yet it is as attractive to deep-pocketed Indian Americans as to other American and international collectors.

On a more mundane level, it is easy to find Indian entrées such as *palak paneer* and *chicken tikka* in the frozen food section of any supermarket in most major or even mid-sized American cities. Indian *chai* has become as much a fixture of the ubiquitous American coffeehouse scene as have lattes and cappuccinos. The American "*dosa* wrap" has expanded the South Indian traditional repertory to include such nontraditional fillings as roast chicken and goat cheese. The *masala bhangra* workout has become the latest fitness craze in California. These transformations and others led *Newsweek* magazine in 2004 to proclaim under the rubric "American Masala" that South Asians in the United States "have changed the way we eat, dress, work and play."

Meanwhile, in India, American culture was transforming the lives of the urban and the affluent and challenging the Indian government to meet the aspirations of the millions of Indians who still live below the poverty level yet can see all around them, and on television, the new affluence of their fellow citizens. Starbucks attempted a foray into the land of Darjeeling and other teas. Pizza Hut, McDonalds, and other fast-food restaurants have set up shop in India, while new shopping malls complete with underground parking, escalators, and multiplex movie theaters feature international brands. Many young urban Indian girls have become Westernized to such a degree that they not only no longer wear traditional Indian dress but need help from mothers or aunts to put on a sari when a social occasion requires one. Indian television, once the lone territory of state-run Doordarshan television, began to broadcast Western popular culture with MTV. MTV simply rebroadcast in India shows designed for American and other Western audiences. Local networks leapt into a deregulated Indian television market with old reruns of *Bewitched* and *Baywatch*, dubbed in Hindi. Today, no television network can survive in India unless it broadcasts locally produced content featuring local talent. An explosion of Indian-produced talk shows, sitcoms, soap operas, and game shows now dominate the television screens of India.

The visibility of India, Indians, and Indian Americans has reached new levels in American media. Major American magazines, such as *Business Week* and *Wired*, now run cover stories on the Indian technology revolution and outsourcing. Indian actress Aishwarya Rai is featured in photo spreads in the *New York Times Sunday Magazine*, proclaimed to be one of the most beautiful women in the world, a rising "international superstar." British Indian actress Parminder Nagra has a role on the television series *ER*, while Indian actors regularly have cameo or even episode-starring roles on major American television network and cable shows. NBC is working on a comedy, *Nevermind Nirvana*, based on the lives of a family of Indian immigrant doctors, the Mehtas, modeled on the British hit series *The Kumars*. Meanwhile, real-life television doctor Sanjay Gupta dispatches medical advice daily to millions of Americans who watch CNN. The increasing visibility of Indian Americans in everyday American life has everyone in the media business talking "crossover." With India predicted by some leading economists to overtake the U.S. economy within the next fifty years, it is looking more and more as if the next American century may be Indian.

Mira Kamdar

See also **Diaspora; Film Industry**

BIBLIOGRAPHY

Breckenridge, Carol Appadurai, Homi K. Bhabha, Dipesh Chakrabarty, and Sheldon Polack, eds. *Cosmopolitanism.* Durham, N.C.: Duke University Press, 2002.
Desai, Jigna. *Beyond Bollywood: The Cultural Politics of South Asian Diasporic Film.* London: Taylor & Francis, 2003.
Dwyer, Rachel, ed. *Pleasure and the Nation: The History, Politics and Consumption of Popular Culture in India.* London: School of Oriental and African Studies, 2003.
Kumar, Amitava. *Passport Photos.* Berkeley: University of California Press, 2000.
Lahiri, Jhumpa. *The Interpreter of Maladies.* New York: Houghton Mifflin, 2000.
Maira, Sunaina Marr. *Desis in the House: Indian American Youth Culture in New York City.* Philadelphia: Temple University Press, 2002.
Mazzarella, William. *Shoveling Smoke: Advertising and Globalization in Contemporary India.* Durham, N.C.: Duke University Press, 2003.
Merchant, Ismail. *My Passage from India: A Filmmaker's Journey from Bollywood to Hollywood.* New York: Viking Studio: 2002.
Page, David, and William Crawley. *Satellites over South Asia: Broadcasting, Culture and the Public Interest.* Oxford: Oxford University Press, 2001.
Prashad, Vijay. *Karma of Brown Folk.* Minneapolis: University of Minnesota Press, 2001.
Rustomji-Kerns, Roshni, ed. *Living in America: Poetry and Fiction by South Asian Writers.* Boulder, Colo.: Westview Press, 1995.
Sharma, Sanjay, John Hutuyk, and Ashwini Sharma, eds. *Dis-Orienting Rhythms: The Politics of the New Asian Dance Music.* London: Zed Books, 1997.
Srikanth, Rajni, Suchen Chan, and David Palumbo-Liu, eds. *World Next Door: South Asian American Literature and the Idea of America.* Philadelphia: Temple University Press, 2004.

INDRA The leading deity in Vedic Hinduism, Indra is evidently a pre-Vedic god, invoked by Mitanni Aryans of northern Syria in their famous treaty with the Hittites about 1380 B.C. Almost one-fourth of the 1,028 hymns of the Rig Veda, composed in verse by 1000 B.C. at the latest, are addressed to Indra as the conqueror of enemies of Indo-Aryans, the Dāsas or Dasyus in particular, at times conflated with *asura*s, mythic enemies of the gods. When destroying demons or human foe, Indra wields his *vajra*, a thunderbolt-mace forged by Tvastā, and becomes a shape-changer by means of his powers of *māyā*. Above all, he is Vritrahan (slayer of Vritra) an epithet cognate to ancient Iranian Verethraghna. This conquest of the serpent demon named "Resistance" is recounted in Rig Veda 1.32 and 1.51. Indra emerges here as a cosmogonic figure, since Vritra held in bondage all the fertilizing waters necessary for life. Not only does the warrior of the gods release those streams, often homologized to captive cows, he also wins the light or the sun, and retrieves the primary sacrificial substance soma from the cloud-mountains. In another cosmogonic feat, he is credited with propping apart heaven and earth. As invincible leader, Indra thus becomes patron deity of Kshatriyas, the warrior *varṇa* (class) that is the source of kingship in ancient and classical India. In sum, he is the heroic champion who in battles of cosmic scale wins the day and the territory—perhaps in the vicinity of the Sarasvati River in southern Afghanistan—for Indo-Aryan nomadic pastoralists.

Of all the deities in Rig Vedic poetry, Indra is described most colorfully. Whereas Varuṇa is *samrāj*, or universal king, simply by his nature, the younger, impetuous Indra is *svarāj*, one who seizes kingship by his prevailing self-rule. Chariot-driving Indra, said to have a hundred powers, is bearded and gigantic in size. Having a thousand testicles, he is a universal fertilizer of females, including the earth; though boastful and intoxicated by soma, he is also generous, designated by poets as *maghavan* (bounteous).

In some fifty hymns, Indra is associated with other gods and goddesses, chiefly Agni, Brihaspati, Varuṇa, Ushas, Vāyu, the Ashvin twins, martial storm-gods known collectively as the Maruts, and Soma, the last as both god and the pressed juice that he voraciously consumes in soma sacrifices. In the extended mythology, more than one perspective unfolds to engage Indra in controversy. He is charged with crimes against the three classes—Brahmans, Kshatriyas (his own *varṇa*), and Vaishyas—and in consequence suffers diminution of his seemingly invincible power. The terrible dragon Vritra is identified as a Brahman, and therefore Indra is guilty of Brahmanicide, a dreadful sin. In violation of the code of courageous warriors, he is accused of cowardly flight from combat, including his initial confrontation with Vritra. And in a sexual crime against the Vaishya class, society's producers, he assumes the guise of Gautama to trick and violate his wife, Ahalyā, while sage Gautama performs his morning prayers.

In the later era of the Sanskrit epics and Purāṇas, Indra's worship and centrality as divine sovereign dwindle in favor of Shiva and Vishnu. Preserved, however, are countless aspects of his warrior career. Tamil epics, for example, situate the self-offerings of martial heroes, and victory for their king, in the festival of Indra. Also perpetuated are Vedic myths that ridicule his sexual prowess in accounts of castration and substitution of his genitals with those of a ram or goat. In one variant, the body of Indra sprouts a thousand vaginas. Shiva in particular sustains many of Indra's famous roles. Shiva, Vishnu, and emerging cults of major goddesses gradually take center stage, just as Indra himself in an earlier era had replaced Varuṇa as king of the gods.

David M. Knipe

See also **Agni; Hinduism (Dharma); Soma; Varuṇa; Vedic Aryan India**

BIBLIOGRAPHY

Dumézil, Georges. *The Destiny of the Warrior*. Translated by Alf Hiltebeitel. Chicago: University of Chicago, 1970. Situates Indra in comparative Indo-European motif of the warrior's three sins.

Gonda, Jan. *The Indra Hymns of the Ṛgveda*. Leiden and New York: E. J. Brill, 1989. Analysis of cosmogonic and other central and enduring myths.

O'Flaherty, Wendy Doniger. *Hindu Myths*. Baltimore: Penguin, 1975. Ch. 2 translates, annotates key episodes, Rig Veda to epics and Purāṇas.

INDUSTRIAL CHANGE SINCE 1956 When India achieved independence in 1947, the national consensus was in favor of rapid industrialization, which was seen not only as the key to economic development but also to economic sovereignty. In the subsequent years, India's industrial policy evolved through successive industrial policy resolutions and industrial policy statements. Specific priorities for industrial development were also set forth in the successive Five-Year Plans.

Early Industrial Development

Building on the so-called Bombay Plan prepared by leading Indian industrialists in 1944–1945, the first Industrial Policy Resolution in 1948 laid down the broad contours of the strategy of industrial development. At that time the Constitution of India had not taken final shape, nor had the Planning Commission been constituted. Moreover, the necessary legal framework had not yet been put in place. Not surprisingly, therefore, the resolution was somewhat broad in its scope and direction. Yet, an important distinction was made between industries to be kept under the exclusive ownership of government (public sector) and those reserved for the private sector. Subsequently, the Constitution of India was adopted in January 1950, the Planning Commission was constituted in March 1950, and the Industrial (Department and Regulation) Act (IDR Act) was enacted in 1951, with the objective of empowering the government to take the necessary steps to regulate the pattern of industrial development through licensing. This paved the way for the Industrial Policy Resolution of 1956, which was the first comprehensive statement on the strategy for industrial development in India.

Industrial Policy Resolution of 1956. The Industrial Policy Resolution of 1956 was shaped by the Mahalanobis model of growth, which suggested that an emphasis on heavy industries would create long-term higher growth. The resolution widened the scope of the public sector. Its objective, following socialist theory, was to accelerate economic growth and boost the process of industrialization to achieve social benefits. Given the scarce capital and inadequate entrepreneurial base, the resolution accorded the state a predominant role in industrial development. All industries of basic and strategic importance and those in public utility services, as well as those requiring large-scale investment, were reserved for the public sector.

The Industrial Policy Resolution of 1956 classified industries into three categories. The first category comprised seventeen industries (included in Schedule A of the resolution) exclusively under the domain of the government, including, among others, railways, air transportation, arms and ammunition, iron and steel, and atomic energy. The second category comprised twelve industries (included in Schedule B of the resolution), which were envisaged to be progressively state owned, with the private sector supplementing the efforts of the state. The third category contained all the remaining industries, and it was expected that the private sector would initiate development of these industries, though they would remain open to the state as well. The government was to facilitate and encourage development of these industries in the private sector, in accordance with the programs formulated under the Five-Year Plans, by appropriate fiscal measures and by ensuring adequate infrastructure. Despite the demarcation of industries into separate categories, the resolution was flexible enough to allow adjustments and modifications in the national interest.

Another objective specified in the Industrial Policy Resolution of 1956 was the removal of regional disparities through the development of regions with a low industrial base. Accordingly, adequate infrastructure for industrial development of such regions was duly emphasized. Given the potential to provide large-scale employment, the resolution reiterated the government's determination to provide various forms of assistance to small and cottage industries for a wider dispersal of the industrial base and a more equitable distribution of income. The resolution, in fact, reflected the prevalent value system of India in the early 1950s, which was centered around self-sufficiency in industrial production. The Industrial Policy Resolution of 1956 was a landmark policy statement, and it formed the basis of subsequent policy announcements.

Industrial Policy Measures, 1964–1980

The Monopolies Inquiry Commission (MIC) was set up in 1964 to review various aspects pertaining to the concentration of economic power and the operation of industrial licensing under the IDR Act of 1951. While emphasizing that the planned economy contributed to the growth of industry, the report by the MIC concluded that the industrial licensing system enabled large business firms to obtain a disproportionately large share of licenses, which had led to preemption and foreclosure of capacity. Subsequently, the Industrial Licensing Policy Inquiry Committee (Dutt Committee), constituted in 1967, recommended that larger industrial firms be given licenses only for setting up industry in core and heavy investment sectors, thereby necessitating the reorientation of industrial licensing policy.

In 1969 the Monopolies and Restrictive Trade Practices (MRTP) Act was introduced to enable the government to effectively control the concentration of economic power. The Dutt Committee had defined large business firms as those with assets of more than 350 million rupees. The MRTP Act of 1969 defined large business firms as those with assets of 200 million rupees or more. Large industries were designated as MRTP companies and were eligible to participate in industries that were not reserved for the government or the small-scale sector.

The new Industrial Licensing Policy of 1970 classified industries into four categories. The first category, termed "Core Sector," consisted of basic, critical, and strategic industries. The second category, termed "Heavy Investment Sector," comprised projects involving an investment of more than 50 million rupees. The third category, the "Middle Sector," consisted of projects with investment in the range of 10 million to 50 million rupees. The fourth category, the "De-licensed Sector," in which investment was less than 10 million rupees, was exempted from licensing requirements. The Industrial Licensing Policy of 1970 confined the role of large business firms and foreign companies to the core, heavy, and export-oriented sectors.

The Industrial Policy Statement of 1973. With a view to prevent the excessive concentration of industrial activity in the large industrial firms, this statement gave preference to small and medium entrepreneurs over the large firms and foreign companies in the setting up of new industrial enterprises, particularly for the production of mass-consumption goods. New undertakings of up to 10 million rupees in terms of fixed assets were exempted from licensing requirements for the substantial expansion of assets. This exemption was not allowed to MRTP companies, foreign companies, and existing licensed or registered undertakings having fixed assets of 50 million rupees or more.

The Industrial Policy Statement of 1977. This statement emphasized the decentralization of the industrial sector, with an increased role for small-scale, "tiny," and cottage industries. It also provided for close interaction between industrial and agricultural sectors. The highest priority was accorded to power generation and transmission. It expanded the list of items reserved for exclusive production in the small-scale sector from 180 to more than 500. For the first time, within the small-scale sector, a "tiny" unit was defined as a unit with investment in machinery and equipment up to 0.1 million rupees and situated in towns or villages with a population of less than 50,000 (as per 1971 census). Basic goods, capital goods, and high technology industries important for the development of small-scale and agriculture sectors were clearly delineated for the large-scale sector. It was also stated that foreign companies that diluted their foreign equity up to 40 percent under the Foreign Exchange Regulation Act of 1973 were to be treated on par with Indian companies. The Policy Statement of 1977 also issued a list of industries in which no foreign collaboration of a financial or technical nature was allowed, as indigenous technology was already available. Fully owned foreign companies were allowed only in highly export-oriented sectors or sophisticated technology areas. For all approved foreign investments, companies were completely free to repatriate capital and remit profits, dividends, and royalties. Further, in order to ensure balanced regional development, it was decided not to issue new licenses for setting up new industrial units within certain limits of large metropolitan cities (population of more than 1 million) and urban areas (population of more than 0.5 million).

The Industrial Policy Statement of 1980. The Industrial Policy Statement of 1980 placed emphasis on the promotion of competition in the domestic market, technological upgrade, and the modernization of industries. Some of the socioeconomic objectives defined in the statement were: optimum utilization of installed capacity, higher productivity, higher employment levels, removal of regional disparities, strengthening of the agricultural base, promotion of export oriented industries, and consumer protection against high prices and poor quality.

Policy measures were announced to revive the efficiency of public sector units by developing the management cadres in functional fields such as operations, finance, marketing, and information systems. An automatic expansion of capacity up to 5 percent per annum was allowed, particularly in the core sector and in industries with long-term export potential. Special incentives were granted to industrial units that were engaged in industrial processes and technologies aiming at optimum utilization of energy and the exploitation of alternative sources of energy. In order to boost the development of small-scale industries, the investment limit was raised to 2 million rupees in small-scale units and 2.5 million rupees in ancillary units. In the case of "tiny" units, the investment limit was raised to 0.2 million rupees.

Industrial Policy Measures, 1985–1991

Policy measures initiated in the first three decades following independence facilitated the establishment of basic industries and the growth of a broad-based infrastructure in the country. The Seventh Five-Year Plan (1985–1900) recognized the need for consolidation of these strengths and the initiation of policy measures to prepare Indian industry to respond effectively to emerging challenges. A number of measures were initiated toward technological and managerial modernization to improve productivity and quality, and to reduce costs of production. The public sector was freed from a number of constraints and was provided with greater autonomy. There was some progress in the process of deregulation during the 1980s. In 1988 all industries, except twenty-six industries specified in the negative list, were exempted from licensing. The exemption was, however, subject to investment and locational limitations. The automotive industry, cement, cotton spinning, food processing, and polyester filament yarn industries witnessed modernization and expanded scales of production during the 1980s.

With a view to promote industrialization of the underdeveloped areas of the country, the government of India announced in June 1988 the Growth Centre Scheme, under which seventy-one growth centers were proposed to be created throughout the country. Growth centers were to be endowed with basic infrastructure facilities such as power, water, telecommunications, and banking to enable them to attract industries.

The Industrial Policy Statement of 1991. The Industrial Policy Statement of 1991 stated that "the Government will continue to pursue a sound policy framework encompassing encouragement of entrepreneurship, development of indigenous technology through investment in research and development, bringing in new technology, dismantling of the regulatory system, development of the capital markets and increased competitiveness for the benefit of common man." It further added that "the spread of industrialization to backward areas of the country will be actively promoted through appropriate incentives, institutions and infrastructure investments."

The objectives of the Industrial Policy Statement of 1991 were to maintain sustained growth in productivity, to enhance gainful employment and achieve optimal utilization of human resources, to attain international competitiveness, and to transform India into a major player in the global economy. Quite clearly, the focus of the policy was to unshackle the Indian industry from bureaucratic controls. This called for a number of far-reaching reforms.

A substantial modification of industrial licensing policy was deemed necessary, with a view to ease restraints on capacity creation and to respond to emerging domestic and global opportunities by improving productivity. Accordingly, the policy statement included the abolition of industrial licensing for most industries, barring a handful of industries for reasons of security and strategic concerns, or social and environmental issues. Compulsory licensing was required in only eighteen industries. These included coal and lignite, distillation and brewing of alcoholic drinks, cigars and cigarettes, drugs and pharmaceuticals, household appliances, and hazardous chemicals. The small-scale sector continued to be reserved. Norms for setting up industries (except for industries subject to compulsory licensing) in cities with a population of more than 1 million were further liberalized.

Recognizing the complementarily of domestic and foreign investment, foreign direct investment (FDI) was accorded a significant role in policy announcements of 1991. FDI up to 51 percent foreign equity in high priority industries that required large investments and advanced technology was permitted. Foreign equity up to 51 percent was also allowed in trading companies primarily engaged in export activities. These important initiatives were expected to provide a boost to investment as well as enabling access to the high technology and marketing expertise of foreign companies. To spur the growth of technology in Indian industry, the government provided automatic approval for technological agreements related to high-priority industries and eased procedures for the hiring of foreign technical expertise.

Major initiatives toward the restructuring of public sector units (PSUs) were initiated, to remedy their low productivity, overstaffing, lack of advanced technology, and low rate of return. In order to raise resources and ensure wider public participation in PSUs, it was decided to offer its shareholding stake to mutual funds, financial institutions, the general public, and employees. Similarly, in order to revive and rehabilitate chronically "sick" PSUs, it was decided to refer them to the Board for Industrial and Financial Reconstruction. The policy also called for greater managerial autonomy for the boards of PSUs.

The Industrial Policy Statement of 1991 recognized that the government's intervention in investment decisions of large companies through the MRTP Act had proved deleterious for industrial growth. Accordingly, preentry scrutiny of investment decisions of MRTP companies was abolished. The thrust of policy was more on controlling unfair and restrictive trade practices. The provisions restricting mergers, amalgamations, and takeovers were also repealed.

Industrial Policy Measures since 1991

Since 1991, industrial policy measures and procedural simplifications have been reviewed on an ongoing basis. Currently, there are only six industries that require compulsory licensing. Similarly, there are only three industries reserved for the public sector.

The promotion of FDI has been an integral part of India's economic policy since 1991. The government has ensured a liberal and transparent foreign investment regime in which most activities are opened to foreign investment, without any limit on the extent of foreign ownership. FDI up to 100 percent has also been allowed for most manufacturing activities in special economic zones. More recently, in 2004, the FDI limits were raised in the private banking sector (up to 74 percent), oil exploration (up to 100 percent), petroleum product marketing (up to 100 percent), petroleum product pipelines (up to 100 percent), natural gas and liquified natural gas pipelines (up to 100 percent) and the printing of scientific and technical magazines, periodicals, and journals (up to 100 percent). In February 2005 the FDI ceiling in the telecommunications sector in certain services was increased from 49 percent to 74 percent.

The reservation of items of manufacture exclusively in the small-scale sector has been an important tenet of industrial policy. Realizing the increased import competition with the removal of quantitative restrictions since April 2001, the government has adopted a policy of de-reservation and has gradually pruned the list of items reserved for the small-scale industry sector from 821 items as in March 1999 to 506 items in April 2005. Further, the national budget of 2005–2006 has proposed to de-reserve 108 additional items that were identified by Ministry of Small Scale Industries. The investment limit in plant and machinery of small-scale units has been raised by the government from time to time. To enable some of the small-scale units to achieve required economies of scale, a differential investment limit has been adopted for them since October 2001. As of early 2005, there were 41 reserved items that were allowed an investment limit up to 50 million rupees instead of the limit of 10 million rupees applicable to other small-scale units.

Equity participation up to 24 percent of the total shareholding in small scale units by other industrial undertakings has been allowed. The objective here has been to enable the small sector to access the capital market and to encourage modernization, technological advance, ancillarization, and subcontracting.

In an effort to mitigate regional imbalances, the government announced a new North-East Industrial Policy in December 1997 for promoting industrialization in the Northeastern region. This policy, applicable to the states of Arunachal Pradesh, Assam, Manipur, Meghalaya, Mizoram, Nagaland, and Tripura, has provided various concessions to industrial units in the region, including the development of industrial infrastructure, subsidies under various schemes, and excise and income-tax exemption for a period of ten years. The North Eastern Development Finance Corporation has been designated as the primary disbursing agency under the program.

The focus of the disinvestment process of public sector units has shifted from the sale of minority stakes to strategic sales. Up to December 2004, PSUs had been divested to an extent of 478 billion rupees. Apart from general policy measures, some industry-specific measures have also been initiated. For instance, the Electricity Act of 2003 was designed to de-license power generation and to permit captive power plants. It was also intended to facilitate private-sector participation in the transmission sector and to provide open access to the grid sector. Various policy measures have facilitated an increase in private-sector participation in key infrastructure sectors such as telecommunication, roads, and ports. Foreign equity participation up to 100 percent has been allowed in the construction and maintenance of roads and bridges. MRTP provisions have been relaxed to encourage private-sector financing by large firms in the highway sector.

Evolution and Change

In the evolution of India's industrial policy, governmental intervention has been extensive. Unlike many East Asian countries, which used state intervention to build strong private sector industries, India opted for state control over key industries in its initial phase of development. In order to promote these industries, the government not only levied high tariffs and imposed import restrictions, but also subsidized the nationalized firms, directed investment funds to them, and controlled land use and many prices.

There has long been a consensus in India on the role of the government in providing infrastructure and maintaining stable macroeconomic policies. However, the path to be pursued toward industrial development has evolved over time. The form of government intervention in development strategy must be chosen from two alternatives: "outward-looking development policies" encourage not only free trade but also the free movement of capital, workers, and enterprises; "inward-looking development policies" stress the need for internal development. India initially adopted the latter strategy.

The advocates of import substitution in India believed that imports should be replaced with domestic production of both consumer goods and sophisticated manufactured items, while ensuring the imposition of high tariffs and quotas on imports. These advocates cited the benefits, in the long run, of greater domestic industrial

diversification and the ultimate ability to export previously protected manufactured goods, as economies of scale, low labor costs, and the positive externalities of learning by doing would cause domestic prices to become more competitive than world prices. However, the pursuit of such a policy forced Indian industry to have low and inferior technology. It did not expose the industry to the rigors of competition and therefore resulted in low efficiency. Inferior technology and inefficient production practices, coupled with a focus on traditional sectors, choked further expansion of Indian industry and thereby limited its ability to improve employment opportunities. Considering these inadequacies, the reforms since 1991 have aimed at infusing state-of-the-art technology, increasing domestic and external competition, and diversifying the industrial base so that it can expand and create additional employment opportunities.

In retrospect, the Industrial Policy Resolutions of 1948 and 1956 reflected the desire of the Indian state to achieve self sufficiency in industrial production. Huge investments by the state in heavy industries were designed to put Indian industry on a higher long-term growth trajectory. With the limited availability of foreign exchange, the effort of the government was to encourage domestic production. This basic strategy guided industrialization until the mid-1980s. Until the onset of the reform process in 1991, industrial licensing played a crucial role in channeling investments and controlling entry and expansion of capacity in the Indian industrial sector. Industrialization thus occurred in a protected environment, which led to various distortions. Tariffs and quantitative controls largely kept foreign competition out of the domestic market, and most Indian manufacturers looked on exports only as a residual possibility. Little attention was paid to ensuring product quality, undertaking research and development for technological advancement, or achieving economies of scale. The industrial policy announced in 1991, however, substantially dispensed with industrial licensing and facilitated foreign investment and technology transfers, opening tareas hitherto reserved for the public sector. The policy focus in recent years has been on the deregulation of Indian industry, enabling industrial restructuring, and allowing industry the freedom and flexibility to respond to market forces and provide a business environment that facilitates and fosters overall industrial growth. The future growth of Indian industry, as widely believed, is crucially dependent upon improving the overall productivity of the manufacturing sector, rationalization of the duty structure, technological advancement, the search for export markets through promotional efforts and trade agreements, and the creation of an enabling legal environment.

Narendra Jadhav

See also **Capital Market; Economic Reforms of 1991; Industrial Growth and Diversification; Industrial Policy since 1956; Infrastructure Development and Government Policy since 1950; Small-Scale Industry, since 1947**

BIBLIOGRAPHY

Ahluwalia, I. J. *Productivity and Growth in Indian Manufacturing.* Delhi: Oxford University Press, 1991.
Government of India. *Handbook of Industrial Policy and Statistics–2001.* New Delhi: Ministry of Commerce and Industry, 2001.
———. *Annual Report, 2003–2004.* New Delhi: Ministry of Commerce and Industry, 2004.
———. *Economic Survey, 2004–2005.* New Delhi: Ministry of Finance, 2005.

INDUSTRIAL GROWTH AND DIVERSIFICATION

In 1951, when India embarked on its first five-year plan, the country's industrial base was small, dominated by cotton and jute textiles. Registered manufacturing units, employing ten or more workers, contributed about 4.4 percent of the gross domestic product (GDP) at 1993–1994 prices; the contribution of unregistered units was 4.6 percent. Barely more than fifty years later, India has a highly diversified industrial structure, producing a wide range of goods. Indian industry is now capable of designing and implementing industrial projects using sophisticated technology. In 2000–2001, the GDP share of registered manufacturing was 10.5 percent, and that of total manufacturing 17.2 percent. In terms of manufacturing value added, in 1998 India ranked fifteenth among 87 countries (UNIDO, *Industrial Development Report, 2002/03,* p. 162). Among developing countries, India ranked sixth, behind China, Brazil, Korea, Mexico, and Taiwan.

The industrialization strategy implemented in the second (1956–1957 to 1960–1961) and third (1961–1962 to 1965–1966) plans emphasized rapid growth and diversification through industrialization, considered essential for achieving and maintaining full employment at a rising level of productivity. India's planners believed that in order to industrialize, it was necessary to develop an indigenous heavy industry base, for which the public sector would take prime responsibility. Such thinking shaped the policy environment for Indian industry, and the government invested in heavy industries, primarily iron and steel. During this period and in the next twenty-five years, India pursued an inward-oriented industrialization strategy. There were high import restrictions, combined with strong regulation of domestic industry. Domestic manufacturing enterprises were highly protected against foreign competition. Most production- and investment-related decisions of industrial firms were subject to extensive government controls.

Portrait of Jamnalal Bajaj. Bajaj, an Indian industrialist, was drawn to the teachings of Gandhi. The two men developed a close friendship (Gandhi often publicly referred to Bajaj as "his fifth son"), and the Bajaj family came to play a pivotal, pioneering role in the economic development of India following its independence in 1947. K. L. KAMAT / KAMAT'S POTPOURRI.

In the 1970s, those "protective" industrial and trade policies were clearly having detrimental effects on India's economy, which led to the initiation of a slow process of liberalization of industrial and trade policies that gained momentum in the 1980s. It was the economic crisis of 1991, however, that led to major and far-reaching economic policy reforms in India. The economic reforms undertaken in India since 1991 have unleashed the forces of competition and globalization, providing opportunities for Indian industry to raise its standards of technology, product quality, and efficiency, allowing it to become competitive at home and abroad.

Industrial Growth

Reforms of the 1990s were expected to lead to an accelerated industrial growth, but the growth rate in the first ten years of the postreform period was inferior to that of the 1980s. During 1990–1991 to 2000–2001, the annual growth rates in real value added in registered and total manufacturing were 6.3 and 6.1 percent respectively, both lower than the 7.9 and 7.0 rates achieved in the 1980s. Industrial growth performance was quite poor in the second half of the 1990s; between 1996–1997 and 2000–2001, real value added in total manufacturing grew only at the rate of 3.8 percent.

In the mid-1960s, there had been a sharp fall in the growth rates of basic metals, metal products, nonelectrical machinery, electrical machinery, and transport equipment. During the 1980s, however, the growth rates of these industries recovered, accompanied by accelerated growth in food products, beverages and tobacco products, wood and wood products, paper and printing, textiles, and leather and fur products. Indeed, the 1980s proved to be a period of broad-based industrial growth for India. In the 1990s, there was a fall in the growth rate of real value added in food products, paper and printing, rubber, plastic and petroleum products, and in electrical and nonelectrical machinery. On the other hand, there was an increase in growth rate of real value added in basic metals and metal products.

Factors determining industrial growth. Several econometric studies have been carried out to explain variations in industrial growth, concluding that India's industrial deceleration of the mid-1960s was largely due to the following factors: unsatisfactory agricultural performance affecting agricultural incomes, slowdown in public investment, infrastructure constraints, reduced scope of import substitution, deterioration of intersectoral terms of trade unfavorably affecting industry, and the adverse effects of restrictive industrial and trade policies on industrial costs and efficiency.

The resurgence in industrial growth in the 1980s may be traced more or less to the same set of factors. Growth of per capita agricultural incomes, improvement in the rate and pattern of gross domestic capital formation, particularly in public investment, step-up in investment in infrastructure and better management, less adverse trends in intersectoral terms of trade, and reforms of industrial and trade policies all contributed to the revival of industrial growth.

The deceleration in industrial growth in the postreform period seems to have been caused by stalled reforms. The initial 1991 reforms should have been followed up quickly by sharp reductions in tariffs on imports, while pulling down the remaining restrictions on foreign direct investment and removing all policy-induced rigidities in industrial labor markets. This was not done, however, hence the adverse effect on growth.

One important difference between the industrial growth in the 1990s and that prior to the mid-1980s relates to exports. From 1973–1974 to 1984–1985, the contribution of export expansion to output growth in manufacturing was merely 5 percent, while that in the

period 1989–1990 to 1997–1998 was 24 percent. The ratio of India's manufactured exports to the value of production of the registered manufacturing sector was 6.7 percent in 1980–1981 and 8.4 percent in 1990–1991, and increased to 15.4 percent in 2000–2001. Exports have now become an important source of industrial growth in India, and for this reason international market conditions exert an important influence on industrial growth performance. During 1990–1995, the global exports of manufactures grew at the rate of 8.6 percent; during 1995–2000, that growth rate was only 4.5 percent. With a quarter of India's industrial growth now dependent on export, world markets in the latter half of the 1990s clearly have had a significant adverse effect on India's domestic industrial output.

Diversification

Since self-reliance through the building of heavy industries was the key element of India's industrialization strategy, a major drive for diversification was launched in the mid-1950s, establishing machine tool industries, heavy electricals, machine building, and other branches of heavy industry. The value of production of machine tools increased from Rs. (rupees) 3 million in 1950–1951 to Rs. 8 million in 1960–1961 and Rs. 430 million in 1970–1971. Production of power transformers increased from 0.2 million kilovolt amps (KVA) in 1950–1951 to 8.1 million KVA in 1970–1971. Production of crude steel increased from 1.5 million tons in 1950–1951 to 6.1 million tons in 1970–1971. Production of caustic soda increased from 12 thousand tons in 1950–1951 to 371 thousand tons in 1970–1971, while the production of soda ash increased from 46 to 449 thousand tons in that period. Between 1956–1957 and 1970–1971, the value of chemical industrial production increased at the rate of 12.6 percent per annum.

In spite of the setback to industrial growth after the mid-1960s, the progress in diversification of the industrial structure was maintained. The weight of capital goods in the Index of Industrial Production increased from 4.7 percent in 1956 to 11.8 percent in 1960 and further to 15.2 percent in 1970. The weight of "basic goods" (heavy chemicals, fertilizers, basic metals, and cement) increased from 22.3 percent in 1956 to 32.3 percent in 1970 and further to 39.4 percent in 1980. The weight of consumer goods, on the other hand, declined from 48.4 percent in 1956 to 31.5 percent in 1970 and further to 23.7 percent in 1980.

The diversification achieved by India in its industrial structure is reflected in a relatively high share of high and medium tech industries in manufacturing value added. In 1985 this ratio was 56 percent for India, the foremost position among all the major industrializing countries

(UNIDO, *Industrial Development Report, 2002/03*, p. 164). This ratio was 54 percent for Brazil, 49 percent for China, 47 percent for Korea and Malaysia, 43 percent for Taiwan, 37 percent for Mexico, 25 percent for Indonesia, and 18 percent for Thailand. But, in terms of the share of high and medium tech products in manufactured exports, most of these countries were ahead of India, with the exception of China and Indonesia. By 1998 China had surpassed India, and Indonesia had caught up with India in terms of the level of technological sophistication of manufactured exports.

The fact that the share of medium and high tech industries is relatively high in India's industrial production while the products of such industries constitute only a small part of India's manufactured exports shows that in most cases these industries are not internationally competitive. Since India's initial drive for diversification was directed at attaining self-reliance in a wide range of industrial products, that process neglected cost considerations, which did not receive sufficient attention. Its new industries therefore were not under any strong pressure to improve efficiency and reduce costs until 1991. In such an environment, the global competitiveness of new industries was obviously low.

Technical Change

In the last five decades, the main source of technical change in Indian industry was the purchase of technology from foreign firms against royalty, technical fees and lump-sum payments, and the efforts made by Indian firms to adapt technologies to local conditions. Another important source was the import of capital goods embodying advanced technology. Heavy machinery imports declined as domestic machinery replaced them. While foreign direct investment can potentially be an important source of technical advance, the level of foreign direct investment in India remained very low until the end of the 1980s. In the postreform period, there has been a spurt in foreign direct investment in Indian industries. However, as a ratio to the annual rate of capital formation in manufacturing, foreign investment inflows have remained low (about 5 percent from 1992–1993 to 1998–1999).

A large amount of technology has entered Indian industry through the route of technology imports, that is, the purchase of foreign technology. Three phases can be distinguished in the government policy on foreign collaboration: 1948 to 1968, 1969 to 1979, and 1980 onward. In the first phase, the foreign collaboration policies were liberal, and the annual average number of foreign collaborations increased from a mere 35 during 1948–1955 to 210 during 1964–1970. Technology payments increased from Rs. 12 million in 1956–1957 to Rs. 190 million in

1967–1968. However, in the absence of competitive pressure, there was little incentive to learn, absorb, assimilate, and upgrade the foreign technologies. In the second phase, 1969 to 1979, Indian policies regarding foreign collaboration were highly restrictive. The focus was on technological self-reliance, making use of the infrastructure built in the previous phase. To generate demand for indigenous technologies, the government reversed its policies on foreign technology acquisition. Numerous restrictions were imposed on foreign collaborations. There were lists specifying industries in which foreign investment would be permitted with or without technical collaboration, industries in which only technical collaboration would be permitted, and industries in which no foreign collaboration, financial or technical, would be permitted. There were also elaborate regulations relating to the duration of technology agreements, payment of royalties, and lump-sum transfers for imported technology. Technology sellers had to abide by conditions connected to export restrictions, the use of trademarks, and the importer's rights to sell or sub-license the imported technology. Because of such policies, the growth rate of technology payments fell, as did the level of foreign direct investment. The overall effect of the restrictive technology policies from 1969 to 1979 was that Indian industry could not bring into use internationally competitive technology, with adverse consequences on its export performance.

Since 1980 the policies on foreign collaboration have been progressively liberalized, especially since 1991. For instance, the procedure for approval has been made easier and the ceiling on royalty and lump-sum payments has been raised. This liberalization has led to a dramatic increase in the number of foreign collaborations, from an annual average of 230 in the 1970s to about 550 in the 1980s. The average number of collaborations (technical and financial combined) was about 730 in the 1980s, increasing to about 1,600 in the 1990s.

Royalty and license payments made by India for imported technology were $25.1 million in 1985, increasing to $200.8 million in 1998. As a share of gross national product, this increased from 0.012 percent in 1985 to 0.047 percent in 1998. However, this achievement is still small in comparison with other industrializing countries. In 1998 royalty and license payments for technology was $2,392 million in Malaysia, $2,369 million in Korea, $1,149 million in Taiwan, and $420 million in China.

Productivity Change
Labor and capital productivity. From 1951 to 1970, the average growth rate of labor productivity in Indian

industry was about 5 percent per annum. In the 1970s the growth rate was much lower (about 1% per annum, according to some estimates). In the 1980s and 1990s, the growth rate of labor productivity picked up again to a little over 6 percent per annum. Increases in capital intensity (ratio of fixed capital stock at constant price to employment) made a major contribution to increases in labor productivity. Capital intensity grew at the rate of about 5 percent per annum during the 1950s and 1960s, about 3 percent per annum during the 1970s, and about 7 percent per annum during the 1980s and 1990s.

During the 1950s and 1960s, capital productivity (measured by the ratio of real value added to the value of fixed capital stock at constant prices) in Indian industry declined by about 1.5 percent per annum. During this period, there were major changes in the structure of the industrial sector in favor of metals, machinery, and chemical industries. These industries are relatively more capital intensive and have relatively low capital productivity as compared to traditional industries such as textiles. Therefore, the changes in industrial structure had an adverse effect on capital productivity during the 1950s and 1960s. The downward trend in capital productivity continued in the 1970s, but reversed later.

Total factor productivity. To assess overall production efficiency, the concept of total factor productivity (TFP) is commonly used in productivity studies. TFP may be defined as the ratio of output to total input, a composite measure of the technical change and changes in the efficiency with which technology is applied to production.

During the decades of 1950s and 1960s, the average growth rate of TFP in Indian manufacturing was very low, about 1 percent or a little less than 1 percent per annum. Trade and industrial policies of India's government, especially import control and domestic industrial licensing, curbed competition; the lack of competition protected inefficiency and blunted incentive for cost reduction. Control of foreign exchange and raw materials, policies aimed at control of monopoly, led to industrial fragmentation, which adversely affected efficiency since scale economies could not be exploited. Moreover, India's general economic condition, characterized by shortages of materials and power, as well as transport bottlenecks, was not conducive to productivity growth.

The increased industrial growth rate in the period from 1980–1981 to 1985–1986, as compared to the period from 1965–1966 to 1979–1980, may be attributed to improvement in productivity growth in the first half of the 1980s, thanks to the liberalization of economic policies.

Estimates reported in some recent studies on productivity in Indian industry indicate that the average growth rate during the 1980s was 3 to 4 percent per annum. By comparison, the growth rate in the 1990s was only about 1.5 to 2 percent per annum. The explanation for that deceleration seems to lie mostly in capacity underutilization during the 1990s. As a result of the reforms, India's manufacturing sector had an investment boom in the first half of the 1990s, raising capacity output sharply, though demand did not expand as rapidly, leading to underutilization of capacity, which had an adverse effect on productivity.

B. N. Goldar

See also **Industrial Policy since 1956; Private Industrial Sector, Role of**

BIBLIOGRAPHY

Aggarwal, Aradhna. "Technology Policies and Acquisition of Technological Capabilities in the Industrial Sector: A Comparative Analysis of the Indian and Korean Experiences." *Science, Technology and Society* 6, no. 2 (2001): 255–304.

Ahluwalia, Isher Judge. *Industrial Growth in India: Stagnation since the Mid-Sixties.* Delhi: Oxford University Press, 1985.

———. *Productivity and Growth in Indian Manufacturing.* Delhi: Oxford University Press, 1991.

Balakrishnan, P., and K. Pushpangadan. "Total Factor Productivity Growth in Manufacturing Industry: A Fresh Look." *Economic and Political Weekly* 29, no. 31 (1994): 2028–2035.

———. "What Do We Know about Productivity Growth in Indian Industry." *Economic and Political Weekly* 33, nos. 33–34 (1998): 2241–2246.

———. "TFPG in Manufacturing: The 80s Revisited." *Economic and Political Weekly* 37, no. 4 (2002): 323–325.

Bhagwati, J. N., and T. N. Srinivasan. *Foreign Trade Regimes and Economic Development: India.* New York: Columbia University Press, 1975.

Desai, Ashok V. "A Decade of Reforms." *Economic and Political Weekly* 36, no. 50 (2001): 4627–4630.

Goldar, B. *Productivity Growth in Indian Industry.* New Delhi: Allied Publishers, 1986.

———. "Productivity and Factor Use Efficiency in Indian Industry." In *Indian Industrialization: Structure and Policy Issues,* edited by A. Ghosh, K. K. Subramanian, M. Eapen, and H. A. Drabu. Delhi: Oxford University Press, 1992.

———. "TFP Growth in Indian Manufacturing in 1980s." *Economic and Political Weekly* 37, no. 49 (2002): 4966–4968.

Goldar, B., and Arup Mitra. "Total Factor Productivity Growth in Indian Industry: A Review of Studies." In *National Income Accounts and Data Systems,* edited by B. S. Minhas. New Delhi: Oxford University Press, 2002.

Kumar, Nagesh, and Aradhna Aggarwal. "Liberalization, Outward Orientation and In-house R&D Activity of Multinational and Local Firms: A Quantitative Exploration for Indian Manufacturing." Discussion Paper no. 7. New Delhi: Research and Information System for Nonaligned and Other Developing Countries, 2000.

Kumari, Anita. "Sources of Growth in Indian Engineering Industries." Ph.D. diss., University of Delhi, Delhi, 2003.

Krishna, K. L. "Industrial Growth and Diversification." In *Indian Economy since Independence*, edited by Uma Kapila. 14th ed. New Delhi: Academic Foundation, 2002.

Nagaraj, R. "Industrial Growth: Further Evidence and Towards an Explanation and Issues." *Economic and Political Weekly* 35, no. 41 (1990): 2313–2332.

———. "Industrial Policy and Performance since 1980: Which Way Now?" *Economic and Political Weekly* 38, no. 35 (2003): 3707–3715.

Nayyar, Deepak, ed. *Industrial Growth and Stagnation: The Debate in India*. Mumbai: Oxford University Press, 1994.

Rao, J. M. "Manufacturing Productivity Growth: Method and Measurement." *Economic and Political Weekly* 31, no. 44 (1996): 2927–2936.

Trivedi, P., A. Prakash, and D. Sinate. "Productivity in Major Manufacturing Industries in India: 1973–1974 to 1997–1998." Development Research Group Study no. 20, Department of Economic Analysis and Policy. Mumbai: Reserve Bank of India, 2000.

Uchikawa, S. "Investment Boom and Underutilisation of Capacity in the 1990s." *Economic and Political Weekly* 36, no. 34 (2001): 3247–3754.

Uchikawa, S., ed. *Economic Reforms and Industrial Structure in India*. New Delhi: Manohar Publishers, 2002.

United Nations Industrial Development Organization. *Industrial Development Report, 2002/03*. Vienna: UNIDO, 2003.

INDUSTRIAL LABOR AND WAGES, 1800–1947

Throughout the British colonial period, workers in "unorganized," small-scale units outnumbered those in modern factories, mines, and railroad construction. As late as 1911, 95 percent of industrial workers were employed in units other than registered factories. The level of employment in important industries such as hand-loom manufacture and spinning no doubt declined due to the competition of European imports and to the disappearance of demand from pre-colonial states. But weaving, rice processing, *bidi* (cigarette) rolling, leather work, carpet making, and gold thread manufacture gave work to substantial numbers of people.

Changes in the modes of work and in production relations could be as significant in smaller industries as in large factories. Merchants frequently tightened their control over artisan producers, small workshops using wage labor sometimes replaced family-based units, and workers often had to adjust to new forms of technology.

In the hand-loom industry, there was extensive mobility of labor, as thousands of weavers moved from depressed areas of northern and southeastern India to more dynamic centers of the Bombay presidency. There was also considerable conflict between workers and employers, though often it was expressed in the form of individual, "everyday" acts of resistance, such as slowing the pace of work, embezzling yarn, or absconding with cash advances. There was little collective action by workers against employers in small-scale production until the 1930s and 1940s, when several unions were established and strikes were organized in the hand-loom, *bidi*, and gold thread industries, at least in western India.

Labor in Large-Scale Industry

What most distinguished the "organized" sector was in fact not its degree of organization or, in all cases, its technology, but the size of the pools of labor it required. At the peak of their activity, railway building, cotton textile production in Mumbai (Bombay), jute manufacture in Kolkata (Calcutta), and coal mining in eastern India each gave employment to hundreds of thousands of workers, while industries such as the cotton mills of Ahmedabad and Kanpur, the steel mills of Jamshedpur, and the gold mines of Mysore used tens of thousands. Because of the small number of such industrial enclaves, employment in registered factories was never more than 1 percent of the Indian population. Nonetheless, each industry needed to attract sizable numbers of workers to a concentrated locale, with the largest industries recruiting labor from great distances. Because of constantly fluctuating economic circumstances, many industrialists were unwilling to offer significant prospects for long-term employment to a large portion of their workers, often hiring them instead on a casual daily basis, then discarding them when the workers were no longer needed.

In most cases, migrants to industrial workplaces came from "labor catchment areas," rural regions where marginal farmers often struggled for subsistence on small plots of land. Bihar, Orissa, and parts of the United Provinces in eastern India, Telugu- and Tamil-speaking districts in the Madras presidency, and the Konkan and Deccan regions in the Bombay presidency were all areas marked by significant outflows of labor. In the textile industries of Bombay and Calcutta, ex-artisans provided an important part of the skilled workforce. Workers were often recruited by intermediary contractors and jobbers either in the villages or, more commonly, among people who had already moved to cities. These intermediaries frequently took small payments from the workers in return for the jobs they provided. Migrants looking for employment also relied on relatives and fellow villagers whom they had followed to industrial centers. Workers often retained rural connections to their home regions, in part due to cultural attachments and kin ties, in part because maintaining landholdings provided some insurance against the uncertainties of industrial employment.

Conditions of work in large-scale industry were generally quite difficult. Workers labored as long as fifteen

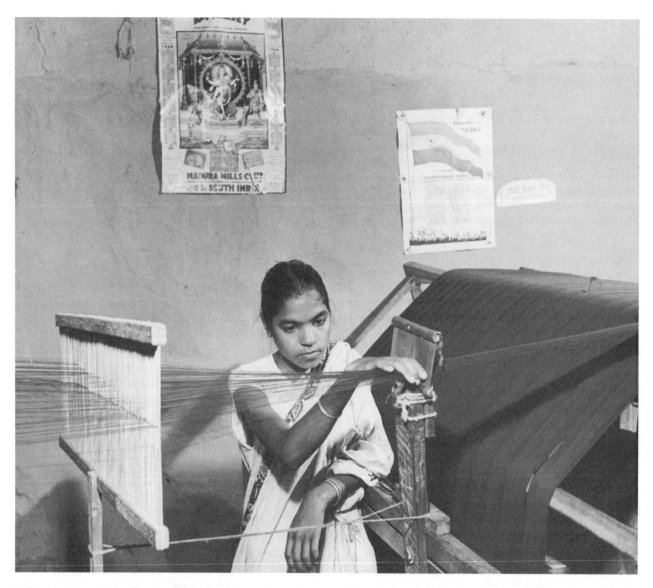

Indian Girl at Loom, 1944. While historians tend to disagree on the veracity of available statistics for laborers' wages in the nineteenth and twentieth centuries, the consensus is that compensation was rarely adequate. This frequently necessitated the employment of all family members, including children. BRADLEY SMITH / CORBIS.

hours daily, for instance, in the Bombay mills, after electricity was introduced in the 1880s and before legislation established a maximum workday of twelve hours in 1911. Jobbers often tyrannized workers, and the sexual harassment of women appears to have been widespread. Health and safety standards remained low. Work rules frequently gave to employers' arbitrary and unlimited authority to punish workers by dismissal or the docking of pay. At the same time, the ability of employers to impose tight discipline in practice was limited by their own internal divisions, their dependence on intermediaries, and their reluctance to develop a permanent workforce. Workers' resistances, whether in the form of collective action or of individual methods of everyday struggle, could affect employers' ability to introduce new technology, to

standardize wages, or to speed up production. In railroad construction managers learned that they needed to offer significant cash advances before they could hire workers. In short, employers often had to make accommodations to workers' social structures and expectations.

Women in Industry

Women's role in modern industry was increasingly marginalized over time. Women constituted 37 percent of mine workers in eastern India in 1920 but only 11 percent in 1938; they composed 25 percent of the workforce in Bombay mills in 1896 but only 12 percent in 1944; their proportions in the jute industry fell from 21 percent in 1901 to little more than 12 percent by 1950. This trend seems to have been caused by a convergence of several factors: the strengthening of norms of social respectability discouraging women's work outside the household (especially in rural north India); British colonial legislation that restricted working hours for women; and the role of jobbers and other middlemen in hiring. There is some evidence of decline in women's industrial role even in informal industry. Spinning of cotton yarn dwindled into virtual economic insignificance, and the use of machinery displaced women in professions such as rice husking and warping of yarn. A few occupations involving women, such as rolling *bidi*s, did expand, but the overall trend toward "de-industrialization" for women seems clear.

Wages and Earnings

Compensation for industrial work was uneven and generally poor. When male workers could find jobs, these positions usually paid better than unskilled agricultural work or employment as hand-loom weavers. There was no single trend for wages in India as a whole. Available statistics seem to suggest that while real wages in the cotton textile industry of Bombay and Ahmedabad rose after World War I, wages in the jute industry were stagnant until the late 1930s, and then increased only to a minor extent. But these general trends mask considerable internal variations and instability.

Most workers received less compensation than they needed to support their families. This sometimes necessitated labor by all family members, including children. Women were paid less for the same work as men when they could get it, but more commonly they were confined to less prestigious forms of employment deemed "supplementary," where payments were particularly poor.

Evidence on wages for workers in small-scale industry is especially scanty, but unpublished research suggests that real earnings of hand-loom weavers in some cases fell over the course of the nineteenth century to levels little higher than those received by unskilled agricultural laborers. Other forms of artisan wage employment, such as carpentry and brick masonry, may have kept better pace with rising prices.

Strikes, Trade Unions, and Workers' Consciousness

Workers in large-scale production took part in collective resistance almost from the inception of the factory system, but sustained participation in trade unions was limited. Nearly every major industry had an extensive history of strikes, and dramatic episodes of confrontation with factory management were not uncommon. There were also several major waves of strikes for India as a whole: in 1919–1920, 1928–1929, 1937–1939, and 1945–1947. Some strikes proved successful in winning higher wages or in defending against wage cuts planned by employers. Strikes sometimes brought into being the organizations necessary to sustain workers' solidarity and to bargain collectively, but such unions often died out after the strikes were broken or workers lost interest. A number of significant trade unions with substantial membership did develop, for instance, the Gandhian Ahmedabad Textile Labour Association after World War I; the Bombay Textile Labour Union in the mid-1920s and the communist Girni Kamgar Union after the later 1920s (both among mill workers of Bombay); and the Jamshedpur Labour Association and the Jamshedpur Labour Federation in the Tata steel mills of Bihar. There were also national organizations of workers, most notably, the All-India Trade Union Congress, founded in 1920. But few of these organizations commanded the support of a majority of workers over long stretches of time. Labor organizations often became torn by internal conflict. The hostility of employers and occasional repression by the colonial government were major causes of the ephemeral character of union organization.

Discussions about workers' consciousness are among the most contentious issues in the labor history of India. Certainly contemporary scholars no longer accept the notion that work experiences in factories and mines led automatically to the formation of broad solidarities among workers. Divisions among the working class were widespread. Often these resulted from ethnic identities that were developing in Indian cities, differential skills and earnings in workplaces, and competing social networks in working class residential areas. Indian workers could be drawn to nationalist, caste-based, and communalist activity as strongly as action on the basis of class. Workers' solidarities often shifted over time as the larger political environment changed. Consciousness of exploitation in the workplace could just as easily give expression to caste- as to class-based assertions of equality. Even nationalist and communalist politics among the urban poor, however, were often colored by uniquely working class perspectives grounded in the experience of deprivation and subordination. As discussion of these issues continues, labor history, once thought to be virtually moribund, now appears to be undergoing a significant revival.

Douglas E. Haynes

See also **Economic Development, Importance of Institutions in and Social Aspects of; Economic Policy and Change, 1800–1947**

BIBLIOGRAPHY

Chakrabarty, Dipesh. *Rethinking Working-Class History: Bengal, 1890–1940.* Princeton, N.J.: Princeton University

Press, 1989. A stimulating work, often seen to epitomize a cultural approach to labor history.

Chakravarty, Lalita. "Emergence of an Industrial Labour Force in a Dual Economy: British India, 1880–1920." *Indian Economic and Social History Review* 15, no. 3 (1978): 249–328. A superb analysis of the rural sources of migration in British India as a whole.

Chandavarkar, Rajnarayan. *The Origins of Industrial Capitalism in India: Business Strategies and the Working Classes in Bombay, 1900–1940.* Cambridge, U.K., and New York: Cambridge University Press, 1994. A magisterial study of capital-labor relations in Bombay, with a special focus on the textile industry.

———. *Imperial Power and Popular Politics: Class, Resistance and the State in India, c. 1850–1950.* Cambridge, U.K.: Cambridge University Press, 1998. A provocative collection of essays on capital, labor, and the colonial state.

De Haan, Arjan. *Unsettled Settlers: Migrant Workers and Industrial Capitalism in Calcutta.* Kolkata: K. P. Bagchi and Company, 1994.

Gooptu, Nandini. *The Politics of the Urban Poor in Early Twentieth Century India.* Cambridge, U.K.: Cambridge University Press, 2001.

Haynes, Douglas. "The Logic of the Artisan Firm in a Capitalist Economy: Handloom Weavers and Technological Change in Western India, 1880–1947." In *Institutions and Economic Change in South Asia,* edited by Burton Stein and Sanjay Subrahmanyam. Delhi: Oxford University Press, 1996.

Kerr, Ian J. *Building the Railways of the Raj, 1850–1900.* Delhi: Oxford University Press, 1995.

Morris, Morris David. *The Emergence of an Industrial Labor Force in India: A Study of the Bombay Cotton Mills, 1854–1947.* Berkeley: University of California Press, 1965. Classic early study of labor in the Bombay textile industry.

Mukherji, K. "Trends in Real Wages in Cotton Textile Mills in Bombay City and Island, from 1900 to 1951"; "Trends in Real Wages in Jute Textile Industry from 1900 to 1951"; and "Trends in Real Wages in Cotton Textile Industry of Ahmedabad from 1900 to 1951," in *Artha Vijnana* 1, no. 1 (1959): 82–96; 2, no. 1 (1960): 57–69; and 3, no. 2 (1961): 124–134. The most important sources of quantitative information on wages in Indian industry.

Nair, Janaki. *Miners and Millhands: Work, Culture and Politics in Princely Mysore.* New Delhi: Sage, 1998.

Roy, Tirthankar. *Traditional Industry in the Economy of Colonial India.* Cambridge, U.K.: Cambridge University Press, 1999. An overview of small-scale industry, one that pays much attention to capital-labor relations.

Sen, Samita. *Women and Labour in Colonial India: The Bengal Jute Industry.* Cambridge, U.K.: Cambridge University Press, 1999. The most wide-ranging study of gender issues in Indian industry.

Simeon, Dilip. *The Politics of Labour under Late Colonialism: Workers, Unions and the State in Chota Nagpur, 1928–1939.* Delhi: Manohar, 1995.

INDUSTRIAL LABOR MARKET, WAGES AND EMPLOYMENT, SINCE 1950

India is a large agrarian economy; as of 1999-2000, 60 percent of its workforce was employed in agriculture, living in rural areas and producing about 25 percent of gross domestic product. In terms of institutional structure, the organized (formal) sector employed slightly less than 10 percent of the total workforce to produce 40 percent of net domestic output, mostly originating in the industrial and services sectors; the rest were in the unorganized (informal) sector. The organized sector consists of public sector, private corporate enterprises and cooperatives, manufacturing firms registered under the Factories Act of 1948, or the Bidi Cigar Workers' Act of 1966, and recognized educational institutions. The public sector constitutes about 66 percent of organized employment.

Worker-population ratio in the economy has remained roughly stable, at around 40 percent; it is about 28 percent for women (with sizable underestimation). The participation of children in the workforce has steadily declined, though in absolute numbers it remains substantial, concentrated in selected labor-intensive industries, often producing goods for export.

About 30 percent of India's population is urban, residing mainly in the metropolitan cities. Rural-urban migration to the cities moderates urban wage growth, and also causes considerable open (as well as disguised) unemployment in the informal sector. The industrial sector's share in the workforce (mining, manufacturing, construction, and utilities) is around 18 percent, producing 27 percent of domestic output. Only about 20 percent of industrial employment is in the organized sector, much of it is in urban areas and is predominantly male.

Changes in Workforce Composition

After remaining roughly constant, at little over 70 percent, from 1950 to 1980, the share of India's workforce in agriculture declined to about 60 percent by 2000. In 1980 both China and India had roughly about the same proportion of workforce engaged in agriculture. Two decades later, while the agricultural share in China declined by 20 percentage points (the majority of whom found employment in manufacturing), the decline in India was only half as great, and the majority of that percentage went into services. In fact, there has been only a marginal rise in the share of manufacturing, while the construction sector has doubled its share, from around 2 percent to 4 percent of the total workforce, between 1983 and 2000.

In 1950 manufacturing employment was concentrated in four states: West Bengal, Maharashtra, Gujarat, and Kerala. Half a century later, Kerala's share has declined, while those of Maharashtra, Gujarat, and West Bengal have increased. Other states that have improved their share in the industrial sector are Karnataka, Andhra Pradesh, Madhya Pradesh, and Haryana.

Household manufacturing has declined in absolute as well as in relative terms, a trend consistent with modern economic growth. However, in contrast, employment has shifted away from the organized (registered or formal) into the unorganized (unregistered) sector. Within the organized sector, employment has shifted to smaller sized factories, as the average factory size has declined from over 140 workers per factory in 1950 to less than 60 in 1976. The trend has persisted in more recent years as well. Proportion of workers employed in factories with 500 or more workers has declined from 55 percent in 1980–1981 to 38 percent in 1997–1998.

Trends in Wages

From 1960 to 1980, real earnings per worker in registered manufacturing grew at about 1.5 percent per year, marginally higher than the growth rate of per capita income during this period. However, in the subsequent two decades (1981–2001) per capita income grew twice as fast as real earnings per worker at 3.6 percent per year. But product wage—nominal earnings deflated by producer prices—grew at a faster rate than real earnings, as a result of the effects of domestic terms of trade. All along, there has been a steady growth of casual and contract labor, and a decline in the share of "permanent" jobs, thus affecting the quality of employment. Despite the wage growth, unit labor cost declined from 1974 to 1998, as labor productivity grew much faster. Moreover, the wage-rental ratio—the ratio of wages to deflator for machinery—also declined during this period. Wage growth in India's public sector, a sizable part of which is industrial, has been consistently faster than that in organized manufacturing. This growth is in part explained by the compensation for higher education and skills required in heavy industry, and in part by the superior bargaining power of public sector employees.

As no official statistics on wages in the urban informal sector exist, wage trends in this sector cannot be directly assessed. It is reasonable to expect, however, that unorganized sector wages lie between those in the organized sector and those in agriculture, subject to education, skill, and experience. Agricultural wages have shown a steady rise since the 1980s; but wages in agriculture as in unorganized urban sector, tend to be too low to overcome poverty.

Labor Market Institutions

State intervention in industrial labor markets began during the colonial period with the introduction of several measures including the restriction of the length of the working day to eight hours, the establishment of a minimum wage, and the right to form trade unions apparently under pressure from British textile interests, who were losing markets to Indian firms. After independence, these efforts were strengthened and their scope widened. However, the scope and effectiveness of labor legislations vary across the states.

The Factories Act of 1948 is the cornerstone of labor regulation in manufacturing, and electricity and gas; the Shops and Establishments Act exists for the tertiary sector. Registration under the Factories Act is mandated for all factories employing ten or more workers using power, and twenty or more workers without using power on a regular basis. As the factory size increases in terms of employment, the act becomes more stringent with respect to benefits for workers.

Minimum wage legislation. India does not have a national minimum wage, or publicly funded universal unemployment insurance. As per the Minimum Wages Act of 1948, the state governments mostly set minimum wages. In some states, like Maharashtra, minimum wages are indexed to the cost of living. Many traditional industries have "Wage Boards," with members drawn from management, unions, and government that periodically determine wages for the industry or region as a whole.

Trade unions and collective bargaining. The Industrial Disputes Act of 1947 is the principal legislation intended to resolve workplace conflicts. The state can intervene in any dispute between employers and employees in the organized sector. Employers or employees are expected to inform the labor commissioner before declaring a lockout or going on strike. In all such disputes, the labor commissioner is, in principle, a party to the decisions. On the face of it, the mechanism is stringent; for instance, to retrench even a single worker, an employer must seek the permission of the state labor commissioner if the factory employs one hundred or more workers.

As in most developed economies in recent decades, union density in India has declined sharply, to about 25 percent among workers in organized manufacturing by 2000. Labor militancy, as measured by workdays lost due to strikes and lockouts, decreased dramatically during this period. Centralized industry- or region-wide collective bargaining mechanisms have given way to decentralized, company based, collective bargaining arrangements.

Public sector. Employment generation in the public sector was accepted as one of implicit objectives. Every ten years, the central government appoints a "pay commission" to determine wages for its employees, arriving at wages (and benefits), based not on the government's ability to pay, or on worker productivity, but on notions of "fair" wages. The pay commission awards tend to become benchmarks for wages in the rest of the public sector. Thus public sector employment generation and wage settlement have become significant determinants of the organized labor market.

Social security. This benefit is largely restricted to the organized sector. Public sector employees have either (indexed) defined benefit pensions or contributory provident fund programs with publicly set interest rates. Central government employees are entitled to health insurance for life, and organized workers have the Employees State Insurance Scheme (a social security plan) that provides health care financed by workers and employers while employed. Some state governments have social security and pension plans for workers belonging to specific industries in the unorganized sector.

Evidence on enforcement of labor laws. As in many developing economies, India's labor legislation tends to be aspirational, with limited effectiveness. Ambiguity in the legal system leaves considerable discretion to the administration and the courts that seem detrimental to the smooth functioning of the labor market. The Factories Act, for instance, is widely violated. In 1990, 58 percent of all manufacturing enterprises employing ten or more workers did not register under the act. The magnitude of underregistration is likely to have gone up further in the 1990s, when the enforcement of many legal provisions was relaxed.

As productive activities are decentralized and geographically dispersed in the unorganized sector, government has little ability to administer minimum wage laws effectively. Even where it is possible, enforcement is problematic, as most of the employment contracts are informal, and unverifiable in courts. Moreover, illiterate workers have little knowledge of their rights; even if they do, they are often too poor to seek redress from administration or courts. Not surprisingly, in factories employing up to one hundred workers, effective trade unions are uncommon, with some states and location excepted.

Development Strategy

Why has industry's share in the workforce remained modest in India compared to fast-growing Asian economies? India's development strategy is believed to have caused the dominance of large, capital-intensive factories that are inconsistent with the economy's resource endowments, compared to East Asia, where small factories dominate. India inherited a skewed distribution of factories for many historical and institutional reasons, including the British managing agency system, a lack of capital market institutions, and the absence of market-based interfirm relationships. Moreover, Indian data overstate large-sized factories in manufacturing, as the data on the size-distribution of factories include generation and distribution of electricity, which tends to be large sized.

Industrial labor in India forms a relatively small proportion of the total workforce; its share has witnessed a modest increase since the 1950s, compared to many rapidly industrializing Asian economies. Household manufacturing's share has declined, both in relative and absolute terms. However, contrary to much of the development experience, Indian industrial employment over the last few decades has diffused into small-sized factory and into nonfactory enterprises. Thus, it is the urban informal (unregistered) manufacturing sector's employment that has been growing.

Regionally, the industrial sector's employment percentage has declined in Kerala, while that in Maharashtra, Gujarat, West Bengal, Karnataka, Andhra Pradesh, and Haryana have increased. Similarly, the shares of urban and male employment probably have declined somewhat in favor of rural and female labor.

Real wages have risen half as fast as the growth in per capita income since the 1980s; the wage share, and wage-rental ratios have declined. Whether the rise in real wages represents compensation for education, skills, and experience or the growing power of organized labor is unclear.

Many believe that India's organized industrial labor market has grown very rigid, as employers must seek the state's permission to retrench even a single worker. Such rigidity is believed to be responsible for rapid wage growth and poor employment growth and increasing substitution of capital for labor. Evidence on the declining strength of unions, the informalization and casualization of the workforce, and the declining unit labor cost are, however, widely adduced to question the rigidity hypothesis.

R. Nagaraj

See also **Agricultural Labor and Wages since 1950; Industrial Policy since 1956**

BIBLIOGRAPHY

Besley, Timothy, and Robin Burgess. "Can Labor Regulations Economic Performance? Evidence from India." *Quarterly Journal of Economics* 69, no. 1 (2004): 91–134.

Bhagwati, Jagdish. *India's Economy: The Shackled Giant.* Oxford: Clarendon Press, 1992.

Bhalotra, Sonia R. "The Puzzle of Jobless Growth in Indian Manufacturing." *Oxford Bulletin of Economics and Statistics* 60, no. 1 (1998): 5–32.

Chadda, G. K., and P. P. Sahu. "Post-Reform Setback in Rural Employment." *Economic and Political Weekly* 37, no. 22 (25 May 2002): 1998–2026.

Dutta Roy, Sudipta. "Job Security Regulation and Worker Turnover: A Study of the Indian Manufacturing Sector." *Indian Economic Review* 37, no. 1 (2002): 141–162.

Ghose, Ajit K. "Employment in Organised Manufacturing in India." *Indian Journal of Labor Economics* 37, no. 2 (April–June 1994): 143–162.

Goldar, Biswanath. "Employment Growth in Organised Manufacturing in India." *Economic and Political Weekly* 35, no. 14 (1 April 2000): 1191–1195.

Mazumdar, Dipak. "Labor Supply in Early Industrialisation." *Economic History Review* 20, no. 3 (1973): 477–494.

Nagaraj, R. "Wages and Employment in Manufacturing Industries: Trends, Hypothesis and Evidence." *Economic and Political Weekly* 29, no. 4 (22 January 1994): 177–186.

———. "Organised Manufacturing Employment." *Economic and Political Weekly* 35, no. 38 (16 September 2000): 3445–3448.

———. "Fall in Organised Manufacturing Employment: A Brief Note." *Economic and Political Weekly* 39, no. 30 (24 July 2004): 3387–3390.

INDUSTRIAL POLICY SINCE 1956 Prior to the economic reforms of the 1990s, industrial policy in India was characterized by an extensive regime of domestic regulation, a strong bias in favor of the public sector (with several industries reserved for the public sector), a restrictive approach to foreign investment, and very heavy protection of domestic industry from foreign competition. Industrial licensing was a major instrument of control of the private sector; under this system, central government permission was needed for both investment in new units (beyond a relatively low threshold) and for substantial expansion of capacity in existing units. Licensing also controlled technology, output mix, capacity location, and import content. Apart from industrial licensing, large industrial firms needed separate permission for investment or expansion under the Monopolies and Restrictive Trade Practices (MRTP) Act, which aimed to prevent the concentration of economic power. There were price and distribution controls in industries such as fertilizers, cement, aluminum, petroleum, and pharmaceuticals. Almost eight hundred items were reserved for production by small-scale units as a way of protecting the small-scale sector from competition from large companies; investment in plant and machinery in any individual unit producing these reserved items could not exceed $250,000.

There were also barriers to industrial restructuring and exit of firms. The Bureau of Industrial and Financial Reconstruction (BIFR) was set up in 1987 and was assigned the task of separating the nonviable "sick" enterprises from the revivable ones and providing rehabilitation packages for the latter and effective solutions for exit to the former. Because the BIFR came into the picture at a fairly advanced stage of "sickness" and because its powers are not mandatory this has meant that it has not been effective in facilitating this exit of the nonviable sick units within the existing institutional constraints. Labor laws have been relatively inflexible, making it difficult for nonviable firms to exit or for firms to reduce labor if needed. As of May 2005, any firm wishing either to close down a plant or to retrench labor in any unit employing more than one hundred workers can do so only with the permission of the state government, and this permission is rarely granted. These provisions discourage employment and are especially onerous for labor-intensive sectors.

The inefficiencies promoted by the regime of industrial controls were supported by India's trade policy regime, which provided very heavy protection to domestic industry from foreign competition. It was characterized by very high and dispersed tariff rates and pervasive import restrictions. Before 1991 India's import tariffs were among the highest in the world, with duty rates above 200 percent being fairly common. Imports of manufactured consumer goods were completely banned. For capital goods, raw materials, and intermediates, some goods were freely importable, but for most items for which domestic substitutes were being produced, imports were only possible with import licenses. The criteria for issuing these licenses was nontransparent, delays were endemic, and corruption unavoidable. Policies toward foreign investment were quite restrictive, reflecting the general protectionist thrust of India's industrial policy.

Domestic Deregulation and Trade Policy Simplification: 1980–1990

Some steps toward reforming the policy regime were taken during the 1980s. Some of the important initiatives in domestic deregulation included the de-licensing of a number of industries, providing flexibility to manufacturing units to produce a range of products rather than a specified product under a given license, encouraging modernization and innovation by exempting such investments from licensing requirements and making it easier to import foreign technology, providing a broader scope for large industrial firms, and encouraging existing industrial undertakings in certain industries to achieve minimum economic levels of operations. These initiatives had the common theme of reducing reliance on physical controls and experimenting with market orientation in domestic regulation. Reforms of the public sector enterprises were limited to providing somewhat greater autonomy to these enterprises from their administrative ministries through signing a series of MoUs (Memoranda of Understanding).

The trade policy changes during the 1980s focused on the simplification of the existing complex procedures; the protectionist thrust nevertheless remained intact. This process was driven by pressures from domestic industry to allow easier access to imported intermediate inputs for capacity utilization and modernization of capital goods. Export subsidies were given to domestic industries in order to offset the anti-export bias of the import substitution regime.

Although the industrial and trade policy reforms of the 1980s were limited, they did lead to significant improvement in productivity in the manufacturing sector; total factor productivity grew at a rate of 2.7 percent per annum in the 1980s, compared with a growth rate of –0.5 percent per annum in the preceding two decades. This experience was to form the basis for much bolder reforms in the industrial and trade policy regime in the1990s.

Economic Reforms since 1991
Domestic deregulation. Industrial policy was radically overhauled during the reforms of the 1990s, with most central government industrial controls being dismantled. Industrial licensing by the central government has been almost done away with, except for a few hazardous and environmentally sensitive industries. The MRTP Act was abolished so that large industrial houses no longer require a separate additional clearance. Instead, the Competition Act of 2002 was put in place on 14 January 2003. It regulates anticompetitive behavior in other ways. The list of industries reserved solely for the public sector has been drastically reduced to three: defense aircraft and warships, atomic energy generation, and railway transportation.

Removal of the reservation in production of items for the small-scale sector started late but gathered momentum after 2000. Even earlier, since some of the reserved items, such as garments, had high export potential, and small-scale limit was a serious constraint to producing in a cost-effective manner for export, exemptions were granted to units if they were substantially engaged in export activity. Beginning with 2001, when fourteen items were removed from the reserved list, a number of such steps were taken, so that by March 2005, 550 items remained on the list. The unreserved items include some important sectors, such as garments, shoes, toys, and auto components, all of which have strong export potential.

Opening up to imports. A process of radical change in trade policy was set in motion in 1991, although progress here was slower than in industrial liberalization. Import licensing was abolished relatively early for capital goods and intermediates, which became freely importable in 1993, coinciding with the switch to a flexible exchange rate regime. For consumer goods, a process of dismantling the quantitative restrictions on imports was started through the introduction of the Special Import License

Scheme, whereby export earnings could be used by exporters to import certain consumer goods. Quantitative restrictions on imports of manufactured consumer goods and agricultural products were finally removed on 1 April 2001, almost exactly ten years after the reforms began.

Progress in reducing tariff protection has been slower and not always steady. The weighted average import duty rate declined from the very high level of 72.5 percent in 1991–1992 to 24.6 percent in 1996–1997. This was followed by a process of slow reversal up to 1999–2000 and a sharp increase in 2000–2001, the latter reflecting the imposition of tariffs on many agricultural commodities in preparation for the removal of quantitative restrictions as part of an obligation to the General Agreement on Tariffs and Trade and the World Trade Organization. In the subsequent years, with the resumption of the reduction in import tariffs, the import-weighted tariff rate was brought down to 18 percent in 2004–2005—still the highest among the developing countries.

A new approach to foreign direct investment. A more liberal approach to foreign direct investment was an important plank of India's reforms during the 1990s. From a policy that was restrictive and selective and that supported mainly technology transfers, foreign investment policy in the 1990s moved toward becoming much more open and proactive. The policy now allows 100 percent foreign ownership in a large number of industries and majority ownership in all except banks, insurance companies, telecommunications, and airlines. A bill to allow up to 74 percent foreign ownership of banks was introduced in Parliament in March 2004. Procedures for obtaining permission have been greatly simplified by listing industries that are eligible for automatic approval up to specified levels of foreign equity (100 percent, 74 percent, and 51 percent). Potential foreign investors investing within these limits need only register with the Reserve Bank of India. For investments in other industries, or for a higher share of equity than is automatically permitted in listed industries, applications are considered by a Foreign Investment Promotion Board that has established a good record of speedy decisions. Beginning in 1993, foreign institutional investors have been allowed to purchase shares of listed Indian companies in the stock market, opening a window for portfolio investment in existing companies.

Public sector reform. Reform of the public sector has been talked about since the 1980s. During the 1990s the government began to undertake sales of minority shares in the better-performing public enterprises, and the enterprises were also given the freedom to access capital markets on the strength of their own performance. They were given more management autonomy in shaping their future. The loss-making enterprises, however, languished for want of budgetary support and political will to close them down.

A Disinvestment Commission was set up in 1997, but privatization was not seriously put on the policy agenda until 2001. The National Democratic Alliance (NDA) government did undertake a few privatizations involving the sale of public sector enterprises with the transfer of management control during the period 2001–2003, the most important being the privatization of Bharat Aluminum Company to a "strategic" private investor. But resistance to privatization was building from within the NDA government when an attempt was made to privatize two oil companies. The United Progressive Alliance (UPA) government, which came to power in 2004, changed the policy to one that is more restrictive. The current policy is that profit-making public sector enterprises will not be privatized, although sale of government equity can continue as long as the government retains 51 percent.

Policies toward infrastructure. Poor infrastructure has been a major constraint on India's industrial performance and competitiveness, especially as the country opens up to foreign competition and seeks to attract investment from abroad. Industrial policy has therefore focused on the need to build better infrastructure, especially electric power generation and distribution, telecommunications, roads, railways, ports, and airports. Prior to 1991, all these infrastructure services were organized as public sector monopolies, and a major challenge of the reforms was how to attract private investment into these sectors in order to meet the enormous investment requirements of upgrading infrastructure. Following the reforms of 1991, these sectors were opened up to private investment at different times with varying degrees of success. Telecommunications is the area in which the effort was most successful. The process was not smooth, and there were many regulatory hiccups on the way. But policy was helped by the fact that the pricing of telecom services (unlike that of power) was not uneconomic; by 2005 there were a handful of strong private sector telecom service suppliers competing effectively with the public sector companies. Access to telecom services has expanded greatly, costs have come down, and quality has improved. Private investment has also been attracted in ports and more recently in airports. In roads, new investment has been dominantly in the public sector, as is the case in most countries, but there has been some limited private sector involvement.

The biggest disappointment has been in the power sector, mainly because both the reform of the incumbent public sector and the setting up of an effective regulatory framework were slow to develop. This was the earliest sector to be opened up, and at one stage there were expectations of being able to attract large investments in generation capacity. These expectations were belied by the continuing financial problems of the distribution segment, which remains unviable because of a combination of unrealistically low tariffs for some sections of consumers (households and farmers) and also very large inefficiencies in collection. Faced with financially bankrupt distribution systems, private investors have been understandably reluctant to invest in generation capacity to supply electricity for which they may not be paid.

In recent years, attempts have been made to depoliticize the process of fixing power tariffs. Following the lead of the central government, a number of state governments have set up independent regulatory commissions for this purpose. Policies are also being directed at improving the efficiency of distribution, both through reforming the existing utilities and by selective privatization. The Electricity Act of 2003 lays out a broad legal framework of regulation for the sector. The act effectively empowers state governments to accelerate power sector reforms by fostering greater competition, increased involvement of the private sector, and better governance. But many details remain to be put in place. The Common Minimum Program of the UPA government has expressed a commitment to review the Electricity Act.

Special economic zones. A May 2005 initiative announced by the government of India is the enactment of a law to establish special economic zones, which would enable industrial units located in the zones to benefit from duty-free entry of imported inputs for production meant for exports, while paying duty on production diverted to the domestic market. The zones will have superior infrastructure and some special facilities, including the possibility of a more liberal labor law regime if the states in which the zones are located request it. Unlike the special regions of China, these zones will be much more compact, but their improved infrastructure should increase their attractiveness to investors.

Role of state governments. Industrial policy reforms by the central government have not always been associated with comparable policy reforms by state governments. Private investors require multiple permissions from state governments to start operations, for example, connections for electricity and water supply, environmental clearances, and other municipal clearances. They also need to interact with the state government administration for their day-to-day operations because of laws governing pollution, sanitation, and workers' welfare and safety. Some states have taken the initiative to ease these interactions and have put in place a process of supportive deregulation to attract private investment. States that have moved faster in this regard have created a better investment climate for private investors and have succeeded in attracting investment. Similarly, states differ in the extent to which they have implemented reform in the power sector, which is a crucial dimension of state policy toward infrastructure. Because liberalization has created a more competitive environment, the payoff from pursuing good policies has increased, thereby increasing the importance of state-level action. It is noteworthy that in one major respect, that is, with regard to modernizing the labor laws to provide the flexibility in shedding labor when necessary, only a few state governments have taken initiatives, while most have resisted reform.

Assessment. The industrial and trade policy regime has come a long way on the road to reform since 1991. However, the gradual pace of reform has meant that important gaps remain. India's tariff levels are still much higher than those in most developing countries. Infrastructure reforms thus far have been far too slow and inadequate. Important areas remain closed to foreign investment or with equity ceilings that are too low. Approach to privatization has been hesitant. Labor laws continue to be rigid.

Notwithstanding these gaps, there is evidence that in recent years Indian industry has been responding to policy reforms by working toward restructuring and reducing costs in a slow but steady manner. Some star performers have emerged on a global scale, particularly the new knowledge-based industries. In addition to information technology, pharmaceuticals and automotive components are two conspicuous examples of manufacturing industries that have successfully developed a global vision and have subsequently penetrated world markets. Biotechnology and animation industries have also been growing very rapidly. However, Indian industry still falls short of the targets set for its growth, presenting a continuing challenge to India's planners and policy makers.

Isher Judge Ahluwalia

See also **Economic Reforms of 1991; Foreign Resources Inflow since 1991; Industrial Growth and Diversification; Infrastructure Development and Government Policy since 1950**

BIBLIOGRAPHY

Ahluwalia, I. J. *Industrial Growth in India: Stagnation since the Mid-Sixties.* Delhi: Oxford University Press, 1985.
———. *India Industrial Development Review.* London: Economist Intelligence Unit; Vienna: UNIDO, 1995.
Ahluwalia, Montek S. "Infrastructure Development in India's Reforms." In *India's Economic Reforms and Development: Essays for Manmohan Singh,* edited by Isher J. Ahluwalia and

I. M. D. Little. Delhi and New York: Oxford University Press, 1998.
Bhagwati, J. N., and P. Desai. *India: Planning for Industrialisation, Industrialization and Trade Policies since 1951.* Delhi: Oxford University Press, 1970.
Bhagwati, J. N., and T. N. Srinivasan. *Foreign Trade Regimes and Economic Development: India.* Delhi: Macmillan, 1975.
Dagli, V. *Report of the Committee on Controls and Subsidies.* Delhi: Ministry of Finance, Government of India, 1979.
Hussain, Abid. *Report of the Committee on Trade Policies.* Delhi: Ministry of Commerce, Government of India, 1984.
———. *Report of the Committee on Small Industries.* Delhi: Ministry of Finance, Government of India, 1993.

INDUS VALLEY CIVILIZATION Also referred to as the Harappa culture, the Indus Valley civilization was the earliest urban, state-level society in South Asia (2600–1900 B.C.) and was contemporaneous with state-level societies in Egypt and Mesopotamia. The core area for settlements of the Indus Civilization has been found in the alluvial plains of the Indus River and its tributaries, as well as along the now dry bed of the Sarasvati-Ghaggar-Hakra-Nara river system that flowed east of the Indus. This eastern river has many modern names but is thought to be associated with the ancient Sarasvati River mentioned in the Rig Veda. Settlements of the Indus Civilization were also established in the rich agricultural regions between the Ganga and the Yamuna rivers and throughout modern Gujarat. Because of its vast extent, the term "Greater Indus Valley" has come to be accepted by most scholars as representing the territories surrounding the Indus River that include sites of this civilization.

In some circles, a new name, the Indus-Sarasvati or Sarasvati civilization, has begun to appear, based on the unsubstantiated argument that a larger proportion of the ancient sites were situated along the bed of the now dry Sarasvati-Ghaggar-Hakra-Nara River. Although the Sarasvati mentioned in the Rig Veda and later Mahābhārata texts is said to be a major river flowing to the sea, with many large and populous cities along its banks, most sites along the dry river channel are relatively small, and even the few large ones are not as large as the major cities on the Indus or its tributaries. Furthermore, the only reason so many small sites have been discovered along the dry river channels is because the region was abandoned and there was very little sedimentation and site disturbance in later times. Most of the smaller settlements along the Indus were covered by flood sediments or buried by later historical villages and cities.

The total geographic area encompassed by sites associated with the Indus Valley civilization is over 262,500 square miles (680,000 sq. km) and includes most of

Brick Wall and Drain Excavated at Mohenjo-Daro. Due to the nature of the topography and the intensity of floods along the Indus and its tributaries, ancient settlements were not able to maintain major canals for irrigation, although they frequently constructed drains for redirecting floodwaters. FOTOMEDIA ARCHIVE.

modern Pakistan and parts of western India and northern Afghanistan. Indus artifacts have been found at sites in Oman and the Persian Gulf region, as well as in Iran, Iraq, and various Central Asian countries, such as Turkmenistan.

Origins and Chronology

The origins of the Indus civilization can be traced to the early Neolithic settlements such as Mehrgarh, located along the borders of the major alluvial plain of the Indus River, and subsequent Chalcolithic cultures that emerged at sites like Harappa, along the Indus and Ghaggar-Hakra river systems. All of these communities appear to be descended from even earlier Paleolithic peoples living in the subcontinent and are not the result of migration from outside regions.

The chronology of the Indus civilization is now based primarily on radiocarbon dates, using charcoal or burned bone from hearths, and undisturbed stratigraphic levels. While the origin and decline of specific Indus sites varies slightly from one region to the next, excavations at the site of Harappa between 1986 and 2001 have provided more than 120 radiocarbon dates that can be used to define the chronology of this major urban center and surrounding regions of the northern Indus Valley. The early Ravi Phase (3500–2800 B.C.) corresponds to the Chalcolithic period, when agricultural settlements were established in the alluvial plains and regional cultures were emerging in different regions of the northern and western subcontinent. The subsequent Kot Diji Phase (2800–2600 B.C.) represents the culmination of regional cultures and the establishment of the first small urban centers. The Harappa Phase (2600–1900 B.C.) is the major period of urban expansion and corresponds to the Bronze Age in Mesopotamia and Egypt. Some scholars refer to the Harappa Phase, which lasts for over seven hundred years, as the Mature Harappan or Mature Indus period. This long time period can now be divided into three subphases on the basis of major rebuilding episodes and site expansion, as well as changes in artifact and writing styles. The Late Harappa Phase represents the final Indus

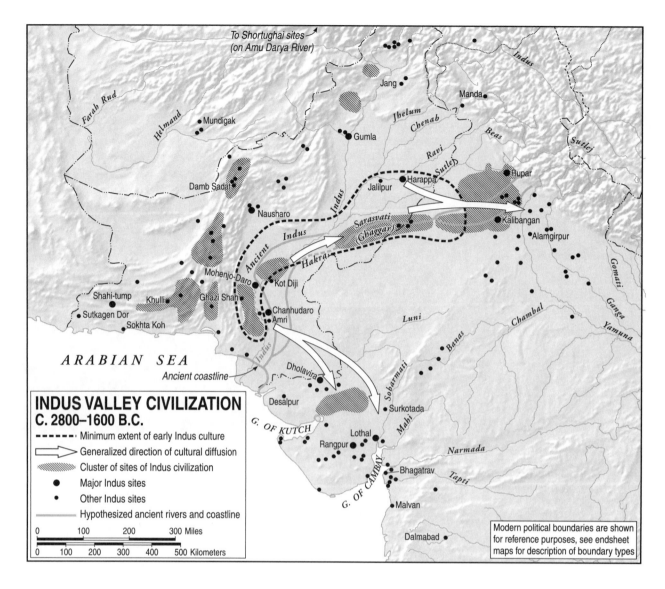

INDUS VALLEY CIVILIZATION
C. 2800–1600 B.C.

- - - - - Minimum extent of early Indus culture

⇨ Generalized direction of cultural diffusion

▨ Cluster of sites of Indus civilization

● Major Indus sites

• Other Indus sites

Hypothesized ancient rivers and coastline

|0   100   200   300 Miles|

|0   100   200   300   400   500 Kilometers|

Modern political boundaries are shown for reference purposes, see endsheet maps for description of boundary types

occupation of the city. From 1900 to 1800 B.C. a transitional phase can be identified, during which pottery traditions, burial practices, and other cultural patterns began to change. What followed was a longer period of transformation and eventual decline that continued until around 1300 B.C. in the region around Harappa, but may have lasted as late as 1000 B.C. in other regions to the east.

Geography and Climate

The geographical setting of the Indus civilization includes the western plateau of Baluchistan and the piedmont zone along the western edge of the Indus. Resources of wood and minerals were obtained from the northern mountains of Afghanistan, Pakistan, and India. Two major river systems, the Indus on the west and the Ghaggar-Hakra on the east, combined to create a vast area for grazing and a fertile alluvial plain for agriculture. This plain can be divided into two regions: the Punjab in

the north has higher rainfall from both the summer monsoon and the winter rains; the region of Sind in the south is flatter and semiarid, with unpredictable rainfall. The eastern border of the civilization extended from the Yamuna and Ganga rivers in the north, to the Aravalli ranges and the Thar Desert of Rajasthan, eventually ending at the mouth of the Narmada River in south Gujarat. The coastal zone bordering the Arabian Sea extended from the rugged Makran hills in the west, through the Indus delta and the Greater and Lesser Rann of Kutch, to the Gulf of Khambhat in the southeast. The large island of Kutch, the peninsula of Saurasthra, and the coastal plains of north and south Gujarat represent several distinct geographical regions, but are generally included as part of the Greater Indus Valley region.

Two major climate systems dominate the greater Indus Valley. The southwest summer monsoon brings rain and floods from June to August, and the winter cyclonic

TABLE 1

General Indus chronology based on radiocarbon dates from Harappa		
Period 1	Ravi aspect of the Hakra Phase	3500 B.C.–c. 2800 B.C.
Period 2	Kot Diji (Early Harappa) Phase	c. 2800 B.C.–c. 2600 B.C.
Period 3A	Harappa Phase A	c. 2600 B.C.–c. 2450 B.C.
Period 3B	Harappa Phase B	c. 2450 B.C.–c. 2200 B.C.
Period 3C	Harappa Phase C	c. 2200 B.C.–c. 1900 B.C.
Period 4	Harappa/Late Harappa Transitional	c. 1900 B.C.–c. 1800 B.C.
Period 5	Late Harappa Phase	c. 1800 B.C.–<1300 B.C.

SOURCE: Courtesy of author.

system contributes snow in the higher elevations and light rains throughout the Punjab and sometimes into Sind. Snow melt in the spring results in major flooding, followed by the summer monsoon and more flooding.

Settlements

Over 2,600 sites have been discovered, and they include major cities (250 to 500 acres, or 100–200 hectares) such as Mohenjo-Daro, Harappa, Dholavira, and Rakhigarhi, as well as smaller urban centers (125 to 250 acres, or 50–100 hectares) like Ganweriwala that are located along the major river systems. Regional towns (25 to 125 acres, or 10–50 hectares) such as Kalibangan and small towns (2 to 25 acres, or 5–10 hectares) like Lothal, Chanhudaro, and Banawali were situated along important tributaries or along major trade routes between the major cities. The hinterland was dotted with villages (2.5 to 12 acres, or 1–5 hectares) such as Kot Diji, Nausharo, Balakot, and Nageshwar, as well as small hamlets (2.5 acres, or 1 hectare) that may have been country estates like Allahdino or coastal outposts such as Surkotada.

Major features of Indus sites. Perimeter walls are found around most settlements, with gateways that allowed for the control of access into and out of the settlement. These walls were probably built for defensive purposes, as well as for control of trade and protection from floods. Standardized bricks with a thickness to width to length ratio of 1:2:4 are a diagnostic feature of the Indus civilization. All domestic and public architecture throughout the Indus Valley and adjacent regions used bricks with this same strict proportion. The standardization of brick size is probably the result of craft specialization, combined with the migration of kin-related masons and brick makers to sites throughout the region, rather than highly centralized state control as proposed by early scholars.

Main streets were not paved and generally range in width from 13 or 16 feet (4–5 m), which would allow two-way cart traffic. Large sewers, sometimes covered with limestone slabs, were placed along the side of major streets and eventually emptied through the main gateways or walls out onto the plain. Many of the large drains were covered with a corbelled arch to allow the drain to pass under streets, walls, or other buildings. Narrow side streets, 6 to 10 feet (2–3 m) wide for one-way cart traffic, led into the major neighborhoods, and smaller lanes for pedestrian traffic created an irregular network linking one house to another. Small drains leading from bathing areas and latrines fed into sump pits and larger drains on the main streets. Rectangular trash bins for dumping solid waste were often located along major streets and would have been cleaned out regularly by city maintenance workers.

Baked brick architecture using standardized bricks is seen at major cities and towns, while smaller settlements used baked brick only for drains, wells, and bathing platforms. Mud brick was used for platforms and smaller dividing walls. Stone architecture is seen in regional sites with locally available stone, and there is evidence for wood and reed architecture at all sites. Gateways and important administrative or ritual structures had columned entryways with large wooden columns set on stone ring bases.

House plans were quite varied with many different styles, but most had a central courtyard and surrounding rooms with a private entrance off the main street. Some houses did open out directly onto the street, and these may have been shops with domestic quarters in the back or on the second story. Most houses had separate bathing and toilet rooms located adjacent to the street. Bathing platforms were made with closely fitted bricks and had drains leading to street drain. Latrines were located next to the bathing area and consisted of reused large storage vessels buried up to the rim, with a few bricks set along one edge of the rim to allow a person to squat more comfortably. A large water vessel with water and a small dipper were often placed next to the commode for washing up after using the latrine.

Wells for providing clean drinking water are common at most Indus sites. Some sites had only one well, but larger cities needed more water, and at Mohenjo-Daro archaeologists have estimated that as many as seven hundred wells would have been scattered throughout the city. Wells were almost always made using specially designed wedge-shaped bricks (or stone at Dholavira) to create a strong cylindrical structure. Some settlements like Harappa had only a few wells and appear to have obtained water from the nearby river or large reservoirs constructed at the edges of the city. Reservoirs found at Lothal and Dholavira were lined with brick or stone with gypsum plaster to make them waterproof. Catchment drains for collecting water to fill reservoirs are found at the site of Dholavira and were separate from the sewerage drains. Drainage channels were constructed at sites like Dholavira and Lothal for directing river flow into the reservoirs.

Public areas for markets are found in front or inside the major gateways and in various neighborhoods at large sites. Large buildings were discovered at Mohenjo-Daro and Harappa that may have been used for public rituals, or by centralized administrators, but there is still much controversy regarding their precise function due to the lack of proper excavation and precise recording during the early excavations. The so-called Great Bath at Mohenjo-Daro may have been used for ritual public bathing, and the large building next to it may have been the foundation of a large hall or possibly even a palace. This building has been commonly referred to as the "Granary," but there is no evidence that it was used to store grain or any other produce.

Specialized architecture has been found at Mohenjo-Daro that may represent a meeting hall and a dyer's shop or laundry; a large building complex with a double staircase entryway may be a palace or temple. At Harappa circular brick platforms were discovered that excavators thought were used for processing grain, but recent excavations do not support this interpretation.

Indus Writing

The Indus script appears to have been developed indigenously and was not borrowed from West Asia. It has its foundation in early written symbols dating to the Ravi Phase (3500–3300 B.C.) at the site of Harappa and at approximately the same time from other sites in the greater Indus Valley region. This script became more standardized during the Kot Diji Phase (c. 2800–2600 B.C.) into what can be called the Early Indus script. By 2600 B.C. a fully developed Indus script was being used throughout the Indus Valley in an area that was twice the size of ancient Mesopotamia or Egypt.

The Indus script was usually written from right to left. This is confirmed through an analysis of sign sequences carved on seals and on the basis of writing on pottery shards that shows the sequence of strokes. More than 4,200 objects containing Indus script have been discovered, and most of these come from the sites of Mohenjo-Daro and Harappa (over 3,700). Scholars have defined between 400 and 450 distinct Indus script signs or graphemes. Most scholars agree that the writing is based on a logo-syllabic system in which each sign means a word, a syllable, or a sound. However, some signs appear to represent pictographs (of a man or a fish, and so on) and when used alone they might represent an idea or an entire story. The use of ideographs with a logo-syllabic

writing system suggests that there were many different ways of using the writing.

The Indus writing has not yet been deciphered, and there is no hope of a breakthrough until a bilingual text or longer inscriptions with Indus script have been discovered. Because the script was no longer used after 1900 B.C., it is not possible to connect it to later writing systems and known historical languages. Dravidian languages are now spoken primarily in South India, but some of the place names and river names, such as the Nara and Porali rivers in Sindh and Baluchistan, may represent Dravidian or Mundari (Austro-Asiatic) languages. Indo-Aryan languages may have been present in the northern Indus region and Baluchistan, while Sino-Tibetan languages may have been spoken in the far north at sites such as Shortughai. Remnants of earlier Neolithic languages that have no relation to any of the four major modern language families also may have been present in the region. Since urban centers are by their very nature places where people from different cultures come together, it would not be surprising to have many different language speakers present in the cities. As was common in Mesopotamia and Egypt, traders and elites from each group could have used the same writing system for inscribing their names or words for commodities. Words and names from any one of these four or five language families may have been written in the Indus script during the seven hundred years when the script was being used.

The production of seals and tablets was a highly specialized craft that was strictly controlled by the elite traders and rulers of the cities. New research at Harappa has been able to provide a new chronology for the writing and to better define the wide range of contexts in which the writing was used by literate elites. The script is found on square seals made of stone, engraved with symbols and animal motifs. The most common animal on the seals is a mythical unicorn, while other seals are carved with a bull, an elephant, or even a rhinoceros. Seals were used to stamp into clay sealings on goods to document and control trade, and also possibly for ritual purposes. Steatite and terra-cotta tokens include script and what appear to be numbers. Some of these tokens may have been used for accounting, and others appear to have been used for ritual purposes. Script is found inscribed on clay lumps that were used as sealings to lock storehouses. Merchants incised messages directly on large jars filled with trade goods to indicate the contents or the destination. Script was also painted or molded on pottery to define ownership or for ritual purposes. Examples of script have been found on tools and personal items that may indicate personal identification or ritual protection. Writing was also used in combination with narrative depictions of myths and religious ceremonies, possibly identifying the main characters or deities, or the name of the ritual. At the two largest cities, Harappa and Mohenjo-Daro, distinctive copper tablets with script and animal motifs may be the earliest evidence for city coinage in South Asia, a thousand years before the introduction of stamp-marked silver coins of the Achaemenid Empire.

Most inscriptions are only five to seven signs long and are very small, ranging in size from .4 to .8 inches (1 to 2 centimeters) in height. However, one example of what appears to be a public signboard has been discovered in a side room of the major northern gateway on the citadel mound at Dholavira. Made with white gypsum inlay, the signboard had ten script signs that are around 14 inches (37 centimeters) high and 10 inches (26 centimeters) wide. The board may have been mounted above the gateway for all to see, but this does not mean that everyone in the city was literate. The distribution of seals and writing in distinct areas of Harappa suggests that only certain segments of the population had seals and that, even though writing was found on artifacts throughout the city, the production of seals and the use of writing were restricted to the elites.

Sociopolitical Organization

Scholars are currently divided on how to best describe the political organization of the Indus cities. Although most agree on the presence of a highly stratified social organization and the presence of multiple urban centers, some feel that these cities were not organized as state-level societies but were basically large chiefdoms. The main argument for chiefdom society is that no large central buildings that could represent temples, palaces, or administrative structures have been identified. Another argument is that there are no royal burials, which are a common feature in the early states of Mesopotamia, Egypt, and China. The opposite position, which is supported by most scholars, is that the Indus was organized as a state-level society, but that it had a decentralized political and ideological organization.

In this model, several competing classes of elites dominated the four or five major cities. In the course of seven hundred years, different individuals and communities would have been dominant, but no single community was able to rule long enough to establish a high degree of centralization. Merchants, ritual specialists, and individuals who owned resources such as land, livestock, and raw materials would have maintained different levels of control in different regions. These communities shared a common ideology and a standardized economic system and used a common script. In contrast to the large cities, the smaller settlements, which included more agriculturalists and herders, may have been less rigidly stratified and segregated than the larger cities. The largest cities,

such as Harappa, Mohenjo-Daro, Dholavira, and Rakhi-garhi, may have been relatively independent city-states with direct political control over their immediate hinterland. Trade and exchange of important socio-ritual status items demonstrate that the cities and villages were politically and economically integrated, and they therefore appear to be integrated on a general ideological level as well.

There is no evidence for the presence of a military or the use of warfare in the integration of the hinterland around the major cities. In contrast to the patterns seen in Mesopotamia and Egypt, there are no depictions of people being captured, attacked, or subjugated. Even though large city walls with impressive gateways surrounded all of the major settlements, there is no evidence that these walled cities were ever attacked or burned. The city walls and gateways were probably guarded by armed watchmen, and the discovery of bronze arrow heads, spears, and daggers indicate that they had the technological capability to protect themselves against bandits and raiders, as well as to wage warfare. The absence of conclusive data for warfare does not support a model for a peaceful civilization, and it is not unlikely that there were occasional battles and violent conflicts.

Indus Religion and Belief Systems

Without the aid of written texts it is difficult to reconstruct the Indus religion. They made clay figurines of animals, men, and women that probably were used in special rituals. Some of the female figurines are thought to represent Mother Goddess images, while others are possibly toys for children. Soft limestone was used to carve small sculptures of deities or important people such as the famous "Priest-King" found at Mohenjo-Daro. Harder stone was carved into nude male sculptures that have been found at the site of Harappa. These images were probably used in special domestic rituals to represent deities.

Many of the seals have narrative scenes that appear to represent ceremonies and mythological scenes. One famous seal from Mohenjo-Daro shows a deity with horned headdress and bangles on both arms, standing in a pipal (sacred fig) tree. Seven figures in procession and a kneeling worshiper sit before the deity, with a human head resting on a small stool. Since no temples have been identified, it is possible that worship took place under trees as depicted on this seal. Some terra-cotta tablets have narrative scenes stamped on both sides. At Harappa, one such tablet shows a figure, possibly a female deity, grasping two tigers by the throat and standing above an elephant. On the reverse is a narrative scene depicting the killing of a water buffalo in the presence of a priest or deity seated in yogic position. Such narrative scenes indicate the presence of a highly developed mythology and iconography, and

Woman Kneading Dough, Terra Cotta Sculpture Unearthed at Harappa. Images of this sort were often used in domestic rituals to represent deities. NATIONAL MUSEUM / FOTOMEDIA.

Trade and Technology

The Indus cities were connected with rural agricultural communities and distant resource and mining areas through strong trade networks. They used pack animals, riverboats, and bullock carts for transport. This trade is reflected in the widespread distribution of exquisite beads and ornaments, metal tools, and pottery that were produced by specialized artisans in the major towns and cities. Cotton, lumber, grain, livestock, and other foodstuffs were probably the major commodities of this internal trade. There was also external trade with Central Asia and Iran by overland routes. Trade with the Arabian Gulf region and the distant Mesopotamian cities, such as Susa and Ur, was conducted by sea and may have been dominated by middlemen living along the Indus coast or Oman.

Indus artisans produced a wide range of utilitarian and decorative objects using specialized techniques of stone working, ceramics, and metallurgy. They did not erect stone sculptures to glorify the power of the elites, and most of the art and symbolic objects were relatively small and in many cases even made in miniature. Objects made with exotic materials and complex technologies were probably produced for the wealthy merchants and the ruling classes, while more simple objects made with local materials and simple technology were presumably for ordinary people. Ranking or stratification within the society as a whole appears to have been reinforced by the use of various raw materials and manufacturing processes that resulted in finished objects with different relative values.

Pottery with a red slip and black painted designs were made in all the major settlements for use in rituals and possibly in marriage ceremonies. Motifs on the pottery are usually arranged in panels and include the intersecting circle, fish-scale, and pipal leaf design, combined with floral and geometric patterns, as well as animals and birds. Plain pottery was produced for everyday use, including disposable goblets with pointed bases that were common in the major cities. Copper and bronze were used to make ornaments, tools, mirrors, pots, and pans. Bone, shell, and ivory were used to make tools, ornaments, gaming pieces, and especially inlay for furniture. Silver and gold utensils and ornaments and fine ceramic objects, such as stoneware bangles and glazed faience ornaments, also were produced. The glazed faience of the Indus is much stronger and more durable than terra-cotta and was used to make beads, bangles, buttons, inlay, and small vessels for holding pigments or perfume. Natural stones were prepared in specific ways to enhance their color and accentuate the natural patterns of the stone. Artificially colored stone, faience, and painted terra-cotta ornaments were created as imitations of the natural stones.

Evidence for wool and cotton textiles is found preserved on copper tools and reveals the presence of a

similar motifs are widespread at sites throughout the larger Indus region. Some of the iconography seen on Indus seals and the use of specific symbols, such as the swastika and *mandalas*, were incorporated into later Vedic, Brahmanical, Jain, and Buddhist religious traditions. Even though there is no direct historical connection, some Indus symbols and narratives do appear to have been incorporated into religious traditions that are today collectively referred to as Hinduism. For example, the famous seal from Mohenjo-Daro with a horned deity seated in yogic position surrounded by wild animals has often been compared to later Hindu representations of Siva as "Lord of the Beasts."

The Indus people buried their dead in wooden coffins along with many pottery vessels that were probably filled with food for the afterlife. Most individuals, both male and female, were buried with some simple ornaments, such as shell bangles or copper rings and agate beads. Elaborate ornaments of gold, silver, and precious stones were never included in the burials and must have been inherited by the living relatives. No royal burials have been found.

Mortar and Pestle from the Mohenjo-Daro Site. The strong network of trade among Indus peoples is reflected in the widespread distribution (among archaeological sites) of tools and pottery produced by specialized artisans in the civilization's major towns and cities. NATIONAL MUSEUM / FOTOMEDIA.

well-developed spinning and weaving tradition. Recent analysis of threads preserved inside copper beads suggests that wild tussar silk was also being used. The textile industry would have been an important source of wealth to large cities that could maintain extensive cotton fields and large numbers of craftsmen and -women.

Weights. The Indus rulers and merchants developed and maintained a highly standardized weight system for taxation and control of trade in specific commodities. Cubical stone weights were usually made from a special type of banded chert or agate and range in weight up to 24 pounds (10,865.0 grams). The smaller weights were probably used in the weighing of precious stones, metals, and perfumes or incense, while the larger weights may have been used for assessing the taxes for larger quantities of grain, foodstuffs, and other commodities. Each graduated weight is double the weight of the previous weight category. These distinctive weights have been found at all

settlements of the Indus region as well as in settlements on the periphery, where Indus merchants may have obtained raw materials or traded finished products.

Agriculture and Animal Husbandry

The Indus subsistence system was highly diverse due to the many different environments in which people lived. Wheat and barley cultivation, supplemented by animal husbandry, was the foundation of the urban centers in the core alluvial regions, but millets and possibly rice were cultivated in Gujarat. Animal husbandry was dominated by humped zebu (*Bos indicus*) cattle, but also included non-humped cattle (*Bos taurus*), water buffalo (*Bubalus bubalis*), sheep, and goats. Fishing, hunting of wild fauna, and the collection of wild fruits supplemented the major crops and animal foods. Wheat and barley agriculture was practiced primarily during the winter growing season, and crops such as cotton and millet were probably cultivated after the summer monsoon. The presence of two growing seasons made it possible to create enough surpluses to support large cities and trade networks.

Due to the nature of the topography and the intensity of floods along the Indus and its tributaries, it was not possible to maintain major canals for irrigation. Most cultivation in the alluvium was based on adequate rainfall and opportunistic agriculture where crops could be planted along the banks of oxbow lakes and slower streams. Along the piedmont zone of Baluchistan, some Indus settlements constructed diversion canals for directing floodwaters to fields, and there is some evidence for the construction of small irrigation canals near the site of Shortughai in northern Afghanistan.

Decline and Legacy

Around 1900 B.C. there is evidence for a transitional phase during which many characteristic features of the Indus civilization begin to fall out of use. This transition represents a reorganization of power among the ruling elites of the Indus cities, but does not reflect the intrusion of new people or the invasions of Indo-Aryans, as has been proposed in the past. The Indus script and square seals with unicorn and other animal motifs gradually disappeared. Cubical weights for taxation and trade were no longer used, possibly because the major trade networks began to break down.

Different factors leading to the decline and reorganization of the Indus civilization have been identified. The overextension of political and trade networks led to eventual fragmentation. In addition, the lack of a military to reinforce integration would have had a direct impact on political and economic organization. The Sarasvati-Ghaggar-Hakra river system in the east began to dry up, and the changing river systems disrupted the agricultural and economic system. Eastern communities began to gradually migrate to the larger urban centers along the Indus or into new agricultural areas of the Gangetic Plain and Gujarat. The processes involved in this transformation were more rapid in some areas, but by around 1300 to 1000 B.C. a new social order emerged, dominated by Vedic communities who used horses for ritual sacrifice and warfare, spoke Indo-Aryan languages, and worshiped new deities.

Although certain distinguishing aspects of the Indus civilization disappeared, many other aspects of Indus craft technology, art, agriculture, and possibly social organization continued among the Late and post-Harappan cultures. These cultural traditions eventually became incorporated in the new urban civilization that arose during the Early Historical period, around 600 B.C.

Jonathan Mark Kenoyer

See also **Chalcolithic (Bronze) Age; Goddess Images; Harappa; Mohenjo-Daro**

BIBLIOGRAPHY

Allchin, Bridget, and F. Raymond Allchin. *The Rise of Civilization in India and Pakistan*. Cambridge, U.K. and New York: Cambridge University Press, 1982.

Bisht, Ranvir S. "Excavations at Banawali, 1974–1977." In *Harappan Civilization: A Contemporary Perspective*, 2nd rev. ed., edited by Gregory L. Possehl. New Delhi: Oxford and IBH Publishing, 1993.

Bisht, Ravindra Singh. "Dholavira and Banawali: Two Different Paradigns for the Harappan Urbis Forma." *Puratattva* 29 (1998–1999): 14–32.

———. "Urban Planning at Dholavira: A Harappan City." In *Ancient Cities, Sacred Skies: Cosmic Geometries and City Planning in Ancient India*, edited by John M. Malville and Lalit M. Gujral. New Delhi: Aryan Books International, 2000.

Gupta, S. P. *The Indus-Saraswati Civilization*. Delhi: Patibha Prakashan, 1996.

———. "The Indus-Sarasvati Civilization: Beginnings and Development." In *The Dawn of Indian Civilization (up to c. 600 B.C.)*, edited by G. C. Pande. Delhi: Munshiram Manoharlal, 1999.

Jansen, Michael. *Mohenjo-Daro, City of Wells and Drains: Water Splendour 4500 Years Ago*. Bergisch Gladbach, Germany: Frontinus Society Publications, 1993.

———. "Settlement Networks of the Indus Civilization." In *Indian Archaeology in Retrospect*, vol. 2: *Protohistory: Archaeology of the Harappan Civilization*, edited by S. Settar and R. Korisettar. New Delhi: Indian Council of Historical Research, 2002.

Jarrige, Catherine. "The Mature Indus Phase at Nausharo: Elements of Urban Infrastructure." In *South Asian Archaeology 1997*, edited by M. Taddei and G. De Marco. Rome: Istituto Italiano per l'Africa e l'Oriente, 2001.

Jarrige, Jean-François. "From Nausharo to Pirak: Continuity and Change in the Kachi/Bolan Region from the 3rd to the 2nd Millennium B.C." In *South Asian Archaeology 1995*, edited by B. Allchin. Mumbai: Oxford and IBH Publishers, 1997.

Kenoyer, Jonathan Mark. "Interaction Systems, Specialized Crafts, and Culture Change: The Indus Valley Tradition and the Indo-Gangetic Tradition in South Asia." In *The Indo-Aryans of Ancient South Asia: Language, Material Culture, and Ethnicity*, edited by G. Erdosy. Berlin: W. DeGruyter, 1995.

———. "Early City-States in South Asia: Comparing the Harappan Phase and the Early Historic Period." In *The Archaeology of City-States: Cross Cultural Approaches*, edited by D. L. Nichols and T. H. Charlton. Washington, D.C.: Smithsonian Institution Press, 1997.

———. *Ancient Cities of the Indus Valley Civilization*. Karachi: Oxford University Press, 1998.

———. "Wealth and Socio-Economic Hierarchies of the Indus Valley Civilization." In *Order, Legitimacy, and Wealth in Early States*, edited by J. Richards and M. Van Buren. Cambridge, U.K.: Cambridge University Press, 2000.

———. "Uncovering the Keys to the Lost Indus Cities." *Scientific American* (July 2003): 67–75.

Lal, Braj Basi. *The Earliest Civilization of South Asia: Rise, Maturity, and Decline.* New Delhi: Aryan Books International, 1997.

Meadow, Richard H., ed. *Harappa Excavations, 1986–1990.* Monographs in World Archaeology. Madison, Wis.: Prehistory Press, 1991.

Meadow, Richard H., and Jonathan Mark Kenoyer. "Excavations at Harappa 1993: The City Walls and Inscribed Materials." In *South Asian Archaeology 1993*, edited by A. Parpola and P. Koskikallio. Helsinki: Suomalainen Tiedeakatemia, 1994.

———. "Excavations at Harappa, 1994–1995: New Perspectives on the Indus Script, Craft Activities, and City Organization." In *South Asian Archaeology 1995*, edited by B. Allchin and R. Allchin. New Delhi: Oxford and IBH Publishers, 1997.

———. "The Indus Valley Mystery." *Discovering Archaeology* (April 2000): 38–43.

Mughal, Mohammad R. "The Decline of The Indus Civilization and the Late Harappan Period in the Indus Valley." *Lahore Museum Bulletin* 3, no. 2 (1990): 1–17.

———. "The Geographical Extent of the Indus Civilization during the Early, Mature, and Late Harappan Times." In *South Asian Archaeology Studies*, edited by G. L. Possehl. New Delhi: Oxford and IBH Publishers, 1992.

Parpola, Asko. *Deciphering the Indus Script.* Cambridge, U.K., and New York: Cambridge University Press, 1994.

Possehl, Gregory L. "The Transformation of the Indus Civilization." *Journal of World Prehistory* 11, no. 4 (1997): 425–472.

———. "Sociocultural Complexity without the State: The Indus Civilization." In *Archaic States*, edited by G. M. Feinman and J. Marcus. Santa Fe, N.Mex.: School of American Research Press, 1998.

———. *The Indus Civilization: A Contemporary Perspective.* Walnut Creek, Calif.: AltaMira Press, 2002.

———, ed. *Harappan Civilization.* New Delhi: Oxford and IBH Publishing, 1982.

Weber, Steven A., and William R. Belcher, eds. *Ethnobiology and the Indus Civilization.* Lanham, Md.: Lexington Books, 2003.

INFORMAL CREDIT MARKETS India has a long history of traditional financiers, or "indigenous bankers" as they came to be called in British times, organized along ethnic community lines. Some of them, such as the networks of Gujarati *shroff*s, accepted deposits, discounted commercial paper, and facilitated trade and remittances, especially to upcountry areas poorly served by the banks. With the spread of modern banking, these indigenous bankers lost much of their share of the market, but many of them evolved into thriving present-day "finance companies." These continue to be important in financing modern India's trade in cloth, grains, and other commodities, including used commercial vehicles, hand looms, and small industries. Rotating local savings and credit groups, called chit funds, also date back at least several centuries in South India.

References to village moneylenders date back to Vedic times. Their dominance began to be broken only near the end of the nineteenth century, when British officials started promoting cooperatives, introducing legislation to restrict the sale of agricultural land. Such restrictions in Punjab, especially, proved effective in ending the large-scale alienation of land that had been taking place for the previous thirty years. The new class of agricultural trader moneylenders started lending against the security of produce, replacing the earlier large farmer moneylenders. These are still widely used by farmers in the Punjab in preference, or in addition to, the banks.

Size and Types of Lenders

With the growth of cooperative credit after independence, and the massive expansion of rural bank branches since the 1970s, following the nationalization of banks, the share of informal credit in total rural credit has steadily declined from about 90 percent of all outstanding debt in 1951 to about 40 percent in 1991. In 1991 moneylenders still accounted for about 16 percent, and interest-free credit from friends and relatives for about 7 percent. Reflecting the declining share of cooperative credit during the 1980s, the share of "other sources" such as chit funds and finance companies almost doubled from 13 to 24 percent between the rural credit surveys of 1981 and 1991.

In contrast, in the urban areas, informal credit was almost as important as formal, even after excluding large flows of tax-evaded "black" money. More than half was used as trade credit, though there were also other important sectors like small-scale industry, road transport, construction (especially residential), and a large number of service sectors.

Informal credit is heterogenous, encompassing the wide range of activities of wholesale traders, commission agents, and chit fund operators, as well as those of local moneylenders, pawnbrokers, village shopkeepers, agricultural input suppliers, itinerant peddlers, and even friends and relatives. What all these lenders have in common is informality, adaptability, and flexibility of operations, a characteristic that reduces "transactions costs" (i.e., the cost of making, monitoring, and recovering loans) and confers on informal lenders their comparative advantage over formal banks and credit associations.

Areas of Comparative Advantage

Formal and informal finance each have their comparative advantages. Formal finance is more readily able to accommodate large and longer-term loans because of its greater reliance on the pooling of deposits and maturity transformation (being able to lend for longer terms than the average tenure of deposits, because deposits are continually replaced). It is better suited to serving the needs of large- and medium-scale industry, organized trade and commerce, large- and medium-scale farmers who can offer the security of the land they own, and well-to-do urban households. It has been less successful in serving the needs of the large unorganized sector of small and micro-entrepreneurs, small traders, tenant farmers and sharecroppers who do not have title to their land, and small and poor borrowers in general.

The lower transactions costs of the informal sector make it particularly well suited to making transactions that are cost intensive, small, and of short duration. Its flexibility regarding collateral enables it to finance a large number of service activities, where fixed assets are not created as security for the loan. The tying of credit with marketing transactions gives informal lenders a comparative advantage in supplying working capital loans for agriculture, as crop production loans, as well as in small industries, such as those using hand looms or making footwear, where the lender is often also a supplier of raw material or a buyer of the final products.

The two sectors are therefore by and large complementary. Policy should proceed on a recognition of this complementarity and facilitate informal finance in its own area of comparative advantage. There are three major aspects to this broad policy orientation. One is to improve market structure, or the degree of competition between lenders in the informal sector by encouraging ease of entry. Licensing and registration should be restricted as far as possible to deposit taking and the main emphasis of regulation should be prudential. An example of inappropriate regulation is the central government's Chit Fund Act, which requires chit funds with as little as 100 rupees to register with the state registrar. However, the costs of registration would render hundreds of thousands of community chit funds unviable, and the limit should be raised. Usury laws are another example. Although interest rate ceilings have largely been removed in the formal sector, they are still being enforced by some state governments for moneylenders and pawnbrokers. Usury laws only drive informal credit transactions underground, and by making contracts legally unenforceable, increase the risk premium that borrowers have to pay through the interest rate.

The second approach, of promoting "linkages," or increasing lending from the banks to informal lenders, applies to parts of the informal sector that are reasonably competitive and in which lenders do not enjoy market power, but where the cost of funds of informal lenders are high. This approach seeks to take advantage of the lower transactions costs or better informational resources of informal lenders by refinancing them, thereby reducing their cost of funds and enabling them to lower their lending rates. In this approach, the formal sector acts as a "wholesaler," while informal lenders "retail" credit to small and poor borrowers. It is suited, for example, to pawnbrokers and potentially to improving the terms and amount of credit available to farmers from agricultural marketing intermediaries such as commission agents, input suppliers, and agro-processors. Thus in Abohar in the Punjab, the largest cotton market in the country, banks refinance the book debts of commission agents, who lend huge amounts to farmers at the standard 2 percent a month against sales through them of cotton and grains. Farmers prefer the one-stop convenience of dealing with commission agents, who pay for purchases of fertilizer, diesel, and other inputs when they come into town, and who pay interest on balances left with them after the season.

A third approach, applicable to parts of the informal sector in which the problem of market power is not amenable to the previous two approaches (because in some markets informal lenders will always have better information ties to poor borrowers, and will earn "rents" or monopoly profits on such information, no matter what their cost of funds) is that of offering stronger competition to the informal sector, and thereby improving its terms. An example is the huge expansion currently taking place of micro-finance through women's self-help groups, bringing down village moneylender rates for small emergency and consumption loans. In the long run the two sectors are expected to become increasingly integrated but specializing in their own area of comparative advantage.

Chit funds (or *kuri*s in Kerala, "committees" in the north, and *bishi*s in the west) is the Indian term for what are generically known worldwide as rotating savings and credit associations, small neighborhood- or workplace-based community organizations whose major attraction is that they are a convenient vehicle for savings. They entail contractual savings, each member committed to saving a particular amount on a particular date, usually once a month, being entitled to the pooled kitty in turn, the sequence of turns being decided by consensus, lottery, and in more evolved business people's chit funds, by a system of bidding for the kitty, the bid amount becoming in effect the interest earned by other members in that round.

Given the widespread ownership of gold and silver ornaments in India and the convenience of ornaments as collateral (being easy to store, value, and sell), borrowing against the security of ornaments is widespread. A large part of the lending by moneylenders is against the security of pledged ornaments. As a shop-based activity, however, pawnbroking is carried out usually as an adjunct to the activities of goldsmiths and jewelry shops. Much of the lending by smaller unlicensed pawnbrokers is for relatively small amounts and for consumption purposes. In a poor tribal district of Rajasthan, thirteen retail shopkeepers lent an estimated 4,500 *bhil*s in the surrounding hamlets, against the security of silver ornaments. Only about 30 percent of the value of the pledge was lent, difficulties were experienced in redeeming the pledges, and interest rates were high. However, an important part of lending by pawnbrokers in other areas is for crop production purposes. Thus in the agricultural district town of Raichur in Karnataka, farmers top up loan requirements after first exhausting limits available from banks and commission agents. The lending of about fifty active pawnbrokers peaks at the start of the *kharif* (autumn) crop and winds down from December, when the loans start to be repaid. Loans range from 500 to 15,000 rupees, at an interest rate of 3 percent a month. This appears to be the standard "institutional" rate in most parts of the country.

The banks also make (cheaper) gold loans, motivated primarily by the need to meet their agricultural lending targets. With the emphasis of modern banking on cash flow rather than security-based lending, the term "pawnshop banking" has come to acquire pejorative connotations. The ambivalence of the official stance may also have something to do with the country's policy of discouraging the hoarding of gold as an unproductive asset. However, in providing essential liquidity against gold, banks enable the savings represented by gold to be invested productively. The major advantages pawnbrokers have over banks is the higher proportion of the value of pledged articles they advance, flexibility about exceeding this margin in appropriate cases, and lower borrower and lender transaction costs generally. The optimum division of responsibility between banks and pawnbrokers might be refinancing arrangements by the banks, based on the repledging of pawns to the banks.

Prabhu Ghate

See also **Banking Sector Reform since 1991; Rural Credit, Evolution of since 1952**

BIBLIOGRAPHY

Bouman, F. J. A. *Small, Short and Unsecured: Informal Rural Finance in India*. New Delhi and New York: Oxford University Press, 1989.

Darling, Malcolm. *The Punjab Peasant in Debt and Prosperity*. 1925. Reprint, New Delhi: Manohar, 1978.

Das-Gupta, Arindam, and C. P. S. Nayar. *Urban Informal Credit Markets in India*. Study prepared for the Asian Development Bank by the National Institute of Public Finance and Policy, New Delhi, 1989.

Ghate, Prabhu, et al. *Informal Finance: Some Findings from Asia*. Hong Kong: Oxford University Press for Asian Development Bank, 1992.

Jones, J. Howard. "Jain Shopkeepers and Moneylenders: Rural Informal Credit Networks in South Rajasthan." In *The Assembly of Listeners: Jainism in Society*, edited by M. Carruthers and C. Humphrey. Cambridge, U.K., and New York: Cambridge University Press, 1991.

Nayar, C. P. S. *Chit Finance: An Exploratory Study on Working of Chit Funds*. Mumbai: Vora, 1973.

Timberg, Thomas, and C. V. Aiyar. *Informal Credit Markets in India*. Annual Number, *Economic and Political Weekly*, February 1980.

INFORMATION AND OTHER TECHNOLOGY DEVELOPMENT

India's information technology industry achieved exports of $12.8 billion in the year ending March 2004, equal to 19.8 percent of India's exports and 10.9 percent of current account receipts. Its total sales of $21.5 billion amounted to 3.5 percent of India's gross domestic product. India's new stellar "industry," information technology (IT) has given India an international reputation for high technology and has boosted Indian self-confidence.

The Early History of the Industry

A number system can be constructed out of three numbers: 0, 1, and any number greater than 1. The decimal system, which uses 10 to build the system, is a historical accident. The simplest number system is one based on powers of 2, the binary system; in this system, for instance, 2 would be represented by 10, 4 by 100, and 7 by 111. This system has been used in computers from the outset, as it is easy to give a physical form to a binary system: all it needs is a device that would give an interruptible power flow. A state in which power was interrupted would represent zero, and a state in which power flowed would represent one.

The first computers, constructed during World War II, employed radio valves, which were switched on and off to represent binary digits. But soon thereafter, the semiconductor was invented; it used much less electricity and thus did not overheat so easily, and it was sturdier. (V. Ramamurti, an Indian scientist, believed that the semiconductor was invented because the Allies feared the loss to Japan of India, the Allies' prime source of mica, which was essential to the making of radio valves.) Technological development of computers and of their multifarious applications has since been driven by the progressive reduction in the size and cost of semiconductors. They have now been so reduced in size that millions of them can be etched onto a small chip; chips are

Infosys Headquarters in Bangalore. In response to the collapse of the Silicon Valley technology boom, India developed a vast IT marketplace catering to the needs of corporations in the West. Infosys is one of the biggest IT providers worldwide. INDIA TODAY.

designed for specialized uses, such as for a laptop or a washing machine.

The first computers in the 1940s were as big as a house; by the 1960s, however, miniaturization of semiconductors had made it possible to create computers that were no bigger than a small room. At that point, IBM began to make a series of standardized computers; its 1620 and 360 series of mainframe computers found users all over the world, including India. The Indian government imported a few computers from the Soviet Union, especially EVS EM, its IBM 360 clone; but they were not popular, even in the government establishments where they were installed. IBM computers dominated the market. They were used for calculation, accounting and data storage in large companies, and in research laboratories. Tata Consultancy Services, India's largest software producer, was established in 1968 to run the computers acquired by the Tata group and to develop uses for them.

Tension has prevailed in relations between India and Pakistan since they were formed by the partition of British India in 1947. In the 1950s Pakistan joined two defense pacts under the aegis of the United States; in response, India moved closer to the Soviet Union. In 1971 a revolt erupted in East Pakistan. A war broke out, in the course of which India supported the separation of East Pakistan; it emerged as a new country, Bangladesh. During this war, the United States ordered its Seventh Fleet to the Bay of Bengal, worsening relations between India and the United States.

In 1973 India passed an amendment to the Foreign Exchange Regulation Act that required foreign companies to reduce their equity holdings in Indian subsidiaries to a minority. The law was initially implemented haltingly. In the 1977 general election, the Indian National Congress was defeated, and the Janata Party formed a coalition government. Its socialist minister of industries,

Users at a Cyber Café. Software development continues to thrive in India's cities, many of which boast state-of-the-art facilities and the presence of a large number of overseas vendors. AKHIL BAKSHI / FOTOMEDIA.

George Fernandes, vigorously began to implement the 1973 act. Most foreign companies fell in line, with the exception of Coca-Cola and IBM, which closed down their operations in India. However, IBM's computers in India needed continued servicing; to ensure this, the government established the Computer Maintenance Corporation (CMC), which took over the erstwhile IBM subsidiary.

A major cost of using mainframe computers was the specialized manpower they required. It was the practice then to write programs for individual operations; when operations changed or expanded, the programs had to be modified. The data were stored in punched cards and tapes. Both were easily damaged, and data often needed to be reconstructed. Thus a mainframe computer had its complement of servicing staff; a small business could not afford such manpower.

By the 1980s, computer chips were becoming small enough to be embodied in almost portable mini-computers, and these were getting cheap enough to be used in small businesses. Manufacturers began to build into minicomputers a selection of programs that performed the most common operations, such as word processing, calculation, and accounting. Over the 1980s, the mini-computers shrank in size and weight and were transformed into personal computers (PCs). Indian agents who sold imported minicomputers and PCs also employed software engineers for sales assistance and service. Thus, in the latter half of 1980s, Indian software engineers were scattered. Some worked in CMC; others serviced the surviving IBM machines in companies, government establishments, and research facilities; and still others serviced minicomputers and PCs.

Meanwhile, in the United States, the computer industry was manufacturing PCs, which embodied standardized software. A great deal of work went into perfecting PC software. Other software companies translated customers' requirements into software packages and sold them off the shelf to be copied into their PCs' hard disks. As PCs developed, so did mainframe computers. The old computers, known as legacy systems, were loaded with data; and a running business, like a bank or an insurance company, could not do without records. The old computer users wanted to keep their old systems while at the same time acquiring new equipment; and they wanted the two to work together seamlessly. So programs had to be written to enable the new and old machines to talk to one another. That required knowledge of old and new languages; and it required patience and application. The work had to be done on systems that were in use; and often the programmer had to try out a number of approaches before achieving a workable solution. It was laborious, often frustrating work.

Growth of the Industry in India and the United States

By the late 1980s, there were many Indian engineers in the United States. The Indian government had expanded engineering education in the 1950s, but its engineering industry could not absorb the number of engineers that its institutes produced. The brightest engineering graduates began to go to the United States to pursue higher degrees and were soon absorbed into the U.S. industry. Graduates of India's five elite Indian Institutes of Technology (IIT) found easy entry into the United States, and over two-thirds of them routinely emigrated. Thus by the 1980s there was a large diaspora of Indian engineers in the United States, and many of them entered the new computer hardware and software industry. When they encountered shortage of programmers, they turned to India for supplementing the supply. They tapped grapevines of their old friends and colleagues in India. Some just went to the Indian metropolitan areas, checked into a hotel, advertised for software engineers and recruited them on the spot. This "body-shopping" deprived Indian employers of their programmers. Indian sellers and manufacturers of PCs and private users of mainframes could not afford to lose their staff. They took a number of defensive steps. First, a number of them went into body-shopping themselves: they began to hire out entire teams of programmers. Today's foremost software exporters, Tata Infotech, Patni Computer Systems, and Wipro, began as computer manufacturers, all between 1977 and 1980. Second, they realigned wages so as to retain their more experienced staff. Third, they developed active and anticipatory recruiting techniques. The standard method was campus recruitment. In response to their demand, the intake into engineering and IT courses increased. Fourth, with the recruitment of fresh graduates, Indian software firms also developed short, focused training programs designed to bring them up to speed quickly. Finally, Indian software firms meticulously recorded the progress of work every day, so that if a worker left a job half done, someone else could immediately pick up the threads.

By 1985 satellite links made the export of software possible without having to send programmers abroad. At that time, however, the Indian government did not allow private links, so Texas Instruments gave it the equipment, which it then proceeded to use from its Bangalore establishment. IBM, which wanted to set up a link in 1988, ran into the same problem: the government insisted on retaining its monopoly in telecommunications, the rates offered by its Department of Telecommunications were exorbitant, and it was inexperienced in running Very Small Aperture Terminal (VSAT) links.

In 1991 the Department of Electronics broke this impasse, creating a corporation called Software Technology Parks of India (STPI) that, being owned by the government, could provide VSAT communications without breaching its monopoly. STPI set up software technology parks in different cities, each of which provided satellite links to be used by firms; the local link was a wireless radio link. In 1993 the government began to allow individual companies their own dedicated links, which allowed work done in India to be transmitted abroad directly. Indian firms soon convinced their American customers that a satellite link was as reliable as a team of programmers working in the clients' office.

Another important change was in the import regime. In the 1980s, an importer of hardware had to get an import license from the chief controller of imports and exports, who in turn required a no-objection certificate from the Department of Electronics. That meant going to Delhi, waiting for an appointment, and then trying to persuade an uncooperative bureaucrat. In 1992 computers were freed from import licensing, and import duties on them were reduced. As a result, it became possible for Indian software firms to work on the same computers as their clients.

Satellites and import liberalization thus made offshore development possible, with a number of implications: It enabled firms to take orders for complete programs, to work for final clients and to market their services directly. Work for final clients also led firms to specialize in work for particular industries or verticals: it led in particular to India's specialization in software for banking, insurance, and airlines. It gave India a brand value and a reputation.

The next big technological change was the World Wide Web. Even when satellite links became available, they could be used only by exporters who had their own satellite disks or shared the STPI ones. The Internet, which gathered pace after 1996, offered the same links on telephone lines, although they were slower; and as the number of firms using the Internet expanded, the potential market for software expanded accordingly. Since it was easier and cheaper to obtain telephone lines than satellite links, the Internet greatly increased the number of potential exporters, bringing many small, resource-poor Indian firms into the market.

The late 1990s saw a surge in the Indian IT industry. To assure potential clients of their permanency, Indian software companies built large, expensive campuses, where they made working conditions as attractive as possible, to help them retain workers. Trees grew and streams flowed inside buildings, and swimming pools, badminton courts, meditation rooms, auditoriums, and restaurants were provided.

The IT boom in the United States was the source of India's software exports. It ended in 2000; the downturn in India was delayed until early 2001. The low-cost Indian programmers' market in the United States expanded. More Indian programmers got an H-1B visa in 2001–2002 than in any previous year. Of the 331,000 H-1B visas issued in the United States that year, 191,000 were issued to software engineers, and 137,000 of those went to Indians. Although export growth slowed down, exports still continued to grow. From an average annual compound rate of 52 percent between 1993–1994 and 2000–2001, export growth fell to 22 percent in the next two years.

However, demand for Indian programmers also fell in 2002. For the first time since body-shopping began in the late 1980s, Indian companies did not face a labor shortage. Body-shopping virtually ceased; and firms that depended on it closed down. So did many small firms, which served local firms.

As realization of low wages in India spread, new services and new companies began to locate in India. Until 2000, most call centers serving the U.S. market were in the United States; the only countries that had offshore call centers were Britain and Ireland. After 2000, both U.S. and Indian firms began to set up call centers in India. Back-office functions, such as record transcription, accounting, and documentation, also began to be moved to India. In 2003–2004, exports of such IT-enabled services were estimated to be $3.6 billion.

Major international IT firms have set up a presence in India, mostly doing work outsourced to them by their head offices. The software industry has grown to a size at which it affects the larger economy, particularly in its major centers in the south: Bangalore, Chennai, Poona, and Hyderabad. The industry's export revenues have added to India's bulging reserves of foreign exchange. As a result, the Indian economy has been flush with liquidity, and interest rates have been halved since the late 1990s.

India's IT development has created a model of placing high international value on India's educated manpower. Some 150 global companies, including General Electric, Oracle, DaimlerChrysler and Hyundai, have set up research and development centers in India. Indian pharmaceutical companies are turning research and development into internationally marketable products, doing research on commission for companies abroad. Indian companies are venturing into bioinformatics. India's hospitals are attracting patients from neighboring countries. The Anglophonic educational system planted decades ago by the British has begun to bear global fruit.

Ashok V. Desai

See also **Indian Institutes of Technology (IITs); Industrial Growth and Diversification; Intellectual Property Rights**

BIBLIOGRAPHY

Arora, Ashish, V. S. Arunachalam, Jai Asundi, and Ronald Fernandes. "The Indian Software Industry." *Research Policy* 30, no. 8 (2001): 1267–1287.

Desai, Ashok V. "2. India." In *The Software Industry in Emerging Markets*, edited by Simon Commander. Cheltenham, U.K., and Northampton, Mass.: Edward Elgar, 2005.

Heeks, Richard. *India's Software Industry: State Policy, Liberalization, and Industrial Development*. Thousand Oaks, Calif.: Sage Publications, 1996.

Kobayashi-Hilary, Mark. *Outsourcing to India*. New Delhi: NASSCOM, 2004.

Kumar, Nagesh. "Developing Countries in International Division of Labour in Software and Service Industries: Lessons from Indian Experience." Background paper, *World Employment Report*. Geneva: International Labour Organization, 2001.

———. "Indian Software Industry Development: International and National Perspective." *Economic and Political Weekly* 36, no. 45 (2001): 4278–4290.

Saxenian, AnnaLee. *Silicon Valley's New Immigrant Entrepreneurs*. San Francisco: Public Policy Institute of California, 1999.

Software Technology Parks of India. *Annual Report, 2003–2004*. Delhi: STPI, 2000. Available at <http://www.stpi.soft.net/areport.html>

Subject Group on Knowledge-based Industries, Prime Minister's Council on Trade and Industry. *Recommendations of the Task Force on Knowledge-based Industries*. New Delhi: Prime Minister's Office, 2000. Available at <http://www.nic.in/pmcouncils/reports/knowl/>

INFRASTRUCTURE AND TRANSPORTATION, 1857–1947 At independence in 1947, the most tangible legacy of British rule in India was the modern infrastructure that the regime had left behind, built to a large extent with British expertise. This legacy included the railways, ports, major irrigation systems, telegraph, sanitation and medical care, universities, postal system, courts of law, information-gathering systems, and scientific research. The immediate motivation behind infrastructure development by the British was governance rather than development or welfare. And yet, once built, such assets did not necessarily serve only imperial interests, but were available as public goods. That said, the absence of a strong welfare or developmental objective imposed unevenness in the way that these assets were created.

The Impetus

In the nineteenth century the main focus of productive investment by the state was irrigation, railways, roads, and the telegraph. Defense interests played a role in the creation of modern communication and transportation networks, but they were not the only factor. Business interests too urged that such systems be set up in India. The influence of Lancashire textile-mill owners behind the construction of a railway in India is an example. Because Britain was a pioneer in these new technologies, the knowledge and capital were more cheaply available to India than to many other developing countries of that time. Famines in the nineteenth century exposed the susceptibility of the economy to shocks, and underscored the importance of irrigation in preventing famines, railways in distributing food, and public works for providing wage work to affected people.

By the interwar period, the drive to create physical infrastructure had spent itself. On the other hand, the demand for welfare expenditure had been gaining ground. The demand for education was connected with movements for social reform. Mass education had thus far been neglected by both public and private institutions. Extreme illiteracy and mortality in India showed rather starkly that fifty years as a British colony had done little to enable India to approach British standards of social development. Yet, given the government's own poverty and political commitments, the change in mind-set made rather little impact on the scale and composition of government investment.

Public investment in railways was regionally well balanced in the long run, but investment in irrigation, roads, and power was unevenly distributed. There was apparently a correlation between the initial inaccessibility of a region, its size, and the share of the region in public investment. Burma (present-day Myanmar), for example, was a major recipient of funds. Within British India, western and southern India received more investment than did eastern and northern India.

Irrigation

When the British East India Company took control of the upper Gangetic Plains, an extensive network of irrigation channels in a state of disrepair was found in the western part of the river Yamuna, attributed to Firoz Shah Tughluq. The "grand anicut" (dam) on the Cauvery, attributed to the Chola rulers, was another large pre-British system. The company administration by and large appreciated the importance of these systems, and restored some of them. From the late nineteenth century, major new constructions consisted of canals taken out of perennial rivers (in Punjab, Sind, and United Provinces), and weirs constructed on major rivers (South India). The Punjab canals spread access to water over formerly water-scarce territories. In the South, canals mainly redistributed monsoon water. The most dramatic effect of the former type of canals was the "colonization" of vast areas of wastes and pastures by migrant cultivators. In Punjab these "canal colonies" arose between 1890 and 1930. The colonists did not come from peasant stock necessarily; many were soldiers of disbanded armies, and many others were former pastoralists. A network of canals thus restructured entirely the rural society and politics in some areas of Punjab.

Acreage irrigated as percentage of cropped area increased from possibly 5 or 6 percent in the early nineteenth century to 22 percent in 1938, about 60 percent of the addition to irrigated areas being served by government canals. Among the largest projects undertaken in British India were Upper and Lower Ganga canals (1854–1878; 3,212,000 acres, or 1.3 million hectares), Sirhind canal (1887; 2,471,000 acres, or 1 million hectares), Cauvery delta system (1889; 1,050,000 acres, or 425,000 hectares), the Western Yamuna canal system (1982; 1,236,000 acres, or 500,000 hectares), the Krishna and Godavari delta systems (1898–1890), together serving about 2,471,000 acres, or close to a million hectares, and Sarda canal (1926; 1,236,000 acres, or 500,000 hectares). Smaller works that had considerable impact in a relatively small area included the Sone canal (1879), the Nira valley system (1938), the Mettur project (1934), and the Upper Bari Doab canal (1879).

In the regime of the company, canal construction was left to the engineering department of the army. From 1854, the Public Works Department became responsible for canal construction. A broad distinction was made between those works that were built for administrative or famine relief purposes ("protective" works) and those built to increase agricultural production ("productive" works). The former class was not expected to yield an income, though they might save the government money that would have to be spent on famine relief if a famine occurred. The latter class could be commercially profitable for the government. The water that raised incomes was charged at a certain rate, paid out of that income. This tax accrued to the Public Works Department, and was calculated in the rate of return on capital invested in irrigation projects. Increased income from a plot of land also increased the rental value of that land. In areas outside the Permanent Settlement, the government could realize

Bhakra Dam. When Nehru dedicated the Bhakra Dam (shown here) in 1963, he referred to it as a "temple of modern India," a symbol of the aspirations of developing countries worldwide. In the early twenty-first century, similar large-scale dam projects in India (at last count more than 23) are the focal point of several well-funded campaigns to protect the millions of ordinary citizens displaced by them. SUJATA KULSHRESHTHA / FOTOMEDIA.

this value. But these benefit-cost estimates were neither quite accurate nor persuasive to the critics, in London, of government investment in India.

In 1878 an influential committee of the India Office declared that irrigation projects were a failure, both commercially and in preventing famines. At the same time, the 1880s Famine Commission claimed that irrigation projects were on average profitable for the government. The difference partly reflected official mindsets in India and Britain. This question of what monetary return the irrigation programs generated for the government remained shrouded in speculation. Nevertheless, private enterprise was never seen as a viable alternative in canals. It was felt that allowing the private sector to construct canals would complicate the question of property rights in canal water.

The private gains from irrigation projects were mixed. Did irrigation projects reduce famines and increase peasant incomes? Canal-irrigated area as a percentage of cropped area was not very different between Madras and Punjab in 1900. Yet, Madras suffered far more from famines. The reason was that canals as such could not prevent water scarcity in the dry months if the region suffered from a general shortage of rains. In other words, the natural supply of water and the capacity of canals to prevent famines were correlated. In several parts of the canal-served agrarian countryside, there were dramatic improvements in the wealth and income of the people. But the negative externalities of extensive canal projects were also large. These costs occurred due to a persistent engineering defect, the poor drainage of excess water, and the resulting malaria epidemics and saline deposits. The net effects of canal irrigation were seemingly larger in the initially more water-scarce Punjab and Sind than in a region like western United Provinces, where canals were an alternative to well irrigation. Uniformly, however, canals intensified rural inequality.

Railways

Until the mid-nineteenth century, the common systems of long-distance transportation of cargo were pack animals and small sailing vessels on navigable rivers. Large trains of pack animals were driven by the nomadic Banjaras on

Railway Train Car. With their construction initiated under British rule, India's railways—still one of the largest transportation networks in the world—provided much needed stimulus to the labor market. AKHIL BAKSHI / FOTOMEDIA.

roads that connected western India with eastern and northern India. For short-distance trade and travel, the common means of transportation were palanquins, small river craft, and bullock carts. The older systems of long-distance trade used a lot of labor and time. The railways destroyed them without much resistance. Comparatively lesser attention was paid by the government to roads and short-distance travel, so in that sphere, traditional means of transportation survived until well after 1947.

In 1849 the Government of India entered an agreement with some British railway companies to construct railways in India on a guaranteed minimum return of 5 percent on paid-up capital. The guarantee was meant to attract investment in a venture that would normally be seen as risky because it consumed so much capital for an uncertain return. The guaranteed profit imposed a fiscal burden on the state. But since many crucial lines in India (nearly all those in South India, for example) ran at a loss for many decades after their construction, it is probable that without the guarantee these would not have been built at all.

Railway construction began on a large scale in the 1850s and continued, almost exclusively by the private sector, until 1870. At 1870, Calcutta, Bombay, Madras, and Delhi had become interconnected by the "broad-gauge" system. Thereafter, the fiscal burden became too heavy to bear due to the depreciation of the rupee and the rise in interest rates on government borrowing abroad to pay for guarantees. Increasingly, therefore, the government itself entered railway construction. The first major "meter-gauge" lines were a product of direct investment. Later in the nineteenth century, the government started buying out some of the "guaranteed companies." During the 1920s, all railways in India were brought under government management.

By then the Indian railway system was one of the largest networks in the world. Between 1860 and 1940, total route miles increased from 838 to 41,852. Route miles per 1,000 square miles increased from 0.5 to 26, and route miles per million persons increased from 3 to 107. Passengers carried by the railways increased from 48 million in 1880 to 604 million in 1940. Clearly, the railways had revolutionized the mobility of people and goods in South Asia.

The economic effects of the railways can be classified into two types. First, the railways had significant forward

Truck Owned by Tata Industries. Road construction was a low-priority area of government investment during the colonial period and beyond. In 2004, however, the National Highways Development Project devised an ambitious plan to repair and convert some 8,000 miles (13,000 km) of road in India to four- and six-lane superhighways. AKHIL BAKSHI / FOTOMEDIA.

and backward linkages with other sectors of the economy. Second, there was great reduction in average transportation costs measured in money and time. Railway construction worldwide stimulated the engineering industry, financial markets, and labor markets. In India the first of these three effects was relatively weak until World War I. Until then, nearly all of the railway material was imported from Britain. The government had built railway workshops in India for repair and production of parts, but they were not intensively used. Coal mining was the only important example of backward linkage of the railways. After the war, a progressive "Indianization" began to occur. The role of the railways as a major source of demand for the basic metal industries in India became significant from that time forward. The financial development effect was weaker still, since the major part of the capital came from London. The effect on stimulating the labor market was of great importance. At 1947 the Indian railways were the single largest employer in the organized sector, a distinction maintained today. And railways facilitated the major channels of internal labor migration. A Chota Nagpur laborer, traveling to the Assam tea plantations for work in the mid-nineteenth century, was awestruck by the railway carriage and composed songs, at

least one of which compared the black locomotive to the image of Krishna, the dark-skinned god.

Import and export trades in real terms increased enormously as a result of reduction in transportation costs. Because these costs became a smaller part of the price, the supply of goods now responded to narrower differences between local and world price than before. Exports of raw cotton and hides and skins quickly expanded. Railways also facilitated the integration of markets. This is evident from declining regional variability in prices of food grains. Some Indian nationalists alleged that by thus increasing the supply response to the world market, the railways intensified local shortages of food during the late-nineteenth-century famines. More recent research, on the other hand, has attributed the remarkable reduction in the incidence of famine after 1900 to easier interregional crop movements that the railways had made possible.

Roads and Inland Waterways

A systematic history of roads and road transportation in India remains to be written. From the little research that is available on the nature of long-distance trade before the British came to India, it is fair to conclude that good and safe roads were scarce in pre-colonial and early colonial India. The poor condition of the roads partly reflected limited engineering capability in bridging the numerous rivers. The East India Company restored and constructed some major roads for military purposes, but regular allocation of funds for roads did not begin until the 1830s.

Even thereafter, roads were a low priority area of government investment. Road length grew at a much slower pace than the railways. In 1931 the length of "metalled" roads per 1,000 persons was as low as 0.4. For a comparison, the ratio was above 1.5 in British Ceylon and Malaya. There were possibly three reasons behind this bias against roads. First, road construction was said to have been too costly in India given the terrain, the rivers, and the high repair costs due to the monsoons. Second, roads brought the government no monetary return, whereas the railways did. Third, the lobbies that pushed the government into investment in modern transportation clearly wanted railways, or cheaper modes of long-distance trade.

In northern and eastern India, and sporadically elsewhere, the major navigable rivers were an important means of transportation of cargo. River traffic was cheaper than roads, and carried larger volumes per head. But the role of rivers in long-distance trade was more or less confined to the Gangetic Plains. This traffic was of great antiquity. It declined in competition with the railways.

Ports

India had a long and rich tradition in mercantile marine and shipbuilding. The advent of the Europeans in the Indian Ocean created competition for the Indians in coastal shipping. However, it also stimulated the business of some of the ancient ports like Masulipatnam or Cambay. The final blow to Indian traditional enterprise in ocean shipping came with the displacement of sailing vessels by steamships in the early to mid-nineteenth century. The major ports that carried the bulk of foreign trade in the colonial period were new sites where railways and modern harbors converged, for example, Bombay, Madras, Calcutta, Karachi, and Rangoon. Each served as an export outlet for the products of a vast hinterland. The two western Indian ports enhanced their trade manifold with the U.S. Civil War (1861–1865) and the opening of the Suez Canal (1869). Thereafter, Calcutta and Bombay also grew to become industrial centers. World War I, while upsetting private business through these ports, emphasized their military importance. Bombay especially saw a modernization drive in the early interwar period.

Posts and Telegraph

The foundations for a government postal system were in place before 1858, but it became a widely used utility only in the late nineteenth century. This expansion was largely driven by the demand for the services of the post office. Migration and money orders had become synonymous. In safety, cost, and wide reach, the postal money order was unprecedented in the history of internal remittance in India. Already in 1849 the East India Company had decided to construct a telegraph system along the railway lines. The telegraph became an urgent necessity on account of the Afghan war and the impending war with Burma. The first line, between Calcutta and Diamond Harbour, opened in 1851 and was used to send shipping news from the coasts to Calcutta. The major lines were completed before 1855. This remarkable speed of construction resulted from both strategic needs and Lord Dalhousie's personal interest in the plan. The telegraph was a private enterprise in England and the United States and a state enterprise in continental Europe. In India it turned out to be a state enterprise for military reasons, despite Dalhousie's general aversion to state monopolies. By 1857 the telegraph had proved itself a critical military tool. Not surprisingly, it symbolized evil for the mutineers. With vengeance, they destroyed telegraph establishments wherever they could (and never used it to their advantage). With this lesson behind itself, the Crown rule saw massive expansion of the telegraph system within the country and between India and Europe. From then onward, the commercial uses of the telegraphs began to overwhelm strategic needs, leading to extremely rapid growth in the use of the system.

Power

Electricity generation in colonial India saw significant private-public coexistence and cooperation. By contrast, in the period after 1947, there was a decisive turn toward state monopoly. The first private firm to produce electricity for Calcutta city was proposed in 1891. In the next ten years, a series of legislation laid down the basic framework of regulation. Electricity was first introduced in 1897 by a small firm in the Darjeeling Municipality utilizing a mountain stream. Two years later, the Calcutta Electricity Supply Undertaking started producing electricity with steam power. Two other large hydroelectric projects came up before World War I: the Sivasamudram on the Cauvery, erected by the Mysore government, and the Khopoli plant of Tata Electric Power. The former supplied power to the Kolar gold mines, and the latter to Bombay city. The report of the Indian Industrial Commission (1918) laid great emphasis on the need for organized exploitation of natural resources, including hydroelectric power. However, efforts in this direction had to wait until the mid-1920s, when the provinces recovered from the initial trauma of "dyarchy" and pursued some of their now exclusive duties, electricity generation for example. In the interwar period a large number of hydroelectric and thermal power units were started, many of these in the territories of the princely states. At 1947 the installed capacity stood at 1.7 million kilowatts.

The process of infrastructure development had inherent inequalities. Irrigation systems remained primitive and undeveloped in large parts, the railways de-prioritized roads, electricity generation was initially drawn toward centers of modern enterprise, and so on. Some of these inequalities were redressed in the post-colonial period, but others continued. Communication and local transportation remain even now of sharply variable quality. The regions poorly endowed have seen a long history of neglect and government failure.

Tirthankar Roy

See also **Economic Policy and Change, 1800–1947; Fiscal System and Policy from 1858 to 1947**

BIBLIOGRAPHY

Derbyshire, I. D. "Economic Change and the Railways in North India." *Modern Asian Studies* 21, no. 3 (1987): 521–545.

Government of India. *The Gazetteer of India: Indian Union*, vol. 3: *Economic Structure and Activities*. Delhi: GOI, 1975.

Hurd, J. "Railways." In *The Cambridge Economic History of India*, vol. 2: *C. 1757–1970*, edited by Dharma Kumar. Cambridge, U.K.: Cambridge University Press, 1983.

Morris, M. D., and C. B. Dudley. "Selected Railway Statistics for the Indian Subcontinent (India, Pakistan and Bangladesh), 1853–1946–47." *Artha Vijnana* 17, no. 3 (1975): 187–298.

Stone, I. *Canal Irrigation in British India*. Cambridge, U.K.: Cambridge University Press, 1984.

Whitcombe, E. "Irrigation." In *The Cambridge Economic History of India*, vol. 2: *C. 1757–1970*, edited by Dharma Kumar. Cambridge, U.K.: Cambridge University Press, 1983.

INFRASTRUCTURE DEVELOPMENT AND GOVERNMENT POLICY SINCE 1950

India's infrastructure services are slowly but steadily moving away from the realm of government control to that of the private sector. Across sectors ranging from telecommunications and roads to power and ports, state-owned agencies are giving way to private sector entities operating in a competitive environment and subjected to economic regulation where necessary. Governments at both central and state levels are actively engaged in managing this transition, devising appropriate policy frameworks and establishing suitable institutions such as the central road fund and independent regulatory authorities in power and telecommunication sectors.

Telecommunications

Since India's independence, its telecommunications sector has continued to be governed by the Indian Telegraph Act of 1885, which placed all telecommunications within the government domain. Telecommunications services were the exclusive monopoly of the Department of Posts and Telegraphs, which had the mandate to regulate and provide these services. Public ownership over the next several decades hampered growth of the sector, leaving India's teledensity (defined as main lines per 100 inhabitants) among the lowest in the world: 0.4 in 1980 and 0.7 in 1990. The extremely high level of unfulfilled demand was evident from the long waiting lists and the willingness of Indian subscribers to pay large up-front payments for telephone connections.

The government initiated partial reforms in 1985, when the Department of Posts and Telegraphs was divided into separate entities, the Department of Posts and the Department of Telecommunications. In 1986 the government spun off basic telephone services in the two metropolitan cities of Delhi and Mumbai into a new public sector entity, the Mahanagar Telephone Nigam Limited. Overseas communication services were transferred to Videsh Sanchar Nigam Limited. Subsequently, the government ushered in the National Telecom Policy of 1994, which allowed private participation in both basic and cellular services. In 1997 the government enacted legislation to establish the Telecom Regulatory Authority of India.

The process of liberalization received further fillip in 1999 with the adoption of the New Telecom Policy of 1999, which permitted the entry of multiple players into all segments, including fixed line, cellular, and long distance telecommunications. Furthermore, the policy-making and service-providing functions of the Department of Telecommunications were separated; the latter were transferred to a new company, Bharat Sanchar Nigam Limited. In addition, the Telecom Regulatory Authority of India Act was amended in 2000, to bring clarity to the authority's functions and powers, and a separate Telecom Disputes Settlement and Appellate Tribunal was established to adjudicate disputes.

In November 2003 the government issued guidelines for converging the hitherto disparate basic and cellular licenses into Unified Access Services Licenses. This process of license unification is likely to be extended to other service segments. Today, most major telecommunications operators are aggressively seeking to expand their operations. These expansion plans will, however, require substantial additional investment, and will prove to be a considerable challenge for private players due to the steep decline in tariffs.

The spectacular progress of India's telecommunications sector has been largely due to the entry of private players. Private participation has resulted in greater competition, better service, increased penetration, and lower prices. By 2002 the average cellular tariffs were reduced by 53 percent, and national long distance and international subscriber dialing tariffs declined, respectively, by 56 percent and 47 percent. Cellular tariffs in India are now among the lowest in the world, and tariffs for cellular-to-cellular calls fell by almost 70 percent. This steep decline, coupled with a significant growth in wireless telephony, resulted in an unprecedented increase in teledensity, from 1.9 in March 1998 to 7 in March 2004. The cellular subscriber base nearly doubled in 2002–2003 to reach 12.7 million, and again in 2003–2004, to 26 million.

Though teledensity has grown at so rapid a pace, much of this growth occurred in urban areas and telephone connectivity in rural areas still remains a cause of concern. In rural areas, where two-thirds of India's population live, about 14 percent of the villages are still without any telephone service. While the costs of rolling out village public telephones are undoubtedly high, it is also widely acknowledged that the absence of credible penalties for nonfulfillment of rural rollout obligations by the licensees has not helped in this regard. The government is, however, committed to expanding the rural telephone network through a universal service fund.

Power

Private sector participation in the power sector is not new to India. In fact, at the time of independence in 1947, private sector utilities and licenses accounted for over 80 percent of all electricity supplied in India. Immediately after independence, the Electricity Supply Act of 1948 vested responsibility for the generation, transmission, and distribution of electricity to State Electricity Boards (SEBs), marking the first shift toward public ownership in the power sector. Within the next decade, the state electricity boards took over almost all private sector power licenses.

By the mid-1970s it had become apparent that SEBs alone would not be able to meet the rapidly increasing demand for power, and the central government established the National Thermal Power Corporation Limited and the National Hydroelectric Power Corporation Limited to enhance generation capacity. To mitigate regional imbalances, the government established the Power Grid Corporation of India Limited to manage the transmission of power between states and regions. By the mid-1980s it was clear that the power sector would not be able to meet India's growing demand without considerable restructuring. In 1991 the government amended the Electricity Supply Act of 1948 to encourage private investment by providing a legal basis for facilitating investment in generation and distribution. This policy was to provide additional generation capacity to complement the rapidly declining public sector resources.

The responsibility for the power sector is currently shared between the central government and the states. At the central level, policy and planning is under the purview of the Ministry of Power and its arm, the Central Electricity Authority. The Central Electricity Regulatory Commission was established in 1998 and deals with inter alia regulation pertaining to the tariffs of generating companies owned or controlled by the central government and those who sell electricity in more than one state, interstate transmission of energy including tariff of transmission utilities, and oversight of the India's Electricity Grid Code. At the state level, there are State Electricity Regulatory Commissions, whose functions include determining the tariff for generation, supply, transmission and wheeling of electricity within the state, issuing transmission, distribution and trading licenses, and facilitating intrastate transmission of electricity. The energy departments of each state address policy and planning issues.

Although the sector was liberalized in 1992, private participation has remained far below expectations. Out of nearly 120 expressions of interest registered to add 69,000 megawatts of capacity amounting to about U.S.$55.5 billion of investment, only a handful of private projects have been implemented.

One of the main factors impeding private participation in generation is the precarious financial condition of the SEBs, which, in turn, is attributable to nonremunerative tariff structures, poor operational and collection practices (which facilitates theft), and dilapidated networks. Despite some improvement over the previous year, the operating losses of state power utilities in 2002–2003 continued to remain high, at an estimated U.S.$4 billion. Aggregate technical and commercial losses are reported to be as high as 40 percent, and, of these, about two-thirds are said to be commercial losses, a euphemism for theft. As a result, private investors and lenders are wary of supporting power projects that have to sell exclusively to financially weak SEBs.

India's per capita electricity consumption is still among the lowest globally (for example, half that of China). It is estimated that over 100,000 megawatts of

Nagarjunasagar Dam. Named after Acharya Nagarjuna, a philosopher who spread Mahayana Buddhism, the Nagarjunasagar Dam was among the earliest hydroelectric projects in India. The largest masonry dam in the world, it straddles a massive manmade lake and has rendered Andhra Pradesh the "rice bowl" of India. JYOTI BANERJEE / FOTOMEDIA.

capacity need to be installed by 2012, which will require additional investments of U.S.$178 billion in the next decade. To meet these requirements, the power sector will have to rely on sizable private sector participation and investment, which in turn is intrinsically linked to reform of the sector.

In order to spur reforms, the central government has undertaken a few key initiatives. Parliament passed the Electricity Act of 2003, which consolidates the existing electricity laws and attempts to usher in a market-based competitive regime and institutionalize appropriate regulatory safeguards. Following the recommendations of an Expert Committee, the Ministry of Power is now providing incentives to the states that manage to reduce the gap between the cost of supply and revenue realization, through the Accelerated Power Development and Reform Programme. The Expert Committee also delineated a reform framework and financial restructuring principles that could potentially form the basis for devising state-specific reform programs. Central Electricity Regulatory Commission has notified and implemented an Availability Based Tariff regime, with a view to make the incentives of the utilities compatible with the merit order requirements of the entire network and thereby improve grid discipline.

At state level too, reforms are progressing, albeit at a varying pace. While Orissa and Delhi have moved furthest by privitizing power distribution in their respective states, quite a few other states have unbundled generation, transmission and distribution functions into separate entities. Twenty one states have constituted State Electricity Regulatory Commissions.

Ports

India has over 3,728 miles (6,000 km) of natural coastline and is strategically well-positioned on global trade routes. India has 13 major ports and over 181 minor ports (of which 139 are operational), which together handle the bulk of India's foreign trade. Most of the major ports in India were established after independence, except for Kolkata (Calcutta) and Mumbai

(Bombay), which were built in the nineteenth century by the British. Responsibility for all major ports has mainly been, and still is, in the domain of the central government. The thirteen major ports handled over 280 million metric tons of cargo in 2001–2002, mostly petroleum, iron ore, and coal; they operate under the jurisdiction of the Ministry of Shipping. The Tariff Authority for Major Ports regulates prices at the major ports, while the remaining ports fall under the jurisdiction of their respective state governments.

While overall cargo traffic grew at approximately 7 percent per annum during the 1990s, most Indian ports are already operating at full capacity and there is a critical need for augmentation of capacity. Globally, increased trade, coupled with enhanced efficiency levels and improved processes, have made it difficult for traditional ports with outdated facilities and systems to compete effectively. Indian ports are plagued by widespread inefficiencies in cargo handling, poor connectivity, a mismatch of facilities and type of cargo traffic, and outdated labor practices. In the last few years, although there has been some improvement in operational performance, with the average turnaround time falling from 8.1 days in 1990–1991 to 3.7 days in 2001–2002, there is still a long way to go to attain international efficiency levels. Indian ports also face growing competition from nearby transshipment ports, such as Colombo, Singapore, Dubai, and Salalah, which offer world-class facilities and quick turnaround times. The mismatch of cargo facilities is further likely to impede future viability of the sector, as global trade is moving increasingly toward containerized cargo, which has been growing at over 10 percent per annum; only 13 percent of India's port capacity is dedicated to container traffic.

In due recognition of the aforementioned deficiencies, the government has sought to usher in market oriented reforms in the sector. As part of this, port trusts have been given the authority to spend up to 1 billion rupees (U.S. $22.2 million) without prior permission of the central government. Ports trusts are also now required to follow a new commercial "profit and loss" accounting system. More significantly, the central government as well as states have initiated measures to attract private participation in the sector. Major port trusts have awarded concessions for container terminals to global port majors such as P&O (Jawaharlal Nehru Port Trust [JNPT] and Chennai) and PSA (Tuticorin) and new international players are entering, viz., Dubai Port Authority in Cochin and Maersk in JNPT and Pipavav. Amidst poor efficiency gains in the port sector as a whole, the performance of some private port terminals has been impressive. The Nhava Sheva International Container Terminal developed by P&O Australia at JNPT initially expected to handle 500,000

TEUs (twenty feet equivalent units) by 2005, had already exceeded 900,000 TEUs by 2002.

It is imperative that Indian ports improve efficiency levels to match international standards. This cannot be achieved in an environment in which state-owned monopoly operators provide port services, since there is little incentive for them to improve efficiency. The experience of the private container terminal at JNPT clearly indicates the benefits that can be achieved through private sector involvement and competition. Accordingly, the government should curtail its involvement in this sector and instead devolve more power to port authorities, and embrace privatisation of various port services. In addition, the government should ensure good connectivity to ports with the rest of India's transportation network, so as to facilitate and enhance interport competition. As intraport and interport competition increases, the government should phase out economic regulation.

Roads

India's total road network, stretching approximately about 2 million miles (3.3 million km), is the second-largest road system in the world, comprising national highways, state highways, major district roads, and rural roads. Since independence the road network has suffered from a lack of funds, poor monitoring, and inadequate supervision of road projects. Maintenance has been a low priority, which has led to appalling safety conditions, resulting in over 70,000 fatalities per year. Only 46 percent of India's roads are paved, and of those only 20 percent are in good condition. The last few years have seen a rapid increase in motor vehicles and a marked deceleration in the development of road capacity, as over 85 percent of passenger traffic and 70 percent of freight traffic is carried by the road network. As a result, roads have become congested, and the quality of road travel has deteriorated substantially.

This problem is especially acute in the case of national highways (36,000 mi., or 58,000 km), which form the backbone of India's transport network. Due to the poor physical condition of roads, traffic speeds are low, leading to increased freight costs. In 1995 the National Highways Authority of India was given a mandate to develop, maintain and manage national highways entrusted to it. The authority is currently implementing the National Highways Development Project (NHDP) comprising of over 8,700 miles (about 14,000 km) of the national highways network, including the 3,600 miles (5,800 km) of roads linking the four major metropolitan cities and 4,500 miles (7,300 km) of the North-South and East-West corridors. The total construction cost of the NHDP has been estimated at about U.S.$13 billion. In addition to NHDP, forty-eight new road projects at an estimated cost of about U.S.$8.8 billion will be undertaken in the coming years.

According to a World Bank study, the completion of the new corridors will result in annual savings of approximately U.S.$1.8 billion in fuel spending, reduced wear and tear of vehicles, and faster transportation. It is noteworthy that, compared to an annual addition of 6.8 miles (11 km) of national highways since independence, about 3,200 miles (5,100 km) of roads have already been four-laned as part of the NHDP.

The high traffic risk and the unwillingness of commuters to pay tolls often impede private investment in this sector. In this regard, the government's decisions to indirectly collect road-user payments through a tax on fuel and to constitute a nonlapsable central road fund appear to be steps in the right direction. However, there remains scope for further improving the existing institutional arrangements. For example, including road-user representatives in the management of the road fund would help impart greater transparency, establish accountability, and ensure that expenditure decisions are more responsive to the user needs. Yet another area of concern is that a substantial portion of the NHDP is being implemented through traditional civil works contracts, which leaves subsequent maintenance of the roads to the vagaries of funds availability and allocation. In order to overcome this limitation, the government could consider adopting approaches such as Build, Operate, and Transfer (BOT), Annuity and Shadow Tolling, which seem to offer better incentives for the operators to adopt optimal life-cycle construction methods and to maintain the roads over the contract duration.

At the state level too, there has been some progress. Several states, including Gujarat, Karnataka, Kerala, Madhya Pradesh, and Maharashtra, are going ahead with their (state) highway development programs, funded by a variety of approaches including toll roads, annuity, and capital subsidies. The last few years have also seen a much-needed thrust by the government toward improving the rural road network in India. In 2000, with a view to enhancing rural connectivity, the government launched the Pradhan Mantri Gram Sadak Yojana, a centrally sponsored program funded by a tax on diesel.

Airports

Airports play a critical role in promoting trade, tourism, and the economic development of a country. The Airports Authority of India was constituted in 1995 to bring about integrated development and the expansion and modernization of operational, terminal, and cargo facilities at India's airports. Out of a total of 400 airports/

airfields/airstrips in the country, the authority manages 94 civil airports (of which 11 are international airports) and 28 civil enclaves at defense airfields. These airports handled over 44 million passengers in 2002–2003 (15 million international and 29 million domestic). The authority is responsible for providing air traffic services over the Indian airspace and adjoining oceanic areas.

Although it may appear that India has considerable airport capacity, it has for the most part lost out in aviation; it missed the global travel boom of the 1990s, ceding its natural geographic and economic advantages as a cargo and courier hub to other countries. Air travel still remains confined to a tiny section of the domestic population. The share of India in total world aviation traffic remains minuscule. India accounted for a mere 2.4 million tourist arrivals in 2002, compared to 715 million worldwide and 130 million in the Asia Pacific region. Worldwide, tourism accounts for about 10 percent of gross domestic product; in India it is less than 5 percent.

There is considerable underutilization of existing capacity, as only 62 of India's airports are in use, with the rest remaining inactive. Moreover, there are a large number of airports where full infrastructure is available, but which operate only a few flights a day. Over 40 percent of the passenger traffic is concentrated in the two main international airports in Delhi and Mumbai, and the limited terminal capacity at these airports has led to increased congestion, bunching of flights, and delays in passenger clearance. This situation is exacerbated by outdated infrastructure, inadequate ground-handling systems and night-landing facilities, and poor passenger amenities. Grossly inadequate cargo-handling procedures at airports result in delays of days in transit from one terminal to another. Only ten airports in the country are profitable, despite airport charges in India being considerably higher than the international average.

India's airports urgently need to improve efficiency and undertake investments for capacity addition. There is an increasing recognition that private participation is the key for achieving both these objectives. The government has recently taken a long-awaited decision on the privatization of the New Delhi and Mumbai airports, approving the proposal to set up joint ventures with 74 percent private ownership and a cap of 49 percent on foreign direct investment. The government has also approved plans for two new airports near Hyderabad and Bangalore, with majority private sector participation.

Railways

The Indian Railways (IR) is over 150 years old. Since independence, the IR has remained a government enterprise and it currently operates the world's second-largest

Indian Airlines Passenger Jet. State-owned Indian Airlines remains the top domestic carrier. In the face of intense competition from budget, no-frills airlines, and the growing number of air travelers (the Centre for Asia Pacific Aviation estimated that the Indian market will add 5 million passengers every year for the next five years), can it continue to manage its high costs while maintaining service standards? AKHIL BAKSHI / FOTOMEDIA.

rail network under single management, with a route length of over 39,500 miles (63,000 km). The railways carry over one million metric tons of freight and transport over 10 million passengers a day (of which over 5 million are in Mumbai's suburban network). The annual revenue of the IR is approximately U.S.$5.5 billion, of which freight transport accounts for 70 percent and the balance is passenger traffic.

IR is now facing strong competition from road transport, pipelines, and air transport. Arbitrary pricing policies by the government, especially after 1985, prevented IR from raising passenger fares in line with rising costs, and led to heavy cross-subsidization by overcharging freight customers. Greater customer orientation, more flexibility, and the lower costs of road transport, contrasted with the slow movement and poor service quality of the railways, induced many freight customers to move to relatively cheaper road transport. IR is also plagued by very high operational expenses. In 2000–2001, operating ratio—that is, ratio of total working expenses to gross

traffic receipts—reached 98.5 percent. Even as IR is unable to generate enough internal resources to contribute to investment plans, the government too reduced its level of financial support to the railways in the last decade.

A combination of the aforementioned factors has placed the IR on the verge of a financial crisis and led to substantial whittling down of fresh investments. The Railway Safety Committee's recommendation to invest U.S.$2.2 billion over the next five years to improve the safety of the aging network through better track maintenance and general improvements has been inordinately delayed. The need to increase investment in rail infrastructure led to a policy decision in 2000 to allow private capital in the railways sector, covering rolling as well as fixed infrastructure. In December 2002, the government announced a scheme—the National Rail Vikas Yojana—aimed at increasing the capacity of the rail golden quadrilateral connecting the four largest cities, providing better connectivity to major ports and building a few critically needed bridges over the Ganges and Brahmaputra rivers. Funds required for this scheme, estimated at U.S. $3 billion, are planned to be raised through an innovative mix of budgetary and nonbudgetary resources, including market borrowings and multilateral funding agencies.

The early 2000s have seen some initiatives involving private sector participation in the railways, one in Gujarat, completed in May 2003, entailing an investment of U.S.$119 million. The project, which aims at providing rail connectivity to Pipavav port, has been developed by Pipavav Rail Corporation, a joint venture between Gujarat Pipavav port and the IR. A similar structure is now planned to connect Krishnapatnam port in Andhra Pradesh. In the southern region, the IR is encouraging private entrepreneurs to set up private goods terminals, which will comprise multi-modal facilities for rail-cum-road links, warehousing facilities, storage facilities, and information technology backup for logistics services.

Sunaina Kilachand
Urjit R. Patel

See also **Information and Other Technology Development**

BIBLIOGRAPHY

Annual Report 2003–2004. Department of Telecommunication, Ministry of Communications and Information Technology, Government of India.
Annual Report 2003–2004. Ministry of Power, Government of India.
Blueprint for Power Sector Development. Ministry of Power, Government of India, 2001.
The Indian Railways Report—2001: Policy Imperatives for Reinvention and Growth, Expert Group on Indian Railways, New Delhi.
India Port Report: Ten Years of Reforms and Challenges Ahead. Navi Mumbai: i-Maritime Consultancy Private Limited, 2003.
National Highways Authority of India. Available at <http://www.nhai.org>
Report of the Committee on a Road Map for the Civil Aviation Sector. Ministry of Civil Aviation, Government of India, 2003.
Structuring of APDRP, Reform Framework and Principles of Financial Restructuring of SEBs. Expert Committee on State-Specific Reforms, Ministry of Power, Government of India, 2002.

INSURANCE INDUSTRY At the time of India's independence, the country had a competitive market both in life and nonlife insurance. After independence, Indian insurance companies started growing faster as competition intensified and as non-Indian insurers were dislodged. In 1956 the government nationalized the life insurance industry, and in 1973 nationalized nonlife insurance businesses. Until 2000 India's government enjoyed a virtual monopoly of the country's insurance industry. Currently, however, competition from many private insurers has been introduced.

Nationalization and Change

When the government of India nationalized all life insurance companies in 1956, it brought together over two hundred private life insurers and provident societies under a single entity, the Life Insurance Corporation of India (LIC). However, the stated mission of the nationalization of life insurance was to mobilize savings for the development of the country and to conduct the business in the spirit of trusteeship, providing protection to the people in every part of the country. The LIC is a public company, owned entirely by the government. Since the LIC's charter specified that only 5 percent of its annual valuation surplus would go to the government (the owner), the remaining 95 percent was returned to policyholders in the form of bonuses and profits. The corporation was thus run almost like a mutual fund. After the nationalization, the life insurance business in the country has been synonymous with the LIC, which has developed a vast network of branches. The number of policyholders has increased from 5.6 million in 1956–1957 to 125.8 million in 2001–2002; the number of branches increased from 240 to over 2,000 during the same period.

The LIC has also been active in the field of group insurance plans for the more vulnerable sections of society since the 1980s. By offering subsidized plans for the unorganized and rural sectors, the LIC has played an important role in supplementing other, state-level efforts in providing social security. In the past, it covered around 5 million lives of people working in diverse occupations, including rickshaw pullers, construction workers, and self-employed women. A significant portion of LIC funds was invested in social projects; in March 1997, the LIC invested 610.74 billion rupees in central, state, and local government guaranteed marketable securities, and in loans to various socially oriented programs to provide for and improve basic amenities such as potable water, drainage, housing, electrification, and transportation.

The LIC's socioeconomic commitment defined its basic thrust. In its formative years, it was engaged in harnessing savings, providing security, and utilizing people's money for their welfare. However, in the 1970s, the LIC branched from its traditional life insurance operations into mass insurance through group insurance, later extended to social security. It further entered the pension field in mid-1980s. These achievements notwithstanding, the LIC has been able to cover only a quarter of India's insurable population. Lack of competition engendered complacency in the insurance industry, and this was reflected in insufficient responsiveness to customer needs, high costs, overstaffing, and a relatively high rate of lapsing policies. The LIC was also slow to adopt new technology. By the 1990s the need for major reforms in the insurance sector seemed clear.

On the nonlife insurance (or "general" insurance) front, the situation was much the same, though the General Insurance Council did frame a code of conduct for fair and sound business practices in 1957. In 1968 the Insurance Act was amended to provide for greater social control over the general insurance business. In 1971 the management of nonlife insurers was taken over by the government, and general insurance was nationalized in 1973. As a result, 107 insurers were amalgamated and grouped into four companies with headquarters in Kolkata, Mumbai, Delhi, and Chennai. The General Insurance Corporation of India (GIC), incorporated in November 1972, was their holding company, commencing business on 1 January 1973. The general insurance business also increased in volume after its nationalization. The net premium income increased from 2.2 billion rupees in 1973 to about 85 billion rupees in 2001–2002. The four public insurers were expected to compete among themselves. But, in reality, there was hardly any competition among them, partly because they all were owned by the government, and partly because the Indian general insurance market was substantially driven by a tariff regime, decided by the Tariff Advisory Committee.

General insurance business is broadly divided into three categories: fire, marine, and miscellaneous. Motor vehicle insurance is a part of miscellaneous, accounting for 35 to 40 percent of the total gross premium collected by the general insurance industry. The fire portfolio accounts for about 20 percent of the total business. Though the industry makes overall profits, the motor vehicle portfolio continues to lose money, mainly due to third-party legal liability claims.

Later Reforms

Reforming the insurance sector has been part of India's economic reforms initiated in the 1990s. The government constituted an insurance reform committee, headed by former finance secretary and central bank governor R. N. Malhotra, in April 1993. In its report submitted to the government in January 1994, the committee highlighted the major weaknesses and problems in the sector, and also recommended opening the sector to competition from private players. Other important recommendations were to restructure the public insurance companies so as to enable them to face competition, and

the setting up of an autonomous statutory regulatory body with independent financing. In response to the Malhotra Committee recommendations, the government in 1996 constituted an Interim Insurance Regulatory Authority to suggest legislative reforms in the insurance industry.

The Insurance Regulatory and Development Authority (IRDA) Bill of 1999 was passed by both houses of Parliament and was later ratified by the president on 29 December 1999. The act provides for the establishment of a statutory IRDA to protect the interests of insurance policy holders and to regulate, promote, and ensure orderly growth of the insurance industry, opening it up to the private sector. The act also stipulated that no insurer be allowed to conduct life insurance or general insurance business in India unless it has a paid-up equity capital of 1 billion rupees. A single company is not allowed to transact both life and nonlife insurance business; foreign equity at present is capped at 26 percent. For banks to enter into the insurance business, prior approval of the central bank is required.

Following the passage of the IRDA Act, private players were allowed into the insurance business in 2000. In the first year, six private insurers were registered: four in life insurance and two in nonlife insurance business. As of 31 March 2002, there were twelve life and ten nonlife insurers registered with IRDA. Most of the new companies in the industry have formed a joint venture with a foreign partner.

The Insurance Amendment Act of 2002 has paved the way for the entry of corporate agents and brokers, for accepting different modes of payment of premiums, and for changes in provisions relating to the distribution of surplus in the life insurance business. The introduction of licensed third-party administrators is expected to give a boost to the health insurance that has remained underdeveloped in the country. In 2001–2002—the first year of operation of four new life insurance companies—the life insurance industry witnessed a growth of 43.03 percent in gross premiums. LIC dominated the life insurance market. On the general insurance front, of the six new nonlife insurers, five have formed joint ventures with foreign equity participation. The general insurance business grew at 12.03 percent during 2001–2002. The share of private insurers was 3.74 percent of the total gross premiums underwritten in the country.

The benefits of a competitive market are becoming visible as the insurance companies are educating customers about the need for buying insurance, advertising their products, and trying to differentiate from those of others. The insurers are adopting creative ways of marketing products and developing unconventional distribution channels, such as establishing links with banks to attract their clientele. The insurance regulator's approach so far is reassuring.

Rajeev Ahuja

See also **Economic Reforms of 1991; Economy since the 1991 Economic Reforms**

BIBLIOGRAPHY

Government of India. "Report of the Committee on Reforms in the Insurance Sector." Delhi: Ministry of Finance, 1994.

Life Insurance Corporation of India. "Saga of Security: Story of Indian Life Insurance 1870–1970." Mumbai: LIC, 1970.

———. "Tryst with Trust: The LIC Story." Mumbai: LIC, 1991.

Niranjan, Pant. "The Insurance Regulation and Development Bill 1999: An Appraisal." *Economic and Political Weekly* 34, no. 45 (6–12 November 1999): 3166–3169.

Ranade, A., and R. Ahuja. "Insurance." In *India Development Report*, edited by Kirit Parikh. New Delhi and New York: Oxford University Press, 1999.

INSURGENCY AND TERRORISM

Insurgency and terrorism are as old as war. These are tactics of the weak, a means by which people with a cause attempt to gain political objectives through violence. Since independence, India has extensively experienced both insurgency and terrorism, essentially of two types. One type is oriented to socioeconomic Marxist revolution, the first of which began at Telengana in present-day Andhra Pradesh, spreading over time to include Nepal. In the 1960s it engulfed parts of West Bengal in violent urban terrorism inspired by the politics of Mao Zedong. These movements were countered essentially by state police forces, subdued but never eliminated. There has been a resurgence in these movements; in 2002 they formed an umbrella organization called the Coordination Committee of Maoist Parties and Organizations of South Asia (CCOMPOSA) to facilitate cooperation and coordination among fourteen Marxist groups. The other form of violence was guerrilla war, or an insurgency, advocating separatism and affecting the peripheral regions of the country. It began at independence among the Naga people in Northeast India and spread elsewhere later. Terrorism evolved and spread in India in the 1990s as an even more intense form of violence.

Insurgency and terrorism have definite characteristics in India. Insurgency may be said to represent a people's movement with a political cause, usually aiming for independence and often settling at some stage for political autonomy. It uses violence as the principal though not the only means to achieve its ends. It targets mainly the state apparatus and particularly the security forces. Legitimacy is sought through popular support; it therefore attempts to create an alternate state structure. Even though violence may be intense, it is neither random nor meant purely for effect. The battle is for the hearts and minds of the people, based on a perceived cause, with the insurgents likely to have an initial advantage. Terrorism, a comparatively recent phenomenon in India, is more likely to be inspired by religious causes. Particularly since 1999, it has also adopted the version of suicide or fedayeen attacks.

The Northeast Insurgencies

Insurgencies in independent India began in the Northeast region of the country, which today comprises seven provinces. The region was deprived of its links with the rest of the nation at partition, with East Pakistan (later Bangladesh) interposed between the two parts. Only a narrow 12 miles (20 km) wide corridor between Bangladesh and Nepal link the two parts. Deprived of an outlet to the sea and with limited access to the outside world, the region was condemned to underdevelopment. Ethnically, the people are immensely diverse, with distinct and separate identities, more akin to those in Southeast Asia, from where many of them originally came. Except for the Brahmaputra River valley and the adjacent low hills suitable for the highly lucrative tea cultivation, the British had left the tribes almost entirely to themselves. It is not surprising that they would ask for independence.

Nagaland. Insurgency in India began in Nagaland on 14 August 1947, when the Naga National Council (NNC) demanded independence from the Indian Union. The movement was initially limited to political action. First, the NNC conducted a "plebiscite" in 1951, which it claimed supported their cause. Next, it launched a boycott against the first general elections, held in 1952. Soon after, the movement turned violent. In September 1954, Naga leader Angami Zapu Phizo announced Nagaland independence and confronted the central government with an armed insurrection. Initially, the Indian government responded with escalating counterviolence, using local police and the Assam Rifles, and in 1956 sending in the regular army. By 1964 an Indian infantry division of some 20,000 soldiers was deployed against a few thousand armed rebel insurgents. Simultaneously, state administrative structures were strengthened, and political actions were initiated, granting statehood to Nagaland in January 1964. A peace initiative was then launched under Jaya Prakash Narayan, B. P. Chaliha, and Michael Scott, a Scottish missionary. This initiated a cease-fire, and after a decade of sporadic violence, peace terms were finally agreed upon. The Shillong Accord was signed in 1975, under which most Nagas agreed to surrender their arms. Two armed Naga groups were, however, enroute to China for military training and arms procurement at the time the agreement was signed, and hence were left out of the peace process. The leaders of this group, S. S. Khaplang, Issak Swu, and T. Muivah, decided to continue the insurgency from adjacent Myanmar. After prolonged discussions they too finally abandoned the insurgency in 2002.

Mizoram. South of Nagaland lie the Mizo Hills, inhabited by a single tribe, the Mizos. Unlike their neighbors in the plains, however, they did not initially demand independence, merely greater autonomy from the state of Assam in order to maintain their identity and traditional culture. Crops failed repeatedly in the area in the early 1960s, leading to acute famine in the hills. The slow response of the Assam government led to deep discontent and finally to insurrection. The Mizo movement, led by Laldenga, commenced with armed attacks throughout the region at midnight on 28 February 1966. India responded in force, sending in an armed division to punish the Mizo tribals. Support was offered to the rebels by East Pakistan (Bangladesh after 1971) and sanctuary in Myanmar. Violence continued for two decades. After prolonged discussions, a peace settlement was finally reached in 1986, with Laldenga finally vowing to accept the Constitution of India. He was made the chief minister of the state of Mizoram the next year. All violence ended with the accord.

Manipur. The plains of Manipur, adjoining Nagaland, saw an outbreak of insurgency in the mid-1970s. Several factions had varied goals, centered around factional and tribal demands. At least one was pro-Communist, its leaders having come in contact with China. Sporadic violence continued during the initial years of independence, but was countered successfully by the army. The state remains prone to law and order problems, though virtually all insurgency ended by the early 1990s.

Assam. Economic stagnation, lack of employment, and a continuous flow of refugees from Bangladesh have posed major challenges to Assam's state government. Prolonged popular student agitation in the late 1970s led to the All Assam Students Union forming its own state government in 1983. Assam's problems did not go away, however, and the resultant instability bred greater discontent, leading to the outbreak of more insurgencies. The principal one, led by indigenous Assamese of the valley under the United Liberation Front for Asom (ULFA), brought out the army in support of the government in Operation Rhino before the end of 1989. The Indian army has remained engaged, though at much lower levels of intensity. The situation in Assam remains disturbed and is countered primarily by central police forces. A number of smaller insurgencies have emerged, opposing ULFA and challenging the Assamese majority. Violence remains in the region and has spread to Bhutan, with armed groups seeking sanctuary there as well as in Bangladesh.

The Punjab

Insurgency came to the heartland of India's in the early 1980s. The Sikhs constitute a vibrant minority in India, with 2 percent of the nation's population. The linguistic reorganization of India's states after 1957 led to the formation of a much smaller state of Punjab, where the Sikhs had a bare majority. Autocratic and interfering policies of the central government led in turn to fundamentalist Sikh aspirations, which soon turned violent under a charismatic religious leader, "Sant" J. S. Bhindranwale. Sharing a border with Pakistan, dissident Sikh groups received arms and support from Islamabad. Armed groups soon established themselves in Sikh religious shrines (*gurdwaras*), with Bhindranwale moving into the holiest of them all, the Golden Temple at Amritsar. They openly challenged Delhi, promising a violent revolution. The Indian state responded with military force, launching Operation Blue Star on the night of 4 June 1984. After an intense overnight battle employing tanks, the army secured the Golden Temple, damaging it seriously in the process and suffering over three hundred casualties. Many Sikh insurgents and some pilgrims perished in the attack. The state was traumatized.

Barely five months later, on 31 October, Prime Minister Indira Gandhi was assassinated by two of her Sikh bodyguards. A riot broke out in Delhi, targeting Sikhs. It is claimed that some mobs were led by political leaders belonging to the ruling Congress Party. Over two thousand innocent Sikhs were murdered and torched in the nation's capital over the next few days. An armed insurgency soon broke out in the Punjab.

The insurgency was intense, violent, sectarian, and indiscriminate. The situation was countered primarily by the state police, with the army remaining always on call and in support. Even though an accord was signed with the moderate Sikh leader of the Akali Party, Sant Gurcharan Singh Longowal, in 1986 and a government installed in the state under him, insurgency continued. Finally, when in desperation the insurgents targeted the families of policemen, they countered with greater violence under the leadership of the director general of police, K. P. S. Gill, himself a Sikh. After prolonged attrition, the situation was controlled by 1992, returning to full normalcy soon afterward.

Jammu and Kashmir

The most complex and intense insurgency that India has faced is the ongoing proxy war in Jammu and Kashmir.

Its origin can be traced to the state's accession to India at partition. The Indian Independence Act promulgated by the British Parliament allowed the rulers of the princely states to decide to which dominion (India or Pakistan) the state would accede. The maharaja of Jammu and Kashmir, Hari Singh, delayed his decision. Only when armed marauders from the North-West Frontier province of Pakistan, led by regular officers from its army, invaded the state did the maharaja seek help from Delhi, signing the Instrument of Accession to India on 25 October 1947. Indian forces flew in the next day and over time stabilized the situation. India referred the question of "Pakistani aggression" to the United Nations Security Council, and a cease-fire was agreed to from 1 January 1949, with Pakistan still in control of about one-third of the state.

Two more wars were fought between India and Pakistan by 1971. Under the Simla Agreement of 1972, both sides agreed to resolve the issue bilaterally. The earlier cease-fire line was replaced by a new "line of control" demarcated after prolonged meetings of senior military commanders of both sides and both countries agreed not to violate it. Peace prevailed in Jammu and Kashmir for the next sixteen years.

Discontent surfaced in the province over the central government's interference with the political process in the state in the 1980s. The Inter Services Intelligence (ISI), a wing of the Pakistan military, seized this opportunity, and with surplus weapons of the Afghan War (supplied to it by the U.S. Central Intelligence Agency) directly sponsored insurgencies in India. The turning point came in December 1989, following new elections to Parliament, when the new home (interior) minister's daughter, a medical doctor, was kidnapped in the state capital at Srinagar. The new government was unable to deal with the situation effectively and released the prisoners sought by the kidnappers unconditionally. Euphoric celebrations followed, expecting a collapse of the government in Jammu and Kashmir. The situation was restored, but only with much martial power, and the state settled in for a prolonged period of insurgency encompassing the entire province.

Two terrorist organizations took up arms. One, led by the Jammu and Kashmir Liberation Front (JKLF), consisted of indigenous insurgents seeking independence. The other group, led by the Hizbul Mujahideen (HM), sought to merge Kashmir with Pakistan. All insurgent groups were supported and supplied by Pakistan and its ISI, with training, weapons, and money from across the border. By the end of 1990, additional formations of the regular Indian army reinforced the police and paramilitary organizations, and intense counterinsurgency repression was launched. Cordon and search, raids, patrols, and special operations formed the bulk of counterinsurgency

operations throughout the state. Borders had to be sealed and the deployment posture along the line of control was shifted from conventional defense to anti-infiltration. Force levels increased over the years, and a new paramilitary organization, the Rashtriya (National) Rifles was formed, consisting of regular soldiers on deputation in Kashmir. By the early 1990s, the JKLF was marginalized, and the HM was slowly replaced by extremist Islamic forces

Kashmiri insurgents continued their terrorist attacks against Indian security forces, which by then were more than half a million strong in Kashmir, as well as against minority Hindu families, forcing the latter to leave the valley. Indigenous militants were replaced by "guest" militants from Pakistan Occupied (Azad) Kashmir, Pakistan itself, and Afghanistan, and by Islamic terrorists from around the world. Advanced training was carried out under the Taliban, supported by Osama bin Laden, in Afghanistan. By the late 1990s, the situation had turned into "cross border terrorism."

Indian Counterinsurgency Strategy and Tactics

Indian counterinsurgency doctrine evolved from the British era "Aid to Civil Authority," the lessons of the Malayan campaign, and its own experiences of what it terms "low intensity conflicts." The premise has always been that operations were against misguided elements within one's own society and therefore justified use of only "minimum force." In very exceptional and rare circumstances, and as a last resort, the Indian army has used tanks or helicopters in such combat. The principal focus has been to win the "hearts and minds" campaign, with civic actions always following coercive tactics.

There has never been any dichotomy or questioning within the army of its use in internal security. A secondary role of the armed forces, enshrined in the Constitution, mandates aid to the government when required. Detailed modalities and procedures are laid down by the government for its implementation. Special legal authority is provided by the Parliament through the Armed Forces Special Powers Act, applicable in specific "Disturbed Areas" as notified and for a fixed duration, which allows the army to search and arrest without warrant.

When called upon for counterinsurgency operations in a rural area, the army would deploy in a grid pattern. A battalion of about 800 soldiers in five companies would operate over an area of about 4 sq. miles (10 square km). About one-third of the force would remain in reserve at all times. The rest would be engaged in patrolling, collecting information, and launching operations. Opening roads and protecting convoys were important initial tasks. Specific search-and-destroy operations would be carried out on known hideouts and weapons caches. Grouping of villages, as in Malaya, was tried in both Nagaland and Mizoram with varying success. A grid system facilitated civic actions, which in turn produced intelligence and also ensured accountability.

Major fedayeen attacks have been frequently launched by terrorists in Jammu and Kashmir since 1999. These terrorists seize hostages, murder innocents, and kidnap and rape at random. India has trained special forces and antiterrorist cells in military and police units to deal with these situations. An elite National Security Guard specializes in hostage rescue and antihijacking operations.

The security forces' record in counterinsurgency has not been without blemish. There have been many cases of human rights violations, deaths in custody, rape, and looting. Perhaps police forces with a less stringent regimental system of discipline are more vulnerable to such behavior. Cases brought to light have been dealt with severely, and exemplary punishments meted out. National and state human rights commissions are vigilant in trying to keep the security forces in check. A notable feature of the Indian counterinsurgency experience has been that, despite their extensive use in India's internal environment, the forces have never attempted to usurp political power. They have consistently maintained their accountability to Indian law and their adherence to the Constitution.

Dipankar Banerjee

See also **Assam; Ethnic Conflict; Ethnic Peace Accords; Jammu and Kashmir; Manipur; Mizoram; Nagas and Nagaland; Northeast States, The; Paramilitary Forces and Internal Security; Punjab**

BIBLIOGRAPHY

Banerjee, Sumanta. *India's Simmering Revolution: The Naxalite Uprising.* London: Zed Books, 1984.
Bhowmick, Subir. *Insurgent Crossfire: North East India.* New Delhi: Lancer, 1996.
Ganguly, Sumit. *Conflict Unending: India-Pakistan Tension since 1947.* New York: Columbia University Press, 2001.
Grewal, S. S., and B. K. Khanna, "Low Intensity Conflict in Indian Context." *Journal of the United Service Institution of India* (July–September 1992): 205–223.
Hazarika, Sanjoy. *Strangers of the Mist: Tales of War and Peace from India's Northeast.* Delhi: Viking, 1994.
Joshi, Manoj. *Combating Terrorism in Punjab: Indian Democracy in Crisis.* Conflict Studies no. 261. London: Research Institute for the Study of Conflict, 1993.
Kalyanraman, Sankaran. "The Indian Way in Counterinsurgency." In *Democracies and Small Wars,* edited by Efraim Inbar. London: F. Cass, 2003.

INTELLECTUAL PROPERTY RIGHTS Intellectual property (IP) awareness in India has recently experienced a sharp increase. From 1972 to the 1990s, research and development expenditure in the country grew more than fifty times, but patent filing remained static at 3,500–4,000 applications per year. Though new inventions were being made, they were not being protected, due to a general distrust of the system, coupled with a lack of awareness.

This situation has now changed. As of 2005, India's Council for Scientific and Industrial Research was the third-largest applicant from developing countries under the Patent Cooperation Treaty. The number of patent applications being filed annually has more than doubled, to over 10,000, as people are recognizing the potential of their creative skills and channeling them into productive resources.

The Indian courts have also started granting substantial damages in IP cases. Initially, the courts were reluctant to grant damages, being more sympathetic to a defendant whose business was restrained through an injunction. There has, however, been a radical change in the approach of the courts.

Legislation

Since 1999 Indian law relating to IP rights has doubled in volume as a result of the requirements of the World Trade Organization agreement on Trade Related Aspects of Intellectual Property Rights (TRIPS). New IP laws have been enacted, including: the Geographical Indications of Goods (Registration and Protection) Act, 1999; the Protection of Plant Variety and Farmers' Act, 2001; the Information Technology Act, 2000; the Semi-Conductor Integrated Circuits Layout Design Act, 2000; and the Bio Diversity Act, 2002.

The Patents (Amendments) Act of 2002 was enacted, taking effect on 20 May 2003, in line with India's phased compliance with its TRIPS obligations. The act established a patent term of twenty years; exclusive marketing rights; patentability of microorganisms; expansion of the list of nonpatentable inventions; and patentability of software-related inventions. The time period for the grant of most patents was reduced from over five years to about two years.

On 26 December 2004 the government of India also promulgated the Patents (Amendment) Ordinance of 2004 to make Indian patents law compliant with TRIPS, (January 2005). This ordinance ushers in a product patent regime for all fields of technology and is of particular relevance to drugs, pharmaceuticals, and chemicals. The ordinance clarifies the Indian position on the patentability of software inventions by stating that

Investigators Visit a Video Store in Seach of Pirated DVDs. There is a well-established statutory and judicial framework in India for safeguarding intellectual property rights, whether they relate to patents, trademarks, copyright, or industrial designs. Accordingly, tougher enforcement measures have been adopted in recent years. INDIA TODAY.

embedded software as well as software/hardware combinations would qualify for patents. However, the provisions relating to exclusive marketing rights have been deleted. The Indian Parliament on 23 March 2005 passed the Patents (Amendment) Bill of 2005, to replace the Patents (Amendment) Ordinance of 2004.

Intellectual Property Litigation

While the Indian courts continue to deal with traditional IP matters pertaining to "passing off" and counterfeiting, an attempt is being made by rightful owners as well as the courts to take IP litigation to the next level. The courts have adopted an innovative and experimental approach, rather than remaining rule-bound. This was achieved by expanding and developing well-established principles and by exploring new legal avenues.

In the first case of its kind, the Delhi High Court in *Emergent Genetics India Pvt. Ltd v. Shailendra Shivam* in 2004 applied principles of the law of confidentiality in giving protection to hybrid cotton seeds that are genotypically identical to those of the plaintiff, and principles of copyright law, to protect unique sequencing information locked inside genes of hybrid varieties of the plaintiff.

The courts have started to grant compensatory damages in IP litigation and have also begun to grant punitive and exemplary damages. The case that set the benchmark was *Time Incorporated v. Lokesh Srivastava & Anr,* in which the High Court of Delhi granted 500,000 rupees as damages to the plaintiff on account of loss of reputation, and punitive and other damages of an additional amount, for a total of 1.6 million rupees. The court held that the defendant's magazine, which used the Hindi transliteration of the word "time" with the word *sanskaran* and a distinctive red border, to be a slavish imitation of the plaintiff's trademark and held the defendant liable for infringement.

This trend was followed in numerous cases, including:

In the case of *Amarnath Sehgal v. Union of India* (1992), the High Court of Delhi ordered the government of India to pay 500,000 rupees of damages to the plaintiff, a world-famous sculptor, for the violation of his moral rights by their act of distortion, damage, and mutilation of his bronze mural, which had been sold to the government, and also directed a return of the mural itself to the sculptor.

In the case of *Buffalo Networks Pvt. Ltd. & Others v. Manish Jain & Others* (2000), the Delhi High Court protected the domain name rights of the plaintiffs, a media and advertising company, by restraining the defendant from using the domain name "www. tehelka.com" or the word "tehelka" on the Internet or otherwise, awarding a sum of 100,000 rupees as damages against the past misuse of the same by the defendants.

In *Tata Sons Limited v. Fashion ID* (2005), the Delhi High Court directed the transfer of the domain name "www.tatainfotecheducation.com" to Tata Infotech Education from a Chinese registrant, and awarded an amount of 100,000 rupees as costs to Tata Infotech.

In *Microsoft Corporation v. Yogesh Popat* (2003), the Delhi High Court awarded a sum of 1.98 million rupees as damages to Microsoft Corporation, with 9 percent interest, for the infringement of its IP rights in its software programs.

Pharmaceutical Patents

The Patents (Amendments) Act of 2002 had had some far-reaching implications for the pharmaceutical sector with the introduction of requirements envisaged by the Doha Declaration of 2001 by the World Trade Organization in the form of a provision for the grant of a license to manufacture generic drugs on notification of the central government in a national health emergency, thus overriding international pharmaceutical patents. The emergency circumstances include "public health crisis relating to Acquired Immuno Deficiency Syndrome (AIDS), Human Immunodeficiency Virus (HIV), Tuberculosis (TB), malaria or other epidemics."

On 26 December 2004 the government of India enacted the Patents (Amendment) Ordinance of 2004, introducing product patents for all fields of technology, including drugs and pharmaceuticals. That ordinance has now been replaced by the Patents (Amendment) Bill of 2005.

Amendments brought about by the new legislation have raised concerns in the pharmaceutical industry that the prices of drugs might increase tremendously. Given the advent of a faster and more effective patent protection regime, the vibrant Indian pharmaceutical industry is gearing up to face challenges. The highly fragmented Indian pharmaceutical sector, with approximately 22,000 registered units employing around 460,000 people, is led by about 250 companies that control 70 percent of the market share. Besides being one of the top five bulk drug

manufacturers in the world, India is also among the top twenty pharmaceutical exporters in the world.

India has also become an attractive destination for clinical trials. India anticipates the gain of a large share of the multi-billion-dollar global business of clinical trials in drugs. In India the clinical research industry is projected to bring in over U.S.$100 million in 2005, and potentially over $1 billion by 2010.

Protection of Small Farmers

Over 200 million Indian farmers and farm workers have been the backbone of India's agriculture. Despite having achieved national food security, the well-being of the farming community continues to be a matter of grave concern for the country. The establishment of an agrarian economy, which ensures food and nutrition for India's billion people, raw materials for its expanding industrial base and surpluses for exports, and an equitable reward system for the farming community for the services it provides to society, will be the mainstay of reforms in the agriculture sector. These concerns led to passage of the Protection of Plant Varieties and Farmers' Rights Act in 2001. The act provides for the establishment of an effective system for the protection of plant varieties, the rights of farmers and plant breeders, and the development of new varieties of plants.

The government of India introduced the Seeds Bill in 2004, in place of the existing Seeds Act of 1966. Although the main purpose of the 2004 Seeds Bill was to address farmers' concerns regarding sowing, use, exchange, and sale of seed, the bill has in turn made it more difficult and cumbersome for a farmer to sell seeds or exchange or reproduce seeds. The bill makes it compulsory for a seed of any kind or variety to be registered if it is sold for the purpose of sowing or planting. Even for bartering of seeds, the person doing so must obtain a registration certificate as a dealer in seeds from the state government.

The bill has obviously made the sale, import, export, and bartering of seeds more transparent by laying down various procedures. However, government intervention has increased. Compensation to farmers in cases where the seed fails to provide the expected performance has been provided for. However, the farmer can claim this from the producer, dealer, distributor, or vendor under the Consumer Protection Act of 1986. Therefore, although there are provisions providing benefits to the farmers, they are cumbersome.

India also has a unique position in the world insofar as it accounts for 7 to 8 percent of Earth's total biodiversity. India is also one of eighteen "mega-diverse" countries, which together possess 60 to 70 percent of the world's biodiversity. For the conservation of its biodiversity, important steps taken by India include enactment of the Biological Diversity Act of 2002 to protect India's rich biodiversity and associated knowledge against their use by foreign individuals and organizations without sharing the benefits arising from such use.

Pravin Anand
Sagar Chandra Anand

See also **Information and Other Technology Development; World Trade Organization (WTO), Relations with**

BIBLIOGRAPHY

"India Can Earn $1B from Clinical Trials." *Times of India*, (New Delhi), 29 March 2005.

Sahai, S. "India's Plant Variety Protection and Farmers' Rights Act, 2001." *Current Science* 84, no. 3 (February 2003).

South Asia Watch on Trade, Economics and Environment. "Protecting Mountain Farmers' Rights in India." Policy brief available at <http://www.sawtee.org>

Watal, Jayashree. *Intellectual Property Rights in the WTO and Developing Countries*. The Hague and Boston: Kluwer Law International, 2001.

INTERNAL PUBLIC DEBT, GROWTH AND COMPOSITION OF

The uninterrupted and rapid growth of India's public debt has been a matter of serious concern. An increasing debt servicing burden and its feedback into further deficits and debt have raised apprehensions about sustainability and solvency. Its adverse impact on economic growth by crowding out private investments has also been a matter for concern. Government finances deteriorated and deficits emerged in the revenue (current) account in 1982, and its rapid increase since has caused India's central government to employ public debt mainly as an instrument to transfer private savings into public consumption and public investment, a considerable proportion of the latter being unproductive. Increasing indebtedness has raised questions about sustainability, and has dampened the growth prospects of the economy by crowding out private investment.

The growth of government indebtedness can be viewed in relation to the development strategy and economic environment in the country, and four distinct phases in the trend can be discerned. Initially, government borrowing was meant to finance public sector investment in keeping with the development strategy of India's first few Five-Year Plans. Thus, public debt as a ratio of gross domestic product (GDP) increased from 30 percent in 1950–1951 to 36 percent in 1960–1961, remaining broadly at that level until 1964–1965. However, inability to generate public savings required financing

further public sector investments, initiating the economic recession of 1965, which forced a suspension of the plan from 1966 to 1968. Subsequently, in the second phase, government indebtedness declined sharply to 26.8 percent of GDP until 1975. The third phase saw the rapid increase in public debt, particularly after 1984–1985. The debt to GDP ratio increased from 37.6 percent in 1980–1981 to 45 percent in 1984–1985 and further to 56.7 percent in 1990–1991. The fiscal expansion in the latter half of the 1980s, and the consequent sharp increase in primary and revenue deficits at both central and state levels resulted in the rapid increase in the debt-GDP ratio. The buildup of fiscal expansion in the 1980s and the persistent fiscal imbalance caused macroeconomic imbalance, creating a crisis in 1991. Thus, the fourth phase in public debt began with fiscal containment, which was, however, short-lived. The inability to contain government expenditures on the one hand and a declining tax-GDP ratio at the central level on the other resulted in the sharp increase in government indebtedness, bringing to the fore serious questions of debt sustainability and solvency.

The increase in indebtedness over the years is due to both central and state governments. The total outstanding debt attributable to the states increased from about 10 percent in 1950–1951 to over 25 percent in 2001–2002. Thus over a quarter of the internal public debt incurred in India is for the state governments, and the remainder is for New Delhi's central government.

The internal debt of the government consists of outstanding loans from the market and other outstanding liabilities. Within the latter, deposits in provident funds, post office savings, and other small savings collections constitute the bulk. Analysis shows that the proportion of other outstanding liabilities has steadily increased over the years, from about 25 percent of total outstanding liabilities in 1950–1951 to over 40 percent in 2001–2002. Transferring private savings for public investment within the regime of financial repression was an inherent part of the planning strategy. Thus, during the first four decades, the interest rate on market borrowing by the government was fixed at substantially below the market rate, and commercial banks were required to invest a significant portion of their lendable resources in government securities as a statutory liquidity ratio.

Traditionally, part of the budget deficit was financed by loans from the Reserve Bank of India. The proportion of such deficit financing increased from 16 percent in the early 1970s to nearly one-third during the latter half of the 1980s. This resulted in unplanned growth in the public debt. The economic crisis of 1991 raised serious questions about the means of financing budget deficits, and in 1995 an agreement was reached between the Reserve

Bank's governor and the finance secretary of the government of India to completely dispense with the practice of monetizing the deficit.

The high and increasing volume of debt raised serious questions of stability and sustainability, and had a dampening effect on economic growth. As much of the borrowing is undertaken to finance current expenditures of the central and state governments, it does not generate direct or indirect returns to the government to meet debt-servicing obligations. Thus, additional borrowing has to be resorted to, and this vicious cycle creates imbalance between savings and investments and spills over into the balance of payments problem. The simple test of sustainability is given by the Domar rule, according to which debt is sustainable as long as the interest rate is lower than the growth rate of the economy. In India, the interest rates were deliberately kept low, and therefore there was no danger of their exceeding the growth rate until the interest rate regime itself was liberalized. Nevertheless, effective interest rates steadily increased from 2.3 percent in 1951–1952 to 5 percent in 1970–1971, to 7.6 percent in 1990–1991, and finally to over 10 percent in 2001–2002. Recent careful analysis of the central government debt shows that the interest rate has been higher than the growth rate of the economy both in 2000–2001 and 2001–2002.

Thus on the one hand, the volume of borrowing has increased at over 20 percent per year since 1991–1992, and on the other, the effective interest rate has shown a sharp increase following the financial liberalization. The effect is rapid increase in debt servicing costs, feeding back into further borrowing. Recent lowering of interest rates and acceleration in growth rate may hold back the growth of indebtedness, but the high volume of borrowing to finance large fiscal deficits continues to be a matter of serious concern. Fiscal consolidation is perhaps the key required to arrest further rapid growth of India's internal indebtedness.

M. Govinda Rao

See also **Fiscal System and Policy since 1952; Public Debt of States since 1950**

BIBLIOGRAPHY

Buiter, Willem H., and Urjit Patel. "Deby, Deficits and Inflation: An Application to the Public Finances in India." *Journal of Public Economics* 47 (March 1992): 172–205.

Moorthy, V., Bhupal Singh, and S. C. Dhal. "Bond Financing and Debt Stability: Theoretical Issues and Empirical Analysis for India." DRG Study no. 19. Mumbai: Reserve Bank of India, 2000.

Rajaraman, Indira, and Abhiroop Mukhopadhyay. "Sustainablity of Public Domestic Debt in India." In *Fiscal Federalism in India—Contemporary Challenges: Issues before the Eleventh Finance Commission*, edited by D. K. Srivastava. New Delhi: Har Anand Publications, 2000.

Rangarajan, C., Anupam Basu, and Naredra Jadhav. "Dynamics of Interaction between Government Deficit and Domestic Debt in India." In *Tax Policy and Planning in Developing Countries*, edited by Amaresh Bagchi and Nicholas Stern. Delhi: Oxford University Press, 1994.

INTERNATIONAL MONETARY FUND (IMF), RELATIONS WITH

The Bretton Woods Conference was convened in 1944 for the purpose of formulating postwar currency plans, as a result of which the International Monetary Fund (IMF) was established. India, though not yet independent, was among the countries whose representatives attended the meeting, and it was therefore counted as one of the founding members of the IMF. India's special concern at the time was about the "embarrassing plentitude" of sterling balances and their multilateral settlement and the inclusion, among the purposes of the IMF, of a clause to assist in the fuller utilization of resources of underdeveloped countries. This concern was not appreciated by the Americans and the British on the ground that the problem of wartime balances was too large for the IMF to tackle, and the development of underdeveloped countries was the responsibility of the World Bank. However, as the deliberations of the conference proceeded, it was conceded that the sterling balances would be freely convertible after the transition period, and also that the Articles of Association governing the IMF would include the development of productive resources of all members as a primary objective of economic policy.

India, which became a formal member of the IMF in December 1945, played a significant role in its formation. Each member's contribution to IMF resources, called its "quota," was made partly in gold and U.S. dollars and partly in its own currency, determining its voting rights and the amount it could borrow in the event of need. The quotas are decided generally on the basis of a member's national income, foreign exchange reserves, and its importance in world trade, though political considerations also weigh heavily. In 1945 India's quota was fixed at U.S.$400 million—sixth largest after those of the United States, the United Kingdom, the Soviet Union, China, and France, which entitled those countries to be five permanent members of the Executive Board of the IMF. As the Soviet Union declined to join the IMF, India moved up to the fifth permanent seat on the Executive Board. The board, the main decision-making body, consisted initially of twelve members. IMF membership expanded from thirty in 1947 to 194 by 2004. India's quota has grown from special drawing rights (SDR) of 400 million in 1947 to SDR4.158 billion in October

2004, though it declined relatively, thereby depriving it of a permanent seat on the board. India has, however, retained membership on the board through biannual elections.

Despite India's junior status as a member of the IMF, it exercised considerable influence in shaping IMF policies, being one of the largest developing countries. This was evident by the role it played in the emergence of the SDR, an artificial device for the creation of international liquidity, the shortage of which was felt since the first half of the 1960s. India also, as a prominent member of the Group of Twenty-Four (a subgroup of the leading developing country members of the IMF) worked assiduously for safeguarding the interests of developing countries in the management of the international monetary system.

India's Use of Fund Resources

The year 1947, when the IMF commenced its operations as a provider of resources to members in need of balance of payments support, coincided with the emergence of India as an independent nation. In March 1948, when India's requirements of foreign exchange exceeded its own receipts, India borrowed from the IMF for the first time, SDR28 million, and again SDR72 million toward the end of the year. The impact of the increasing development activity was felt on the balance of payments during 1956–1957, which sharply deteriorated, and India was required to negotiate borrowing of SDR200 million under the "stand-by" arrangement—one of several kinds of borrowing arrangements of the IMF. India returned to the IMF again in July 1961 for borrowing an additional SDR250 million. The relief afforded by the use of IMF resources, however, was short-lived, and despite the policy measures taken by the Indian government, the reserves continued their downward slide, forcing India to approach the IMF again for a loan of SDR100 million. After an interval of a couple of years of trouble-free times, India resumed further borrowing of SDR237.5 million between March 1964 and March 1966. The stresses and strains arising from the unsustainable size of the plans, the misconceived policies of the government, and the drought of 1965–1966 aggravated India's balance of payments problems. This compelled India to seek a loan of SDR90 million from the IMF under a compensatory financing facility (CFF). Thus, the IMF played an important role, through its lending to India, in stabilizing the Indian economy between 1952 and 1970.

During the early part of the 1970s, the Indian external position was comfortable as a result of a commodity boom facilitated by the international currency realignment. But this respite lasted only for a year or two. With rising inflation, drought depleting food-grain stocks, and rising foreign debt servicing, India resorted to borrowing from the IMF. To begin with, it used the CFF because the conditionality associated with it was mild and less onerous. India was soon overwhelmed by the first oil price shock of 1974–1975, which led to a sharp worsening of its balance of payments. The foreign exchange outlay on oil imports rose to $1.3 billion in 1974–1975, from $625 million in 1973–1974. India had no other alternative than to resort to additional resources from the IMF. First, it used "gold tranche" (i.e., borrowing against its contribution in gold) for SDR76.2 million, and a first tranche of its quota of SDR235 million, called "credit tranche" for its less stringent conditions. But this was not enough to fill the gap in the balance of payments. India, therefore, borrowed $400 million under two special oil facilities of the IMF, specially designed to meet the emergency faced by the developing countries in the wake of an upsurge in oil prices. This meant that India had to follow severely restrictive fiscal and monetary policies to contain both inflation and worsening of the balance of payments position.

India adjusted well to the first oil crisis, and there was a favorable turn in the India's external accounts, with invisible receipts rising sharply. History, however, repeated itself again. In 1979–1980, inflation soared to 20 percent, and the external trade deficit widened sharply. India responded to this by first using the CFF for SDR266 million and then approached the IMF for an additional borrowing of SDR5 billion under the extended financing facility (EFF) arrangement. Intense debate, both at home and abroad, marked the negotiations. Within India, controversy centered around conditionality versus economic sovereignty, whereas criticism abroad revolved around the size and the need for such a massive purchase. In particular, the industrialized members of the IMF were averse to the loan, on the grounds that the adjustment program lacked specificity, the balance of payments need was not established, and the investment plan was more suitable for commercial bank financing than that from the IMF. Despite vehement opposition by prominent members of the board, the SDR5 billion loan was approved, which at that time was the largest commitment for the use of IMF resources in history. However, there was heavy criticism from within India of the IMF conditionality associated with the loan. The Indian government tried to weather the storm, by pleading that it was a case of voluntary adjustment through appropriate stabilization and liberalization measures, though it carried little conviction. Eventually, however, India purchased only SDR3.9 billion until April 1984, and requested cancellation of the remaining part of the arrangement.

The next milestone in the IMF-India relationship was in 1991 following the Gulf War, with an increase in oil prices and a generally adverse turn in global developments. India's foreign reserves dwindled and credit ratings lowered, prompting India to seek again IMF financing. The resources borrowed from the IMF, under standby arrangement, amounted to a total of SDR2.2 billion. With the help of these borrowings, India could ride over the grim balance of payments crisis and move onto the path of structural adjustment in the crucial areas of finance, privatization, dismantling of controls, and liberalization of imports. Treading its way cautiously but firmly, India took several radical measures in the areas of trade, industry, and the public sector, which radically transformed the structure and nature of the Indian economy, thereby placing it firmly on a trajectory of steady and rapid growth. For the first time during the history of the IMF-India relationship, for more than a decade India did not approach the IMF for financing. Notwithstanding frequent differences regarding the conditions underlying loans from the IMF, India's association with the IMF has worked, on the whole, to its benefit; it has helped India to turn its chronically vulnerable economy with acute foreign exchange shortages into a self-sustaining one, globally competitive with high growth, relative price stability, and burgeoning foreign exchange reserves. As a result of this growth, India in 2004 has become a net creditor to the IMF—that is, it lends to the latter more than it borrows. As a consequence, India now has a greater voice in the formulation of IMF policies and in restructuring the international monetary system.

Chandi J. Batliwala

See also **Economic Reforms of 1991; World Bank (WB), Relations with**

BIBLIOGRAPHY

Balachandran, G. *The Reserve Bank of India: 1951–1967.* Delhi: Oxford University Press, 1998.
DeVries, Margaret. *International Monetary Fund, 1972–1978: Cooperation on Trial.* Washington, D.C.: IMF, 1985.
Horsefield, J. Keith. *The International Monetary Fund, 1945–1965.* 3 vols. Washington, D.C.: IMF, 1969.
International Monetary Fund. *Annual Report, 2003.* Washington, D.C.: IMF, 2003.
Reserve Bank of India. *History of the Reserve Bank of India, 1935–1951.* Mumbai: RBI, 1970.

IQBAL, MUHAMMAD *(1877–1938), Indian poet and philosopher.* Muhammad Iqbal was born on 9 November 1877 at Sialkot, a border town of the Punjab. Iqbal's grandfather, Shaykh Muhammad Rafiq, had left Kashmir not long after 1857, as part of a mass migration of Kashmiri Muslims fleeing repression from the British-backed Hindu Dogra rulers installed in Kashmir in 1846. Although the family never returned to Kashmir, the memory of the land and its people never left Iqbal, and he remained dedicated to the principle of self-determination for the people of Kashmir.

Life

Iqbal's parents raised him in a deeply Islamic environment. After Iqbal finished high school, he enrolled in the Scotch Mission College (later renamed Murray College). After two years he went on to the Government College in Lahore. By this time, Iqbal had mastered Urdu, Arabic, and Farsi under the guidance of Sayyid Mir Hasan (1844–1929), who had been markedly influenced by the Aligarh Movement of Sir Sayyid Ahmed Khan (1817–1898). Under Sayyid Mir Hasan, Iqbal studied classical Urdu and Persian poetry, and his own poetic genius blossomed early. Iqbal then found a master of Urdu poetry in Navab Mirza Khan Dagh (1831–1905). Iqbal was on the creative path that was to bring him success and international fame; however, his personal life was marred by unhappiness that was to follow him for much of his life. In 1892 his parents had arranged his marriage to Karim Bibi, the daughter of an affluent physician in the city of Gujarat. Two children were born to the couple, but soon differences developed, and they separated. Iqbal married again and also had two children with his second wife.

Iqbal graduated cum laude from the Government College at Lahore and was also awarded a scholarship for further study toward a master's degree in philosophy. During his studies at the Government College, Iqbal was strongly influenced by Sir Thomas Arnold, an accomplished scholar who combined a profound knowledge of Western philosophy with a deep understanding of Islamic culture and Arabic literature. Arnold helped to instill a blending of Eastern and Western sensibilities in Iqbal, and inspired him to pursue higher graduate studies in Europe. In May 1899, a few months after Iqbal received a master's degree in philosophy, he was appointed the Macleod-Punjab Reader of Arabic at the University Oriental College in Lahore. From January 1901 to March 1904, he taught English intermittently at Islamia College at the Government College of Lahore.

In 1905 Iqbal went to Europe, studying in both Britain and Germany. In London he studied law at Lincoln's Inn. There he received the Bar-at-Law degree on 1 July 1908. At Trinity College of Cambridge University, he enrolled as a student of philosophy while simultaneously preparing a doctoral dissertation in philosophy for Munich University. The German university exempted him from a mandatory stay of two terms on campus before submitting his dissertation, "The Development of Metaphysics in Persia," and he was awarded a doctorate in philosophy on 4 November 1907. Iqbal's dissertation was published the following year in London. In Cambridge, Iqbal came under the influence of the neo-Hegelians John McTaggart and James Ward. Two outstanding Orientalists at Cambridge, E. G. Brown and Reynold A. Nicholson, also became his mentors; the latter translated Iqbal's Persian masterpiece *Asrar-i Khudi* when it was first published in 1915.

Iqbal never felt at home in politics, but he was invariably drawn into it. In May 1908 he joined the British Committee of the All-India Muslim League, to which he belonged for most of this life. Iqbal was elected a member of the Punjab Legislative Assembly from 1926 to 1930. In 1930 the All-India Muslim League invited him to preside over its annual meeting, and his presidential address became a landmark in the Muslim national movement anticipating the creation of Pakistan. Iqbal called for "the formation of a consolidated North-West Indian Muslim state" as "the final destiny of the Muslims, at least of North-West India."

Iqbal returned to England to attend the second (1931) and third (1932) London Round Table Conferences, called by the British government to consult with Indian leaders on constitutional reforms for India. In February 1933 Iqbal was back in Lahore. Seven months later, Muhammad Nadir Shah, the king of Afghanistan, invited him to visit Kabul to advise the Afghani government concerning the establishment of a new university utilizing the best of modern Western and traditional Islamic values.

After his return from Afghanistan, Iqbal's health steadily deteriorated. His intellect remained sharp, however, and during this time he conceived many new projects, including proposed studies on Islamic jurisprudence and the study of the Qur'an. During this period Iqbal also invited a younger Muslim scholar, Sayyid Abu al-A'la Mawdudi, to the Punjab, where he began to publish his well known journal, *Tarjuman al-Qur'an*. Iqbal had hoped that Mawdudi would become a modernist scholar who would update Islamic ideas. Just before the creation of Pakistan in 1947, Mawdudi established Jamat-i-Islami; after 1947, he moved to Lahore and involved himself in the struggle for power in Pakistan, presenting a very conservative paradigm of Islamic polity.

By 1938 Iqbal's health had sharply declined, and he died on 20 April. He was buried to the left of the steps leading to the Badshahi Mosque in Lahore; construction of the mausoleum over his grave was started in 1946, its marble provided by the government of Afghanistan.

Religious and Political Thought

Iqbal lived exclusively under British colonial rule, a period during which Muslims in the Indian subcontinent were profoundly influenced by the religious thought of Shah Wali Allah (1703–1762) and Sir Sayyid Ahmed Khan. Shah Wali Allah was the first Muslim thinker to realize that Muslims were encountering a modern age in which old religious assumptions and beliefs would be challenged. His monumental study *Hujjat Allah al-balighah* provided the intellectual foundations for updating Islam. Sir Sayyid, who lived through the life of the last Mughal emperor, was profoundly influenced by British political culture. He engendered an intellectual movement that came to be known as the Aligarh movement; it attempted to update Islam, popularize Western education, modernize Muslim culture, and encourage Muslims to cooperate with the British government in order to gain a fair share in the administration and political framework of India. This was the intellectual legacy inherited by Iqbal.

Iqbal's most notable philosophical and political prose works were: *The Development of Metaphysics in Persia* (Cambridge, U.K., 1908); *The Reconstruction of Religious Thought in Islam* (Lahore, 1930); and his *Presidential Address to the Annual Meeting of the All-India Muslim League, 1930*. Iqbal here expounded the concept of two nations in India. Subsequently, his address came to be known as the conceptual basis for the state of Pakistan, although he did not use the name "Pakistan." The emphasis was on Muslim nationalism, giving shape and content to the national liberation movement of Muslims in India. Iqbal stressed the necessity of self-determination for the Muslims: "I'd like to see the Punjab, North-West Frontier Province (NWFP), Sindh and Baluchistan amalgamated into a single state. Self-government within the British empire or without the British empire, and the formation of a consolidated North-West Muslim Indian State appears to be the final destiny of the Muslims, at least of North-West India."

Intellectually, however, Iqbal was not an enthusiastic supporter of nationalism, and especially nationalism among Muslims. He attempted to resolve this dilemma in a letter to Jawaharlal Nehru, his younger contemporary, writing:

Nationalism in the sense of love of one's country and even readiness to die for its honor is part of the Muslim faith; it comes into conflict with Islam only when it begins to play the role of a political concept and claims . . . that Islam should recede to the background of a mere private opinion and cease to be a living factor in the national life. Nationalism was an independent problem for Muslims only in those countries where they were in the minority. In countries with a Muslim majority, nationalism and Islam are practically identical, but in countries where Muslims are in the minority, their demands for self-determination as cultural unification is completely justified. ("Reply to Questions Raised by Jawaharlal Nehru," in S. A. Vahid, ed., *Thoughts and Reflections of Iqbal*, Lahore, 1964)

Iqbal composed his poetry in both Persian and Urdu. His six Persian works include: *Asrar-i khudi wa Rumuz-i Bikhudi* (Secrets of the self and mysteries of selflessness, 1915); *Payam-i Mashriq* (Message of the East, 1923); *Zabur-i 'Ajam* (Scripture of the East, 1927); *Javid-namah* (Book of eternity, 1932); *Pas chih bayad kard, ay aqvam-i sharq* (What should be done, oh nations of the East, 1926); and *Armaghan-i Hijaz* (A gift of the Hejaz, 1938). His Urdu works, which are primarily responsible for his popularity in Pakistan as well as in India, are: *Bang-i dara* (Voice of the caravan, 1924); *Bal-i Jibril* (Gabriel's wing, 1935); and *Zarb-i Kalim* (The rod of Moses, 1936). Poetry, like visual art, is susceptible to varied interpretations; consequently his admirers, relying primarily on his poetry, have variously attempted to prove him a Pakistani nationalist, a Muslim nationalist, a Muslim socialist, and even a secularist.

Relations with Jinnah and the Emergence of Pakistan

Iqbal remained a steady supporter of the founder of Pakistan, Mohammad Ali Jinnah. During 1936 and 1937, Iqbal wrote eight letters to Jinnah, emphasizing the partition of India into two states; earlier, during the 1920s, Jinnah was still groping for coexistence with the Indian National Congress, and Iqbal had opposed Jinnah's policies.

Reluctantly but steadily, Iqbal had supported the establishment of a separate Muslim identity in the Indian subcontinent, while to the British and the Congress he often extended tactical cooperation. In the 1920s, Jinnah was willing to compromise with the Congress by abolishing separate electorates for Muslims in the provincial legislatures. Jinnah had agreed with the president of the Congress on 20 March 1927 to accept the joint electorates under certain conditions. Muslim seats in the central legislature were to be no less than one-third of the total seats. This agreement came to be known as the Delhi Proposals. In May 1927 the Punjab Muslim League, under the leadership of Mian Muhammad Shafi, Mian Fazl-i-Husein, and Iqbal, denounced the Delhi Proposals. The Punjab's opposition seriously weakened Jinnah's bargaining position with the Congress, which nevertheless participated in the All Parties Conference from 12 February to 15 March 1928, which produced the revisions of the Nehru Report. This proposal granted Muslims only 25 percent of the legislative representation. The Congress adopted the Nehru Report and decided to initiate a policy of nonviolent noncooperation

against the British if they did not accept it by 31 December 1929.

This reflected the Congress's determination to defy the British government for not including an Indian in the Simon Commission, which was established to make recommendations for future constitutional reforms in India. The appointment of the Simon Commission split the All-India Muslim League into two factions, one led by Jinnah and Saif-ud-Din Kitchlew and the other by Mian Muhammad Shafi and Iqbal. The Shafi League met in 1928 in Lahore, rejected the Delhi Proposals, and offered cooperation to the Simon Commission.

At Calcutta in 1928, the Jinnah League disavowed the Punjab Muslim League, adopting the Delhi Proposals and accepting the Nehru Report, subject to four amendments; all four proposed amendments were rejected by the Congress. The Jinnah League was thus repudiated by the Congress and simultaneously alienated from significant Muslim opinion. The split in the ranks of the Muslim League did not end until 1934, when Jinnah was finally elected president of the united Muslim League.

In the interim period, 1930 to 1934, Iqbal provided ideological leadership, articulating the Muslims' demand for a separate Muslim state. It is in light of this political split within the ranks of the League that Iqbal's presidential address of 1930 should be examined. That Allahabad address formulated the two-nation theory, which Jinnah finally accepted when he presided over the Muslim League's annual meeting in Lahore in 1940. He then demanded that India should be partitioned. Even though Iqbal was by no means a skillful politician, he nevertheless may thus be seen as a political guide of Jinnah in regard to the creation of Pakistan.

Hafeez Malik

See also **Jinnah, Mohammad Ali; Pakistan; Sayyid Ahmed Khan and the Aligarh Movement**

BIBLIOGRAPHY

Aziz, Ahmad. *Studies in Islamic Culture in the Indian Environment*. Oxford and New York: Clarendon, 1964.

Beg, Abdullah Anwar. *The Poet of the East: The Life and Works of Dr. Sir Muhammad Iqbal*. Lahore: Quami Kutub Khana, 1939.

Iqbal, Javid. *Zindah-Rud*, Lahore: Shaikh Gulam Ali, 1979.

Iqbal, Muhammad. *The Reconstruction of Religious Thought in Islam*. 1934. Reprint, Lahore: Institute of Islamic Culture, 1986.

Malik, Hafeez, ed. *Iqbal: Poet-Philosopher of Pakistan*. New York: Columbia University Press, 1971.

Schimmel, Annemarie. *Gabriel's Wing: A Study into the Religious Ideas of Sir Muhammad Iqbal*. Leiden: E. J. Brill, 1963.

Williams, L. F. Rushbrook, ed. *Great Men of India*. Delhi: Shubhi, 1999.

IRON AND STEEL INDUSTRY. *See* **Tata, Jamsetji N.**

IRWIN, LORD *(1881–1959), the first baron Irwin, first earl of Halifax, viceroy and governor-general of India (1926–1931).* Edward Frederick Lindley Wood was a respected Conservative member of Parliament (1910–1925) who served as president of the Board of Education (1922) and minister of Agriculture (1923) before being raised to the peerage as Lord Irwin and named to succeed Lord Reading as viceroy of India. From the outset of his viceroyalty, Irwin was not unsympathetic to Indian political aspirations, and he admired the religious spirit that animated Mahatma Gandhi's politics: that both men were devout helped smooth their subsequent face-to-face negotiations.

On 31 October 1929, with the tacit approval of the home government and over some resistance from of his own council, Irwin announced that "the natural issue of India's constitutional progress was the attainment of Dominion status," and that a Round Table Conference in London would follow the Report of the Simon Commission to lay the groundwork for further political devolution of power to Indians. Without Indian representation, however, the Simon Commission was greeted with black flags and boycott wherever it went in India. India's National Congress responded by boycotting the first Round Table Conference, calling for *purna swaraj* (complete independence) on 30 January 1930. On 6 April at Dandi, Gandhi launched his famous march to the sea against the salt tax, which turned world opinion against the Raj. That action had been preceded on 2 March by Gandhi's direct appeal to Irwin, announcing his intention to resist the salt tax and urging the viceroy to act to remove the manifold inequities of British rule that left Indians no choice but civil disobedience. Irwin, however, would not countenance violations of the law, even in the furtherance of a cause he respected. His arrest of Gandhi, the Congress's entire Working Committee, and over ninety thousand Indians during the subsequent *satyagraha* (nonviolent resistance campaign) led to widespread violence and brutal police atrocities.

British prime minister J. Ramsay MacDonald, recoiling from the damage the *satyagraha* and its subsequent repression had done to British prestige, expressed the hope that Congress would attend a second "all-party" conference in London, something Congress leaders could hardly do from prison. Accordingly, Irwin released Gandhi, and the two met eight times beginning on 17 February 1930. Winston Churchill decried the "nauseating and humiliating spectacle of this once inner-temple lawyer [Gandhi], now seditious fakir, striding half-naked up the steps of the viceroy's palace there to negotiate and parley on equal terms with the

representative of the King Emperor." But the meeting of "the two Mahatmas," as Sarojini Naidu, the Indian poet and nationalist, referred to these encounters, proved amicable. The resultant Gandhi-Irwin Pact, agreed to on 5 March 1931, was the subject of much debate. It ended the civil disobedience campaign in return for minor British political concessions, but it did allow Gandhi to attend the Second London Round Table Conference. His insistence on serving as the sole representative of India's National Congress, however, proved to be a serious strategic mistake.

Irwin left India in April 1931 and held increasingly responsible posts, culminating in 1938 with his appointment as foreign secretary. His association with Britain's failed policy of appeasement toward Hitler's Nazi regime, however, damaged his reputation. He ultimately accepted appointment as ambassador to the United States, and his wartime service there earned him an earldom in 1944.

Marc Jason Gilbert

See also **British Crown Raj; Congress Party; Gandhi, Mahatma M. K.; Satyagraha**

BIBLIOGRAPHY

Birkenhead, Earl of. *The Life of Lord Halifax.* London: Hamish Hamilton, 1965.
Gopal, Sarvepalli. *The Vice-Royalty of Lord Irwin: 1926–1931.* Oxford: Clarendon Press, 1957.
Halifax, Earl of. *Fulness of Days.* London: Collins, 1957.

ISLAM Islam is a monotheistic religion that arose in Arabia in the early seventh century as a movement for social and spiritual reform. It began with Muhammad (571–632), regarded by Muslims as a prophet, who received revelations from God (*Allah* in Arabic) through Archangel Gabriel.

Islam means peaceful submission to God, and a Muslim is one who acknowledges the need of such a submission and commits to required practices identified as the Five Pillars or acts of faith. These include: the acknowledgment of the one God and of Muhammad as the Prophet of God; ritual prayer five times a day; fasting during Ramadan, the ninth month of the Islamic calendar; almsgiving according to one's capabilities; and pilgrimage to Mecca, if means permit.

In Islam, God has no representation, although the practice of making calligraphic imagery of the many names of God is fairly common and can be seen in mosques and in the homes of many Muslims. The revelations God sent to Muhammad were collected and now form the sacred text of the Qur'an. Islam does not prescribe priesthood, and there is no clergy. Muslims rely on

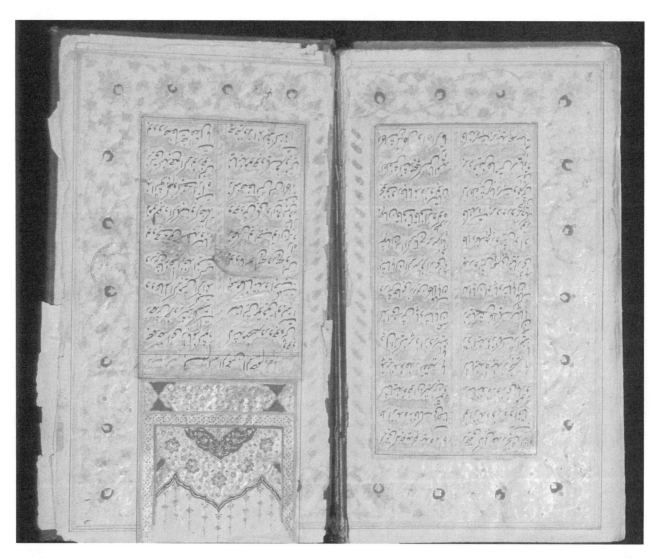

Muslim Manuscript. Throughout the Middle Ages and into the modern period, Islam's presence in India has been so pervasive that it may be regarded as an intrinsic part of India's cultural heritage. Here, a rare illuminated Muslim manuscript dating to medieval times. From the collection of the Arabic and Persian Research Institute, Tonk, Rajasthan. ADITYA PATANKAR / FOTOMEDIA.

the learning from ulama (religious scholars) who strive to understand and teach the Quran, the *hadith* (sayings of the prophet Muhammad), and Shari'a (Islamic law) to others. There are five major schools of law. Most Muslims in India follow the Hanafi school, prevalent in the north, and the Shafi'i school, which is more popular in the south.

The majority of Muslims in the world are Sunni, but a smaller percentage belong to the second major branch of Islam, Shi'ism. There is a significant population of Sh'ia in India, which includes the Isma'ilis, concentrated in the western states and in Mumbai, and the Twelvers, who are more scattered. One of the major festivals in India in which both the Sunni and Sh'ia Muslims come together is the celebration of Ashura, the day of remembrance of the martyrdom of Husain, the grandson of the

Prophet. This takes place each year on the tenth day of the first Islamic month, Muharram.

Sufism and the Growth of Islam in India

Islam spread rapidly throughout Arabia and its environs during the lifetime of the prophet Muhammad. Within a century of his death, Muslim armies were present in the farthest regions of North Africa in the west and among the Hindus and Buddhists of Sind in the east. It is through the conquest of Sind that Islam first came to North India. At the same time, Islam grew peacefully among the natives in the south through the Arab merchants who had been part of a thriving trade between Indian western coastal regions and the Muslim world since pre-Islamic times.

While Islam is not indigenous to India, Islam in India is as authentically Indian as are Indian Buddhism and Indian Christianity. A significant majority of Muslims in India descend from the native Indians who converted to Islam from the eighth century onward. They share ethnic and cultural as well as linguistic traits with Indians of other religious traditions. According to the 2001 census, there were approximately 138 million Muslims in India, 13.4 percent of the country's population. Unofficial estimates, however, range from 150 million to 180 million. Indian Muslims are culturally diverse, economically disparate, and geographically they are spread all across the country. The areas of concentration of Muslims can be found in the northern and eastern states of Jammu and Kashmir, Uttar Pradesh, Bihar, and West Bengal.

Since its arrival in the seventh and eighth centuries, Islam has continued to spread in India due to multiple factors. The most significant reason for this rise is the mediation of Sufis and scholars who are engaged in teaching, healing, and general spiritual guidance. The conversions themselves were a gradual process, spanned over centuries, thus indicating that they occurred partly through the assimilation of cultural and religious ideas. A major factor in the growth of Muslim communities in India was emigration from other Muslim lands.

The Sufis, or the mystics of Islam, were themselves of various origins. Many had emigrated from other Muslim lands; others simply emerged as Islam developed its roots in India. Many immigrants came because they were enchanted by the notion of "Hind" (Persian for India) as the land of ancient wisdom as well as of spices and silk. They intermarried and adopted those local customs that did not conflict with their faith obligations. There were also missionaries among them. Among the first Muslim missionaries to come to India were the Isma'ilis. Arriving in the northwest, they tried to convert the natives to Islam through preaching. With the help of the Fatimids, the ruling dynasty in Egypt at the time, the Isma'ilis exercised political control in the northwestern region for a brief period.

The second major thrust in conversions came from the Sufis, who were largely Sunnis. Sufism speaks of *tariqa* (mystical path), which has many varieties worldwide, and India certainly has its share of them. Authentic Sufism is based on the Qur'an and basic principles of Islam, but sometimes in actual practice these principles are interpreted in unorthodox ways. This becomes a cause for tension between what the textually explicit, orthodox tradition teaches and how a particular mystical seeker interprets those teachings and incorporates them into practice. Sufis often claim to have a direct experience of the oneness of God. From the eighth century, Sufis were organized in various orders, many of which were

brought to India by traveling scholars and saints with their disciples.

Among these was the Sufi Ali bin Uthman al-Hujviri, popularly known as Data Ganj Bakhsh (died c. 1073), revered to this day in parts of the northwest. He was the author of *Kashf al-Mahjub*, a major treatise on the lives of Sufi saints, which offered spiritual advice. Traveling throughout the Muslim world, he chose Lahore as his final destination, which is where his tomb lies today, visited by thousands of seekers each year.

Another major Sufi movement that established its foundations in India was the Chishti Order, introduced by Khwaja Muin al-Din Chishti (1142–1236) in the thirteenth century. Mu'in al-Din (or, as he is often called, Khwaja Gharib Nawaz) is associated with countless stories of spiritual miracles, which make him one of the most famous of all saints in India. His shrine in Ajmer is a major center of pilgrimage for Hindus and Muslims alike.

The memory and traditions of these and other Sufis are still kept alive through a chain of successors to the *shaykh* or *pir* (Sufi master), and their shrines have become sites of prayers and community gatherings for disciples and lay people alike. They believe that the *shaykh*'s spiritual blessings are continuously available to all who come to seek it at their *dargah*. Such shrines exist throughout India. In the south, the shrine of Banda Nawaz (1321–1422) is known as the *dargah* of Gulbarga and is a place of pilgrimage for both Hindus and Muslims. The importance of shrines attached to the memory of Sufi saints is a significant aspect of Indian Islam because it is strong evidence against the cliché classification of fixed religious behavior belonging to either Hinduism or Islam.

The Sufis' main approach was devotionalism, which included, among other things, the practical arts of healing the physical and the spiritual together. The devotional culture promoted by the Sufis and the Hindu *bhakti* movement gave rise to all forms of "religious" or spiritual trends, some syncretistic, others eclectic. Devotional music was introduced by the Chishti Sufis in the thirteenth century as a means of achieving the state of ecstasy. They believed that the harmony of sounds stirs the heart of the listener, arousing a deeper love for God. Sufis wrote in and used other major languages besides Persian and Arabic. Sufi devotional literature is found in Punjabi, Sindi, Bengali, and Urdu in particular, which became the language of the masses throughout North India.

Development of Urdu

Muslims over the centuries introduced several languages to India. Besides Arabic, the language of the Qur'an, Persian was the main medium of literary and political discourse. Many of the rulers during the Sultanate period were of Turkish origins, hence elements of their language became part of the local dialects. It seems probable that the interaction of the local languages of North India with Persian, which was used by the ruling classes, gave rise to a "proto-language" during the period of the Delhi Sultanate. As the Sultanate became well established in the twelfth century, the emerging proto-language further coalesced with the Brij Bhasha spoken in Delhi and other local dialects of the surrounding regions, and gave rise to Urdu.

Spoken by the ruling classes, the language soon evolved as the forerunner of modern Urdu. In the fourteenth century Urdu was picked up and further developed in the south under Bahmani rulers, becoming known as Daccani. Like other languages, Urdu began its literature with poetry. In the south it flourished as the ruler of Golconda, Sultan Quli Qutb Shah (1565–1610), was himself a poet who wrote in Persian, Telgu, and Urdu.

While Urdu developed in the south, it was not so in Delhi, where Persian continued to dominate the literary scene. One major poet from the south, Wali Deccani (1644–1707), shook the city with his Urdu poetry while visiting Delhi. Wali thus became the reviver of Urdu in the north. This gave rise to a new and invigorating period in Urdu literature with the emergence of the so-called Delhi school, with Mir Taqi Mir (1723–1810) and Mir Dard (1720–1784), two of its pillars, developing different genres of poetry.

The towering figure of Asadullah Khan Ghalib (1789–1869) is another major poet who contributed to Urdu's honored status. His also wrote letters, and his style was regarded by many as groundbreaking and innovative, liberating Urdu from the clutches of formalism and setting it apart from its "superior" rival, Persian. Ghalib wrote mostly in Persian, but his Urdu *divan* (collection of poems) is considered a classic.

In the twentieth century, Urdu poetry has served as a medium of expression for social critics, literary trendsetters, and even secularists and humorists, giving rise to figures such as Ali Sardar Jafri (1913–2000), Quratul Ain Haider (b. 1926), and Majrooh Sultanpuri (1919–2000). Urdu continues to be the language in which much of Islamic religious and secular literature is published, and it is also the national language of Pakistan.

Music, Architecture, and Art

For centuries, Islamic and Hindu cultures developed in relation to each other. There is a long history shared by the members of these two traditions with regard to Indian classical music, art, and architecture. India Muslim devotional music is a blend of *bhakti*-style poetry and music from Muslim regions brought to India by travelers and immigrants. The sharing of musical traditions

can be traced back as early as the eighth century. Musical traditions originating in Persia and Central Asia can still be found in the Kashmiri and Punjabi art forms. Many Indian musical instruments also developed as a result of Islamic influences. For example, the *santoor* as well as the *tabla* evolved during the Muslim period. Amir Khusrau (1253–1325) was a composer and a literary giant who wrote prolific poetry. He is credited with developing Hindustani classical music as well as Qawwali, a genre of Sufi devotional music that continues to be popular in South Asia today.

Islamic architecture in India is a reflection of the synthesis of Hindu and Muslim cultures. As these influenced one another, an unparalleled style developed out of the two seemingly contradictory cultural traditions. The Qutub Minar and the Jami Masjid in Delhi are classical masterpieces of Muslim architecture. The Mughals, connoisseurs as well as patrons of art and architectural masterpieces, built great monuments throughout India. One of the finest examples is the Taj Mahal at Agra, built during Shah Jahan's reign (1628–1658) as a mausoleum for his wife Mumtaz Mahal.

The Mughals were also patrons of the literary arts, which thrived during this period. Historiography reached new heights with the writing of *Akbarnamah* by Abul Fazl (1551–1602). Persian and later Urdu were refined, spurring the production of numerous literary works. During the Mughal period, the art of miniature painting was also prevalent. These and other Mughal cultural traditions were replicated at various levels among the nobility and in the larger society in general, affecting Hindu and Muslim communities alike.

Islamic Modernism

Muslims are the largest minority in India, and Indian Muslims have influenced the world of Islam in several ways, most notably by creating a unique form of Islam that expanded the intellectual and spiritual horizons of Muslims everywhere. India was the land of enchantment for many in the Muslim world. Muslims learned from Indian wisdom and transferred it, as faithfully as they could, to other centers of learning around the world. It was Muslims who gave India its fundamental sense of self and defined it as a civilization, setting it apart conceptually as well as geographically. As André Wink notes in his magnificent study *Al-Hind: The Making of the Indo-Islamic World*, it was the Arabs and Muslims who first applied the word "Hind" to the entire subcontinent as well as the archipelago. In later writings India was referred to as "Hindustan," the land of the Hindus.

Through the Middle Ages and into the modern period, Islam's involvement in India has been so intricate that it has become an inseparable part of the fabric of India's cultural heritage. The long presence of Muslims in India entitles them to be part of both Indian and Islamic civilizations, hence, Muslims are as much Indian as any other community in India. Muslims of India can be faithful to both their nationalistic aspirations as well as their religio-cultural traditions, without having to choose between the two. This is the message, echoed by many modern Muslim reformers, of Sayyid Ahmed Khan (1817–1898), founder of the Aligarh Muslim University.

Another early modernist Muslim thinker was Sayyid Ameer Ali (1849–1928), who appreciated the importance of scientific learning, earlier advanced by Sayyid Ahmed Khan. Ali studied abroad and practiced law upon his return to India. An orthodox Shi'a, he presented Islam in a nonsectarian framework. He produced a number of books, including a major influential work on Islam, *The Spirit of Islam* (1922).

Muhammad Iqbal (1877–1938) is perhaps the most revered modernist Muslim thinker of the twentieth century. He was a philosopher by training and studied in the West. He published a major philosophical work, *The Reconstruction of Religious Thought in Islam*, in 1934. Iqbal believed that the decline of Muslims had been caused not by the failure of Islam but by a lack of adherence to the spirit of Islam. His poetry, written mostly in Farsi and Urdu, inspired not only religious but also sociopolitical activism among Muslims.

Another major thinker of the twentieth century was Abu'l 'Ala Maududi (1903–1979). He founded the Jama'at-i Islami in 1941, which has been proactively promoting Islam as a "way of life" and advocating the establishment of an overtly Islamic government through peaceful means by way of political processes.

During the same period, Maulana Muhammad Ilyas (1885–1944) founded a humble organization, now known worldwide, called the Tablighi Jama'at, a society of missionaries. Ilyas and his followers became active in the 1940s as teachers of the basics of Islamic practice to rural illiterate Muslims, and they encouraged personal renewal of faith.

Challenges in the Twenty-first Century

Before the nineteenth century, Muslims and Hindus did not consider each other merely in religious terms. Religious differences were clearly present, but class differences, geography, and language were greater factors in determining identity than was religion. At the level of the common person, for most of their history in India, Muslims and Hindus have experienced a common culture, language, and even ethnic makeup. Religion as the determinant of identity is a very recent construct and one that

has been exploited by political leaders of both communities since the heightened awareness of their separateness was reflected in the policies of the British Raj.

Indeed, Hindus and Muslims are different and they have always seen each other as such. The Muslim religious elite, especially in the early twentieth century, highlighted these differences in clearly religious terms, some even attributing the term *kafir* (used as a derogatory term) to denote Hindus. Similarly, since the rise of Hindutva, the politics of the Sangh Parivar, Muslims and other minorities have been subjected to communal riots, frequently since 1947, in which their economic, social, and personal interests have suffered. The height of this religious tension was reached in the 1992 destruction of the Babri Mosque in Ayodhya by members of right-wing Hindu groups, who continue to be vocal about their plans to build a Ram temple on the site. Many more Muslims and Hindus were affected throughout India by the violence that ensued. Then in 2002, a systematic persecution of Muslim communities was carried out in several towns and villages in Gujarat with the help of the state apparatus.

Islam in India is unique in many ways, and cultural traditions, both homegrown as well as those borrowed from Hinduism, are major factors in its uniqueness. Indian Muslims have "indianized" Islam in such a way that often many local customs (and they differ from community to community) have lost the puritanical Islamic status in their extended and parochial forms.

Indian Muslims also differ in cuisine and attire, as well as in their general attitude toward Pakistan and other Islamic countries. Furthermore, the process of Indian Islamization has allowed Muslim communities to legitimize social customs and practices on the basis of the Shari'a, hence remaining firmly rooted within both their cultural and religious traditions. Islam in India is hardly monolithic. It is as varied as Indians themselves.

Irfan A. Omar

See also **Ayodhya; Hindutva and Politics; Islam's Impact on India; Mughal Painting; Muslims; Sayyid Ahmed Khan and the Aligarh Movement**

BIBLIOGRAPHY

Ahmad, Aziz. *Studies in Islamic Culture in the Indian Environment.* Oxford: Clarendon Press, 1966.

Ahmad, Imtiaz, ed. *Ritual and Religion among Muslims in India.* New Delhi: Manohar, 1981.

Brass, Paul. *The Production of Hindu-Muslim Violence in Contemporary India.* Seattle: University of Washington Press, 2003.

Chand, M. A. Tara. *Influence of Islam on Indian Culture.* Allahabad: Indian Press Private Limited, 1963.

Eaton, Richard M. *The Rise of Islam and the Bengal Frontier, 1204–1760*. Berkeley: University of California Press, 1993.

Engineer, Asghar Ali. *Communalism in India: A Historical and Empirical Study*. New Delhi: Vikas Publishing House, 1995.

Haq, Mushir-ul. *Islam in Secular India*. Simla, India: Indian Institute of Advanced Study, 1972.

Mujeeb, Muhammad. *The Indian Muslims*. New Delhi: Munshiram Manoharlal, 1995.

Nizami, Khaliq Ahmad. *Religion and Politics in India during the Thirteenth Century*. New Delhi: Oxford University Press, 2002.

Schimmel, Annemarie. *Islam in the Indian Subcontinent*. Leiden: E. J. Brill, 1980.

Sinha, N. K. P. *Islam in India: Synthesis of Cultures*. Patna: Khuda Bakhsh Oriental Public Library, 1996.

Smith, Wilfred Cantwell. *Modern Islam in India*. New York: AMS Press, 1974.

Troll, Christian W., ed. *Muslim Shrines in India: Their Character, History, and Significance*. New Delhi: Oxford University Press, 2003.

Wink, André. *Al-Hind: The Making of the Indo-Islamic World*, vol. 1: *Early Medieval India and the Expansion of Islam*. Leiden: E. J. Brill, 1991.

ISLAM'S IMPACT ON INDIA Islam exploded from the Arabian Peninsula eastward and westward after the Prophet's death in A.D. 632 By the start of the next century, Islam would reach Spain in the West and India in the East. What did the early Muslims find in these societies?

In the West, Muslims came across Christian and Jewish communities with whom they were already familiar. These were faiths within the Abrahamic tradition. Muslims were aware that their God was the same, their prophets were shared and indeed many of their values and customs were familiar. In the East, however, Muslims were to encounter wholly different challenges in territory that had never been influenced by the Abrahamic tradition. In Persia, Muslims encountered a society in which people appeared to worship fire; further east, the Buddhists in Central Asia appeared to have no concept of a divine being; to the southeast, in what they would call Hindustan, or the land of the Hindus, societies appeared to worship numerous gods taking different forms. In Hindustan or India, a name derived from the river Indus, Islam came face to face with Hinduism—a polytheistic, ancient, and sophisticated religion.

In the encounters in the East, Islam's response tended to be one of two extremes: that of the military commanders, who believed that the Hindu and Buddhist idols were to be destroyed and the people who worshiped them to be converted; or that of the Sufi scholars, who preached the essential oneness of humanity on the basis of *sulh-i-kul* (peace with all). The former advocated a

Entrance to Ajmer Sharif, Tomb of Muin al-Din Chishti. Every year thousands make a pilgrimage here to honor the revered Sufi saint who came to Ajmer, in the heart of Hindu India, in the twelfth century. ADITYA PATANKAR / FOTOMEDIA.

jihad, which ignored moral elevation and emphasized religious war against the *kafir*, or nonbelievers, and an imposition of the *jizya*, or head tax. The image of one of the earliest invaders, Mahmud of Ghazni (971–1030), "notorious" as an idol breaker, is therefore only one aspect of Islam in South Asia.

India presented what seemed to be intractable problems to the Muslims. The encounter changed the nature of Islam and was sometimes expressed in extravagant forms: Akbar, the great Mughal ruler, creating a new religion, the Din-i-Illahi; Ali, the son-in-law of the Prophet of Islam, almost worshiped as a Hindu avatar with four arms; Duldul, the Prophet's mule, equated to Hanuman, the monkey god. Islam in India was meeting its most interesting set of challenges.

For Hindus, the religion of Islam, too, was equally perplexing. In India people who were accustomed to looking for the divine in a stone or in a snake were now expected to believe in one God, who was also invisible. Individuals who were expected to be reborn in unending cycles of life now faced the prospect of a judgment day at the end of their lives when they would be sent either to heaven or hell. Finally, societies that had been divided rigidly into a hierarchy of castes were expected to accept the notion that all human beings were essentially the same and that their deeds, not their birth, determined their merit.

In the stereotype created by the critics of Islam, the conversion of large parts of the population in India to Islam was effected by fanatical medieval warriors from Central Asia waving a sword in one hand and the holy Qur'an in the other. This is not entirely a correct picture. Conversions and their lasting impact on society came from Sufi scholars and saints. The first response rested in the strength of the sinew; the second in the enlightenment of the heart. It was the second Islamic response that in time would develop into a specific South Asian brand of Islamic mysticism. Nonetheless, Muslims are aware of the tensions that the stereotype implies. Muhammad Iqbal (1877–1938), who best symbolizes the response of Islam to modernity, reflects the dilemmas in his popular poems *Shikwa* (Complaint) and *Jawab-i-Shikwa* (Response to complaint). He talks of *quwat-i-ishq*, or the power of love, while at the same time reminding God that it was the Muslims who—through the power of the sword—forced the infidel to acknowledge monotheism.

Sometimes alone and sometimes with a few disciples, these Sufis settled in and went about their business in small towns and villages. Universalist, gentle, and visibly rejecting the material world, these Sufis reached out to ordinary people with their message of *sulh-i-kul*. Sufism was the attractive face of Islam in India.

Perhaps the most famous Sufi saint of India is Muin al-Din Chishti (1142–1236). He came to Ajmer in the heart of Hindu India to preach *sulh-i-kul* and is buried in that town. His shrine attracts thousand of pilgrims annually. Many of these are Hindus who believe in the goodness of the saint. The annual anniversary of his death is the occasion for festivities and attracts hundreds of thousands of people.

Ali Hujwiri, popularly called Datta Sahib, is buried in Lahore and came to India even before Muin-al-Din Chisti. He is the most renowned Sufi saint of Pakistan. His shrine in Lahore is the center of social and religious activity. The tradition of devotional singing is maintained at both shrines.

From the time of Mahmud of Ghazni in the eleventh century to that of the establishment of the Mughal dynasty in the early sixteenth century, Delhi was ruled by several Muslim dynasties of Afghan/Turkic background. Serious attempts were made at establishing a permanent administration and a permanent viable presence in India.

But it was with the arrival of Babur (Zahir-ud-Din Muhammad), originally from Farghana in Central Asia, that Muslims established what would be their most successful and famous dynasty, that of the Mughals.

The Mughals of India

Babur conquered Delhi and established the Mughal empire early in the sixteenth century. It became one of the largest and most successful centralized states in early modern world history—greater in extent than the other great Muslim empires, the Ottoman and the Safavid. At the height of their power, the Mughals ruled what in effect are the modern countries of India, Pakistan, Bangladesh, Afghanistan, and parts of Myanmar.

Six remarkable emperors ruled the empire over the span of three centuries from the time of Babur to Aurangzeb, his direct descendant. The Mughal empire would last until the uprisings against the British in 1857, although by then it was a shadow of its former self and its rulers mere puppets. The British would then step in as direct rulers, and Queen Victoria would be declared the empress of India.

Akbar (1542–1605), the grandson of Babur, consolidated the empire during his fifty-year reign. Administrative, financial, and diplomatic structures were put in place that would convert the empire into one of the most powerful in the world. In particular, Akbar reached out to the majority population of the Hindus. Hindu warrior groups who had been excluded from power by the previous Muslim dynasty, the Lodhis, were favored by Akbar. Of these, the powerful Rajput chieftains now served the Mughal emperors, even giving wives to the emperors (as in the case of Akbar).

Indian, Iranian, and Central Asian influences combined to create eclecticism and synthesis in the arts, architecture, literature, and music. The creation in the next century of the Taj Mahal at Agra by Shah Jahan (1592–1666), Akbar's grandson, is to be understood in this context. One of the finest glories of Mughal architecture, it is also one of the most recognized buildings in the world. Indeed, the Taj Mahal, the tomb Shah Jahan built for his wife Mumtaz Mahal, has come to symbolize romantic love. Shah Jahan also built the Red Fort and the Jumma Masjid in Delhi. The latter was then the largest communal mosque in India. Alongside these buildings he built colleges and hospitals.

The mutual intellectual and artistic stimulation and synthesis between Hinduism and Islam reached a peak during the time of the great Mughal emperors. But from the late seventeenth century onward, Muslims became aware of their predicament as a minority, faced with two choices: they could either draw rigid boundaries around

Islam, or allow the boundaries to become porous to the point where Islam itself became compromised. The first strategy emphasized an orthodox, formal, and legal interpretation of Islam; the second advocated synthesis, eclecticism, and informality. It is no historical accident that the two opposed forms of Indian Islam were embodied in the sons of Shah Jahan, Dara Shikoh (1615–1659) and Aurangzeb (1618–1707).

The clash between Dara Shikoh and Aurangzeb was more than a clash for succession. The victory of one over the other would influence the course of history and cast shadows on events today in South Asia. Here are the differentiating characteristics of the two princes: Dara Shikoh believed in a universalist humanity, encouraged art, and was known to dislike religious clerics (as is clear from his quotation "Paradise is there, where there is no Mullah"). He kept the company of Sufis and Hindu yogis, and the ring he wore bore the legend *Prabhu*, Sanskrit for "god." He helped translate the classic Hindu texts, the Upanishads and the Bhagavad Gītā, into Persian. He argued that Hinduism and Islam were not theologically incompatible and, as an example, he equated Adam with Brahman.

Aurangzeb, in contrast, emphasized his commitment to the *ummah*, the Muslim community, discouraged art, and supported the clergy. He maintained the outward signs of orthodoxy, rejecting silk clothes and gold vessels. He patronized the *Fatwa-i-Alamgiri*, the most comprehensive digest of Muslim jurisprudence ever compiled. His favorite reading was the Qur'an, the holy book of Islam, which he learned by heart. He abandoned many of Akbar's liberal practices. The hated *jizya* tax was imposed on non-Muslims. Aurangzeb's understanding of Islam did not prevent him from ruthlessly executing his brothers and cruelly imprisoning his father Shah Jahan until his death in 1666.

In the end, Aurangzeb would succeed to the throne of India, and Dara Shikoh would lose his life. Dara Shikoh was paraded in rags through the streets of Delhi and was executed in prison on the grounds that he was an apostate on 30 August 1659. The tension between the two brothers around the opposed forms and interpretations of Islam is reflected in modern South Asian society. It has been argued that the clash between General Zia ul-Haq and Zulfikar Ali Bhutto, leaders of modern Pakistan, reflected the earlier clash between the two opposed models of Islam. Zia was more like Aurangzeb and Bhutto like Dara Shikoh in their approaches to Islam. Bhutto's death at the hands of Zia suggests that there is little compromise between the two positions. The death warrants signed by Aurangzeb and Zia, sealing the deaths of Dara Shikoh and Bhutto, reflect the unresolved dilemmas and tensions of South Asian Islam.

Muslim Crisis and Renaissance

By the middle of the nineteenth century, Muslim power in Delhi, however symbolic, was finally snuffed out after the uprisings against the British in 1857 and 1858. This was a major turning point in history for the Muslims of India. Delhi, their capital, was almost razed to the ground. The Red Fort and the Jumma Mosque, the two central symbols of Muslim rule, were almost blown up. To be Muslim was to be seen as an enemy of the British.

The savagery on both sides was startling. Here is Robert Montgomery, a well-known British official, writing to Hodson, a colleague, congratulating him on a deed that found few defenders, even among the British. Hodson had cold-bloodedly shot the male members of the family of the last king of Delhi, the frail and old poet Bahadur Shah Zafar, the last of the Mughals: "My dear Hodson, All honour to you (and to your 'Horse') for catching the king and slaying his sons. I hope you will bag many more."

It appeared that Islam in India was the prime target of the new masters of the land. This was a depressing time for Muslims. A letter written shortly after 1857 by one of the greatest Urdu poets, Mirza Ghalib, in Delhi, once the mighty and flourishing capital of the Mughals, captures the mood.

> At two separate points in your letter yesterday I see that you have written that Delhi is a big city and there must be plenty of people with all sorts of qualifications there. Alas, my dear boy, this is not the Delhi in which you were born, not the Delhi in which you got your schooling, not the Delhi in which you used to come to your lessons with me to Shaban Beg's mansion, not the Delhi in which I have passed fifty-one years of my life. It is a camp. The only Muslims here are artisans or servants of the British authorities. All the rest are Hindus. The male descendants of the deposed King—such as survived the sword—draw allowances of five rupees a month. The female descendants, if old, are bawds, and if young, prostitutes. . . . Agha Sultan, son of Paymaster Muhammad Ali Khan, who has himself held the rank of Paymaster, fell ill; without medicine, without food, at last he died. Your uncle provided for his shroud and his burial. (Russell and Islam, *Ghalib: 1797–1869*, 1969, p. 269)

In not so subtle ways, the British now ridiculed the main figures of Islam, its kings and saints. Rulers such as Siraj-ud-Dawla (1733–1757) (notorious for the Black Hole of Calcutta in which many Britons were killed) and Shah Shuja-ul-Mulk (1780–1842) became "Sir Roger Dowler" and "Cha, Sugar and Milk," respectively. The saintly leader, the Akhund of Swat (1794–1877), became part of a "nonsense rhyme" in Edward Lear's poem, "Who or why, or which or what, is the Akond of Swat?" Religious leaders of revolts against the British were simply dismissed as the "Mad Mullah." The British Empire's most renowned writers reflected the prejudice: for Rudyard Kipling, South Asian "natives" were a "blackfaced crew" ("Gunga Din"), "half devil and half child" ("The White Man's Burden") and the women of the east, "funny an' yellow" ("The Ladies").

Muslim society itself was affected. Professor Imtiaz Ahmad, in Delhi, has documented the growth of caste-like structures. The *ashraf*—especially the Sayyids and Pukhtuns—considered themselves superior to the *ajlaf*, the recently converted Muslims. But these divisions are to be taken with a pinch of salt: a well-known proverb tells of the recently self-elevated sheikh who calculates that if crops are good again next year he will elevate himself to Sayyid category. In society it appears as if leadership after the collapse of the Mughal empire in India was provided by the *ashraf*, by men like Sir Sayyid Ahmed Khan. But the most prominent leaders, including Muhammad Iqbal and M. A. Jinnah, were not from *ashraf* families.

Macaulay's Minute and Muslim Society

Confronting the diverse mass of humanity in India that it was their destiny and intention to rule, the British outlined a strategy. British colonial philosophy would embrace the upper layers of society and encourage them to become as much as possible like their masters. T. B. Macaulay's "Minute on Education" in 1835 established English as the medium of instruction in India. When English replaced Persian, the court language of the Mughals, ordinary Muslims found themselves at a crippling disadvantage. With this one crucial step, Macaulay aimed to create a social class "who may be interpreters between us and the millions whom we govern; a class of persons, Indian in blood and colour, but English in taste, in opinions, in morals, and in intellect."

The Indian generation after Macaulay, who would be "English in taste," was mainly Hindu. Schools, colleges, and service in the army and civil administration encouraged this process. Among the Muslims, the man who came closest to representing Macaulay's new ideal Indian was Sir Sayyid Ahmed Khan, "loyal servant of the Crown."

Islam in India had constantly faced the challenges posed by the majority Hindu population and as a result developed inner tensions within society. Now it also faced a hostile British presence. The result was a constant renewal and continuous vitality, which produced remarkable leaders in thought and action. The decline of Muslim power in the eighteenth century helped to sharpen sensibilities. This process began when the Mughal empire was still ruling from Delhi. It came with Shah Waliullah (1703–1762), who promoted the puritanical Muhammadia movement, which aimed to purge Islam of non-Islamic influences, in particular Hindu ones. Other reformers soon took to arms in different parts of the subcontinent: Sayyid Ahmad of Bareli (1781–1831) died waging jihad, or holy war, against the Sikhs in North India; and in Bengal, Haji Shariatullah (1781–1840) led the Faraizi movement to revive the teachings of Islam at the village level. Sir Sayyid Ahmed Khan (1817–1898) fought the jihad, but in a different form: he opened a college at Aligarh.

The Aligarh Model

Sir Sayyid argued that if Muslims continued to shut out modern—by which he meant British—civilization they would be reduced to *khansamas* (cooks) and *khidmatgars* (attendants/servants). The Muslim tendency to ignore the present and wallow in past glory was, he argued, a dangerous opiate. His bluntly expressed views outraged religious circles.

In *The Loyal Muhammadans of India*, Sir Sayyid defended Muslim loyalty to the British. Muslims, he argued, were as loyal as the most faithful Hindus. The college that he founded at Aligarh in 1875 was called the Muhammadan Anglo-Oriental College, its very name illustrating the synthesis he wished to effect. His models were the universities at Oxford and Cambridge. The Muhammadan Anglo-Oriental College was later upgraded to a university. Its main buildings, the clock tower, and the cricket fields all reflected nineteenth-century ideas of British architecture in alliance with Islam. Resigning from government service in 1876, Sir Sayyid lived in Aligarh, promoting the college until his death in 1898. His success affected the future course of events in India.

The emblem of the college at Aligarh expressed its Islamic stance. In the center stood a date palm, a reminder of Arabia and the origins of Islam, on the right the book of learning—no doubt the Qur'an—and on the left a crescent, a widely recognized symbol of Islam. The emblem seems oddly out of tune with present-day India, which is undergoing Hindu cultural and religious revivalism.

The college at Aligarh was to be the Muslim answer to modernity, introducing the study of mathematics, science, and modern languages in a syllabus in which Islam was also prominent. It offered Muslims from all over India a sense of direction and revived confidence. It educated those Muslims who would eventually lead the community in the movement that would create Pakistan. Indeed, it produced several presidents and prime ministers.

Macaulay's vision and Sir Sayyid's ethos would bear triumphant fruit in one of the most influential and popular books written on Islam in the early part of the twentieth century, Justice Sayyid Amir Ali's *The Spirit of Islam*. Translated into numerous languages, including Arabic and Turkish, it was written in English. *The Spirit of Islam* reflects pride in Islam while placing it in a modern context, though Muslim critics cited it as too apologetic.

Amir Ali's book inspired men like Mohammad Ali Jinnah (1876–1948) who represented the political response of Islam to modern times. Jinnah argued for rights and security for his community. Upon failing to achieve them, he demanded a separate homeland. What is important to point out is that Jinnah fought for the Pakistan movement through constitutional means, using his skills as a trained lawyer. It was this response that gave the Muslims their most notable triumph in the twentieth century: the creation of Pakistan, then the largest Muslim nation on Earth.

Aligarh was not the only Muslim model produced in India as a response to the modern era. Another educational center was opened in Deoband at around the same time as the college in Aligarh. However, in this case, lines would be rigidly drawn around Muslim identity and practice. Deoband has remained an important source of inspiration for many contemporary Islamic parties and movements, including the Taliban.

The Pakistan Movement

Although Jinnah skillfully and successfully led the Muslim League to the creation of Pakistan in 1947, he was representing an intellectual movement begun in the last century and one that was clear in the writings of Sir Sayyid Ahmed Khan. Sir Sayyid's discussion of two distinct communities in India, both needing to live in harmony but as separate entities, had already outlined the idea of a separate Muslim polity. This argument culminated in the poetic vision of Iqbal, which saw a distinct geographical area for the Muslims of North India. Chaudhri Rahmat Ali in Cambridge gave the name Pakistan to the area—letters of the alphabet representing a distinct Muslim area and together forming the word Pakistan—thus "P" for Punjab, "A" for Afghanistan, "K" for Kashmir, "S" for Sind and "tan" for Baluchistan. Pakistan also means the land of the "pure," from *pak*. Jinnah, then, was expressing the sentiments of Muslims, not creating them.

Early in his career, Jinnah had advocated dialogue and understanding with the Hindus. Indeed, Gopal Krishna Gokhale, a leading Hindu politician, called him "the best ambassador of Hindu-Muslim unity." Later Jinnah began to believe that, once in power, the Hindus would not

honor their commitments to the Muslims. But Jinnah aimed high. In an inspiring speech that he made to the newly formed Constituent Assembly of Pakistan in August 1947, he underlined the tolerant and compassionate nature of the new Muslim state.

But even Iqbal the visionary poet, or Jinnah the humanist, could not have envisioned the extent of disruption at the creation of Pakistan. A communal madness gripped the land in 1947. Centuries of fear and hatred exploded into savagery. No one was spared—young or old, male or female, high or low. The massacre and migration were unprecedented. It has been estimated that possibly 2 million people were killed, and 10 to possibly 15 million migrated from their homes, Muslims fleeing to Pakistan, Hindus and Sikhs to India. Not all Muslims in India could or indeed wished to migrate to Pakistan.

Although the creation of Pakistan had solved one problem, that of establishing a separate homeland for Muslims, it did not solve the problem of identity. The debate about religious and political identity in Pakistan ensured stormy and unsettled politics; the periods of martial law were almost inevitable. Corruption and nepotism were also widespread. Bengalis in East Pakistan complained of being treated like colonial subjects by West Pakistanis and, in 1971, broke away to form Bangladesh—the "nation of Bengalis." After 1971, what remained of Pakistan was plunged more directly than ever before into attempts to resolve the dilemma of identity. Zulfikar Ali Bhutto and later his daughter Benazir wished for a "democratic" Pakistan, while generals like Zia ul-Haq wanted a fundamentalist Islamic Pakistan, ruled by the army.

There have been gains over the years. The number of universities and medical colleges has increased. Agriculture and the textile industry have shown development. Income per capita has risen to twice that of India. The Soviet invasion of Afghanistan in the 1980s and the U.S. "war on terrorism" in the aftermath of 11 September 2001 have allowed Pakistan to play a major role in the region. Pakistan's self-conscious Islamic posture has assured it an important voice in the Muslim world.

But Pakistan faces the new century with uncertainty. Ethnic tensions, breakdown of law and order, and an unpredictable international climate have created problems. India and Pakistan have so far fought three wars. The rise of the communal party, the Bharatiya Janata Party (BJP), in India and its campaigns against Muslims, including the destruction of the mosque at Ayodhya and its support of riots (like the especially savage ones in Gujarat in 2002) confirm in Pakistani minds their worst fears of "Hindu domination"; for them, in retrospect, the orthodox Aurangzeb, not the tolerant Akbar nor Dara

Shikoh, seems vindicated. The BJP recognize this, almost as in a mirror, and have a contemptuous title for the Muslims of India: *Aurangzeb ki aulad*, "the children of Aurangzeb." The failure of Pakistan to develop Jinnah's vision and its subsequent spiral into violence has meant that the community is pushed further away from the tolerant and compassionate model of Islam.

The Creation of Bangladesh

While Bengali leadership enthusiastically embraced the idea of a separate homeland for the Muslims in the first half of the twentieth century, once Pakistan was created, the Bengalis felt, rightly, that although they formed the majority of Pakistan's population, the more powerful West Pakistanis had sidelined them. West Pakistanis controlled the two key instruments of government, the civil service and the army. Bengali political and cultural feelings of alienation developed into an irresistible ethnic movement for independence, which was given its final shape in 1971, when the mainly West Pakistani army posted in East Pakistan attempted to control that province by force. Atrocities were committed, as West Pakistani soldiers sought to suppress Bengali demands for "autonomy" and full democratic control of a new national assembly, reflecting the victory won in the 1970 elections by Sheikh Mujibur Rahman's Awami League. Adverse international public opinion against Pakistan, despite support from U.S. president Richard M. Nixon, further isolated it. India, with strong Soviet military assistance, easily won the war it fought with Pakistan toward the end of the year, ensuring the birth of Bangladesh, quickly recognized as an independent nation.

Although Bengalis shared Islam with West Pakistan, they looked to Calcutta (Kolkata) for their poetry and literature. Their ideas were laced with the intellectual arguments emanating from the coffee shops and salons of Calcutta. They were also more politically sophisticated than the people of West Pakistan who, until then, were largely led by the feudal lords of Sind and Punjab and by tribal chiefs in the North-West Frontier province and Baluchistan. The breakup of Pakistan would act as a catalyst and help challenge this feudal and tribal way of thinking.

The creation of Bangladesh meant that the Muslims of South Asia were now divided into three bodies increasingly isolated from one another. Yet each remains aware of the mutual predicament of living in South Asia with and in the presence of a far larger majority, that of the Hindus concentrated in India.

The Muslims of India

Muslim leadership in India disintegrated in 1947 as millions fled to Pakistan. The next decades were traumatic.

Muslims appeared uncertain and unsure. It has been a slow struggle to reestablish an Indian Muslim identity. The events and dates are clearly etched in the Muslim mind: the uprisings of 1857 and 1858, the partition of 1947, and then, at the turn of the century, the dramatic rise of communal violence.

Muslims are aware of the cruel irony of history in the splendid monuments that lie scattered over India's landscape: the Taj Mahal, the Red Fort, the Jumma Mosque, the Qutb Minar. It is precisely at this point where they are most threatened, for there is a growing movement among Hindus who claim that these monuments were built not by Muslims but by Hindus themselves, out of more ancient Hindu temples, that will be "restored" by force if necessary. Hindus argue that the now demolished Babri Masjid (Babur's mosque) in Ayodhya was just the first of these conversions.

India's Muslims desperately cling to some sort of identity in the face of massive cultural and media onslaught. It is this desperation that partly explains their rallying behind three major cases which they saw as Muslim causes from the 1980s onward, but which led to deaths and further alienated them from the majority: the Shah Bano case, in which Muslims succeeded in overturning a Supreme Court decision granting better financial rights to Shah Bano than provided by her husband who had divorced her under Muslim personal law; the banning of *The Satanic Verses* in India; and the Babri Mosque controversy in Ayodhya. India's problems with Pakistan act as further pressure on the Muslims as communalist Hindu leaders accuse them of being secret supporters of Pakistan.

So as they cling to their identity they are castigated for being isolationist, backward, and marginal; accusations of a "ghetto mentality" create the ghetto and reinforce it. It is a cycle in which they appear to be trapped and from which, for the time being, there appears little escape. On the bright side, individual Muslims have done very well in India, several of them becoming heads of state.

The Muslims of South Asia

Pakistan, Bangladesh, and India together have about one-third of the world's Muslim population. About 95 percent of Pakistan's population of 145 million, about 90 percent of Bangladesh's population of 135 million, and about 13 percent of India's 1 billion people are Muslim. It is estimated—and figures for population on the basis of religion are invariably "estimates"—that the total Muslim population in South Asia may well be over 400 million people.

Muslims in South Asia have produced a remarkable modern Muslim renaissance. Some of the most renowned and influential modern Muslim intellectuals—including

Iqbal, Maulana Azad, and Maulana Maududi—have lived there. The Muslims of South Asia have won international prizes, and they have produced world-class figures in sports, especially in cricket, hockey, and squash. South Asians have created a coherent and rich cultural legacy, starting from the time of Amir Khusrau (1253–1325), one of the earliest Sufi poets, who synthesized Hindu and Muslim cultures. They have created one of the most powerful and impressive empires of world history, the Mughals; achieved architectural excellence in the Taj Mahal; touched the highest peaks of literature in the verses of Mirza Ghalib, Iqbal, and Faiz Ahmed Faiz; and have led the most significant and successful Muslim political movement of the twentieth century, resulting in the creation of Pakistan in 1947.

Women have always played an important role in South Asian Muslim society—from the time when Razia Sultana actually ruled over Delhi's sultanate in the thirteenth century, to the remarkable empress Nur Jehan, who ruled along with her husband, Mughal emperor Jahangir, in the seventeenth century, to modern times, when female prime ministers have been elected both in Pakistan and Bangladesh.

The main communities, Hindus and Muslims, see history differently. If Muslims in Pakistan were asked to name their favorite historical figures, most would probably say: Mahmud of Ghazni (one of the earliest warriors to invade India from what is now modern Afghanistan); Aurangzeb, the last great Mughal emperor; and Mohammad Ali Jinnah, the founder of Pakistan. Most Hindus would respond to the question "who are your least favorite historical figures?" by giving the same names. Mahmud is associated with brutal military raids into India, smashing Hindu temples and statues; Aurangzeb with a harshly violent, triumphant Islamic rule and a narrow interpretation of Islamic law; and Jinnah is blamed for splitting Mother India in two.

History is never far from the surface in contemporary India. Newspaper articles and letters constantly cite Mahmud, Aurangzeb, or Jinnah as a hero among some Muslims but a villain for most Hindus. Few mention that on the whole Muslims were sensitive to their Hindu compatriots. From the start, Babur abolished cow slaughter, and up to the last Mughal emperor it was banned in Delhi as a gesture toward the Hindus. Sir Sayyid did the same at Aligarh. The contribution to Hindu culture of rulers like Akbar and Dara Shikoh is forgotten.

Bazaar sociology does not stop with the past; it feeds into the writing and perception of modern history. In India, if Muslim rulers are depicted in the stereotype as alien invaders, mainly drunk and destroying temples, in Pakistan the Hindu past simply does not exist. Hindus are dismissed as cowardly and mean. History in Pakistan begins in the seventh century, after the advent of Islam and the Muslim invasion of Sind; the great pre-Islamic civilizations of Mohenjo-Daro, Harappa, and Taxila are more or less ignored.

Trends in the Future

The events of partition still haunt South Asia: for India the nightmare of disintegration; for Pakistan the terror of the violence. This mutual hatred still feeds into the complex political configuration of contemporary India and Pakistan. Three wars with India and now a nuclear confrontation further underscore the importance of reaching enduring agreements to ensure a peaceful future for South Asia. India and Pakistan's nuclear explosions, the struggle for independence among the Muslims of Kashmir, the exorbitant cost of keeping large armies and the geopolitics of the region all reflect the dreadful dangers and inordinate price of communal conflicts, rooted in history.

Nuclear weapons on the one hand and starving peasants on the other are the reality of South Asia today. As a result one-fifth of humanity is mired in poverty (incomes per capita range between $200 and $400 in these countries). South Asia has produced world scientists and writers—including Nobel Prize winners—and yet seems incapable of improving its poor record on poverty and peace. The true enemies of South Asia are poverty, illiteracy, and communal hatred. Until this dawns upon all communities, South Asia will not enjoy peace, nor will it benefit from the uniqueness of its cultural legacy of synthesis and harmony.

At the start of the twenty-first century, we could well ask which model of Muslim political action triumphed in South Asia for over a thousand years—the model called fanatical by its critics, or that of peace? The answer lies in the demographic figures of the subcontinent. The vast majority of the population is still Hindu. Had Muslim rulers been ruthless tyrants, they could have converted the people they ruled, virtually unchallenged, for the better part of a millennium.

Jinnah's Pakistan anticipated the global questions that would be asked about modern Muslim states and societies in the aftermath of 11 September 2001: Is Islam compatible with democracy? Does Islam always subjugate women? Does Islam preach violence?

Jinnah's vision of a tolerant and modern Muslim Pakistan had provided the answer to the first of those questions in the affirmative, while rejecting the second and third as totally biased and untrue. Current Indian and Pakistani "cease-fire" agreements in Jammu and Kashmir and plans to meet to discuss ways of further opening closed borders to help achieve permanent South Asian peace and stimulate economic trade suggest the possibility of hope for the more than 1 billion people of this long-suffering region.

Akbar Ahmed

See also **Bangladesh; Iqbal, Muhammad; Jinnah, Mohammad Ali**

BIBLIOGRAPHY

Ahmed, Akbar S. *Jinnah, Pakistan, and Islamic Identity: The Search for Saladin.* London and New York: Routledge, 1997.
———. *Discovering Islam: Making Sense of Muslim History and Society.* 1988. Rev. ed., London and New York: Routledge, 2002.
———. *Islam under Siege: Living Dangerously in a Post-Honor World.* Cambridge, U.K.: Polity, 2003.
Johnson, Gordon. *Cultural Atlas of India.* New York: Facts on File, 1996.
Russell, Ralph and Khurshidul Islam. *Ghalib: 1797–1869,* vol. I: *Life and Letters,* translated and edited. Cambridge, Mass.: Harvard University Press, 1969.
Wolpert, Stanley. *Jinnah of Pakistan.* Oxford and New York: Oxford University Press, 1984.
———. *A New History of India.* Oxford and New York: Oxford University Press, 2000.

ISRAEL, RELATIONS WITH The attitude of Indian nationalists toward their Israeli counterparts largely influenced India's policy toward Israel. Since the early 1920s, Indian nationalists strongly supported Arab rights in Palestine and were unwilling to endorse Zionist aspirations for a Jewish national home there. British India had the largest Muslim population in the world, and this, coupled with the ongoing rivalry with the Muslim League, forced the Indian National Congress to perceive the Arab-Jewish controversy through an Islamic prism. The tiny Jewish presence in India and the limited interests shown by the prestate Zionist leadership toward the subcontinent had also contributed to an unsympathetic Indian position. According to Mahatma Gandhi, "Palestine belongs to the Arabs in the same sense that England belongs to the English or France to the French." Similarly, Jawaharlal Nehru, felt that Palestine "is essentially an Arab country and no decision can be made without the consent of the Arabs." Despite these positions, in March 1947, a ten-member Jewish delegation from Palestine was invited to the Asian Relations Conference hosted by Nehru. The political impact of the visit, however, was marginal.

In April 1947 the United Nations (UN) convened a special session of the General Assembly to discuss the British request to determine the future of Mandate Palestine. After two weeks of deliberations, on 15 May 1947 an eleven-member United Nations Special Committee on Palestine (UNSCOP) was formed, and India was elected to the committee as an Asian member. Nehru, who was then heading the interim government, nominated Sir Abdur Rahman, a judge at the Punjab High Court in Lahore, as the Indian representative.

On 1 September 1947 UNSCOP submitted its recommendations. A seven-member majority advocated partition as the solution for Palestine, while India (supported by Iran and erstwhile Yugoslavia) proposed a minority plan that called for a federal Palestine with adequate internal autonomy for the Jewish population. India perceived the partition of Palestine to be an unjust, unviable option. In an extension of the Congress Party's position vis-à-vis the Muslim League's two-nation theory, India refused to endorse any religious basis for modern statehood. It argued that since Palestine was a predominantly Arab country, any solution of the conflict should not be to the disadvantage of the Arabs.

Both Arabs and Jews found the Indian proposal inadequate and were unanimous in rejecting it, however; hence the UN never discussed that federal plan. On 29 November 1947 the General Assembly approved to partition Palestine into independent Jewish and Arab states. Joining the Arab and Islamic countries, India voted against the partition plan.

Recognition without Relations

The establishment of Israel on 14 May 1948 created a new political reality in the Middle East. For a while, India continued to argue its former position, and in May 1949 voted against Israel's admission to the UN. After protracted deliberations, on 17 September 1950 India extended de jure recognition to the Jewish state. This decision was not accompanied by any formal announcement concerning diplomatic relations. For the next four decades, recognition without normalization characterized Indo-Israeli relations.

In May 1950 or nearly five months prior to Indian recognition, Israel appointed a Bombay (Mumbai)-based Indian national, F. W. Pollack, as its trade commissioner of Southeast Asia; in December 1950 he was redesignated as trade commissioner for India and South East Asia. In the same month, a temporary *aliya* (immigration) office was opened in Bombay to facilitate the immigration of Jewish refugees stranded in India during World War II. In June 1951 Pollack was concurrently appointed Israel's consular agent in India, and in October 1952 he was made honorary consul for India. In January 1953 this position was upgraded to a full-fledged Israeli consulate, and in

L. K. Advani and Shimon Peres. Indian Deputy Prime Minister Advani (left) and Israeli Prime Minister Peres during the former's official state visit, June 2000. Since the normalization of diplomatic relations in 1992, the two nations have regularly conferred on military matters, as they share similar concerns about terrorism and security. INDIA TODAY.

June 1953 career diplomat Gabriel Doron took over as the first Israeli consul in India. Between July 1953 and January 1992, fifteen officials headed the Israeli mission in Bombay. Despite their lower official status, Israeli consuls had direct access to the foreign minister and often met the prime minister. They also enjoyed unrestricted freedom of movement, except in sensitive border areas, but their consular jurisdiction was largely restricted to the state of Maharashtra.

Meanwhile, concerned over delays in the establishment of normal diplomatic relations, Israeli Foreign Ministry Director-General Walter Eytan paid an official visit to India in early 1952, and Prime Minister Nehru informed the visitor that India was favorably disposed toward normalization. Following this visit, an Indian official was asked to prepare the budget and other financial details for a resident Indian mission in Tel Aviv.

At first, the absence of relations was attributed to financial constraints, scarcity of personnel, and India's desire not to overstretch its meager resources. India's

concerns over Pakistan, particularly its desire to neutralize Pakistani efforts and influence in the Middle East, resulted in a cautious approach toward Israel. India felt that an early "resolution" of the Kashmir dispute would enable it to modify its position toward Israel. There were apprehensions that diplomatic ties with Israel might displease Arab countries. Perceived opposition by India's Muslim population also played an important role in its reluctance to establish relations with Israel, and in private discussions with Israelis, Indian leaders candidly referred to their fears of inflaming Muslim sentiments. When Prime Minister Narasimha Rao decided to normalize relations with Israel in January 1992, his senior cabinet colleagues warned him of possible negative reactions from Muslims. Speaking in Jerusalem in June 2000, Foreign Minister Jaswant Singh attributed prolonged nonrelations to the feelings of Indian Muslims.

The Afro-Asian Conference in Bandung in April 1955 marked an ominous trend for Israel-India relations. Bowing to Arab pressures, India went along with others and opted to exclude Israel from the conference, thereby legitimizing the exclusion of Israel from subsequent Afro-Asian and third world meetings.

The Suez crisis of 1956, in which Israel joined hands with Britain and France and invaded the Sinai Peninsula, marked a shift in India's Israel policy. Afro-Asian solidarity, based on anticolonialism, as well as Israel's identification with imperial powers and the growing friendship between Nehru and Egyptian leader Gamal Abdel Nasser, influenced Indian calculations. Strongly condemning the Israeli aggression against Egypt, on 20 November 1956 Nehru told the Indian Lok Sabha that "in view of the existing passion" diplomatic exchanges between India and Israel were not possible. Since then, "the time is not ripe" remained the standard Indian refrain to explain the absence of relations with Israel, up until January 1992.

Despite the absence of diplomatic relations, Indian and Israeli diplomats met regularly in a number of places, including Washington, New York, Ottawa, London, Ankara, and Rangoon. There were many regular visits between leaders of both countries, including former Israeli foreign ministers Moshe Sharett (1956) and Yigal Allon (1959 and 1964), who visited India and met with Nehru.

Since the mid-1960s, the general warmth of the earlier years began to wane, and Indo-Israeli relations deteriorated. The preemptive strike launched by Israel against its Arab neighbors on 5 June 1967 resulted in the deaths of a number of Indian soldiers serving in the Gaza Strip as part of the United Nations Emergency Force (UNEF). Infuriated, India ruled out diplomatic relations, blaming Israel's "wrong" policies. The emergence of the Palestine Liberation Organization (PLO) in 1964 further alienated India from Israel; in January 1975, India recognized the PLO as the "sole legitimate representative of the Palestinian people." The formation of the Organization of Islamic Conference in 1969, India's growing dependence on the Middle East for energy resources, and the presence of substantial numbers of Indian laborers in the oil-rich Gulf states further entrenched India's pro-Arab policy.

When Morarji Desai's Janata government was in power, Israeli foreign minister Moshe Dayan paid an unsuccessful incognito visit to India in August 1977 to explore the possibilities of diplomatic relations. Continuing India's pro-Arab policy in March 1980, Prime Minister Indira Gandhi granted full diplomatic status to the PLO mission in Delhi, while Israel's consulate languished in Maharashtra. In 1982 in a media interview, Yossef Hasseen, Israeli consul in Mumbai, accused India of trying to compete with Pakistan to curry favors with the Arabs. Coming as it did against the backdrop of increasing international criticism of Israel, he was declared persona non grata. Moreover, since the late 1970s, a number of Israeli delegations were denied visas to attend various international conferences and sports events hosted by India.

Indo-Israeli relations began to improve after Rajiv Gandhi became prime minister in October 1984. The issue of normalization figured prominently in his discussions with U.S. officials. He also met with Israeli prime minister Shimon Peres during the fortieth annual session of the UN in 1985; facilitated the Indo-Israeli Davis Cup tennis match in New Delhi in July 1987; restored consul status to the Israeli mission in Mumbai in August 1988; hosted a pro-Israeli delegation from the Anti-Defamation League in January 1989; extended Israeli consular jurisdiction to the South Indian state of Kerala, which has a significant Jewish population; and relaxed visa procedures for holders of Israeli passports.

The outbreak of the Palestinian *intifada* (uprising) in December 1987 and subsequent Israeli isolation curtailed India's options. Israeli involvement in the Sri Lankan ethnic conflict, especially its military-intelligence cooperation, generated suspicion and anger in India. Rapid erosion of his own popularity and a string of electoral reverses suffered by his Congress Party limited Rajiv Gandhi's ability to complete the process he had initiated to establish full diplomatic ties with Israel. Nevertheless, these measures proved useful to Narasimha Rao, who became prime minister soon after Rajiv Gandhi's assassination in 1991.

Normalization

Within days after Rao assumed office, a group of Israeli tourists was kidnapped in the state of Jammu and Kashmir. A senior Israeli diplomat came to India to "coordinate" their release, and during this brief visit, he met a number of senior Indian officials. In a well-publicized gesture on 16 December 1991, India voted with the majority in repealing the 1975 UN General Assembly resolution that equated Zionism with racism. As India had been one of the resolution's original sponsors, this move marked a significant departure from the past.

Shortly afterward, high-level Indo-Israeli diplomatic consultations were held in Washington. On 29 January 1992, Foreign Secretary J. N. Dixit formally announced India's decision to establish full and complete diplomatic relations with Israel. India became the last major non-Arab or non-Islamic state to establish formal diplomatic relations with the Jewish state. Within weeks, the Israeli consul in Bombay, Giora Becher, moved to New Delhi and opened the Israeli embassy, and on 15 May, India opened its embassy in Tel Aviv.

A host of domestic and international developments enabled Rao to complete a process that began in September 1950. These developments included: the end of the cold war and the collapse of the Soviet Union; the weakening of the Non-Aligned Movement (NAM), which had consistently adopted an anti-Israeli posture; India's policy of economic liberation, which required strong American backing; the inauguration of the Middle East peace process in Madrid in October 1991, which signaled the willingness of the Arabs and Palestinians to seek a political settlement with Israel through direct negotiations; and the formal termination of Israel's prolonged political and diplomatic isolation.

Contrary to prolonged apprehensions, domestic or regional opposition to normalization of relations were marginal. Some Arab countries were displeased with India's development of security cooperation with Israel, but the overall response in the Middle East was subdued. Contrary to past apprehensions, the newly established relations did not inhibit India from pursuing productive relations with a number of countries in the region. The warming of Indo-Iranian relations and growing economic ties between India and the Gulf states underscore that normalization has not prevented India from improving its ties with countries pronouncedly hostile toward Israel.

Since the opening of the diplomatic missions, a host of official, semiofficial and nonofficial delegations have visited one another. A number of Israeli cabinet ministers, senior officials, and businesspersons visited India, including Foreign Minister Shimon Peres, and President Ezer Weizmann (December 1996). Indian Home Minister L. K. Advani visited Israel in June 2000, with Foreign Minister Jaswant Singh.

Diplomatic relations with Israel now have bipartisan support in India. The Bharatiya Janata Party has been enthusiastic in its support for the pro-Israeli policy initiated by Congress. Even parties such as Janata Dal, which opposed Rao's decision in 1992, have endorsed bilateral cooperation. The visit to Israel of veteran communist leader and West Bengal chief minister Jyoti Basu in the summer of 2000 signaled that even India's communists are no longer opposed to closer ties with Israel. India's position in the UN–sponsored World Conference against Racism in Durban in August–September 2001 underscored India's newly found self-assertion toward the Middle East. Despite pressures from the region, it refused to join Arab and Islamic countries in equating Zionism with racism.

Since normalization, both countries have established extensive relations and cooperation in the military-security arena. Because of increasing acts of terrorism and border infiltrations, India has sought Israeli expertise in intelligence gathering, innovative and pro-active counter-terrorism policies, and electronic surveillance along international borders, adapting some of the Israeli methods to combat threats emanating from India's borders with Pakistan. Moreover, in the political arena, India has gradually distanced itself from its past postures and has been less critical of Israel and its policies.

National security advisers of both countries meet periodically, holding high-level consultations, and both countries have set up a joint working group on counter-terrorism. A number of senior officials belonging to intelligence and internal security officials accompanied Deputy Prime Minister Advani when he visited Israel. On 11 September 2001, the day terrorists attacked the World Trade Center and the Pentagon in the United States, Israeli national security adviser Major General Uzi Dayan was holding high-level counter-terrorism discussions with top Indian officials in New Delhi. As part of a new approach toward Israel, India has contributed troops to the United Nations Interim Forces in Lebanon.

Conscious of the potentials, both sides have depoliticized defense-related cooperation. Less than a decade after normalization, Israel emerged as the second-largest military supplier (after Russia) to India, and the latter is now Israel's largest market for military exports. Israel is actively involved in upgrading India's aging Soviet-made MiG aircraft. Green Pine radars, remotely piloted vehicles, Barak ship-borne antimissile systems for the navy, and ammunition for Bofors guns, used during the Kargil operations, are some of the prominent defense deals. In August 2001, after months of negotiations, India signed a series of defense contracts with Israel, estimated at $2 billion, for the supply of long-range surveillance equipment, night-vision hardware, and ammunition. An Israeli consortium has been awarded the contract to upgrade India's 130-mm artillery guns into 150-mm howitzers. In late 2003 Israel agreed to supply Phalcon airborne early warning systems to India, estimated to cost over $1 billion. Growing Indo-Israeli military ties are developing against the background of increasing Indo–U.S. cooperation, leading to suggestions of a friendly triangle involving India, Israel, and the United States.

The pace of bilateral trade since the establishment of diplomatic relations gives the impression that India and Israel have determined to make up for lost decades. Bilateral trade stood at just $200 million in 1992 and has crossed the billion-dollar mark in less than a decade. Diamonds and precious stones, which accounted for nearly 90 percent of the trade in 1992, now constitute just over 50 percent. Both countries have signed a number of agreements pertaining to agriculture, trade, investments, scientific cooperation, and double taxation.

Even though increasing Indo-Israeli security contacts are often presented as a strategic partnership, one cannot ignore that on such sensitive issues as Indo-Iranian relations or Pakistan's role in international terrorism, India and Israel have fundamental differences. Similarly, India has been less enthusiastic in endorsing Israeli positions concerning Islamic fundamentalism, especially since the outbreak of the *al-Aqsa intifada* in September 2000. The Congress Party expressed its displeasure at what it perceived to be an abandonment of India's historic support for the Palestinian cause, and a section of the opposition called for a reassessment of India's growing ties with Israel.

Seen in this context, the high-profile state visit of Israeli prime minister Ariel Sharon in September 2003 was a watershed in Indo-Israeli relations. Despite controversies and protests in New Delhi, the visit marked a new high level of Indo-Israeli relations, underscoring the willingness and determination of both countries to give greater visibility to their diplomatic relations.

P. R. Kumaraswamy

See also **United States, Relations with**

BIBLIOGRAPHY

Agwani, M. S. "The Palestine Conflict in Asian Perspective." In *The Transformation of Palestine*, edited by Ibrahim Abu-Laghod. Evanston, Ill.: Northwestern University Press, 1971.

Chatterjee, Margaret. *Gandhi and His Jewish Friends*. Houndmills, Basingstoke, U.K.: Macmillan, 1992.

Government of India. Ministry of External Affairs. *India and Palestine: The Evolution of Policy*. New Delhi: Ministry of External Affairs, n.d.

India's Campaign against Israel: ADL International Report. New York: ADL, 1987.

Kumaraswamy P. R., "Mahatma Gandhi and the Jewish National Home." *Asian and African Studies* 26, no. 1 (March 1992): 1–13.

———. "India and Israel: Prelude to Normalization." *Journal of South-Asian and Middle Eastern Studies* 19, no. 2 (Winter 1995): 53–73.

———. "India's Recognition of Israel, September 1950." *Middle Eastern Studies* 31, no. 1 (January 1995): 124–138.

———. "Sardar K. M. Panikkar and India-Israel Relations." *International Studies* 32, no. 3 (July 1995): 327–337.

———. *India and Israel: Evolving Strategic Partnership*. Security and Policy Studies, no. 40. Ramat Gan: BESA Centre for Strategic Studies, September 1998.

———. "India and the Holocaust: Perceptions of the Indian National Congress." *Journal of Indo-Judaic Studies* 3 (April 2000): 117–125.

———. "India, Israel and the Davis Cup Tie 1987." *Journal of Indo-Judaic Studies* 5 (June 2002): 29–39.

———. "India and Israel: Emerging Partnership." *Journal of Strategic Studies* 1.25, no. 4 (December 2002): 192–206.

Shimoni, Gideon. *Gandhi, Satyagraha and the Jews: A Formative Factor in India's Policy toward Israel*. Jerusalem: Leonard Davis Institute for International Relations, 1977.

IVORY CARVING   There is a long and rich history of ivory carving in India. Over the course of its millennia of artistic expression, several natural sources of ivory, antler, and bone were utilized interchangeably to fashion a wide variety of objects. Many of these works can easily be classified as decorative art, such as various containers, combs and other personal grooming items, ornaments, jewelry, writing implements and manuscript covers, hookah mouthpieces, dice and other nonfigural gaming pieces, nonfigural weapon hilts, and musical instruments. Many other extant examples are clearly sculpture, such as religious images of Buddhist, Hindu, and Christian subjects (but not Jain), and secular representations of royalty, the privileged class, and ethnographic or occupational types. Intriguingly, however, there are also several types of Indian carved ivory objects for which the traditional boundaries between figural sculpture and decorative art objects are blurred. For instance, numerous ivory plaques survive that were originally used in a decorative context by being affixed to various containers as ornamental facades. These plaques typically feature figures carved in intaglio, low relief, and in the round against a pierced background. Certainly the best-known South Asian ivory plaques are the hoard of about 600 extraordinary examples dating from the Kushana period (1st–3rd centuries A.D.) found at Begram in Afghanistan, the summer capital of the Kushana kings. These world heritage treasures now survive primarily in the Museé Guimet, Paris, as many of those in the collection of the Kabul Museum in Afghanistan have been looted and are in danger of perishing. The tradition of using ivory facade plaques for decorative purposes continued in India for centuries. Particularly accomplished examples were created in South India during the seventeenth and eighteenth centuries; one of the finest surviving such works is an exquisitely rendered tripartite panel, depicting amorous couples, now in the Virginia Museum of Fine Arts.

In addition to the ivory plaques, which were primarily carved in relief, there was also an extensive tradition of ivory carving in the round, featuring decorative throne legs, object handles, weaponry hilts, containers fashioned in figural forms, chessmen, and sundry representations of animals, humans, and conveyances that primarily served a decorative purpose. Ultimately, the classification of ivories depends upon the viewer's perspective—whether primacy is given to form or function. Given the extraordinarily high artistic level and extremely long history of Indian ivory carving, its classification should clearly not be determined on the basis of size or whether the medium of ivory is considered a "minor art" in comparison to works made of metal or stone.

Ivory Carving of Krishna and Rādhā. Dating to seventeenth-century Orissa, Krishna and Rādhā, his divine love. Though many ivory carvings were created in the image of religious deities, as here, many more proliferated in the decorative arts, with the distinction between the two often blurring. NATIONAL MUSEUM / FOTOMEDIA.

Typology of Decorative Ivory Carvings

Myriad decorative ivory object types were carved in the Indian subcontinent, beginning at least as early as the Indus Valley Civilization (mature phase, dating from c. 2600 to 1900 B.C.), and continuing to the present day. Extensive evidence of the extent and socioeconomic importance of premodern ivory carving is provided by a plethora of extant ivory objects and numerous references to ivory carvers and their products contained within the vast corpus of Indian epigraphical records and literary works. In the earlier periods of Indian history, a wide range of domestic artifacts were made of ivory and bone, including pins, needles, hooks, awls, styli, pegs, rods, arrowheads, and gaming pieces. These everyday objects were generally unadorned or partially embellished with rudimentary cross-hatching and geometric designs sawed or drilled into the surface.

Personal grooming aids made of ivory, particularly combs and hairpins, were also common, and examples survive from many periods of Indian and greater South Asian history. Early ivory combs, typified by the Kushana examples found near Taxila in modern Pakistan, have fine or occasionally coarse teeth on one side and rectangular or round-edged flat handles decorated with incised animal and human figures and auspicious symbols. Later ivory combs, especially those made during the seventeenth through the nineteenth centuries in South India and Sri Lanka, typically have fine teeth on the top and bottom with a central grip area often decorated with painted female figures and animals carved in bas-relief. Early ivory hairpins usually have a single tapering shaft with an animal-shaped or animal-headed terminal. Later ivory hairpins can sometimes have as many as several thick tapering prongs, and a flat handle carved in the form of an animal such as a rearing lion.

Indian ceremonial throne legs carved of ivory are prime examples of utilitarian objects that can be classified as both decorative and sculptural. The earliest and best known such Indian ivory is a throne or perhaps stool leg (once thought to be a mirror handle) in the form of an elegantly coiffured and adorned female figure. This ivory, now in the Archaeological Museum of Naples, was unearthed from the ruins of Pompeii, where it was buried in A.D. 79 following the eruption of Mount Vesuvius. A similar ivory female figure was discovered at Ter in modern Maharashtra, which in ancient times was the important trade city of Tagara, mentioned in the first-century merchant account *The Periplus of the Erythraean Sea*. Thus, in addition to their artistic importance, these ivory female figures are significant for documenting the international trade in ancient Indian luxury items. The early use of female figures as subjects for furniture legs was generally supplanted in the sixteenth through the nineteenth centuries by representations of lions, elephants, and mythical beasts (*vyāla* and *śārdūla*). With the introduction of British artistic influence, furniture legs often terminated in stylized lion paws. The tradition of making ivory ceremonial thrones continued in India at least until the mid-twentieth century. Many different types of ivory and ivory-veneered furniture and cabinets were created in India, each embellished with a different regional decorative style. The major centers of production were in Delhi, Orissa, Gujarat, Murshidabad in Bangla (West Bengal), Mysore in Karnataka, Vishakhapatnam (Vizagapatam) in Andhra Pradesh, and Travancore in Kerala. One of the finest and most famous examples of an Indian ivory-veneered throne, now in the Royal Collection, London, is the ornate one presented to Queen Victoria (r. 1837–1901) by Maharaja Martanda Varma (r. 1847–1860) of Travancore, which was displayed in the Great Exhibition of 1851 in London.

Only a few different types and sizes of Indian containers were made of ivory, presumably because of the dimensional limitations inherent in the medium. Cups, bowls, decorative storage vessels, jewelry caskets, pen boxes, and rosewater sprinklers were among the most frequently fashioned objects. The most distinctive type of Indian ivory container was the powder primer flask, which was used to prime the flash pan and touchhole of early firearms. A number of these important weaponry accoutrements survive from the mid-seventeenth and eighteenth centuries. Most powder primer flasks are fashioned in the form of an antelope, its head at the mouth of the container, with a bird at the other end. They typically have a bipartite, gracefully curved body enlivened with hunt scenes, animals of prey, and fowl.

The largest Indian carved ivory objects—sometimes utilizing an entire tusk and more—are the ivory boats mounted on display stands that were made during the late nineteenth and early twentieth centuries in Murshidabad, the great Bengali center of ivory carving. These are ivory models of royal pleasure boats, called peacock barges (*mayūra-pankhī* or *morpankhī*) because their prow was shaped in the form of a peacock, which were enjoyed by Siraj-ud-Dawla, the governor (*nawāb*) of Bengal (r. 1756–1757), and his guests during festivals on the Ganges River. The ivory models, made in varying sizes, depict the elaborate peacock barges in detail. They typically feature one or two covered pavilions in the forward section that were used for entertaining the ruler and his guests with musicians, dancers, and a communal hookah. A number of servants are often in attendance, including one whose job was to pull the cord of the swinging ceiling fan (*pankhā*). The stern has several pairs of rowers and a helmsman. Intriguingly, these ivory boats could also be customized for a Hindu clientele by omitting the *pankhā*-servant and adding in its place a small shrine of the goddess Durgā Slaying the Buffalo Demon. Once graced with the divine image, the ivory boats may have been used for ritual immersion during the Durgā Pūjā festival.

The Murshidabad ivory carvers produced many other popular subjects, including bullock carts, elephants with canopied howdahs, and colonial personages such as Indian civil servants. Regrettably, the artistic glories of Murshidabad and other Indian centers of ivory production faded with the dawn of the modern age. The multipurpose use of ivory was supplanted by the introduction of plastic, and despite the 1972 ban on the trade in ivory under the Indian Wild Life (Protection) Act, some formulaic carvings of limited subjects are still being created for the indiscriminate tourist market.

Stephen Markel

See also **Metalware**

BIBLIOGRAPHY

Born, Wolfgang. "Ivory Powder Flasks from the Mughal Period." *Ars Islamica* 9 (1942): 93–111.
Chandra, Moti. "Ancient Indian Ivories." *Bulletin of the Prince of Wales Museum* 6 (1957–1959): 4–63.
———. "An Ivory Figure from Ter." *Lalit Kala* 8 (October 1960): 7–14.
Collin, Francis. "The Good Shepherd Ivory Carvings of Goa and Their Symbolism." *Apollo* 120, no. 271 (September 1984): 170–175.
During Caspers, E. C. L. "The Indian Ivory Furniture from Pompeii: A Reconsideration of Its Functional Use." In *South Asian Archaeology 1979: Papers from the Fifth International Conference of the Association of South Asian Archaeologists in Western Europe Held in the Museum für Indische Kunst der Staatlichen Museen Preussischer Kulturbesitz Berlin*, pp. 341–353, edited by Herbert Härtel. Berlin: D. Reimar Verlag, 1981.
Dwivedi, Vinod Prakash. *Indian Ivories*. Delhi: Agam Prakashan, 1976.
Jaffer, Amin. *Furniture from British India and Ceylon: A Catalogue of the Collections in the Victoria and Albert Museum and the Peabody Essex Museum*. London: V & A Publications; Salem, Mass.: Peabody Essex Museum, 2001.
———. *Luxury Goods from India: The Art of the Indian Cabinet-Maker*. London: V & A Publications, 2002.
Jain, Jyotindra. "Indian 'Folk Art': Tradition, Revival, and Transformation." In *2000: Reflections on the Arts in India*, edited by Pratapaditya Pal. Mumbai: Marg Publications, 2000.
Kramrisch, Stella. "Early Indian Ivory Carving." *Philadelphia Museum of Art Bulletin* 54, no. 261 (Spring 1959): 55–66.
Lynch, Brendan. "The Near East, India." In *Ivory: An International History and Illustrated Survey*, pp. 188–225, edited by Fiona St. Aubyn. New York: Harry N. Abrams, 1987.
Nandi, Sipra. "Art of Ivory in Murshidabad." *Indian Museum Bulletin* (January 1969): 93–99.
Pal, Pratapaditya. *Elephants and Ivories in South Asia*. Los Angeles: Los Angeles County Museum of Art, 1981.
———. "Murshidabad: Capital of Fleeting Glory." In *Bengal: Sites and Sights*, edited by Pratapaditya Pal and Enamul Haque. Mumbai: Marg Publications, 2003.
Rosen, Elizabeth S. "The Begram Ivories." *Marsyas* 17 (1974–1975): 39–48.
van Lohuizen-de Leeuw, J. E. "Indian Ivories with Special Reference to a Mediaeval Throne Leg from Orissa." *Arts Asiatiques* 6, no. 3 (1959): 195–216.
Willis, Michael. "Early Indian Ivory." *Arts of Asia* 28, no. 2 (March–April 1998): 112–119.

JAHANGIR (1569–1627), Mughal emperor (1605–1627).

Jahangir ("World Grasper") was born Muhammad Salim. Married at fifteen, ultimately over eight hundred women occupied his harem, and his strong constitution was ruined by alcohol and opium. In 1600 he revolted against his father, Akbar, declared himself emperor, and refused to march on Kandahar to stave off the Persians. In 1602 he had the last of his father's great ministers, Abul Fazl, murdered. He was, nonetheless, forgiven by his father and was named as his successor.

As emperor, Jahangir promulgated twelve regulations that continued his father's policies of conciliation, religious tolerance, and justice, although he was a more orthodox Muslim than his father. Under Jahangir, the bureaucracy expanded dramatically, but the empire did not. In 1606 his eldest son, the popular Khusrau, revolted, and in suppressing that Punjab-based rebellion, Jahangir initiated a brutal conflict with the Sikhs. Khusrau was partly blinded and imprisoned for life, and was murdered in 1622 by his younger brother, Prince Khurram, the future emperor Shah Jahan.

Jahangir's reign changed dramatically with his marriage in 1611 to the Persian princess Nur Jahan ("Light of the World"), a beautiful, intelligent, and highly cultured and ambitious woman who set the fashions for the age and soon ruled the empire in all but name. Jahangir may have ordered the murder of her husband in 1607 in order to marry her. Nur Jahan, her father, and her brother, along with Prince Khurram, dominated the faction-ridden court until Prince Khurram rebelled in 1623, and the final years of Jahangir's reign were riven with conflict. With Nur Jahan came a greater infusion of Persian culture to Jahangir's court, especially miniature painting. Nur Jahan married her daughter by her first husband to Jahangir's youngest son, Shahryar. She and Jahangir had no children together.

Jahangir did not have his father's energy or drive, and his long desultory war against Mewar was concluded unfavorably in 1615. His campaigns from 1610 against Ahmednagar were also conducted fitfully and unsuccessfully. His son Prince Khurram was more successful in 1616, and he obtained the surrender of Ahmednagar, though it remained independent until 1629. Prince Khurram also captured Kangra in 1620. In 1622, however, Kandahar was lost to the Persians.

During the day Jahangir carried out his imperial duties, met with people, and was capable of great energy; at night he loved pleasure, and was an alcoholic with a mercurial and violent temper. In 1623 Shah Jahan rebelled, and he and his father were not reconciled for two years.

Jahangir allowed the British East India Company to establish a trading post at Surat, where the representative, Captain William Hawkins, arrived in 1608 and spent three years at Jahangir's court. The British ambassador, Sir Thomas Roe, served at his court between 1615 and 1619. This was of historical importance because it allowed the Europeans to make inroads into India. Jahangir wrote his memoirs, *Tuzuk-i-Jahangiri*, but in his last year his health was broken. He tried to restore it by visiting his Shalimar Gardens in Kashmir. He died on his return and was buried in Lahore.

Roger D. Long

See also **Akbar; Babur; Shah Jahan**

BIBLIOGRAPHY

Eraly, Abraham. *The Mughal Throne: The Saga of India's Great Emperors.* London: Weidenfeld & Nicolson, 2003.

Mitchell, Colin Paul. *Sir Thomas Roe and the Mughal Empire.* Karachi: Oxford University Press, 2000.

Richards, John. *The Mughal Empire.* Cambridge, U.K.: Cambridge University Press, 1993.

JAIN AND BUDDHIST MANUSCRIPT PAINTING

Buddhism and Jainism played an important role in generating written culture in a society where the oral transmission of knowledge has long been predominant. The production of Buddhist texts could have been inspired by the fear of forgetting the Buddha, who had already entered Nirvāna, and his teachings. Although much later in its date, Jain literature clearly records such fears as a reason for having written texts. When a terrible famine in the fifth century A.D. killed the majority of the Jain monks well versed in the sacred knowledge, the body of this knowledge was committed to writing for fear of losing the tradition forever. Books have been treasured in both Buddhism and Jainism not only as texts that record otherwise lost teachings of the venerable ones, but also as sacred objects that should be duly venerated. The books belonging to the latter category of sacred objects often contain paintings that contribute to their religious efficacy.

Buddhist Manuscript Painting

Historical background. The earliest illustrated Buddhist manuscript of the Indian subcontinent is the manuscript of the Astasāhasrikā Prajnāpāramitā (Perfection of wisdom in eight thousand lines) now in the Cambridge University Library. Its colophon tells us that the manuscript was made in the fourth regnal year of Mahīpāla I (c. 992–1042). The Pālas ruled in the ancient land of Magadha and adjacent regions (the present-day Indian state of Bihar and parts of Bengal) from the eighth to the early thirteenth centuries. The reign of Mahīpāla I marks a turning point in Pāla history because he is responsible for stabilizing and recovering the territory that was lost during the successions of weak kings before him. The heightened religious activities and the degree of royal patronage of the Buddhist institutions exemplified by the inscriptions bearing his regnal years suggest the perfect atmosphere for commissioning beautifully illustrated Buddhist manuscripts. A tradition of illustrating Buddhist books must have existed before Mahīpāla's reign, but the surviving body of manuscripts suggests a heyday of Buddhist book production, especially books with illustrations, during the eleventh and twelfth centuries in eastern India. Illustrated Buddhist manuscripts were made in regions outside Pāla territory in eastern India, and we have manuscripts dated with the regnal years of the Candras and the Varmans, who ruled parts of eastern India during this period. The popularity of illustrated Buddhist manuscripts was also witnessed in Kathmandu Valley, Nepal, a region that seems to have been culturally interconnected with eastern India during this time.

Manuscript production and the Buddhist monasteries in eastern India. The colophon of the Cambridge University Library manuscript mentioned above does not tell us where it was prepared, but the use of Mahīpāla's regnal year suggests that the site of its production must have been one of the famous Buddhist monasteries that prospered under the Pāla rule. Even though only a few of the Pāla kings were devout Buddhists, they continued to support the internationally well-known monastery of Nalanda and founded other grand monasteries, such as Vikramashīla, located in Antichak, near Bhagalpur in Bihar. We know from different colophons that manuscripts were actually made in these famous monasteries of eastern India. For example, a beautifully written manuscript of Astasāhasrikā Prajnāpāramitā that includes eighteen illustrations and painted wooden covers (now in the Bodleian Library, Oxford) was, the colophon tells us, prepared by a scribe Ahunakunda of Sri Nalanda in Magadha in the fifteenth year of the king Rāmapāla (c. 1087–1141). Another manuscript of Astasāhasrikā Prajnāpāramitā written in ornamental Kutila (hooked) scripts (now in the British Library) was made in Vikramashīla during the fifteenth year of King Gopāla III (c. 1143–1158).

Along with the accounts of later Tibetan monks visiting these sites, the ruins at the excavated sites of Nalanda and Vikramashīla suggest a blow of destruction by the Muslim army in the early thirteenth century, and such an attack must have destroyed thousands of manuscripts kept at the monasteries. This full-scale destruction of the Buddhist establishments in eastern India may have nevertheless contributed to the preservation of Buddhist manuscripts of the Pāla period: as the monks fled to Nepal and Tibet, these manuscripts were transported to a more hospitable climate for their fragile leaves, which otherwise may not have withstood almost a thousand years of harsh weather.

Material and production. Buddhist manuscripts of eastern India and Nepal were made with the leaves of the talipot (*Corypha umbraculifera*), a type of palm tree. The use of paper in Buddhist manuscript production was known in the Kathmandu Valley as early as the twelfth century, but palm leaf was the most commonly used material for writing. The palm-leaf manuscripts usually measure about 21–21.5 inches (53–55 cm) by 2–2.5 inches (5–6 cm) and come with a pair of wooden covers protecting the leaves. The pile of leaves and the wooden covers are strung together by a cord through prebored holes. A reed pen with black ink was used to write on the leaves, which had been rubbed to create smooth surfaces for writing. The colophons suggest that the scribe was

Illustrated Folio of Kalkacarya Katha. Illustration accompanying the Kālakāchāryakathā (Story of the teacher Kālaka), Jain manuscript from Western India, c. 1450–1500. By the time this watercolor was created, the introduction of paper had led to bolder stylization in Jain paintings. Note also the characteristic exaggerated linear depictions of figures. SURESH NEOTIA COLLECTION. JNANA PRAVAHA, VARANASI, INDIA.

usually a resident monk of the monastery where the project was commissioned.

When the donor's request included paintings in the manuscript, all the spaces for paintings were laid out at the commencement of the project. We do not know much about who undertook the paintings because the colophons are silent about the painters. It is most likely that there were specially trained painters at the monasteries, but there is also a possibility that a skillful scribe was the illustrator of the manuscript. Provided with a very small space of 2–2.5 inches (5–6 cm) square, the painters of the earliest illustrated manuscripts tended to abbreviate and simplify both lines and colors to create spontaneous and lively representations. By the late eleventh century, the manuscript painting style of eastern India and Nepal was as refined as that of Ajanta wall paintings, employing a fine yet sinuous line and color gradation to achieve a graceful and delicate modeling of each figure. Sometimes, if the donation fell short of the budget or the project was hurried to meet the deadline, these spaces for paintings were left empty. As long as the writing was finished, the manuscript was ready to be used and worshiped.

Book cult and paintings. Out of hundreds of Mahayana Buddhist texts, only a few enjoyed a great zeal of patronage during the Pāla period: the Astasāhasrikā Prajnāpāramitā, the Pancarakshā Sūtra of five protection goddesses, and occasionally the Kārandavyūha Sūtra, in eulogy of Avalokiteshvara. The most famous was the Astasāhasrikā Prajnāpāramitā, a philosophical treatise that expounds the Mahayana doctrine of *shuūnyataā* (emptiness) and a book of the Buddhist book cult in which the text promotes its own worship. As such, over two-thirds of the surviving illustrated manuscripts from this period are of the Asta.

The paintings in the Astasāhasrikā Prajnāpāramitā manuscripts often depict the eight scenes of the Buddha's life, even though we find no reference to such scenes in its text. Scholars who acknowledged such disjuncture between the text and images have argued that the paintings in the manuscripts of the Astasāhasrikā Prajnāpāramitā have no relation to the text, and that they serve as mere decorations that help the manuscript donor to accrue more religious merit. However, a careful look at the text-image relationship seems to prove otherwise. If the text of the Astasāhasrikā Prajnāpāramitā tries to explain the nonexistence of existence or the existence of nonexistence, disjuncture between the text and images may be said to illustrate the text by being elusive. Moreover, a systematic placement of images suggests that the paintings serve a more important role than mere decorations and merit making.

In a typical manuscript of the Astasāhasrikā Prajnāpāramitā, we have either twelve or eighteen painted panels, sized about 2–2.5 inches (5–6 cm) square. Three panels that appear on one side of a folio usually face another set on the next folio. Each set of two folios, with six paintings, marks the beginning and the end of the text. In the case of manuscripts with eighteen panels, paintings will also appear in the middle. Four of the eight panels depicting the Buddha's life scenes usually appear in the beginning, and the other four at the end. The rest are representations of different deities and *bodhisattva*s, such as Prajnāpāramitā, Avalokiteshvara, Manjushri, and Tārā. As a collective unit, these paintings become the icon of the book that can open and close the path to the core teaching of the Astasāhasrikā Prajnāpāramitā. The paintings are the indexical signs of the contents of the book.

Jain Manuscript Painting

Historical background. Jain manuscripts were mainly produced and kept in the Jnāna Bhandārs, a comprehensive library usually found underground, attached to Jain temples. According to the Jain literature, the foundation of the Jain Jnāna Bhandārs began at the same time as the writing of the Jain texts in the fifth century A.D. From the tenth century these libraries began to enjoy prosperity, thanks to support from the Jain kings, who ruled Gujarat and parts of Rajasthan, their ministers, and the merchant-bankers of the Jain communities. Such support partly originated from the interest in religious merits one could attain with the donation of a book. The event of donating a carefully made book to a Jnāna Bhandārs came with the opportunity for hearing the recitation of their sacred teachings. Such a book could be taken up for Jnanapuja, the worship of the book, as in Buddhist tradition. The survival of numerous palm-leaf and paper manuscripts made in western India is indebted to the Bhandārs of the Svetāmbara (clad in white) sect. The most famous Jain Jnāna Bhandārs are now found in Patan, Cambay, and Jaisalmer.

Scholars have suggested that the earliest illustrated Jain manuscript is the palm-leaf manuscript of the Nishīthachūrnī now in the collection of the Sanghavīnā Pādānā Bhandār, Patan, dated 1157 Vikramasamvat (A.D. 1100). This manuscript contains only floral and geometric patterned roundels and small figural drawings on the margins, whose purpose seems to be to decorate the manuscript. During the twelfth century we find Jain manuscripts of various canonical texts with illustrations of deities and other figures, as in the Buddhist examples. The illustrated manuscript on paper first emerged around the mid-fourteenth century, coinciding with the advent of the Sultanate rule in Gujarat, as exemplified by a paper manuscript of Kalpa Sūtra dated 1346, now in a private collection in Mumbai. Palm leaf continued to be used for manuscript production until about 1450.

The development of Jain manuscript painting.

The Kalpa Sūtra (Book of the ritual), often paired with Kālakāchāryakathā (Story of the teacher Kālaka), seems to have been the most favored Jain text for commissioning an illustrated manuscript. Apart from being recited once a year at the time of the Paryushana festival, both contain stories popular among Jains. The first two sections of the Kalpa Sūtra provide interesting narratives for illustrations, telling the life stories of the Tīrthānkaras and the genealogy of the elders, as does the Kālakāchāryakathā, a text about the adventure of a Jain monk, Kālaka, who saves his abducted sister with the help of the King Sāhi of the Saka tribes. Early makers of the Jain manuscripts paid little attention to the pictorial depiction of narratives. As in the illustrated manuscripts of other canonical texts of the twelfth and thirteenth centuries, the paintings in the Kalpa Sūtra portrayed the Tīrthānkaras, Jain monks, and lay devotees, probably the donors of the manuscripts.

The stories of the Kalpa Sūtra and the Kālakāchāryakathā began to be illustrated around the mid-fourteenth century, and once the iconography for each narrative scene was established, little deviation was made in their representations. It has been suggested that the introduction of paper during the fourteenth century led to stronger stylization and distortion of the figures. More exaggerated, linear, and flat depictions of figures with protruding eyes continued. During the fifteenth century, border decorations became more sumptuous and opulent, possibly influenced by contemporaneous Islamic manuscripts. The unusual manuscript of the Kalpa Sūtra of the Devasano Pādo Bhandār has very lavish illuminations on its borders. The application of new colors, such as ultramarine, lapis lazuli blue, and crimson red, with the occasional application of gold and silver, also contributed to the more elaborately decorated and illustrated Jain manuscripts of the fifteenth century. The unique figural style of the Jain manuscript paintings endured until the late sixteenth century, when the interest in Kalpa Sūtra suddenly dropped. In its place, other texts were commissioned for illustration in a completely different style, concurrent with that of Hindu manuscript paintings.

Jinah Kim

See also **Ajanta; Miniatures**

BIBLIOGRAPHY

Chandra, Moti. *Jain Miniature Paintings from Western India.* Ahmedabad: Sarabhai Manilal Nawab, 1949.
Foucher, Alfred. *Étude sur l'iconographie Bouddhique de l'Inde d'après des documents nouveaux.* Paris: Ernest Leroux, 1900.
Losty, J. P. *The Art of the Book in India.* London: British Library, 1982.
Nawab, Sarabhai. *Jain Paintings.* Vols. I–II. Ahmedabad: Sarabhai Manilal Nawab, 1980, 1985.
Pal, P. *Indian Painting.* Los Angeles: Los Angeles County Museum of Art, 1993.

Pal, P., and J. Meech-Pekarik. *Buddhist Book Illuminations*. New York: Ravi Kumar Publishers; Hurstpierpoint, U.K.: Richard Lyon-Chimera Books, 1988.

JAINISM Jainism is one of the oldest living religions of India. Older than Buddhism, its origins date before 3000 B.C. Though Mahāvīra (599–527 B.C.) is popularly perceived as the founder of Jainism, he was actually the last of the spiritual lineage of twenty-four Tīrthānkars recognized under Jainism. Jainism had existed before Mahāvīra, who was more a reformer and propagator of Jainism, reviving the Jain philosophy preached by his predecessor, Parshva (c. 950–850 B.C.).

Jainism is a religion of purely human origin. The twenty-four Tīrthānkars recognized under Jainism are those who have attained perfect perception, perfect knowledge, and perfect conduct—the golden trinity. In ancient times, Jainism was also known as the religion of *jina*, which literally means "conqueror," one who has conquered worldly passions such as, desire, hatred, anger, and greed. To Jains, all human beings have the potential to become *jinas*. The *jina* is not a supernatural entity, an incarnation, or almighty God, but a liberated soul, freed from the bonds of worldly existence and the cycle of rebirth.

Under Jainism, the concept of God as a creator, protector, and destroyer does not exist, nor does the idea of God's reincarnation as a human being to destroy the forces of evil. Jainism does not believe in God as a creator, yet it is not immune to the idea of gods. Under Jainism, the *jina*s are viewed as gods. As such, there can be many gods in Jainism. Recent research claims that one of the twenty-four Tīrthānkars, Mallinath, could be female. Under Jainism, each soul can attain enlightenment and become a Paramatma, a divine soul. Jainism presents an enlightened perspective of the "equality of souls" irrespective of physical form, ranging from human beings to microscopic living organisms. Jainism thus remains an original system, quite distinct and independent from other systems of Indian philosophy.

Buddhism became much more popular outside India, but Jainism remained confined to India. The Jains were the first to withdraw from the mainstream of Hinduism by refusing to entertain all the deities of the Hindu pantheon, but today they are being reabsorbed into mainstream Hinduism. Most Jains have started worshiping the Hindu deities simultaneously. While some Jains call themselves Hindus, others are fighting for minority status in order to avail themselves of the special protections and benefits reserved exclusively for minorities under Indian law.

One of the answers to the question of why Buddhism became more popular than Jainism outside India may be that the former received royal patronage. Emperor (Samrat) Ashoka, the great Mauryan monarch, embraced Buddhism after he became disillusioned over massive violence and death during the Kalinga war. During his reign, the empire covered nearly all of India, and Ashoka, who is believed to have converted to Buddhism before he died, sent his disciples to promote Buddhism within India and beyond. Jainism did not benefit from such royal patronage. Moreover, Jains adhered to strict vegetarianism, whereas Buddhists could be nonvegetarians.

The Theory of Karma and Rebirth

The theory of karma and rebirth forms the foundation of Jainism. The ultimate goal of each soul is to seek emancipation, *nirvāna*, or *kaivalya*. But it is not possible to achieve this emancipation during the present lifetime. Hence, under Jainism, a number of births are required for its realization. This provides the metaphysics of rebirth, which is also inseparable from karma. If rebirth is accepted as a fact, the idea of prebirth cannot be rejected, as every event must have a cause, and every cause must have its effects. This is the law of karma, which governs the universe. Karma is rebirth latent, and rebirth is karma manifest, under the indivisible unity of cause and effect. The Jains despise all forms of karma, whether good or bad, since they cause bondage. In other Hindu doctrines, good karmas are encouraged, as they yield good results.

Under Jainism, it is assumed that every act must have its consequences, and if these are not worked out in one's lifetime, another life is required for their fruition. The karma theory also seeks to provide an explanation for the widespread diversities and inequalities prevailing throughout the universe. To Jains, karma does not simply mean "work" or "deed" but signifies an aggregate of very tiny particulars attached to the soul, which are not even perceivable by the senses. The Jains believe in the material and formless nature of karma, crystallized as the effect of past deeds. They also believe in the doctrine of the soul as the possessor of material karma. To Jains, the karmas pervade all cosmic space in the form of a substantive force or matter in subtle form, mixing with the soul as milk mixes with water.

Jainism assumes that the universe is without a beginning or an end. It is everlasting and eternal. There are six *dravaya* (fundamental entities): *jiva* (soul or consciousness), *pudgal* (matter), *dharma* (medium of motion), *adharma* (medium of rest), *aakash* (space), and *kaal* (time). These entities are eternal but undergo continuous and countless changes. During the changes, nothing is lost or destroyed; everything is recycled into another form.

Coconuts Being Prepared for Jain Ceremony. Most of the 8 million to 10 million followers of Jainism (traditionally known as Jain Dharma) worldwide live in India. FRANCOIS GAUTIER / FOTOMEDIA.

The proper knowledge of the six *dravaya* and nine *tattva* (fundamental truths) form the basis of right perception and right conduct. The nine *tattva* are: *jiva* (living beings), *ajiva* (non living substances), *aasrava* (causes of the influx of karma to the soul), *bandha* (bondage of karma to the soul), *sanvara* (stoppage of the influx of the karma), *nirjhara* (exhaustion or falling of the accumulated karma due to self-purification, penance, and meditation), *moksha* (complete liberation from karma responsible for rebirth), *paap* (sin), and *punya* (virtue). The knowledge of these *dravaya* and *tattva* paves the way for salvation.

Right conduct comprises the following five ideals: *ahimsa* (nonviolence), *satya* (truthfulness), *asteya* (not stealing), *brahmacharya* (chastity), and *aparigraha* (non-possessiveness). The main slogans under Jainism as a religion are *ahimsa parmodharma* (nonviolence is the supreme religion) and "live and let live." Within Jainism, the concept of *ahimsa* is very profound. It does not refer merely to abstaining from physical acts of violence, but also to abstaining from violence in thought. According to ancient Jain texts, violence is not defined by actual harm but by the intention to harm. Without violent thought, violent action is not possible.

The Jain Symbol and Sects

The comprehensive Jain symbol consists of a digit of the moon, three dots, the swastika, the palm of the human hand with a wheel inset, and a figure outlining all. The moon symbolizes the region beyond the three worlds where the liberated souls reside. The three dots symbolize the path of liberation: right perception, right knowledge, and right conduct. The swastika symbolizes the cycle of birth and death, divided due to karma into four forms: heaven, human, *tiryanch* (animals, birds, and plants), and hell. The palm signifies that one need not be afraid of sufferings from karmic bondage. The wheel with twenty-four spokes represents the Jain religion, preached by the twenty-four Tīrthānkaras.

Mahāvīra, the last of the twenty-four Tīrthānkaras, organized his followers into four sects: *sadhu* (monks), *sadhvi* (nuns), *shravak* (male devotees), and *shravika* (female devotees). With the passage of time, Jainism as a religion grew more complex. Eventually, two major sects were established, the Digambaris and the Svetambaris. The Digambari (sky-clad) monks do not wear any clothes, and the Svetambari monks wear only unstitched white cloths. Both believe in basic values and principles of Jainism. Both believe in *kshmavani* (forgiveness), a ritual that is performed annually in the month of August–September. On this day, Jains seek forgiveness from fellow Jains for any misdeed or bad thought during the past year, whether intentional or unintentional. It promotes universal friendliness, universal forgiveness, and universal fearlessness.

The Cardinal Principles of Jainism

Ahimsa (nonviolence), *anekantavada* (non-one-sidedness) and *aparigraha* (nonpossessiveness) form the distinguishing features of Jainism. It is not easy to explain the doctrine of *anekantavada* and *syadavada* (maybe). It is also known as the philosophy of nonabsolutism, the theory of manifoldness, and the theory of many-sided nature. It is nearer to the Western theory of relativism. To understand *anekantavada*, or "non-one-sidedness," it is imperative to understand *ekantavada*, or "one-sidedness." One-sidedness signifies only one point of view as absolute truth, often leading to dogmatism and intolerance. Jains view it as falsehood, false knowledge, and false perception. To Jains, the truth can be manifold. The doctrine of *anekantavada* and *syadavada* helps in understanding divergent viewpoints and in reconciling apparent contradictions.

Under Jainism, there can be many ways of looking at an object or an idea, all of which may be valid at the same time. This moral can be derived easily from the story of six blind men in the *Panchtantra*, who each tried to describe an elephant. Each of the six blind men caught hold of a different part of the elephant's body and formed his own image of the huge animal. The man who caught the tail of the elephant thought it to be like a long rope. The one who held the leg thought it to be like a pillar. The one who touched the ear thought it to be like a huge fan. The one who held the trunk thought it to be like a python, and the one who held the stomach thought it to be like a drum. The one who touched the back thought it to be like a platform. Each of the six blind men considered his viewpoint to be absolutely true and the views held by others as absolutely false, resulting in a fight. At that critical juncture a wise man made them feel the other parts of the elephant. They then realized that although each one of them was partially correct in his imagination of the elephant, the others were equally correct. The *anekantavadi*, or multifaceted approach, helped them realize the truth.

The theory of *syadavada*, or the "maybe" approach, prepares one to accept other's viewpoints as true by demonstrating that the human capability to learn and act accordingly is necessarily limited. Our perceptions can be partially true, and they can be true only conditionally. As such, it is always desirable under Jainism to add qualifying words, such as "perhaps" or "maybe." This doctrine thus includes the respect of the viewpoints of others.

The theory of *anekant* and *syadavada* is also called a doctrine of reconciliation and assimilation, on the one hand, and tolerance and understanding, on the other. It holds the opening of one's mind and one's heart to the notion and complete picture of truth. It is the first condition of human well-being and happiness. It provides the binding force to other cardinal principles of Jainism: nonviolence and nonpossessiveness.

Jainism is an important ideological phenomenon in the religious history of humankind. The entire edifice of Jainism rests on one principle: live and let live. It is based on positive love, a principle that was propagated by Jesus and Mahatma Gandhi as well. The doctrine of *anekantavada*, or non-one-sidedness, can be seen as an extension of the doctrine of nonviolence. Jainism is adept at providing a theoretical basis for the practical beliefs of its followers. It emphasizes the dictum: "do not injure, abuse, oppress, enslave, insult, torment, torture or kill any living being." Jainism does not advocate suicide, assisted suicide, mercy killing, or the removal of life-supporting devices. However, Jainism allows *sallekhana*, a "holy suicide by starvation," to spiritually very advanced persons. They can terminate their lives, as Mahāvīra did, under specified circumstances under the supervision of the Acharyas—the *sadhu*s, teachers and role models.

According to Jainism, each soul is innately pure and inherently perfect, but the karmas attached to it, due to past thoughts and deeds, make it imperfect and obscure. When the soul is freed from karmic influences, it becomes liberated. The contribution of Jainism toward human omniscience is very significant. Equally significant is the Jain philosophy of *anekantavada* and *syadavada* which not only help in acquiring true knowledge from different perspectives but also help in reconciling different points of views amicably.

The cardinal principles of Jainism—nonviolence, nonpossessiveness, and non-one-sidedness—are important not only because they are ancient Indian in philosophy but because they are universal. They stress reconciliation rather than reputation, cooperation rather than confrontation, and coexistence rather than mutual annihilation. Jain philosophy, if understood, may help humankind to emerge from its modern moral crisis, emotional emptiness, and violence.

Asha Gupta

See also **Jain and Buddhist Manuscript Painting; Jain Sculpture**

BIBLIOGRAPHY

Birodkar, Sudheer. "Jainism—Gave Us Non-violence as an Ethical Outlook." Available at <http://india.coolatlanta.com/GreatPages/sudheer/book2/jainism.html>

Chatterjee, Asim Kumar. *A Comprehensive History of Jainism.* 2 vols. Delhi: Munshiram Manoharlal, 2000.

Kothari, Ajay P. *The Concept of Divinity in Jainism.* Jaipur: Prakrit Bharti Academy, 2000.

Mardia, K. V., ed. *The Scientific Foundations of Jainism.* Delhi: Motilal Banarsidass. 1996.

Mukherjee, Asha, ed. *Cognition Man and the World: Perspectives in Jaina Philosophy.* Delhi: Kalinga, 2004.

Prasad, Sital. *A Comparative Study of Jainism and Buddhism.* Delhi: Satguru, 2003.

Sancheti, Asoo Lal, and Manak Lal Bhandari. "The Central Philosophy of Jainism: Anekantavad, the Doctrine of Non-one-sidedness." Available at <http://www.jainworld.com/jainbooks/firstep-2/anekantavad.htm>

Sangave, Vilas Adinath. *Facets of Jainology: Selected Research Papers on Jain Society, Religion and Culture.* Mumbai: Popular Prakashan, 2001.

Singh, Nagendra Kumar, ed. *Encyclopedia of Jainism.* 30 vols. New Delhi: Anmol Publications, 2001.

JAIN SCULPTURE Jain sculpture is identifiable as Jain only by subject matter, iconography, or inscription. Otherwise, in terms of style, ornament, and in many cases, subsidiary figures, Jain sculpture is indistinguishable from sculpture made for other Indian religious groups, as they were all produced by artists from the same workshops. Nevertheless, as early as the second century B.C., the Jains continuously have been active patrons in many regions of the Indian subcontinent, and the sculpture they worship and use to adorn their sacred sites is of major importance in the history of Indian art. Movements and innovations within the Jain religious communities often found expression in sculpture, which in turn proved influential to members of the other religious traditions with which they regularly came in contact. Conversely, aspects of the literature, art, and practices of Buddhism, Hinduism, and popular local cults were absorbed and adapted by the Jains, since the Jain religion and its art existed not in isolation, but partook of a broad cultural and social network that was constantly interacting.

Some features of Jain sculpture are distinctively Jain, unmistakable from imagery associated with other sects, and they serve to identify the work as Jain in orientation. They include representations of the twenty-four Tīrthānkaras ("crossers of the ford," also called Jinas, or "conquerors"), who are the liberated beings of Jainism and the primary objects of veneration. Also distinctively Jain are the tonsured monks and nuns, usually shown carrying the accoutrements of their strict adherence to *ahimsa*, which refers to their practice of refraining from killing or harming any living being. Another means of distinguishing Jain sculpture is by identifying narrative sequences that are found only in Jain devotional texts. Most popular are scenes from the lives of the Tīrthānkaras, particularly

Mahāvīra, Pārshvanātha, or Rishavanātha. Finally, inscriptions, generally written in a vulgate (Prakrit) derived from Sanskrit, with distinctively Jain content or formulaic wording, can be used to identify a sculpture as Jain.

Icons for Veneration

A fundamental aspect of Jainism, regardless of sect, is that during the current epoch, twenty-four people have achieved supreme knowledge (*kevala jñāna*) through strict asceticism and meditation, which allows them upon death to be liberated from our world of endless cycling from one birth and death to another. These liberated beings are called Tirthankaras, and they dwell in an eternal state of meditative bliss in a realm above our universe, and hence they are depicted in sculpture in postures denoting meditation. Their presence is known in our world through the dissemination of their teachings and through the veneration of their images in temples. Most Jain iconic sculptures are images of a Tirthankara, which would be placed on an altar in a shrine or temple.

Other types of icons are also set up for veneration in a Jain context. Goddesses and other divinities play crucial roles in Jainism. The goddess of learning, Sarasvatī, is frequently found in association with Jain monuments, and the Jain mother goddess Ambikā becomes ubiquitous by the eighth century A.D. The goat-headed divinity Naigameshin, who transported the embryo of the twenty-fourth Tirthankara, Mahāvīra, to the womb of Queen Trishalā, remains an important figure in the Jain pantheon from the first century A.D. onward. Finally, saints and important teachers of Jainism can be venerated as objects of worship as well.

Iconography of Tīrthānkaras

The most recognizable type of Jain sculpture is that of the seated or standing Tīrthānkara icon. Rigidly axial and usually totally nude (until after the sixth century, when some sects provide them with a lower garment), sculptures of Tīrthānkaras embody the ideal of rigorous asceticism that is so central to the practice of Jainism. When standing, their arms are held stiffly by their sides, not touching the body, in a posture called *kāyotsarga*. Seated Tīrthānkara figures have crossed legs, and their hands are positioned one atop the other in the lap in the gesture of meditation (*dhyāna*). Often they will have the auspicious *shrīvatsa* symbol on the chest, denoting the beneficial results that can ensue from veneration of the image.

Most of the Tīrthānkaras are visually indistinguishable from one another, except for two of them that have distinctive characteristics. The first, Rishavanātha (also called Ādinātha), is the only Tīrthānkara depicted with long hair. Otherwise, all Tīrthānkaras are fully tonsured

DONORS AND THE PROCESS OF DONATION

Donors who give the images and the worshipers who venerate them earn valuable spiritual merit, which aids in a favorable rebirth and moves them closer to the liberated state. Many of the icons have valuable donative inscriptions that yield information regarding the structure of the Jain monastic and lay communities of the region. The thriving Jain monasteries had many monks and nuns, and they would serve as spiritual advisers to laypeople, who, acting under the instigation of the monastic adviser, would pay for the creation of an image and its installation within the sanctuary. This would be done for the sake of honoring the Tīrthānkaras, often called arhats (or "qualified ones") in the inscriptions. During the pre-Kushana and Kushana periods (c. 150 B.C.–A.D. 250), many of the donors of Jain icons were laywomen, thus indicating that wealthy women were prominent supporters of the Jain establishments at Mathura.

with no cranial protuberance (*ushnisha*), until the fifth century A.D., after which Tīrthānkaras could be shown with the protrusion atop the head, like a Buddha. The twenty-third Tīrthānkara, Pārshvanātha (or simply Pārshva), is shown with a five-hooded serpent behind him, which makes reference to a specific event in his biography. By the mid-second century A.D., Neminātha (also Arishtanemi) can be identified by his being flanked by Krishna and Balarāma, the well-known Hindu gods whom the Jains consider to have been his cousins. Specific Tīrthānkaras were often provided with an animal or other cognizance that serves as a means of signifying which Tīrthānkara is being represented. Ajitanātha, for example, has an elephant for his cognizance, while Mahāvīra has the lion, and Rishavanātha the bull. As iconographies became more elaborate and codified, in keeping with pan-Indian trends of the medieval period, each Tīrthānkara was assigned further identifying attributes, such that by the eighth century they were provided with identifying colors, particular trees under which they achieved *kevala jñāna* (the highest knowledge leading to final liberation), and specifically named male and female attendants who serve as messengers (*shāsanadevatā*) between them and their devotees.

Early History of the Tīrthānkara Icon

Some fragmentary examples of nude male figures resembling Tīrthānkaras standing frontally have been discovered that are attributed to the earliest phases of stone sculptural production in India. However, there is no indication that Jainism as we know it existed before the time of Mahāvīra, who is credited with founding the Jain religion in the sixth century B.C. Moreover, other iconic images of unidentified nude male figures attributed on the basis of style to the next phase of stone carving (third century B.C.) possess no distinguishing inscription or iconographic mark to prove they are necessarily Jain.

The earliest known icon of an identifiable Tīrthānkara is a stone image of Pārshvanātha, made in the city of Mathura, Uttar Pradesh, in northern India, and datable on the basis of style to around 100–75 B.C. For the next three hundred years, Mathura figures as the most prominent center for the manufacture of Jain sculpture.

Most of the earliest Jain Tīrthānkaras, from the first century B.C. and first century A.D., are carved in low relief on stone plaques called *āyāgapata*, which functioned as objects of worship in Jain sanctuaries. The Tīrthānkara imagery on these plaques seems to have played an important role in the formulation of the anthropomorphic Buddha icon, which was initiated in Mathura in the first decades of the first century A.D. During this period, Jainism at Mathura flourished, and Jain foundations enjoyed much better financial support from the laity than did their non-Hindu monastic rivals, the Buddhists. The inhabitants of Mathura evidently favored the worship of anthropomorphic icons, and the particular heterodox sect of Jainism, called Ardhaphālaka, known primarily from sculptures and inscriptions and active only in Mathura, appear to have been eager to accommodate this regional predilection.

Hundreds of Tīrthānkara icons have been recovered from Mathura, dating predominantly to the Kushana period of the second and third centuries A.D.; such mass production often led to repetitive and conventional modes of representation. Once the Ardhaphālakas were completely subsumed within the more mainstream Shvetāmbara branch of Jainism by the fourth century, the production of Jain sculptures at Mathura dropped off to be more in step with the number and type of images made for Jains in other regions.

Jain Icons of the Guptan and Medieval Periods

Some of the most sublime Jain Tīrthānkara icons were carved during the Guptan period of the fifth century A.D. Less mass-produced than during the preceding Kushāna period, the softly naturalistic Guptan Tīrthānkaras exude the peaceful idealization characteristic of all sculpture produced during this classical age. They still maintain the total nudity and stiff frontal postures, whether standing or seated in meditation.

RĀMAGUPTA TĪRTHĀNKARAS OF VIDISHA

At times Jain sculptures serve as important documents of Indian history and art history. Three stone images of Jain Tīrthānkaras were recovered near Vidisha, Madhya Pradesh. They are all inscribed with lengthy donative inscriptions stating that they were made during the time of King Rāmagupta, a monarch of the Guptan empire of northern India, who, until the discovery of these images, was thought to be apocryphal. He had a short and calumnious reign in the A.D. 370s, and hence these three images are rare examples of stone sculpture dated to the fourth century. They have thus become benchmarks for the understanding of sculptural styles of the fourth century, a time to which very little art from any region can be firmly attributed. The Rāmagupta Tīrthānkaras are key examples of the stylistic transition from the boldness and extroversion of Kushāna sculpture (second–third centuries) to the softer surfaces and gentle introspection of the Guptan period (fifth century).

After the Guptan period, a proliferation of Jain sculpture and icons can be found throughout the Indian subcontinent, as is the case with the arts of other religious traditions as well, since it is a time generally marked by multiplicity, elaboration, and more surviving examples. Some of the most important works of Jain sculpture from the sixth through the thirteenth centuries are cast in bronze, to be used as objects of worship in smaller shrines or for personal devotion. The tradition of casting Jina icons in bronze dates as early as the second century A.D., as known from a rare early hoard discovered at Chausa, Bihar, in eastern India, which includes images made during the Kushāna and Guptan periods. Dating from the sixth to tenth centuries are the extraordinary group of bronzes from Akota, Gujarat, in western India, including icons and shrines not only of Tīrthānkaras, but also of Jain goddesses, such as Ambikā.

From the eighth to thirteenth centuries, the most prominent center for the production of Jain sculpture, particularly in bronze, is in the south, both in Karnataka and in Tamil Nadu, where the Jain community flourished intermittently between major persecutions. The unusually magnificent tenth-century freestanding stone colossus of the Jain saint Bahubali (also known as Gomateshvara) in Shravana Belgola, Karnataka, in southwestern India, is to this day a major pilgrimage site for Jains. Bahubali, a son of the first Tīrthānkara, Rishavanātha, renounced his princely life after a duel with his brother. He stood for so long in meditation that vines grew up around him, and depictions of Bahubali are readily recognizable by the distinctive feature of vines curling around his body. This sculpture measures about 60 feet (18 m) in height and is said to be the tallest freestanding monolithic sculpture in the world.

Jain Sculpture and Temple Architecture

Jain sculpture surviving on intact monuments are valuable documents for understanding how the imagery was used in its religious context. While the Tīrthānkara icon served as the focal object of worship, a profusion of other kinds of imagery adorn other areas of sacred structures.

Cave temples. On the hills known as Udayagiri and Khandagiri near Bhubaneshvara, Orissa, in eastern India are the ruins of an apsidal temple and a number of rock-cut shelters in which Jain mendicants stay during the rainy season. In running friezes along the tops of the rear walls of the verandas, in tympana, on exterior walls of outdoor cells, and on pillar capitals are a great variety of relief sculptures. The first phase of carving dates to the second and first centuries B.C. Many of them are complex narratives that remain unidentified but testify to the rich literary tradition of the early Jains, which is now lost. Some reliefs depict intriguing scenes of worship, such as a royal couple venerating a nonanthropomorphic symbol on an altar. Other imagery includes pan-Indian motifs such as animals, nature divinities (*yaksha* and *yakshī*), Sūrya the sun god, and Lakshmī the goddess of good fortune. About a thousand years later, images of Tīrthānkaras and their messenger divinities were added to the walls of the caves, and during the nineteenth and twentieth centuries, a Jain temple and Tīrthānkara sculptures further augmented the site.

It is remarkable that a number of major Hindu cave temple sites of the Guptan and post-Guptan periods (fifth and sixth centuries A.D.) include several Jain sanctuaries. Of note are the caves at Udayagiri, Madhya Pradesh (early fifth century) in central India; Badami, Karnataka (late sixth century) and Ellora, Maharashtra (eighth century), in the Deccan of western India. These Jain caves have received very little attention, overshadowed as they are by the Hindu caves at the same sites. The sculptural program primarily includes multiple Tīrthānkara icons and subsidiary divinities.

Structural temples. The inclusion of Jain temples at otherwise predominantly Hindu sites continues into the medieval period, even in structural temple complexes. At the famed temple site of Khajuraho, Madhya Pradesh, Jain temples are among the predominantly Hindu monuments. Visually, the Jain Pārshvanātha temple at Khajuraho is virtually indistinguishable from the other temples in the area, and it is just as lavish, but with less emphasis on erotic imagery.

Some of the finest Jain temples are in Gujarat and Rajasthan in western India. The temple to the Jain mother goddess Ambikā at Jagat in Rajasthan is dated to A.D. 961, and it is an exemplar of the pure North Indian temple style at its height. The exterior is replete with figural and vegetal imagery. An explosion of sculptural imagery can be found on the interior of the Vimala temple at Mount Abu, a major pilgrimage Jain pilgrimage site atop a sacred mountain in Rajasthan. Carved completely of polished white marble in the eleventh and thirteenth centuries, the Tīrthānkara icons remain austere, but the dizzying array of figural and lacelike ornamental sculpture that adorns the ceilings, pillars, and archways testifies to the wealth of the Jain community in western India. Major donations from Vimala, the temple's patron and a minister to the Solanki king, supported the construction and embellishment of this stunning temple, including the famous spectacular ceilings made of concentric rings of intricately carved marble and images of female directional divinities, dancers, and celestial musicians. The voluptuous figures of the divinities and the exuberant ornamentation of Jain monuments such as the Vimala temple seem to be at odds with the doctrines propounding austerity and detachment for Jain practitioners. These temples, however, are reflections of the activities of the wealthy Jain laity, primarily of the mercantile class, and donations to Jain monuments in order to beautify them was one of the chief means of accruing spiritual merit without renouncing society.

Sonya Quintanilla

See also **Guptan Period Art; Jainism**

BIBLIOGRAPHY

Ghosh, A. *Jaina Art and Architecture.* 3 vols. New Delhi: Bharatiya Jnanpith, 1974.

Jaini, Padmanabh S. *Jaina Path of Purification.* 1979. Reprint, Delhi: Motilal Banarsidass, 2001.

Mathur, Asha Rani, and Karl J. Khandalavala, eds. *Indian Bronze Masterpieces.* New Delhi: Festival of India, 1988.

Mitra, Debala. *Udayagiri and Khandagiri.* New Delhi: Archaeological Survey of India, 1975.

Pal, Pratapaditya. *The Peaceful Liberators: Jain Art from India.* Los Angeles: Los Angeles County Museum of Art, 1994.

Quintanilla, Sonya Rhie. "*Āyāgapata*s: Characteristics, Symbolism, and Chronology." *Artibus Asiae* 60, no. 1 (2000): 79–137.

Shah, U. P. *Studies in Jaina Art.* Banaras: Jaina Cultural Research Society, 1955.

———. *Jaina Rūpa Mandana: Jaina Iconography.* New Delhi: Abhinav, 1987.

Shah, U. P., and M. A. Dhaky, eds. *Aspects of Jaina Art and Architecture.* Ahmedabad: Gujarat State Committee for Celebration of 2500th Announcement of Bhagavan Mahavira Nirvana, 1975.

JAMDANI *Jamdani*, a figured muslin, is a very fine, textured fabric. Considered the most sophisticated of the Indian hand-loomed textiles, it reveals the dexterity and genius of its makers. *Jamdani* is woven by varying the thickness of the yarn, in tones of white, bringing about a unique effect of light and shade, opaqueness and transparency. The resulting nuances of white in five different shades convey a highly developed aesthetic.

The origin of *jamdani* muslin is not clear. There is mention of this fabric as having been worn by Lakshmī, the goddess of wealth, in Bana Bhatta's treatise *Harsha Charita*, which is a rich source of knowledge of ancient Indian textiles. There is also a reference in the Sanskrit literature of the Gupta period (4th to 6th centuries A.D.). *Jamdani* appears to have been derived from the ancient Persian technique of twill weaving. The term, which applied both to the woolen weaves of Kashmir as well as to the cotton floral weaves of the Gangetic Plain, also seems to have been known as figured or loom-embroidered muslin. While the technique of weaving and the nature of the textile are considered ancient, it was not until very late that the term *jamdani* appeared, probably derived from *jama*, or "coat."

The Gangetic Plain was noted for its fine muslins since earliest times; the important centers were Banaras (Varanasi, in Uttar Pradesh), Tanda (in Faizabad district, Uttar Pradesh) and Dacca (Dhaka, the present-day capital of Bangladesh). In Banaras, gold thread was used along with bleached and unbleached white; in Tanda, only white yarn was used; and in Dacca, colored cotton thread was used in addition to white and gold. The finest and best *jamdani* textiles from Banaras are referred as *kasi vastra*. The development of these fine fabrics was attributed to the growing of high-grade cotton, the proficiency of the spinners and weavers, and the quality of water used for washing and bleaching, combined with the conditions of humidity in the atmosphere.

It was during the Great Mughal period (1556–1707) that royal patronage was extended and royal workshops were established for the manufacture of these fabrics for the court, giving further impetus to the production of the finest muslins. Tanda and Dacca became important centers of production. The spinners and weavers seemed to have migrated to Tanda from Banaras in the early sixteenth century. Under Mughal influence, there were two fundamental changes in the design of the textiles produced in the royal workshops. The existing figural designs of birds and animals were eliminated and were

A Weaver Designs a *Jamdani* Sari. *Jamdani* is considered the most sophisticated woven product among Indian hand looms. In this photo, a Bangladeshi works its delicate weave. AFP / GETTY IMAGES.

replaced by floral ornaments in the cloth. This practice, which originated in the Islamic prohibition of the use of imagery, existed in all textiles worn on the body. The color scheme also underwent a change, with no use of tones of white. The unbleached cloth, which had a ritual significance for Hindus, was replaced by the bleached *jamdani* worn in Mughal courts. In Banaras, there was no mention of royal workshops. The *jamdani* of Tanda, under the patronage of Oudh rulers, reached a level of excellence and became a monopoly of the government. The various techniques are said to have reached the weavers of the East Godavari and Nellore districts of Andhra Pradesh by way of West Bengal and Oudh.

The East India Company established a trading center in Dacca during the eighteenth century. Indian and European merchants had to purchase the muslins through brokers appointed by the British government. Under the British, many changes occurred in the production of muslin fabrics in Tanda. For the first time,

domestic products like tablecloths and towels were woven for the European market.

The feature of Tanda muslin that distinguishes it from other ornamental weaves is the use of the twill tapestry technique to weave without any additional devices or attachments. Historian John Irwin traces the origin of twill tapestry technique in India to the time of Zain-ul-Abidin (A.D. 420–470) and the weavers of Turkistan. The weavers were Muslims, and the spinners were Hindus; both had the capability and skill to produce and spin yarn in thread count ranging from 150 to over 200. Hand-spun cotton yarn was used to weave the *jamdani* cloth, containing threads of 90 to 120 ends in the warp and 80 to 110 in the weft. The weavers used the traditional type of pit loom. This technique of weaving is akin to embroidery, but in place of the needle, the weavers use a bamboo spindle directly on the loom, articulating the design from memory. Spindles made of small bamboo or maize stocks, about 2 inches (5 cm) long, were used for extra weft threads. The number of bamboo splits required were as many as there were floral ornaments across the width of the cloth. To weave the ornamental figures, two threads of the same count as in the background were introduced, using extra spools where the threads were passed under and over the ornament as required to form the design. The threads were manually selected and lifted for this purpose. The weavers sat at the loom with one or two assistants, though there was no "draw boy" sitting near the loom to pull the cords to maintain the harness. In the *jamdani* of Dacca and Tanda, the weavers used only weft threads to make a pattern on the warp threads to create the ornamentation.

With the introduction of the new function of *naqsha-band* (making of jacquard) and the practice of tying the *naqsha* (pattern on the loom) by the Muslim conquerors of Persia and Central Asia to the *jamdani* weavers, both design and color underwent a change. More and more complicated designs and a large number of colored threads were included in the fabrics. The weavers adapted to the range of new techniques and continued to develop their fine product in the traditional *jamdani* centers, catering to the needs of different communities and different markets. Because of the great degree of skill required and time consumed, the number of *jamdani* weavers began to decline. Today *jamdani* fabrics are still being woven, though with a lesser degree of skill, in parts of Uttar Pradesh, Andhra Pradesh, and Dhaka, mostly using mill-made yarn of a silk-cotton blend, for garments and other items on demand. Some of the weavers of Andhra Pradesh in the district of Srikakulam are still employing this ancient twill tapestry technique without any additional attachments, with hand-spun yarn, into the twenty-first century.

Jagada Rajappa

BIBLIOGRAPHY

Chandra, Moti. *Kashmir Shawls.* Bulletin of the Prince of Wales Museum of Western India. No. 3: 4.

Forbes, Watson J. *Textile Manufacturers and Costumes of India.* London: n.p., 1866.

Ghosh, Ajit. "Figured Fabrics of Old Bengal." *Marg* 3, no. 1: 38.

Irwin, John. *Shawls: A Study in Indo-European Influences.* London: Her Majesty's Stationery Office, 1955.

JAMMU AND KASHMIR Jammu and Kashmir State consists of different ethnic, linguistic, and religious groups. Its three broad regions are: Jammu, which has a Hindu majority; Kashmir, with a Muslim majority; and Ladakh and Kargil, which is split between Buddhists and Muslims. A little over half of the population of the state is concentrated in the Valley of Kashmir, which accounts for only 10 percent of the area. Ladakh, Gilgit, and Baltistan are very sparsely populated.

History

Kashmir is at the center of Purānic geography. In the Purānic conception, Earth's continents are arranged in the form of a lotus flower. Mount Meru stands at the center of the world, the pericarp or seed vessel of the flower, as it were, surrounded by circular ranges of mountains. Around Mount Meru, like the petals of the lotus, are arranged four island-continents (*dvīpa*s), aligned to the four points of the compass: Uttarakuru to the north, Ketumāla to the west, Bhadrāshva to the east, and Bharata or Jambudvīpa to the south. The meeting point of the continents is the Meru mountain, which is the high Himalayan region around Kashmir.

Kashmir's proximity to rich trade routes brought it considerable wealth, and Kashmirs spread Sanskrit culture as missionaries. Kashmiris also became interpreters of the Indian civilization, and they authored many fundamental synthesizing and expository works.

Buddhism was introduced into the Vale by the missionaries of the emperor Ashoka (r. 268–231 B.C.). The Kushān emperor Kanishka (c. A.D. 100) convened a Buddhist council in Kashmir, which led to the foundation of Mahāyāna Buddhism. Kashmiri missionaries played a leading role in the spread of Buddhism into Central Asia and China.

The Kārkota dynasty of the seventh and eighth centuries provides the first authentic accounts of the government in the Valley. Lalitāditya (724–761), the outstanding king of this dynasty, built the famed Sun temple of Mārtand. In the ninth century Avantivarman built a grand capital south of Srinagar; the ruins can still be seen.

Muslim rule was first established in Kashmir in the fourteenth century. Kashmir became a part of the Mughal empire under Akbar in 1587. In 1752, with the collapse of Mughal power, Kashmir came under control of Afghans, who lost it to the Sikhs in 1819. In 1846, following the defeat of the Sikhs by the British—when Jammu's Ghulab Singh turned against his Sikh allies—Singh reaped the Valley of Kashmir as a reward to add to his fiefdom of Jammu.

The movement for independence in British India spilled over to Kashmir as well. The maharaja tried to hold out for independence in August 1947 when India was partitioned. But in late October of that year Pathan tribesmen, led by military officers in civilian clothes, tried to take the valley by force. Maharaja Hari Singh, Ghulab's grandson, hastily acceded to the Indian Union. Soldiers of the Indian army were immediately flown into

Supporters of the Ruling National Conference Party Campaign in Jammu and Kashmir. Supporters of the ruling National Conference Party hours before the September 2002 elections in the troubled states of Jammu and Kashmir. The long-entrenched party was ousted, but tensions between the Hindu majority in Jammu and the Muslim majority in Kashmir persist. AMIT BHARGAVA / CORBIS.

Srinagar, and they turned the tide of the tribal invasion. Pakistani regulars were sent in, and the Kashmir war raged throughout 1948. Finally, under the supervision of the United Nations Security Council, a cease-fire was declared on 1 January 1949. Pakistan still controls about one-third of the Jammu and Kashmir State, mostly the northwest parts of Jammu and Baltistan, and the Gilgit region. The Security Council called upon both India and Pakistan to allow the United Nations to hold a plebiscite in Kashmir to ascertain the will of its people; the two countries could never agree to do so in over half a century, fighting three wars instead.

The political boundaries of Kashmir have on occasion extended much beyond the valley and the adjoining regions. According to the seventh-century Chinese Buddhist monk Hsieun Tsang, the adjacent territories to the west and south down to the plains were also under the direct control of the king of Kashmir. With Durlabhavardhana of the Kārkota dynasty, the power of Kashmir extended to parts of Punjab and Afghanistan. It appears that during this period of Kashmiri expansion, the ruling

elite, if not the general population, of Gilgit, Baltistan, and West Tibet spoke Kashmiri-related languages. Later, as Kashmir's political power declined, these groups were displaced by Tibetan-speaking people.

In the eighth century, Lalitāditya conquered most of north India, Central Asia, and Tibet. His vision and exertions mark a new phase of Indian empire-building.

Religious and Cultural Influence

Kashmir had a very strong tradition of Sanskrit scholarship. Patanjali, the great author of the Mahābhāshya, the commentary on Pānini grammar, was a Kashmiri. He is said to have made contributions also to yoga and to Āyurveda. Some scholars believe that Bharata Muni of the Nātya Shastra was a Kashmiri. Durgā, the commentator on the Nirukta of Yāska, was from the Jammu hills.

Tantra: Shaivism and Vaishnavism. The Kashmiri approach to the world is part of the tantric thought of both Shaivism and Vaishnavism. The Tantras stress the equivalence of the universe and the body and look for divinity within the person. Although the Vaishnavite Pāncharātra now survives only in South India, the earliest teachers looked to Kashmir as the seat of learning and spiritual culture.

According to Kalhana, the twelfth-century Kashmiri historian, author of *Rajatarangini* (Chronicle of kings), one of India's oldest histories, the worship of Shiva in Kashmir dates prior to Mauryan King Ashoka. The Tantras were enshrined in texts known as the Āgamas, most of which are now lost.

Contributions to Buddhism. Kashmir became an early center of Buddhist scholarship. In the first century, the Kushān emperor Kanishka chose Kashmir as the venue of a major Buddhist Council comprising over five hundred monks and scholars. At this meeting, the previously uncodified portions of Buddha's discourses and the theoretical portions of the canon were codified. The entire canon (*Tripitaka*) was inscribed on copper plates and deposited in a stupa, the location of which is now unknown.

Kashmiris were tireless in the spread of Buddhist ideas to Central Asia. Attracted by Kashmir's reputation as a great center of scholarship, many Buddhist monks came from distant lands to learn Sanskrit and to train as translators and teachers. Among these was Kumarajiva (344–413), the son of the Kuchean princess who, when his mother became a nun, followed her into monastic life at the age of seven.

Buddhist Tantric teachers were associated with Kashmir. According to some Tibetan sources, Naropa and Padmasambhava (who introduced Tantric Buddhism to Tibet) were Kashmiris. The Tibetan script is derived from the Kashmiri Shāradā script. It was brought to Tibet by Thonmi-Sambhota, who was sent to Kashmir during the reign of Durlabhavardhana (seventh century) to study with Devatītasimha.

Architecture and the Arts

The ancient temple ruins in Kashmir are some of the oldest standing temples in India today. The sculptures found here are significant and exquisite. The Mārtanda temple, built by Lalitāditya, is one of the earliest and yet largest stone temples to have been built in Kashmir. Lalitāditya also built an enormous *chaitya* in the town of Parihāsapura which housed an enormous Buddha. Only the plinth of this huge monument survives, although one of the paintings at Alchi is believed to be its representation. There was also an enormous stupa in Parihāsapura built by Lalitāditya's minister Chankuna, which may have been even larger than the *chaitya*. The Parihāsapura monuments became models for Buddhist architecture from Afghanistan to Japan. The Pandrethan temple, as well as

the Avantipur complex, provide further examples of the excellence of Kashmiri architecture and art. Kashmiri ivories and metal images are outstanding and are generally considered to be among the best in the world.

Kashmir also had a flourishing tradition of painting, which was used to decorate the temples walls. The earliest surviving examples of these paintings come from Gilgit and date from about the eighth century. Kashmiri artisans were famed for their work, and their hand can be seen in many works of art in Central Asia and Tibet. Painted figures of Bodhisattva Padmapāni from Gilgit demonstrate the mingling of the Gāndhāran and the Gupta Indian conventions with local elements.

After Lalitāditya, Kashmiri style appears to have changed, and the new style endured until the tenth or eleventh century. This phase is the most developed stage of Kashmiri art, and its fame spread into the remote Himalayas. The ninth-century complex of Avantipura built by King Avantivarman (855–883) is an amalgam of various earlier forms from India and regions beyond. The best example of this style is found in the bronzes dated from the ninth to the eleventh century cast by Kashmiri craftsmen for Tibetan patrons. The style of such bronzes presents a remarkable affinity to the wall paintings dating to the tenth or eleventh century that decorate the Buddhist temples of Western Tibet. The wall paintings of Mangnang and the manuscript paintings of Tholing, discovered in Western Tibet, are generally acknowledged to have been created by Kashmiri painters.

One of the best sites to see the Kashmiri painting style is in the five temples comprising the *dharma-mandala* at Alchi in Ladakh, which escaped the destruction that other temples suffered at the hands of a Ladakhi king who embraced Islam. The earliest of these buildings is the Du-khang, where one can see well-preserved *mandala*s that document not only the Kashmiri Buddhist pantheon but the Buddhist representation of the Hindu pantheon as well.

Pahārī painting. Outside Kashmir, there was a new flowering of painting in Basohli in the Jammu hills. By the closing decades of the seventeenth century, these paintings emerged in a steady stream, when a depiction of the Rasa-manjarī, a fifteenth-century poem, was painted during the rule of Kripāl Pāl.

Dance and music. The paintings in Kashmiri style depict the temple dances that prevailed in Kashmir at the time the paintings were made (tenth–eleventh centuries). The only extant complete commentary on the *Nātya Shāstra* is the one by Abhinavagupta. The massive thirteenth-century text *Sangīta-ratnākara* (Ocean of music and dance), composed by the Kashmiri theorist Shārngadeva, is one of the most important landmarks in Indian music history.

Literature. The ninth-century scholar Ānandavardhana, who was a member of the court of the king Avantivarman, wrote the *Dhvanyāloka*, (Light of suggestion), which is a masterpiece of aesthetic theory. Ānandavardhana was the first to note that *rasa*, identified by Bharata in his *Nātya Shāstra* as the "essence" of artistic expression, cannot be communicated directly. This can be done only by *dhvani*, or "suggestion." Abhinavagupta, who lived about a hundred years after Ānandavardhana, wrote a famous commentary on the *Dhvanyāloka* called the *Lochana*. His work on Tantra, the *Tantrāloka* (Light of the Tantras), is one of the most important on the subject. In all, he wrote more than sixty works.

Kshemendra was a philosopher, a poet, and a pupil of Abhinavagupta. Among his books is the *Brihat-kathāmanjari*, which is a summary of Gunādhya's *Brihat-kathā* in 7,500 stanzas. Somadeva's *Kathā-sarit-sāgara* is another version of Gunādhya's *Brihat-kathā*. Somadeva's collection of stories, in 22,000 stanzas with additional prose passages, were written for Queen Sūryamatī, the wife of King Ananta (1028–1063).

The classic arts and the sciences of Kashmir came to an abrupt end when Islam became the dominant force in Kashmir in the fourteenth century. Sculpture, painting, dance, and music could no longer be practiced. The next centuries saw preoccupation with devotion and its expression through the Kashmiri language, as in the poetry of Lalleshvarī.

Many Kashmiris emigrated, as in the case of the musicologist Shārngadeva and the poet Bilhana. Although Kashmir had sunk to a state of conflict and misery, outsiders continued to pay homage to the memory of Kashmir as the land of learning, and Shāradā, the presiding mother goddess of Kashmir, became synonymous with Sarasvatī.

The major poets who followed Lalleshvarī include Habbā Khātūn (c. sixteenth century) and, more recently, Mahjūr (1885–1952), Abdul Ahad Āzād (1903–1948), and Zinda Kaul (1884–1965). Habbā Khātūn is credited with originating the *lol* style of poetry, in which the predominant mood is that of longing and romantic love. Mahjūr, Āzād, and Zinda Kaul and their successors have tried to forge a new sensibility in their poems, but the mystical and the *lol* continue to be the dominant ethos.

The theory and philosophy behind Kashmiri classical music, called Sūfiyāna, is described in two books from the seventeenth and the eighteenth centuries, written in Persian: the anonymous *Karāmat-e mujrā* (The flowering of munificence), and Dayā Rām Kāchroo Khushdil's *Tarānā-e-Sarūr* (The song of joy).

Subhash Kak

See also **Kashmir; Pakistan**

BIBLIOGRAPHY

Bamzai, Prithivi Nath Kaul. *A History of Kashmir*. Delhi: Metropolitan, 1962.
Dyczkowski, Mark S. F. *The Doctrine of Vibration*. Albany: State University of New York Press, 1987.
Huntington, Susan. *The Art of Ancient India*. New York: Weatherhill, 1985.
Jaitly, Jaya, ed. *Crafts of Kashmir, Jammu, and Ladakh*. New York: Abbeville Press, 1990.
Kak, Ram Chandra. *Ancient Monuments of Kashmir*. London: India Society, 1933.
Stein, M. Aurel. *Kalhana's* Rajatarangini. 1900. Reprint, Delhi: Motilal Banarsidass, 1979.

JAMMU AND LADAKH The Valley of Kashmir frequently occupies a central place in discussions about the political status of Jammu and Kashmir, whether within or outside India. However, the valley is only one of three regions of the state—each defined by distinct geographical, historical, and cultural backgrounds. Since the partition of India and the accession of the state of Jammu and Kashmir to the Indian state, the regions of Jammu and Ladakh have consistently pursued their own politics of identity in relation to the valley, yet they remain shadowed by the latter's demands for autonomy and freedom from the Indian state.

According to the Census of India of 2001, the total population of Jammu and Kashmir stood at 10.07 million. As no regular census was held in the state due to the secessionist movement, the population figures were "interpolated" by the Office of the Registrar General of India. According to these 2001 census estimates, 54 percent of the state's population resides in the valley, 43.7 percent in the Jammu region, and 2.3 percent in Ladakh. While the valley's population is 94 percent Muslim, the populations of the other two regions are less homogeneous. Jammu is 66 percent Hindu, 30 percent Muslim, and 4 percent Sikh. Dogri is its major language, although Gojari, Pahari, and Punjabi are also spoken. In Ladakh, Buddhists and Muslims are almost evenly divided. Buddhists, who constitute 52 percent of its population, are concentrated in the Leh district, while Muslims (48 percent; largely Shi'a), live in the district of Kargil. The major language of Ladakh is Ladakhi or Bodhi. Other languages spoken are Balti, Dardi, and Shina.

In 1947, after Indian independence and the partition of India, the Indian state faced the challenging task of nation building and integrating the princely states into the nation-state. In the process, the Indian political elite arrogated to itself the power to define Kashmiri identity and in so doing profoundly affected the process by which the collective identities of the Kashmir's Hindus and Muslims, Ladakh's Buddhists, and Jammu's Hindus were

Ladakh Landscape. With one of the lowest population densities in the world, Ladakh is a land of bewitching silence, its rocky desert framed by the imposing, seemingly inhospitable, Karakorams to the north and Himalayas to the south. IPSHITA BARUA.

constructed and maintained. The maharaja of Kashmir signed the Instrument of Accession in October 1947 when his troops were no longer able to defend the state from tribal aggression from the North-West Frontier province of Pakistan. The Indian state created two legal categories in its Constitution in Article 370, affirming a special status for the state of Jammu and Kashmir in the Indian federation and reaffirming the state-subject requirements whereby employment and ownership of property were to remain the exclusive prerogative of citizens of Jammu and Kashmir. The origin of these legal categories lay in the nationalist discourse developed by Sheikh Mohammad Abdullah's 1939 mass-based, secular, and socialist nationalist movement against the Dogra ruler. Through the legal and constitutional categories underlined in the Delhi Agreement and finally in Article 370 of the Indian Constitution, the Indian state simultaneously embraced and denied its differences from Kashmiri society. While it recognized the cultural and political identity of the Kashmiri people and defined them as distinct, it also asserted that the similarities between Kashmir and the Indian state were based on their compatible secular, socialist, and democratic agendas.

Jammu

In the construction of the Kashmir nation, however, the Indian state privileged the collective memory and history of the Kashmiri Muslims at the cost of denying the history and stifling the politics of the Hindu and Buddhist populations of Jammu and Ladakh, respectively. India's political leadership completely ignored the latter regions' desire for full integration with India. As far as Jammu was concerned, there were two underlying reasons for that. First, the ruler against whom the Kashmiri nationalist movement was carried out was a (Hindu) Dogra, and guilt by association certainly played a part in the Indian state's indifferent attitude toward Jammu. Second, Jammu's loyalty to India was taken for granted. Given its large Hindu population and its awkward geographical location, Jammu had no choice but loyalty to the Indian state, since its future was secure only within Hindu-dominated India.

Jammu's response to the denial of political and legal space to its Hindu community within the articulated Kashmiri identity has been twofold. On the one hand, a minority has expressed itself through Hindu nationalist symbols and has actively supported the Indian Hindu party (Bharatiya Jan Sangh, later the Bharatiya Janata Party) in the cause of fully integrating Kashmir within the Indian state by abolishing Article 370 of the Indian Constitution. According to these Hindu nationalists, Article 370 disallows Kashmiri citizens from being emotionally attached to the Indian nation. On the other hand, a much larger group also seeks emotional and political recognition and a space for itself within the formally articulated and constructed Kashmiri identity, but has supported the Kashmiri demand for the recognition and maintenance of its distinctness. However, it is not willing to sever Jammu and Kashmir state's links with India.

The Jammu and Kashmir Praja Parishad, which had been formed in 1947 with the support of leading RSS (Rashtriya Swayamsevak Sangh) workers, took up Jammu's cause for the state's complete accession to and total integration with India. By 1951 Praja Parishad had emerged as the principal opposition party, and the only party representing Jammu's Hindus as well as the refugees who had migrated from West Pakistan and Pakistan-occupied Kashmir. The party drew support from the leading Hindu nationalist parties in India such as Hindu Mahasabha, Ram Rajya Parishad, and Bharatiya Jan Sangh. In 1952 it began its most vocal and aggressive agitation demanding the abrogation of Article 370, full integration of the state into the Indian union, full application of the Indian Constitution, complete jurisdiction of the Supreme Court, and removal of customs barriers between Kashmir and India. Over the next few months, Jammu's streets echoed with Praja Parishad's slogan of *Ek Vidhan, Ek Nishan, Aur Ek Pradhan* (One constitution, one flag and one head of the state). Jammu's Hindu population was effectively mobilized by Praja Parishad. Consequently, when the first assembly elections took place in 1957 (after the promulgation of the new constitution for the state), the Praja Parishad received 52 and 43 percent of the total votes polled in the urban constituencies of Jammu and Udhampur, respectively, the party's strongholds. The National Conference, Abdullah's ruling party, successfully competed for Jammu's votes, however, and was able to secure twenty-four out of its thirty seats.

Since then, Jammu's main grievance has been that the state government has consistently discriminated against Jammu in favor of Kashmir in terms of development, representation in the civil service and the Cabinet, and the provision of higher educational facilities. Since the mid-1960s, both the Kashmir and Indian governments have taken note of Jammu's grievances. The Gajendragadhar Commission was appointed in 1967 to inquire into complaints of regional imbalance in developmental programs and recruitment policies. The commission, in its 1968 report, recommended equal representation of Jammu in the state cabinet, the establishment of a full-fledged university, medical college, and regional engineering college in Jammu, the establishment of a statutory State Development Board, and the creation of regional development boards for each of the three regions. Except for the establishment of Jammu University and a medical college, none of the commission's recommendations was implemented. In 1979 the state government appointed the Sikri Commission to review Jammu's consistent complaints of discrimination. In August 1980 the commission once again recognized regional imbalances and made specific recommendations in developmental policies and programs, recruitment policies, and admission to professional institutions. Since that time, several of Jammu's demands have been met, particularly in regard to development, political representation in the state government, and the establishment of professional institutions; a strong feeling still prevails among Jammu's population, however, that the central government in India has largely taken for granted their unflagging patriotism and Indian nationalism.

Ladakh

Despite knowledge of the cultural identity of the Buddhist population of Ladakh, India's leaders, in determining the Indian state's relations with Jammu and Kashmir, have consistently tended to ignore that region's aspirations. After the partition of India, the Buddhists in Ladakh perceived their historic association with the state of Jammu and Kashmir as having come to an end: they had been annexed by the Dogras in 1842, and now, with the maharaja's transfer of power to the National Conference, they felt they deserved to reacquire their full sovereignty. However, in their own larger interests and those of India, they agreed to continue to remain part of the state. The demands of Ladakh's Buddhist population have ranged from recognition of the community as scheduled tribes, to the granting of quasi-autonomous Frontier, Union Territory, or Autonomous Hill Region status.

During the very early days of the interim regime of Sheikh Abdullah, the relationship between the Buddhist population of Ladakh and the Kashmir government turned both acrimonious and fragile. The Buddhist Ladakhis have consistently complained about the Kashmir government's discriminatory attitude toward the region in terms of administrative and political representation in state institutions, a lack of economic development, and the denial of their cultural and linguistic identity. In addition, they have accused the state government of communalizing their politics by dividing the region into two districts, a Buddhist majority Leh and a Muslim majority Kargil. Fearing their assimilation into a

Muslim-dominated state and the conversion of their status into a minority, the Buddhists have consequently insisted upon the protection of their distinct religion and culture by seeking closer relations with India's central government.

On 4 May 1949, Chhewang Rgzin Kloan, president of the Buddhist Association, presented a memorandum to Prime Minister Jawaharlal Nehru, unequivocally declaring that Ladakh could not be bound by the decision of a plebiscite that might be held to decide Kashmir's accession to India. Kaushok Bakola, the head lama and the most vocal advocate of central administration for Ladakh, challenged the legality of the state government's jurisdiction over the region. In general, Ladakh complained of discrimination, police brutality (most of the police force was from the Kashmir region), conversion of the Buddhist population to Islam and Christianity, and finally, threats to the *gompa*s (Buddhist monasteries) through the implementation of land reforms.

During the 1960s, the Kashmir government made some efforts to respond to some specific Ladakhi demands, but the communal divide between Buddhists and Muslims had begun to sharpen. In April 1969, when a Buddist flag was desecrated by a Muslim, the Buddhist Action committee started an agitation for the central government to grant Union Territory status to Ladahk, a demand completely opposed by Kashmir's chief minister G. M. Sadiq. Continued communal problems between the two religious communities caused Bakola to reassert his demand that the region be centrally administered, while Chief Minister Sadiq, in turn, minimized the Ladakhi agitation as merely a "law and order" problem. The government and the Buddhist leaders attempted to negotiate Ladakh's demands for proper educational and health facilities and an increased share of the administrative and economic budget. The Jammu and Kashmir government acknowledged that there was a need to invest more resources in the region and, in 1973, Mir Kasim became the first chief minister of the state to visit Ladakh. The situation changed in 1977 with the reentry into Kashmir politics of Sheikh Abdullah. The Ladakhi Buddhists intensified their demands for the region to be centrally administered. The situation got much worse in 1979, when Ladakh was bifurcated into two districts, Leh and Kargil, for administrative purposes. The Buddhist leaders blamed Sheikh Abdullah for destroying the cohesiveness and the secular image of the region. The two districts began to select candidates from their respective majority religious faiths. The Buddhist-majority Leh chose the Congress candidate, supporting Ladakh's integration with India, and the Muslim-majority Kargil elected the National Conference candidate, supporting the cause of the valley's Muslims.

The All-Party Ladakh Action Committee launched an agitation in 1981 and 1982 for the declaration of the entire people of Ladakh as a "scheduled tribe." It was only in 1984 that G. M. Shah, in his brief stint as Kashmir's chief minister, recommended to the government of India to grant tribal status to eight selected Ladakhi ethnic groups, and it was not until 1991, in response to another serious agitation by the Buddhist community two years earlier, that the formal order to implement the decision was issued. Finally, after prolonged talks between the government of India, the state government, and the Ladakh Buddhist Association, an Autonomous Hill council was approved on 9 October 1993 for Leh, and a similar one for Kargil, which would be operational only when the population of the latter desired. On the whole, as the Indian state constructed the Kashmiri nation on the narrow premise of the Kashmiri Muslim identity, the economic and identity-related demands of the Ladakhi Buddhists and Jammu's Hindus remain less than fully satisfied.

Reeta Chowdhari Tremblay

See also **Kashmir**

BIBLIOGRAPHY

Behera, Navnita Chadha. *State, Identity and Violence: Jammu and Kashmir and Ladakh*. New Delhi: Manohar, 2000.

Kaul, Shridar, and H. N. Kaul. *Ladakh through the Ages: Towards a New Identity*. New Delhi: Indus Publishing Company, 1995.

Puri, Balraj. *Simmering Volcano: Study of Jammu's Relations with Kashmir*. New Delhi: Reliance Publishing House, 1983.

———. *Jammu and Kashmi: Regional Autonomy (A Report)*. Jammu: Jay Kay Book House, 1999.

Tremblay, Reeta Chowdhari. "Jammu: Autonomy within an Autonomus Kashmir?" In *Perspectives on Kashmir: The Roots of Conflict in South Asia*, edited by Raju G. C. Thomas. Boulder, Colo.: Westview Press, 1992.

JAMSHEDPUR A city in the state of Jharkhand, Jamshedpur's population was 1 million in 2001. It is named after Jamsetji N. Tata, a Parsi industrialist. Tata had built several cotton textile mills before deciding to take the risk of establishing a steel mill in India. Since India is rich in coal and iron ore, it presented a natural advantage for the development of steel industry. Because British steel dominated the Indian market, Tata turned to U.S. engineers for advice on setting up his mill. Though he died before the mill was started, his sons Dorab and Ratan managed to raise the huge amount of capital required for the enterprise. Fifteen Indian maharajas were among the investors. Tata Iron and Steel Company (TISCO) was founded in 1907; the village

Sakchi in Singbhum District, close to the iron ore deposits, was chosen as the site for the mill. In 1908 TISCO acquired 3,584 acres around Sakchi and thus became a large landowner. For the future development of the steel city, this was a great boon, as municipal government and city planning remained under control of the company.

TISCO started operating its first blast furnace in 1911. The venture could still have turned out to be a costly flop, but then World War I cut off trade links with Europe. TISCO now had to supply the entire Indian market; it also received British orders, for example for the Mesopotamian railway that was built for strategic reasons during the war. In 1919 Sakchi was given its new name, Jamshedpur, and became a veritable boom town. Wartime profits were invested in an expansion of the steel mill. But then a new challenge emerged, as cheap Belgian and German steel flooded the Indian market. In 1924 the British government of India imposed a protective tariff on steel with a preferential rate for British steel. TISCO survived and prospered once more during World War II. Since the supply of locomotives for Indian railways was cut off during the war, TELCO (Tata Engine and Locomotive Co.) was established at Jamshedpur in 1944. Later, TELCO became the major producer of trucks in India, initially in cooperation with Daimler-Benz (Mercedes), but then expanding rapidly on its own. In independent India, heavy industry was reserved for the public sector. TISCO was not nationalized, but it was not permitted to expand. This also constrained the growth of Jamshedpur, which could otherwise have emerged as an industrial metropolis even earlier than Bangalore.

Dietmar Rothermund

BIBLIOGRAPHY

Dutta, Maya. *Jamshedpur: The Growth of the City and Its Regions.* Kolkata: Asiatic Society, 1977.
Misra, Babu Ram. *Report on Socio-Economic Survey of Jamshedpur City.* Patna: Patna University, 1959.
Vishwakarma, Y. B. *Industrialization and Tribal Ecology: Jamshedpur and Its Environs.* Jaipur: Rawat, 1991.

JANATA DAL. *See* **Political System.**

JAPAN, RELATIONS WITH India and Japan had little mutual knowledge or appreciation of one another before the 1990s. India's policy of nonalignment—with a Moscow tilt—contrasted sharply with Japan's role as the bastion of U.S. forward deployment in the Asia-Pacific region. The Japanese were irritated at what they perceived as airs of sanctimonious superiority among Indians; the Indians were unimpressed by Japan's materialistic drive to economic growth. The persistence of poverty in India and the successful drive to prosperity in Japan changed the basis of their bilateral relationship. A more recent economic slump in Japan and the reemergence of India as a formidable power are once again redefining their relations.

The relative aloofness between the two countries is evident in the paucity of prime ministerial visits. Japanese prime ministers Nobusuke Kishi and Hayato Ikeda visited India in 1957 and 1961, respectively. The next such visit, by Yasuhiro Nakasone, did not take place until 1984, followed by Toshiki Kaifu in 1990, and Yoshiro Mori ten years later. In the other direction, Indian prime ministers Jawaharlal Nehru and Indira Gandhi visited Japan in 1957 and 1969, respectively, Rajiv Gandhi in 1985 and 1988, P. V. Narasimha Rao in 1992, and Atal Bihari Vajpayee in 2002.

Political and Security Relations

Japan's presence in South Asia is not constrained by memories of wartime hostilities and atrocities. Since India has been relevant neither to Japan's security nor to its international economic strategy, New Delhi has figured little in Tokyo's foreign policy priorities. Yet some of India's diplomatic endeavors have ensured that it would not be totally ignored by Japan: its support for reintegrating Japan into the world community after World War II, its invitation to Japan to take part in the first Asian games in New Delhi in 1951, and the establishment of diplomatic relations in 1952.

India interpreted Japan's role in the Asia-Pacific region from a macrostrategic perspective, as a regional balancer to China. Not having shared the rest of Asia-Pacific's experience of aggressive Japanese militarism, India was more welcoming of the prospect of a militarily resurgent Japan that would keep China's attention focused to its east. Even at the Tokyo War Crimes Tribunal after World War II, the Indian judge dissented from the verdict that Japanese leaders were guilty of having committed war crimes. But the Indian wish for a Japanese strategic counterweight to China remained unfulfilled because of the carefully nurtured relationship between Beijing and Tokyo, which is more important to both than either's relationship with India.

India's nuclear explosions in 1988 at Pokhran-II cast a long shadow on Delhi-Tokyo relations. While Japan has supported the antinuclear cause from within the nuclear Nonproliferation Treaty (NPT), India has been the NPT's most prominent critic. Indians underestimate the depth and breadth of Japanese nuclear revulsion and the sense of sadness and betrayal that the land of the

Prime Minister A. B. Vajpayee with Prime Minister Yoshiro Mori of Japan. Then Prime Minister A. B. Vajpayee (left) welcomes Prime Minister Yoshiro Mori of Japan. Mori's five-day visit to India in August 2000 helped to soften the diplomatic impasse that had long existed between the two nations. INDIA TODAY.

Buddha, Mahatma Gandhi, and Nehru should have embraced nuclear weapons. India insists, however, that each country must make its own decision on reconciling tensions between its commitment to international idealism and the requirements of national security. Prime Minister Mori's five-day visit to India in August 2000 helped to soften the impasse. Opinion toward India became a bit more sympathetic in 2003, when reports of Pakistan's export of nuclear technology to North Korea (in return for long-range missile technology, whose object could only be India) were published.

The competition between New Delhi and Tokyo for permanent membership on the United Nations (UN) Security Council could be converted into cooperation, since their credentials and political constituencies are complementary. Japan is an industrialized nonnuclear country whose status as the world's largest aid donor is in contrast to constitutional restrictions on the use of military force abroad. India, a developing country with nuclear weapons, has contributed more personnel to UN peacekeeping than any other country. While Japan relies principally on economic instruments to pursue foreign policy, India has developed diplomatic tools to offset its

lack of economic muscle in world affairs. In the annual session of the UN General Assembly in September 2004, India and Japan joined Brazil and Germany in pressing for permanent membership of the Security Council for all four countries.

Trade and Economic Relations

Historical and linguistic ties to the West, economic policies of import-substitution and protectionism, and a foreign policy of close relations with the Soviet Union kept India at a distance from Japan, whose importance increased with its enlarged role as an aid donor. Official aid to India has been part of a broader long-term government strategy of promoting Japanese business interests through a policy of maintaining low-cost official contacts in developing countries, until such time as they become more hospitable to foreign trade and investment.

While Japanese foreign aid to India increased, there was no commensurate increase in Japanese trade and investment, despite Japan's status as the world's largest capital exporter. By the 1990s, Japanese investment in China was about twenty times more than in India; only

0.3 percent of Japan's direct investment abroad in 1990 had gone to India. Ambassador Shunji Kobayashi delivered an unusually blunt address to an Indian audience in 1991. Noting that trade with India had fallen from 2.5 percent of total Japanese trade in 1960 to 0.7 percent in 1990, he urged India toward greater domestic and international competition. The Japanese were discouraged in part by the social and political instability of South Asia, but the main deterrents were India's restrictive foreign capital laws and the miles of "red tape" that confronted foreign investors.

The Indian economy has since then been progressively opened to international competition, of course, and has grown at a rate second only to China among the major countries. Complementary economic needs and strengths could provide a firm basis for substantial strengthening of bilateral relations. India's vast middle class offers a stable and expanding market, and its thriving information technology sector is of great interest to Japan. India also has a track record of adapting its management styles to match new technology. For India, Japan continues to be attractive as a major aid donor, a capital surplus economy, and a large trading nation with a huge export market.

On the security side, Tokyo's defense establishment awoke to the potential for military cooperation with India after a Japanese cargo ship, captured by pirates in the Indian Ocean, was rescued by Indian naval forces in 1999. India could thus prove helpful in safeguarding critical sea-lanes for Japan's oil imports across the Indian Ocean. In September 2003 the two countries held their fourth annual joint maritime search-and-rescue and anti-piracy exercises. The future of Indo-Japanese relations thus appears to be much more vital than in the past.

Ramesh Thakur

BIBLIOGRAPHY

Jain, Purnendra. "Japan and South Asia: Between Cooperation and Confrontation." In *Japan's Foreign Policy Today: A Reader*, edited by Inoguchi Takashi and Purnendra Jain. London: Palgrave Macmillan, 2000.

Jaishankar, S. "India-Japan Relations after Pokhran II." *Seminar* 487 (March 2000): 44–55.

Kesavan, K. V., and Lalima Verma, eds. *Japan and South Asia*. New Delhi: Har-Anand Publications, 2000.

Narasimhamurthy, P. A. *India and Japan: Dimensions of Their Relations*. 3 vols. New Delhi: ABC Publication House, 1998.

Shigeyuki, Abe. "Contributing to Development in South Asia." *Japan Echo* 20 (1993): 64–71.

Thakur, Ramesh, and Dipankar Banerjee. "India: Democratic, Poor, Internationalist." In *Democratic Accountability and the Use of Force in International Law*, edited by Charlotte Ku. Cambridge, U.K., and New York: Cambridge University Press, 2003.

JATI. *See* **Caste System.**

JESUITS. *See* **Christian Impact on India, History of.**

JEWELRY Several countries can boast of a period when their culture produced outstanding jewelry, but none can surpass the vitality of India's output, which has spanned over three thousand years. Physical evidence brought to light at Indian archaeological sites in the Indus Valley, such as Mohenjo-Daro (2500–1700 B.C.), support this claim. Necklaces, bracelets, bangles, rings, beads, and other forms of ornaments made in gold, silver, copper, stone, ceramic, proto-glass, and other materials were unearthed there, revealing that the material culture at that early period included an extensive use of personal ornaments. Other finds elsewhere in the Indian subcontinent support the premise that Indians adopted the concept of body ornamentation at an even earlier date. To these physical remains we must add the many later literary references to jewelry, highly sophisticated written treatises on gemstones, and the existence of epigraphic inscriptions concerning the donation of jewelry to a temple, such as those that occur in profusion on the eighth-century Rajaraja temple at Thanjavur in South India.

Ethnic Jewelry

The unique creative genius that constitutes Indian civilization permeates all aspects of its expressive arts, including jewelry. Following a recognized pattern of development, over time, the contributions of many individual artisans coalesce, and the results take on a unique character that becomes identifiable with the group or place where they were initiated. When, in the creation of artifacts, governing concepts of technology, form, and design are retained, repeated, and developed, the results become a physical aspect of the material culture in which they originated. When seen by others outside that culture, such concepts are perceived to possess original and unique qualities, and these become associated with the creators. Such a group is designated as a specific ethnic entity, which can consist of relatively few (a tribal group), many (a regional class), or an entire nation. The traditional jewelry of India is an outstanding example of ethnic jewelry characterized by unique, unmistakable regional styles.

Religion and Jewelry

Religion has always been a dominant factor in the use of Indian jewelry, and its attributed protective purpose was probably its original function. This is especially apparent in the widespread practice of wearing amulets

Gold Necklace. Nineteenth-century gold necklace (*kazhuththu uru*), from Pudukkottai, Tamil Nadu, South India. Worn by a Chettiar bride at her wedding and again on celebrating the 60th birthday of her husband. Unique in its traditional use by the mercantile Chettiar community. TOMMY CARAWAY, NEW YORK.

and using rosaries, both of which are normally carried visibly on the body. Their use is universal and stems from a common belief in the supernatural, whose dire effects the amulet is meant to repel or control. The most usual amuletic function is to counteract potentially disastrous encounters with the evil eye. Made in many materials, amulets must be consecrated and activated by a priest. They can then be worn on the body and put to use. Thereafter they are normally never removed.

Another example, the rosary, is a handheld prayer counting device in the form of strung beads. When not in use, it may be worn on the neck or coiled around the left wrist. Widely used by the followers of all religions in India, the rosary is a means of acquiring merit by the recitation of prayers invoking a specific deity. Count of the recitations is noted by means of passing the beads through the fingers. Prayer recitation is a daily practice necessary to earn the ultimate reward of a future existence in the postmortal world (Nirvāna for Hindus, Paradise for Muslims, and the Western Paradise for Buddhists). Hindu rosaries have 100 beads; those of Muslims have 99, and Buddhists, 108. All these are made in a variety of materials that among Hindus and Buddhists is often one related by tradition to a particular deity and chosen for use for that or other reasons. Rosary materials include natural organic substances, such as sections of dried basilica stems (a plant sacred to Vishnu), various hard seeds, stones (including gemstones), glass, silver, and even gold.

Social Identity and Practices

Certain forms of jewelry are worn by particular groups to indicate to others their religion and caste, the latter concept still operative in India though legally banned. These forms become familiar to others, as is their significance. Aside from form, the particular material used for jewelry also becomes an important factor because ideas and specific symbolism are associated with them. Thus a wearer of gold jewelry automatically acquires a higher social status than one using silver, a less precious metal. This is most evident in making a distinction between the gold-wearing urban and silver-wearing rural people. Using a traditional jewelry form, normally made in silver, but ordered by the user to be made in gold, is another way of achieving and indicating high social status.

Until recent times, it was common to see rural women publicly wearing considerable amounts of jewelry. In effect, these possessions represented the surplus earnings of the family, transformed into ornaments acquired when economic circumstances permitted and, for reasons of safety, worn on the body. Rural economy, however, is subject to vicissitudes of reliability, often depending on natural causes such as monsoon success or failure. Investment in jewelry is a form of family security; when necessary, jewelry can be sold to assure survival from a natural or man-made disaster.

According to texts such as the Kāma Sūtra, which among other subjects discusses concepts of feminine beauty, the ideal woman must wear the types of ornament prescribed for her social condition. As a means of achieving this, the dowry system evolved and became a necessity at the time of marriage, an event considered to be the most important of one's lifetime. By universal practice, the two families must arrive at a mutually acceptable agreement, which in most Indian societies involves providing a bride with a specified weight of precious metal jewelry. The amount varies according to the economic condition of the families involved. This jewelry is generally termed the bride's *stridana* (*stri*, meaning "woman"; *dana*, meaning gifts). In theory it remains her sole property to dispose of as she wishes. In practice it may be used as a means of family survival when by necessity, the wife may allow it to be sold.

Indian jewelry can be classified into typological groups based upon broad geographic areas (Himalayan, North Indian, South Indian) and within these places classes that use it. These divisions simultaneously reveal the overall hieratic organization and complexity of Indian society. Each group has its own characteristic cultural concepts, resides in communally or geographically concentrated locations, and employs its own culturally evolved types of traditional ornaments. The most primitive groups, whose culture until recently harkens back to Neolithic times, are tribal peoples, who generally live in relatively isolated locations. By far the largest group, comprising at least 70 percent of the over 1 billion total population of India, is the rural agriculturalist contingent. At the economic apex of Indian society are the growing middle and upper classes, the latter in former days the royal sector. In reality, a degree of interaction of jewelry design concepts occurs among these categories which at times results in the appearance of some hybrid artifacts.

Materials Used and Their Origins

In the history of the development of personal ornament by humankind, the earliest materials used are believed to have been substances available in the immediate environment. These include many types of fibers, grasses, wood, flowers, seeds, mica, shells, gourds, feathers, stones, and sometimes metals. In modern times in India, the use of such materials characterizes the ornaments of tribal groups such as the Nagas of northeastern India Though tribal groups usually reside in remote areas, they were never totally isolated, and other nonindigenous materials, such as metals, came to them by trade. In some cases, unique metal tribal ornaments were made to their specifications by nontribal artisans who worked in or near tribal territory and catered to tribal demands. Glass beads of various types are also widely used; these also arrived through trade from their centers of manufacture, which were often great distances away from the place of their eventual use.

An example of the above is a special material and an important ornamental element used by most tribal people, but especially by Naga groups: hard-stone beads. For more than two thousand years, utilizing an unchanged manual technology, the manufacture of drilled hard-stone beads of a variety of stones and forms continues in many workshops of bead-making artisans at Khambat, Gujarat, in western India, and have since antiquity been widely distributed.

Metals. Metals of several kinds are a major element of jewelry in general. India is rich in iron (in very limited use, however, for ornaments in India), but the inadequate indigenous production of copper and its alloys, brass and bronze (widely used by tribal people for ornament), had to be supplemented by the import trade. The precious metals, silver and gold, whose local production was never sufficient to meet the enormous demand, since antiquity have constituted important foreign import products. As long ago as Roman times, and probably longer, the much sought after Indian spices and textiles were, by the demand of Indian merchants, paid for in foreign silver

Nineteenth-Century Gold Hand Ornament (*hathphul*) with Diamonds. The hand ornament's ring (*arsi*) is mounted with a small round mirror. Typically, such a piece is elaborately polychrome-enameled with an intricate floral and bird design on the reverse side (never seen), which is characteristic of work crafted in this North Indian Rajput-Mughal style. COURTESY AIR INDIA, MUMBAI.

and gold bullion or coinage, hidden hoards of which have been uncovered in archaeological excavations. Voluminous import of the precious metals continues even today, giving India the reputation of being the world's largest consumer of the precious metals, most of which are converted into jewelry.

Gemstones. Hard stones used in Indian jewelry are divided into two categories: the semiprecious variety, in Sanskrit termed *uparatnani* (minor gemstones); and the precious ones, termed *maharatnani* (major gemstones). India is fortunate in its natural possession of many of both kinds. Deposits of semiprecious hard stones such as agates (which include carnelian, bloodstone, chalcedony, moss agate, and onyx), garnet (almandite and uvarovite), rose quartz, apatite, rhodonite, and tourmaline exist in quantity. Most of these are used for beads, and less frequently are set to ornament jewelry.

Beryl (emerald) and corundum (sapphire) also exist, but of the precious gemstones, the most important is diamond (which, followed by ruby, emerald, sapphire, and pearl, comprise the five classical gemstones used in upper-class Indian jewelry, especially since Mughal

times). Until 1726, when diamond deposits were discovered in Brazil, India was the world's principal producer of diamonds. Jean-Baptiste Tavernier, a seventeenth-century French gemstone merchant who made six journeys to India mainly to purchase diamonds, recorded that enormous quantities came from several highly productive mines located in the Kingdom of Golconda in the Deccan. These mines were intensely worked until their exhaustion in the eighteenth century. Eventually South Africa and Russia emerged as the main diamond producers while Indian production today is negligible. The regular faceting of diamonds, on the other hand, has become an important industry centered in Mumbai and Surat. This technology now provides India with a means of earning foreign exchange. India today is a world leader in diamond faceting, exceeded only by the Netherlands and Israel.

Other gemstones that were not available domestically were regularly imported. Of primary importance among these is ruby, followed by emerald (found only recently in India) and the prolific pearl. In an annual monsoon-dependent trade, rubies came to India from the Mogok mines of Burma (Myanmar), which are still active. This trade originated in South India, from where wind-borne boats regularly seasonally crossed the Bay of Bengal. Mostly small rubies, rounded by attrition, became available in prodigious amounts, and as a result, with minimal polishing could be profusely used in a single ornament. This circumstance to a great extent determined the character of an extensively produced class of South Indian gold jewelry. Today, because of trade difficulties and high cost, synthetic ruby manufacture has been firmly established in India to supply the ongoing demand.

Emeralds have always been utilized in Indian ornament. Their original main source was Egypt, but in the sixteenth century, Spanish and Portuguese conquistadores in the New World discovered and exploited the highly productive Chivor and other emerald mines of Colombia, still the world's main source. Exported in extraordinary amounts to Europe, they were then brought to the colonial Portuguese-Indian enclave of Goa, which, with its existing Indian diamond trade, became a precious gemstone entrepôt. Indian Mughal dynasty rulers and their courtiers especially favored the intense green of emerald (a propitious color associated with Islam), endowed this gemstone with mystical, prophylactic powers, and utilized it widely in their highly idiomatic style of jewelry.

Pearls, a ready-made, popular natural mollusk product needing only to be drilled, have been extensively used in Indian jewelry from ancient times through the present. The proximity of their prolific sources in the Gulf of

Manar, between India and Sri Lanka (Ceylon), and Basra in the Persian Gulf facilitated their availability.

Semiprecious gemstones were also in wide use. Contributing to their employment is the concept of the nine planetary gemstones (*nava ratna*), in which the nine different stones were frequently used as a group, mounted in one object. References to this concept occur as early as the thirteenth century. In this belief system, each of the nine planetary or celestial entities in the then known universe is assigned a gemstone. According to the widespread belief in astrology, every planet is thought to exert a positive or negative influence on the life of every individual born at the time of its ascendancy, a fact calculated by an astrologer for every child at birth and carefully preserved on paper thereafter. This calculation of compatibility becomes a strong factor in choosing jewelry that contains a gemstone.

For those unable to afford ornaments set with gemstones, glass substitutes are treated in the same manner as precious stones, that is, cut into cabochon, rounded, or dome shapes, but not faceted forms. To heighten their brilliance, such transparent "stones" were backed by a polished, shining metal foil, sometimes colored to increase its resemblance to a genuine gemstone. Glass mirrors are also set as gemstones, an outstanding example being their use in a ring (*arsi*) generally worn on the left thumb.

Gemstone settings. India developed a unique system for the setting of gemstones, which when present can serve to identify the origin of some Indian jewelry. Known as the *kundan* style (meaning "pure gold"), the system is used to set gemstones in metal or stone substrates such as jade. In this technique, a depression or opening is made to conform to the shape of the gemstone (or glass "stone") being set. This depression is filled with lac (the Indian term for a natural resin exuded by an insect—*tachardia lacca*—on the branches of its host tree during its life cycle). A backing sheet of polished metal foil is placed over the lac. While the stone is held in the depression, a strip of pure gold (*kundun*) is forced around its perimeter with a stylus. Because pure gold is soft enough to be manipulated simply by pressure, the result, a raised surrounding ridge of gold, firmly fixes the gemstone in place

Jewelry Making

Jewelry making starts with the training of an apprentice. Until recent times, this was probably a boy belonging to a jeweler's family, or a relative whose caste was that of the jeweler (*sonar*). Beginning at an early childhood age, the apprentice is trained by his family in the simpler tasks, which increase in complexity with his acquisition of

skills. Ultimately, after several years, the trainee becomes a full-fledged gold- or silversmith. Each workshop, whether a family unit or, as in recent times, a cooperative of many workers, is headed by a leader (*ustad*) or master craftsman, under whose direction work proceeds. Large workshops are often owned by an entrepreneur (Mahajan or Saraf) who decides what is to be made according to demand, provides his hired workers with materials, and either sells the results directly or wholesale to other jewelry dealers. There are believed to be over 2 million artisans currently making jewelry in India.

Fabrication techniques. The nature of metal jewelry fabrication is such that the basic techniques employed have not changed since the time when this technology began. Indian jewelers work with what their Western counterparts consider to be the most elemental tools. Yet, despite this seeming limitation, through the ages they have produced, and continue to make, masterpieces of the jeweler's art.

Jewelry fabrication processes have developed from the necessity to employ the elemental forms of metal available to every jeweler: wire, sheet metal, and bulk metal, the latter used for the casting process. The dominating use of the first two forms, wire or sheet metal, at specific locations has resulted in jewelry designs that exploit the possibilities inherent in these forms of metal. Thus, for example, torques constructed totally of wrapped and coiled wire are made in Rajasthan and Gujarat; and low relief repoussage transforms flat sheet metal into decorated dimensional forms in Uttar Pradesh and places too numerous to mention here.

Some uniquely Indian specialized decorative metalwork processes have evolved, and their use in many cases has become associated with a particular place of manufacture. Among these are the granulation technique used in Gujarat; the *babul kam* ("acacia thorn work," small projecting gold "thorns" that cover a surface) of the Punjab; *thewa* work (pierced gold foil units fused on glass) of Partabgarh, Rajasthan; the enamel work of Jaipur, Rajasthan; and the aforementioned, widely practiced *kundan* style of gemstone setting in universal use.

Mughal Style Jewelry

The styles of jewelry produced in India are extremely varied, and as mentioned, many can be associated with the geographic area of their origin. Thus the jewelry of the Himalayan area, North India, and South India are stylistically distinctive. Only recently have these general differences been recognized and given the attention they deserve. One North Indian style of design also practiced as far south as the Deccan is the so-called Mughal style. This today should rightfully be designated the

Silver Headband from South India. From South India, silver headband (*thalaikkachchu*) to adorn a sacred bull (Nandi). Madras (Chennai), Tamil Nadu, nineteenth century. Its sections are ornamented with repoussage and chasing, and set with glass "stones." TIMO RIPATTI, HELSINKI.

Mughal-Rajput style since it originated during the Mughal period but is now practiced in places such as Jaipur, Jodhpur, and Bikaner (all in Rajasthan). This style has become so well known worldwide that for most Western people it represents Indian style in general to the exclusion of other, lesser known but equally interesting styles. Accounting for this popularity may be its prolific use of gemstones as well as the highly skillful application of polychrome enamel (usually on the reverse, unseen side of the ornament), resulting in objects of seductive opulence. Perhaps also operative in this world perception of what constitutes Indian design is the romanticized association of this style with the fabled wealth of the Mughal court, reflected in the rich appearance of new work in this design idiom. Its perpetuation in India and elsewhere attests to the endless design possibilities it allows.

Late Developments and Modern Trends

For millennia, Indian jewelers have cultivated their own systems of work production. With the invasion of Europeans, bent on commercial and colonial exploitation, that started in the sixteenth century and ended with Indian independence in 1947 inevitably, new concepts exotic to indigenous practice were introduced. In the jewelry field, of significant importance was the Western use of regularly faceted, calibrated sized gemstones, and claw settings for them developed to increase gemstone brilliance. Previously, the time-honored Indian approach to the use of gemstones, especially diamonds, was to retain their initial weight as much as possible by limited polishing. As a result, gemstones of many dissimilar, irregular forms were used in the same object. Stone form irregularity is probably what motivated the invention of the *kundan* gemstone setting process, as it permitted and facilitated the setting of stones of any perimeter form, thus eliminating the painstaking work of producing many exactly measured collet-type bezels, which are required when calibrated gemstones are used.

The claw or open-backed setting was another innovation, though rare examples from the past do exist. Prior to this, Indian gemstones were set into the *kundan* foil-backed, closed settings. In these settings, light was reflected through the stone from the backing foil to the visible front only. Open-backed settings, as in the case of claws that hold the stone in air, permit light penetration from all directions, which considerably increases gemstone brilliance. Both methods are in practice in India since the mid-nineteenth century. The Western use of regularly faceted gemstones and claw settings in an otherwise traditionally styled ornament probably are indications of a relatively recent manufacture.

The Influence of Indian Jewelry Design on the West

Conversely, the impact of Indian jewelry design on the jewelry of the Western world became strongly evident after the Great Exhibition at the Crystal Palace in London in 1851, when traditional Indian jewelry was first presented in quantity to the general public. Its earliest subsequent influence is seen in the jewelry design of the so-called Arts and Crafts Movement in Great Britain in the late nineteenth century. Indian forms and motifs of ornament were widely adopted by Western craftsmen who, in sympathy with Indian handwork methods, admired the organic, handmade appearance characteristic of Indian jewelry, as contrasted with the more mechanical-looking perfection of most contemporary Western jewelry.

Especially dramatic was the adoption of Indian styles, especially inspired by that of the Mughal period, by the grand jewelers of France and Great Britain, such as Cartier, Van Cleef and Arpels, Chaumet, and others. This occurred coincidentally with the universal acceptance of platinum in jewelry at the turn of the nineteenth century into the early years of the twentieth. The reign of Queen Victoria and that of her son, King Edward VII, both of whom bore the additional title, respectively, of Empress and Emperor of India, brought about a surge of interest in Indian culture. This period also attracted to Great Britain and Europe many Indian maharajas and their retinues to participate in political events such as the celebration of Queen Victoria's Jubilee of 1877 (when she was designated empress of India) and the coronation of Edward VII in 1907 (when he became emperor of India). Their magnificent appearance, particularly the opulence of their elaborate jewelry display, was widely reported in the newspapers and magazines. Upon their exposure to high fashion Western jewelry and its refined technology, Indian royalty soon became important clients to the famous European jewelry houses. The result was an active intercultural jewelry design exchange.

Western jewelry that either exhibits an obvious stylistic similarity to Indian jewelry, or that uses typical elements of traditional Indian design, is still produced by the workshops of the major jewelry fabrication houses of the world. This artistic homage, a form of flattery to Indian culture, is but one instance of evidence of the inexhaustible design inspiration that Indian jewelry has provided to the world.

Oppi Untracht

BIBLIOGRAPHY

Allami, Abu'l-Fazl. *The Ain-i-Akbari.* 3 vols. Reprint, New Delhi: Oriental Books, 1977.

Aziz, Abdul. *The Imperial Treasury of the Mughals.* Lahore: Published by the author, 1942.

Borel, France. *The Splendor of Ethnic Jewelry: The Colette and Jean-Pierre Ghysels Collection.* New York: Harry N. Abrams, 1994.

Brijbhushan, Jamila. *Indian Jewellery, Ornaments and Decorative Designs.* Mumbai: D. B. Taraporevala, 1964.

Butor, Michel. *Adornment: The Jean-Paul and Monique Barbier-Mueller Collection.* London: Thames and Hudson, 1994.

Chandra, Rai Govind. *Studies in the Development of Ornaments and Jewellery in Proto-Historic India.* Chowkhamba Sanskrit Series Studies, vol. 41. Varanasi: Chowkhamba Sanskrit Series Office, 1964.

Filliozat, J., and P. Z. Pattabiramin. *Parures divines du sud de l'Inde.* Pondicherry: Institut français d'indologie, 1966.

Hasson, Rachel. *Early Islamic Jewellery.* 2 vols. Jerusalem: L. A. Mayer Memorial Institute for Islamic Art, 1987.

Hendley, Thomas Holbein. "Indian Jewellery." In *Reprints of Journal of Indian Art.* 2 vols. New Delhi: Cultural Publishing House, 1989.

Hendley, Thomas Holbein, and Swinton S. Jacob. *Jeypore Enamels.* London: William Griggs and Sons, 1886.

Jacobson, Doranne. "Women and Jewellery in Rural India." In *Main Currents in Indian Sociology,* vol. 2: *Family and Social Change in India,* edited by Giri Raj Gupta. New Delhi: Vikas, 1976.

Kautilya. *The Arthasastra of Kautiliya.* Translated by R. Shamasastry. 8th ed. Mysore: Mysore Printing and Publishing House, 1967.

Nadelhoffer, Hans. *Cartier: Jewelers Extraordinary.* New York: Harry N. Abrams, 1984.

Nandagopal, Chudamani. "The Traditional Jewellery of Karnataka." In *Decorative Arts of India,* edited by M. L. Nagam. Hyderabad: Salar Jung Museum, 1987.

Postel, Michel. *Ear Ornaments of Ancient India.* Mumbai: Franco-Indian Pharmaceuticals, 1989.

Pressmar, Emma. *Indian Rings.* Ahmedabad: New Order, 1986.

Stronge, Susan, Nima Smith, and J. C. Harle. *A Golden Treasury: Jewellery from the Indian Subcontinent.* London: Victoria and Albert Museum, 1988.

Tavernier, Jean-Baptiste. *Travels in India by Jean-Baptiste Tavernier, Baron of Aubonne.* Translated from the French edition of 1676 by Valentine Ball. 2 vols. London: Macmillan, 1889.

Untracht. Oppi. *Jewelry Concepts and Technology.* Garden City, N.Y.: Doubleday; London: Robert Hale, 1982.

———. *Traditional Jewelry of India.* New York: Harry N. Abrams; London: Thames and Hudson, 1997.

JEWS OF INDIA

JEWS OF INDIA The Jewish population of India is diverse—much like that of India itself—with histories extending over hundreds, if not thousands, of years. The Jews reached India by various routes and means, settling at different times, often in separate areas of the subcontinent, where they successfully adapted to the local environment. The Jews of India have lived peacefully with their neighbors in the subcontinent. Indian social paradigms allowed these groups to thrive unhindered and to survive into the twenty-first century, unlike the Jews of China, whose ancient communities had largely disappeared by the early twentieth century. Though small in size, the Jewish communities produced individuals and institutions that have enriched the substance of Indian society.

The Bene Israel, the largest group of Indian Jews, first settled on the Konkan Coast, on the shores of the Arabian Sea, south of the region that would eventually become Bombay (Mumbai). Arriving by sea from a place to the north, their traditional account mentions a shipwreck in which all their possessions were lost while several passengers survived. Eventually, as their numbers grew, their descendants spread to locations throughout the state of Maharashtra and beyond in the subcontinent. The other group claiming great longevity in India is based farther to the south, along the Malabar coast in the modern state of Kerala. They are known as the Cochin or Shingly Jews. The most recently arrived group of Indian Jews is that of the Iraqi or Baghdadi Jews, who can be found primarily in Mumbai, Pune, and Kolkata in ever dwindling numbers. This group includes Jews from other Arab lands, including Syria and Yemen. The most recently emerged group is that of the Jews of Assam. The latter, also known as the B'nei Menashe, from the northeast reaches of the subcontinent, have taken their place in Indian Jewish history only during the last several decades of the twentieth century. In addition, there are European Jews, primarily those who sought refuge in India before and during World War II.

The Bene Israel

The Bene Israel of Maharashtra state and the Jews of Kerala claim title to being among the first Jews on Indian soil. According to their folk tradition, the ancestors of the Bene Israel arrived at the village of Naveder Navgaon on the Konkan coast as the result of a storm at sea, which blew their ship far from their destination (perhaps Broach, a busy port to the north). As the story goes, the seven couples who miraculously survived the shipwreck

Man Holding Brass Insignia of the Pardesi Synagogue. As of 2004, fewer than twenty Jewish families remained in Cochin, Kerala. Still standing in the Mattancheri section of the town is the Pardesi Synagogue. At approximately 438 years, it is the oldest synagogue outside Israel. PALLAVA BAGLA / CORBIS.

made their way to shore and became the nucleus of the Bene Israel community. A memorial monument designed by a member of the community—Joshua Benjamin, (b. 1920) former chief architect to the government of India—stands on the shore near the village. The survivors took up the craft of oil pressing, which required little overhead and created a commodity much needed in that tropical region. In the villages, where they were known as *teli* (oil pressers), the Bene Israel came to be called the *shaniwar teli*, or those oil pressers who did not work on Saturday, in distinction from other *teli* of the area. As such, the Bene Israel can be traced in the local archives of the Hindu and Muslim rulers of the region. For example, two men named Aron and Sileman Israil are listed in the tax records for the coastal town of Revdanda in 1759. It is only in the British records that Bene Israel recruits are designated as being members of the "Jew Caste." The community had remained largely in the villages and towns of the Konkan until the advent of the European powers in the 1700s, when they began migrating to British-controlled territories. It was also during the eighteenth century that a traveler named

David Rahabi is thought to have visited the Konkan, though this date is disputed by some historians as too recent. Rahabi (whose name might reveal Egyptian origin) was happy to have found an Indian community that observed the Sabbath by not working, recited the *Kriyat Shema* (the credo "Hear, O Israel, the Lord our God is one") on auspicious occasions, and followed the laws of *kashrut* (dietary purity). The impact of caste consciousness on the Bene Israel community is evident in its division into Gora (white) Israel and Kala (black) Israel. Individuals in each group maintain that the terms have nothing to do with color, but rather refer to children of "mixed marriages" with members of the surrounding population.

In the period during which Bombay was growing as a port for the goods of British traders, the Bene Israel began to move out of the Konkan. Since some of the men of the community had already served in the military forces of the local leaders, the Marathas, enlisting in the British East India Company's forces was, perhaps, a natural choice. Others, who had served as contractors (suppliers) for the armed forces of the local rulers, moved to the city seeking business opportunities. Life in the expanding city of Bombay and in Pune (the traditional seat of Hindu power on the Deccan Plateau) brought about changes in social and economic patterns among the Bene Israel. Throughout the nineteenth and into the twentieth centuries, military recruits fanned out over British India, settling in the regions of their posting from Karachi to Rangoon. When, in 1813, the British allowed Christian missionaries into India to preach and teach, the first group to arrive was the American Marathi Mission, which sent its members into the Konkan. Since they were well acquainted with the concept of monotheism, the Bene Israel were among the first to obtain positions as teachers in the American Marathi Mission schools. Hoping to convert the locals by means of Bible study, the impact of missionary education on the Bene Israel had precisely the opposite effect. By disseminating Hebrew bibles, along with those translated into Marathi, and in pioneering Hebrew language education among the Bene Israel, the missionaries provided the catalyst for a rejuvenated Jewish community in the Konkan and in Bombay.

Another catalyst came from Bene Israel contact with the Kerala Jews from the Malabar coast. In the second half of the eighteenth century, during the Mysore wars, a commander in the British East India Company Army was captured by the enemy, Tipu Sultan, the Muslim ruler of Mysore. According to the oral tradition of the Bene Israel, Commandant Samaji (Samuel) Hassaji (Ezekiel) Divekar, after having revealed his Bene Israel origins, was released as a result of the intervention on his behalf by the sultan's mother. A very pious woman, she prevailed

upon her son to show mercy to Divekar, as he was of *Israil* stock—a people she knew of from the Qur'an, but whom she had never seen. Following what he considered a miraculous escape, Divekar returned to Bombay via Cochin, where he saw and admired several synagogues. As a gesture of thanks, Divekar constructed the first synagogue in Bombay in 1796; it is known as the Sha'ar Harachamim (Gate of Mercy) Synagogue. Throughout the course of the next century, synagogues were built in twelve towns and villages of the Konkan.

The contributions of the Bene Israel to India are found in politics, economics, the arts, and sciences. Beyond their original participation in military life—unique among Jewish diasporas—the Bene Israel continued to forge careers in the armed services. Several who actively engaged in politics during India's freedom struggle include Abraham Erulkar (1887–1960), who was dean of Bombay University's Faculty of Medicine as well as president of the Indian Medical Council; he tended Mahatma Gandhi during several of his fasts. His brother, David Erulkar (1891–1970), was part of the defense team (with Mohammad Ali Jinnah) during the trial of the radical Indian nationalist Bal Gangadhar Tilak in 1916. Elijah Moses served as mayor of Bombay in 1937. Jerusha Jhirad (1890–1984) was among Bombay's most distinguished gynecologists, in addition to serving her community as a religious innovator by helping to bring liberal Judaism to India. Bene Israel original literary works in Marathi began with Samuel Shalom Kurulkar's novel *Gooldhusta*, published in 1878. Meera Jacob Mahadevan (1930–1979) instituted the Mobile Creche network, which supplied child care for poor and migrant construction workers. She also authored a novel in Hindi (*Apna Ghar* [Our home], 1961) interpreting the impact on the Bene Israel community of the nearly simultaneous independence from British rule of both Israel and India. Perhaps the most prominent author in Jewish India is the poet Nissim Ezekiel (1924–2004). A professor of American and English literature at Bombay University, Ezekiel published *A Time to Change and Other Poems, The Unfinished Man,* and *Hymns in Darkness,* along with articles and literary criticism. His works, written in English, reflect the modern, post-colonial, urban Indian ethos. Another modern author is Esther David (b. 1945), whose novels include *The Walled City* and *Book of Esther,* along with the short stories in *By the Sabarmati.*

The Kerala Jews

The Kerala Jews in South India also claim ancient origins for their communities. Linguistic research has produced a connection between some Hebrew words and both Sanskrit and Tamil. As the southern portion of the Indian subcontinent has long been rich in spices—particularly pepper—it is not surprising that sailors from southwest Asia might have risked the long voyage from southern Israel or Yemen to India. King Solomon is reported to have imported *tukki* (peacocks) to his palace court. *Tukki* is a Tamil word. The Hebrew word for ivory (*shenhav*), another luxury item, is related to its Sanskrit term (*ibha dana*). There are also literary concepts, such as courtly love poetry, that suggest a link between ancient Israel and India.

According to the traditions of the Kerala Jews, early settlers built a synagogue in the town of Cranganore (also known as Shingly). A tombstone in the region is dated to the thirteenth century. Another item attesting to the antiquity of the communities is a foundation stone inscribed in Hebrew, dated 1344, from Kochangadi. The local raja had given a grant of land and privileges to a man named Joseph Rabban, written on copper plates in archaic script; various scholars have dated the plates from the fourth to the eleventh century A.D.

During the fourteenth century, as a series of storms silted up the port of Cranganore, that community fled south. There they met other Jews who had migrated from Arab lands, as well as descendants of refugees from Spain and Portugal. The Portuguese nobleman Martim Pinhiero (perhaps a *converso*, a crypto-Jew) sold Hebrew books in Cochin in 1506. Another source reports Jewish traders in Cochin in 1518. Cochin Jews played important roles in the business enterprises of both the Portuguese and Dutch traders who brought their political and military might to bear on India. Ezekiel Rahabi (1694–1771), a wealthy trader, served simultaneously as leader of the Cochin community, advisor to the maharaja, and agent for the Dutch. Ultimately, when the British arrived to oust the latter, the Jews of Kerala found new benefactors. With ancestors reaching back to the Portuguese and Dutch periods in Cochin, the most prominent family of Jews in the late twentieth century was that of Koder. Wealthy and influential, the Koders, as leaders of the White Jewish community, had participated in Cochin's municipal government, directed the electricity board, and operated the ferry transport company. Changes in Kerala's political environment reduced the economic and political authority of the Koders, but in the Jewish life of Cochin and beyond, the Koder family name still reverberates.

The gem of Cochin Jewish life, known as the Pardesi (Foreigners') Synagogue, was built in Matttancheri (in an area now called Jew town) in 1568; those responsible for its construction included refugees from the Iberian Peninsula who had arrived in India by various routes. The site, a gift from the maharaja, is located adjacent to his palace. Inside the Pardesi Synagogue are the treasures of Cochin Jewish heritage: the delicately painted blue willow Chinese tiles (1762) that cover the floor of the sanctuary, and the copper grant given to Joseph Rabban

by the raja. The copper plates lie at the core of the continuing conflict among Kerala Jews, which is expressed in the community's division into three groups: White Jews, Black Jews, and the *meshuchrarim* (manumitted). Members of both the White and Black groups claim to be descendants of the first Jewish settlers in India, hence the dispute over the origins of Joseph Rabban. The *meshuchrarim* (also known as Brown Jews) are considered the descendants of local people who served the White Jews and, upon release, adopted Judaism. Well into the twentieth century, these groups were exogamous. However, since Indian independence and the creation of the state of Israel, the considerable number of people lost to all Cochin Jewish communities because of emigration has led to a softening of the lines, and—out of necessity—intermarriage among the groups. The White Jews make great efforts to bring Black Jews to their synagogues for holidays in order to ensure a *minyan* (quorum required for public prayer). The tiny communities remaining in Kerala see their days numbered; the Paradesi Synagogue has been designated a national treasure by the government of India. On the occasion of its quarter-centenary celebrations in 1968, a postage stamp featuring the interior of the building was issued and Prime Minister Indira Gandhi participated in the festivities.

The Iraqi Jews

The third major Jewish group, known as Baghdadi or Iraqi Jews, comprises the most recent arrivals to British India. Perhaps a more accurate name for this group would be "Jews of Arab lands" because the Arabic language and later English were the common links among the members of this community. The first Arabic-speaking Jew to settle in India was probably Joseph Semach from Syria, who arrived at Surat in 1730, later settling in Bombay. Shalom Cohen reached India and settled in Calcutta in 1798. The arrival of Baghdadi Jews infused new vigor into Jewish life in India, bringing a vibrant religious energy with which they constructed synagogues and community institutions wherever they settled.

David Sassoon (1792–1864) established a far-flung mercantile empire stretching from Bombay to Singapore, via Calcutta (Kolkata) and Rangoon. David Sassoon Enterprises consistently employed family and community members in its network of factories, warehouses, and shipyards. His great wealth enabled Sassoon to be a major philanthropist for both the larger Jewish community as well as the cities in which he lived and or had major establishments. After building the Magen David (Shield of David) Synagogue (1861) in Bombay, he went on to construct the Ohel David (Tent of David) synagogue in Pune in 1863, known locally as the "Red Temple" (Lal Deul). Throughout the nineteenth century it was a city landmark, as it was the tallest building in Pune. He also funded the construction of the Sassoon Hospital there. The Sassoon family were great benefactors of the city of Bombay, where they constructed the Sassoon Docks (1870). They also established the David Sassoon Benevolent Institution near Bombay University, which now houses the Sassoon Library, where a life-size marble statue of David Sassoon stands near the entrance.

Calcutta's Iraqi community eventually supported three synagogues and two Jewish schools. The community's prosperity was so well known that an emissary was sent from Jerusalem (then part of the Ottoman Empire) to seek funds for the poor Jews of the Holy Land. Unlike the other Jewish communities of India, the Baghdadis, or Iraqis, never felt quite at home in India. They continued speaking Judeo-Arabic at home and even published a community newspaper in that language. From the second generation, they took to wearing Western dress and identified more with the British than with their Indian neighbors. For the most part, they were in India but not of it. This led the Baghdadi community to maintain a distinction, as far as possible, from the other communities of Indian Jews. Hence, there were separate sections for Bene Israel graves in the Baghdadi Jewish cemeteries. In Bombay, where the Iraqis had at first prayed together with the Bene Israel, synagogue separation was instituted as soon as the size of the Baghdadi population allowed for it. Following Indian independence and the creation of the state of Israel—with the consequent diminishment of both the Baghdadi and Bene Israel communities—members of the latter group were regularly, actively encouraged to join the Iraqis in their synagogues in order to form the *minyan*.

By the late twentieth century, the number of Baghdadi Jews in India was small, but a few individuals made vital contributions to Indian life. One of the most prominent is General J. F. R. Jacob (b. 1921), who played an important role as chief of staff in the 1971 conflict with Pakistan that resulted in the creation of Bangladesh. Subsequently, he served as the appointed governor of the Indian states of Goa, Haryana, and Punjab.

The Jews of Assam: B'nei Menasha (Children of Menasseh)

In the mid-twentieth century a group claiming to be descendants of the tribe of Menasseh (the son of the biblical Joseph) emerged in eastern India in the regions of Manipur and Mizoram, where prayer halls serving the communities dot the region. After several young members of the B'nei Menasha, also known as Shinlung, had reached the Jewish ORT Technical School in Bombay, and were accepted there, they forged a path to Israel, which many of their coreligionists have since followed.

European Jews in India

Although there have probably been Jews from the northern Mediterranean in India since Greek and Roman times, their numbers have been small and their names have been erased over the years. It is, therefore, interesting to note that two individuals in particular—both scientists—stand out: one in the sixteenth century, at the dawn of European exploration and involvement with the subcontinent, the other in the early twentieth century.

Garcia da Orta (1499/1500–1568) was born in Portugal, educated in Spain, and taught at Lisbon University before sailing for India in 1534. In Goa, he treated the viceroys, along with other Christian dignitaries, as well as the local Muslim ruler, Burhan al-Din Nizām al-Mulk. In acknowledgment of his services, da Orta was granted the island Mumbai, a small fishing village at that time (1554/1555). Da Orta's real interest lay in India's wealth of medicinal herbs, which he investigated for nearly thirty years, ultimately producing his vast work in Portuguese, *Colloquies on the Simples, Drugs and Medical Applications in India*, publishing it in Goa in 1563. After St. Francis Xavier in 1560 introduced the Inquisition in Goa, da Orta—a *converso*—moved his residence to Mumbai, where he died in 1568. However, after his sister had, under torture, admitted that the family were crypto-Jews, Garcia da Orta's remains were exhumed and burned at the stake alongside his sister and his treasured books.

Another European Jew came to India after having been denied a teaching position because of his religion. Waldemar Mordecai Haffkine (1860–1930), born in Odessa, developed the first effective cholera vaccine, which he introduced in India in 1893. Three years later, when plague broke out in Bombay, Haffkine worked there to develop a vaccine, which he produced within three months. After being honored by Queen Victoria and receiving British citizenship in 1899, Haffkine returned to India. He lived and worked in Calcutta for several years until ultimately settling in Paris. His contribution to India was recognized in 1925, when the Plague Research Laboratory he had established in Bombay was renamed the Haffkine Institute.

In the years surrounding World War II, Jewish refugees fleeing the Holocaust made their way to India, which provided them a haven from the horrors of Europe. Many of them were professionals or businessmen who, in the aftermath of the war and India's independence, left the subcontinent. Yet, as evidenced by Anita Desai's novel, *Baumgartner's Bombay* (2000), traces of this vanished group survive.

Brenda Ness

See also **Bene Israel; Rabban, Joseph; Sassoon, David**

BIBLIOGRAPHY

Fischel, Walter J. "Bombay in Jewish History: In the Light of New Documents from the Indian Archive." *Proceedings of the American Academy for Jewish Research* (New York) 40 (1972–1973).

Isenberg, Shirley Berry. *India's Bene Israel: A Comprehensive Inquiry and Sourcebook.* Mumbai: Popular Prakashan, 1988.

Israel, Benjamin D. *The Bene Israel of India: Some Studies.* London: Sangam Books, 1984.

Jacob, J. F. R. (Lt. Gen.). *Surrender at Dacca: Birth of a Nation.* New Delhi: Manohar, 1997.

Katz, Nathan, and Ellen S. Goldberg. *The Last Jews of Cochin: Jewish Identity in Hindu India.* Columbia: University of South Carolina Press, 1993.

Ness, Brenda Joseph. "The Children of Jacob: The Bene Israel of Maharashtra." Ph.D. diss., University of California, Los Angeles, 1996.

Roland, Joan G. *Jews in British India: Identity in a Colonial Era.* Hanover, N.H. and London: University Press of New England (for Brandeis University Press), 1989.

Slapak, Orpah, ed. *The Jews of India: A Story of Three Communities.* Jerusalem: Israel Museum, 2003.

JINNAH, MOHAMMAD ALI (1876–1948), *first governor-general of Pakistan.*

Quaid-i-Azam ("Great Leader") Mohammad Ali Jinnah, considered the father of Pakistan, was its first governor-general. Reared in Sind's port of Karachi, the eldest son of a wealthy Muslim merchant, Jinnah was shipped off to London at sixteen to study British management methods. His brilliantly vital young mind was magnetized more by bustling London's exciting politics, theaters, and Inns of Court, however, than the dull routine of business bookkeeping.

Impact of London

Soon after settling down in London, Jinnah met India's "grand old man" of Congress politics, Parsi Dadabhai Naoroji, one of the first Indians elected to Britain's Parliament. Dadabhai's maiden speech in the House of Commons, to which Jinnah listened from the balcony, inspired him to join India's National Congress as President Naoroji's secretary. But it was the Shakespearean performances at the Old Vic that youthful Jinnah found most fascinating, inspiring him to hone innate theatrical skills of rhetoric that would serve him so well for the rest of his life as one of British India's greatest barristers. Jinnah abandoned his business apprenticeship and completed legal studies at Lincoln's Inn in 1896, when he was admitted to London's Bar.

Bombay Barrister

After London, Jinnah found Karachi much too provincial a town in which to start his legal practice. He moved to British India's booming commercial capital, Bombay,

Pandit Jawaharlal Nehru and Mohammad Ali Jinnah. Jinnah with Jawaharlal Nehru (right), leader of the Congress Party, 1946. At this time Britain, as represented by Lord Mountbatten, still hoped for a diplomatic end to hostilities between warring Hindu and Muslim factions, but partition, not unity, was inevitable. A year later the separate nations of India and Pakistan were formed. BETTMANN / CORBIS.

where he felt more at home. Bombay's posh residential community atop Malabar Hill would soon become and, for most of the remaining years of Jinnah's life, remain his primary residence. Brilliant barrister that he was, Jinnah earned such high fees for his legal services that he could well afford the luxury of devoting much of his time to public political service. He joined India's National Congress in 1906 as President Dadabhai's secretary, and he worked closely with Gopal Krishna Gokhale, the previous year's Congress president, as well. Gokhale was so impressed with Jinnah's legal brilliance, eloquence, integrity, and singular command of English Common Law that he dubbed him India's "best ambassador of Hindu-Muslim unity," grooming him, as he also did Mahatma Gandhi, as one of his potential successors to Congress leadership. But moderate Gokhale died in 1915, too soon to permit him to see which of them would become his successor. World War I, and Mahatma Gandhi's return from South Africa soon after it started, radically changed the nature of India's political aspirations and popular nationalist demands. Moderate "Mister" Jinnah was driven out of the Congress in the aftermath of that global conflagration, while Mahatma Gandhi captured the hopes and support of India's Congress majority with his revolutionary *satyagraha* ("hold fast to the truth") proposals.

Muslim League Leadership

In 1913 Jinnah joined India's Muslim League, premier political organization of British India's Muslims, founded in 1906. At Lucknow in 1916, Jinnah won both Congress and Muslim League support for the nationalist reform platform he drafted, calling upon Great Britain's Cabinet to grant virtual Dominion status to British India after the war's end. That "Lucknow Pact" marked the high point of Hindu-Muslim political agreement and seemed to augur well for the emergence of a united independent Dominion of British India, three decades before partition shattered South Asia's unity with the birth of a bifurcated Pakistan and a diminished India in 1947.

Soon after leaving Congress in 1920, Jinnah had considered moving permanently to London. He bought a grand home on Hampstead Heath, rented chambers in the city, and pleaded princely probate appeals before the Privy Council. He even thought of running for Parliament, following Dadabhai's lead, but he was unable to convince either of Britain's major parties to nominate him as a candidate. So when several ardent young Muslim League leaders—among them Liaquat Ali Khan, who was to become Jinnah's lieutenant and Pakistan's first prime minister—passionately appealed to him to return "home" to revitalize their dispirited Muslim League, Jinnah agreed. Elected Muslim member from Bombay on the Viceroy's Council, Jinnah's eloquent brilliance won the admiration and friendship of British viceroys and secretaries of state for India, as well as of Prime Ministers J. Ramsay MacDonald and Winston Churchill.

The Muslim League was so inspired by Jinnah's return that they elected him their permanent president, and by 1937 he was hailed as their "great leader," Quaid-i-Azam, by thousands of Muslim followers. That was when Jinnah cast off his Saville Row suit, donning instead a black Punjabi *sherwani* and astrakhan cap (which came to be known as a "Jinnah cap"), symbolizing Jinnah's Islamic faith and his unique powers as the leader of South Asia's Muslim "nation" waiting to be born. Jinnah by now believed that Mahatma Gandhi had alienated not only himself but all Muslims from the Indian National Congress by transforming it from the moderate political movement it once was into a chauvinistic "Hindu" revolutionary organization. Congress leaders all disagreed, of course, but Jinnah claimed that Gandhi had "alienated eighty million Muslims . . . by pursuing a policy which is exclusively Hindu."

The Pakistan Idea

In 1930 Choudhry Rahmat Ali, a Muslim student in Cambridge, first called for the creation of a South Asian Muslim national "homeland" to be carved out of the Muslim-majority provinces of British India. He named it Pakistan (Land of the Pure), which could also be an acrostic of its major provinces: Punjab, Afghania (North-West Frontier), Kashmir, Sind, and the last few letters of Baluchistan. Bengal, the eastern half of which later became East Pakistan, was never even an initial in the new national name. In 1930 Punjab's great Muslim poet-philosopher, Muhammad Iqbal, also called for a consolidated "North-West Indian Muslim state" at the League's annual meeting, but Jinnah did not support either of those early Pakistan suggestions from London's Round Table Conference, which he was attending at that time.

Not until after his Muslim League passed its own "Pakistan" Resolution in Lahore in March of 1940 would Jinnah be committed to Pakistan as his League's primary demand. The year before, after Congress had won provincial elections in which the League did poorly, Jinnah lost all faith in Congress leadership, and any hope of Congress-League coalition-cooperation in jointly governing British India. At the historic Lahore League meeting in his presidential address, Jinnah thundered: "The Musalmans are not a minority. . . . The Musalmans are a nation." After that he never changed his mind, nor would he ever abandon his ultimate goal—Pakistan—though at times he proved wise enough to be willing to work with all parties, Congress as well as the British Raj, seeking the most peaceful path to Muslim national independence from "Hindu dominance."

Jinnah never lost faith in democratic governance based on Britain's parliamentary constitutional model. He always admired and adhered to "justice and fair play" under the "rule of law," as his personal ethical code. "The Muslim League stands more firmly for the freedom and independence of the country than any other party," Jinnah assured Stafford Cripps on his mission to India in 1942. "We have no designs upon our sister communities. We want to live in this land as a free and independent nation."

Last Years and Legacy

Jinnah pressed his political suit for the creation of Pakistan with single-minded determination throughout the last decade of his life. He never wavered, nor did he reveal how pain-filled his life had become because of the fatal lung disease that half a century of heavy cigarette smoking had inflicted on him. Only his sister Fatima, who faithfully nursed him, his loyal Parsi physician in Bombay, who remained scrupulously silent about his greatest patient's pneumonia and lung cancer, and his leading lieutenant, Liaquat Ali Khan, realized during the last years of the British Raj just how near death Jinnah was, for he remained stoical till his final hour. Little more than a year before Pakistan was born, Jinnah informed his Muslim League colleagues in Delhi that the Pakistan they were "fighting for" was "not a theocracy," for he believed in equal rights and legal protection for people of every faith, which was why he so intensely opposed what he called "Hindu domination."

In his first address to Pakistan's Constituent Assembly on 11 August 1947 in Karachi, Governor-General Jinnah told his new nation's elected representatives that their "first duty" as Pakistan's supreme governing body was to "maintain law and order, so that the life property and religious beliefs of its subjects are fully protected." Next, he warned them against twin "curses" of "bribery and corruption." Jinnah himself was never tempted by either "poison," those common temptations of power. "Unpurchasable," Liaquat rightly called his great leader. "Black-marketing is another curse," Jinnah warned his young nation, adding that they must also remain vigilant against "the evil of nepotism and jobbery." Perhaps most important of all that Jinnah said in this wise speech to his newborn nation's representatives was his reminder that "You are free; you are free to go to your temples, you are free to go to your mosques or to any other place of worship in this State of Pakistan. . . . You may belong to any religion or caste or creed . . . there is no discrimination, no distinction between one community and another . . . we are all citizens and equal citizens of one State."

Had he lived a decade longer, instead of merely fourteen more months—many so painful he was forced to spend them lying on a sick bed in Baluchistan's hill station, Ziarat—Jinnah might well have led Pakistan to achieve those noble goals. "Now, if we want to make this great State of Pakistan happy and prosperous," Quaid-i-Azam Jinnah told his people, "we should wholly and solely concentrate on the well-being of the . . . masses and the poor . . . work together in a spirit that everyone of you is . . . first, second and last a citizen of this State with equal rights." But just two months after Pakistan was born in August 1947, it was bogged down in a costly war with India over the former princely state of Jammu and Kashmir. That was only the first round in more than half a century of conflict, costing South Asia some 50,000 lives and billions of dollars in scarce resources, keeping India and Pakistan constantly mistrustful of one another, if not locked in mortal combat. India's first governor-general, Lord Mountbatten, came to dine with Governor-General Jinnah in Karachi in August 1947. Jinnah "assured" him then that "we shall not be wanting in friendly spirit with our neighbours and with all nations of the world."

The last time Jinnah and Mountbatten met, however, was in early November in Lahore, after the first Indo-Pak War had started. Jinnah angrily accused India of grabbing Kashmir, which with its Muslim majority he believed "justly belonged" to Pakistan, by "fraud and violence." Mountbatten replied that Maharaja Hari Singh's "accession" to India was "perfectly legal and valid." But Jinnah never forgave Mountbatten, and he felt "betrayed" by the British Commonwealth, which Pakistan had freely and hopefully joined.

"That freedom can never be attained by a nation without suffering and sacrifice, has been amply borne out by the recent tragic happenings in this subcontinent," Jinnah told his compatriots. His coughing made it difficult for him to speak, and though doctors hoped that Ziarat's hill-cooled air might ease his pain, nothing could stop the cancer that consumed his lungs. On 11 September 1948, Quaid-i-Azam Jinnah, then weighing only 70 pounds, was flown home to Karachi, the teeming city of his birth, where his body now lies buried inside a marble-domed monument.

Stanley Wolpert

See also **Gokhale, Gopak Krishna; Iqbal, Muhammad; Khan, Liaquat Ali; Naoroji, Dadabhai; Pakistan**

BIBLIOGRAPHY

Ahmad, Riaz, ed. *The Works of Quaid-i-Azam Mohammad Ali Jinnah*, vol. I (1893–1912) and vol. II (1913–1916). Islamabad: Quaid-i-Azam University, 1996, 1997.

Ahmed, Akbar S. *Jinnah, Pakistan, and Islamic Identity: The Search for Saladin.* London: Routledge, 1997.

Hasan, Syed Shamsul, ed. *Plain Mr. Jinnah.* Karachi: Royal Book, 1976.

Ispahani, M. A. Hasan. *Quaid-i-Azam Jinnah as I Knew Him.* Karachi: Forward Publications,1966.

Mujahid, Sharif al. *Quaid-i-Azam Jinnah: Studies in Interpretation.* Karachi: Quaid-i-Azam Academy, 1981.

Pirzada, Syed Sharifuddin, ed. *Quaid-i-Azam Jinnah's Correspondence.* 3rd ed. Karachi: East & West Publishing, 1977.

Waheed-uz-Zaman. *Quaid-i-Azam Muhammad Ali Jinnah: Myth and Reality.* Islamabad: Centenary Celebrations National Committee, 1976.

Wolpert, Stanley. *Jinnah of Pakistan.* New York and Karachi: Oxford University Press, 1984.

JIVA. *See* **Jainism.**

JODHPUR A city in Rajasthan, Jodhpur was earlier the capital of the princely state of Jodhpur. In 2001 its population was 860,400. Jodhpur is the center of a region called Marwar (Land of Death), which borders the Thar Desert. Since its barren soil does not offer much scope for agriculture, many of its inhabitants have migrated to other parts of India, particularly the traders, who are mostly Jains by religious affiliation, and are kown as Marwaris throughout India. Many of the Marwaris are financial wizards, including the famous Birla family. The Birlas have made a mark as industrialists and have built many large Hindu temples; they long sponsored and hosted Mahatma Gandhi, who lived in their Delhi mansion during his last months in 1947–1948. The fact that Marwar has produced such enterprising traders is probably due to its location at the center of an important trade route linking Delhi and Agra with the ports of Gujarat.

The princely state of Jodhpur was founded in 1212 and was locked in constant conflict with the sultans of Delhi at that time. The city of Jodhpur was founded by Rao Jodha of the Rathor clan of Rajputs in 1459. In 1561 Jodhpur was conquered by the Mughals, and later the Marathas captured this area. Under British colonial rule, the maharaja of Jodhpur survived, as had several other Rajput princes. Umaid Bhavan, the enormous city palace of Jodhpur, built with "golden" (yellowish) local sandstone in the twentieth century is a symbol of princely splendor in the twilight of the British Raj.

Jodhpur houses a university and the High Court of Rajasthan. In recent years it has also attracted some minor industries. As a railway station and a shopping center, it services a vast region, as it is located at a distance of about 185 miles (300 kilometers) from Jaipur to the northeast and 125 miles (200 kilometers) from Udaipur to the southeast.

Dietmar Rothermund

BIBLIOGRAPHY

Upadhyaya, Nirmala M. *The Administration of Jodhpur State, 1800–1947*. Jodhpur: International Publishers, 1973.

JUDICIAL SYSTEM, MODERN The judicial system in India today has generally won laurels for safeguarding the basic spirit of the Constitution and protecting the fundamental rights of common citizens. But it has also come under severe criticism for exhibiting extra activism. The judiciary is an important organ of the Indian state, and it has a vital role in the proper functioning of the state as a democracy based on rule of law. Without courts, laws remain dead letters; it is the courts that expound and define the true meaning and operation of the laws. The framers of India's Constitution had firm faith in the supremacy of law, and held that it was the only security for the disciplined and orderly growth of Indian democracy. They further stated that the judiciary had to perform a crucial role in a federal polity like India, where power was divided between the central government and the governments of the constituent units, and disputes concerning the range of their power and authority were likely to arise. Disputes between citizens as well as those between citizens and the state had to be resolved by litigation. Only an independent and impartial judiciary could settle such disputes effectively and decisively. Initially, Indian judges were influenced by the British concept of justice. But as the socioeconomic and political climates of the country began to change, the judiciary had to refashion itself accordingly. It dispensed with many stereotypes and started entertaining public interest litigations, passing strictures against the malfunctioning of the executive. It issued cautions and held that the legislature had no right to destroy the basic spirit of the Constitution. Thus the judiciary emerged as the guardian of the Constitution and the protector of the rights of Indian citizens.

Pre-independence Judicial Systems

It is only partly true that the modern judicial system was British. It also had deep roots in India's sociopolitical soil. India had various sets of laws, and its people were governed by different systems. Ancient scriptures, especially the Dharma Shāstra, took the dispensation of justice seriously. The king was entrusted with the supreme authority of the administration of justice. His palace court was the highest court of appeal, as well as an original court in cases of vital importance. He was assisted by a chief justice, and a host of other judges. The judges came from the upper castes, usually Brahmans. No Shūdra (a member of a lower caste) or woman could become a judge. Officers under the authority of the king presided over the town and district courts. Trade guilds (*srenis*) and corporations were authorized to exercise an effective jurisdiction over their members. *Pūgā* (commercial organization that was less powerful than *Sreni*, or guild) decided civil disputes among family members. Local village councils, or *kulani*, played an important role in solving simple civil and criminal cases. Decisions of each higher court superseded that of the court below. Each lower court respected the decision of each higher court.

Justice was not administered by a single individual. A bench of two or more judges was preferred. There were no lawyers, though persons well-versed in the laws of the *smriti*s (law books) could represent a party in court. The rulings of the Dharma Shāstra were given precedence in criminal cases. In both civil and criminal cases, the social status of the accused, as well as that of the witness, was considered. The accused was allowed to provide witnesses in

High Court Building at Chennai (Madras), India. The High Court in Chennai. In the twentieth and twenty-first centuries, with the socioeconomic conditions and political currents in India ever-evolving, the judiciary has had to continually redefine its role while interpreting and upholding a complex body of law. ABBEI ENOCK; TRAVEL INK / CORBIS.

his defense to prove his innocence. People of higher castes received lighter punishments than lower caste offenders.

During the time of Muslim rule, dispensation of justice continued to be a matter of utmost concern for the state. Islamic law, or Shari'a, was the basis of the administration of justice. It was considered the duty of rulers to punish criminals and to maintain law and order.

The British exploited India's traditional judicial systems to their own advantage for some time. In 1772 Warren Hastings took responsibility for dispensing both civil and criminal justice. He established a civil court (Diwani Adalat) and a criminal court (Faujdari Adalat) in every district. The civil court was presided over by a collector, who administered justice with the help of Indian subordinates. An Indian officer presided over the criminal court; *qazi*s (judges) and *muftis* (theologians) assisted him. In the civil courts, Hindu law was applied in cases concerning Hindus, and Muslim law was applied in cases that involved Muslims. In the criminal courts, only Muslim law applied. For a while, the judges of the Supreme Court, established in 1774, tried to uniformly apply English law. However,

this move was opposed bitterly by Indians. Thus the Act of 1781 restricted the application of English law to Englishmen in India only. But soon conditions changed, and the need for definite codes, applicable to all Indian subjects, was urgent. Lord Cornwallis took the initiative in applying British laws in India, implying the spirit of equality for all before law. He is also credited with introducing a secular judicial system in India. The Cornwallis Code, or Bengal Regulations, bound the courts to make decisions on the rights of persons and the property of the Indians according to the provisions of the regulations. To a great extent the regulations accommodated the personal laws of Hindus and Muslims, stating them in clear terms. The regulations were published in English and in Indian languages. Thus the administration of justice based on written laws and regulations, rather than vague customs and the will of the ruler, was initiated. This was a landmark in the history of India's modern judicial system.

Cornwallis also separated the judiciary from the executive. One person could not control both wings honestly and efficiently. To make the judicial system more effective, provincial circuit criminal courts were established. Provincial civil courts were initially established at Dhaka, Murshidabad, Kolkata, and Patna. Both district level courts were presided over by English judges. *Munsif* courts (local courts that dealt with civil matters) and registrar's courts (local courts that dealt with the purchase and sale of land) were introduced with Indians at their head. Sadr Diwani (an apex court that dealt with civil matters) and Sadr Nizamat courts (the highest criminal court) were the highest courts in Kolkata, and the governor-general was to preside over both. Capital punishment could be awarded only by the Sadr Nizamat court, just as the King's court, or Privy Council, in England was the highest court of appeal.

Governor-General William Bentinck abolished circuit courts. In 1833 an Indian Law Commission was appointed under T. B. Macaulay to codify the Indian system of law and court procedures. The Indian Penal Code was introduced in 1861. The Criminal Procedure Code was promulgated in 1872. The British Parliament passed the Indian High Courts Act in 1861, after which a number of High Courts were established in provinces. The Federal Court of India was established under the Government of India Act of 1935. This court was inaugurated in New Delhi on 1 October 1937. It was given all three kinds of jurisdiction: original, appellate, and advisory.

The British thus introduced a judicial system in India, which helped Indians in many ways. In theory, everyone was equal in the eye of law. In British India, however, this was never true in practice. The British living in India, suffering from their affliction of racial superiority, opposed any move by which they could be tried by Indian judges. The British bureaucracy and the police enjoyed arbitrary powers. In practice, therefore, the system failed to achieve its objectives of establishing a rule of law and equality before the law.

After Independence

India attained independence on 15 August 1947, and its Constitution was adopted on 26 January 1950. A single integrated system of courts for the union and the states, to administer both union and state laws, was accepted.

The Supreme Court. At the apex of the entire judicial system is the Supreme Court. This court is given independent status, and all laws declared by this court are binding on all courts in India. Initially, this court had a chief justice and seven other judges. The number of judges, however, has gone up to twenty-five. The chief justice is appointed by the president of India, as are the other judges, in consultation with the chief justice. Judges hold office only until they reach sixty-five years of age. They can also be removed by the president, but only when impeached by both houses of Parliament.

The Supreme Court enjoys original, appellate, and advisory jurisdiction. It is given exclusive jurisdiction in disputes between the central government and a state, or between one state and another. The Supreme Court also has exclusive jurisdiction over matters arising in the territories in India, and it is the custodian of fundamental rights, a power that is widely exercised. It has extended its powerful, long hands to protect any person whose fundamental rights have been violated. It has also started entertaining public interest litigation.

The primary task of the Supreme Court is appellate. It plays the role of final arbiter in constitutional questions. It can hear appeals against the judgments of the High Courts, tribunals, and special tribunals, and its judgment is final and can be reviewed only by itself.

The Supreme Court can render advice on any question of law or fact of public interest as might be referred to it for consideration by the president. The Supreme Court is a court of record, and its proceedings are recorded for perpetual verification and testimony. The Supreme Court enjoys the power of judicial review. It can pronounce upon the constitutional validity of laws passed by the legislature and actions taken by administrative authorities.

The High Court. At the state level, the Constitution provided a High Court, which is highest judicial administrative body in the state. The chief justice of the High Court is appointed by the president, and other judges with his consultation. A citizen of India who has held a judicial post for ten years or who has been a lawyer for two years can be appointed a judge of the High Court. Judges of the High Court hold office until age sixty-two. The mode of their removal is the same as that of a judge of the Supreme Court. They can be transferred from one High Court to another.

The High Court exercises supervision over all courts and tribunals within its jurisdiction. It can take steps to ensure that the lower courts discharge their function properly. It can transfer cases from one lower court to other lower courts. The High Court can issue writs for the enforcement of fundamental rights. It can issue writs even in cases where an ordinary legal right has been infringed. The High Court is a court of record and is the highest court of appeal in the state in both civil and criminal cases. The High Court has advisory power, and the governor seeks its advice on some important issues.

The lower courts. Barring some local variations, the subordinate courts throughout the country are structured uniformly. They function under the supervision of High

Courts. There are civil and criminal courts in each district. When the judge hears the civil suits, he is called district judge, and when he presides over the criminal court, he is called the session judge. Apart from these courts, Sub-judges Court (courts subordinate to the district judge), Munsif Court, and other courts also appear at the district level. At the subdivision level, similar courts function smoothly.

The *panchayat*s, or village councils, also play a vital role at the local level. The Mukhiya (head of the village council) and the Sarpanch (figure who looks after judicial matters at the village level) are armed with some judicial powers. Inquiries are to be conducted, and punishments are imposed on the offenders.

The attorney-general is appointed by the president of India. It is his duty to give advice to the government of India on legal matters. He also gives advice to the president on legal matters. He can appear in any court in the territory of India. He has the right to speak in either house of Parliament, or in any committee. The solicitor-general and the additional solicitor-general are two other important legal authorities who advise the government of India on legal matters. They can appear in the Supreme Court or any High Court on behalf of the government of India.

Later Developments

India's courts of law, however, were unable to meet the challenges posed by modern socioeconomic developments. As a result, various tribunals have been established that are not strictly courts in the traditional sense. A member of a tribunal takes a functional rather than a theoretical and legalistic approach. Tribunals do their work more expeditiously, inexpensively, and effectively. The Central Administrative Tribunals were formed to deal with the service matters of the employees of the central government. The president of India appoints the chairman and vice-chairman of these tribunals, in consultation with the chief justice of the Supreme Court. Other important tribunals include: the Customs and Excise Revenue Appellate Tribunal, Monopolies and Restrictive Trade Practices Commission, National Consumer Disputes Redressal Commission, States Cooperative Appellate Courts and Tribunals, Foreign Exchange Appellate, and Industrial Tribunals. The Election Commission has been constituted to hold free and fair elections in the country. Martial law courts at various levels have been constituted to handle cases related to military personnel.

Family courts have been established to dispose cases of divorce and promote conciliation in securing speedy settlement of disputes relating to marriages. Cases are also solved by the arbitration courts. Lok Adalats, initially started and encouraged by a few judges of the Supreme Court, promote the voluntary settlement of disputes inexpensively and expeditiously.

To make justice more democratic, Legal Aid was created for citizens whose annual income does not exceed a certain sum. The Legal Aid and Advice Boards were also constituted. Another advance was the emergence of the public interest litigation movement in the 1970s, with its goal of making the judicial system accessible to the lower socioeconomic strata of the society. Socially conscious individuals and action groups helped bring justice to people whose rights had been violated and who on their own could not approach the court. Complaints filed against authorities were looked into by commissions appointed by the court. On the basis of their reports, cases were filed in the High Court as well as the Supreme Court.

The Supreme Court shifted from a detached positivist institution to one that was an active player. Hence it was accused of activism. Judicial activism was an assertion of judicial power in cases where the judiciary came face to face with legislative arbitrations or executive abuses. The famous 1975 prime minister election judgment unseating Indira Gandhi and holding her election to parliament as null and void was one such case. The High Courts and Supreme Court on many occasions passed strictures on the functioning of the executive. It was argued that the judiciary was encroaching upon the jurisdiction of the executive, the legislature, and other institutions. However, an essential aspect of a constitutional judicial system is the duty of the courts to safeguard the interests of the common citizen.

As a result of public interest litigation, the weaker sections of the populace are now looking to the courts as their protectors. The courts, once inaccessible to them, are now seen as a source of justice. Still, despite these positive developments, litigation expenses and inordinate delays in deciding cases still plague modern judicial system.

The nature of the judicial process is very tiresome. Examination, cross-examination, and reexamination of witnesses in court takes too much time. Generally, the offenders and influential people manage lawyers and waste too much of the court's time. In this process, justice is delayed, and often, justice is denied. The high incidence of acquittals points to the failure of the judicial system. The judicial process has become technical and cumbersome; lawyers take full advantage of this complexity, and exploit the litigants financially as well.

Pramoda Nand Das
Yuvaraj Deva Prasad

See also **Bentinck, Lord William; Cornwallis, Lord; Dharma Shāstra; Hastings, Warren**

BIBLIOGRAPHY

Austin, Granville. *Working a Democratic Constitution: The Indian Experience*. New Delhi and New York: Oxford University Press, 2000.

Epp, Charles. *The Rights Revolution: Lawyers, Activists, and Supreme Courts in Comparative Perspective*. Chicago: University of Chicago, 1998.

Garlander, Marc. *Competing Equalities*. Berkeley: University of California Press, 1984.

Kirpal, B. N., Ashok H. Desai, Gopal Subramanium, Rajeev Dhawan, and Raju Ramachandran. *Supreme but not Infallible*. Delhi: Oxford University Press, 2000.

Kohli, Atul. *The Success of India's Democracy*. Cambridge, U.K.: Cambridge University Press, 2001.

Kulshreshtha, V. D. *Landmarks in Indian Legal and Constitutional History*. Lucknow: Eastern Book Company, 1984.

Verma, S. K., and Kusum. *Fifty Years of the Supreme Court of India: Its Grasp and Reach*. New Delhi and New York: Oxford University Press, 2000.

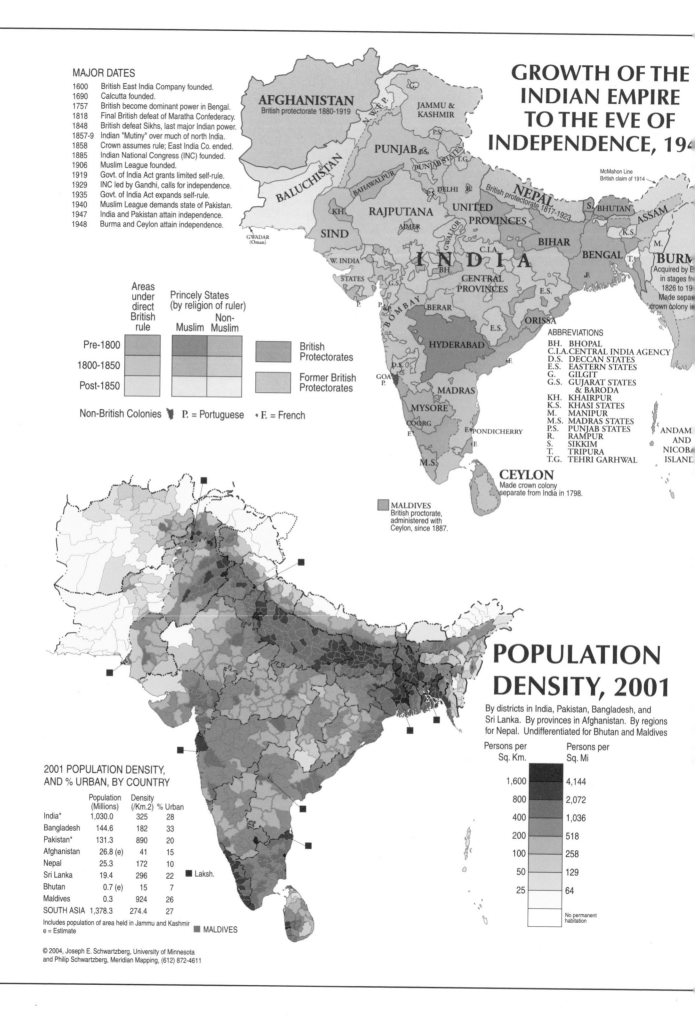

GROWTH OF THE INDIAN EMPIRE TO THE EVE OF INDEPENDENCE, 194[7]

MAJOR DATES

1600	British East India Company founded.
1690	Calcutta founded.
1757	British become dominant power in Bengal.
1818	Final British defeat of Maratha Confederacy.
1848	British defeat Sikhs, last major Indian power.
1857-9	Indian "Mutiny" over much of north India.
1858	Crown assumes rule; East India Co. ended.
1885	Indian National Congress (INC) founded.
1906	Muslim League founded.
1919	Govt. of India Act grants limited self-rule.
1929	INC led by Gandhi, calls for independence.
1935	Govt. of India Act expands self-rule.
1940	Muslim League demands state of Pakistan.
1947	India and Pakistan attain independence.
1948	Burma and Ceylon attain independence.

Legend

Areas under direct British rule:
- Pre-1800
- 1800-1850
- Post-1850

Princely States (by religion of ruler):
- Muslim
- Non-Muslim

British Protectorates

Former British Protectorates

Non-British Colonies   P. = Portuguese   F. = French

AFGHANISTAN
British protectorate 1880-1919

McMahon Line
British claim of 1914

NEPAL British protectorate 1817-1923

CEYLON
Made crown colony
separate from India in 1798.

BURMA
Acquired by B[ritain]
in stages fro[m]
1826 to 19[...]
Made separ[ate]
crown colony i[n ...]

MALDIVES
British proctorate,
administered with
Ceylon, since 1887.

ABBREVIATIONS

BH.	BHOPAL
C.I.A.	CENTRAL INDIA AGENCY
D.S.	DECCAN STATES
E.S.	EASTERN STATES
G.	GILGIT
G.S.	GUJARAT STATES & BARODA
KH.	KHAIRPUR
K.S.	KHASI STATES
M.	MANIPUR
M.S.	MADRAS STATES
P.S.	PUNJAB STATES
R.	RAMPUR
S.	SIKKIM
T.	TRIPURA
T.G.	TEHRI GARHWAL

POPULATION DENSITY, 2001

By districts in India, Pakistan, Bangladesh, and Sri Lanka. By provinces in Afghanistan. By regions for Nepal. Undifferentiated for Bhutan and Maldives

Laksh.

MALDIVES

2001 POPULATION DENSITY, AND % URBAN, BY COUNTRY

	Population (Millions)	Density (/Km.2)	% Urban
India*	1,030.0	325	28
Bangladesh	144.6	182	33
Pakistan*	131.3	890	20
Afghanistan	26.8 (e)	41	15
Nepal	25.3	172	10
Sri Lanka	19.4	296	22
Bhutan	0.7 (e)	15	7
Maldives	0.3	924	26
SOUTH ASIA	1,378.3	274.4	27

*Includes population of area held in Jammu and Kashmir
e = Estimate

Density Legend

Persons per Sq. Km.	Persons per Sq. Mi
1,600	4,144
800	2,072
400	1,036
200	518
100	258
50	129
25	64
No permanent habitation	